Organization an
Economic Beha

CW00616653

Anna Grandori

London and New York

First published 1995 as *L'organizzazione delle attività economiche*
by Il Mulino, Bologna
Second edition 1999 as *Organizzazione e comportamento economico*

English edition published 2001
by Routledge
11 New Fetter Lane, London EC4P 4EE

Simultaneously published in the USA and Canada
by Routledge
29 West 35th Street, New York, NY 10001

Routledge is an imprint of the Taylor & Francis Group

Typeset in Times by RefineCatch Limited, Bungay, Suffolk

British Library Cataloguing in Publication Data
A catalogue record for this book is available from the British Library

Library of Congress Cataloging in Publication Data
Grandori, Anna.
  [Organizzazione delle attività economiche. English]
  Organization and economic behavior / Anna Grandori.
    p. cm.
  Includes bibliographical references and index.
    1. Organizational behavior I. Title.
  HD58.7 .G68313 2000
  302.3′5 – dc21   00–038261

ISBN 0–415–16407–9 (hbk)
ISBN 0–415–16408–7 (pbk)

Contents

Preface

∙∙

This book is a revised version of a volume originally published in Italian in 1995, now published both in Italian and in English. It formalizes an exposition of what I think are the main tenets of organization science, it is based on both teaching and research experiences, and it is directed to both students and scholars, who can read it according to their different interests.

To intermediate/advanced business students it intends to offer a unitary and problem-solving oriented treatment of the field. The challenges of using as few as possible key concepts and of not changing assumptions implicitly according to the problem at hand, are taken to heart. The need for "flexible minds" capable of creating suitable and if necessary new solutions to organizational problems is responded to by focusing on learning what type of causal relations govern the organizational world rather than on providing recipes and pre-defined solutions which are likely to be quite short lived. Active learning is sustained by case studies, simulations, and exercises; this material can be adapted, integrated, or substituted easily with analogues more suitable to particular times and places. For example, at Bocconi University, where the book has been used on a large scale in Italy, not only teachers but even students each year produce dozens of new and stimulating empirical cases which serve as examples for the discussion of and the application of the main propositions.

To Ph.D. students and researchers the book proposes a conceptual integration of a discipline which has become highly fragmented in "schools" and perspectives. This integration is conducted by building on a revisited theory of rationality that goes beyond the divides between "global" and "bounded rationality," between farsightedness and habit, between calculativeness and appropriateness, to understand how decision-makers are capable of multiple rationalities depending on their knowledge of self and others. Consistently economic behavior is analyzed as struggling with problems of knowledge validity and growth and not only with problems of costs – hence, both knowledge-based and cost-based theories of governance and organization are used.

This view has led me to extend and generalize the available models of "organization design," in at least two directions:

- organizing is not just a matter of classification and selection of "types" of structures and processes that are known to be "adequate" in certain circumstances; is not only an "assessment" exercise; it is a design and engineering exercise, in the strong sense of being able to draw solutions for new problems;

- both the design and the assessment of organizational solutions are – more as a rule than as an exception – multi-actor, multi-objective problems calling for solutions that are not only effective in relating outcomes to preferences and efficient in using scarce resources, but also equitable in allocating and dividing rights.

My debts and acknowledgments go to entire collectives of people. All the groups in organization which have adopted the book in Italian universities since 1995, have provided enormously precious experiences, suggestions, and teaching solutions. In particular I am grateful to Bocconi's students and colleagues in organization for making the book a living and evolving experience through the ongoing production of new cases and incidents.

The anonymous Routledge reviewers have had a fundamental influence in challenging and pushing me to clarify and to explain the conceptual innovations which were, at the beginning of the process, often tacit.

Whenever in writing this book I had to cope with theory-building and interdisciplinary integration efforts, I had the opportunity to draw on years of tight and illuminating debate within a wide network of European (and extra-European) scholars who became involved, especially thanks to a five-year research program supported by the European Science Foundation (the "EMOT" – European Management and Organization in Transition – program) of which I was one of the two scientific directors. Many contributions from this community are used and quoted in the references.

The funds provided by the Italian Ministery of University and Scientific Research have made this editorial project financially feasible. The English translation grew out of step-wise work: I thank Jene Chaloux and Bryan Mundell for having produced the first English version of the original 1995 Italian book, and Professor Timothy Keates for having corrected the whole new text after my revisions.

A special thanks is due to those who have had a direct individual involvement in the genesis of the book, in different ways. I do not know if I would ever have undertaken such a venture without the encouragement and support I received from Andrea Rugiadini – one of the founders of the organizational scientific community in Italy, my former professor and mentor.

Most of the case study materials in the book are original and have been produced specifically for the book by colleagues at Bocconi University, at the University of Modena and Reggio Emilia, and in other universities – Luigi Golzio, Massino Neri, Giuseppe Soda, Giuseppe Delmestri, Silvia Bagdadli, Roberto Ravagnani, Davide Ravasi, Ferdinando Pennarola, Massimo Pilati, Francesco Paoletti – as well as by some former students who graduated with me – Federico Mazzoli, Christian Montermini, Massimiliano Mollona. Authorship is acknowledged in each box.

Barbara Balbiani – secretary at the Bocconi's Center of Research on Business Organization – contributed with her usual patience and common sense in handling the most delicate graphical problems.

To what extent so many valuable contributions are successfully integrated into the text is naturally only my responsibility.

Anna Grandori
March 2000

Organization: A Problem, a Discipline

● ●

PURPOSE OF THE BOOK

A first answer to the question "What kind of book is this?" can be given by declaring what kind of book it is *not*. This is not a handbook of organization, it is not a manual, it is not a "textbook" as usually intended, although it has also been written for teaching purposes (and on the basis of teaching experience). Instead, this volume is intended to be a unitary and basic treatise on the organization of economic action and interaction as a disciplinary area and as a problem, a "primer" in economic organization. This type of book has matured in response to at least two kinds of need.

In the first place, it intends to offer, in universities and other educational or research institutions, a base level but scientific education, aimed more at understanding key concepts that "open many doors" than at furnishing a series of notions or a complete survey of themes, research, and techniques in various areas. In these ways, it responds to the needs of those teachers and readers who might find the traditional textbooks too short on theory and too rigid in use. From this perspective, there are many European and American professors in our field who seem to have the opinion that a useful mix of educational tools should include a *primer* or basic text that can be flexibly integrated with other resources (articles, essays, anthologies, collections of cases, and exercises) according to particular educational needs and personal styles.

In the second place, the book aims at integrating, or re-integrating, a discipline that has always been "interdisciplinary," but that has in the last decades become fragmented in "schools" with heavy disciplinary characterization. After a long period of separation, if not mutual exclusion, today it seems once again time for dialogue between the main disciplinary "souls" of the interdisciplinary field of organization. A unitary approach actually characterized early founding works in the discipline, mainly in the 1950s and 1960s, such as those by Herbert Simon, James March, and James Thompson. They viewed administrative science as a distinct discipline that "should stand approximately in relation to the basic social sciences as engineering stands with respect to physical sciences or medicine to the biological" (Thompson 1956). However, the 1970s and 1980s witnessed a development of theories and research approaches more and more connected to the different social sciences, to the point where it is difficult to identify an organization science. There are models in the economics of organization, sociology of organization, psychology of

1

organization. "The organization" is conceived as an object – the firm, the political party, the public administration agency – not as a problem and a discipline.

This situation creates problems in research and many problems in teaching. To start with, in teaching, learners are more interested in being able to understand, predict, and manage organizational structures and behaviors than becoming erudite about the differences among schools of thought. In addition, learners are confused by the fact that, in many textbooks available, the underlying conceptual and methodological apparatus changes according to whether it deals with "micro-structure" (e.g. job design) or with "macro-structure" (e.g. firm organization structure), with individual motivation or the design of incentive systems, with organization internal to a firm or with coordination among firms. In research, on the other hand, the fragmentation of the field has produced duplications of research efforts and a blockage of the cumulative component in the growth of knowledge. In research-oriented books, organization is often seen as a complex and multidimensional construct that can only be approached by looking from one perspective at a time. This is not to deny the importance of theoretical variety; on the contrary, fruitful exercises in theory integration need theoretical differentiation. The distinction lies in how differences are treated and in whether inter-theoretical and even interdisciplinary dialogue and integration are considered possible or not. Among the main available perspectives and models of organizational analysis, we shall focus particular attention on integrating organization theory and organizational behavior (that were developed in close connection with cognitive psychology, social psychology, and sociology), and the streams of studies of "organizational economics" that have forcefully entered the field of organization studies since the mid-1970s. Some scholars have begged for a similar integration (Barney 1990), and others have cast doubt on its feasibility (Donaldson 1990). This book proposes one way in which it can be done.

Intended audience and reading suggestions

Since the treatment is problem-oriented, it may be difficult to infer from the text all the methodological ideas on which the conceptual integration between perspectives is based. Therefore we set out these methodological options in a dedicated introduction, especially addressed to teachers and research-oriented readers (Introduction II).

Beyond the two introductions, there are other elements in this book that are directed at different audiences. The book aims at fulfilling both teaching needs and theory development needs; hence (encouraged by some literary examples) I have tried to write it so that it can be profitably read at the two different levels.

For those who already have an education in organization, who know the models and the state of the art, this can be read almost as a monograph integrating many of these models. *This type of research-oriented reading is supported by notes, which can be skipped by students.*

For those approaching the field, reading can be done favoring learning of basic concepts and schemes to respond to problems. To support this type of reading, the text is organized in a format that can sustain teaching and learning, and more precisely active teaching and critical learning, both in the case of a self-managing reader and in the case of mentored readers. There are cases and exercises, simulations and problems that, in my personal teaching, I use as entrances to any of the treated topics before offering conceptualizations. For reasons of space, however, case studies and illustrations have been limited to those that are more specific to the argument developed in this text. *The boxes support a teaching-oriented use of the book and can be skipped in many cases by expert readers. However, almost all of them are based on empirical research, and are not hypothetical situations. Hence, they also provide some empirical support for the theses expounded, especially in the less conventional passages.*

This book is not meant as exclusive material for specialists of organization in the professional sense (such as personnel managers) but is directed to all persons interested in understanding and reshaping organization arrangements, in the broader field of *business administration*. It offers more interpretative and design models than techniques, though, taking seriously the idea that contemporary education needs to form "flexible cultures" – minds that are not programmed to act in particular ways, but that are equipped to change the way of acting. The themes are those that one could find anywhere in organized action: when to set up an authority? when and how to use groups? how to evaluate and reward work services? why are some firms big and others small? what problems might we expect in a firm organized by divisions? is it better to make or buy? how can these problems "be governed?"

Lastly, the book can be read from the perspective of any actor participating in organized systems and not only from a "governance" perspective. To that extent, the book speaks both to people or groups who are trying to find strategies to live in organized systems as well as to those who have or will have the responsibility of governing larger or smaller systems.

AN EXTENDED DEFINITION OF ECONOMIC ORGANIZATION

The aim of this section is to reconstruct a definition of organization – that will thereafter be used throughout the text – that responds to questions that may reasonably arise on the matter.

Teaching traditionally prefers a deductive path: here are the definitions, consider them as postulates or assumptions. These definitions lead to arguments, given those assumptions theorems are proved and laws are empirically checked. However, the process of constructing the definitions and learning the laws does not actually go ahead in that way at all, either for the scientific researcher who has produced that knowledge or for the student or reader who seeks to learn by critical understanding.

Definitions are, for their part, conjectures, hypotheses. What is a polyhedron? What is a mammal? What is salgemma? The definitions are propositions that "forbid" or "allow" access to phenomena or objects in our conceptual categories. Anything that "enters" a category will then be subject to a series of laws supposed to have been discovered for that type of object. The definitions, in turn, are historically constructed in a "piece-meal" way, in order to generate propositions that are scientifically valid and useful (Lakatos 1970). Without wishing to labor the point or needlessly complicate it with a discourse on method, we wish merely to justify and clarify the origins and motives of an approach to definition different from the usual. *In order to define the central concept, organization, dealt with in this book, one is invited to try generating definitions of organization and to discuss them, before reading this section.* The following dialogue simulates in a highly stylized fashion a possible debate among some basic arguments (eventually actually used in the history of organizational thought) which can contribute to delimiting a concept of organization that is sufficiently ample as to include the varieties of current forms and problems of organization, but sufficiently confined and precise so as to enable the formulation of theories with a good explicative and design capacity.[1] We trust that the reader will appreciate this approach, rather than demanding a ready-to-use (or memorize) definition starting from page one.

A dialogue on organization

Coordinator ((C)):   Now, how would you reply to the question "what is organization?" Let's start out from some minimal elements. On the one hand, the origin of the word "organization" refers at the very least to "an ordered and connected set of organs or parts of a whole." Is this an acceptable and sufficient definition? On the other hand, we can consider examples of problems that we would define as organizational: is it better to structure a firm in organs specializing by product or by technical function? is it better to pay salaries according to position or performance? why do some firms manufacture their components in-house while others make (more and more) use of outsourcing? why do some hotel chains belong to a single ownership (they are a firm) whereas others are run on franchising? why is there a return to and diffusion of "atypical" forms of work contract, neither fully dependent or autonomous?

(d):   Looking up in the dictionary, I see that "organ," "order," "coordinate" have connected meanings. . . . An organ is defined as a part of a whole, of a composite unit or system, linked with others and supplying a positive contribution to the working or survival of the system. The notion of co-ordinating also implies a concept of effectiveness, an ordering by one or more parties of the components into something different and better than other orders or random combinations. Organization, then, means giving form to, or putting in order, all these things: organs and linkages among organs.

(C):   Nice. For example, Marturana and Varela (1980), working on the borderline between biological and cognitive sciences, state that "*the relations between the components that define a composite unit (system) as composite unit of a particular type constitute its organization.*" Moreover, your concept also fits well with a core traditional notion of organization, according to which "organizing" is a concept that integrates two operations: "to divide" – to identify parts, components, organs; to divide activities and resources among organs, units, actors, or systems – and "to link" – to define, govern, regulate, give a particular shape to the relations among those parts or nodes (Mintzberg 1979). Hence, in very general terms, *the organization of a system is a selection of modes of partitioning the system and of modes of linking the parts.*

(a):   If we work on this first definition and on the examples of organization problems you have given, I also get the feeling that the meaning of organization is not that of an entity, such as a firm, an association, a hospital, and so on. If a subcontracting or franchising agreement is viewed as a form of organization, then the concept must be enlarged. There may be organization both "within" these entities (among their parts) and "among" them, considered as parts of a broader system.

(C):   Splendid! So an actor is not an organization, and not even a set of actors. We

shall refer to not to "organizations" (plural) but to the "organization" (singular). And since we shan't speak of "organizations" as that which lies "within," neither shall we speak of "environments" as that which lies "outside" and is defined by being excluded from the organization. *Organization appears to be a "way" of doing something rather than one "thing."* But doing what? Organization as a way-of-doing requires a predicate: organization of . . .?

(b): It seems to me that one often speaks of "organization of labor": organization is a way of working, dividing labor, controlling it, linking the various tasks.

(d): Hm . . .? Historically speaking, *labor* carries the meaning of exaction of energy, of effort, of human toil. I don't think it's the right predicate . . . it's too restrictive. For instance, there are other resources than human ones that combine to generate activity. I think that the combination of different resources to generate valuable activities and outputs is an organizational problem *par excellence*. Wouldn't "*organization of resources and activities*" be better?

(e): In that case, one should also add the organization of *rel-ations*, of *cooper-ations*, of *trans-actions* . . .

(C): Well then, let's speak of *actions* and *relations* among persons, groups, firms. But are we speaking of all the kinds of actions and relations? Affective life? Enjoyment? The organization we are speaking of here does not include the organization of biological systems or the organization of the life of a couple, or that of churches. In effect, certain differences among disciplines stem precisely from the fact that one is dealing with the organization of different systems. Some abstract and basic ideas on the nature of organization – as a special configuration of nodes and relations – may be common to different natural and

social sciences, but the models able to explain and predict the structure and behavior of different systems diverge in their content and method. For example, what is the precise meaning of to "divide" and "link" organs, if the latter also consist of persons, and not merely material or natural resources? And what if we are talking of economic activities, rather than of any activity?

(f): In this connection, I call to mind a topic I studied at high school, the "apology of Menenius Agrippa": the speech with which the Roman consul convinced the plebs, who had withdrawn in protest against the patricians on the Aventine, to return to the city and fulfill their role, comparing them to the members of a human body in revolt against the stomach, with serious damage to the body as a whole. The plebs returned, but succeeded in instituting the "tribunes of the people." I think that, if the organs consist of people, then "*rights*" and "*obligations*" come into play – which would not be the case with organs of biological systems.

(C): Fine. So, you see, the idea that an "organ" or "organizational unit" can be defined by a set of rights and obligations is compatible with the fact that the "parts" of social systems are "*actors*" as well as "*organs*" (Crozier and Friedberg 1977; Aoki *et al.* 1990; Keeley 1988). What about the meaning and consequences of considering *economic activities*?

(d): I go on looking up the origins of the words. "Economy" is made up of two Greek terms, *oikos* (house) and *nomia* (government, regulation). The word originally indicated administration and government of the household. In common language and meaning, the words "economy" and "economic" often refer to phenomena connected with money, saving, or increase in wealth. It seems to me that neither of these

two meanings (the original one and the common one) correspond well to the one we would like to specify.

(C): In fact, today economists would consider the notion of utility central, rather than that of wealth: they would try to analyze what the utility of money is for various individuals, as well as to measure the different utilities that may derive from satisfying different needs – consumption, cultural, environmental, and housing quality; plus the degree of freedom that an individual has in choosing which interests to satisfy and what effects this will have on the opportunity for other individuals to satisfy their interests.[2]

So the meaning of "economic" has indeed been expanded and rarefied to the point where it indicates the general problem of *allocation of scarce resources to alternative uses*, a problem in which it is therefore useful to reply to the question: which allocation is superior?

Thus, in order to define an activity as *economic* it is not essential that it is appraisable in monetary terms; it is important that it absorbs *scarce resources* in order to produce an *output of value*. In this sense, for an economic activity "costs" as opposed to "benefits" (neither of them necessarily translatable into money) can be defined.

Well then, we shall use the adjective "economic" to refer to activities and behaviors in this sense. On the contrary, we shall not adopt an "economic approach" in the disciplinary sense of the term. This is not a book about the economics of organization, it is a book on the organization of economic activities. For there is a discrete difference between explaining actions that have consequences endowed with economic value with the most adequate variables (also "cognitive," "social," etc.) and explaining social phenomena (and even the actions

having no important economic consequences) as though they stemmed from calculations of costs and earnings.[3]

(f): Ah, yes, at a debate I remember hearing someone remark that an economist is one who would marry Liz Taylor for her money . . .

(C): Good! Let us then only retain the focus on economic activities, for which the modes of organizing can be evaluated in terms of utility and performance. This focus leads to a diagnostic, prescriptive, design perspective. . . . Not a description of everything that happens; rather, a distinction between good and less good solutions: more or less efficient, more or less effective, more or less fair, but in any case more or less "useful" for the actors.

(b): If these "actors" and their utility are so important, at this point I should like to know what is meant by actors. Are they "behind" or "inside" the organization? How do they deal with their utility? Are they always aware of it? What about actions that are chosen for certain motives and turn out to have different and unexpected consequences?

(e): . . . dear me . . . we'll never get to the end of this . . .

(C): . . . and *e* is right to complain. . . . In hunting for definitions, you inevitably run up against a problem of infinite regression of terms. . . . So at a certain point you have to stop. The questions asked by *a* have led us to a problem of defining the elementary unit of analysis, the actor, to whom the actions, relations, and allocation of resources and rights must be referred. *A model of the economic actor and his behavior*, rooted in the research on models of rationality and "decision," will therefore be our starting point, in Chapter 1. The map for the subsequent path, which will guide us from actor to organization – backwards with

respect to the direction we have taken in this discussion, from organization to actors – is outlined in Figure I.1. In the course of the book, each part will be enlarged and enriched with details.

ORGANIZATION OF THE BOOK

As can be inferred from Figure I.1, the point of departure is the configuration of actors as unit of analysis; then the problem of multiple interdependent actors and of coordination mechanisms is introduced; finally, organization forms are analyzed as combinations between configurations of actors and of coordination mechanisms.

Part I is dedicated to the construction of a model of actor, including structural aspects – the structure of knowledge and preference relevant for understanding economic behavior and the organizational arrangements governing it (Chapter 1) – and process aspects – the processes of decision and motivation through which behavior is generated (Chapter 2).

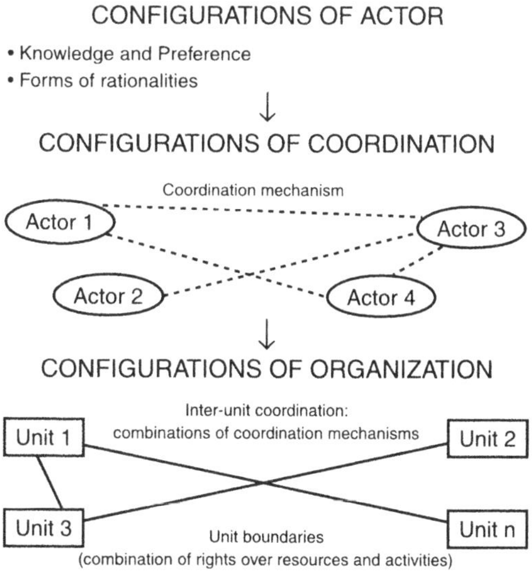

Figure I.1 From actor to organization: a map

In Part II, the problem of interdependent action by more than one actor, and of the main ways of coordinating it, is introduced. Coordination mechanisms are distinguished and assessed on the basis of the logic of the multi-party decision they imply: models based on unilateral decisions, such as pricing and voting (in Chapter 3); models based on decision rights sharing to different extents: authority and agency, teaming and negotiation mechanisms (in Chapters 4, 5, and 6 respectively); and models based on automatic decisions, taken by following norms, rules, and conventions (in Chapter 7).

Part III illustrates how different configurations of actors and different combinations of coordination mechanisms configure different *forms of organization*. The modes of division of resources and activities among actors and the coordination among these at various levels (persons and job, groups and organizational units, firms and clusters of firms) are analyzed in their nature of rights and obligations relative to action, information, decision, control, rewards, and ownership allocated (formally and informally) to the different actors. The first part of each chapter in Part III is devoted to presenting *a procedure for organization design* – in the sense of finding, constructing, generating suitable solutions – at different levels and in different areas of organising. The second part of each chapter considers the *comparative assessment of a set of "given" alternative configurations* – in the sense of recurrent, known, and codified forms of organization.

Chapter 8 performs a founding function for the whole of Part III. The chapter defines the main variables that are utilized in the analysis, design, and assessment of organizational forms. In this chapter, the effort of integrating the many, often overlapping, relevant variables present in different organization design models, is conducted at a general and conceptual level. The other chapters in Part III apply the general framework as relevant to different problems and levels of analysis. Chapters 9 and 10 address the problem at the "micro" level of the organization of work; Chapter 11 at the level of the "macro-structure" of the firm; and Chapter 12 at the level of interfirm boundaries and interfirm coordination.

The Conclusions to each Part build on all the material previously discussed and on the conclusions of previous parts. Therefore, the Conclusions to the three parts can be read together as building up the Conclusions to the whole book.

Introduction II

Methodological Options for an Integrated Perspective

For Research-oriented Readers

••

This introduction is especially directed to those who already have a perception of the field and may otherwise find unusual the way in which the material they know is employed in the book, or may wonder why some perspectives and ideas are included and some are not. Students interested in gaining a deeper understanding of the conceptual texture of the field can eventually read it *after* the book.

FROM UNIVERSAL LAWS TO CONDITIONAL PROPOSITIONS

Consider some of the laws of organization formulated by the forefathers of organization theory: "The higher the degree of division of labor among workers, the higher the level of work productivity" (Smith 1776; Taylor 1947) or "The higher the level of job satisfaction, the higher the level of work productivity," where "the lower the degree of division of labor, the higher the level of job satisfaction" (Roethlisberger 1942; Mayo 1945); "Bureaucracy is the most efficient form of organization in an industrial economy" (Weber 1922) or "Peer group organization is superior to other forms in an industrial economy" (Marx 1867). The error of the ancestors of organization theory was one of universalism. Their discoveries about the advantages of specialization, the relevance of workers' preferences,

and the coordination properties of hierarchy or peer groups were in good part valid, and, for those parts, were in fact resurrected in later models and are all still in use. But the specification of the conditions under which those laws and properties are valid were at best very weak or absent in those classics. For quite a long time, and sometimes even now, then, what were hypotheses valid under different circumstances were treated as irreconcilable paradigms.

This error of universalism was denounced in organization studies, especially in the 1960s and 1970s, by what is known as "contingency theory" of organization (Woodward 1965; Thompson 1967; Lawrence and Lorsch 1967; Pugh *et al.* 1969a), trying to specify what are the best forms of organizing given what types of technology are used, what tasks are performed, and what types of environmental uncertainties and interdependencies are faced. But this criticism was either not deep enough, or partially flawed, or not listened to enough, or all these things together, because the temptation to announce the discovery of unconditioned best ways of organizing keeps reappearing. For example, together with an enriching attention to the problem of the allocation of property rights – formerly somewhat neglected in mainstream organization studies – organizational economists brought into the organization field the never-ending polemics about the universal superiority of "capitalist" or non-capitalist forms of organizing work; or, new polemics about the superiority of certain organization structures (e.g. multidivisional structures) in the organization of the firm (Williamson 1975, 1981b).

In fact, the criticism leveled at the possibility of formulating valid universal laws did not go far enough. Contingency theories ended by substituting the idea that "one best way of organizing" can be identified in general, with the idea that one best way of organizing can be identified in correspondence to each among a few different configurations of environmental and technological variables (Butera 1972; Child 1982; Grandori 1987). Hence it underrated other important sources of "organizational choice" (Trist *et al.* 1963): the degrees of freedom existing in organizing even in similar technical or institutional conditions, which may certainly rule out the feasibility or convenience of some solutions, but rarely determine a single optimal one.

In this book, *the integration between the different perspectives and results of research is performed, in the first place, on the basis of (1) the transformation of universal laws into conditioned laws (if ... then ...); and (2) the admission that the laws of organization are, usually, not laws of one-to-one and deterministic correspondence between conditions and organization solutions (there is normally more than one "best solution" even in "given conditions").*

FROM "BEHAVIORAL ASSUMPTIONS" TO BEHAVIORS TO BE EXPLAINED

The field is, however, broken up by deeper divides. The most serious of these is certainly the

"model of rationality" that economic actors are "assumed" to follow.

In the social sciences the term "assumption" refers to those statements that are accepted as true by definition and convention, and that specify the conditions under which a theory holds. Hence, an assumption differs from a hypothesis: hypotheses can and must be subjected to proof and refutation, or to empirical control, in the conditions specified by the assumptions under which a theory holds. A good rule for research, then, would require that the "assumptions" be as limited and sparing as possible; and that one should not "assume" what can be explained.

These differences in assumptions mainly derive from the background disciplines from which organizational perspectives have emerged. For example, the difference between the "free" and "calculative" decision-makers assumed in economics, and the "constrained" and non-calculative behaviors of actors portrayed in a large part of classic sociology, has been so striking as to provoke sarcastic remarks: for example, the aphorism – attributed to Vilfredo Pareto – that "economics is the science of how to make decisions, sociology is the science explaining how there is no choice to make"; or the now increasingly popular charge made, on the one hand, against economics for having constructed an "under-socialized model of man" and, on the other hand, against sociology for having postulated an "over-socialized model of man" (Wrong 1961; Granovetter 1985).

Between these two extreme models, as well established as clearly incapable of explaining many interesting economic and social behaviors, the "theory of bounded rationality" formulated by Herbert Simon (1947, 1955b) and primarily grounded in cognitive psychology, provided a "third way" and middle ground, a model of an actor who "is rational, but only intendedly so." Bounded rationality theory provided the cognitive foundations for the development of a relatively autonomous organizational and behavioral science. However, it has ended by sharpening unnecessary divisions with its contrast between "absolute" and "bounded" rationality. For the concept of bounded rationality is very vast and in certain respects ambiguous, for two reasons: (1) various components and sub-models were intermingled in Simon's elaborations, from which, in fact, different perspectives have developed; (2) in Simon's original work there was some ambiguity as to whether bounded rationality should be considered a universal assumption, rival and alternative to that of economic optimizing rationality, or a model of decision behavior contingently – albeit frequently – observed outside of the restrictive conditions required by value maximizing. Unfortunately, the most common interpretation has been the first universalistic one, with the result of sharpening the divide between economic and behavioral models of organization, and between forms of organization based on the two contrasting models of "economic man" and "administrative man." These two difficulties are resolved in this book as follows.

1 Among the bounds or limits to human rationality considered by Simon there was not only the finite computational capacity of the human brain, considered the most precious scarce resource that can be allocated to different uses, which has become the most widely used notion of bounded rationality. There was also the acknowledgment of some more epistemic problems that echoed and in some cases anticipated other contributions on the nature of rationality in general and economic rationality in particular: the recognition of the intrinsic fallibility of human judgments and knowledge, of the models of the world that decision-makers are acting upon (Popper 1935; Simon 1947), of the unavoidable imperfection in knowledge codification and transmission (Simon 1947; Polany 1958), of the logical necessity of "decision premises" and "background knowledge" considered "out of discussion" providing a framework and a language for starting any decision process (Simon 1947; Khun 1962; Lakatos 1970). These are sources of complexity and difficulties in *knowing* rather than in *calculating*. Subsequent perspectives have often paid attention only to partial aspects of bounded rationality. For example, this is the case of the divide between those organizational economics perspectives interpreting bounded rationality mainly as a problem of information costs (as information cost economics and transaction costs economics) (Arrow 1974; Williamson 1975) and those interpreting it mainly as a problem of constructing valid knowledge for economic action (as the competence and knowledge based theories of the firm) (Foss 1993).

In this book, both these sources of decisional problems and of uncertainty will be acknowledged, and their organizational consequences will be specified: a problem of *computational complexity*, mainly reflecting the needs for limiting search and calculation costs (such as looking for a good candidate for a given job, or for good equipment to buy) – and a problem of *epistemic uncertainty*, mainly reflecting the need for constructing a valid model of what action alternatives are available and of what consequences can be expected (such as discovering which new combinations of human and technical resources can generate value-creating activities).

2 Simon's way of presenting his theory of "bounded" rationality as a rival theory to the model of "absolute" or "global" rationality

of economics, charged with being less "real-istic" and less "predictive" of observed eco-nomic behaviors, has contributed to creating what will be considered here an unnecessarily profound divide. For there is no such thing as an "absolute knowledge" or "absolute rationality," to the extent that all human knowledge is fallible and any form of ration-ality is "bounded" (Popper 1935; Russell 1948; Simon 1977). There can be different decision behaviors, or strategies, which treat information in different ways and therefore are applicable under different circumstances (Grandori 1984). In particular, as von Hayek (1945) stated with impressive clarity, decentralized profit-maximizing decisions based on quantified information condensed into prices, can be highly efficient – under appropriate circumstances – exactly because this "economizes on bounded rationality" (Williamson 1975), rather than because it realizes some form of global or objective rationality. In fact, the immensely complex problem of the coordination of an economy is thereby decoupled into very simple ones, a huge amount of information can be neg-lected, and communication can be avoided altogether. The most interesting question is, then, under what circumstances can value maximizing decision strategies be predicted and prescribed, and under what circum-stances do other strategies become not only more likely but also more advisable?

James March is perhaps the sole "*maître à penser*" in organization who clearly sug-gested that rationality is polymorphic and contingent (1978: 604): "Calculated rational-ity . . . is only one of several forms of intelli-gence, each with claim of legitimacy. Learned behavior, with its claim to summar-ize an irretrievable but relevant personal history, or conventional behavior and rules, with their claims to capture the intelligence

of survival over long histories of experience more relevant than that susceptible to immediate calculation, are clear alternative contenders [. . .] The superiority of learned or conventional behavior depends, in general, on the amount of experience it summarizes and the similarity between the world in which the experience was accumulated and the current world."

The integration between perspectives that "assume" different models of rationality will be performed here by treating these models as behaviors to be explained rather than assumed, and by specifying the conditions under which those models can be expected to be applicable or superior.

This same methodological stratagem – that may be called "the endogenization of assumptions" – can and should be applied also to other controversies. For example, the content of preferences has been often treated as a matter of "assumption." Some models have "assumed" that labor effort is a cost for agents (such as, recently, agency theory and in the past the Taylorist school) and have been opposed by others who wished to "assume" that labor is a natural activity and can be intrinsically rewarding (McGregor 1960; Argyris 1964; Pfeffer 1994). Or, there are models that have included a propensity toward "opportunism" (self-interest seeking with guile and deception) among their found-ing "behavioral assumptions" (Williamson 1975). They have often been harshly opposed by the observation that "trust," instead, often prevails; leading them to pose "loyalty" or even "altruism" as rival assumptions (Simon 1997). By contrast, opportunistic or trustful conducts, instrumental or intrinsic motiv-ation – as well as other "propensities" and motives, such as those toward risk, achieve-ment or power – will be treated in this book as behaviors to be explained, or at least as empirical regularities to be discovered and documented, rather than as assumptions on which theories can be based.

TRANSLATIONS BETWEEN "PARADIGMS"

Description and prescription

In many cases, important and possibly complementary perspectives on organization and economic behavior "do not talk" to each other and generate incomparable predictions because they talk different languages: the descriptive language of how things are (descriptive laws), or the prescriptive language of how things should be if they are to produce certain consequences (prescriptive laws). Some economists usually argue that they do not describe how decisions are made, they prescribe how they should be made in order to achieve superior results. Other economists are willing to go as far as to assert that in economic action those behaviors and structures that generate inferior results will be selected out and disappear, so that their prescriptive theories are also supposed to describe the world as it is likely to exist (in the long run) (normative laws). By contrast, in other social sciences, a descriptive or "positive" language is used: e.g. gender, age, nationality "influence" behavior; activities "influence" structures; stimuli "influence" responses; etc.

However, it is always possible to reformulate prescriptive (and even normative) propositions – provided that they have an empirical basis – in descriptive propositions, in the form: "if x is a necessary and/or sufficient cause of y, if one wishes to observe y, then it is necessary and/or sufficient to observe x" (Simon 1977). On the other hand, many regularities expressed in a descriptive language in organizational studies – such as "system size

is correlated to decentralization" – are in fact valid only under some conditions of effectiveness. Hence they can be translated into prescriptive statements, such as "decentralize in large systems to improve performance."

These translations are often used in the book in order to connect otherwise incomparable statements.

Efficiency and power

The lack of translation between descriptive and prescriptive models has merged with a controversy about the content of the "objectives" pursued by economic actors to generate another and possibly the most wrongly defined conflict among organizational perspectives – the contrast between "power" and "efficiency" explanations of organization. Are resources allocated in firms according to efficiency or according to the power of offices (Bower 1970; Pfeffer and Salancick 1974a)? Did the capitalist form of enterprise appear because it was more efficient or because capitalists found it convenient to gain more power over workers (Marglin 1974; Francis 1983)? Are interfirm alliances formed for producing new products at lower costs or for reducing competition and increasing market power (Jaquemin 1985)? But what do "power" and "efficiency" mean exactly? Both are multidimensional and complex concepts (Turk 1983) and, descending into their operative definitions, one discovers that they are rather overlapping concepts (Grandori 1993). These different definitions are briefly recalled here, indicating how each of them will be treated in the book.

Efficiency is the generation of valuable outcomes through the use of the minimum possible amount of resources. This may seem simple but it entails several complications.

Encompassing the two components of benefits and costs, efficiency can be augmented not only by reducing costs, but also, and often more easily and productively, by creating more value (Dietrich 1993). In practice this is quite important, as it may make the difference between, say, cutting personnel in order to be more efficient in one production or making an alliance to open a new line of production; or between accepting the first satisfactory partner for forming an alliance, for reducing search and negotiation costs, or investing more resources for finding a partnership that creates more surplus. In fact, the value-increasing component of efficiency is commonly distinguished by the term *effectiveness* (capacity to reach valued outcomes).

In addition, efficiency is ill-defined unless the subjects bearing benefits and costs are defined and the time horizon is defined. *Short- and long-term efficiency* are almost proverbially conflicting criteria. When there are many subjects, efficient solutions are all those (and usually they are more than one) with respect to which no improvement for one or more party is possible without subtracting something from other parties (*Pareto-efficiency*). Furthermore, efficiency criteria can be applied in a *static* way (for example, in terms of comparative costs, it is more efficient to make rather than to buy a component) or in a *dynamic* way (for example, the marginal costs of adding one more item to internal production may be higher than the marginal costs of adding a procurement relation). Therefore, in the first place, different organizational solutions to the same problem can be explained by different efficiency criteria. Does power explain further differences?

Power is an even more multifaceted concept. As used in organization studies, it has been used in at least the following meanings, with quite different implications.

1 Power has been used as a synonym for particularistic objectives – that is, for differentiating the interests of a system from those of its parts (e.g. Pfeffer and Salancick 1974a, 1974b, 1978). In this case, just to recognize that there is a problem of *"locus" of efficiency* and that different parties may receive different benefits and bear different costs has many advantages over contrasting efficiency and power. In particular, it enables one to solve the problem (being prescriptive) rather than just describing that there is something going on that differs from standard system efficiency criteria. *Pareto-efficiency and fairness criteria* can be employed (and are both necessary) to the purpose, as will be shown in all the parts of this book devoted to enlarging current approaches to organization design in order to deal with the presence of different interests over organizational arrangements.

2 Power has been used as a synonym for *freedom of action* and "control of uncertainty" (Crozier and Friedberg 1977). In this meaning it amounts to a procedural way of defining expected utility (Grandori 1987; Friedberg 1993). Economic actors should not be assumed to be necessarily interested in accumulating valuable resources of a particular type – money, status, free time, influence on others – but can be supposed to be more generally interested in being free to act so as to get whatever they might prize (Sen 1992). In this sense, in most economic action problems they usually *prefer more rights of action (and of decision over actions) rather than fewer. In addition, they can usually be supposed to be interested in reducing the costs of negotiation with others to achieve those results (in economic language, in reducing transaction costs).*

3 Power has been used as a synonym for *dominance*: the reduction of the freedom of action and of the resources of other actors in order to make them dependent on one's own

will and redistribute resources to one's own advantage (Marglin 1974; Francis 1983). In this sense, a power criterion does make a difference with respect to efficiency and fairness criteria. Supposing that there is no incentive to impose a solution that can be improved both for oneself and for others, still one party (typically because it is much less substitutable than others) may be able to impose an arrangement in which it captures all the surplus created by cooperation or exchange and gives others their minimum acceptable reward rather than their fair share. These arrangements undoubtedly can exist. However, if and when this is the diagnosis, scholars of *almost all perspectives would agree that these arrangements are to be proscribed rather than prescribed* and that remedies should be found. The point of disagreement is not in the theoretical model – whether organization is shaped by power or efficiency – but in the substantive and empirical assessment of whether a particular organizational solution at a particular time does or does not have efficiency and fairness properties. For example, it has been harshly debated whether the substitution of putting-out relations for the integrated factory in the nineteenth century has led to a more efficient system of production or to the establishment of a dominance relationship and the redistribution of surplus to one party. By an irony of history, the more recent return to putting-out in many modern mass production industries has raised the same question: whether the "externalization" of production, rather than its internalization, has led to superior efficiency or has merely allowed large firms to avoid unionization costs and reappropriate larger surplus shares by squeezing subcontractors and putter-outers. Whatever the response may be, it must be empirical, because these are observational propositions. And whatever the response may

be, it would not test a power-based against an efficiency-based theory of organization, but merely establish to what extent, under what conditions, in what combinations and under what contractual provisions an integrated firm or a subcontracting system can be defended as a relatively superior mode of organization.

Lastly, part of the confusion on the issue of power and efficiency stems from a lack of perception of the difference between the *motives* leading to an action (its "teleological explanation") and the *properties* that this action has (its "functionalist explanation"). For example, for what motives, say, was the multidivisional structure first adopted? Has it been the chance result of a merger and acquisition process, the negotiated outcome of an internal bargaining process, the move through which top managers hoped to get rid of information overload, the plan of owners trying to reduce managerial opportunism? Independently of the motives leading to its adoption, it is possible to ask the completely different question of what advantages the divisional form turned out to have – in sociological language, what functions it performed in the wider economic system (Williamson 1986). On this latter ground – privileged in the book – a dialogue between economic and sociological perspectives is easier and more fruitful than a debate on the "real motives" that drive organizational choices.

Learning and natural selection

The issue of natural selection has recently received increasing attention in organization studies not only because of the growing influence of economic models in the field, but also because of the development of an influential research program in organizational sociology applying the concepts and tools of biological

15

models (birth and death rates, organization forms like "genes," competition among populations of organizations for scarce resources and Darwinian selection of the less adapted forms of organization) to study the evolution of populations of firms characterized by different organization forms (Hannan and Freeman 1977, 1989). In their first proposal of the new approach, Hannan and Freeman insightfully and understandably contrasted a change process based on natural selection with one based on learning, arguing that organization studies overrated the importance of the latter and neglected the former. In the first case "it is the environment which optimizes" (the firm chooses an organization form and the environment "chooses" a state which may be favorable or not), while in the second case individual firms change their internal structure to adapt to a changing environment. Initially, then, this was a methodological distinction between processes of variation and selection of organizational solutions occurring at different levels – within a single actor (a firm in the case) through competition among alternative solutions, or among actors through competition among subjects "incorporating" different solutions. This was the origin of the hypothesis of "structural inertia" at the level of individual subjects: in order to see the effects of natural selection, let us "assume" that organization structures and behaviors, once adopted, cannot be further adapted by an actor but are exposed to competition with other choices.

In subsequent developments and debates, however, these "assumptions," that were and should have remained methodological conventions for isolating the effects of natural selection from those of learning, became interpreted as substantive predictions about whether organizational structures and behaviors are in fact inert or not, as assumptions on the "nature" of organization in this respect, thereby causing another mistitled division in organization studies. In fact, not only do both individual learning and natural selection processes obviously exist in reality, but, more importantly, *they interplay rather than being mutually exclusive, so that one cannot be well understood without the other in social systems.* Natural selection needs variation in structures and behaviors, but is fairly indifferent toward the origins of these organizational variations (inertia, random trials, intelligent adaptation, etc.) (Campbell 1969; Aldrich 1979). Furthermore, if economic actors, firms in particular, were permanently marked by an organizational "blueprint" from their birth to their death (like biological individuals), the rate of change and evolution would be as slow as in the evolution of natural species. Such a strict biological analogy would lead one to underestimate the rate of change and the importance and effect of natural selection itself on social constructs. In fact, conversely, competition and the *possibility* of natural selection are fundamental incentives for learning and adaptation, precisely because they are a "credible threat" but not a certain sanction. This is the way in which both learning and selection will be taken into account in this book.

Part I

The Actor

....

The Actor

Introduction to Part I

A Definition of the Actor

• •

A theory of the organization of economic action calls for a model of how human beings are believed to behave in economic actions. In fact, the concept of *actor* is widely used in organization. But why do we speak of actors and not more simply of individuals – of persons? There is a reason, and it relates to a basic methodological aspect of a discipline – the elementary unit of analysis.

Economics is very clear in this regard. The elementary unit of analysis is the individual. Individuals are in fact the legitimate owners of interests and rights. These are also deemed to be the not further divisible units in which preferences and subjective utilities are formed. It is the principle of methodological individualism: every socio-economic formation that is more complex than the individual must be explained and justified starting from individuals who are "free" to order alternatives and "states of the world" according to preference, on the basis of the consequences for their own interests (Schumpeter 1942; Arrow 1951).

From sociology there have arisen methodological conceptions that are opposed to methodological individualism. In a famous essay, Wrong (1961) contrasted the "undersocialized" view of actors in economics with an "oversocialized" conception prevailing in sociological studies: individuals are not free to act, their actions are in large measure determined by the social environment in which they find themselves, by groups (more or less large), by social norms and inherited culture, and by resource constraints. To that extent, the sociology of organization has often assumed aggregated units of analysis (the family, the firm, and the national society).

Psychological accounts of behavior, including economic behavior, usually interested in the most micro and individual level of analysis, have often found it necessary to introduce an infra-individual notion of self (Elster 1985). Contradictory beliefs and conflicting desires need not be considered as irrational as they may stem from the different, equally legitimate interests of the same physical person as projected through time, or across different contexts, or at different hierarchical levels of cognition (for example, the immediately sensible and the more immaterial and constructed, the agent and the controller).

Organizational analysis has been characterized by the assumption of a unit of analysis that is (1) variable according to the scope of the study and (2) often at the "meso" level (greater than the individual but less than the system analyzed – Tosi 1992; Grandori 1995). A great number of organization theorists is in fact reluctant to adopt monolithic conceptions of systems composed of many people, sensitive to the problem of the potential differentiation of interests, and inclined to concede that people have the capability for choice and strategic behavior. On the other hand, organization theorists have a distinct awareness of the limits of cognition and individual rationality, of influence processes in small groups, and of the homogenization of perceptions and judgments produced from having access to the same information. To that extent, organization theory usually accepts the idea that the interpretation of one's own interest and the formation of preferences on the part of individuals happens often, even if not always, in groups. For example, for many analytical purposes, a group of workers employed in the same firm and in the same position in the productive process and in the organization structure can be considered to be an actor, characterized by homogenous perceptions, interests, and preferences. Groups of decision-makers responsible for different firm functions (production, marketing, and research, etc.) can be seen as single actors participating in an inter-functional project.

What matters for defining a unit of analysis, then, are analytical purposes. Depending on what problem is studied, some distinctions may become negligible – for example, intra-individual or small group differentiations if interfirm alliances are studied: if the formation of a joint venture is studied, firms can be defined and modeled as actors. Therefore in this text we define an actor as *a social entity in which no problem of inter-personal comparison of utility and of information transmission is considered to be relevant in relation to the problem being examined.* For example, the actors will typically be individuals when we are dealing with motivations and incentives or of job design; the actors will typically be interest groups or organization units when we are dealing with the analysis and design of the macrostructure of the firm; and the actors will typically be firms when we are dealing with networks of firms.

Chapter 1 is dedicated to developing a model of actor, focusing on its "endowment" of knowledge and interests. Chapter 2 presents a process model of decision and motivation, integrating the different "models of rationality" in a multiple rationality model.

If we look in more detail at the box of the configuration of actor in Figure I.1, we obtain Figure I.2, summarizing the structural and processual elements relevant for understanding the economic behavior of actors.

RESOURCES

• Knowledge and competences
• Self-efficacy judgments

PREFERENCES

• Interests and needs
• Probability and expectancy judgments

DECISION AND MOTIVATION PROCESSES

• Expected value maximization
• Satisfaction of acceptability levels
• Replication of appropriate actions

Figure I.2 Elements of the configuration of actors

Chapter 1

Knowledge and Preference

· ·

Two main structural features of actors can explain economic behavior – in so far as it depends on actors: what they know and are capable of doing (knowledge and competence) and what they want (their preferences and interests). These two elements substantiate the *identity* of an actor – the response to the questions: Who am I? What can I do? What do I wish to do? – whether the actor is individual or collective. In this perspective, an entity can be treated as an actor if it perceives itself as, or acts as if it were, on a certain matter, a unit of preference and knowledge.[1] Figure 1.1 outlines the conceptual structure of the chapter.

THE ECONOMIC ACTOR AND THE STRUCTURE OF KNOWLEDGE

Data, information, and knowledge

The "material" which is transformed in a decision-making process consists of information. This is the basic element that constitutes all the decision components that will be described. For example, in a decision-making process concerning the purchase of a car, all the following observations are information: the fact that the car we currently own no longer works well, the data relative to the performance of alternative vehicles, prices,

the image of the car with respect to the image we have of ourselves, the level of aspiration concerning the type of car desired, and the experience and the evaluations formulated on the performance of that car once acquired.

First, there is a distinction to be made between the notions of "information" and that of "data." Data (news, facts, numbers, reports, etc.) must be perceived by a subject, interpreted, and stored in relation to others in order to become information. Second, different bits of information should be put in relation to one another in order to guide choice and learning: this is the network of relationships between cognitions that constitutes the "knowledge" of the subject. As Bateson (1972) evocatively illustrates: "Those of you who believe to see me, raise their hand. I see a lot of hands raised . . . I deduce that folly likes to stay in company. Naturally you do not 'really' see me: what you 'see' is a bunch of information about me, that you synthesize into a visual image of me. You construct that image."

Types of knowledge and competence

On the basis of contributions to the theory of knowledge in various fields (Simon 1960, 1990; Kuhn 1962; Polanyi 1967; Nelson and Winter 1982; Bandura 1986; Grant 1996),

KNOWLEDGE AND COMPETENCE   **PREFERENCE**

<u>DIMENSIONS AND TYPES</u>

- Complexity   - Clarity and precision
- Generative potential   - Difficulty, ambitiousness

   - Generality:

  – Paradigmatic   – Values and needs
  – Procedural   – Motives and interests
  – Substantive-declarative   – Goals and objectives

<u>LEARNING AND IMPROVEMENT</u>

- Framing problems
- Generating alternatives and consequences
- Assessing probabilities
- Learning from experience

<u>CONSEQUENCES</u>

- Communication and decision premises

Figure 1.1 Knowledge and preference

knowledge relevant for economic action can be represented along some dimensions with important organizational implications. In this chapter we consider those dimensions that qualify the type of knowledge used by an actor in relation to an economic world: (1) the hierarchical organization of knowledge and competence; (2) the extent to which actors are aware and can transfer these resources (tacitness); (3) the quantitative and qualitative characteristics of information which make knowledge more or less *complex* and more or less *incomplete*, thereby generating a state of uncertainty in the subject; (4) the *combinative and generative potential* of knowledge and competence with respect to activities.

Those dimensions of knowledge and competence that characterize the *relations* among actors (in particular as deriving from the division of labor, as specialization and specificity) will be considered in the opening and founding chapter of Part III (Chapter 8), after having analyzed the problem of inter-

dependence and coordination between multiple actors (Part II).

In addition, here the focus is on actors as subjects endowed with knowledge and competence resources. In Chapter 8, the relation between actors and the resources they "possess" – distinguished in human resources (human knowledge and competence) and technical resources (machine-embodied knowledge and competence) – will be taken as problematic, as a relation that can be organized in various ways, depending, among other things, on the nature of knowledge as described below.

THE HIERARCHICAL STRUCTURE OF KNOWLEDGE

"Paradigmatic" and "critical" knowledge

A first and framing component of actors' knowledge consists of underlying concepts and theories that enable them to make sense of observed phenomena, hypothesize correlations among phenomena, and define economic problems; and of cognitive schemes which direct their attention, defining categories of subjects and objects and evaluating them positively or negatively.

Examples of basic assumptions about economic behavior are: Is the economic environment an external given, or can it be modified? Is work a costly activity or is it beneficial for the person who does it? Are other economic actors potential competitors or potential partners? (Schein 1985). Why is this type of knowledge present? Does it have any positive property? What are its organizational consequences? What are its limits?

Logicians and cognitive scientists have stressed the technical impossibility or the disproportionate cost of insisting on directly and knowingly checking all information and options on which human beings in general, and economic actors in particular, base their own conduct. It is sensible to trust teachers, to rely on past experience, to accept good "rules of thumb." It would be neither convenient nor feasible to start from scratch each time, rechecking all the information and assumptions on which inherited knowledge is based; and if it were attempted, it would entail enormous risks of error and inferior performance with respect to other actors (Bandura 1986). On this basis, a process of natural selection could even be expected to occur, in which unreceptive subjects would be eliminated in economic action while the number of "docile" ones in the population would increase (Simon 1990). In this way, a "species" of economic actors possessing the trait of "docility," or a capacity to accept a cumulated knowledge base, would even be privileged in the competition for survival.

However, each of us, as human beings, economic actors, and "informal scientists" in everyday life, has come up against the very difficult problem of drawing a boundary between the knowledge we are willing to accept as non-problematic, and the knowledge we wish to scrutinize critically and subject to conscious learning processes. Not by chance is this also a core dilemma in science (Kuhn 1962; Lakatos 1970). Indeed, the dilemma is typical of all processes involving knowledge acquisition and learning. On this basis, the nature and dynamics of economic and organizational knowledge can be and have been assimilated to the much more extensively studied nature of scientific knowledge: *a "core" of knowledge "assumed" to be outside discussion – called here "paradigmatic"*[2] – surrounded by a "belt" of hypotheses which is subject to critical examination (Argyris and Schön 1978; Duncan and Weiss 1978; Weick 1979b).

This schematization of knowledge can help to predict which economic actions will be more "inert" and which are more adaptive: economic actions that come into being as a result of "paradigmatic" knowledge will show a high level of inertia and will be more subject to natural selection processes than learning processes. Moreover, the "platform" of an actor's paradigmatic knowledge helps to predict the learning trajectories that can be followed by starting from that basis, or by working within that frame. An illustration of the dependence of learning paths and solutions found on paradigmatic and framing knowledge is given here in Box 1.1.

Beyond predicting and understanding behaviors, if knowledge is so structured, a *knowledge engineering* problem can be posed: Is there an "efficient boundary" of paradigmatic knowledge? How wide a set of shared and taken-for-granted beliefs should there be? Consider that this component of economic knowledge is scarcely modifiable

Box 1.1
Physicians, generals, and
videotapes

How can the knowledge of a particular battle tactic help us to solve a medical problem? Gick and Holyoak conducted important experiments on the effectiveness of transferring knowledge and models to solve new problems. The following is a well-known experiment: suppose that you are a doctor and you are dealing with a patient who has been diagnosed with stomach cancer. It is impossible to operate; however, there is a kind of radiation that can destroy the tumor if administered at high intensity. Unfortunately the high intensity of the radiation would at the same time destroy the good organs and tissues affected by the radiation; at a lower intensity, good tissues would not be damaged but the radiation would not be enough to cure the patient. How do you cure the patient without damaging the good organs and tissues?

In their experiment, Gick and Holyoak posed this problem to groups of subjects. In order to provide these groups with source models, they were told different versions of a military incident. A general wants to capture a fort centrally located in a region. There are several roads that lead to the fort but they are all mined, so although small groups could go through with few risks, a larger contingent would certainly cause the mines to explode. However, the general needs all his troops in order to launch the winning attack against the fort. The different versions of the story offer different conclusions. In one version, for example, the general discovers an unguarded road that leads to the fort and sends all his troops along that route. In another version, the general divides his troops into several small groups and sends them simultaneously along all the routes so that they finally meet at the fort.

The subjects in the experiment turned out to be particularly sensitive to the source model that was presented to them in the form of a military incident. For example, about 75 percent of those who heard the version of the story where the general divides his troops came up with the correct solution to the medical problem – apply low-intensity radiation to the stomach from several directions, so as to pass only a limited amount of radiation through each healthy organ. On the other hand, only 10 percent of those people who were not told about the source model came up with the correct solution. It is interesting to note that all those who were presented with various versions of the story tended to develop different solutions. For example, those who read the version of the "unattended route" tended to suggest solutions based on the identification of an open passage – i.e. the esophagus – through which the high-intensity radiation could be given.

The Gick and Holyoak experiment enables us to understand the structure of competence transfer, as well as giving us a language to describe and analyze it. We can use these initial tools to reconstruct a richer and more complex example that might be faced by firms on a daily basis. The case of the development of the market for videotapes has gained a lot of attention, because of the disparity of competitive results among those firms that had first invested in product research, and the others that came into the market as technological followers. The video cassette recorder (VCR) case can be interpreted as a parable on the advantages of arriving late, and on the risks faced by technological pioneers. However, in light of the concept of knowledge transfer, the case can be interpreted in a very different way.

> The two largest groups of firms that have created the VCR market highlight two different source models concerning innovation processes which led these organizations to focus their efforts very differently. On the one hand, because of their own previous experience in radio and television broadcasting, the first VCR pioneers (RCA and Ampex) initially concentrated their efforts on high-performance and high-cost recording tools aimed primarily at the market for technical instruments for television broadcasting. Later, however, they found themselves unable to reconvert such technologies to products for the large consumer market (primarily owing to manufacturing innovation problems.) On the other hand, the first followers in the development process (JVC, Sony, Matsushita) focused their efforts on developing a product aimed at the mass consumer market. As a result of these different objectives (reflecting the different routines, competences, and experiences of the firms), RCA and Ampex concentrated their efforts on sporadic research on important technological breakthroughs. JVC, Sony, and Matsushita, instead, continuously focused the process on developing a product that could be produced cheaply and on market research, owing to their experience as manufacturers of mass-produced electronics. As a result of these different technological strategies, RCA and Ampex found themselves excluded from the "window of opportunity" when it was effectively open during the second half of 1970.
>
> The VCR case illustrates the sensitivity of strategic decisions of firms on their competences and accumulated experience (Prahalad and Hamler 1990.) Like the experimental subjects of Gick and Holyoak, firms have been exposed to different source models and have thus developed different representations of the problem to be solved and different behavioral strategies. The future of firms largely depends on their ability to use their own past intelligently.
>
> *Source*: Warglien (1990).

because it is learned in an uncritical and unconscious way, or because it is believed to be "self-evident" and "outside discussion," or because it is made unmodifiable by convention. It will change very slowly or, rarely, through difficult "revolutions." Hence, *there is a trade-off between the informational efficiencies it brings about and the inertia it generates.* On one side, an actor should be able to exploit a basis of learned lessons and to act without verifying all assumptions on which action is based; on the other side, it should be able to question those assumptions and to explore radically new hypotheses of action, at least from time to time, for generating innovations (March 1992). Learning processes and organizational solutions can be shaped so as

to achieve these capabilities. This issue is addressed in the next section on decision and learning processes, as well as in the second and third part of the book on coordination mechanisms and organization forms.

"Substantive" and "procedural" knowledge

Another distinction contributing to the hierarchical structuring of knowledge is that between "substantive" and "procedural" knowledge. "Substantive" knowledge consists of substantive propositions about what is observed and what to do, while "procedural" knowledge consists of rules on how to observe and how to find out what to do (Simon 1976; Anderson 1983). Hence procedural knowledge is a "higher order" set of "mental programs" which governs the more operative notions of substantive knowledge.[3] For example, to possess knowledge about electronics and mechanics does not make an expert electromechanical technician; or to know that substituting a certain component of a broken machine usually fixes it is different from knowing how to search for other alternatives if the machine does not start again. The relative incidence of substantive or procedural knowledge in the endowment of a subject, therefore, is a determinant of the degree of discretion and expertise of the actor.

"Tacit" and "explicit" knowledge

People know more, and are able to do more, than they can explain. This component of knowledge is defined as the "tacit" knowledge of an actor (Polanyi 1972). The notion of tacit knowledge does not point at those components of know-how that have *not yet* been analyzed and made explicit, but could be codified without loss of information. For example, in the transformation of wood, skilled workers may apply sequences and procedures which have been learned through time and never been declared in an explicit procedure. However, suppose that the combinations of pace, motion, materials, tools, and remedies for problems encountered could be observed or reconstructed by the master worker so as to be communicated to others. In this case, the difference would be between unexpressed/informal knowledge and codified knowledge, and the organizational issue would be simply whether it pays off to structure information (for example, to allow production on a larger scale). By contrast, *knowledge is tacit if it is intrinsically difficult to identify which information and procedures* *are applied in successful processes.* Art, sport, and research and development are examples of activities largely based on tacit knowledge. An example of tacit economic knowledge is that used by a master artisan, as illustrated in Box 1.2.

The presence of tacit knowledge in many economic activities has far-reaching consequencies for their organization (illustrated in Parts III and IV). Knowledge of this type can be incorporated in human resources, in technical instruments, or in the organizational routines of a collective actor as a firm. By definition, however, it is difficult to diffuse or transfer it without common practice and reciprocal observation; therefore, economic action and interaction, where tacit knowledge is involved, cannot be effectively organized by mechanisms that do not allow this type of information exchange or learning.

Competences

The notion of competence further contributes to an understanding of the distinction between tacit and explicit knowledge, and the hierarchical organization of actor's resources that are relevant for organizing. The concept of competence is used in economic and organizational analyses as a wider construct, *including the notion of knowledge as well as those of skills and capabilities: a component of expertise that is "embodied"* in the whole body of the actor – the actor's force, senses, equilibrium, responsiveness – and not only in the actor's brain. Although the terms just used are typical of physical persons, it is common now to speak of "a firm's competences," precisely indicating not only its knowledge base, but also those capabilities that are embodied in its people, organization, and technologies (Richardson 1972).

Different types of competence can be

Box 1.2
The potter

Imagine observing a potter at work. On the shelves we can admire vases of various colors and shapes. To produce these pieces, the potter's job consists of various steps: s/he works the clay with the hands in order to obtain a lump, making sure that it is of the right consistency and has the appropriate degree of moisture; s/he then works the clay on the wheel to the desired shape, using the hands to correct small imperfections; in order to create spouts and handles, s/he uses special spatulas and tools; s/he then puts the vase into the oven for the first firing, taking care that the temperature is set correctly and that the vase is at the proper distance from the fire. If necessary, s/he fires the vase a second time. S/he then proceeds to decorate the vase, picking and choosing various colors. The potter evaluates the results obtained during each step of the work; if the piece is not satisfactory in terms of quality or shape, it is discarded. We label the potter as having a practical knowledge which allows him/her to "feel" the quality of the material that s/he uses, the consistency of the mixture of clay, the appropriateness of a decoration, and the effects that colors have on the clay. S/he knows that for different kinds of products and shapes, different kinds of clay are necessary, or alternatively that the mixture may change. The potter has a varied portfolio of models to choose from which can, however, be adapted to various needs upon request. When s/he works at the wheel, s/he knows what the pressure of his/her hands should be in shaping a piece and how to allow, with hands and fingers, for any possible imperfection; s/he also knows how best to synchronize and coordinate the various steps in such a way as to make the most efficient use of time. S/he is able to achieve the goal of producing a good piece based on certain design criteria, the characteristics of the material used, and the kinds of tools utilized. As in the case of the ski-instructor (see Box 1.3), the potter is an example of someone perfectly in synchronization with a continuous cycle of actions and steps, in which the material, the tools, the hand movements, the knowledge, and the actions constitute a single, consistent system.

Source: Lanzara (1992).

defined according to the extent and depth at which they are incorporated in actors.

Spencer and Spencer (1993) propose the image of an iceberg or of Chinese boxes to represent the idea that, in addition to visible layers, competence has "sunk" layers that are very difficult to distinguish from the identity of actors themselves and difficult to change. The traits and talents with which a person is gifted, the person's physical and cultural heritage, and personality, constitute the core, or deepest layer, of human competences; the knowledge and energy incorporated in technical assets can be seen as a complementary component of the "core competences" of a firm (Prahalad and Hamler 1990).

An intermediate component is seen as constituted by *skills or capabilities*. This layer of competence is seen not only as a set of resources but also as operating knowledge capable of dictating actions in response to the circumstances encountered, a set of "if–then" rules that connects repertories of possible actions to types of problems and conditions (Nelson and Winter 1982). This layer of competences then parallels (and includes) that of procedural knowledge. For example, a person who is very knowledgeable in a given subject area may be very competent in terms of notions, but may not necessarily have the capability to act well on that knowledge. It is important that *competence as a stock of resources be coupled with application routines or action programs*. The "database" made up of substantive knowledge should be made operational by a procedural, action-oriented component. Habitualization and interioriza-tion should transform calculated action into automatic action. Competence in sports is often cited as an example of this dynamic and procedural component of competence, as shown in Box 1.3.

The most explicit, codified, and manageable layer of competence is identified with explicit knowledge and codifiable expertise. For example, the ensemble of technical notions and symptom-diagnosis relations employed by a financial analyst or a physician to solve standard problems of investment or health care may be examples of this layer of codifiable competence, based on explicit knowledge.

Box 1.3
The ski-instructor

By observing a ski-instructor descending a slope we can evaluate – without hesita-tion – the instructor's level of ability, and thus we know that we are not dealing with an amateur. We appreciate the correctness of the instructor's position, the harmony and the fluidity of the movements, the smoothness with which the turns are coordinated, and the way the instructor controls and maneuvers skis and poles according to the characteristics and the difficulty of the slope (steepness, curves, etc.) We also notice the expert skier's ability to correct any mistakes or react to difficult moments. What impresses us is the elegance and the spontaneous way in which such experts ski, as well as their lightness, which makes it all seem effortless. The skier's practical knowledge – what is referred to as "knowing how to ski" – is in part codified within the sensory-motor skills, in such a way that the skier's muscle behavior responds instantly and almost automatically to the signs and the characteristics of the slope. Thus, one could almost say that the skier's behavior functionally "complements" the technical characteristics of the tools employed (skis, poles, booths) and the morphological peculiarities of the slope. However, the skier's competence also lies in the ability to anticipate what comes next, such as identifying what the toughest sections of the slope are, evaluating snow conditions, and choosing the easiest and least dangerous route to descend the hill. It is obvious that the skier who "really knows how to ski" must possess an explicit knowledge about a physical activity called "skiing," but the cognitive activity that distinguishes the competence of the skier is directed at the production of the skill during the action itself.

Source: Lanzara (1993).

Individual and collective competence and knowledge

The example of sport competence is also useful in highlighting how competences are more closely incorporated in actors and have a larger tacit component with respect to knowledge: therefore they are less easily modified and, in order to be transferred, may require more intense reciprocal interaction and observation between various subjects. However, it would be wrong to conclude that competence (let alone knowledge) is an exclusive or typical patrimony of the individual. On the contrary, if individual actors were to develop their competences only on the basis of direct experience, without taking advantage of the experience of others, learning processes would be extremely costly, slow, and boring. In addition to "inherited" knowledge and competence, many capabilities develop because the experience of other actors believed to be comparable is observed and these experiences are imitated or re-elaborated (Bandura 1986). This process of "social cognition" is fundamental in explaining the efficient development of sophisticated individual capabilities, which would be somewhat improbable without the support of collective capabilities, understood as reciprocal learning networks.

Second, not all types of competences require the same degree of interaction to be effectively transferred. For example, skiing capabilities can be taught fairly smoothly and even transferred on a competence market. This is not true for other competences that, however tacit or explicit, are nonetheless very personal, particular, and applicable only in a single environment – very "specific" to a use or a user (Williamson 1981a; Chapter 8).

Combinative and generative potential

Following a conceptual, primogenital path, the first important instance where the economic actor was modeled as a set of resources – and particularly of competences – is usually recognized in the work of Edith Penrose (1959). Looking for answers to classic economic questions on the nature of the firm and the reason for, the direction of, and the potential for its growth, Penrose identified a powerful explanatory factor in the capacity of both technical and human resources to deliver a wide range of potential services, and, in particular, a range that is often wider than the sum of their actual uses.

> Strictly speaking, it is never the resources in and of themselves that constitute the input of productive processes, but only the services that the resources can deliver. . . . The resources consist in a set of potential services and can, in large part, be defined independently of their use, in contrast to the services themselves that imply an activity or function. As we shall see, the source of the uniqueness of every firm lies, in large part, in this distinction.
>
> (Penrose 1959: 25)

At the individual actor level, its set of talents and competences is seen as capital that can be put to different uses, and hence as an input to the definition of new tasks and services rather than a consequence of task requirements (a resource-driven approach). At the level of collective actors, it is the combination of the uses that resources are put to that becomes of prime importance, since the variety of the possible combinations makes collective competence "distinctive," unique, and imitated only with difficulty to a much greater degree than individual competence, and, from an economic point of view, creates a possible additional source of uniqueness and "competitive advantage" (Penrose 1959; Barney 1990).

The very fact that competences are not easily divisible from the actors possessing them contributes to creating surpluses of competences with respect to the particular uses for which the resource was acquired. Competences, and more precisely the possible combinations and recombinations of competences, are a formidable base of value creation and task design (Chapter 8). Let us call this dimension *a competence "generative potential"* – *applicable to both human and technical resources.*

Complexity and incompleteness

Knowledge may often be in short supply – with respect to what would be necessary for complete coverage of all the relevant information for solving problems. Problems obviously can be more or less complex. As they grow larger – including many elements and relations among them – the knowledge required for solving them becomes *"computationally complex,"* as in the prototypical example of the game of chess. As problems include difficulties in diagnosing what is observed, what actions cause what results, or even what is a positive or negative consquence, the knowledge required for solving them becomes *"epistemically complex"* – as in the prototypical example of the game of scientific discovery. This growth in knowledge complexity at a certain point will succumb to incompleteness, given the existence of limits to human rationality. The *lack of knowledge* about some elements in decision-making gives rise to a state of *uncertainty. This contingency is of core importance for understanding and designing which decision process to follow.*

For example, Thompson and Tuden (1959) in a seminal contribution hypothesized that different decision strategies are feasible contingent to the initial state of knowledge of two main decision inputs: objectives and cause–effect relationships. Developing this approach further, *knowledge relevant for decision-making* can be characterized as a system of conjectures regarding at least the following four fundamental classes of decision inputs:

- *objectives* (hypotheses about what is desired and perceived to be obtainable)
- *cause–effect relationships* (hypotheses about which actions or alternatives are related to which desired results)
- *probability judgments* on the likelihood of consequences
- *observational judgments* (estimates and measures about what events and "data" are observed).

The next section will examine how knowledge of these elements can be improved. The next chapter on decision and motivation processes addresses the problem of what decision strategy is applicable if uncertainty on some or all the elements cannot be further reduced.

IMPROVING JUDGMENT UNDER UNCERTAINTY

The processes of perception and judgment on the basis of which decisional inputs are defined are subjective and fallible. This consideration would, however, have few practical consequences if one were not able to identify some of the systematic weaknesses of human judgments and how to overcome them. A vast area of research in cognitive psychology has generated a mass of reliable and interesting results in this respect, especially on individual and group decision-making (Carroll and Payne 1976; Nisbett and Ross 1980; Einhorn and Hogarth 1981; Kahneman *et al.* 1982; Bandura 1986).

On the basis of these researches, it is

possible to make a sort of inventory of the principal systematic distortions of human judgment (obviously a limited inventory, not an exhaustive or absolute one). The term "biases" is used because it refers to undesired effects, optical illusions, and unconscious errors that, if only they were "seen" by decision-makers, would be willingly corrected.

These corrections cannot and should not be interpreted as the restoration of an impossible absolute or global rationality. They can and should be seen as a guide to an improved use of our inescapably fallible and bounded rationality, to the capacity for discerning between "good" and "bad" heuristics as a function of the decision situation, to the development of capabilities useful in making judgments under uncertainty, and to improving the quality of decision inputs.

"Heuristics"

The term "heuristics" refers to any mental rule or procedure capable of generating or finding something that is being sought. In other words, it is a method of search, which may be more or less well grounded in experience, more or less structured, and more or less "substantive" (prescribing an action) or "procedural" (prescribing a method), more or less "tacit" or "explicit." For example, all of the following rules indicating how to act or how to process information are heuristics: "Take an umbrella if you go out when it is cloudy," or "Hit the tennis ball at the highest point of the parabola after it bounces" (Russo and Schoemaker 1989); when searching, apply the principle of scanning "breadth first" and go "in depth" next (Newell and Simon 1976); "Look where information is readily available" (Tversky and Kahneman 1974); "Lower expectations if it is difficult to

find an alternative that is satisfactory" (Simon 1955a); "Infer that A is the cause of B, if B is always observed after having observed A" (Nisbett and Ross 1980).

The use of heuristics is necessary in all problems where search is important. Still, there are important differences among heuristics. The difference between an expert and efficient decision-maker and a novice in a field depends to a large extent on the variety of heuristics they possess, on their degree of general validity, and on the awareness of possible distortions (Simon 1987, 1977; Kahneman, *et al.* 1982).

In this section we will present a selection of main distortions arising from the use of heuristics related to four main decision inputs and to their formulation processes:

- the definition of problems
- the search for information and alternatives
- the calibration of probability judgments
- the making of inferences based on observed experience.

Defining problems and interpreting observations: "framing" and "cognitive distance"

Many, if not all, decision processes begin with problems. However, no problem really exists in nature. It is always the fruit of a mental model, a series of perceptions and interpretations by an actor. For example, to state that "there are investment opportunites to be found in new technologies" defines a problem and a possible course of action, but implies several judgments and mental operations: allocating attention to technological innovations rather than to other aspects of reality; explicitly or implicitly defining desirability criteria, i.e. parameters for evaluating outcomes; diagnosing that the current state of affairs is not satisfactory or could be improved, i.e. that there are "performance gaps" (Simon 1947, 1955a; March and Simon 1958).

Merton (1949) said that any way of seeing is also a way of not seeing. Defining problems is not only subjective but also selective in that it implies considering certain aspects of reality and ignoring others, stating what is "in" the problem and what is "outside" the problem. Real phenomena have infinite aspects and no decision-maker could consider them all. There is a considerable difference, however, between a decision-maker who considers one or a few aspects of a problem and one who considers many (Payne 1976), as illustrated by the study described in Box 1.4.

"Structured" and "unstructured" problems

The fact that the definition of a problem always implies building a model of the reality (Simon 1955a) does not imply that the nature of reality has no influence whatsoever on the complexity of the problem. The analogy between problem-solving in economic action and in scientific discovery (Simon *et al.* 1981) has shed light on the reasons why, in some areas, problems are typically "well structured" (well defined, with clear boundaries, a finite number of potential alternatives and a single best solution), while in other areas they are "ill structured" (Simon 1973). For example, physics problems lend themselves to a higher degree of structuring, on average, than those in medicine or sociology. Therefore, it is not true that the wider the definition of problems, the better – nor conversely. The ability to choose the least number of aspects that, at the same time, includes the largest number of relevant factors for an effective

---

Box 1.4
Framing investment decisions
in information technology

In a research project about the decision processes related to the purchase and introduction of automated information systems, the decision-makers in various firms were found to define the problem in at least three ways, depending on the breadth of their perspective. For some, the problem concerned investing in technologies (equipment, software, and data elaboration techniques); for others, it included the issue of which informational sub-systems within the firm could use computerized information system services (order management, personnel management, general accounting, etc.) and how they could use those services. In the broadest formulation of the problem, issues related to information technology investments were considered to be problems connected to the evolution of the information systems of the firm as a whole; they therefore had an impact not only on all of the firm's activities, but also on the decisions and motivation of the people. The capacity to define problems in a wide rather than a narrow way was found to be related to the level of actors' experience in the decision area; this was consistent with the theoretical proposition that people learn the consequences of the action and their own preferences (judgments of desirability) on the basis of experimentation.

Source: Research described in C. De Vecchi and A. Grandori (1983) *I processi decisionali d'imprese*, Milan: Giuffrè.

solution, is a fundamental cognitive capability (in scientific activity as well as in decision-making). There is a trade-off between effort and accuracy, and between completeness and manageability, in the definition and structuring of problems.

Beyond the awareness of these trade-offs, problem-formulation may be improved by the awareness of some fundamental biases that can influence it. Two classes of biases have shown to be particularly important in framing problems: *cognitive dissonance* and *prospect effects.*

Consider the image drawn in Figure 1.2. What do you see?

The lines that make up the drawing can be interpreted in two different ways. For example, a curve can be interpreted as a chin

Figure 1.2 Gestaltic figures

or a nose depending on how it is related to other elements in reconstructing the meaning of the whole image – that could be an old and a young woman simultaneously. Typically, after one interpretation has been adopted, it becomes difficult to see other possibilities. An explanation of this phenomenon is that our mind is geared or "programed" to eliminate inconsistencies, contradictions, and incoherent information, discarding or even not seeing those elements which do not fit or have no significance according to one's own scheme of interpretation. Cognitive psychologists have called it a tendency to reduce cognitive dissonance (Festinger 1957). The implication of this cognitive tendency for problem-formulation is that once a point of view, an interpretation of observed "data," has been accepted, the ability to see alternative interpretations is inhibited and this can lead to rigidity and conflicts.

Other important framing effects are generated by even more subtle shifts of meaning with respect to the choice of language and reference systems. A famous experiment designed to show these effects (Tversky and Kahneman 1981) is reported in Appendix 1. It should be played in a large enough group (such as a standard classroom); half of the participants solve the problem in Appendix 1.1A and the other half the problem in Appendix 1.1B.

On average, the choices made regarding the problem as formulated in the two ways are systematically different. In the 1.1A formulation, decision-makers tend to be risk prone: the majority select the uncertain alternative over the certain alternative, even though the expected value of the two alternatives is the same, in terms of expected saved lives. In the 1.1B formulation, decision-makers tend to be risk averse: the majority prefer the sure alternative over the uncertain alternative of equal-expected value. Nonetheless, if the two formulations of the problem are compared, one realizes that they have identical characteristics with respect to the number of lives saved or lost as a result of the two restructuring plans. Tversky and Kahneman attributed the systematic difference in choices to a "prospect" effect. Decision-makers assess consequences with respect to some reference point – for example, the current situation, a "neutral" outcome, the best or the worst that can happen to them. They can then perceive or express the consequences as losses or gains with respect to that point of reference. Adopting a "positive frame" (see consequences as possible gains) or a "negative frame" (see consequences as possible losses) has a significant impact on the choices made: for example, other things being equal, positive frames make people more flexible in accepting solutions, less demanding, and less innovative; while negative frames encourage one to take risks and to flee from current states of affairs.

Frames are frequently adopted unconsciously, or by chance, or people are simply not aware they may exist. It is not difficult to imagine the potential for biases and conflicts that this may entail. For example, part of the systematic conflict that exists between technical functions and units – such as manufacturing – and commercial functions – such as marketing – is due to the different mental schemes that have been formed as a result of working in different information environments: production plants and raw materials, customers, new techniques, or scientific discoveries; and to the resulting inability to see other aspects of the shared reality within the firm (March and Simon 1958; Lawrence and Lorsch 1967; Chapter 11). In economic negotiations, the framing of consequences in terms of potential "concessions" (losses) or as potential gains with respect to not reaching an agreement has a paramount impact on which agreement will be reached, and on whether it will be reached (Chapter 6).

Cognitive differentiation and distance

The establishment and consolidation of actor-specific frames favor the differentiation between cognitive endowments and styles. In other words, the systematic differences in the type of information that actors take into consideration and the way of interconnecting them become fixed in their minds as a sort of mental software.[4] The consolidation and relative inertia of frames give rise to significant, predictable, and relatively stable "cognitive differentiation" (Lawrence and Lorsch 1967) or "cognitive distance" (Nooteboom 1999) among actors. The diversity of cognitive frames is sustained at the individual and collective level in economic action by the separation between units (groups, departments, or entire firms) that perform activities of different informational nature, which, in turn, attract and reinforce cognitive personalities whose traits are consistent with the nature of the activities and information (Tosi 1992). The specialization of knowledge and tasks, and its advantages, sustains it. Cognitive differentiation in itself must therefore be considered physiological. However, some of its consequences are undesirable such as the rigidity of frames and the inability to see new aspects of reality; or the misunderstandings and conflicts among actors with different mental outlooks.[5]

Antidotes

Communication difficulties do not imply and should not lead to total incommunicability.

As among people who speak different languages, the difficulties diminish as reciprocal exposition and communication intensity increase (provided there are no underlying conflicts of interest). Indeed, the investment in communication channels or "intermediaries" among actors using different mental schemes and styles is traditionally considered to be a good antidote to interfunctional and interpersonal conflicts (Lewin 1948; Lawrence and Lorsch 1967) and has been recently recommended to sustain knowledge transfers between business units (Grant 1996) or different firms in alliances (Lutz 1999).

A second type of antidote is multiplying the number of frames available to a decision-maker (Russo and Schoemaker 1989). An "open mentality" can be acquired and formed, in this perspective, by broadening individual cognitions and using groups. Individuals can cultivate additional areas of interest that differ from their principal fields of action. They can reduce their degree of specialization and focalization on particular tasks and information. All this helps to reduce the undesirable effects of framing and of the differentiation between cognitive styles. However, it may be difficult for all this to occur at individual level; and, if it does, it may remove the desirable effects of specialization and focalization. As a result, multiple competences' group problem-solving, or the use of third parties with an intermediate orientation, is often a more effective antidote than individual poly-valence, especially in unstructured and important activities (Lawrence and Lorsch 1967; Chapter 11).

"Local knowledge"

Research is a costly and difficult process. Therefore, actors might deliberately choose to limit it, as will be illustrated in the next chapter. Here, instead, the unconscious and spontaneous tendency of mind to orient and restrict attention in certain directions will be considered.

Tversky and Kahneman (1974), in their most influential and seminal work on the subject, identified three basic heuristics which tend systematically to restrict and bias the type of information we tend to consider, by catching us in a "local knowledge" trap: "availability," "representativeness," and "anchoring."

Availability

Consider the experiment described in Box 1.5. This judgment can be said to be "under uncertainty" because subjects do not usually possess all the relevant information for expressing an opinion. The usual process for generating information is then to generate examples and try to recall instances of the phenomenon. As a result, the judgment on which factor is more important turns out to be influenced (and biased) by the ease of retrieval of information. What are the characteristics of easily retrievable information? Not only the frequency with which one is exposed to it, but also its salience: its familiarity, vividness, and cognitive and emotional intensity.

In the example in Box 1.5, the vividness of information derived from journalistic sources and its frequency – biased in favor of impressive deaths – systematically bias respondents' judgments on the relative importance of different causes of death. The availability heuristics can therefore have important consequences on economic action. Insurance may or may not be bought depending on the salience of risks. Investments may or may not be made depending on how close and familiar the cases of failure and success are; staff

---

Box 1.5
An experiment on availability

Here are some possible causes of death, listed in sets:

Set 1	Lung cancer	vs	Car accidents
Set 2	Emphysema	vs	Murder
Set 3	Tuberculosis	vs	Fires

For each set, please select the item that it is believed will cause the most deaths in a year's time. The average percentages of the answers by the people interviewed by Russo and Schoemaker are shown in Appendix 1.2.

Source: Experiment described in Russo and Schoemaker (1989).

---

promotions may favor more visible rather than better performers; project costs and times are usually underestimated because it is more difficult to imagine what can go wrong rather than a sequence of normal activities.

Representativeness

Now try the question posed in the problem described in Box 1.6, before continuing with reading the rest of the chapter. Typically, in answering this question, people vastly over-estimate the probability that Stefano is a librarian. Why?

On the basis of self-reports on mental operations by subjects, it appears that what governs assignments to categories is, above all, a judgment on the similarity between the qualitative description of the individual and the stereotype of that category, i.e. on how "representative" the individual case is of the category. Background information, such as the incidence of occupational categories in the population, or what is the presence of shy and introverted people in any profession, is scarcely taken into consideration, if at all (Tversky and Kahneman 1974).

More generally, the effects of chance and stochastic phenonema are poorly understood

and little considered by decision-makers. This leads to believing in predictions and estimates with unjustified confidence. For example, evaluations of the probability of success of a person in a job, made on the basis of the correspondence between candidate profiles and job descriptions, are vulnerable to a representativeness bias .

Anchoring

No estimate or judgment is possible without reference points. Nonetheless, depending on the type of reference point employed, rather diverse estimates and different actions are produced. They should therefore be used knowingly.

For example, submit the following two estimating tasks to two different groups of people. What is the estimated product of $1 \times 2 \times 3 \times 4 \times 5 \times 6 \times 7 \times 8$, in 5 seconds? And what is the estimated product of $8 \times 7 \times 6 \times 5 \times 4 \times 3 \times 2 \times 1$, in 5 seconds? Tversky and Kahneman (1974) report that the average estimate for the ascending sequence is 512, and for the descending sequence 2,250 (the correct answer is 40,320).

Another experiment, conducted by Russo and Schoemaker (1989), is described in Box

Box 1.6
An experiment on
representativeness

This is a description of a person made by someone who knows him best: "Stefano is very shy and reserved, always available but showing little interest in people and the world in general. He is submissive and has a need for order and structure; he is very detail-oriented."

Question: what would you say the probability is that Stefano is:

- a farmer   %
- a salesman   %
- a librarian   %
- a physician   %

(Time allotted to answer: 2 minutes.)

The sum of the four probabilities does not necessarily have to add up to 100.

Source: Experiment described in Tversky and Kahneman (1974).

Box 1.7
An anchoring experiment

Russo and Schoemaker (1989) asked about 100 managers the following question: What do you think the prime rate will be in 3 months? The average answer (this happened in 1983 when prime rate was around 11 percent) was 10.9 percent.

Later, they put the following two questions, in sequence, to another group of managers: Do you think that in a 3 month period the prime rate will be more or less than 8 percent? What do you think it will be? The goal was to verify if the first question, aimed at anchoring the managers to 8 percent, would have lowered the estimates compared to the ones expressed by the anchored group. The average response was 10.5 percent.

The following question was then posed to a third group: Do you think that in a 3 month period the prime rate will be more or less than 14 percent, and what will it be? The average estimate was 11.2 percent.

Source: Experiment described in Russo and Schoemaker (1989).

1.7. People frequently make estimates starting from a known initial value and adjust them in the direction that they believe to be correct. For example, what will sales amount to in the next budget period? It is reasonable to begin with current sales and "adjust" in the right direction (is there economic expansion or contraction?). Empirical research has shown, in general, that adjustment is not sufficient. If estimates are anchored, they tend to be systematically biased toward the anchor and not sensitive enough to the corrective factors that should have been taken into consideration. If estimates involve many related variables rather than just one, the effect is likely to be stronger. As Tversky and Kahneman note, anchoring contributes to explaining why people often badly underestimate, for example, the probability of failure of complex systems and actions – such as a nuclear plant, the human body, or the launch of a new product. In fact, people anchor their estimates to the failure probability of each single component, which may be low. If, however, the number of components is high, the estimate of the joint probability of failure is not sufficiently adjusted.

Antidotes

Many aspects of organizational systems and structures provide a response to these fundamental biases in judgments, and offer tools for improving the validity and reliability of the knowledge used in organizational decision-making. For example:

- The use of checklists on "factors to be considered" and *decision-support systems* is not a useless overhead invented by experts to squash "intuition." Intuitive decision-making in situations of uncertainty is subject to systematic error.
- *Explicit and codified personnel evaluation systems* are useful for reducing the above biases – and the unequities which are likely to go with them.
- "Zero-based budgeting" and other "zero-based" management techniques – "starting from zero" the analysis of activities and of resources needed – are corrections to the anchoring effect in the growth of activities and of the resources allocated to them, that in each period tend to be anchored to what was done in the previous period.
- When making important decisions it is useful to consider the apparently "unuseful"

and boring output of information system services on "base-rate" information, and on the probability distributions of the variables at hand.
- If adequately varied in their composition and free in their dynamics, the use of groups can reduce the local search trap, generating richer and more varied information.

Overconfidence and underconfidence

All the three heuristics described so far may intervene, and intermingle, when a judgment on one's own knowledge and competence is involved. This judgment is usually called a "confidence" judgment: assessing how much one knows with respect to what one does not know on a matter.

Try to make an estimate of the size of a variable that, under normal information conditions, implies a judgment under uncertainty: for example, try to estimate the unemployment rate or the percentage of women in important positions in a foreign country, or the time it takes to manufacture a car. In order to control the experiment, choose examples of variables on which statistics are available for subsequent control of the quality of estimates. Then, attempt to estimate the probability or confidence that the estimate made was correct, using one of the following two methods:

- set an interval in which the value of the variable should fall, and express the probability that the estimates made will fall within the interval
- alternatively, set a level of confidence to reach, say 80 percent, and then estimate how large a value interval should be in order that, in eight out of ten cases, the estimate will be correct.

Both statistics can be constructed either by the same person on many estimates, or by several persons on even a single estimate.

In order to control how well "calibrated" the probability estimates are, one can compare the subjective probabilities of being right, or the subjects' degree of confidence, with the observed frequency of correct responses. The usual outcome of these experiments is that the average subjective confidence in one's own judgment is far greater than the frequency of correct answers (Lichtenstein *et al.* 1982). For example, in an experiment that we conducted with MBA students, they were asked to put in order three management schools, in terms of the overall number of course participants on an annual basis. The average subjective probability of having given the right order was about 60 percent, whereas the correct ordering was actually produced by only four students out of 120. The reason for such a wide discrepency can be traced to a combination of distortions, arising from qualitative information about schools being more available than quantitative, considering image and fame as "representative" of size, regardless of structural factors, such as market structure (for example, the number of comparable schools in the national market) and the school strategy (for example, the breadth of the course portfolio).

Underconfidence and self-efficacy

Confidence judgments are inescapably involved in the application of an actor's knowledge and competence in order to reach certain performances. Possessing competence does not necessarily mean using it. An intermediate variable of great importance for explaining performance differences, which plays a role even before expected benefits are considered, is an actor's perception of his/ her own competence and of its expected link with performance ("self-efficacy" judgments – Bandura 1986). This perception may easily be uncalibrated. Experienced subjects are easily overconfident, because they assimilate new tasks to those in which they have already succeeded, or even develop a self-confidence that is independent from the task in hand; while the lack of experience and "noviceness" tends to produce underconfidence (Lichtenstein, *et al.* 1982; Bandura 1986).

Antidotes

The management of self-efficacy and the antidotes to uncalibrated confidence are a problem of sustaining and correcting learning processes. Different types of learning processes can contribute, depending on the possibility of direct experience and on the complexity of the task.

Direct experimentation

"Enactive attainments" – i.e. the direct experience of one's own success – "constitute the most influential source of information on effectiveness because they are based on authentic mastery experiences" (Bandura 1986: 399). In fact, it has been empirically shown that regular access to feedback on one's own performance is the most systematic factor in the calibration of probability and confidence judgments (Lichtenstein *et al.* 1982). Direct feedback is not, however, always so clear and objective as in the example of the long jump. In economic activity, the availability of feedback frequently depends on the potential and capacity of others – teachers, bosses, clients – to give it.

Vicarious learning

Actors adjust their own confidence judgments by observing how other actors who have comparable resources and competence succeed or fail. Observation and imitation are of course particularly important in activities that are new to the subject, or in activities where performance has few objective measurements and depends above all on comparison with others (Bandura 1986). However, learning through imitation requires similar and stable conditions, and is not likely to lead to discovering talents and competences of special quality and level.

Modeling

A more ambitious approach, more likely to enhance success chances and perceptions of chance in complex and new activities, involves the use of experiences for the construction of models of behavior correlated to success in the task, which can then be applied to the specific initial condition and starting competences available to the subject ("*modeling*"). This approach could be seen as an effort to construct causal explanations of performance in specific action fields. Box 1.8 describes an example of how to construct a model of the activities and behaviors that can lead to the completion of a challenging and complex task, and can help in building confidence.

Learning traps

As John Stuart Mill said: the logic of science is also the logic of economics and life. This thesis was more recently reinforced by similar opinions expressed by Karl Popper (1989), Herbert Simon (Simon *et al* 1981), and Karl Weick (1979b). To understand fully the difficulties of learning in economic and organ-

ized activities, however, some complications should be considered. While learning, economic actors pursue desired results. This can make learning from experience more difficult – for example, because there is interaction between the observer and the observed, or because actors face trade-offs between acquiring knowledge (on what actions are most fruitful for example) and short-term pay-offs. In this section, three fundamental types of obstacles typical to the learning processes in economic action will be illustrated.

The first and most important learning trap is generally valid for any process of research, while the other traps are more specific to economic learning. Consider the experiment described in Box 1.9.

The most frequent response by subjects in this experiment is to "test" series of numbers that conform or are deduced from the rule they have in mind. For example, if the rule is thought to be "a difference of two units," one would tend to try a series such as 10–12–14; or if the rule is thought to be a constant difference, one would try 10–15–20. The answer is always favorable, and no experiment is particularly informative. Confirming one's own hypothesis could go on forever. This would increase a psychological sense of confidence that the right rule has been found, whereas knowledge does not increase at all. For example, in Wason's experiment (1960), only 6 out of 29 participants had actually discovered the right rule the first time they thought they knew the answer. The most informative experiments are, on the contrary, "falsifying" experiments such as: supposing that the rule is "all numbers are even," try odd numbers; supposing that the law is that numbers should be ascending, try a descending series. The answers to these "falsifying experiments" are highly informative because, at least on structured tasks, they

Box 1.8
Tenure track modeling

Suppose you are the chairperson of an academic department and you want to help a new assistant professor to get tenure. Let us further assume that it is a publish-or-perish university and that the assistant professor is in the summer of her fourth year with a below-average, but not hopeless, record for scholarship. You sit down with her and go over her record. So far she has had two articles published in good journals, one in a mediocre journal, and has four papers under review. She also has six more projects in the pipeline, which can be submitted in the next year. The first task is to figure out what will be needed to make tenure. Let's say she will need about 10 papers, eight in good journals. Since tenure review will occur in two years, and since all projects do not work out, you would suggest that she has all six of the "in the pipeline" projects submitted by January of her last year (i.e. in the next 18 months.) This is to allow time to revise and resubmit before the September deadline. Furthermore, you advise that all "revise and resubmit" revisions on these and the "under review" manuscripts be done within 30 to 60 days. These are the goals. How do you get commitment? If the professor decides that she does not really want to be an academic in this institution, suggest that she look for work elsewhere. But if she does want to succeed, then the main issue is confidence-building. Express confidence based on the work to date. Suggest role models. Be supportive: ask her what you can do to help (for example, some extra assistants for data analysis; time off in the summer; reduced committee work). If previous rejections of papers have been demoralizing, suggest some alternative strategies (for example, reframe and submit to a different journal, combine two papers into one, etc.).

To insure careful tracking (feedback regarding progress), have her make a schedule indicating when each in-process manuscript will be submitted. Go over time-utilization issues (goal priorities) and strategies (for example, has she delegated as much of the busy work as possible? Is she going overboard on teaching? Is she working enough hours? Is she going to too many professional meetings? Is she spending too much time writing conference papers?).

To further help develop effective plans, have her consult with other junior and senior faculty members to see if they have any tips for her. Persuade her to let colleagues (expeditiously) review her papers before submission and also help to interpret letters from editors. Finally, tell her you want her to make it (if you do) and the reasons why.

Source: Locke (1996).

allow potential rules to be excluded or eliminated with certainty. (Wason's experiment is usually played with the coordinator applying a rule of "strictly ascending whole numbers.")

The indications of this experiment coincide with the single most important prescription of scientific research methodology which is taught to any professional researcher: no series of favorable cases can prove that a theory is true; there is more information in the confutation of hypotheses than there is in their confirmation; even though many hypotheses

> ### Box 1.9
> #### Wason's experiment
>
> Suppose that a pre-defined rule is used to create triples of numbers. Among all possible triples, some obey the rule and some don't.
>
> The following triple obeys the rule: 2, 4, 6.
>
> Suppose you are a scientist, or a person interested in studying that rule, and you are trying to understand what is the law that links the numbers.
>
> Based on triples you have created, you can ask the game leader if those triples obey the rule or not; you would get fair and honest answers.
>
> Continue to test triples until you have defined a rule about which you feel reasonably certain.
>
> *Source*: Experiment described in Wason (1960).

and conjectures are initially formulated by observing and recognizing empirical regularities, they can be improved or corroborated only by falsifying rival hypotheses, or parts of the initial hypothesis that are contradicted by the data and are substituted (Popper 1935; Hanson 1958; Simon 1977).

The tendency to search for confirmatory examples does not run the risk of being overestimated. For example, the fact that actors tend to judge the strength of a relationship between two variables, X and Y, based only on the frequency of favorable evidence is well documented (Einhorn and Hogarth, 1978). Decisions commonly involve hypotheses of this type. Consider any decision rule such as: if an alternative meets certain requirements, it is accepted; if not it is discarded, like rules used for hiring or promoting personnel, admitting students to schools, or granting credits. They are hypotheses that a relationship between (at least) two variables exists: if alternatives with sufficiently high values on an X property are accepted (people hired, credit granted), positive consequences will follow on certain result variables Y (for example, performance, credit repayment). For example, suppose that a new rule for promo-

tion to sales management positions is adopted in a firm. Assume that 80 percent of those promoted are successful because, for example, they meet budgeted targets. What conclusions could be drawn on the validity of the promotion procedure, i.e. on the hypothesis that high values of X (the positively evaluated candidate characteristics) are correlated with high levels of Y (performance measurements)? Actually, no conclusion. To draw conclusions about that hypothesis, it would be necessary to consider what the success and failure rates would have been for candidates promoted according to alternative rules (an alternative hypothesis) or even randomly selected (a null hypothesis).

As Einhorn and Hogarth observed, decision-makers tend not to consider the entire four-cell quadrant of information (X acceptable/not acceptable; Y successful/not successful) even when this information is available at low cost. In addition, in economic activity, this full experimental information is often quite costly to obtain, because it may imply lower results (produced by the application of the hypotheses that turn out to be "wrong"), or because discarded alternatives may be no longer available, or because causal attributions when actors' deliberate action is involved are particularly difficult, as illustrated below.

Therefore, distinctive complications of learning processes in economic action are: that often discarded alternatives disappear (partial feedback); that an actor's hypotheses influence observed behaviors (interaction effects); and that hypothesis-testing can imply a loss of income. All these factors accentuate the self-confirmation trap.

Partial feedback

Situations where feedback is partial are, for example, those in which it is not possible to control what would have happened if the discarded alternatives had been accepted: the people not hired, the trading offers rejected, the partners with whom a deal is not concluded.

Treatment effects and income losses

Treatment effects and income loss effects are well exemplified by the decision-making process of a waiter hoping for a tip (Einhorn and Hogarth 1978) (analogous examples could be a firm trying to learn which clients to target with higher discounts, or a tax office trying to choose which taxpayer to audit). The waiter has a theory regarding which characteristics of clients are good predictors of the size of the tip. However, since tipping is influenced by the quality of service provided and action is costly, the waiter has an incentive to provide a superior service to those clients with good prospects of giving a tip, and inferior service to those without (according to his theory about what tip predictors are). In this way, theories of an acting learner easily become self-fulfilling prophecies. How would it be possible for the waiter to discover whether his theory is valid? He should be willing to test different predictors, with the risk of obtaining a lower income, in case his initial theory might be right.

Attribution errors

Learning economic actors are often active and interested subjects, also as far as causal attribution processes and the ability to correct mistakes are concerned.

Nisbett and Ross (1980) identified a general tendency, when social phenomena are considered, to hypothesize that subjects, actors, and decision-makers – their will and action – are "causes" of events and results, rather than other more structural and more "exogenous" factors. Management decisions are believed to influence firm profits more than economic and sectoral trends. Managers are rewarded according to results, often regardless of the extent to which the results stem from their actions. The principal cause of the success of the Japanese economy is often sought in some attribute of Japanese mentality, for example.

This bias of "illusion of control" (Langer 1975) has received various psychological explanations, including the fact that people participate in social phenomena as actors and that information on actors' purposes and actions is more "available" than information on structural trends. Knowing that this bias is at work in causal attributions, one would be advised to force oneself to consider alternative, more structural, explanations of action outcomes, before attributing them directly to actors' will.

Self-serving biases

A complication in following this prescription may arise when considering that actors may assign positive or negative preferences to

> **Box 1.10**
> An experiment on
> commitment
>
> Assume that you are a loan director at a bank. A customer comes in and asks for a $100,000 loan to start a business. After a thorough analysis of the request, you personally decide to grant the loan. Six months later, the customer comes back and says: "I have some good news and some bad news. The bad news is that the company is facing some problems. As a matter of fact, without any further help we will not be able to pay back the loan. The good news is that I am quite confident that if you lend us another $100,000, we could turn the situation around." Would you grant the loan?
>
> *Source*: Experiment described in Bazerman (1986).

different causal attributions. Examine the problem posed in Box 1.10.

In this case, it is probable that the decision-maker will not consider the outcome as a personal failure and will renew the loan. For, if the results linked to the action are negative, then the decision-maker has an incentive to attribute the cause to other factors, and continue the action, however risky, rather than accepting certain losses (reputation, position, income) (Staw 1976b).

Antidotes

As appears particularly clear from the last examples considered, the possibility for *effective learning* is linked, first of all, to the presence of an organizational climate where *experimentation and errors are not immediately and readily punished* (for example, because of a mythicization of the principle that "only results count") (Chapter 9). This is a condition for people not washing their hands of mistakes but discussing them (Staw 1980; Popper 1989).

Second, effective learning is linked to the availability of many theories and hypotheses that can feed the processes of falsification and improvement of hypotheses. Examples of these contexts can be, both within and between firms, *multicompetence groups* (Chapter 5; Part III).

Third, it is important to remember to observe and evaluate action results, maintain systematic records on feedback, and not get rid of decisions as soon as they are "made." Obvious as it may seem, it is not rare to find actors who do not learn from experience simply because they have no available attention to pay to it. Firm *performance evaluation systems* do have this important memory function.

Fourth, it is important that actors be endowed with resources – time, attention, and material resources – that exceed those required in performing currently known actions (*slack resources*), in order to allocate some resource to the search for and test of new actions, and to finance the eventual diseconomies (expected income losses) of learning.

Fifth, if the idea that research and learning activities are an important – and ever more important – part of economic action is taken seriously, training in research and learning methods would not be out of place in economic education, along with the more traditional training in decision methods.

PREFERENCE

Human behavior, and economic behavior in particular, can and should be explained by taking into account that actors can be purposeful and can have "motives" (Elster 1985).

Early psychological approaches to motives emphasized a deep natural and emotional level of analysis and explanation of behavior, in terms of instincts. A psychoanalytical approach to motivation falls outside the scope of this book, and is anyway considered "antiquated" and "outdated" by psychologists as well, owing to various methodological limitations: for example, "the disturbing fact that the list of the instincts has continued to grow, reaching a number of approximately six thousand" and the difficulty in testing instincts empirically in a way that does not imply inferring them precisely from the behaviors that they should explain (Bandura 1986: 11).

Early economic theories of motivation suffered from the opposite problem: they had a very "narrow" view of preference, supposing that economic actors are motivated by (1) individual self-interest (rather than, for example, the interests of a community they identify with); and (2) wealth (rather than, for example, the access to a variety of resources) (Smith 1776; Taylor 1947).

Subsequently, in both fields there has been a gradual shift from content-based, substantive models of interests, to content-free and "procedural" notions of utility and purposeful action.

From substantive to procedural models of preference

Early social psychology models of motivation based on the content of "needs" opened up the "portfolio" of preferences, suggesting that people in organized settings assign positive preferences to resources that are not easily valued in monetary terms. On the other hand, they suffer from the same methodological limitation of early psychological perspectives: the unachievable goal of listing all the relevant content of interests. This is the case of the much criticized, but much used typology of needs developed by Maslow (1964). In contrast to an instinct, a "need" is a conscious drive to action, and consists in the perception of a "deficit," or of a "gap" "to be filled." It is supposed that it is the non-satisfaction of a need that drives toward an action that will re-establish equilibrium (Maslow 1953; March and Simon 1958). In other words, a need can be seen as a very particular type of goal: regarding its contents, it is defined over goods and services that by their nature or social convention are perceived to be necessary; regarding its logical form, it is an aspiration level, a target (Chapter 2) since subjects look for a quantity of such goods sufficient to fill the perceived deficit, not the maximum possible quantity.

A first part of Maslow's model arranges needs in five classes based on content:

- physiological needs (such as sleep or hunger)
- security needs (not being threatened and subject to risk)
- needs for belongingness (to be accepted and to have an identity in relation to a reference group)
- needs for esteem (to have confirmation of one's worth)
- self-actualization needs (to realize one's competence and preferences in intrinsically rewarding activities).

A second part of the model hypothesizes that needs are hierarchically ordered and that this order helps to predict behavior: "lower level" needs must be sufficiently satisfied before "higher level" needs can be perceived in a way strong enough to drive action and orient behavior.

Both parts of the model can be and have been widely criticized. On the one hand, it appears intuitively attractive, and favorable examples can be found to confirm it, especially at levels of relative deprivation and dissatisfaction of primary needs (for example, if one has nothing to eat, all energy will be employed to satisfy that need; only when primary needs are settled, can attention be turned to other objectives). On the other hand, many objections and counter-examples to Maslow's hypothesis can be easily found and they actually led to revisions and modifications of needs theory. As a preparation for a better appreciation of these revised models, it may be useful to try to formulate a list of possible criticisms and counter-examples. An example of such a "list" of objections based on classroom discussion on this question is reported in Box 1.11.

Many subsequent revisions of Maslow's model have reacted to those possible criticisms – leveled against the content of classes as well as the hierarchical hypothesis – by trying to clarify the underlying cognitive processes.

Box 1.11
Counter-examples and objections to the needs hierarchy model

- Needs are culturally determined. It would be necessary to have different models for different cultures and countries and for different periods in history in order to be able to predict and explain behavior.
- Satisfaction levels for each category of needs are extremely different from person to person. It would be necessary to have different need hierarchies for different types of actor in order to explain and predict behavior.
- Rather than a scale, one often finds oneself facing a dilemma: more security, or greater development and self-realization? More esteem and socialization, or more consumption and more individual success? The actions required often conflict.
- When one cannot satisfy a better need – for example, self-realization – other needs are re-evaluated; for example, one invests in sociality.
- Altruistic behavior, "pride" in giving up even primary goods, even by "poor" people, would be inexplicable if the hierarchical hypothesis were true.
- Needs change over the course of one's working life so that a young person has different needs from a person at a later point in the life cycle.
- Needs depend on experience. A person who has had little, expects little. One who is used to receiving a lot, needs a lot.
- The same person, in the same time period, may have different needs when "active" in different activities or tasks.
- Why not the need for power, for fairness, or for novelty and change? Why not simply one need for freedom to choose what material and immaterial goods to look for, and in what measure?

Dual preference structures

One group of important studies tried to make the model compatible with the empirical observation that actors are normally able to perceive higher order needs, even though they do not feel lower order needs are satisfied (Lawler and Suttle 1972). In addition, these researchers were concerned with the potentially unfair consequences of the original formulation in terms of resource allocation (if primary needs are not satisfied, it is useless to offer people benefits that respond to higher level needs, i.e. the less one has, the less one receives). Herzberg and colleagues (Herzberg *et al.* 1959; Herzberg 1966) demonstrated how people are simultaneously sensitive to "lower" and "higher" needs, but interpret them in different ways. On the one hand, the needs for material resources, consumption, security, and affiliation are perceived as "deficits" and create dissatisfaction if left unanswered. On the other hand, the needs for growth, professional development, and self-actualization in work are perceived as "surpluses" and generate positive incentives to act so as to reach high levels of satisfaction, rather than to correct a negative situation. This result was reached through a special interview technique (called "critical incident"), in which people were asked to describe situations in their work life where they felt "particularly satisfied" and "particularly dissatisfied" and to describe in detail the causes and conditions that solicited those perceptions and judgments. The results showed that the factors mentioned as a cause of satisfaction were qualitatively different from those mentioned as a cause of dissatisfaction. Reaching objectives, the recognition of results attained, the content of work, the level of responsibility, and the possibility of promotion and professional advancement were predominantly mentioned as causes of satisfaction. They were therefore grouped in a single category and called *motivator factors.* Organizational procedures, the style of supervision, the quality of interpersonal relations, the physical working environment, compensation, physical conditions, and personal safety were predominantly mentioned as causes of dissatisfaction and were grouped as *hygiene factors.*

The hypothesis that preference structures are "dual," that they are compounded by a "positive" and a "negative" field which are treated differently, finds support in more recent cognitive research. Economic actors have been found to perceive utility in different ways depending on whether consequences are classified as possible losses or possible gains with respect to a situation subjectively believed to be neutral or balanced (Kahneman and Tversky 1979) (see above).

In the light of subsequent research, however, the perception of a particular content or resource as a hygiene or a motivator factor appears to be contingent rather than universal. For example, work satisfaction may vary as a function of age, instruction level, level of experience, and past results (Lawler 1973). Or again, the surprising placement of compensation among hygiene factors, in Herzberg's studies, may well have stemmed from having conducted a test on categories of employees (accountants and engineers) whose pay was predominantly fixed and relatively low; in all likelihood, different results would have been obtained had incentives contingent to performance been important, or had monetary rewards been very high and connected to status and social consideration.

Learned preferences

McClelland's theory of learned needs (1961, 1965, 1987) marked a clear departure from an innate concept of needs. Based on behavioral experiments mainly conducted in the laboratory, it showed that subjects acquire and learn certain needs rather than others, both by inheritance from societal culture and by direct experience. For example, people who realize they are able to develop high level task-oriented competence with ease will acquire a high need for achievement.

These results are broadly consistent with those obtained in cognitive research on preference learning and the perception of utility. Preferences should be explained rather than assumed, and they can be explained as outcomes of learning processes (March 1994). As for any knowledge, actors partly "receive" and partly construct, on the basis of experience, their knowledge of what they prefer. They accept as a matter of social inheritance a variety of basic values on what are "positive" and what are "negative" things (Schein 1985). But value-sharing and identification with given models contribute in defining only a deep and basic level of identity. Most economic actors, individual and collective, are capable of constructing an original identity, not only of identifying with a larger community or with given models. Actors evaluate their direct experience and the experiences of comparable others in order to learn what they can seek for and what they can praise (Bandura 1986).

In conclusion, it can be observed how the more valid and enduring parts of the so-called "content models" of motivation sought their foundations in cognitive learning process models underlying the formation of needs. As was argued for competence content classifications, the possibility of explaining and predicting behavior well on the basis of content typologies seems limited for various reasons including the following:

- the list of contents tends to expand indefinitely
- content typologies say something about what people prefer, and the procedure of "assuming" rather than surveying the content of preferences is of dubious legitimacy
- needs are primary and profound interests, and therefore are rather remote from action: they require to be operationalized in order to guide action and be predictive.

A logical hierarchy of preferences

In fact, more recent approaches to motivation structures favor the analysis of the logical structure of preferences conceived as layers of knowledge about oneself, rather than the listing of possible contents. If a hierarchy of needs exists, it may be the general logical hierarchy that organizes and "operationalizes" an actor's knowledge. According to more recent motivation theory (Locke 1991), needs and values are deep preferences that, even though partly learned in a task-specific way, are internalized as a characteristic of an actor as a whole. In the light of this, the affirmation that they are difficult to change may be justified. Moreover, it can be understood why they are only weakly correlated with specific behavior patterns. For many other passages are necessary in order to move from those primary options to actions, as shown in Figure 1.3. An intermediate judgment is that of attributing weights or values or degrees of utility to categories of desired (or shunned) outcomes, in order to understand what one's own *interests* in given situations are (for example, how one feels about a job that is more self-actualizing but offers

Needs and values   ➡   Interests and motives   ➡   Goals, positions, and objectives

Figure 1.3 A logical hierarchy of preferences
Source: Adapted from Locke (1991).

relatively low monetary rewards). A second kind of judgment is to define specific *positions or goals* that indicate what operative objectives are being pursued (for example, a job position that offers at least a certain level of income, based in one's home town, and not overflowing into weekends).

Among the advantages of this logical or "content-free" framework there are the following:

- the content of utility may be quite different according to the problem at hand, the perception of external constraints and the nature of the game being played, the type of actor considered – individual or collective, acting as a person or in an organizational role
- the framework is compatible with economic ideas of motivation because in economic thinking there has also been an evolution from content-laden views toward content-free and processual views.

Utility as content-free preference

In fact, in economic thinking, the early notion of motivation based on self-interest as profit-seeking (Smith 1776) has been supplanted by notions of motivation based on subjective utility, in which not only the particular content of money and profit but even that of self-interest is not essential. In support of this contention, in a recent revisitation of the concept of rationality, Simon (1997) quotes Marshall's words that what is characteristic of the motivation of economic actions is "a *free choice* by each individual of that line of conduct that, after careful deliberation,

seems to him the best suited *for attaining his ends, whether they are selfish or unselfish.*"

Hence, in economic and cognitive research, economic actors are seen as utility-seekers, capable of translating into their subjective rankings of alternatives all the relevant outcomes they might value (Raiffa 1968; Simon 1996).

Only in particular cases, in highly structured and competitive situations, the relevant outcomes may be well represented by "profit" or net monetary rewards (Chapters 2 and 3). In most situations system efficiency does not coincide with profit or shareholder value maximization (Radner 1987). In addition, individual actors as well as firms can viably pursue a variety of other objectives, such as: growth (Marris 1964); "slack resources" (time, staff, equipment, money, or other resources that are in excess with respect to current productive needs and can be used at discretion (Williamson 1964, 1970); rents (from a variety of sources of monopolistic positioning) (Barney 1991); productive missions and the utility of final consumers under a constraint of economic viability of the producer (Masini 1978; Coda 1996).

Most economic contributions, in fact, employ the procedural notion of "utility maximization" for constructing models of optimal behavior, given some assumptions on the content of objectives that are relevant in solving a given problem. The content of utility can vary: if the problem is a technical investment, it may be the monetary return on investment; if the problem is the choice of a marketing technique, utility may be substantiated by customer satisfaction; if the problem is product innovation, utility may be operationalized as the number of patents.

This variety in utility content is not without implications for the feasible processes of decision-making, however. "Utility maximization" is one possibility, which is feasible if utility and information are structured in a particular way. The next chapter discusses that model of decision in detail and a variety of legitimate alternatives to it.

SUMMARY

Chapter 1 presents a structural model of the economic actor, defined as a subject endowed with knowledge and preferences. In the first part of the chapter, some basic features of economic actors' knowledge with important organizational consequences were identified:

- *Knowledge is hierarchically structured*, whereby a core of basic principles and theories are articulated in operational and testable propositions, and a body of "substantive" notions is made operational by a body of "procedural" know-how. This dimension of knowledge governs the *degree of innovativeness* of economic behavior through the capacity and possibility to put into question and change "higher order" layers of knowledge; and to the extent behavior is constrained by detailed operational rules of action.
- *Knowledge is differentiated* into a *"tacit"* component (difficult to explain and communicate) and an *explicit* component (declarable, codifiable). This dimension governs the degree of transferability of the body of knowledge on which a certain class of actions is based, and influences the types of organizational mechanisms which can support the transfer.

- *Knowledge and competence* can possess higher or lower *combinative and generative potential*. This dimension influences the effective path of evolution and growth of knowledge and activities based on it
- *Knowledge* can be more or less complex. Complexity can be a matter of the quantity of inter-related information (*computational complexity*) or a matter of observational and causal ambiguity (*epistemic complexity*). The former component can be handled by investing in documental and information technology support, and by some organizational attributes (decentralization, formalization); the second component can be helped by direct experimentation and hypothesis testing, and by other organizational means (teaming, discretion).
- *Knowledge is always fallible*, and economic knowledge is no exception. In the second part of the chapter, the rich inventory of available tools that can *improve the validity and reliability of observations, judgments, estimates, and inferences under uncertainty* was examined. The principal cognitive biases in problem-formulation (for example, framing effects), in the selective perception of information on alternatives and probabilities (for example, "local knowledge" and "over-/underconfidence" effects), and in learning from experience (for example, self-confirmation and causal attribution errors) were considered and their possible individual and organizational antidotes examined (such as forming groups, using "management systems" which provide checklists of relevant information and alternatives, and avoiding incentive systems which punish "errors").

The third part of the chapter presents elements for the analysis of *preference*. Early theories attempting to model the content of preference were mentioned, but it is argued that they have been overcome by logical and procedural (learned) conceptualizations of preferences. It is shown that the logical structure of utility judgments – as a form of knowledge of the self – exhibits the same hierarchical stucture of knowledge in general: there are *basic value judgments*, assessments of what the *interests* of an actor and the actor's *motives* for action are in a specified situation, and operational *goals* setting *objectives* to be reached. The more operational and precise utility judgments are, the more they constrain and orient behavior (see Chapters 2 and 7).

Exercise: The palimpsest decider

For some years, channel 1 of the Italian public television company, RAI, has decided to produce and broadcast the program *Carramba che Sorpresa* in the early evening. The new director of RAI1 must decide the palimpsest for the next season. He comes from an important magazine and he wonders what can have persuaded the previous management to confirm this program for three whole years.

Our young director seems to have understood: you choose the program that gives you the best audience. Easy enough – says an elderly director who has survived any amount of restructuring – because RAI is a "generalist" television station and, as such, must succeed in getting mass audiences: "The more people Fra [Francesco Sgobbi, the new director] can catch, the better."

If *Carramba* gets an audience, the problem of decision is thus very simple since the preference function of the decider (to maximize the audience) is circumscribed. Moreover, the result can easily be measured (audience data are provided at intervals of 15 minutes!). In the space of a few weeks at RAI they can tell whether a program is successful, or whether it's a classic flop and they must take the appropriate steps. However, before broadcasting a program, it must be planned, contracts must be drawn up and, often, the production and infrastructures must be set up. All this involves a lot of expense. Thus, as our director immediately learnt, it is necessary to limit as far as possible cancellation of programs as a result of lower than expected audience ratings. On the other hand, it is anything but easy to predict exactly what audience a certain program will get. In general, the deciders base their decision on the intervals: for example, say the experts, *Carramba* might oscillate between 28 percent and 34 percent of audience share. Anyway, at RAI as with other television companies, they are well aware that surprises are all too frequent.

Our new director thinks that you couldn't do better than *Carramba* for a Thursday evening. It's his opinion that "Over these last years *Carramba* has always done well [even with the old director] so why shouldn't it go well for me?" And then, seven million viewers means lots of advertising. This is very important for the RAI as advertising accounts for about half of its annual available revenue (the other half comes from TV licences). Our young director has no doubts: go for *Carramba*.

Convinced of the rightness of his decision, the director of the network is leafing through a newspaper and, in the show pages, he comes across the following headline: "Does RAI1 intend to serve up junk TV once again this year?" According to the journalist: "Aside from the audience ratings, RAI performs, or ought to perform, a public service." "People," he says, "pay the license fee and have the right to a proper service, not just to programs that gratify firms interested merely in advertising." The week before, too, that journal printed an article saying that RAI1 on Thursday evenings "resembled a South American TV station rather than a European one." And yet, recalls the director, when RAI1 decided to broadcast a program on religions in peak time there was a slump in audience ratings and some newspapers talked of "public money used to finance programs watched by a mere handful of pseudo-intellectuals; when people work, and pay, they want to relax a bit in the evening." In addition, the advertisers were enraged and, brandishing their contracts, they demanded a refund of part of the money they had spent.

The preference functions seem to have become at least two in number and could even be in conflict with one another. The same problem has been rendered all the more critical by the fact that, alas, for a television program there is no clearcut criterion for calculating the level of a public service. Our director thinks: "Audience ratings, advertising, public service, orientation of the watchdog commission of the Chamber of Deputies, and we've yet to take account of the opinions of the media and the TV critics . . ."

Our decider is more and more confused, and he decides that the public service interest is best served if many people make use of the service; so, better *Carramba* than the philosophy lecture or the history program that almost nobody would watch. And yet, when he discusses the matter with the head of "educational" programs, he is told: "Look, if a philosophy lecture in peak evening time scores a resounding success, that means that you've stimulated a million ordinary Italians to do a bit of thinking." This sounds convincing enough, but the director who called him "a Fra," and who seemed to know his onions, had taught him that a generalist television must get as high ratings as possible, so even if the philosophy lecture attracts a million viewers, it's no good because the competition from a swimming contest or a comedian turns that million into ten!

What with all these pressures, plus his own confusion, our decider has opted to shoulder his own responsibilities and, thinking only of the audience, he states his decision to the palimpsest meeting to confirm *Carramba*. Unexpectedly, during this meeting all hell breaks out.

The director of RAI's channel 3 says: "Come on now, this is the only evening when I try with my program to reach the target of elderly and middle-aged viewers and you stick *Carramba* in my way. Very good, is this war then?" The director of RAI's channel 2 echoes him: "We're in the same firm, so don't toy with the idea of shifting *Carramba* to Fridays, that's our most important evening, otherwise that'll be the end of everything."

Our decider thinks to himself: "Why in heaven's name did I ever take on this job!?"

By Giuseppe Soda

Questions

- Who are the relevant actors in the matter?
- What type of knowledge can they act upon?
- How can they define their objectives and preferences, in content and form?
- What are the likely consequences, for the decision at hand, of different ways of framing the problem?

Appendix 1.1A

A matter of life and death

A dangerous disease is spreading throughout the region where you are the Assessor of Public Health. It is estimated that 600 people are risking their life in the course of the year.
   You can choose between two possible plans for intervention:

- Under Plan A, 400 lives would be lost.
- Under Plan B, with a probability of 1 out of 3, no one would die; with a probability of 2 out of 3, all 600 would be lost.

   Which plan would you pick?

Appendix 1.1B

A matter of life and death

A dangerous disease is spreading throughout the region where you are the Assessor of Public Health. It is estimated that 600 people are risking their lives in the course of the year.
   You can choose between two possible plans for intervention:

- Under Plan A, 200 people of those exposed to the risk will surely be saved.
- Under Plan B, with a probability of 1 out of 3,600 people will be saved; with a probability of 2 out of 3, no one would be saved.

   Which plan would you pick?

Appendix 1.2

Results of the experiment on "availability"

The table in Appendix 1.2 shows for each couple of causes of death the average response, the real frequency, and the frequency with which two typical daily newspapers published episodes regarding the various causes over a period of a year.

Cause of death	Responses for each couple (%)	Total no. of cases in the USA (in thousands)	Episodes reported by newspapers per year
Lung cancer	43	140	3
Car accidents	57	46	127
Emphysema	45	22	1
Homicides	55	19	264
Tuberculosis	23	4	0
Fires	77	7	24

Source: Russo and Schoemaker (1989).

Chapter 2

Decision and Motivation

....

Knowledge and interests are to be "processed" for leading to action. This can be done in different ways. Beyond all improvements in hypotheses, conjectures, and initial knowledge, problems differ as to the incompleteness of ex ante knowledge, or degree of "uncertainty" about relevant objectives, relevant alternatives, outcome probabilities, or even the very "data observed" and therefore different decision behaviors are comparatively more effective in solving them.

The first section of the chapter shows how decision-making research leads us to conceive an actor capable of adopting different decision strategies as a function of the state of knowledge on decision matters.

The second section of the chapter shows how the available models of motivation processes repropose substantially the same differentiation between modes of taking decisions about economic behaviors, with specific reference to work behaviors. This homology helps in comparing different motivation processes in terms of applicabilty and effectiveness conditions – a prescriptive and comparative approach currently undeveloped in motivation studies.

The third section uses justice and equity theories to show how decision and motivation about economic behaviors are, and need to be, driven not only by effectiveness and effi-

ciency criteria but also by equity criteria. In all these three sections and fields, the three basic forms of value maximizing, heuristic, and non-calculative automatic rationality are found to represent the fundamental logical strategies available, outlined in Figure 2.1 along with the type of information required for their application, illustrated throughout the chapter.

DECISION STRATEGIES

Rationality can assume different configurations, that, in economic behavior, materialize in different decision processes or strategies. These decision strategies are formulated here in a way conducive to comparative evaluation according to three criteria:

- to what extent are they able to link actions – and the results those actions are expected to produce – to the preferences and objectives of decision-makers (effectiveness)
- to what extent do they economize on the scarce resource of cognitive capacity and effort (efficiency)
- to what extent are they able to resolve conflicts between different actors with different objectives using that strategy (conflict resolution capacity).

The main decision-making models that have

CONFIGURATION OF KNOWLEDGE AND
PREFERENCE
- Structured problems
- Complete and clear preference ordering
- Unrepeated action

DECISION LOGIC

- Value maximizing

- Unstructured problems
- Incomplete preference orderings
- Unrepeated action

- Heuristic problem solving

- Unknown cause–effect relations
- Unclear preferences
- Repeated action

- Non-calculative appropriateness

Figure 2.1 Types of decision and motivation processes

been identified in economics, organization, and management can be described as particular, salient, and effective *combinations or configurations of rules and procedures for defining and modifying the fundamental decision inputs: procedures for defining objectives, for generating and evaluating alternatives, and for learning from experience.* In other words, one decision model or strategy differs from another if it is characterized by a different approach to any of these fundamental cognitive activities. The initial information conditions that make these diverse approaches or strategies applicable can be and will be specified.

On the basis of the vast research on economic decision behavior, three basic models can be reconstructed:

- models of deductive rationality based on "optimization" rules
- models of "heuristic" rationality based on acceptability rules
- models of "programmed" rationality based on automatic action.

They can be evaluated according to their capacity to link results to objectives in problems characterized by different levels of information complexity and by different degrees of conflict among interests.[1]

Deductive rationality and optimizing strategies

Consider the following problems:

- Find the sequence of operations a production department must perform to reach a desired level of output with the lowest costs and in the shortest time.
- Given a finite series of stocks and bonds with known interest rates, and an investment budget, define the best portfolio in terms of expected return on investment.
- Calculate the optimal production level of a standard good, given its market-determined price, knowing production costs.

Known objectives and alternatives

These problems are defined in a highly structured way. Interests and objectives are known, clear, and measurable. Alternatives are finite and defined; problem boundaries are defined by the specification of these relevant alternatives. Within these boundaries, an optimization strategy is not only feasible but superior to other strategies because it evaluates all relevant information for finding the best action in terms of the actor's utility.

An optimizing or value-maximizing

strategy can be defined as a combination of particular rules of search and choice. These rules prescribe the decision-maker to examine alternatives until the marginal returns from search are positive and, among the generated alternatives, to pick up those producing the maximum net utility (benefits minus costs). The rules do not require costs and benefits to be expressed in monetary terms, nor do they require that utility is measured "cardinally" (assigning numbers). Utility can be defined "ordinally," expressing a comparative judgment of superiority or inferiority in net benefits (Savage 1954). The decision-maker must at least be able to order alternatives according to preference.

Most times, the task is not easy. If one thinks even of a simple problem, such as buying a car, only where the quality of cars is perfectly standard and price covers all relevant information (say within a power category) can the buyer select the lowest priced car within the category. Almost no one buys a car in this manner, however. For cars today are now differentiated products, whose qualities and images are not perfectly comparable. In addition, people think that many evaluation parameters are significant. Many of them are subjective and not easily measurable. Space, speed, and security may matter, but the status the car confers and the association with the owner's personality may matter even more. How can we build a function which associates each alternative with an overall level of utility? In principle, each attribute can be ranked on a utility scale (as people are sometimes requested to do in questionnaires). Furthermore, it is necessary to specify what "weight" each attribute has in an actor's utility function. Suppose that the decision-maker is able to define these weighted utilities, and that the decision-maker can do so for "all relevant alterna-

tives," assuming that the relevant alternatives are the cars of a certain class.

Further complications may arise. Suppose that used cars are also considered. In this case, the car's performance will depend not only on the decision-maker's choice, but also on external factors: how diligent the mechanic was in overhauling the car, what replacement parts were used, what the real state of those parts that cannot easily be checked, such as electrical components, will turn out to be. These two elements can be represented as in Figure 2.2. $U (p_1 e_1)$ is the utility of an alternative expressed as a function of its sure attributes and of the possible states of uncertain attributes or of external factors that will influence actual performance (Feldman and Kanter 1965).

If this is the situation, applying a fully fledged, value-maximizing strategy would require one to specify with what probability the outcomes would assume different values – for example, what is the probability that the car will be a "lemon," a good bargain, or a gem in its class?

Multiplying utilities by the respective probability, a new single indicator to be maximized would be obtained: subjective expected utility (SEU). Many economic decision models currently in use apply this particularly sophisticated optimization rule, which allows

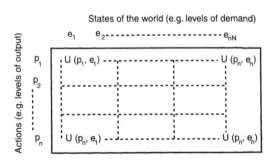

Figure 2.2 Expected utility matrix
Source: Feldman and Kanter (1965).

this strategy of decision also to be applied under conditions of *risk* – consequences are uncertain with a known probability – and even under a certain type of *limited uncertainty* – probabilities are not known but the relevant alternatives and the observable consequences are known. This may be totally appropriate in sufficiently structured problems, where decision parameters are known and quantifiable. Even though not all decision-makers actually decide on structured problems by value maximizing, those who do so can be expected to obtain superior results.

Limits of value maximization

It has been objected that a SEU model does not describe particularly well how people behave, or at least how they behave when facing unstructured problems. The core issue, however, is not that in practice people behave differently on average (perhaps mistakenly) but that it is doubtful whether the model prescribes well how they *should behave* in unstructured problems – or, in other words, whether it describes well the "best processes" under certain conditions. Why?

Optimization fails if uncertainty involves the definition of the relevant alternatives and consequences, rather than just the probabilities of outcomes, i.e. if the problem is unstructured, as in the case illustrated in Box 2.1 (see also the Palimpsest decider case).

Search costs and information losses

The usual defense of optimization rules for all seasons observes that, if information is difficult and costly to find and process, one should take those *search costs* into account in cost and benefit calculations: search should be stopped when its expected marginal costs are superior to its expected marginal benefits. This rule, however, can in turn be applied only when search is very structured and its costs and benefits can be assessed (such as in looking for a new spare part to repair a given machine). In more complex situations (such as in designing a new machine), those cost and benefit calculations would be even more difficult than the evaluation of alternatives. There is *a problem of knowledge (rather than just costs) which can bring an optimizing strategy to failure.* Compelling a quantification or semi-quantification of objectives and information on a utility scale or function can lead to *information losses*, at an increasing rate with the complexity of information to be processed. Utilities and expectations are not measured for choosing partners, mates, and not even for choosing cars, jobs, or new projects or products, because they are multi-dimensional entities, with aspects that are difficult to appraise and are highly incomparable, and because the relevant alternatives are potentially infinite. As a result, even though in principle it is possible to construct such measures and judgments, the *reliability and validity* of preference assessments and utility judgments such as those required by the SEU model would be extremely low in those situations.

Wealth effects

In addition to availability of information, a far-reaching condition for an SEU model to be applicable is availability of resources. Even if one knew how to assess the probability that a deal would be good or a "lemon," one might not have the resources to afford the failure. Resource scarcity easily leads to risk aversion. Whenever the level of wealth of a decision-maker influences the deals the decision-maker is willing to accept, it is said that there are

> **Box 2.1**
> Failure of a hyper-rational system
>
> Let's take into consideration a very specific city service: fire fighting. Its goal is to reduce losses caused by fires and its results will be calculated based on these losses.
>
> The number of losses caused by fires is calculated on the basis of several indicators. Among these there are natural ones (wind, heavy snowfall, hard winters, hot and dry summers, thunderstorms, hurricanes, earthquakes, and floods), structural and environmental factors (buildings, population density, and types of construction and rooftops), factors related to moral character (negligence and arson), and lastly either the efficiency or inefficiency of the fire department. Losses therefore depend on all of these variables including the work standard of the fire department. The fire chief needs to be aware of how the activities of the fire department can affect the losses whenever the fire chief is in a position to make a decision.
>
> How does the fire department carry out its task? It performs inspections of various buildings to reduce the risk of fires, it promotes education campaigns against negligence, it fights fires, it trains firemen, and it will carry out research whenever there are arson charges.
>
> But we could analyze this further. How is the battle against fire carried out? The necessary equipment has to be driven to the site, the hoses have to be ready, the water needs to be pumped and targeted toward the flames, the ladders need to be set in such a way so as not to be damaged by water. Again, each of these activities could be further analyzed. What does it take to unroll a hose? The rubber hose needs to be purchased and maintained, the equipment to carry it also needs to be purchased and maintained. Firemen need to be hired and trained. Firemen also have to spend time and energy in unrolling the hose.
>
> One could analyze each of these factors involved in carrying out one of the tasks described above.
>
> Efficiency can be measured by calculating the cost of each single factor involved in the task as well as the contribution made by that element to meeting the goal of the department. Whenever these costs and contributions are clearly known, the elements of the process can be combined so as to reach the maximum possible reduction of losses caused by fires.
>
> The complexity of this decisional process is clearly such that even if it were possible to standardize it, its full capacity would be subject to unforeseeable events. And, in the meantime, most probably the city would burn down.
>
> *Source*: Simon (1947).

wealth effects. An "expected value maximizer" is supposed to be risk-neutral and not subject to wealth effects (Raiffa 1968; Milgrom and Roberts 1992).

Conflict resolution limitations

And what if there were multiple conflicting actors and objectives? If these objectives were measurable and comparable, it would be possible to make trade-offs, to build "indifference curves" between objectives (combinations of valued resources bringing the same level of utility to the actor), and to find solutions that maximize utility.

If objectives are not directly comparable – for example, because they belong to different actors – the application of value-maximizing rules becomes more difficult, but not impossible. Consider, for example, some alternative ways of restructuring a plant, evaluated in terms of implications for employment and for structure costs: the lower the generated unemployment and the greater the reduction in costs, the better the solutions, as represented in Figure 2.3.

If comparison of the two parameters is believed to be difficult, it becomes problematic to establish a preference order among alternatives. It would be possible to say that D is preferable to A and B, and that E is preferable to B, but it would be necessary to establish more complex rules in order to compare D, E, and C with each other. They are all, in fact, *Pareto-optimal solutions*, i.e. they are such that no improvement with respect to them is possible for both players simultaneously (or for one with equal benefits for the other). To compare multiple Pareto-optimal solutions among themselves, some additional criterion for maximizing joint utility is needed, such as an equity criterion.

Nevertheless, there are particularly conflict-

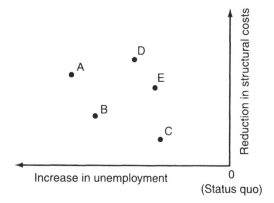

Figure 2.3 Comparing alternatives without comparing objectives

ing configurations of interests that cannot be resolved within a value-maximizing scheme.

For example, preferences may be patterned in a cyclical way so that no one of them is preferred by a majority of players, as in the following case (a case in the "voting paradox"). Suppose that there are three alternatives, A, B, C, and three players, 1, 2, 3 and that the preference order for actor 1 is A over B over C, for 2 is B over C over A, and for 3 is C over A over B. Then a majority prefers A to B, a majority prefers B to C, and a majority prefers C to A.

There are also other types of "encounters" between "optimizing players" that are not solvable, owing to the presence of particularly strong conflict among interests. For example, in "Prisoner's Dilemma" games (see Figure 2.4), two optimizing players who have no

		B		B	
		Cooperate		Compete	
A	Cooperate	Good,	Good	Awful,	Optimal
	Compete	Opitmal,	Awful	Bad,	Bad

Results for A before the commas, for B after the commas

Figure 2.4 Ordinal structure of the generic pay-off matrix of a Prisoner's Dilemma

chance to play repeatedly and to acquire specific information about a partner's behavior, typically end up in the dominated (non-Pareto-optimal) outcome brought about by the combination of the two competitive strategies. In fact, for both players, the choice to "compete" – which can result in an "optimal" or "bad" result – is superior to the choice of "cooperate" – which can result in a "good" or "awful"result.

It can therefore be remarked that the use of optimizing strategies by multiple actors may contribute to creating situations of unresolvable conflict. It could then be argued that in those situations a shift to non-optimizing strategies may be advisable and valuable, even though objectives and alternatives are clear.

Heuristic rationality and "satisficing" strategies

Consider the following problems:

- Which new product is it better to develop and launch?
- Which person is it better to hire as a marketing manager?
- Which public education program is it better to finance?

Objectives and alternatives as "hypotheses"

These are unstructured problems. Relevant objectives are numerous and not easily measurable, and it is wise to test them during the process. Alternatives must be sought. Problem boundaries are potentially infinite, in terms of series of sets of potentially relevant alternatives. For example, if a car acquisition problem is redefined as a broader time-saving and life-management problem, "the sets of relevant alternatives" – hence problem boundaries – become very numerous, potentially infinite, and cannot "all" be considered

simultaneously. For example, instead of choosing the vehicle with maximum utility, one could "evoke a different set of alternatives" (March and Simon 1958) and discover that it is better to buy a house close to work and no car at all, or to change one's job.

In these circumstances, the problem cannot be effectively and efficiently addressed by using an optimizing strategy. The best alternative decision strategy is a heuristic one, based on research. It is the best among other possible strategies (described below) in terms of its ability to link results to objectives (hence to fulfill actors' preferences).

A heuristic strategy formulates objectives as hypotheses to be empirically checked with regard to the existence of acceptable alternatives. Decision-makers can and should be willing to modify all decision inputs in the course of the process, thereby improving their hypotheses. Faced with evidence that falsifies or contradicts their expectations, decision-makers can modify cause-and-effect theories, objectives, the sets of considered alternatives, or the tools for information gathering. For example, not finding a candidate possessing the hypothesized profile for a managerial position, the decision-maker can: change the evaluation parameters (add or eliminate some, lower their level); look elsewhere for alternatives (for example, abroad or in other industry sectors if this has not already been done); change the test being used to measure candidates' characteristics (the possibility of measurement errors is often neglected, but always present).

This decision strategy can be defined as "heuristic" (Grandori 1984) because its basic rules consist of research methods and procedures (Lakatos 1970; Newell and Simon 1972; Kahneman *et al.* 1982).[2] It is able to treat and solve problems of very high information complexity, while maintaining a rather strong tie between actions and object-ives. In fact, each potential action is evaluated in terms of the acceptability of expected results with respect to those aspired to by the decision-maker.

Research activities may concentrate on different phases of a decision process and be more or less intensive, as illustrated below.

Research strategies

An important distinction among research strategies regards the extent to which search is innovative and problem boundaries are allowed to change, or not. Research and learning have often been distingushed as "normal" or "revolutionary"; "incremental" or "radical"; "local" or "not local"; "exploit-ative" or "exploratory" (Kuhn 1962; Cyert and March, 1963; Argyris and Schön 1978; Tuschman and Romanelli 1985; March 1992). These dichotomies underline the difference between a limited research that focuses only on alternatives of the same kind, which look "close" to known solutions; as against research which calls into question cause-and-effect theories, the content of utility, and "paradigmatic knowledge."

Box 2.2
Incremental and radical learning

An example of alternating forms of incremental and radical learning is given by the evolution of car models produced by Ford, and specifically the improvement between the model T and the model A.

The model T represented the first example of a mass-produced car at a reasonable cost and contributed to Ford's great success. The innovation linked to the success of the model T represented a successful radical learning experiment: the goal of the car producer was to move from traditional scale production to mass production. This intuition was the basis of the thorough study of the industrial transformation process that later created an incremental learning track based on the steps highlighted by the scientific management school. Learning stimulated by this innovation gave birth to several other process innovations including the almost forced choice to standardize single parts of the car (for example, nuts, bolts). Ford's original intuition and the learning process that followed rapidly allowed the producer to save on costs and develop mass car production.

The introduction of the later model A followed the thinking that enabled the devel-opment of the model T, i.e. standardization and cost reduction without taking into consideration, however, the constantly changing needs and tastes of the consumers who had begun to appreciate the car not only for its usefulness and relative cost, but also for its immaterial characteristics such as its color or its optionals. Therefore, the model A, although based on the model T's success, was a failure and was overtaken by the competition from General Motors' cars that, while mass-produced like Ford's, were nevertheless supplied in different colors. General Motors' success marked the beginning of a new radical learning process.

Source: By Luca Solari.

The case described in Box 2.2 shows the importance of this difference in an economic decision-making process. If the problem is stable and important consequences can be predicted in advance, analysis of the problem as far as possible before acting is likely to be an effective heuristics. Examples are strategic problems in which there is time for analysis, but once action is taken long-standing and poorly reversible effects are generated.

In other problems this research strategy is not effective, because much relevant knowledge can be generated only by initiating the process of analyzing and comparing alternatives; even by experimenting with them, action can be separated into "small" steps, and consequences are not irreversible. Human resource management decisions, for example, are often of this kind. Personnel search and hiring are especially illustrative of decision processes that should be started if relevant information is to be generated on what is "easy" or "difficult" to find at a certain time. These experiences reorient the search for alternatives and allow objectives to be readjusted: if it is difficult to find the hypothesized alternatives, the objectives will be reduced or qualitatively adapted to what can be found; if search is easy, they can be raised and become more ambitious (Simon 1955a).

Ex post learning

Ex post learning may be the only resort if ex ante hypotheses-making is very hazardous. In decisions regarding people, this is often the case with promotion to new and complex jobs, because the reliability of ex ante information on the relevant characteristics of people is fairly low and the hypotheses on the relationships between these characteristics and performances are even more tentative. More generally, it is typically the case of undertakings of a new kind, from which it is important to draw significant positive results, but it is not very clear which classes of result will materialize. For example, a frequently encountered problem in the evaluation of public administration social programs is that they often prove to be ineffective in attaining previously stated objectives. Only if new objective dimensions are created ex post, on the basis of observed consequences, can many programs receive the deserved evaluation (Chen and Rossi 1981).

Research is not only a very costly activity but is also intrinsically unbounded. Research should be "stopped," but when to stop is not a trivial question: in particular, it is not only a matter of costs but also a matter of validity of knowledge. In a structured, narrowly defined problem (such as the search for a needle in a haystack), the search may be truncated according to the optimizing principle of marginal expected return from the effort. But in unstructured problems (such as the search for ways of improving product quality or of increasing product innovation capacity), the main issue is whether a reliable and valid model of the problem has been produced. Acceptability rules play a fundamental role in this judgment.

Acceptability rules

In heuristic decisions, any hypothesis is judged in terms of its acceptability. As applied to alternatives, the processes of search are "truncated" by comparing the attributes of found alternatives with the actor's hypotheses on acceptable attributes (or "*aspiration levels*").

As a rule of choice, acceptability poses lower information requirements than an optimizing rule. A precise evaluation of the expected benefits of an alternative is not required; a comparison between the alternatives is not required; and, above all, a trade-off between objectives is not required. Only ordinal comparisons between the levels of aspiration and the levels of expected pay-off from each single alternative are necessary. For example, if two objectives are considered, the logical structure of the acceptability judgment can be represented as in Figure 2. 5.[3]

For example, if one were evaluating candidates for a managerial position and the considered objectives were the expected sales performance and the potential for professional development, the necessary judgment would only be an evaluation of whether the performances expected from the candidate profile meet or surpass the levels deemed acceptable.

Quasi-resolution of conflict

Acceptability rules are also able to resolve difficult conflicts and incomparabilities between objectives, even when they refer to different actors, in a more efficient and often more effective way than optimizing rules can. Indeed, decision-makers should evaluate whether there are alternatives that satisfy a series of aspiration levels or constraints, rather than identify the alternatives that maximize a joint utility function reflecting all objectives. Naturally, conflicts between objectives are solved in a weaker manner; and this has in fact been called a "quasi-resolution of conflict" (Cyert and March 1963).

In concluding this assessment of the properties of heuristic and satisficing strategies it should be mentioned that economists have observed that "satisficing" is a form of optimizing in which search costs have been factored in, and that a repeated application of acceptability rules and aspiration level adjustments will slowly discover "all relevant information" and "converge" to optimizing, i.e. it will produce similar decisions (actions) (Baumol and Quandt 1964). This can be demonstrated for structured problems. But in complex problems, experience and learning may lead to the definition of a more comprehensive set of objectives, to improved research heuristics, to a greater ability to predict effects, and to solutions that are superior to those previously generated – but not "optimal" (and even by chance if they were so, nobody could know it).

Non-calculative rationality and the logic of appropriateness

A large area of economic behavior is guided by non-calculative decision logic, which does not imply a forecast of costs and benefits and not even the definition of articulated preferences. Actions are taken by matching the observed situation to the "appropriate" action for the acting system (Nelson and Winter 1982; March 1994). This type of "programmed rationality" involves at least three judgments, which may be more or less complicated and subjective:

- A pattern recognition judgment – What kind of situation is this? What is the state of the relevant "world?"

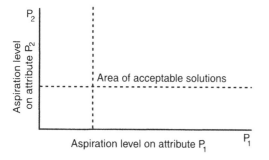

Figure 2.5 Structure of acceptability judgments
Source: Simon (1955a).

- A self-recognition judgment – What kind of actor am I? What is the state of the deciding system?
- A rule of correspondence between (1) the match of the two former elements and (2) a set of "appropriate" actions: what a certain type of actor, in given circumstances, "has to do."

The above judgments can range from the very simple and mechanistic application of a repertoire – such as the "right way" to fill out an administrative form – to the very complex and ambiguous assessment of "identity" and of "correct conduct" – such as the "right" type of intervention of a personnel director in a work dispute. As in the case of heuristic and optimizing decisions, various sub-models of programmed rationality have been identified. Two particular configurations that have been shown to be diffused in important decision fields and have been well specified in their cognitive components are the "incremental" and "cybernetic" models.

Incremental models

Consider the following descriptions of decision processes mainly found in economic activity in particular settings, such as public administration, universities, and research:

- The best predictor of a year's budget for a program or activity in local government is the budget of the preceeding year (Wildavsky 1964).
- How are sales budgets formulated? See if demand is expanding or contracting and modify the current budget by a small percentage in that direction.
- When a new company is acquired, especially in a foreign country and in a different industry sector, organizational changes drawn up by the parent company run the

risk of "breaking the toy." If it is known that the current arrangement works, but it is not known exactly why, it is a good idea to change little and slowly.

The above examples illustrate decision processes that have been defined as "incremental" (Lindblom 1959; Davis *et al.* 1974; Quinn 1980). The most interesting property of an incremental strategy is that it generates sensible action "without" clear objectives. The decision-maker is assumed to have only rather rudimentary experience and preferences concerning the problem: either because the problem itself is too vast and complicated (as in collective political action) or because the decision-maker does not have sufficient experience.

The decision system is able to discern where it wants to go: increase rather than reduce production capacity, improve levels of education, increase well-being. However, no reliable theories are available on the cause–effect relationships that regulate how the action system works and changes. A reasonable decision strategy in similar circumstances is to try "incremental" solutions that differ marginally from those in use (Lindblom 1959).

A rational justification of this rule could be that, since they entail small variations, incremental alternatives also create small consequences and, in particular, "small risks" defined, as decision-makers often do, as small possible negative consequences. In this interpretation, the incremental decision process is a particular variation on a "satisficing" strategy – for example, accept only alternatives with small consequences or "bland alternatives" (March and Simon 1958) – or even a particular case of an optimizing strategy – for example, choose alternatives that minimize risk. Cyert *et al.* (1978) have suggested that in a new area of investment, where it is difficult to assign probabilities to different levels of return on investment, an incremental approach is advisable, when investments are divisible, so that at each step it is possible to observe consequences and to update the probability judgments to be used in the next step. But, as in the case of interpreting satisficing as a particular case of optimizing, it is a reductive interpretation in that it only grasps a problem of information costs and not the problem of the limits of knowledge. An incremental rule can be applied *without* any calculation or prediction of results, not to mention calculations of risk and process costs; hence it is applicable where these calculations are unfeasible altogether, and both optimizing and heuristic strategies are too demanding.

Only if the accumulation of knowledge is based on addressing repeatedly "the same" problem can the problem itself become more structured and the incremental decision process become a more aware, satisficing (or optimizing) kind of process (Padgett 1980).

Linear rules of choice

In other areas of action, it is the type of conflict and the incompatibility between diverse objectives that is difficult to resolve with more comprehensive decision strategies. Is it better to allocate resources to research on cancer or on cardiovascular disease? Is it better to expand the faculty of engineering or that of economics? In these problems, experience probably does not lead to a greater clarification of objectives, which remain essentially elusive, conflictual, and incompatible. As a result, it is not objectives and their consequences which are learned, but decision rules for dividing and allocating resources to different uses. For example, what establishes

the share of resource allocated to different university departments is often a simple linear rule such as that of maintaining the relative shares constant as the budget grows. The result is that current actions depend simply and linearly on past actions (Davis *et al.* 1974).

Tacit objectives

This property of incremental decision rules makes them particularly efficient in resolving conflicts between many, incompatible, or unclear objectives. As Lindblom (1959) noted, an incremental logic does not require that alternatives be evaluated with respect to multiple conflicting objectives. In reality, in an incremental process, objectives come into the game relatively little, and consequently there is little risk of the process being blocked by their incompatibility or vagueness.

The limits of incrementalism

The weakest point of incremental rationality is that *incremental actions do not always produce incremental results* (Padgett 1980). It is quite possible that small variations cause a reaction chain that leads to "major variations" (Weick 1979a). To take a simple example, think of the stability of a boat whose exact carrying capacity is not known when another person gets on: the effect will be incremental if the limit is far off, but could be disastrous if the boat is close to the limit. Similarly, in economic action, a manufacturer's decision to join other producers in a new industrial sector (an incremental variation) will have an incremental effect if saturation is far off, but the closer the sector is to its maximum "carrying capacity," the larger the effect on firms' death rates (Hannan and Freeman 1989).

Cybernetic models

An incremental strategy does not require knowledge and agreement on objectives but does require the capacity to formulate judgments of "similarity" and "marginal difference" between new possibilities for action and current actions, as well as the ability to generate (find, define) such alternatives or increments.

A "cybernetic" strategy (Steinbruner 1974) envisages a fully automatic model of decision. In fact, it can be used not only by human beings, but could be followed by simple machines such as thermostats or by animals (Weiner 1948; Ashby 1952).

A cybernetic decision strategy implies only the following kinds of judgment: the capacity to recognize situations (a certain temperature; a configuration of costs); the capacity to recognize performance gaps with respect to a standard (works/ does not work; positive/ negative); possessing a repertory of possible actions that are applicable to eliminate the gap or respond to the situation as in the example in Box 2.3.

As Steinbruner (1974) notes "in the cyber-netic paradigm, values are articulated at a minimal level ... Therefore, the cybernetic decision-making criterion is not the highest value nor an approximation of it. Rather, the essential criterion is simply survival." Soldiers knew how to identify a "non-working" state from a "working" state of a jeep. This is what defines the problem. Alternatives are not evaluated ex ante, they are simply applied or tested sequentially, in as far as they belong to a repertory of potential solutions. As a result, cybernetic processes can be applied in extremely uncertain circumstances; but it is necessary to be aware that they handle uncertainty by avoiding it, to a much greater degree than do other decision models.

> Cybernetic mechanisms that are able to handle uncertainty do so by focusing on a few entry variables and completely eliminating all serious calculations of probable results. It is assumed that the decision-maker has a smaller set of "answers" and decision rules that predetermine the course of action ... that are of the nature of "recipes" established by preceding experience.
>
> (Steinbruner 1974: 66)

Box 2.3
A cybernetic decision process

A simple illustration can be taken from informal observations of an army maintenance unit staffed with men who knew next to nothing about the vehicles they were charged with repairing, and hence were decision-makers under uncertainty. They responded with a cybernetic decision process. Faced with a broken-down jeep, they replaced the battery and tested the jeep to see if it then ran. If that did not work, they would change the spark plugs and test again, then the distributor, then the carburettor. If all these actions failed, they declared the jeep inoperable and junked it. They proceeded thus for a substantial period of time, with the order of the sequence of actions reflecting roughly (by the principle of reinforcement) the frequency with which each action proved successful.

The men never did develop more elaborate causal understanding of the operations of jeeps or internal combustion engines.

Source: Steinbruner (1974).

The principle of reinforcement and the rule of imitation

Cybernetic learning is driven by the "principle of reinforcement." Actions that produce positive effects (a car starts up again; in behavioral experiments on animals, food arrives; a tentative and exploratory proposal or attitude elicits praise or rewards) are held in the memory as correct and are repeated (imitated) on subsequent occasions – they become recipes and routines. Those actions that produce negative effects are discarded for solving the problem at hand and lose importance in the repertory to the point where they are no longer repeated even on subsequent occasions. This principle allows a certain degree of dynamics and learning, fundamentally based on the *imitation of successful solutions*, without ever understanding why success is achieved. An imitative choice rule only requires that situations be recognized as belonging to certain classes (pattern recognition) and that a particular repertory of actions corresponds to that class of situations (matching rule). This principle can be applied to one's own direct experience, or, vicariously, to the experience of other actors believed to be similar (Cyert and March 1963; Bandura 1986). Rules of choice such as: "do as the most successful firm in the industry does," "do that which was done successfully in the past," "do as the average actor similar to us does under similar conditions," are imitative choice rules. Surprisingly or not, important processes in economic innovation, especially the diffusion of observable and codified technological as well as organizational innovations, can be predicted fairly well as simple imitative processes (Rogers 1962; Hannan and Freeman 1977; Aldrich 1979; Teece 1980b). Imitation is all the more relevant for explaining many facets of individual economic behavior as work choices (Lomi 1997).

Homeostatic processes

A *stationary version* of cybernetic behavior is also possible and not so rare in economic action.

If a deciding system obeys the principle of maintaining a stable state, the result is a stationary version of a cybernetic model (Ashby 1952; Beer 1972). Its logical structure is represented in Figure 2.6. Not only repeated structured decisions such as inventory management are taken on the basis of these types of programs. As will be seen in the next chapter, even elusive phenomena such as motivational processes can be modeled, in some respects, as homeostatic cybernetic processes.

Assets and liabilities of cybernetic models

The great advantage of cybernetic decision-making lies in the economies of cognitive energy and in the applicability of cybernetic

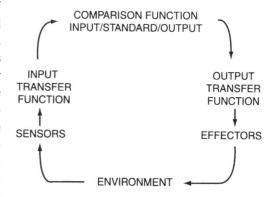

Figure 2.6 A homeostatic cybernetic model
Source: Adapted from Ashby (1952), Beer (1972), and Klein (1989).

rules even when the decision-maker possesses very little relevant information with respect to the complexity of the problem. Causal explanations of why tried and imitated actions should lead or have led to positive results could sometimes be reconstructed, if looked for. Nonetheless, a cybernetic logic is interestingly different and sometime advantageous with respect to other decision strategies, precisely by not looking for these explanations in problems where it would be too costly or too difficult to do so. On the other hand, the effectiveness of cybernetic strategies is limited to situations that repeat themselves over time and across subjects with similar characteristics and in which actions are easily reversible – so that learning by doing is not destructive.

MOTIVATION PROCESSES

The various models of motivation processes that have been proposed can be presented and understood as different models of decision processes. Although they have been elaborated largely independently of decision-process research, and have been applied mainly to work activities, their underlying logic repropounds the basic types of cognitive processes that seem to characterize rationality in general. Hence, the comparative assessment framework developed for evaluating decision strategies can be applied to motivation models as well.

Maximizing expected valence

This perspective is commonly defined as "expectancy theory," and the best known of these models is that developed by Vroom (1964). "Expectancy" is an actor's subjective probability assessment concerning the chances of obtaining certain results, through

the allocation of the actor's efforts and competences to certain tasks or activities. "Valence" is the subjective utility, the value assigned by the actor to results. Vroom suggested measuring valence on a utility scale ranging from +1 (maximum utility, value of the best outcome, at a given time in a given place – for example, for a white-collar worker becoming a manager) to −1 (the consequence of maximum disutility, such as the loss of one's job). An alternative approach to measuring valence could be to quantify the monetary value of results (costs/benefits), providing measurement is not too difficult. More generally, subsequent work in the area has indicated that, if the model is to be reasonably predictive, it should include separate evaluations not only of the extrinsic valence linked to results (the value of monetary and non-monetary rewards), but also of the intrinsic valence that can be generated by performance (sense of competence, interest in the activity), as well as of the negative valence that can be a consequence of effort (House and Wohba 1972).

As regards the operationalization and measurement of expectancy, Vroom distinguished judgments on the probability of producing a given performance by applying certain efforts and competences (effort–performance expectancy) from judgments on the probability that certain results will be produced by that performance (performance–outcome expectancy). The first type of evaluation includes a self-efficacy judgment and a weighting of the incidence of external factors on performance, while the second evaluation concerns the probability of obtaining rewards.

Consider, for example, the situation of a sales executive who formulates all the above judgments as follows. The sales executive can decide whether to go to visit some clients to promote a given product line or remain in the office. Each alternative (not to make a sales call, make an average, run-of-the-mill sales call, or make a carefully planned and well-prepared sales call) entails a different expenditure of effort (quantified as 0 ML, 3 ML, and 5.5 ML respectively) and a different probability of increasing sales by a targeted amount (0.1, 0.4, and 0.7 respectively). If sales do increase by the specified amount, the sales executive will earn a 10 ML bonus (extrinsic valence), with an estimated probability of 0.8 (this expectancy may be less than one, for example, because there might be competition with other sales executives for the bonus). In addition, if the sales executive makes a carefully planned, well-prepared visit, the executive could gain intrinsic benefits in terms of social relationships with clients and of personal image that could be capitalized (assessed current value: 1 ML).

To solve a problem perceived in these terms, the sales executive can apply an expected value-maximizing logic. As a result, the sales executive will not be motivated to make mediocre sales calls (whose expected value is low), but neither will the executive be particularly motivated to make well-prepared

ones, because their expected benefit is equal to the expected value of making no sales call at all, as shown in Figure 2.7. A prescriptive conclusion that can also be drawn from the analysis is that, given these valence and expectancy judgments, only sales bonuses over 10ML will motivate high levels of performance.

The *situational conditions* where one can expect motivation processes to be configured according to expectancy theory can be derived from the general applicative conditions of value-maximizing decision processes. Consequences should be evaluated on a utility scale. Alternatives must be known and comparable. There must be enough information to be able to estimate a probability for each single outcome value. In addition, the analytic process itself may entail appreciable additional costs that may discourage its application if consequences are not important enough. Therefore, processes of this kind can be expected to be applicable and effective in structured activities, and to be enacted by actors sensitive to economic benefits and extrinsic rewards (which are more measurable) and endowed with relatively high competences and responsibilities (owing to process costs).

Action alternative	Cost of effort	Effort → perfor- mance expec- tancy	Intrinsic valence of perfor- mance	Perfor- mance → outcome expec- tancy	Valence of outcome	Net expected valence		
1 No visit	0	0.1	0	0.8	10	10 (.8) (.1)	=	0.8
2 Average visit	3	0.4	0	0.8	10	10 (.8) (.4) −3	=	0.2
3 Well-prepared visit	5.5	0.7	1	0.8	10	10 (.8) (.7)		
						−5.5 + 1 (.7)	=	0.8
						1 (.7) − 5.5	=	0.8

Figure 2.7 An application of the valence/expectancy model (costs and benefits in thousand dollars)

Goal-setting

A second type of motivation process can be retraced to the general characteristics of decision-making based on aspiration levels and acceptability judgments (March and Simon 1958; Chapter 1). Instead of taking into account utility functions to be maximized, actors can allocate effort and competence according to targets and goals to be reached. Hence, the informational requirements of this strategy of effort allocation are less ambitious than those of an expectancy-based strategy. The core question about motivation then becomes: *Are performance levels related to the type of goals actors formulate?* Originally, March and Simon formulated this problem as one of "optimal tension": low aspiration levels reduce search and lead to accepting low results; very high aspiration levels lead to lower success probability estimates, so that above certain levels action is inhibited. Therefore, the relationship between the goal difficulty and performance can be represented by a curve of the type represented in Figure 2.8, where the highest performances are stimulated by objectives of

"reasonable" difficulty. Subsequent studies in the field of "goal-setting" (Locke and Latham 1990) have repeatedly confirmed this hypothesis.[4]

Goal difficulty and precision

An objective or goal is defined as a "pre-specified performance level" that guides the choice of actions for reaching it (Sims and Lorenzi 1992: 117). Numerous laboratory studies have shown that performance is systematically influenced not only by goal difficulty, but also by goal specificity: i.e. the extent to which a measurement scale for results is specified (quantitative or nominal, i.e. an enumeration of things to be done) and a specific level to be reached on that scale is set (for example, a firm's division results are measured by rate of increase and a 5 percent increase should be attained next year). In other words, it has been shown that generic purposes such as "do your best" (or let us do our best) often pave the way for actually doing worse than one could.

The relationship between setting high-level objectives and getting high-level performance has been shown to be particularly robust. Nonetheless, it is mediated by competence and by self-efficacy judgments; and its form depends on the nature of activities. In a task where the actor is clearly perceived to have the required competence and uncertainty is perceived to be low – for example, log-loading on a truck by trained porters – the relationship between goal difficulty – reaching at least 60 percent, or at least 80 percent, or at least 95 percent of a truck capacity utilization – and performance is positive and linear (Tosi *et al.* 1986; Locke 1996). On the contrary, raising a sales budgetary target will improve performance

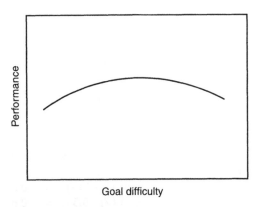

Figure 2.8 The relationship between goal difficulty and performance level

levels only up to a point beyond which they are offset by the downward adjustment of success probability judgments (the relationship has the inverted U shape represented in Figure 2.7).

Task complexity has a significant impact also on the optimal degree of goal precision or specificity. The more complex an activity (i.e. the less the path-to-goal is known), the less a priori information on attainable outcomes will be available, and the more arbitrary and risky the setting of specific goals will be, because it will engender a "tunnel vision which inhibits effective search procedures" (Locke 1996). For example, if the task is to produce innovations in applied marketing techniques, it is not a good idea to set precise and specific goals (how much to improve market share, contribution margins, client portfolio, or the size of discounts). Or, if the task is uncertain because it requires getting other actors' consent, as in sales negotiations, behavior will become rigid if precise and specific targets are defined. Effective goal-setting in complex tasks should not, however, imply reducing difficulties or ambitions, because this would simply lead to low performance. Rather, it should imply a more general, less detailed, and operational definition of goals, a shift from setting goals as specific-result parameters, positions, and targets to setting goals as interests that lie behind those parameters, going a step higher in the logical hierarchy of preferences. Examples and cases abound – especially in fields like budgeting, sales force motivation, and product division performance evaluation – of how narrowly defined performance and rigidly pre-defined targets can become a restricting and distorting factor in the learning of attainable objectives and an appreciable consideration of the multiplicity of consequences of complex economic action.[5]

Participation in goal-setting

Lastly, the process through which goals are set is obviously important and has been much studied. The results, however, are less obvious and clear than one might expect. The relationship between actors' performance and their participation in goal-setting processes is very complicated. The ties connecting the specificity and the difficulty of the objectives with the performance described above are valid both when the actor autonomously sets personal objectives, and when the actor accepts objectives set by others. Participation generates two contrasting effects: on the one hand, self-set objectives may not be as high as those which, in equal circumstances, would be set by others (a self-serving bias); on the other hand, the self-determination may solicit stronger conviction and dedication to goals (commitment) (Locke 1996). But it has also been demonstrated that high levels of commitment are also obtainable when the objectives assigned by others are convincingly explained and understood and are connected to interesting rewards, and regular feedback is provided on the progress of the performance toward the objective. Participation is fundamental, however, when the performers themselves possess the relevant knowledge for formulating valid and accurate hypotheses on attainable objectives – i.e. "participating in goal setting is necessary for cognitive reasons and not motivational ones" (Locke 1996).

The reinforcement of behaviors

A third class of models hypothesizes that motivation processes are regulated by automatic, ex post adjustments upon action feedback, rather than by expectations and predictions of outcomes. These models –

deriving from the behaviorist tradition or even from cybernetic control theories – have been harshly criticized by cognitivist scholars. Nonetheless, accepting the idea that a decision process proceeds automatically does not imply that there is necessarily little or no cognition, nor that the subject is not aware of the process. Automatic motivation is compatible with cognition, albeit with a particular form of cognition (see above, on programmed rationality).

Types of reinforcement

Reinforcement theory, as applied to motivation, maintains that when consequences are attributed to one's own actions and are perceived as positive, the probability that those actions will be repeated increases; whereas the perception of negative consequences of one's own actions diminishes this probability. Reinforcements can be direct (rewards or punishments connected to actions) or indirect (abstention or absence of rewards and punishments). Hence, the model considers four

typical situations, called positive reinforcement, negative reinforcement, punishment, and extinction, as represented in Table 2.1, which shows the model applied to an example of secretarial work and feedback supplied by the boss.

Applying reinforcement theory to motivation has contributed notably to explaining apparently irrational behavior and developing "positive-reinforcement programs" oriented toward correcting such behaviors and improving the relational climate (Komaki *et al.* 1996). In fact, one of the characteristics of reinforcement processes is that of regulating (often inadvertently) behaviors that are given little explicit attention and analysis, such as those requiring quick interactions: interpersonal relationships, aspects of work that have not (yet) been analyzed because they have never constituted a problem, and habitual actions. The fact that these processes take place automatically does not, however, mean that they have consequences of little significance, whether in terms of the quality of inter-

Table 2.1 Motivation through reinforcement

	Action	Stimulus	Response
Positive reinforcement	Letter in English taken down in good shorthand.	Boss: "Great work. You ought to think about taking a course."	Increases the probability that the behavior will be repeated.
Negative reinforcement	Letter in English taken down in good shorthand.	Boss, who normally criticizes anything that is not perfect, is silent.	Increases the probability that the behavior will be repeated.
Punishment	Letter in English with many errors.	Criticism.	Reduces the probability that the behavior will be repeated.
Extinction	Letter in English with many errors.	Boss, who normally praises anything well done, is silent.	Reduces the probability that the behavior will be repeated.

Source: Adapted from Tosi *et al.* (1986).

Box 2.4
Reinforcing A hoping for B

The deadline for presenting the project to the client nears. The project group procrastinates and underestimates the timing. When the deadline is already too close and it is clear that they cannot make it, the group is given extra staff. (*Positive reinforcement of undesirable behavior*)

The rule was clear and written on a poster: wear protective gloves when working in the vicinity of the ovens. Despite this warning, no-one did so. The workers remembered when many wore gloves back in the plant's early days, then some began to get fed up, and nothing special seemed to happen: the bosses did not object and which of the workers were aware of the damage to their hands that only now begins to be manifest? (*Negative reinforcement of an undesirable behavior*)

Young surgeons in a famous clinic are constantly exhorted to study, attend conferences, and develop new surgical techniques. Nonetheless, when they try to experiment with some of their new ideas, they face tiresome discussions explaining or trying to convince their equals and their superiors. And heaven forbid saying no to an extra shift on duty or to an operation commitment, because they want extra time for studying. (*Punishment of desired behavior*)

Everything went along smoothly in the maintenance office. As a result, no one had anything to say. The other departments made no comments. The production department did not protest. The head of the plant rarely dropped by the office because he had other "irons in the fire." It was as if maintenance did not exist. (*Extinction of desirable behavior*)

personal relationships, or in terms of direct impact on economic results.

Pathologies and unintended consequences of reinforcement

The examples in Box 2.4 illustrate some of the typical distortions generated by uncontrolled reinforcement mechanisms, in particular the inadvertent reinforcement of undesirable behavior or the unintended punishment or extinction of desired behavior (Kerr 1975). The reinforcement model helps to make visible other important pathologies, such as the trap of governing mainly through punishment and negative reinforcement, thereby giving indications only of what should not be done, creating negative "frames," and giving no clear indication of what to do.

Control models of motivation

A second type of automatic model of motivation applies cybernetic theory to motivation (Klein 1989). This kind of model assumes automatic adjustment processes oriented toward maintaining a stable state, the positive and negative deviations from which are perceived as performance gaps to be corrected (as in the case of correct temperature). This type of motivational process can effectively explain some types of work actions. For example, if a person has accepted the standard time of 1 hour for completing a particular task, and if the worker observes that after half an hour, less than half of the work has been completed, then the worker will put additional effort into bringing the performance back on track. Homeostatic motivational models, then, can be effective and efficient only in stable activities where maintaining a normal or standard result is more important than striving for better results.

A condition for the effectiveness of reinforcement models in general (homeostatic or not) in a cognitive interpretation is that actors see their own action as a deterministic and systematic cause of the observed consequences. Whenever this hypothesis does not hold, as easily occurs in uncertain and unstable activities, reinforcement models no longer predict behavioral responses well (Kelley 1971; Weiner, 1974).

EFFICIENCY, EFFECTIVENESS, AND EQUITY

The approaches to decision and motivation analyzed so far focus on the relationship between preferences and outcomes. Effectiveness and efficiency, therefore, have been implied as regulatory principles capable of orienting action: the capacity of actions to produce desired consequences (effectiveness) and their ability to do so while saving cognitive and material resources (efficiency). However, these two criteria are insufficient not only for explaining but also for designing organization structures and behaviors well. For example, suppose that a plant manager has the opportunity to participate in a project

to open a new production facility, and the manager is evaluating it by looking at the expected economic benefits, the amount of travel requested, the career potential, and the additional work commitment. What level of overall benefit is sufficient to motivate the manager to take part in the project? Weighing up incentives and contributions (efficiency) alone is not enough; in general, this will not produce enough information. Even assuming that contributions and benefits can be quantified and compared, and that the positive values balance out the negative ones, how can the manager evaluate what level of net benefit is sufficient or adequate to induce the manager to act? Different forms of rationality can be used in making this judgment, but it generally implies at least the following two elements:

- a process of social comparison or interpersonal comparison: actors not only compare their benefits with costs, but will compare their expected net benefits both with those of comparable others and with the net benefits of their exchange counterpart
- an equity judgment on how "just" or "fair" is the share of resources they are getting with respect to other actors' shares.

There are also other reasons why equity criteria should be systematically used in the analysis of economic organization and behavior, even without considering the empirical fact that people often employ them in practice, and even without considering an ethical dimension. The point is that *efficiency and effectiveness criteria are not sufficient, logically speaking, to determine one superior solution (act, contract, structure) in most action problems involving more than one decision-maker.* Most often there are many "superior" (Pareto-efficient) solutions, with respect to which no further improvement of benefits for one or more actors without losses for anyone else can be found (Luce and Raiffa 1958). Therefore, an additional choice criterion which says something on the distributional problem is needed for selecting an action.

It helps to consider all the various branches of research that have analyzed the nature of equity and fairness judgments together in order to reconstruct a variety of equity criteria and their reasons and application conditions.[6]

A first result of general interest has to do with the very existence and importance of fairness concerns in economic action. Consider the problem described in Box 2.5. A game-theory, profit-maximizing solution to this experiment would be for the allocator to propose a minimal "token" payment to the recipient, who should accept any positive offer. However, empirical evidence shows that many allocators offer much more than a token (minimal positive) payment, and that recipients sometimes reject positive but small offers. Cognitivist researchers conclude that fairness criteria are applied by decision-makers even in structured problems where market exchange and unilateral profit maximization criteria were applicable in principle,

and even at the price of renouncing part of their pay-off when they have no obligation or compensation for doing so (Kahneman *et al.* 1986a, b).

An interesting question at this point would be when, and under what conditions, should we expect this behavior to be likely. Clearly it is not to be expected that fairness will always obtain, just as we cannot expect behavior always to be efficient or effective. The discussion conducted in this paragraph on the different possible fairness criteria and of their properties will help in answering this question. An introduction to the issue can be provided by an analysis of a work situation, among the many with which the reader may be familiar, that is considered unmotivating because it is unfair, and a discussion or elaboration of which fairness criteria could be applied in order to improve it (see, for example, the exerciser at the end of the chapter).

Outcome-based equity

Various criteria for fair resource allocation have been elaborated both in economic and sociological perspectives. They all try to translate into applicable criteria a philosophical concept of justice according to

---

Box 2.5
The ultimatum game

The critical laboratory experiment used for discovering to what extent fairness considerations come into play in economic decisions is an "ultimatum game": one player (the allocator) is asked to propose that a sum of money be divided between him/herself and another player (the recipient), who in turn can either accept the offer or reject it, in which case both players receive nothing. The experiment can be run on various dyads with varying amounts of money.

Source: Experiment described in Kahneman *et al.* (1986a).

which a just solution is not necessarily a "Salomonic" one – in which resources are divided equally – but is one that all parties could accept if they did not know what their own share will be, if they agree on the criterion for division behind a "veil of ignorance" about their specific position (Rawls 1971; Brennan and Buchanan 1985).

In an economic perspective, all benefits and costs should be reflected in the utility evaluations that actors make about the outcomes of available alternatives (bundles of resources or combinations of actions). If those different evaluations could be weighted and summed, a possible criterion would be to select as a fair option that for which the sum of utility is higher. This would be a way of taking into account the utility of all the parties involved, and in that sense it involves a notion of fairness. However, what weight is it fair for each party to have? Is one "point" of utility on one party's value scale worth the same as another actor's point? The problem is only shifted and it is usually accepted that there is no legitimate and rational way to perform those "interpersonal comparisons of utility".

Fairness criteria not involving interpersonal comparisons of utility have been proposed by game theorists and economic analysts.

The most widely used fairness rule in economic analyses is probably the Nash (1950) criterion, or the *maximum product of the parties' utilities*. According to this criterion, actors take into account the preferences of their counterparts in exchanges and, among all available Pareto-superior solutions, will give priority to those solutions where benefits are allocated in balanced ways – for which the product of the utilities is generally larger – over those in which some parties turn out close to the maximum they could achieve and

others turn out close to their minimum (see also Chapter 6).

Among the limits of these fairness rules based on the pay-off for the different parties, there is the possibility that they will increase the initial inequality among partners' resources (which does not adequately achieve a philosophical principle of justice) (Sen 1992). Allocating resources according to the subjective utility function of players, in fact, may end up by giving more resources to the "rich" party (which assigns less utility to a marginal increase in resources) and less to the "poor" one (which assigns high value to even a small improvement in their position), thereby reinforcing the initial differences.

In addition, these criteria need a lot of justification, discussion, calculation, and bargaining. Therefore, more egalitarian and less calculative solutions can reasonably be preferred by all parties because they save information-processing costs and losses of "atmosphere," at least up to a certain level of importance of the pay-offs and consequences of the decision.

Lastly, outcome-based criteria require a clear assessment of preferences and interests. As extensively discussed in these first two chapters, this condition is by no means ubiquitous. A master of game and utility theory himself wrote

> To some extent, the complexity of the real situation softens the intensity of the bargaining dynamics. The parties are not clear about what is in their own interest, and their knowledge about the interests of others is likewise vague. Compromise is often easier to arrange in a situation of ambiguity ... many real world negotiations are happily not as divisive as starkly simple laboratory games, because in the real world it is difficult to see clearly what is in one's own best interest.
>
> (Raiffa 1982: 274)

In sociological studies an outcome-based "theory of equity" has also been developed, asserting that people consider a resource assignment to be fair if the pay-off received by each party is proportional to the contribution given (Adams 1965). This principle was made operational in the following fair division rule (Walster and Walster 1975):

(Output – Input)/Input   (for   the   actor) = (Output – Input)/Input (for comparable other actors).

In an early interpretation, this principle of equal returns on investments was thought to be so strong as to be applied by people even against their own interests: i.e. actors try to modify the elements of the equation in order to restore balance both when they believe themselves to be "underpaid" and when they believe they are "overpaid." These "altruistic" behaviors have been observed and are more likely if the actor and his/her "comparable others" perform similar and structured activities (so that social comparison is easy) and the actor who is overcompensated perceives that his/her extra benefits are taken out of the fair share because of other members of the group (Campbell and Pritchard 1976) – for example, in a group of blue-collar co-workers. In fact, in such cases, the losses in status, social acceptance, or even just self-acceptance may well compensate for the extra gain.

   In other situations, it is probable that the actors will modify different elements according to whether they perceive their own position as a deficit rather than as a surplus. It is easy for "overpaid" subjects to react by raising their opinion of their own competence in order to justify what they are paid, and for those who believe themselves to be underpaid to reduce their contribution. Studies conducted by Staw (1982) have illustrated other ways of reacting to the perception of being insufficiently or redundantly compensated, guided by the cognitive tendency toward self-confirmation and self-justification. For example, in order to "justify" staying in a low-paying position at work too long, one tends to re-evaluate other elements and advantages of that job (for example, social relations, intrinsic interest). Symmetrically, if an actor is overpaid for a job that still offers sufficiently high intrinsic compensation to repay efforts and contributions, the actor could become convinced that pay (rather than intrinsic rewards) is necessary to motivate him to perform.

   Fairness rules based on proportionality to contributions are all the more demanding in terms of information required. To be applicable, both contributions (inputs) and results (outputs) must be distinctly measurable and comparable. If work contributions and rewards are considered as examples of "inputs" and "outputs," one can easily see that this is often not the case. Only where resource and competences are relatively standardized and measurable throughout a group of actors and where actors can assess each other's contributions, can those perceived equity judgments on contributions and outcomes be reliably formulated. For example, in interfirm – rather than interpersonal – allocations of resources, whereas the value of the contribution of each firm can be measured (for example, the value of technical and financial assets contributed in a joint venture), the rights to rewards can be made proportional to investments (Grandori and Neri 1999).

Need-based equity and mutual acceptability

A different way to assess interests and preferences, rather than ordering all possible outcomes according to preference, is to consider one's own needs and aspirations. As seen above, need is considered to arise for matters the lack of which would threaten balanced existence. The assessment of needs may then be less difficult and ambiguous than the assessment of the value of contributions and outcomes (Albin 1993). Indeed, if not for their clarity, needs may be easier to assess because they are rooted in the actor itself rather than in what the environment can offer as reward, or with what other subjects receive. In addition, needs and aspiration levels call for "being satisfied" rather than for being maximized. Therefore, fairness judgments based on need satisfaction (rather than on the maximization or equalization of parties' returns) will require less information processing.

Given that needs and aspiration levels are quasi-independent of contributions, need-based equity should be legitimized by the players' mutual acknowledgement of what is essential to the existence of the relationship or to the satisfaction of others (Pruitt 1972).

In economic thought, Sen's definition of needs and distributive justice comes quite close to that used in organization studies: needs are vectors of "acquisitions" that "can vary from elementary things such as being adequately nurtured, being in good health, escaping avoidable morbidity and premature death, to more complex acquisitions such as being happy, having self-esteem and participating in the life of the community" and *justice resides primarily in actors' freedom of access to these acquisitions* (Sen 1992).

Among the advantages and application conditions of needs-based criteria, therefore, there are:

- a redistributive effect to the advantage of the parties who are more in need of resources, which seems to fit with a general concept of justice, especially in conditions of relative scarcity and deprivation
- a reduction of calculation and bargaining costs with respect to joint utility maximization criteria.

These advantages, however, are likely to be realized only under circumstances that facilitate the mutual recognition of needs. They include personal acquaintance and the longevity of relationships (Albin 1993) and the extent to which parties are poorly substitutable or contribute resources that are highly specific to their relationship and critical for its existence (Grandori and Neri 1999).

Non-calculative fairness

In repeated and/or ambiguous situations, learned behaviors and automatic decision rules may substitute for too costly or cognitively complex calculations, of either the optimizing or the satisficing kind. Decisions about fair division of resources make no exception. Two kinds of fairness rules that have the nature of "blind" heuristics are especially important in practice, and they also exemplify two different major sources of legitimacy of automatic rationality: the reduction of information-processing costs and the availability of applicable past experience.

An *equal share rule* expresses an absolute egalitarian principle: different actors receive the same share of resources, regardless of their utilities, contributions, and needs. Among the advantages of this apparently insensitive rule are: a capacity to improve a climate of harmony and trust between actors, a drastic reduction of information-processing costs, especially when these are not justified by the amount of differential expected benefits, and the capacity to produce solutions where it is difficult to measure inputs and preferences over outcomes are not so clear. For example, what are the equitable rewards for each member cooperating in a group where there is no division of labor, and the task is complex, such as developing a new product or a new transformation process? In cases like individual actors cooperating in a team or firms cooperating in a joint venture, we can observe that rewards are often distributed evenly.

An alternative form of automatic and non-calculative fairness is the use of custom and "good practice" as a source of "good right." In this case, the decision is made using historical precedent (Pruitt 1981) as a reference point and making adjustments from status quo situations. On the basis of our previous discussion and assessment of non-calculative rationality, we would expect these "*fairness heuristics*" to be frequently and effectively practiced on many recurrent matters in a stable, long-lasting relationship.

"Substantive" and "procedural" justice

All the equity criteria discussed thus far are criteria that serve to find a point of agreement on how to allocate or apportion resources. They are therefore called *distributive justice* criteria (Greenberg 1987). Each criterion has its own limits and, when there is a decision that is uncertain and important, on the one hand actors could reasonably wish to avoid relying on blind rules, but on the other hand they might not have enough information to divide resources according to inputs or outcomes. In conditions of high information complexity, the fairness of the procedures and of the process followed to

determine what each actor will get, can become especially important, even more important than the amount of resources received. This type of fairness has been called *procedural justice* (Greenberg 1987). Its effectiveness under uncertainty can be supported with the general arguments that make "procedural rationality" (how to arrive at a decision) more interesting than "substantive rationality" (methods prescribing what solution to choose) in solving uncertain problems (Simon 1976). The notion of "fair procedure," inspired by that of procedural justice in law, includes the following traits or properties: fair procedures are consistent across parties and time (the rules of the game remain the same during the process), represent concerns of all parties, provide opportunity to exert influence and revise decisions, and are based on accurate information (Leventhal 1980).

In addition to answering the question as to when these various criteria of fairness should be applied, one may now also legitimately inquire when fairness criteria can be expected to be actually applied to regulating economic activity. Based on all the studies considered, the following list of conditions is the minimal answer to the question. It is more likely that fairness rules will be used, independently of individual propensities toward being fair, when:

- *the set of possible effective and efficient solutions to a problem is wide*, so that there is still a choice to be made among them (as in complex transactions or joint actions involving several matters)
- there is *uncertainty regarding the counterparts' best alternatives* to an agreement, and therefore it would be cognitively difficult to push a counterpart "close" to its minimum acceptable pay-off

- the *exchange relationship is multilateral* rather than bilateral, and is repeated many times with the same features, so that the "comparable others," who invite and sustain equity judgments, can actually be compared and even call for comparison (as in processes involving equal opportunities or equal treatment issues)
- the *relationship is repeated* and expected to be long-lasting, so that each party has incentives to adopt rules of resource allocation which can be accepted independently of its own particular position in an individual exchange
- actors are acquainted with and have a *personal knowledge* of each other
- the *need level of actors' preference structures is at stake* (i.e. the problem concerns resources that nurture actors' continued balanced existence).

For example, the field of labor relations fits all of the above conditions and is, in fact, the economic relationship in which equity concerns are probably densest (see Chapters 9 and 10).

SUMMARY

The first section presented a process model of economic actor rationality. On the basis of available interdisciplinary research on decision processes, the model of rationality on which economic behavior seems to be founded is a multiple or pluralistic model in which different forms of rationality can be expected to be applicable under specifiable circumstances. Therefore, none of these forms is treated in this book as an "assumption" about human rationality (as in mainstream economics and utility theory) or as a universalistic theory of how people behave in

practice (as in classic behavioral decision theory).

It was shown how different combinations of search, choice, and learning rules configure different "strategies" of decision. Three main types of strategies – or models of rationality – are defined (articulated in various submodels):

- a *deductive model*, that can be articulated in various *"optimizing" strategies*, applicable and superior in the solution of *structured problems*
- a *heuristic model*, that can be articulated in various *"satisficing"* and *acceptability-based strategies*, applicable and superior in the solution of *unstructured problems*, where objectives, cause–effect relations, relevant alternatives, and possible consequences are treated as hypotheses to be tested
- a *non-calculative model*, in which behavior is determined by rules indicating *"appropriate" actions* contingent to the situation, to the identity, and to the state of the system. Non-calculative learning processes are sustained by the principle of reinforcement (in direct learning by doing) and the rules of imitation (in vicarious learning). The distinctive advantage of this decision mode is that it is *applicable in the absence of defined objectives and of consequences prediction.*

The second section presented the available process models of motivation, showing that they are no different from decision processes applied to the allocation of one actor's own efforts and actions. Motivation process models considered include:

- *"expectancy theory"* as a model of acting according to the maximization of subjective expected value

- *"goal-setting theory"* as a model based on setting aspiration levels to be satisfied
- *"reinforcement theory"* and *"control models"* of motivation as variants of automatic and non-calculative models of decision-making.

This connection between motivation and decision models has enabled us to specify the *conditions* under which we can expect the different types of motivation processes to occur, as a function of the clarity of preferences and the state of knowledge on action alternatives – whereas they are usually presented just as "different" (or "rival") models of how motivation works.

Lastly, equity theory and the concept of fairness were introduced. They had a special development in the analysis of motivation to work, but it has been argued that *economic behavior in general cannot be completely assessed or designed employing effectiveness and efficiency criteria only*. Using notions of fairness elaborated in different disciplinary fields, it was shown how different conditions of uncertainty can be dealt with by these different equity criteria, which incorporate different forms of rationality: *criteria incorporating some principle of maximization of joint utility; criteria based on the satisfaction of needs; and "blind" or automatic rules of fairness based on symmetries, repertories, or precedents*. The importance of *"procedural justice,"* especially in uncertain and important decisions, in which the fairnes of any substantive distribution of benefits is difficult to judge, was highlighted.

Exercise: BluCer

BluCer is located in the ceramic district of Sassuolo, and produces large ceramic items, primarily tiles and vases.

At the beginning of 1998, the chief executive officer (CEO), Franca Gabrielli, decided to create an autonomous Information Technology (IT) department. "We want to computerize all the ceramics," she said at the time of the decision. The objective of the new department was (in the words of the CEO): "injecting information technology throughout the firm, designing systems to manage the warehouse, the orders, the billing, etc., based on requests by every single department." This needed to be done without forgetting the management of the electronically controlled machines that were already used in production activities (machines regulating movement, the kilns, etc.). This last activity of management/technical assistance (up to then outsourced) had turned out to be particularly costly and inefficient, and this had slowed the process of improving the quality of the product/service to the final client.

Carlo Rossi (an ambitious computer engineer) had been named the director of the new IT department. In total, the new unit included twenty-two people, of whom seven came from different parts of the firm where they had performed IT support activities, even if they had not been effectively coordinated, and instead worked as trouble shooters on problems and/or projects of immediate concern, in collaboration with external technicians and consultants. New staff chosen by BluCer were technicians, mostly with engineering backgrounds, who had been hired primarily to perform research activities. The initial compensation was not high, but they were told that there would be an incentive plan based on the development of new informational projects that would take them to the pay levels of specialized technicians.

At the end of the third month, the results seemed to confirm the appropriateness of the plan. The firm's management took comfort in several indicators, including the more than twenty

81

weekly interventions in the production department that had been performed quickly, and the launch of *Project Blue* (aimed at creating an integrated information system).

After little more than 10 months, the situation seemed to have definitely deteriorated: although the interventions had remained at more or less the same level, *Project Blue* had not taken off and there were conflicts inside the department, based on the distribution of the workload. In addition, in the production department (as in others), there was some grumbling about the quality of the services offered.

For their part, the technicians seemed to demonstrate intolerance and a lack of motivation related to the way in which things were going. First, there was the problem of the "economic return" or lack thereof, from the activities performed. With respect to pay, this had remained unchanged, i.e. it was stuck at a level below the average for information technologists, and the prospects did not seem encouraging.

The technicians complained: "We have not heard any more talk of incentive plans. We earn very little, both with respect to the workload and to our colleagues in other firms. There are no career prospects and we are certainly not treated like researchers," and said confidentially, "we now understand that the evaluation of our work depends on how quickly we intervene, and does not depend so much on whether the work is done or explained well . . . It does not seem to matter if they need to call us the day after to resolve problems caused by yesterday's intervention."

In contrast, regarding the need of various departments for new programming, the slowness of the response was interpreted to be a sign of work that was well done: "On delivery of a program finished 2 months after being requested, I heard that because the preceding one had taken a year, the new one could not possibly be better. It is useless to even talk with people like that!"

The technicians in the IT department were therefore encouraged to overlook the requests of the different departments, keeping busy with simple work instead of doing the complex work which meant delaying delivery of the complex work and giving priority to the frequent demands of the production department.

There was also great frustration about the recognition of the needs – material and otherwise – of the IT department. The budget to buy information technology seemed insufficient but, more importantly, ineffective in the management of technicians' time: "From the day I was hired, I have not had two days in a row to develop new projects," and "One has to understand that this is not a production activity like the others. We need more flexibility in our working hours and opportunities to participate in training courses and to work with other firms (clearly not our competitors) to learn new competences."

Finally, there was a strong sense that the relations among the members of the department were very fragile, in contrast to what had always characterized BluCer, which had always been perceived by its employees as a big family despite its large size. This dissatisfaction was fed by the fact that in other departments the firm had traditionally considered and resolved problems of individual workers, as long as they were compatible with the firm's workload (from shift work to vacations, advance pay to buy a house, "sponsored" hiring). In contrast, the attempt to consolidate the IT department and to make it an autonomous laboratory had led to an "aseptic" management that seemed distant from the problems of individuals.

In brief, the situation seemed critical after only a few months from the start of the project.

The CEO, looking at the data on the activity of the IT department, was asking herself whether to close the new department or to reconvert it for the exclusive management of the productive process and then to evaluate it only in terms of productivity and responsiveness. At the same time, Carlo Rossi had heard that top management was aware of the problems, and had begun to act in defense of his position: he was ready to "save his head" by attributing responsibility for the failure to the lack of information technology culture diffused throughout the firm, and the lack of motivation of the employees.

Questions

- How was the problem of setting up the new information system defined? How could it have been improved? How can the definition of the current failure problem be improved?
- What type of decision process could the CEO effectively follow in dealing with the current problem?
- Why are people "dissatisfied?" How could the equity of the process and of the solution be enhanced?

By Massimo Neri

Conclusion to Part I

An Actor with Multiple Rationalities

....

The model of actor and actor's behavior that can be assumed as a basis for the development of more complex models of organized economic action is a meta-model composed of many. These submodels are conceivable as salient and "discrete" on a continuum of feasible behaviors. They have been shown to be comparable, provided that they are considered as feasible alternative models, whose informative requirements and application domains can be specified. An advantage of this approach is that it captures an important but neglected capacity of decision-makers: to shift from one decision strategy to another according to the nature of problems. A theoretical implication of the developed framework is that it goes beyond the contrast between "global" and "bound" rationality, and between prescriptive and descriptive theories of choice, which has become an obstacle to dialogue and cross fertilization between studies of organization with economic and psychological underpinnings (and to a more general and empirically based explanation of economic behavior).

The plurality of rationalities

Three basic forms of rationality have been reconstructed based on the existing vast theoretical and empirical literature on decision processes in general, and on decision

processes relative to work in particular. It has been shown that the general cognitive model of actor knowledge and behavior developed here is powerful enough to encompass as particular cases the main models of decision and motivation that have been developed in a partially independent way.

The fundamental traits of this model are summarized in Figure I.3 – as far as process models are concerned – and in Figure I.4 – as far as knowledge and preference structures are concerned. The two elements are related, in that decision and motivation processes can be activated only starting from a structure of knowledge, competencies, and preferences that are in turn fed and modified by each process.

Three basic forms of rationality can be distinguished and assessed:

- an expected value, valence/expectancy-maximizing form, which is "deductive" in the sense that solutions are derived logically from sufficient a priori knowledge of relevant objectives, alternatives and consequences
- an acceptability-based, goal-setting form, which is "heuristic" in the sense that the relevant alternatives, objectives, and consequences should be searched and tested
- an appropriateness-based, reinforcement-driven form, which is "non-calculative" in

	Decision strategies		
State of knowledge and preference	Deductive value maximizing	Heuristic problem solving	Non-calculative appropriateness
• Known objectives alternatives and consequences • Complete preference orderings	**All applicable** • Strategy selection, a function of: — effort/accuracy trade-offs — existence of Pareto-optimal solution		
• Conjunctural objectives alternatives and consequences • Incomplete pref. orderings	**Not applicable**	• **Both applicable** • Strategy selection as a function of: — repeatedness and importance of decisions — existence of intersections among acceptability judgments	
• Unknown cause–effect relations and/or unclear preferences	**Not applicable**		• Applicable, in repeated situations • Unrepeatedness leaves with random trial and error

Figure I.3 A decision failure framework

the sense that given a recognition of the type of situation and the identity of the actor in it, actions to be taken follow from a rule of correspondence, which is adapted ex post upon observation of results.

The comparative framework developed in Chapter 2 and summarized in Figure I.3 specifies the maximum level of uncertainty that each strategy can deal with. As such, it is a *"decision strategy failure framework"*: it asserts that if it is cognitively unfeasible or too costly to acquire the requisite knowledge about objectives, alternatives, and cause–effect relations ex ante to a decision process for a given strategy to be applied properly, alternative strategies become superior. This does not mean that, conversely, simpler strat-

egies cannot be applied when more information than required by them is available. However, it does imply that less analytic strategies will usually be inferior in those circumstances because they do not make use of the available information (taking into account the costs of information). More generally, in structured problems all decision strategies are applicable, and their selection can be based on trade-offs between effort and accuracy; or tested against the existence of Pareto-optimal solutions. In unstructured problems, value-maximizing approaches fail; heuristic strategies will be superior on important or new issues, provided that an intersection among the sets of acceptable alternatives for different actors exists. Non-calculative appropriateness is applicable even if the actor is not farsighted and has unarticulated preferences, but the formation and effectiveness of "programs of action" are conditioned to repeated action and consistency among relevant rules: uniqueness of problems or conflict among rules are expected to call for analysis and ad hoc problem-solving.

If those are important configurations of decision processes, they are not the only ones. *Other effective combinations of search, choice, and learning rules can be defined.* For example, in many complex and important problems, a heuristic approach is necessary to generate relevant alternatives and to envisage possible consequences. Once these elements are defined, a value-maximizing choice rule can be adopted for selecting the superior solution (among those available) rather than just the first acceptable solution. The design of organization itself, for those aspects in which it can be designed, can typically be addressed following this mixed, two-stage, decision strategy (Part III).

The fallibility of judgments and their improvement

The admission that human judgment is fallible, and that this is relevant in economic action as elsewhere, has led to the problem of improving judgment being taken seriously, irrespective of which decision strategy is used. A wide inventory of systematic cognitive biases has been presented, including framing effects, local knowledge traps, overconfidence and self-confirmation distortions. Examining the possible "antidotes" and remedies, some aspects of *organization structure and systems*, in particular the use of teams, structured checklists and decision support systems, control systems which do not conceive performance as lack of errors, formal evaluation systems turn out to be *important leverages for sustaining the generation and use of more valid and reliable knowledge.*

The hierarchical structure of knowledge and preference

Streams of study as different as the theory of scientific and technical knowledge, the economic and organizational analysis of competences and the theory of needs converge in the identification of a logical hierarchy in the structure of actors' competences and preferences, as suggested in Figure I.4, deriving from the need for "operationalizing" them in order to act, and from the different processes that lead to the formation of their different layers.

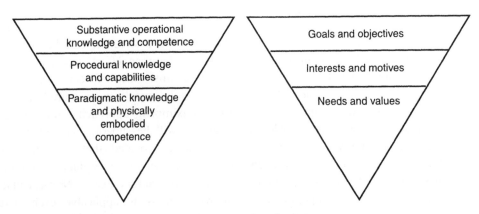

Figure I.4 Logical structure of actor knowledge and preferences

Both the inter-related and interpreted sets of information that make up an actor's knowledge and the wider set of skills that concur to make up an actor's competence have profound, highly embodied layers, in part inherited (socially and genetically) – in which case they are rather difficult to change – and in part accepted by convention. These elements are quite removed from action. There are many ways of applying them. At least two other components of knowledge and competence link paradigmatic competence to action: a substantive, domain-specific "database" of know-that propositions or repertoires (for example, content notions in the field of chemistry, repertories of action in the work process of steel transformation) and a set of "programs," of know-how notions, of procedures that govern the application of substantive competence (for example, experience in chemical research, learned sensibility about when to apply which productive correction as a function of a diagnosed state of melted steel). The relative incidence of the different layers of knowledge and competence have important consequences for the degree of change and discretion that is present in a system of action (Chapter 7).

A preference is a value-laden judgment, expressed (explicitly or implicitly) over alternatives. As a form of knowledge (about reality and about the self), a set of preferences exhibits a hierarchical structure, in which fundamental values and needs can be distinguished from assessments of what an actor's interests in a situation are; and interests can in turn be distinguished from the setting of objectives and goals to be reached. These distinctions are important because the less abstract and more operational the definition of preferences becomes, the more action is constrained. The *degree of precision and operationalization* of goals is therefore an important determinant of the degree of discretion and of the possibility to be creative. Another relevant dimension of the preference structure of an actor is the *ambitiousness or difficulty of goals*, the setting of which is fundamental in sustaining motivation.

Effectiveness, efficiency, and the need for equity judgments

The content of preferences is difficult to predict, and "content models" of motivation can be easily criticized. It can be more reliably supposed that actors are interested in linking actions' consequences to their ends – whatever they might be. This is a criterion of *effectiveness*. Most often, in economic action, actors are also interested in pursuing their interests while saving resources for other possible interesting uses – a criterion of *efficiency*. In many situations these two criteria are not sufficient for evaluating possible actions – the core reasons being that the resources employed and the benefits gained may not be comparable, and that the utilities of different actors should not be assumed to be comparable in a straightforward way (for example, through sums and differences) in most conditions. This creates an indeterminacy as to what the best action is. The notion of "best action," if one wishes to retain it, should include some "joint best" principle, i.e. some criterion of *equity*.

Part II

Coordination Mechanisms

....

Introduction to Part II

A Definition of Coordination

••

Most economic activities generate *interdependences* among actors. For example, the minimum efficient scale to produce most goods and services is greater than one person; different individuals can derive benefits by exchanging resources and the knowledge that differentiates them; economic and social activities derive benefits from the use of common infrastructure (transport, urban locations, communication). All this creates interdependences, and the *effective* regulation of those interdependences requires *coordination*.

Coordination and effectiveness

The technical meaning in which the term coordination will be used here does not go far from its common language one: "to order together; to deploy many things or elements in the most appropriate order for the purposes that one wants to achieve." Then, *the concept of coordination implies an evaluation of effectiveness*, of the desired results. In fact, if we were not interested in results, it would be useless to coordinate: the instruments of an orchestra could each freely express themselves according to the inspiration of the moment, as for the players and the listeners the resulting cacaphony would be as valuable as the symphony. In this sense, it can be said

that *coordination is a set of modes for Pareto-improving collective action* (Casson 1991).

Coordination, influence, and power

Second, *the concept of coordination implies an exercise of influence* among interdependent actors, although according to modalities that can be very different. In fact, the coordination of many actors, whatever the motive for which the actors need to be coordinated, implies processes of *reciprocal modification of behavior.* In the social sciences, normally the processes of modification of behaviors among actors is indicated by the term *influence.*

However, not all influence is coordination. In this text, to the extent that we are concerned with how coordination of collective action is achieved, and not with collective action in general, we will focus mainly on the modes through which actors influence each other in a desired direction. For example, if we physically hit a person on a bus (or psychologically hurt a colleague in the office), it is possible that the person hit or hurt will react by complaining or protesting. Even in this case we have exercised influence, i.e. we have modified the behavior of another person, but not in a desired direction. This does not mean that the "unforeseen consequences" of action are not important; actually these are an integral part of it and essential for understanding the positive and negative properties of various modes of coordination (Merton 1949; Boudon 1977; Giddens 1984). The unforeseen consequences of coordinated or organized action will be treated here in relation to the modality of coordination that generates them: if positive, it will be treated as an opportunity for changing the collective activities and their organization; if negative, it will be treated as a limit, paradox, or "cost" associated with the modality of coordination.

The capacity to exercise influence on the behavior of others in a desired direction has sometimes been a definition of *power* (Dahl, 1957). All the modalities of coordination analyzed here imply that one or more actors have power and exercise influence on others. However, not all power is coordination. The concept of coordination implies an evaluation of results from the point of view of all the players involved, albeit each with its own interests, and no assumption about the content of the pursued interests. For example, in price-based coordination, consumers have power over

producers, in so far as they can influence the types of product offered; in authority systems, one or more parties agree to take actions indicated by other parties; in teams and negotiations, different actors exert influence reciprocally.

Coordination with and without communication

It could be thought that coordination implies communication. This is not true, if coordination is intended as Pareto-improvement. There are situations in which it is possible to increase the pay-offs for everybody without bearing the cost of communication (Schelling 1960). Some concepts from game theory can help to distinguish those situations in which communication is useless from those in which it is worthwhile and to show when coordination mechanisms stronger than communication are necessary for effective multiparty action.

The structure of the game in Box II.1 could be interpreted as follows: company A has more competence in developing product 2

Box II.1
Choosing a "competitive strategy" . . . without competition

Suppose that two firms are evaluating alternative investments to develop products for which the demand is correlated, for example antibiotics and vitamins. Let us further suppose that each firm could bet on one or the other product at a given moment, and that the predictions for the possible outcomes are as follows:

		Company B	
		Product 1	Product 2
Company A	Product 1	3, 4	7, 6
	Product 2	12, 10	6, 5

Note: Numbers before commas = Pay-offs for company A. Numbers after commas = Pay-offs for company B.

and company B in the production of product 1; and for neither of them is it appropriate to develop and launch the same product at the same time. The combination of the strategies by which company A develops product 2 and B develops product 1 is the best for both parties.

Once those involved have seen that the consequences are of this type – i.e. that it is in everybody's best interest for each party to adopt behavior that is also in the best interests of the others involved – the solution of the game does not require any further communication or agreement. This type of game structure, where the best result obtainable for one party is attainable when the other players also get their best outcome, is the opposite of a "purely competitive" structure of a zero sum game – see Box II.2.

Which advertising strategy would you pick if you were player A in the problem presented in Box II. 2?

Looking to achieve the best results for yourself, you could begin by taking into consideration A1, which would allow you to increase your market share by 8 points. However, this outcome is dependent on player B picking B3. But would you pick B3 if you were player B? Probably not, because you would run the risk of big losses in two out of three cases; not only that, if you choose B3 in the hope of gaining 7 points, this outcome is improbable because it is possible only if player A picks A3: also improbable, given that A runs the risk of suffering the greatest losses with that choice. In effect, the game is problematic because the results for A and for B are diametrically opposed: in each cell, that which one gains, the other loses – it is a "zero sum" game. If you were A, then you could consider A2, the line where the worst that could happen to you is higher (a "maximin" strategy) – in this case to gain nothing. If B

used the same reasoning, he would pick column B1. The final outcome for both would be the "least of all evils" that could result from the various actions, represented in this game by the result, 0, 0. Unappealing as this seems, it should be noted that neither of the two players could get a better outcome by unilaterally changing strategy: A can only do worse by picking A1 or A2 and the same is true for B by picking B2 or B3; this characteristic is true only for cell A2, B1. Therefore, this solution is said to be an equilibrium.

The interesting aspect of this situation is that players can coordinate their choices, so as to attain the equilibrium solution, without having to communicate. *In a zero sum game, communication is not only unnecessary but useless*: there is no information or resource to offer in order to improve the result for all parties (Luce and Raiffa 1958).[1]

According to a curious law of symmetry, other conditions being equal, *communication is not necessary for either of these two extreme configurations of interests* – neither for perfect competition, nor for perfect cooperation. Both can be tacit.

Games with communication potential

For the great variety of games which fall between these two extremes, instead, communication is a fundamental mechanism for participants to obtain superior solutions.

The simplest, most obvious instance of the need for interdependent actors to communicate occurs when those actions which are convenient for everybody are in danger of being lost, either owing to *error* or to *chance*. For example, if two professors of different subjects arrive to give a lecture in the same classroom at the same time, it is presumed that communication has been insufficient or unclear – supposing that the professors do

You are the marketing director in a firm that distributes replacement parts for diesel engines. Your firm operates in the northern regions of your country and the firm has only one competitor of any importance which distributes the same product. Total demand for replacement parts has been stable for several years and you do not foresee any changes in it in the near future. However, the market shares controlled by company A and company B have always been subject to notable variations. Advertising is the principal variable that could influence these variations in market share, given that there are scant possibilities for technical differentiation in the product.

One of the principal distribution channels used by both companies is the magazine *Diesel Design*, the primary publication specializing in diesel engines and replacement parts. Each November, the editor of the magazine meets separately with you and with the marketing director of your competitor to define a package of advertising for the issues in the coming year.

The magazine editor usually proposes three different types of package to each firm. Each package specifies the format, placement in the magazine, and the number of pages in the advertising inserts. Each firm can choose any one of the three packages proposed. The advantages of one package over another may be: placement and more space towards the beginning of the magazine as opposed to placement close to an article which deals with a theme relative to the replacement parts market. Each firm knows which three packages have been proposed to its competitor.

Imagine you have just seen the three packages offered to your firm and those offered to your competitor (company B) and have evaluated the effect each combination of choices would have on respective market shares, as shown in the table below. For example, in your estimation, if A chooses package A1 and B chooses B3, A's market share will increase by 8 percent and B's will drop by 8 percent.

Changes in A's market share according to the different advertising packages chosen by A and B:

		Package chosen by B		
Package	A1	−1, 1	−4, 4	8, −8
chosen	A2	0, 0	3, −3	6, −6
by A	A3	−3, 3	5, −5	−7, 7

Note: Net results for A before the comma, net results for B after the comma.

Which package would you choose if you were A? And if you were B?

Source: Grandori (1986).

not care which classroom they go to, but merely that they go to different classrooms and find the right students present. These situations arise, typically, because, in the absence of a conflict between interests in the matter, there is more than one course of action that could lead to a coordinated outcome, but the parties involved cannot know a priori which it is unless they communicate it. This type of situation in a business problem is illustrated in Box II.3.

In this case, it can be calculated whether it is suitable or not to communicate in order to guarantee that the combinations A1, B2 or A3, B3 be chosen rather than any other, based on the difference between the differential benefits that can be obtained and the cost of coordination.

A different structure of the game emerges when the parties involved have conflictual preferences concerning actions (for example, both professors from the example above want classroom A and do not want classroom B), but would suffer even more negative consequences (going to the same classroom) if they *both* chose their preferred alternative.

This type of game structure is known as the "Battle of the Sexes." In the traditional version, the husband prefers vacationing in the mountains, the wife prefers the seaside, but both prefer to go together, rather than go separately to his or her preferred location (in an updated version, both might prefer to vacation in the mountains, but both prefer not to clash with their spouse or ex-spouse over the preferred destination). The way to coordinate the situation effectively does not change: a unilateral decision is ineffective, because it frequently leads to an inferior solution for all involved. *There is a need for communication, created by the potential for error, and if conflicts of interest are added in, coordination mechanisms stronger than communication, such as negotiation, are superior.* (How would you solve your "battles" on vacation destination with friends or family members, for example?)

Games with opportunism potential

Now think about and play the game described in Box II.4. The structure of the

---

Box II.3
Game with error potential

A group of decision-makers having the same preferences and knowing the outcomes which can be obtained is eventually able to calculate what is the optimal amount of communication, bearing in mind the cost of these activities. Suppose, for example, that choosing the level of output of a firm depends on the actions chosen by two subunits A and B and that the pay-off matrix is as follows:

		Player B		
		B1	B2	B3
Player A	A1	0, 0	9, 9	−10, −10
	A2	0, 0	0, 0	0, 0
	A3	0, 0	−10, −10	9, 9

Source: Feldman and Kanter (1965).

game is mixed: there are both conflictual elements and elements of potential cooperation. The difficult problem to solve is that, in this case, the benefits to be obtained by unilaterally choosing a "conflictual" strategy are superior to those which can be obtained through a "cooperative strategy." The results for A are better if Y is chosen, than if X, independently of what B will do. The same is true for B in choosing K. Y and K are dominant strategies. However, if both parties choose their own dominant strategy, the outcome will be negative for both. Not only that: if they communicate and agree to play the two cooperative strategies X and J, there is an even stronger incentive to break the agreement unilaterally. Therefore, not only coordination by unilateral interdependent decisions, but also coordination by simple communication and negotiation are likely to fail in games with high opportunism potential, such as Prisoner's Dilemmas (especially if the possible gains and losses are high).

What coordination mechanisms could then be used to reach the collectively desirable outcome X, Y? For example, the involved parties could "tie their hands" reciprocally through obligations and commitments setting penalties that would be greater than possible gains, if they acted opportunistically (for example, public declarations which could cause a loss of *reputation*, or *pledges*). Or the parties could establish *control and inspection mechanisms* concerning putting an achieved cooperative agreement into effect (such as has been done in disarmament). Or a *monitoring and arbitrating authority* could be nominated to check that each party is respecting cooperative behaviors, if reciprocal control is difficult (as is common in taxation games). Whatever the case, we are far removed from situations where unilateral decision-making, tacit coordination, or simple communication is effective. Interdependence situations where elements of competition are mixed with elements of cooperation and, in particular, situations where there is potential for opportunism, should be coordinated by tighter mechanisms, such as *joint decision-making, authority, and rules.*[2]

Box II.4
Prisoner's dilemmas with different potential for opportunism

		B	
		Strategy J	Strategy K
A	Strategy X	5, 5	−5, 10
	Strategy Y	10, −5	−3, −3

Play the game by unilaterally choosing your own moves (X or Y if you are A; J or K, if you are B), hypothesising that the game is played only once. Then try playing the same scheme with the hypothesis that you have many turns available, for example, ten, and you are able to communicate with and agree with the other player. Then try both schemes but put a 30 instead of a 10 as a maximum positive gain; or a −30 as a worst possible result (instead of −5).

The above discussion sets out some basic implications of different configurations of interests for effective coordination mechanisms. It also serves to introduce some basic types of mechanisms, which differ according to the type of information shared or exchanged and to the types of decision rights shared or exchanged. The various mechanisms are shown in Figure II.1.

These mechanisms have different coordination properties not only in conflict resolution respects, but also in information-processing respects. Think of different persons, or groups, or firms as knowledge and competence nodes – suspending the problem of different interests. Again, in certain cases information sharing and exchange are not necessary; in other cases, they would occur directly and "spontaneously" among parties – just setting up a communication infrastructure; in still other cases, no information and knowledge transfer or sharing occurs unless tighter and more powerful coordination structures are set up.

For certain products and some services, the knowledge employed for production can be separated from that necessary for selling or using them. Coordination between production, sale, and consumption can be achieved through *prices*, and goods can be transferred without sustaining the costs of exchanging the specialized or local knowledge of the different actors (Demsetz 1988). There are instead products that cannot be transferred unless the recipient knows a lot about how they have been constructed and work, for example, a consultancy report. Communication is necessary to coordinate exchanges effectively if the application of outputs requires specific and complex knowledge of that output. For example, usually the transfers of industrial goods require more communication than that of standardized large consumption goods. But even communication would not suffice, if the knowledge employed in the different activities is tacit and involves difficult causal diagnosis and problem-solving: a salesperson, or a supplier

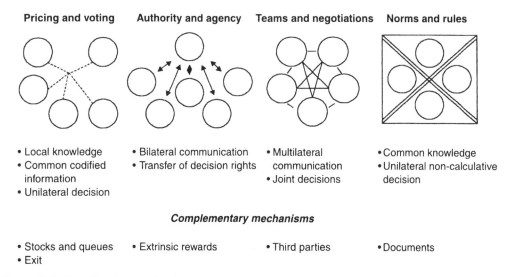

Pricing and voting	Authority and agency	Teams and negotiations	Norms and rules
• Local knowledge • Common codified information • Unilateral decision	• Bilateral communication • Transfer of decision rights	• Multilateral communication • Joint decisions	• Common knowledge • Unilateral non-calculative decision

Complementary mechanisms

• Stocks and queues • Exit	• Extrinsic rewards	• Third parties	• Documents

Figure II.1 Coordination mechanisms

of components, has to "go" to see what the production problems are if actions are to be coordinated. *Groups* are formed and coordinating roles are appointed in these situations. But if it happens that someone knows better than any other what the best design of a product should be for solving all production and sales problems (if knowledge were concentrated rather than distributed), then it is better that that actor decides for all – by *authority*.

The classification illustrated in Figure II.1 is useful for comparing the capacity (and costs) of different mechanisms in governing the diversity of interests and knowledge among economic actors, under varying conditions of uncertainty. This analysis and comparison will be discussed throughout Part II.[3]

The first category of mechanisms is capable of orienting collective action toward effective results without direct communication and without joint decision among actors. This category includes the mechanisms of pricing and voting (Chapter 3).

The second category of mechanisms (including authority and agency relations) is based on the sharing or trading of some decision rights and on partner-specific communication (Chapter 4).

A third type of coordination mechanisms involves an agreement between actors on which actions to undertake, as in teams and negotiations (Chapters 5 and 6).

Finally there are mechanisms which guide behavior without requiring ad hoc decision-making. A large part of the coordination of economic behaviors is "automatic": it is undertaken in accordance with precepts and conventions, rules, and programs (Chapter 7).

The conclusions to Part II will reconsider and summarize the results of the detailed analysis of each mechanism conducted in the following chapters, showing how to compare and combine different mechanisms to govern specific interdependence situations.

Chapter 3

Pricing and Voting

· ·

This chapter outlines the conditions under which coordination can be achieved by means of unilateral decision-making, without direct communication between parties. Pricing and voting systems are mechanisms which convey the relevant information allowing this decentralized and decoupled coordination to take place. We are not concerned here with a substantive theory of equilibrium choices, with what prices or which distribution of votes will emerge. We are concerned with the properties of these devices as modes of organizing or coordinating the actions of different players.

The outline of the chapter, specifying the common and different attributes in the profile of those mechanisms, the type of relations that can be effectively governed by them, and some salient sub-types of pricing and voting systems are summarized in Figure 3.1.

PRICING

How and when people discovered the power of a pricing system as a mechanism for coordinating economic activity is an interesting, historical, and very open question (White 1981). To be sure, once discovered, it became a widely diffused mechanism, applied in the most diverse industrial sectors, between and within firms, and assuming a primary role in regulating national and international economic systems.

The fact that scarce resources need to be distributed to various actors and allocated to various productive activities while keeping information and knowledge exchanges to a minimum (Smith 1776; von Hayek 1945), has certainly been one of the main reasons why the price mechanism has been so widely affirmed as a system for coordinating and governing economic systems.

Box 3.1 presents von Hayek's authoritative and interesting description of coordination systems based on prices as a system which economizes information-processing costs. This interpretation of prices as pieces of highly codified information sheds light on the connection between prices and knowledge. In von Hayek's description, rather than belonging to a world of perfect knowledge and absolute rationality, prices appear as ingenious heuristics, helping to solve complex problems without much analysis. As is the case for all heuristics, however, a lot of information is sacrificed in judging by prices; and one can legitimately ask when the knowledge costs of this procedure outweigh the efficiency gains. This consideration should therefore enter into the evaluation of when coordination by prices is superior to other forms of coordination.

	PRICING	VOTING
CONDITIONS:	• Structured problems • Large members of actors • Local knowledge	
	• Exchange opportunities |	• Collective action opportunities
MECHANISM PROFILE:	• Common general information on alternatives • Unilateral decisions (no partner-specific communication)	
	• Independent actions |	• Aggregation of preference orderings
TYPES:	• Administered • Discovered	• One actor-one vote • Weighted

Figure 3.1 Pricing and voting

Local information and utility maximization

Producers and consumers take decisions on the basis of their local information: they know what resources are available to them – for example, for a consumer it could be the family budget; for a producer, the production technologies to which the firm has access. And they know their preferences – for example, consumers must know if they prefer a combination of more travel and less food expenses, or vice versa (that is to say, they know their "indifference curves" on goods and services). Prices are the only type of information available to everybody, and signal the exchange value and the relative scarcity of an item. If prices are "sufficient statistics" (Williamson 1975) of these variables, and no single actor can exert significant influence on them unilaterally, then profitability can be a clear, synthetic, and locally available yardstick for measuring how good production decisions have been, and for guiding action. As long as profit performs this measurement and incentive function accurately, it can be said that the efficient actions of producers can be predicted well "as if" they were pursuing profit (Friedman 1953). In fact, at the local level, and in each micro-decision on

what to offer and demand, actors face a structured and limited problem in which it is possible to apply a value-maximizing decision strategy. If not able to envisage all possible production and consumption alternatives, they will sequentially choose alternatives with superior expected pay-off, eventually discovering the optimal attainable position. Consumers will discover consumption plans that yield them the maximum utility. Producers will discover profit-maximizing production levels. Investors will discover optimal allocations for financial resources. When that happens, and to the extent to which it can happen, the price mechanism optimizes resource allocation.

The process through which local optimizing decisions lead to a general "optimal" allocation of resources can differ sharply, however, according to how prices themselves are defined. They can be "discovered" incrementally – through a "tatonnement" process (Walras 1874). Or they can be "calculated" as a solution to an optimization problem for a given system – provided that the system is not too large and ever-changing to make these calculations unfeasible. Therefore we can distinguish between types of price systems, in particular between discovered or "free" prices

Box 3.1
Prices as codified information

If we possess all the relevant information, if we can start out from a given system of preferences, and if we command complete knowledge of available means, the problem which remains is purely one of logic. That is, the answer to the question of what is the best use of the available means is implicit in our assumptions. . . . This, however, is emphatically not the economic problem which society faces. . . . The peculiar character of the problem of a rational economic order is determined precisely by the fact that the knowledge of the circumstances of which we must make use never exists in concentrated or integrated form, but solely as the dispersed bits of incomplete and frequently contradictory knowledge which all the separate individuals possess.

Practically every individual has some advantage over all others in that he possesses unique information of which beneficial use might be made, but which can be used only if the decisions depending on it are left to him or are made with his active cooperation. We need to remember only how much we have to learn in any occupation after we have completed our theoretical training, and how valuable an asset in all walks of life is knowledge of people, of local conditions, and special circumstances.

If detailed economic plans could be laid down for fairly long periods in advance and then closely adhered to, so that no further economic decisions of importance would be required, the task of drawing up a comprehensive plan governing all economic activity would appear much less formidable. It is, perhaps, worth stressing that economic problems arise always and only as a consequence of change.

If we can agree that the economic problem of society is mainly one of rapid adaptation to changes in the particular circumstances of time and place, it would seem to follow that the ultimate decisions must be left to the people who are familiar with these circumstances, who know directly of the relevant changes and of the resources immediately available to meet them. . . . We must solve it by some form of decentralization. . . . Fundamentally, in a system where the knowledge of the relevant facts is dispersed among many people, prices can act to coordinate the separate actions. . . . We must look at the price system as such a mechanism for communicating information. The most significant fact about this system is the economy of knowledge with which it operates, or how little the individual participants need to know in order to be able to take the right action. In abbreviated form, by a kind of symbol, only the most essential information is passed on. . . . The marvel is that in a case like that of a scarcity of one raw material, without an order being issued, without more than perhaps a handful of people knowing the cause, tens of thousands of people whose identity could not be ascertained by months of investigation, are made to use the material or its products more sparingly; i.e., they move in the right direction.

Source: von Hayek (1945).

and calculated and regulated prices. Thanks to these differences, price-based coordination can be used efficiently as a constitutive mechanism in different types of institutions, in particular *both in markets and firms.*

"Discovered" prices

In conditions of change and diffused information, as is clearly illustrated in the citation from von Hayek, prices cannot be "calculated" as in an accounting system, but have to be discovered themselves. On the supply side, prices and quantities are adjusted in the "obvious direction" as indicated by observed disequilibria (if demand exceeds supply, then the price will be increased and vice versa). In these conditions, an efficient search process is a series of small sequential moves raising or lowering prices and quantities until supply equals demand (Hayek 1945).

Exit

On the demand side, consumers send information about the "correctness" of producers' moves through "*exit.*" As Hirschman (1970) effectively illustrated, exit is the core sanction or control mechanism which accompanies the information mechanism of price to constitute a market system of governance. If a firm does not produce goods that a consumer is willing to buy, or produces poor quality items, or demands prices that are too high given the current supply and demand relationship, it will gradually begin to lose more and more customers. This is a valuable signal for the firm that has undertaken misdirected actions. When is this signal effective?

Substitutability

For economic actors to be able to generate

informative messages through exit, it is necessary that they be able to find alternative trading partners, without significant costs. For example, a firm transforming steel into other products must be able to buy steel from various suppliers; a person offering services, such as a secretary, must have the possibility of considering various job offers; a manufacturing company that is unsatisfied with the service furnished by one of its distributors must be able to find other wholesalers to replace that partner easily; a user who is unsatisfied with a service provided by its company's internal printing office should be able to buy the service outside; and so forth.

In order for this to happen, conditions of high *substitutability* among trading partners should be sustainable.

On the other hand, if substitutability were perfect and exit without any attrition, the system would learn very slowly (Hirschman 1970). In fact, if a producer made "wrong" offers (in quality, quantity, or price) "some" consumers would begin to exit, thereby signaling the "mistake" to the supplier. If all the clients of a firm reacted immediately by suddenly exiting, the firm would not have time to receive the signal and correct its action. It would die. If the market mechanism worked in this way, its information-processing efficiency would be bought at the cost of a very low efficiency in learning: the system would be able to change only via the slow and resource-wasting process of natural selection (death and substitution of misfit subjects) rather than by taking advantage of human actors' capability to learn individually (change their own actions).

Therefore, the mechanism of "natural selection" is to be considered a complementary mechanism that, combined with incrementally discovered prices and incremental exit sanctions, is constitutive of an efficient competitive market. Actors may be unable to perceive or may ignore weak signals. Or, product and process innovations may create discontinuities to which continuous or incremental adjustment is not possible. In these cases, natural selection is likely to drive the system toward "correct" actions (inappropriate subjects are substituted) rather than learning (subjects substitute inappropriate behaviors).

Therefore, different types of market can be defined, according to the degree of substitutability of players, the extent to which prices are learned incrementally or directly influenced by firms, and the incidence of natural selection with respect to learning. In fact, as the theorists of imperfect competition have stressed in developed economies, many sources of insubstitutability and monopoly have added to the traditional "natural monopoly" and small market size causes (Chapter 8). The supply and demand of differentiated, complex, customized, and innovative goods, which have become increasingly important, systematically reduce the comparability and perceived substitutability of players. Think of fashion articles, management consulting services, new software designed for particular applications. It is difficult to regulate the production and exchange of goods and services of this type by using only a combination of price and exit: either because it is difficult to compare different producers'outputs; or because evaluating the quality and value of goods and services is difficult; or because the value of partners' contributions is higher in some matches than in others, so that exit and substitution are costly.

Pricing will be used as an important coordination mechanism, in all kinds of markets, but it will be combined with other mechanisms, such as tacit coordination, regulation, and negotiation, the incidence of which, in addition to the price mechanism, may qualify a variety of market governance forms (Grandori 1997a; Chapter 12).

"Administered" prices

Consider the coordination problem described in Box 3.2: which coordination mechanisms are employed? Coordination in large firms is often ensured by prices. There are, increasingly, "internal markets" of services (Alchian and Demsetz 1972), of capital (Williamson 1970), of knowledge (Davenport and Prusak 1998). Pricing is applicable, provided that information can be structured and relevant alternatives are known. "Transfer prices" are set for regulating exchanges among firms' divisions. Other mechanisms too have the nature of internal prices. "Incentives" for inducing agents to take particular actions are an example: they are amounts of money paid for particular services; they orient action by rewarding actions that will be adopted by unilateral decision, without the interventions of plans, communication, and controls.

Stocks and queues

The situation described in Box 3.2 also helps to illustrate another coordination mechanism that is often (but not always) associated with monetary prices and exit: stocks and queues.

The adjustment of offer to demand takes time. The greater the possibility of constituting inventories of products to be delivered when demand peaks, the easier the adjustment (though at a cost). Conversely, to the extent to which it is difficult or costly to use stocks (as occurs in many service activities), it is demand that piles up: and the time a customer is willing to wait for a good or service performs the function of a price, conveying

Box 3.2
Pricing internal services: the
charge back of information
system costs

The IT director of MBP Distributions, a leading firm in the distribution of books (from publishers to bookstores) and periodicals (from publishers to news-stands) is concerned with the figures of his IT budget for next year. During the annual November meeting, when all executives would present the final budgets for their areas, he was expected to justify a 30 percent cost increase even though he knew he could not match a similar increase in service performance.

As regards internal company politics, this fact was seen as a negative in that it showed that one of the central units "that did nothing but spend" should instead come forward to clients with high customer service standards. His colleagues would not therefore have understood his request for a budget increase, and that would have forced the IT function to cut the following year's costs.

The reasons for the increase in costs were numerous and diverse: they concerned technical, personnel, delivery, as well as exogenous and endogenous issues. Without that additional 30 percent the director would not be able to guarantee the productivity levels necessary for the firm in its dealing with information resources (circulation of books, logistics, shipping, truck-loading arrangements, improved delivery routes). As in other firms, staff IT skills were very inconsistent: sometimes the IT technicians were called on to solve simple problems ("the printer does not print" or "the computer does not boot up") only to realize later – for example – that the users did not connect the machines to the network. The users' requests for help were indeed most unusual and diverse.

The director attended a conference on the issue: how to manage an increased IT budget and offer a good level of service. A solution was possible: charge service costs to the users or rather to the organizational units that they belonged to. In order to accomplish this, it was necessary to:

- define an internal pricing system for each function and each product (both hardware and software) that would be competitive with similar external pricing systems. This would imply the creation of a price list that would entail all the typical updating and quality evaluation problems related to quantities requested and consumed. For example: "Would you like to change your office PC? If you are happy with Alfa, Beta, and Gamma models that have already been configured for the average users within the company, you could have it on your desk within 10 days from the order date and with a discount of 30 percent on the market price." In these cases the company could purchase large volumes of equipment of those models that were most in demand in order to offer better discounts to its users.
- purchase and install the necessary software on the company servers that would be able to assess who is connected, for how long, what software packages he/she uses, how many reports he/she has requested.
- match a price list to all IT resources with the company network in order to be able to calculate the monthly cost for each user.

- change the accounting system so that an "internal charges" line would be tracked within the IT budget. The line would be an "income generator" within the functions that would come from purchases of goods and services by the users throughout the year. In exchange, it would be necessary to modify the budget structure of all other functions in order to allow for a new line related to costs that would represent purchases of IT goods and services.
- rearrange the overall IT resources of the firm in order to be able always to guarantee careful support. This is necessary because when dealing with paying customers, it is impossible to refuse the service, and one must always be able to find a solution. The transfer of the IT costs to the customer is nothing but a transfer of the evaluation of priorities from the function headquarters to the final users (the demand). Up to now this activity had only been partially successful and was the source of conflict.

These IT charge back procedures were of some concern to the director. What would the users' reactions be? What competences would the IT personnel need to have? What would happen if benchmarking of the service with company suppliers took place?

Source: By Ferdinando Pennarola.

information of the relative worth of that item for different customers (Barzel 1989).

"Buffers" of resources are also a way of reducing the degree of continuous alignement between the "offer" and "demand" sides of a transfer of goods or services (Galbraith 1977). They reduce the need for "just-in-time" coordination between different activities. As the "just-in-time" management philosophy has stressed, on the other hand, one should consider the costs of stocks and queues, in terms of immobilized, "non-working" capital.

In conclusion, *prices, exit, and buffers, hence, may combine in different ways. They can be applied, if information can be structured sufficiently, and if there are many players*, in conjunction or separately with respect to each other and with respect to other coordination mechanisms. A price system per se could be used in a system in which the ownership of production means is centralized, such as a large multidivisional firm or a state-owned sector. In combination with exit, it could still

be used in a conglomerate decentralized firm whose units were profit centers free to buy and and sell either internally or externally. "The market," as a governance system, is constituted by a larger and more complicated set of coordination mechanisms than just price, exit, and buffers; just as different forms of internal organization are characterized by different combinations of price-like mechanisms with others – such as voting, authority, joint decision-making, and rules (Chapters 11 and 12).

VOTING

Voting is a mechanism for coordinating collective action that has much in common with the pricing mechanism (Buchanan and Tullock 1962; Lindblom 1977). The two means of coordination do indeed share some important features and applicative conditions.

- Voting is based on an exit principle

(Hirschman 1970). Actors interested in a particular problem are to be free to choose between the various competing solutions.

- A menu of alternatives should be known, structured, and mutually exclusive.
- Voting is capable of coordinating large numbers of actors, because the exchange of information is reduced to very low levels: actors communicate chosen alternatives to a processing center; the processing center communicates the collective choice, expressed as an aggregation of individual unilateral choices. Where there are large numbers of actors, voting is a *feasible* coordination mechanism, where any of the other potential alternative systems based on the direct, reciprocal influence between the parties involved would be difficult to apply. Voting is also a system which *requires* large numbers of decision-makers to work well (and a limited number of action alternatives) (Tullock 1967). In fact, in small groups, voting is not a very attractive option, unless rather extreme voting rules are used, such as a unanimity principle. In this case, however, it is not the voting mechanism itself which may resolve conflicts, but the processes of reciprocal persuasion taking place in the group. For example, in a group of 5 people, a majority of 3 out of 5 reduces to a simple majority and to a difference of only 1 vote from the minority; whereas in a large group, say 100 people, a majority of 3/5 is a qualified majority, well above 51 percent or the advantage of one vote.

These are some of the important similarities between voting and pricing mechanisms; but there are also other important differences that make each mechanism suited to solving different coordination problems.

Exchange of complementary resources among pairs of actors and competition among actors offering or demanding similar resources is the type of interdependence that prices can coordinate. Not all multiple actor coordination problems are of this kind, however. Opportunities for *common or aligned action*, to *share rather than exchange resources*, can also arise and constitute another form of interdependence to be coordinated. While recognizing the advantages of coordinated action, parties can order action alternatives according to preference in different ways. Voting is an interesting mechanism for constructing "collective preferences, " if the number of actors is sufficiently high and the number of possible actions is sufficiently low. Even under these conditions, though, voting entails its particular costs and is not certain to lead to a solution. What are these limits and costs?

The trade-off between equity and efficiency

An organizational economics view of voting has been developed by applying the political economists' analytical tools to the problem of collective choice and democratic coordination. Among the results there have been elements for the comparative assessment of voting schemes and the comparative assessment of voting with respect to other coordination mechanisms (Arrow 1951; Buchanan and Tullock 1962).

The definition of an optimal voting rule has been addressed as being conditioned by the simultaneous presence of the following two contrasting needs: the more accurately the voting scheme represents the preferences of all actors – that is, the closer it comes to a unanimity requirement under which all are represented – the more costly the process will be: by reason of the process of discussion and persuasion, and the risk of not reaching a consensus. In other words, there is a trade-off between the costs of lack of representation of some actors (an equity criterion), and decision process costs (an efficiency criterion). One can therefore pose the question: how large should the required consensus on decision be for minimizing the total "costs" of a collective decision. Buchanan and Tullock (1962) have called the two cost functions "internal costs" and "external costs." Assuming there is a group of N decision-makers aiming to reach an agreement on a decision that applies to the whole group, and that K represents the number of actors needed to reach a consensus for making the decision (the voting rule), the costs of representation loss decrease with K and are zero for K = N. Decision process costs are zero for an imposition of one actor and increase with K, as represented in Figure 3.2. If the two functions have this shape, then the sum function, that takes into account both the costs of representing preferences completely and the costs of formulating representative decisions, will have a U form: that is, there will be a point K', falling between O and N, for which the costs are minimal. This number defines the optimal voting rule.

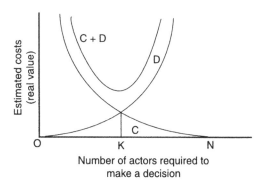

Figure 3.2 The comparative assessment of voting rules

Effectiveness and the quality of decisions

Stable groups may become very efficient in discussion, and find ways to settle conflicts in advance before resorting to voting; or they may share norms and values to such an extent that they are able most times to decide almost unanimously.

The situation described in Box 3.3 illustrates such a situation, and some of its perils, in spite of the impressive performance in terms both of high representativeness and low decision costs. The example stresses the practical importance of the requirements that problems be structured, alternatives be known, and research and confrontation for developing new solutions be relatively unimportant in order for voting to be effective. Plainly, in the relatively unstructured problem of forming a research consortium, it would have been better to suspend voting in order to make room for group problem-solving.

Other difficulties may arise because "calculating the optimal consensus" can be difficult in practice: that is, it may be difficult to quantify and compare internal and external costs to find an optimal K. The costs of lack of representativeness may be simple to evaluate, if expressed as the fraction of actors that can determine the decision. Decision process costs are experienced in quite different terms: people time, investments in logistic facilities, or communication channels (and the monetary costs of these resources). How much is the loss of one vote worth in terms of process costs? This judgment is prohibitively difficult. This may help to explain why the simple majority rule (50 percent plus one) is so much used. It may be seen as a good "heuristic" for reaching a reasonable approximation of a balanced trade-off between the two cost functions, without actually calculating

> **Box 3.3**
> How to make bad decisions
> with an optimal decision rule
>
> The Faculty Council meets exactly on time at 9.00 a.m. All professors are very busy at the University of Alfa and delays are not well tolerated. Discussions and decisions are very well prepared: almost every problem has its committee! For the Council is now made up of hundreds of people, and the formation of consensus at the meetings could thus be quite difficult In addition, by statute, the Faculty Council is a deliberating and voting organ. An unwritten law, however, prescribes that it is desirable that consensus be very large – in practice, that it is preferable that decisions be taken unanimously. Only in exceptional cases and overt impasses is a majority rule actually applied. What is surprising is that not only are most decisions taken with a maximum of consensus, they are also taken very efficiently.
>
> That morning a vote was required about the proposal to join in an international consortium with other universities. The international relations committee had examined all the credentials of the universities proposing the association, the study curricula, published research, etc. The decision was taken unanimously in 15 minutes.
>
> Unfortunately, later on, the agreement remained a dead letter. The energies of Faculty members were too absorbed in other matters to manage the time-consuming coordination, the real competences of researchers turned out to be difficult to integrate and, more importantly, the real working ties of scientific collaboration had been established with other people in other universities. The opportunity to form different types of agreement with different partners had not been considered, however, at the time the decision was taken.
>
> (This situation is possible but purely hypothetical and illustrative. Any reference to real cases is accidental.)

the trade-off: with respect to a situation of collective indifference, with the same number of votes in favor of and against an action, simple majority is the most efficient decision-making rule.

One actor, one vote?

In the discussion up to this point, it has been supposed that each actor having the right to contribute to making a decision on collective choice could express only one vote, as is normally assumed in models of political decision-making. This assumption is also adequate for many economic coordination problems: suffice it to recall the voting mechanisms on a university faculty board, on an administration board, in a union, or in trade associations and other organizations representing economic interests. However, many situations of organizational democracy are complicated by the fact that the actors whose interests must be represented, are collective actors who contribute in quite different degrees to the realization of common action. The typical area where these problems are manifested is in organizing the relationships between distinct economic units, such as different firms. For in coordinating common action among firms, the diverse interests with claims of representation and the need for transparency in multi-actor decision-making, make voting an adequate mechanism. On the other hand, firms can vary in size, importance, and amounts of technical and economic resources conferred.

In these circumstances, both in practice and in organization theory, a weighted voting principle has been re-evaluated (Lammers 1993). Weighting criteria may be represented, for example, by the number of people who make up the collective voting actor or by the resources which it contributes. For example, tying voting rights not to the person, but to the number of shares held in limited stock companies, is a way of weighting votes according to the entity of financial contributions.

Clear and fair weighting criteria should be devisable, however, for applying this coordination mechanism. If actors are internal organization units rather than firms, for example, measurement difficulties may be greater. If the preferences of various managers or stakeholders diverge, mechanisms for representing them within the overall utility function of the firm would be needed (Marschack 1954). But what should the weight of a unit or a manager be, as compared to others? One possibility is to allocate rights as a function of contributions, or of the intensity of preferences, or both (Chapter 2; Williamson 1964). However, it is all too often quite difficult and unreliable to discern how much one contributes in a collective activity and how much net utility one derives from having decision rights (and obligations) on it.

The difficulties in assessing the strength of preferences and the amount of contributions of cooperating actors help to explain why simple, unweighted voting schemes are often also applied in economic organization.

Another reason in favor of symmetrical, equality-based voting schemes is that, even though actors may differ in size and the value of conferred assets may be different, they may be considered as equally unreplaceable and indispensable for performing the considered joint activity. For example, a trade association could consider the affiliation of small enterprises to be just as important as that of large companies; or, in realizing a joint venture, the participation of the various partner firms may be just as necessary to the success of the common activity irrespective of the size or the market value of the resources they contribute. In these circumstances, voting rights are assigned prevalently or completely according to an equal shares principle (Grandori and Neri 1999).

Limits and paradoxes of voting

Voting does not solve all the problems of collective choice, not even within its distinctive areas of application – large numbers of actors and a small number of structured alternatives. For example, if preferences are represented by using a simplified system in which each actor can choose only one action, situations where each course of action is preferred by a very small group of actors could easily emerge. If, in an attempt to avoid this problem, or to represent the preferences more accurately, each actor is given the opportunity to order all the alternatives according to preference, other problems arise. In particular, if it is supposed that actors are free to order alternatives in any way, there is no guarantee that a voting scheme exists capable of leading to a collectively preferred action. Arrow's "general possibility theorem" supplies the most famous proof of this difficulty and is summarized briefly in Box 3.4.

Arrow's theorem has been highly influential

Box 3.4
Arrow's "general possibility
theorem"

Arrow proposes accepting some reasonable assumptions about actors' preferences: that group preferences satisfy transitive properties (if A is preferred to B, and B to C, then A is preferred to C) and that alternatives are comparable (either A is preferred to B, or B to A, or the two are indifferent). Then, the author posits that the group preferences should satisfy the following conditions:

- *Free actors*: the group consists of at least three people who are free to order at least three alternatives in whatever way;
- *Positive association of social and individual values*: the group preferences must be positively correlated to the individual ones;
- *Independence of irrelevant alternatives*: the choice is made on a fixed set of alternatives S and should be independent of alternatives outside S;
- *Citizens' sovereignty*: the collective preference order must not be imposed (it must not depend on external constraints, but only on actors' preferences);
- *Non-dictatorship*: the collective preference order must not be dictatorial (it must not depend on the preferences of one of the group members independently of those of the others).

Arrow proves that, if interpersonal comparisons of utility are not admitted, and "if no *a priori* assumptions are made about the nature of individual orderings," there is no voting scheme guaranteeing that these conditions are simultaneously satisfied.

Source: Arrow (1951).

and very useful for exploring the paradoxes and the limitations of voting. However, it has subsequently been observed that it is not very likely that combining individual preference ordering will actually lead to situations where no majority for one of the alternatives can be found, especially if there are many voters (Tullock 1967).

Moreover, actors' preference orderings are unlikely to be completely independent and free, for at least two classes of reason. The first is that the structure and the very characteristics of alternatives make certain orders improbable. In economic, social, and political decisions, alternatives are evaluated on the basis of various attributes or dimensions: for example, how innovative or conservative a policy is; where a political or economic party stands between the extreme right and left; how aggressive or risky a competitive plan or strategy is. Since decision-makers order alternatives in terms of their utility, certain orders are highly improbable (for example, a motion from the extreme left, first; from the extreme right, second; from the center, third).

The second important source of interdependence among actors' preference orders is reciprocal influence. Empirically grounded hypotheses on the nature of preferences can be done. The studies on the formation of preferences indicate that when actors are embedded in the same information context, and are connected with each other, the same "taboos" are likely to exist for everybody –

making certain courses of action unattractive for everybody – and preferences are learned on the basis of the same experience, so that the gap between preference orders narrows (March and Shapira 1982; Bandura 1986; Etzioni 1988).

Therefore, in conclusion, it should be noted that, much as pricing is not equivalent to a market, so voting should not be equated with a democracy. Voting is a mechanism that can be employed to solve particular coordination problems, not an organization or "governance" form. It can and should be combined with other mechanisms – a framework of rules and norms, the use of appropriate forms of authority to enforce decisions; the possibility to resort to direct influence and adjustment between actors, when appropriate, through group problem-solving or negotiation.

SUMMARY

In the first part of the chapter, the properties of pricing, exit, and other related mechanisms (like stocks and queues) as mechanisms for coordinating economic relations with minimal information exchange are described. Their requirements in terms of the *structurability of information* and the *substitutability of resources* are illustrated. Conversely, the non-comparability and non-measurability of value of resources lead to "price failures" (ineffectiveness of prices as a coordination device).

The second section illustrates how the voting mechanism has some properties that are similar to those of pricing, in so far as coordination among high numbers of players is achieved through unilateral decision-making, over structurable action alternatives. Voting is applicable in distinct instances of interdependence due to opportunities for *common action* rather than to opportunities for *exchange*. It has been shown how the complexity of information leads to "vote failures" due to poor decision quality; and that it is possible that collective preferences cannot be defined through voting under some particular configurations of the member actors'preferences.

It has been shown how *both pricing and voting can be employed either within or between firms* to solve specific coordination problems – for example, a transfer of raw material from one division to another can be regulated by prices; while the cooperation between different firms in an association can be regulated by voting.

Exercise: Investments in formation

An international institution financing training and research is faced with the problem of how to call for training projects for young researchers and how to allocate resources to them. Resources, inevitably, are scarce, and sufficient for financing one or two projects only that have the chance to produce sensible results. The evaluation committee is formed by seven members, each representative of one country; and, by statute, it decides by majority. Projects should indicate objectives and expected benefits, as well as the program of training interventions, the human resources needed, and a financial budget.

The committee divides up in the following two "parties" as to the coordination of the process.

- To issue a call for projects so as to solicit the maximum possible number of submissions from groups of academicians in various countries, and finance the best alternative (or the two first best). "After all – one of the proponents declares – we teach that the market works!"

- To invite the interested research group to communicate and integrate their proposals, so as to present the minimum possible number of high quality and significant projects. "After all – another committee member objects – we teach that the market doesn't always work!"

Questions

- Which features of the projects are relevant for choosing between the two options? Would the problem be different if the investment were to be made in equipment? Why?
- What type of information is encoded in the "price" of the projects? Is it sufficient information for choosing between alternative training services?
- Given the situation, is voting an effective and efficient coordination mechanism? What factors in the described situation may undermine the effectiveness, efficiency, or fairness of voting?

Chapter 4

Authority and Agency

In authority and agency relationships, two or more interdependent actors coordinate themselves by agreeing on a range of actions that could be adopted and on a way for selecting which one to adopt as a function of the state of the world. These modes of coordination require *some communication between identified parties and involve the transfer of some decision rights*. In both authority and agency relations decision rights are allocated in an asymmetrical way, involving the presence of "central agents, " of super-ordinate and sub-ordinate parties. The extent of communication and the agreement on the allocation of decision rights is however different under an authority regime and an agency regime – which consequently have different coordination properties and capabilities.

Among the forms of communication-based coordination, *authority* has received particular attention and wide application. Some of the more influential comparative analyses of the modes of coordination of economic activity have considered systems based on authority and central planning as the most important alternative to systems based on price, exit, and unilateral decision (Coase 1937; von Hayek 1945; Williamson 1975). In effect, these two types of system seem to work in opposite ways: in one case coordination is based on exit and on decentralized decisions; in the other case, coordination is ensured by the centralized decision and control of a central actor. However, these two coordination systems share at least one important common property: that of greatly reducing the cost of coordinating complex systems by reducing the amount of information exchanged. With respect to at least one alternative potential coordination scheme – that in which everyone communicates with everyone to reach a joint decision – coordination systems based both on unilateral and on centralized decisions imply lower costs of information gathering and transmission, of discussion, negotiation, and monitoring. Authority and agency relations are less radical than price-based systems in cutting down communication ties. Seen as stylized communication networks (Figure II.1), a hierarchy (either authority-based or agency-based) is a partially connected network – only some nodes are connected with many others – while in price coordination there is no specific inter-actor communication, and in a group all actors are connected. This chapter examines the mechanisms through which authority and agency relations work and the conditions under which they can be accepted as effective, efficient, and fair by the parties involved.[1] The outline of the chapter, specifying the common and different attributes in the profile of those mechanisms,

	AUTHORITY	AGENCY
CONDITIONS:	• Recurrent non instantaneous exchange or cooperation	
	• Concentrated knowledge • Observable inputs • Small numbers	• Distributed knowledge • Observable output • Large numbers
MECHANISM PROFILE:	• One central agent • Decision and control rights transfers (disjointed decision-making)	
	• Centralized decision and control • Centralized risk-bearing and residual rewards (if any)	• Centralized residual control and reward rights • Partially decentralized decision rights, risk-bearing and residual reward rights
TYPES:	• Competence-based • Decision-based • Control-based • Arbitration-based • Exchange-based	• Incentive-based • Monitoring-based

Figure 4.1 Authority and agency mechanisms

the type of relations that can be effectively governed by them, and some salient sub-types of authority and agency systems are summarized in Figure 4.1.

FORMS OF AUTHORITY

A relationship of authority between two actors exists when one of the parties consents to behave according to the decisions of the other party relative to an agreed area of behaviors (Barnard 1938; Simon 1951). Such a relationship can involve more than two actors: a group of people can accept the authority of one or more leaders.

Many economic and social relationships are authority relations. For example, workers hired by a firm agree to use the facilities and tools belonging to the owners of the firm and to apply their own skills in modes and times defined by the owners or their delegated rep-

resentatives; passengers who board an airplane accept the authority of the pilot relative to the behaviors that can effect the security of the flight; patients accept the authority of their doctors about health problems; members of a union accept the authority of their leaders. All of these are authority relationships. They have in common two essential characteristics – one actor *suspending* his or her own decision rights and *accepting* the decisions of another actor. In other words, authority is an asymmetric relationship of power that is accepted by all the parties involved as *legitimate* (Weber 1922).

Legitimation

If for example we obey the orders of someone who is pointing a gun at our head, the modification of our behavior would be induced by our perception of higher expected loss if we do not obey than if we do. In this case, we act due to an extreme form of asymmetric negotiation, resulting in an imposition, not due to a relationship of legitimate authority.

There are several reasons for the legitimization of authority. Max Weber, who began comparative studies of authority types, distinguished between three basic models: traditional, charismatic, and "rational–legal." In the first two types of authority relationships, the individual does not decide to accept the authority for some reason linked to his own utility. He accepts it uncalculatedly, either because it has always been so and is the right thing to do even if he does not understand why, or because he is emotionally attracted to or affected by the leader. Weber in fact contextualized these two forms of authority as typical of pre-modern and/or non-utilitarian social systems, such as in societies like feudal or religious orders. In systems of collective action in which the participants are aware of their own preferences and their own individual interests, the relationships of authority are often based on more calculative and explicit sources of legitimation or acceptance. For example, all the above-mentioned examples of authority – that of the employer, the expert, or the representative – are normally founded on a judgment that accepting the authority is better than not. Weber defined such authority relationships as *rational* and considered them typical of utilitarian societies in general and of capitalism in particular.

This chapter is concerned with the *properties* of authority, irrespective of the calculated or non-calculated decision processes leading to acceptance of it: it aims at explaining why and when authority is a superior way of coordinating a system of interdependent actors.

Either before or after having undertaken the first section of this chapter, depending on whether one prefers a more inductive or deductive learning style, the readers can elaborate on and discuss what mix of rational bases may explain why the following figures have authority: a university professor in a class, the captain on an airplane, a union leader, the chairman of a conference, a fiscal inspector, a production line supervisor, an owner of technical and financial resources employing human resources.

The motives for which authority comes to be accepted in the above examples are different. At least six different fundamental reasons for the formation of authority relationships can be distinguished and are explained below. As for all other coordination mechanisms dealt with in Part II, they are treated here as "stand alone" modes of governing a relationship. In reality, any mechanism, and authority in particular, will usually appear in combination with other mechanisms: for example, authority is employed "by exception" or in a "residual" way when negotiations or group decision-making fail, regulates matters that cannot be specified in a price-based contract, enforces rules. Either by itself or in residual ways with respect to other mechanisms authority is likely to be employed whenever any one of the following conditions occur.

Competence-based authority

A young researcher in a chemical-pharmaceutical laboratory with a difficult problem to resolve decides to choose the most promising method of experimentation based on the advice of a researcher with more recognized experience. A group of friends in a sailboat appoints the one most expert to be the captain. Among the workers of a production unit, all of equal formal rank, there are two leaders: one is able to influence others in the resolution of technical problems because she is believed to be more competent due to her personal capacity, long-lasting experience and recent formal training; another exerts influence thanks to his particular sensitivity to interpersonal relations, and his talents at communicating, reducing tension, and mediating conflicts.

The word authority does not necessarily refer to kings or to industrial magnates. Nor does it necessarily refer to a stable or formalized relationship. Even in minor influence relationships that develop around particular problems, relationships of authority can emerge.

In fact, starting from these "simple" relationships helps us to clearly distinguish *competence* as one source of authority in more complex relationships, where it is often commingled with other sources. In the examples above, the basis of the authority relationship is exclusively competence. This competence can be technical or social, but the competence of the leader must be considered as not only *relatively* higher than that of the person agreeing to submit to the leader's influence, but also as *absolutely* sufficient to successfully resolve the problem in question.

For competence-based authority to function effectively, there must be no conflicts of interest between the one submitting to influence and the one exercising it. Even if we believe that a person is extremely competent, we will not entrust ourselves to that person's authority if we believe that his or her advice could be self-interested according to diverging motives.

Authority based on decision-making efficiency

A group of friends who are equally expert in sailing name a captain in difficult sailing conditions. A group of associated firms name one firm as the point of contact with the local government agency for which they are executing a construction project. In a firm where production occurs in separate locations, it will often be more efficient for every factory to send their own production data to a central unit and receive instructions on how many products of a certain type to deliver than arrange a production plan for the whole firm by everybody talking and deciding with everybody else.

Number of actors

In these cases the emergence of authority is due to its capacity to align the actions of many interdependent players with a minimum expenditure of resources (time and number of communication ties). Again, it should be hypothesized that the situation is not complicated by the presence of conflicts between interests or between interpretations and judgments about the best actions to undertake. If this is the case, then a decision scheme in which all actors were to directly exchange their local information and knowledge and collectively decide on the best combination of actions, would be very costly.

However, the relative efficiency of a decentralized versus a centralized decision scheme does not depend only on the number of actors and by the time pressure on them. Some important and early experiments in organizational behavior, described in Box 4.1 have revealed another independent variable, *information complexity*.

Information complexity

The implications of the described findings are clear for understanding the domain of effective application of authority. "Authority, the centralization of decisions, serves to economize on the transmission and the

Box 4.1
Bavelas' networks

Bavelas (1951) compared the performance of a group of five or six individuals in completing tasks using different decision-making and communication schemes.

Each individual was given local information: for example, a card with various symbols. A first type of task consisted in determining which one symbol was present in all of the cards. In different groups, individuals were permitted to communicate in different modes, being allowed to send messages to other actors according to the following schemes or *communication networks*. In each network the nodes represent the actors and the lines represent the possibility to be in contact (i.e. the existence of a channel of communication between two specific actors).

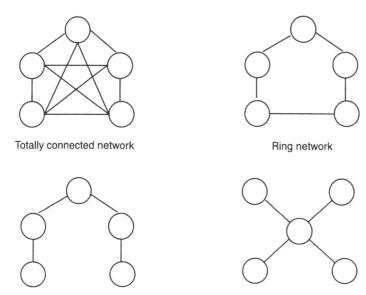

Totally connected network   Ring network

Chain network   Star network

The groups most efficient in performing the task, measured in terms of time needed and number of transmissions of messages, were those in which a centralized scheme was assigned, either star-shaped or chain.

However, in successive experiments Bavelas' communication networks were used to study groups assigned to perform more complex tasks, such as to resolve a math problem or to identify stimulus colors that were ambiguous, unusual, and hard to define. *With these types of complex tasks, the results of the experiment were the opposite: the groups which were assigned decentralized communication schemes achieved better results.*

treatment of information" (Arrow 1974); but this proposition is valid *if information is structured, and if a single actor has the competence necessary to resolve the problem once in possession of that information.*

Returning to one of our initial examples, then, if authority will often be an effective and efficient means of integrating the relevant information for defining the production plans of different plants, typically it will not be so for integrating the contributions of marketing, production, and R&D professionals, or for integrating a firm divisions' knowledge of different markets, in order to define new products.

Arbitration authority

The former two reasons for creating an authority relationship are sufficient to explain the emergence of simple hierarchies in teams, in groups of people with homogeneous interests. An additional reason to create authority relations is the possibility that the interdependent actors have *conflicting interests* and that they cannot always resolve that conflict directly.

Interest conflicts

It has been argued that one of the reasons for the existence of hierarchy in economic action systems is the convenience of establishing a "court of last resort" for the regulation of potential conflicts between parties that are linked by contracts that are too ambiguous, incomplete, and specific to be guaranteed by the legal system and the public authority (Williamson 1991). It can in fact be observed that one function exercised by upper hierarchical levels with respect to lower ones in firms is the resolution of conflicts and exceptions to the rules, when these cannot be effect-

ively resolved directly by the parties involved, or deferred to external courts. Also independent economic actors (that is, those not in the same firm) who write complex contracts, open to many interpretations, often employ commercial arbitrators who can guarantee resolution in case of a dispute.

In order to have legitimate arbitration authority, the arbiter must be recognized as neutral with respect to the parties in conflict (Bazerman and Lewicki 1983). For example, a government department of labor must be seen as neutral by both labor unions and management in order to be effective in arbitrating industrial conflict. Furthermore, an arbiter should be competent about the matter in contention, although not necessarily as competent as the parties in conflict.

Exchange-based authority

Authority relations can become established also when there are differences between the interests of actors exercising it and of those who submit to it. When these different motives are in the particular configuration that will be described in this section, cooperation can be regulated effectively by an *exchange agreement* that includes an authority relationship.

Why would a free actor agree to follow the instructions of another regarding a series of his or her own behaviors, if the motives and the preferences of the other are known to be different from his or her own? The acceptability of a relationship of this type is based on an *exchange*. The fundamental features of this model of authority were originally described by Simon (1951), and have since been developed further. An actor can grant to another the right to direct a specified range of his own behaviors in exchange for something. Naturally, the exchange will be attractive to the extent that it is in the interest of a counterpart to buy this right.

A type of economic relationship in which these conditions typically occur is work relationships. A work relationship implies that it is in someone's interest to work in exchange for compensation and that it is in someone's interest to buy such work services. If all of the services in question can be exchanged instantaneously – as in shopping (Alchian and Demsetz 1972) – or completely foreseen and predetermined in advance (Williamson 1979), then the regulation of this relationship can occur through a contract that specifies the type of service and the compensation. No authority would be involved. However, in most work situations it is cognitively unfeasible or too costly to write complete contracts of this type (Simon 1951).

Uncertainty and knowledge

Over time, the needs for work services may vary due to unforeseeable contingencies and the best way of assigning a task to people often needs to be discovered. The customer may buy product B instead of product A. The type of primary material may vary for both technical and economic reasons. For all non-standard goods and services, the optimal configuration of the workers in the transformation process changes as a function of the clients' needs.

In other words, *uncertainty* would lead to a continuous renegotiation of the employment contracts. Hence, the actor who buys labor services under conditions of uncertainty is interested in having the flexibility to determine the mode of work; that is, the employer prefers a decision-making system where tasks can be assigned as needed in order to adapt the work to the circumstances. Suppose further that the employer has also the *knowledge* (information and competence) and the *resources* (time and attention) necessary to identify the best mode to employ labor. In this case, he is interested in acquiring not only the services of workers but also the rights of decision on how their work is carried out.

Risk aversion

Now let us look at the problem from the point of view of the one who sells the work service. The worker is interested in the compensation, but normally not *only* in this. In fact, actors conferring work as an input to an economic activity are usually interested in *not* bearing the entire *risk* to which the results may be exposed (Arrow 1971; Jensen and Meckling 1976; Aoki 1984). The basic problem is that an investment of work cannot usually be easily diversified. Furthermore, usually the compensation derived from the work significantly influences the total wealth of the worker. Together, these circumstances are important reasons why workers are often *risk averse* regarding the compensation and prefer to receive a fixed, risk-free compensation.

Indifference zones

In addition, at least for some types of obligations and for some possible variations in the employment of his or her work, the worker might not have definite preferences about the particular tasks and actions required: for example red or blue sweaters; sweaters or skirts; more client search or more contract acquisitions. In this case, the worker is indifferent about what tasks s/he is called to perform, even if they vary in an unforeseen way, within a defined field of variation (or s/he may even value this variations positively; Chapter 10). This field of behaviors that the worker can accept to vary "at zero cost," or with a benefit, as indicated by another actor, has been defined as the *"zone of indifference"* or *"zone of acceptance"* of a subject toward an authority relation (Barnard 1938; March and Simon 1958).

The "treaty" of authority

In sum, a risk-averse worker, indifferent over a range of alternative ways to use his work, delegates the right of decision and of control over his behavior within a zone of acceptance and receives a fixed risk-free compensation. An employer buys the right to decide which actions to ask of the worker and to control what will be effectively undertaken; plus the right to retain the residual results (after having paid inputs) derived from such actions and to bear the relative risk. If the employer is conferring capital and he can diversify investments, so as to approximate neutrality toward risk, this "treaty of authority" represents a Pareto-efficient exchange both in terms of risk bearing and in terms of incentives to participate and to produce.

Monitoring authority

Centralized decision-making can be conceptually distinguished from centralized *monitoring*. Often these are found together, but not always. For example, democratic organizations that take their own decisions by voting may still monitor the application of majority decisions by a central structure.

Why monitoring is useful?

Conflicting interests represent the core factor. If all actors were holding homogeneous preferences, once the best combinations of actions were found, all would have the incentives to collaborate to implement those

actions. For example, the members of a small firm in an industry crisis are likely to be equally motivated to maximize the firm's survival chances and are likely to contribute without external control. Or the members of a small group of engineers collaborating on a project that they would all sign would be equally motivated to contribute to the realization of a safe project by using their own skills best. However, in economic collective action a frequent cause of diverging interests is the *"cost of effort"* to produce an action (Alchian and Demsetz 1972). Even where actors had agreed upon a joint action, it is possible that they have definite and negative preferences about the consumption of personal and organizational resources for the taking of that action. *When* preference structures assume this configuration, and *if* a lower effort brings a cost reduction greater than the lost share of benefits, there is a *"free riding potential"* – an incentive to reduce one's individual effort, letting others generate the collective benefits.

Team production

Free-riding is a real threat if there is the belief that opportunistic actions will not be discovered and/or will not be punished. The *non-observability of individual contributions in a collective output* is one of the most studied conditions of this type (Alchian and Demsetz 1972; Holmstrom 1982). In this case, the contribution of each team member is not discernible in a collective production result, such as in an operation of hand-carrying a weight involving more than one person (a "team production" situation).

The magnitude of the free-riding potential is directly related to the number of team members, because the effect of any single actor on the collective result decreases with team size. However, if many actors in the team behave in this way, output may decline below acceptable levels. How can this situation be resolved?

If individual outputs are not observable within team results, a reasonable alternative could be to observe *input behaviors* (Alchian and Demsetz 1972). One can observe the actions that the people take instead of measuring the results of those actions. For example, instead of counting the number of pieces transported by a group of people unloading a truck, one could observe whether or not the individuals are active, follow the recommended procedures, and help the other members of the team when there is a need.

But who will observe these behaviors? If the team is small, team members may directly monitor each other and in fact have an interest in doing so. If, by contrast, the team is large, the number of monitoring relations grow exponentially, and – other things being equal – it becomes more efficient to entrust to one central agent the specialized task of monitoring all others. This cost efficiency property of control authorities contributes in explaining the recourse to supervision in industrial transformation processes with common facilities and tools; or in coordinating service delivery at many outlets under a common brand name (such as occurs in franchising).

Controlling the controllers

But who will control the controller? One response has been to use *incentive mechanisms* instead of control mechanisms. The solution is that the controller will be directly and economically interested in maximizing the result of the team. The supervisor is given the right to a portion of the economic residual result of the team's activity (i.e., the surplus

after having compensated the other input factors).

This argument contributes in explaining why the centralization of control rights is often accompanied by the centralization of residual rewards rights in classical firms (Alchian and Demstz 1972), but it holds only under certain conditions. Particularly important conditions of failure of centralized control are: task complexity and unmeasurable collective results.

Task complexity

How does one monitor the level and the type of effort expended by a researcher, by an auditor, or by a "creative" in the preparation and realization of their outputs? Direct control of behaviors would imply the controller doing the work with the person being monitored (Alchian and Demsetz 1972), thereby duplicating efforts and making collective action as the union of more efforts and resources futile. In addition, if the knowledge required to perform an activity is complex, specialization is likely to pay off and no single agent may be able to command the competence required to control all others.

Measurability of joint outputs

Joint gains should be observable and measurable in order to apportion "residual rewards" to a central agent. There should be a sufficient and reliable signal of the overall performance of the team, so that the actors interested in its maximization are led to make decisions that are correct for the system. Profit provides that signal in "perfectly" competitive situations – or approximately so (Radner 1997). Other positively evaluated results in modern economies, such as innovation or consumer satisfaction can be translated into quantitative performance parameters in order to define incentives contingent on them (Chapter 9).

In fact, in activities with poorly measureable results – to take extreme examples, judiciary activities, or health-care services – a plurality of control centers external to and independent of the controlled system and specialized in different dimensions of performance is usually established. Large firms with multiple objectives and functions, hence, are also likely to require monitoring systems involving checks and balances divided among different centers of power (e.g. auditors, representatives of shareholders, managers, workers, public interests).

A partial solution to the limits posed by task complexity and by distributed knowledge is the substitution of an authority relation for an "agency" relationship. Address and solve, for example, the coordination problem described in Box 4.2 and then discuss the solution in the light of the following section on agency relationships.

AGENCY RELATIONSHIPS

Some of the coordination problems that cannot be resolved by authority relationships in all of the forms described above can be resolved through an agency relationship. An agency relationship is an exchange relation between one actor (*the principal*) who delegates to another actor (*the agent*) the *discretionary power to act in the interest of the principal* (Jensen and Meckling 1976). For example, firm owners delegate to managers the power to make decisions in their interest, the parties to a civil suit delegate the defense of

---

Box 4.2
Alcide's fleet

Alcide Mariolo is a small ship owner on the island of Ponza. He owns six fishing boats and the equipment for tuna fishing. Each fishing boat is entrusted to an expert sailor, called captain. The captain enjoys full autonomy in fishing and in the choice of crew and participates in the results realized by the ship owner by receiving 15 percent of the profit derived from the fish brought in by his crew. The costs, including labor, maintenance of the fleet and the equipment, diesel fuel, etc., are paid by the ship owner.

After a few unpleasant events, Alcide Mariolo decides to reorganize the activity of his little fleet. The problem is the fishing area: it is not divided into exclusive zones and the captains "compete" for the most fertile zones because there they fish the same quantity of fish for much less work.

Some months ago, a fishing net worth 25 million lire owned by Mariolo was damaged by the propeller of a fishing boat to the point of being unserviceable. In town rumors have it that the incident is the result of a vendetta within Mariolo's group. The work climate among the captains is very tense, with much mutual suspicion and strong feelings. It is clear that each crew prefers to continue fishing in the nearest and most fertile zones behind the island of Ponza. Alcide Mariolo, worried about the future of his firm is thinking, nautical charts to hand, of gathering all the captains to find a solution.

Source: By Giuseppe Soda.

their interests to lawyers, workers delegate the power to negotiate in their interest to union representatives, a production firm delegates the power to sell its products to sales agents.

There are similarities and differences between agency and authority. Both relations involve the exchange of decision rights. In an authority relation one actor is obligated to act in the interest of another, but the rights of decision and control on actions remain with the interested party (i.e. the "employer" or "principal"). In contrast, in agency relationships, the one who acts in the interest of another (i.e. the agent) is also entitled to decide what actions are in the best interest of the principal. The motives for this request normally reside in the principal lacking resources, time, or knowledge to be able to directly carry out the activity.

Observable behaviors

This difference would not be fundamental if the principal could observe and perfectly evaluate the behavior of the agent. In fact, if the behavior were completely understandable by the principal and he had the competence to judge whether or not the behaviors were the most effective in his best interest, then the relationship would be reduced to a more decentralized version of authority: the central actor would direct action ex post, evaluating and rewarding observed "good" behaviors, rather than ex ante, by dictating them.

On the other hand, if the agent's behaviors were not directly observable but the results were clear, and such results depended *only* on the actions of the agent, then the principal would have perfect information on the effort of the agent. In this case, an efficient agency contract would be simply a contract contingent to performance, with no fundamental difference from a market exchange.

Incomplete information

The distinctive contribution of agency theory, and the definition of agency as a distinct mode of coordination, different from price-based exchange and from authority, came about relative to conditions of *incomplete information* on behaviors *and* results. Assume that the behavior of the agent is not observable by the principal and that the results may also depend on exogenous factors (level of demand, actions of others) beyond the actions of the agent. Agency theory addresses the problem of how to regulate this relationship in the most adverse conditions: under the hypothesis that the agent positively values compensation in terms of utility or benefit and negatively values effort in terms of disutility or cost. Under these conditions, there are two possible ways to insure that the contract will be respected and that the agent will act in the interest of the principal. The first mechanism is that of resorting to an *incentive system* contingent on results; the second is that of investing in *performance monitoring systems*. Under the conditions hypothesized, both of these solutions are costly for the following reasons.

Residual reward rights

An incentive system that links compensation to results has the advantage of "aligning" the agent's interests with those of the principal. In practice, for example, managers can be compensated on firm's earnings, or sales staff can be compensated on realised sales. However, the problem with these compensation schemes – highlighted by agency theorists – is that they transfer part of the risk from a risk-neutral actor to a risk-averse actor. Thus the contract involves extra costs equal to the premium necessary to induce the risk-averse agent to accept such exposure to risk.

Therefore, agency contracts must be constructed so as to resolve a *trade-off between the benefits of incentives (due to objectives realignment) and the costs of an inefficient allocation of risk* (Levinthal 1988; Douma and Schreuder 1992; Milgrom and Roberts, 1992). This point of equilibrium, i.e. the optimal level of incentive or risk transfer to the agent, will depend on various factors – discussed in detail in Chapter 10. It is however useful for our discussion here to highlight one of these factors – the extent to which the results observed depend on factors other than the actions of the agent. The less the results depend on the agent's actions, the less useful it is to transfer risk to the agent. This means that *uncertainty* figures among the possible causes of failure of agency relations.

Residual control rights

In situations where it is not convenient to transfer risk, an alternative is to invest in monitoring systems. One can put in place systems of indicators of the effort expended or signals of the actions taken, as distinct from information obtainable by observing the results. But we are considering the case of imperfectly observable behaviors, hence only imperfect indicators are supposed to be available. For example, counting the hours spent at the workplace is an indicator possibly relevant to the work done, but it is a very imperfect measure, informative only to the extent that there is a correlation between hours of presence and efforts expended. So even monitoring is costly and imperfect under the assumed conditions. Therefore a second *trade-off is always necessary between the costs of the two potential coordination alternatives – an incentive system and a monitoring system.*

In conclusion, agency relationships and contracts, under the conditions in which they are distinctively applicable (incomplete and asymmetric information) represent a mode of coordination that is contiguous to that of authority, but more *decentralized*. Part of the decision rights about coordinating actions is transferred to the one who holds the action rights – the agent. Along with these rights, part of the risk to which action consequences are exposed is transferred to the agent in the form of residual rewards rights. Residual control rights remain with the principal; but in general, monitoring is costly and the returns on investments in monitoring decrease with the complexity of activities. Due to the presence of these trade-offs, in the conditions of asymmetric information described above, mixed solutions will often be superior, consisting of a *mix of incentives and of monitoring mechanisms.*[2]

THE SOCIAL DYNAMIC OF AUTHORITY AND AGENCY

Authority and agency, involving reciprocal and direct influence between actors, have a more pervasive social dimension than coordination mechanisms based on unilateral decisions. The studies on authority and leadership in a social psychology perspective have been focused on these aspects and have shown how these relationships in practice often are not effective, not because they are the wrong coordination mechanism to apply, but because they are not played and managed competently on an interpersonal ground.

To effectively take advantage of the strengths of authority and agency as coordination mechanisms, the relationship should be balanced at the interpersonal level. Let us first illustrate the main errors and distortions that can cause the relationship to degenerate; then the main antidotes that can limit those distortions.

Pathologies

Authoritarianism

The most common and serious error in the management of authority relationships is the error of *authoritarianism* (Follett 1925; Argyris 1957, 1964; McGregor 1960; Blake and Mouton 1964; Merton 1965;). Its components are varied:

- An authoritarian behavior confuses the right to prescribe certain tasks with an aggressive stance toward people, the right to expect certain services from others with the right to be personally served, the right and duty to identify and indicate the best actions for the system of cooperation and exchange with a right to make arbitrary decisions.
- An authoritarian behavior pretends that the delegation of decision rights by whoever accepts the authority in a certain zone of behavior becomes a general right to direct any (or a much larger zone of) behavior.
- An authoritarian behavior overlooks the exchanges of social goods that necessarily derive from the exercise of authority – approval, esteem, sociability; orders are issued but positive feedback for a job well done is forgotten; attention is paid only to tasks and large losses in social atmosphere are incurred for even small performance improvements.

Manipulation

The principal – or the agent – can provide disguised information to the other party so as to intentionally shape the counterpart's judgment in a self-serving way. It may go as far as to exploit social relations for personally productive ends.

Manipulation is thus a form of opportunism that violates the spirit of an agreement and includes informative traps and declarations that are not believed. Affective manipulation is a particularly extreme form of opportunism, which usually is not included in the expectations of a "normal" strategic use of the information between parties holding different objectives.

Authority and agency relations, resting on an asymmetric distribution of information, are prone to manipulative distortions, orchestrated both by leaders and subordinates.[3] The former can misrepresent information on economic and technological conditions, on accounting data, on the constraints coming down from upper levels. The latter can disclose their "local" information – on clients, productive processes, their own performance – in selective ways so as to maximize their benefits (Crozier and Friedberg 1977).

Paternalism

In spite of having been an important manifestation of authority in industrial history, in modern economic contexts *paternalism* is considered a "degenerated" form of authority, unacceptable for not respecting the maturity and the capacity for self-determination of psychologically healthy adults and for the element of manipulation and authoritarianism that it includes (Argyris 1957; Likert 1961). The charges leveled at paternalism include that it confuses exchange-based authority or agency relationships, which are based on different interests, with a father–son relationship in which the father is the competent decision-maker who foresees everything, in the interests of a son who is not yet able to exercise judgment. The school of *transactional analysis* (of psychological and linguistic transactions) (Bern 1964; Watzlavick *et al.* 1967) has, for example, shown how the dialogue between a leader who plays the role of a parent (speaks from top down, continuously expresses judgments and evaluations about what is good and bad, solicits consensus and adaptation to his own opinion) is possible only with a partner who agrees to play the role of a child (speaks from below up, asks for advice and opinions, does not have autonomy of judgment, is gregarious and insecure). If, on the contrary, authority is accepted as a social contract within clear limits, then the only sustainable interpersonal relationship is an adult–adult dialogue (I have my goals and objectives and you have yours; we are different people who exchange something or cooperate on specific issues; we both have other relationships and other interests).

Permissivism

The monitoring and supervisory activities implied in authority and agency can make the role stressful for the super-ordinate. In particular, if the social and interpersonal relationships are good, it can be difficult to give negative feedback and to point out lack of achievement. Although those types of monitoring behavior may improve the efficiency of the system, they can also bring about personal losses of friendship, affection, and emotional support. On top of that, negative feedback is often not the most well received, and monitoring in itself will always raise a certain resistance. Thus, control may not be exercised and positive feedback may be routinely given irrespectively of performance.

Leadership style

Given those pathologies, some prescriptive principles have been set out in order to sustain agency and authority relations interpersonally.

- An effective leadership behavior requires a *positive orientation toward people*. This means that "principals" have to be concerned with interpersonal relations (Blake and Mouton 1964); and have to be able to distinguish "knowing what to do about a problem or activity" from "commanding people" (Fisher and Ury 1981). They should be aware that their "assumptions" about the motivation of collaborators are likely to become "self-fulfilling prophecies": if a leader behaves as if he believes that people are shirkers and wish to minimize their work effort, he encourages them to conform to that expectation (McGregor 1960).

- An effective leadership behavior requires *the capacity to give both positive and negative feedback* to people about their performance (Tosi *et al.* 1986). This aspect is fundamental for the exercise of competence-based authority inasmuch as it makes it possible for the less competent party to learn and develop their own competence. It is also fundamental in exchange-based authority because if remuneration is fixed, feedback can provide the only relevant information on how to improve performance.

- An effective leader is aware of the type of authority or agency relation that is the basis of his role. An effective leader knows when and to what extent his or her influence is based on technical or social competence; or on control functions in the enforcement of pre-established decisions or rules; or on an exchange of resources; or on arbitration functions; or on the need to efficiently coordinate people under the pressure of time. Given that in practice and in thick cooperation relations a mix of those sources is often present, the activation of different types of authority according to people and tasks is also crucial, i.e. the capacity to play multiple and multidimensional leadership roles (Quinn 1988).

• An effective leader is capable of discerning *the degree of delegation* that is effective in different activities (Tannenbaum and Schmidt 1958; Vroom and Yetton 1973). The conditions under which authority and agency are viable and efficient do not come in packages nor in simple yes or no alternatives. Each antecedent of authority and agency effectiveness is a variable which can assume different values, and there are various possible combinations of these values.

The fine tuning of directive behavior to this mix of conditions entails so many elements that it is difficult to address it analytically (rather than through heuristic experience). However, it can be said that *the greater the degree of diffusion of competences, the greater the degree of acceptance and consensus required, and the harder it is to observe behavior, the greater will be the effective degree of decentralization*: the use of agency rather than authority relationships, and the degree of recourse to consultation, discussion, or even joint decision with the people who work "under the shadow of hierarchy."

Let us experiment with some of the described social dynamics, possible pathologies, and the problem of choosing an appropriate "degree" of centralization in coordination and role play with the situation described in Box 4.3 and attached appendices.

The case in Box 4.3 leads to comparing authority with other coordination mechanisms – as joint decision-making through persuasion and negotiation – and to designing an appropriate mix of them. Also this meta-decision over coordination and decision modes can be seen as a very important com-

ponent of managerial and leadership competence. It will be possible to fully develop this discussion, however, at the end of Part II, once all the basic coordination mechanisms have been presented.

THE COSTS OF AUTHORITY AND AGENCY

Information and communication costs

Authority and agency relationships imply acquiring information about local situations, elaborating action plans, transmitting descriptions of activities to execute or that have been executed, and gathering information on performance. Therefore the costs of information and communication will be greater in an authority relationship and – to a more limited extent – also in agency relations, than in a system of coordination based on unilateral decisions.

On the other hand, the communication and information costs of authority and agency-based hierarchies are lower than those of joint decision-making mechanisms. Authority and agency entail some other typical costs, however.

Influence costs

In exchange-based authority and agency relationships, the monetary and non-monetary rewards obtained by the subordinate or agent depend in variable but often large measure on the judgment of the monitor. By definition, the monitor is responsible for observing and evaluating work, or for feeding a monitoring system with data, or for interpreting those data and attaching reward consequences to behaviors. To the extent that these judgments and evaluations are never "objective, " it is likely that subordinates and agents will make special efforts to influence

Box 4.3
Role playing: Petrolix

Background

Petrolix is one division of the Petrol oil company. The division's main activities include the distribution of heating oil for private and commercial uses.

The Problem

Mr Montes, the Sales Director of Petrolix, was asked at 2.25 p.m. on April 9 by the management of Petrolcasa to "urgently" recommend one of his subordinates for a position in a "Project Team." The job involves evaluating an opportunity to acquire a distribution network currently owned by a competitor who is having financial difficulties.

To be chosen, the candidate must have good professional skills and will be eligible for promotion within the Sales Office in six months.

Mr Montes is 40 years old and has sixteen years of seniority with the group. He has been the Sales Director since 1975. Among his direct subordinates (each in charge of a specific geographical area), three seem to fit the profile of the position requested by the top management.

The Three Candidates Are

- Robert Jordan, 34 years old, has an engineering degree and eight years seniority with the group. During his five years at Petrolix, he has acquired a good experience in sales. He has been in charge of the eastern area within the sales office. Together with Mr Tink, he has supervised the training of some newly hired salespeople and recently, again with Mr Tink, he has worked on a project to increase efficiency within the distribution network of Petrolix.

  He has been studying the problems of relationships between oil firms and the market for some time, taking a different approach to understanding the changes in choices made by final consumers.

  He is intelligent, creative, conscientious, and very keen to work in teams. He feels comfortable in groups, even though he does not seem to have much in common with other colleagues.
- Mark Airat, 31 years old, has a high school degree in bookkeeping and seven years of seniority with the group. He comes from the Petrolix purchasing office where he worked for three years. He is now chief of the central area and is currently working on restructuring the sales territories in his area. He is a very good employee and has a pleasant personality. He is well liked by his colleagues and seems to enjoy their respect. He is also intelligent and is very creative. He has an aptitude for research and has been able to accomplish significant results with innovative projects entrusted to him. He loves mathematics and considers it a hobby.

- Paul Tink, 36 years old, has a vocational degree in chemistry, and has twelve years seniority with the group. He has been working in the sales office for six years. He was very helpful when Mr Montes had to be out of the office for medical reasons for a few months last year.

    He has managed, and still does, the western area, and is personally involved in the definition of training programs for the managers who report to him. He also trained Jordan and Airat so as to facilitate their smooth insertion in the sales office. Tink is a solid replacement for Montes when the latter is out of the office; the sales office staff has a lot of respect for him. He does not make it a secret that he is looking to fill new and challenging responsibilities. Although very competitive in nature, Tink is not easy to deal with: he lacks "tact" and tends to state his opinion without worrying what effect it may have on others.

Today, April 10, Montes decides to meet Tink. (Role details for Tink and Montes are reported in Appendices 4.1a and 4.1b. Do not read both of them before playing).

Source: By Severino Salvemini; Grandori (1986).

the judgment of their superior or monitor: for example, presenting their positive results in the most visible and cognitively "available" way, maintaining close personal relations, justifying their actions, offering pledges and material or non-material guarantees (such as reputation) to assure the correctness and quality of their own work. The costs of these processes have been called "influence costs" (Milgrom and Roberts 1992), and in the particular case of agency relationships, "reassurance costs" (Jensen and Meckling 1976).

Structural costs

With respect to coordination systems where the actors decide, act, and directly control the results of their actions, a hierarchical system carries with it the maintenance of one or more people specialized at least in part in coordination activities. These costs grow in proportion to the number of possible combinations between actors rather than with the number of actors. Therefore, since early organization studies it has been noticed that there is an upper limit to the number of actors that can be supervised, to the "*span of control*" (Graicunas 1937; Woodward 1965). This limit may be very low if activities are to be governed only by the case-by-case decision-making of the central agent. It can be higher if activities are in part rule guided. Therefore – other things being equal – the more complex the task (i.e. the more discretionary decision-making is required) the lower the optimal span of control is, down to reach the small group size. The efficient span of control decreases not only for reasons of information costs and required knowledge, but also for reasons of diverging interests. If subordinates are not indifferent toward tasks and the "rate of compliance" with received orders decreases, the efficient span of control decreases (Williamson 1970). Therefore, if the number of interdependent actors to be coordinated by authority or agency is high, a system of superimposed layers of hierarchy emerges.

Control losses

However, the greater the number of decision and monitoring levels superimposed, and the greater the span of control, other conditions being equal, the greater will be the imperfections and the "loss of control" in the system (Williamson 1970).

First, the episodes of non-compliance, due to residual unresolved divergences in interests in the system accumulate. Second, messages tend to decay and become distorted through many processes of emission/reception. The more information is qualitative rather than codified and formalized, the higher the expected intensity of information distortions is (as in the game of wireless telephone).

In agency relationships monitoring presents peculiar costs due to the delegation of decision power. These costs mount with: (1) the level of discretion granted to the agent (for example in the case in which the agent has to identify and define the relevant action alternatives, rather than merely choose between pre-defined alternatives or levels of effort), (2) the difficulty of observing the agent's behavior, (3) the imperfection of the signals on which the monitoring process is based, and (4) the extent to which parties' preferences over actions diverge.

Control losses have been considered exclusively as a cost in economic-oriented works. However, they can have positive, although unplanned, consequences. In effect, a perfect control system of whatever kind – by exit, authority, or group – would have a low capacity to learn and evolve. In fact some "errors" can turn out to be discoveries of new more effective ways to act, with unforeseen but positive effects, revealed as innovations without research costs (Merton 1949). The flexible interpretation of the spirit of author-ity and agency contracts is often more effective than the perfect execution of orders or initially expected actions. The growth of "control loss" can also be read as a signal that the nature of the activities is no longer appropriate for an authority or agency relationship, and therefore should not necessarily be seen as a cost to be reduced but as a signal that the coordination mechanism should be changed.

Adaptation costs

Authority and agency relations are supposed to be able to regulate (among other things) activities that are not totally predictable, in which the central actor decides or controls the best allocation of efforts according to varying circumstances. However, this does not reduce to zero the time between decisions, implementation, and monitoring. The possibility remains that circumstances may change during the implementation, and that subordinates could behave unexpectedly. If that happens, agents may respond in at least two opposite and interesting ways. They could hold strictly to their instructions – and for this reason not succeed in implementing the "spirit" of those instructions in the observed circumstances. This is a defect or cost of *rigidity* of a system based on authority (Gouldner 1954). Think, for example, of a nurse who follows an order given by a doctor to transfer a patient based on certain information, even when conditions have changed in the meantime so as to make movement of the patient no longer advisable. Alternatively, the subordinate agent (for example, the nurse) can "take responsibility" to interpret the spirit of the orders and to choose actions different from those ordered: with this they can improve the efficiency of the action system, but they do it by exceeding the boundaries of an authority relationship in the narrow sense.

In addition, an imperfect adaptation of actions to plans can occur by mistake, lack of resources, or other inconsistencies between the work required and the possibility of doing it at a particular moment. The costs of errors are not in themselves specific to authority or agency mechanisms, but the *costs of correct-ing errors and of adapting actions* are. In fact, the correction of actions through a cen-tral agent requires additional activities of information transmission to the center and of reception of corrected plans. Hence, hier-archical regimes are not particularly adaptive. Given that the possibility of error and of the obsolescence of plans is greater in more complex and difficult activities, this is another reason why hierachy is not an efficient mechanism in that domain. In practice, the re-evaluation of "flat" structures for coordin-ating dynamic activities – such as those at the interface between firms and clients – is largely due to this type of cost.

Indifference, indulgency, and alienation

Other costs of authority and agency relations stem from the conditions of indifference over actions (or even the disutility of actions) and the suspension of critical judgment.

With reference to exchange-based author-ity, the indifference of the subordinate about the possible use of his work services within a defined zone, is a condition that makes the exchange feasible and efficient. However, this circumstance is not free from costs. A person who is indifferent to the content of her own activity, not having particular incentives to avoid following orders, also does not even have any incentive to act beyond the orders received, to improve them and integrate them as opportunities arise. Combined with the

lack of direct connection between action and results, and with control losses, this condition may make the authority relationship an "*indulgent*" and weakly encouraging coordin-ation system (Williamson 1975, 1991).

Critics of authority systems from various perspectives have highlighted how the divorce between man and the governance of his own activity, even if voluntarily accepted, is a psy-chologically unnatural situation and is a potentially damaging source of "alienation," reducing his general capacity to make a con-tribution to the society in which he takes part. People who agree to act without deciding for an extended part of their time, can later find it difficult to behave independently even when this is necessary or appropriate. Authority in this respect is a relationship that presents particular risks of becoming self-reproducing and self-fullfilling beyond its inherent limits.[4]

Agency relations have less alienation potential and superior incentive power, due to the delegation of decision power and to the transfer of risk. On the other hand, being a more loosely coupled form of coordination, they entail higher opportunism potential and error potential.

SUMMARY

In this chapter we have examined authority and agency as distinct mechanisms of coordination of economic relationships.

Five *different sources of legitimate authority* have been identified: competence, decision-making efficiency, control efficiency, arbitra-tion functions, and the efficient exchange of work services against risk-free reward.

The limits of authority have been analyzed: the heavy requirements about the central actor information and knowledge, and the particu-lar requirements about the configuration of interests and orientations of other actors (risk-aversion and task-indifference). The limits of applicability of authority for coordinating actions based on complex knowledge were also stressed.

Agency relationships, based on the delegation of decision power by a "principal" to an "agent" to act on the interest of the former, to the extent it is a distinctive coordination mechanism, are more decentralized and capable of governing conditions that are not manageable by authority: when it is difficult and costly for a central agent to observe agents' behaviors, to evaluate ex ante which action is superior (even for his own interests), and results are clearly observable and measurable but are subject to risk. Hence, agency can govern more variable and uncertain activities than authority can; it does not require indifference over tasks but resolves preference diversity by modifying the payoffs of the different single acts (thereby "realigning" preferences). However, it does require that action problems are structured, that action alternatives and possible results are known.

Given that authority and agency involve communication between identified parties and rest upon asymmetric information and decision rights, these mechanisms entail particular types of social dynamics and distinctive costs. In the third and fourth parts of the chapter, these two problems were analyzed and solutions to them indicated. We described the social and interpersonal dynamics that can sustain an effective use of authority and agency relationships (separate actions from people, provide feedback, design the division of decision rights situationally); and we described some recurrent pathologies that can obstruct or corrupt them (authoritarianism, paternalism, manipulation, and permissivism). The costs of information transmission, influence costs, control losses, adaptation costs, and opportunism potential have been examined as the main intrinsic costs to be taken into account when using authority and agency relations.

Exercise: Pots of trouble

In Europe, Kook Matic markets steel cooking pots produced in the United States. These are so-called "batteries de cuisine," i.e. complete ranges of saucepans comprising from 12 to 36 items. The problem the firm is now facing is to restructure the sales areas. The marketing is done through area chiefs (direct sellers) responsible for groups of indirect sellers operating within the provinces of a European country. The indirect sellers are paid a commission on their sales gross of traveling expenses. Unfortunately, problems of territorial overlap between the sellers often arise since the clients are contacted on the basis of geographic distance and quality (essentially depending on the sales volumes a client can assure) rather than on the territory of competence (province). In other words, there are areas that may belong to another seller's province but are nearer and more convenient from the point of view of costs (above all, transport). Sellers do not think twice about "invading" these territories, and this causes considerable tension within the marketing management of Kook Matic. Each area chief is, of course, intent on keeping the best clients under his control, and this inevitably produces conflicts.

In the firm's first years of activity, it was decided not to formalize competence by territory, in order to create a minimum of competition among the sellers. Now, the situation has altered and the firm wishes to expand its activities, *inter alia* through better penetration into the territory.

The marketing manager does not have available all the information needed to take an "objective" decision; moreover, the area chiefs are afraid of competition from colleagues and therefore jealously preserve certain "secrets" and do not disclose all the potentialities of the market. Relations between the marketing manager and area chiefs have always been excellent, many of the latter consider themselves "pupils" of the old manager, and the latter has always devoted an important part of his activity to the professional development of *"his boys"*. The area chiefs are all very well prepared and play a crucial role, such as being responsible for the firm's image to the clients and governing unstable relations with the indirect sellers.

By Giuseppe Soda

Questions

- Which aspects of the transactions described can be effectively governed through forms of authority?
- Which others through an agency relationship? Integrated by which mechanisms of control and incentive?

Appendix 4.1A

Role of Mr Montes

After a careful selection, you have decided that the perfect candidate is Jordan. Your choice was especially dictated by the fact that this position requires someone with a high potential. All three of your collaborators would fit the profile of the project team leader but Jordan, of the three, is the one who can offer the most at this time.

You realise that Airat has the necessary technical skills, but they are not as good as Jordan's.

Tink's strong point is his seniority and there are no particular weaknesses that you could point out about him. His personality is similar to that of the others, although he is rough in presenting his opinions and you think that, although in a group one needs to act firmly, it is also true that diplomacy and care are key factors.

His candidacy has been reviewed and accepted by the top management although no official announcement has yet been made. You have spoken to Jordan about it privately and in confidence.

Your goal is to persuade him to accept your decision; at the same time, though, you do not want to disappoint Tink (who is useful to you!), to whom, among other things, has been assigned the job of staffing a Petrolix stand at the upcoming Frankfurt Fair for a week. This task would have been handled by Jordan in the absence of his promotion.

Appendix 4.1B

Role of Mr Tink

Through the grapevine you have heard that corporate headquarters is creating a team of staff who would carry out a study on the possibility of acquiring a new distribution network. You think you may be called to fill one of the positions within the working group because of your good standing in the sales division; at the same time, you are not 100 percent confident that you will get the job given that you have had bad luck in the past.

Given that in the past you have worked on marketing and distribution problems (during the training period of your colleagues), you are not excluding the possibility of being chosen. The new responsibility would allow you to build on your marketing experience and, at the end of the project, better manage your resources.

In case you are not chosen, you think that the best fit for the position is Airat; his background in statistics is strong. With regard to Jordan, you think that he is a flatterer, who is always around the boss, and who claims credit for the knowledge that you taught him when he first arrived at the sales office and that he acquired from you thanks to collaborative projects. In addition, you do not get along with Jordan any more, since he has become closer to Montes. Finally, you think that Jordan is not liked by the group, contrary to Airat.

You are getting ready to meet Montes and you suspect that the meeting agenda is the "project team" position.

You are afraid that the outcome of the meeting may disappoint you, but you have reminded yourself that you do not need to be bothered with such issues.

You deem Montes as one of the best bosses you have ever had; however, you are not happy at the idea of picking up the slack left by Jordan.

Chapter 5

Teams

∙∙

Direct and reciprocal adjustment among interdependent actors is in many respects the most immediate and ancient mode of coordination, for many reasons. Even in economic activities, barter and economic networks and associations were much diffused in the middle ages and before. Interestingly, there has been a revival of the group as a coordination device in modern complex economies: work groups, quality circles, task forces, problem-solving groups, committees and meetings, and partnership structures. In this revival, sometimes the virtues of groups are recalled more easily than the drawbacks. This chapter will examine:

- What the *distinctive mechanisms* of communication, decision, and control thanks to which team coordination is achieved, actually are. As throughout Part II of the book, we shall not consider all aspects of the real life and structure of groups – if those are intended as ensembles of people who collaborate thanks to a variety of mechanisms – leadership, negotiation, voting, in addition to group decision and control. This is the main reason why in this chapter the term "*team*" is preferred: *an ensemble of actors with homogeneous preferences, differentiated knowledge and approximately equally valuable resources*

("peers"), who decide and control collective actions in a joint mode. When the term "group" is used here, it is used as a synonym for team.

- What types of team can be distinguished according to different decision and control properties.
- Under what conditions the different forms of team coordination are effective, efficient, and fair.

The outline of the chapter, specifying the profile of team mechanisms, the type of relations that can be effectively governed by them, and some salient sub-types of team-like coordination are summarized in Figure 5.1.

TEAM COMMUNICATION AND DECISION

Attributes and properties

Group problem-solving

A series of laboratory experiments on solving problems in groups has provided the empirical basis for understanding how groups work in defining common, coordinated action. Typically, the classic design for these experiments entails assigning a task to a small group of five to six people: for example, evaluating a series of personal profiles in

TEAMING	
CONDITIONS	• Distributed knowledge • Homogeneous preferences • Equally valuable resources • Small numbers of actors
MECHANISM PROFILE:	• All to all communication • Knowledge sharing and integration • Reciprocal control • Joint decision-making
TYPES:	• Primitive (communication-oriented) • Relational (control-oriented) • Communitarian (knowledge-oriented)

Figure 5.1 Team coordination

order to select a candidate for a given organizational position; designing the publicity campaign for a new product; solving an accounting problem; choosing between alternative investment plans, and so forth. The experiments allow us to observe the processes whereby a joint decision is produced. Since evaluating the effectiveness of these processes is also of interest, tasks and problems that have a "correct" answer have often been used, so that the solution the group arrives at can be compared/measured against a standard – even though as far as the participants are concerned, the solution to the problem is uncertain. For example, a complicated accounting problem can be difficult to solve for people without a specialist background in the subject; nonetheless, it does have a technically correct answer. Group solutions can be instructively compared, not only with correct answers, but also with the solutions that those same individuals, having the same background, are able to produce alone, before being able to consult with others. The most famous experiment of this type was run by the training experts at NASA and widely repeated with groups of managers and students. It is described in Box 5.1. (Box 5.4 illustrates another problem that could also be used in this way.)

Knowledge sharing and integration

By what miracle does the group work so that the sum of individual quasi-incompetences (or semi-competences) produces collective competence? And when can we expect this to happen?

The key mechanism is *knowledge sharing*: putting everything out in the open, integrating information and the different and partial competences available. Thus, people have the possibility of seeing aspects of a problem not previously considered and of having access to new information, of rethinking their own perceptions, judgments, and opinions, persuading themselves and each other. Each person exerts his own influence based on his own information and competence. In the ideal group model, no single person has enough information or competence to solve the problem on his own. If one or more members of the group have these capabilities, then it would be equally effective and more efficient to ask one of those people to define the collective action for the group.

> **Box 5.1**
> The NASA moon survival task
>
> Imagine belonging to the crew of a space ship that must make an emergency landing on the moon. The crew members are able to bring with them a series of potentially useful instruments for survival and for reaching a space base located 30 kilometers away on the moon's surface.
>
> The members of the group must decide which objects to bring with them; working on the hypothesis that they cannot bring them all, they must define a scale of usefulness of the objects for the trip: for example, water, matches, compass, etc.
>
> There is a "correct" solution, as defined by the technical experts at NASA. Some objects are of primary necessity for survival, while others could eventually be of use, and yet others may seem useful but aren't at all, in view of the geophysical conditions on the moon (absence of magnetic poles, absence of oxygen, etc.) It is with regard to this third class that the contribution of the group is distinctly measured. In a first stage of the experiment, the participants are asked to define a scale individually, and the difference between the order of importance given on average by the individual decision-makers and the NASA experts is fairly high. Once the individuals are allowed to meet as a group, however, with the tasking of discussing and producing an agreed scale, the solutions produced by the group are, on average, much better than those produced by the individuals.
>
> *Source*: Exercise described in various sources, e.g. Lau (1975).

Problem complexity

Typically, it is the new, complex, multi- and inter-disciplinary problems that benefit most from the use of group decision processes: for example, entrusting the creation of a new product line to a group made up of specialists coming from diverse technical functions (such as marketing, research and development, production); assigning to ad hoc groups of workers the quality improvement of an industrial transformation process; defining complex industrial projects that include many different aspects (technical, financial, commercial, legal, etc.) by appointing a group or delegation, rather than a single individual.

Increasing information-processing capacity

A team can realize significant cognitive advantages over other mechanisms in dealing

with complex problems. Rather than working to reduce the quantity of information processed and exchanged, as pricing, voting, authority and agency do in different ways, a team's distinctive method of dealing with uncertainty and knowledge complexity is to amplify the capacity for processing information, the cognitive power of the decision systems.

In effect, in cognitive pyschology there is a wealth of experimental research that corroborates the hypothesis that the group, if properly structured and functioning, is an extremely important tool for reducing the cognitive biases typical of individual rationality. For example, "availability" biases are reduced by the capacity to process more information from diverse sources. "Framing" distortions are reduced by comparing different perceptual schemes and different interpretations of information. Overconfidence and risk-prone behavior may be reduced by group discussion which typically creates a list of pros and cons regarding the various alternatives and favors learning (Lichtenstein *et al.* 1982).[1]

It must, however, be emphasized that group problem-solving enables benefits to be acheived only if it works "well": if, as in the case of price-based exchange or authority, certain conditions regarding the structure of interests and knowledge are respected.

Features of team coordination

Many different disciplines – sociology, social and cognitive psychology, and economics – have studied group relations. This has undoubtedly enriched our vision of the phenomenon, but the distinctive attributes and properties of group mechanisms as alternative to other coordination mechanisms has been blurred. What are the attributes of the group decision-making process as a distinctive coordination mechanism?

First, a *total communication network* is required, in which everybody can communicate with everybody else and, in effect, does so. A group in which some members are not able to express themselves, contributing their own competences and information, will not realize all of the quality improvements that this form of collective decision-making can achieve.

In order for there to be an open and parity-based information exchange and for it to be effective, it is important that *members' resources,* in particular their information and competence, be more or less *of the same importance for the problem or activity in question,* i.e. that they have balanced capacities to influence, that *members are "peers."* For example, in a commission of geophysical,

engineering and regional planning experts created by a ministry to prepare norms for civil protection, each specialty should be equally able to influence the process and the solution; as it is the case for any interfunctional team in firms. Or a "quality circle" created to improve the production process can effectively create a superior level of quality, if all the workers involved in different parts of the process are present and can express themselves freely.

In the third place, reaching a consensus through confrontation and persuasion is possible only if the *potential conflicts between members are not conflicts among interests.* If participants have a personal interest in one or another alternative, if enacting one or another solution changes the allocation of benefits, then knowledge sharing and the comparison of different views would not solve the problem. Negotiation would be needed. The group as defined here is a collective tied to *common interests,* a *"team"* (Marschack 1955). The athletic metaphor of a team accurately captures the distinctiveness of this condition. All members of a team are interested in winning the game they are playing. There can be conflicts concerning the best ways of doing so, over interpreting information, making judgments and diagnoses, and over identifying the causal relationships between action and results. These are conflicts of judgment, differences of opinions, that can and should be resolved by open discussion and information sharing, not conflict between interests.

Team coordination and team production

In this part of the book, we are not considering the team as an operative or productive device but as a coordination device. Actions decided in groups may be implemented individually as well as the reverse. Team production may be governed by the team, or by other mechanisms (authority, rules) (Chapter 4).

There are types of actions, however, in which this separation is not feasible or is costly. Typically, in complex activities joint action cannot be separated from joint coordination because only those who act have the information necessary to select effective actions: the skills of a medical team during an operation, the work of a group of researchers in solving a technical problem, the industry of a team of furniture craftsmen.

Team coordinating is also relevant for those actions which can be performed separately (so that there is no group action) but the definition of which requires solving complex problems and sharing knowledge held by various parties – such as defining strategic plans by cross-functional or inter-divisional committees or coordinating complementary strategic actions by multiple firms.

Group pathologies

The group is a double-edged sword. It can work as a "super-human decision-maker," reducing the limits and biases of individual judgment. But it can also take the opposite track, whenever certain conditions regarding its composition and internal functioning are not met. In the wise words found in one of the managerial classics: "Gentlemen, I take it we are all in complete agreement on the decision here. Then I propose we postpone further discussion of this matter until our next meeting to give ourselves time to develop disagreement and perhaps gain some understanding of what the decision is all about" (Sloan 1963).

Here we examine these conditions and processes of "team failure"; in the next sec-

tion we consider the conditions and the techniques that may sustain a fruitful group dynamics.

Group pressure

One well-known experiment – described in Box 5.2 – clarified long ago how powerful cognitive pressure could be in groups, and how listening to others can lead to blind acquiescence rather than to better decision-making. Given the experiment design, the "pressure" can be attributed entirely to cognitive factors. In other words, in Asch's experiments, people find it difficult to express their own opinion and/or change their opinion owing to the mere fact that others, and more precisely all others, have a different opinion. They are not afraid to offend, to be punished by a superior, to be excluded from the group – all social factors which can make the situation even worse in the real world. Even in a task where ambiguity is minimal, people lose faith in their own evaluations, and begin to think of all possible clues, contrary elements, and contradictions that other people evidently see where they themselves do not. While this process of doubt would be positive in an open, differentatied environment, in one where unaminity or a single vision clearly prevails it is destructive.

"Groupthink"

Cognitive group pressure may result in a pathology that has been called "groupthink" (Janis 1972). It has been studied in cases and real organizational situations and used as one possible explanation of certain disastrous group decisions such as the 1986 Challenger tragedy in which the spacecraft exploded in the air shortly after takeoff, or General Motors' introduction of the model Corvair

Box 5.2
Asch's experiments

The following experiment, known as Asch's experiment, named after its inventor Solomon Asch (1955), clearly shows how difficult it can be for a member of a group to support his own ideas.

The experiment consists in showing the subjects tested the three lines A, B, and C, and asking which of them is the same length as the reference line.

Reference line | A | B | C |

Usually 99 percent of the participants that are tested individually reply correctly.

Asch then tried to conduct the same experiment by forming various groups and having each member of the same group reply one after another. Asch set up the groups in such a way that each group contained a certain number of people to respond uniformly, but incorrectly (for example A). When only one person was instructed to reply incorrectly, the error rate in the person tested immediately afterwards increased from 1 percent to 3 percent; if two people precede the subject tested and respond A, the rate at which the third person will also reply A increases to 13 percent; if three or more people precede the subject tested and answer A, the error rises to 33 percent.

In other experiments, the group was told that everybody would receive a monetary reward as a function of the number of correct answers given by the same group, and the error rate reached 47 percent.

If reciprocal influence created these results in a simple and structured problem like the one outlined, you can imagine what effect group pressure could have in much more complex situations.

However, in the case where even more than three people (six) were instructed to answer A, but at least one was instructed to reply B, the error rate in the person following dropped to 6 percent.

car which incorporated several serious design errors and led to a spate of accidents (Russo and Schoemaker 1989). In all these cases, even though there were signals that the projects had technical limitations and there were some dissenting opinions, the external and internal expectations of results and the collective enthusiasm behind the effort induced those groups to turn a blind eye and relax their critical sense to a much greater extent than is normally present in group members as individuals.

Risk propensity

As the cases described illustrate, groupthink and group pressure are likely to produce risky decisions. Probably no single decision-maker, if s/he had received information regarding the defects that surfaced in testing and trials and which, in effect, was available beforehand, would have taken the responsibility of personally guaranteeing those actions. One of the least desirable consequences of group decision-making, a disadvantage of this type of coordination which is frequently noted, is that individual contributions to decisions are not discernible within the group decision. As a result, each single group member is only partially responsible for the consequences of choice – unless explicit mechanisms are installed to make members separately responsible. In the absence of these corrections, compared to individual decision-makers, who are entirely responsible, decision-making groups are likely to be more risk-prone. It must be remembered, however, that this *incentive effect* may be offset by the greater ability of groups to build a more valid model of the problem, to consider many reasons for and against the various alternatives, to see potential negative consequences (a *knowledge effect*).

Conditions for effective group decision

Considering the pathologies and the advantages, it can be concluded that the following set of variables has significant effects on the effectiveness of teams as a coordination mechanism:

- the degree of differentiation of the knowledge held by members
- the degree of internal motivational pressure to fulfill given team goals
- the degree of external pressure for results
- the degree of rivalry among groups.

The relationship these variables have with group effectiveness and the quality of solutions is not linear. The effective group needs high levels of internal differentiation and a lot of time to decide. On the other hand, if these attributes reach extreme levels, the group could be placed in difficulty or not be sufficiently stimulated or motivated. Communication becomes difficult if cognitive differentiation is too high; consensus building by

confrontation needs common values and interests; internal efficiency is sustained by external pressure and external competition. Consequently, the relationship between the variables mentioned and group effectiveness is an upside-down U-shaped curve, as represented in Figure 5.2.

These predictions can be partly experienced directly by role-playing the many group problem-solving exercises available or easy to construct according to the particular relationship one wishes to test. For example, submit the problem in Box 5.3 to different groups under varying conditions of internal differentiation or pressure on results (and ask for individual solutions before group solutions). Group solutions are more frequently correct unless expert accountants are present (solution in the Appendix). In addition, observing and discussing the different discussion dynamics in the different groups can introduce and clarify the role of group decision supports, illustrated in the next paragraph.

Group decision supports

Just as competition needs support and defense mechanisms and is unlikely to live

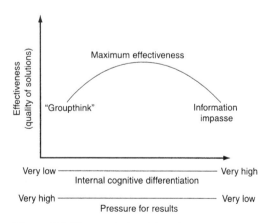

Figure 5.2 The relationship between team attributes and decision effectiveness

Box 5.3
The jeweler's problem

Consider the following accounting puzzle:

A woman buys a $78 necklace at a jewelry store. She gives the jeweler a check for $100. Because he does not have the $22 change to hand, he goes to another merchant next door. There he exchanges the woman's check for $100 in cash. He returns and gives the woman the necklace and her change. Later, the check bounces and he must make it good to the other merchant. He originally paid $39 for the necklace. What is the total out-of-pocket loss?

Source: Russo and Schoemaker (1989).

spontaneously, just as authority needs specific capabilities in order not to degenerate into authoritarianism or imposition, so teams needs behavioral competences to work positively and not degenerate into pathologies or deadlocks. A good part of organizational behavior studies on groups is devoted to developing techniques for maintaining "correct" group dynamics (Lickert 1961; Schein 1965; Maier 1967). The following main prescriptions offered by these studies should be recalled:

• *Involvement in problem definition.* Information processing sub-activities can be identified in decision-making processes, such as defining problems, searching for information and alternatives, evaluating alternatives, and choosing (Chapter 2). The extent to which the whole group is involved in these various activities has a large impact on group dynamics.

Many meetings and group decision processes do not end well because the participants have somewhat different ideas on what the problem to be solved is. For example, discussing the best investment in an information system may not lead to a solution, because information system experts may see it as a problem of memory size, whereas sales forces see it as a problem of data timeliness, and the personnel department sees it as a problem of reorganizing work. Assigning a group the activity of defining the problem, instead of just discussing and evaluating alternatives, is important because it allows the group to establish itself with reference to a common perception and objective.

• *Independent and free generation of alternatives.* What was said regarding the definition of the problem does not rule out group members reducing their interdependence in generating options in order to achieve greater creativity. One frequently used tactic is to form subgroups. Once the problem has been defined as launching a new product, a group of marketing people could be divided into subgroups in order to create various advertising ideas without influencing each other in the phase dedicated to increasing the variety of input information. A second tactic, with similar objectives, is that of "*brainstorming*", or the free-wheeling generation of alternatives under a suspension of evaluative judgment. How is it possible to improve an assembly line; or to improve the traditional process of conducting a university examination; or to improve the process of evaluating personnel? The effort dominating the initial part of an effective creative decision process is to think of something that diverges from the existing situation, of something "distant," of something radical, of not easily "available" solutions. Only later will these ideas be judged in terms of their feasibility and, even if discarded, some of their elements may be incorporated in the accepted solutions. Other techniques for supporting the variety of inputs are: to design groups to include members who have different mental outlooks, cognitive styles, or experiences (external experts, people coming from different firms, industries, or countries); or people called in specifically to play a criticism role such as "discussants" or "devil advocates."

- *Conflicts on the problem not against people.* Discussion and confrontation are intense social and emotional dynamics. Conflict should even be created if conflict resolution is to bring high-quality decisions. However, people are not always used to criticizing or being criticized constructively.

  The pathology of interpersonal conflict is the principal focus in social psychology studies on group processes (Bales 1950). In this perspective, they cite and banish a series of unconstructive but frequent behaviors, such as interrupting, being aggressive toward other people, trying to lower other people's status, not recognizing the legitimacy of different opinions, or isolating. As a support technique, behavioral training for group work has a fundamental role in facilitating effective group processes and is, indeed, widely applied in activities that rely heavily on group work (from military task forces to medical teams, to technical design task forces, to interfunctional or international committees).

- *Role differentiation.* Frequently it is both effective and efficient to have group members assume different, yet complementary roles. Both the differentiation of group members' competences and the convenience of internally dividing labor are conducive to this. For example, creating different roles is useful for coordinating the diverse phases or sub-activities of group decision-making (study, search, elaborating plans or scenarios, comparative evaluation of alternatives, diffusion of results). Recurring differentiated roles in group coordination are, for example, the moderator, the technical expert, the disseminator of information, the linking-pin with other groups.

- *Common knowledge.* Group members should share a sufficiently extended background knowledge, in terms of languages, competences, and values to understand each other and being able to engage in joint elaborations or cross-fertilization of ideas (Schein 1985; Grant 1996).

In conclusion, it can be observed that group coordination has both positive and negative relationships with other coordination mechanisms. Group decision-making can be partially supported by and mixed with other coordination mechanisms to create a viable "group-like" organization form. On the other hand, confrontation can easily be killed if the use of such mechanisms exceeds certain limits. Important mechanisms which reinforce effective group processes are, for example:

- the use of procedural authority to manage the discussion process, but not of substantive authority to assess the merits of decisions;

- the sharing of a basic (paradigmatic) common culture, but not of identical perceptions and judgments, of identical theories, of similar heuristics (Chapter 7);

- the use of social exchange – reciprocal reward through the exchange of "social goods" such as status, esteem, belonging and sociability (Homans 1950) – but not of bargaining over ideas and exchange of technical solutions for side payments (monetary or social).

Costs and limits of team communication and decision

System size

Coordinating collective action through confrontation and the construction of consent is the most costly mechanism in terms of time needed, information exchanged, and resources used. Moreover, these costs increase in proportion to the number of possible connections among actors, and not simply in proportion to the number of actors to be coordinated. As a result, one of the foremost causes of "team failure" is the size of the system to be coordinated. There are firms that are governed extensively by peer group mechanisms – e.g. a group of professionals – but system size affects the mix with other mechanisms. As it grows large, even if activities are complex and competences and power continue to be largely and symmetrically distributed among the members, joint group decision-making will no longer be viable as a prime or stand-alone coordination mechanism. Shared decision rights will usually be complemented by shared property rights, ensuring coordination and control of behavior by incentives rather than by mutual adjustment. Group coordination will be supported by other coordination mechanisms more suitable to large numbers, such as consultation, voting, and internal markets of

activities and resources. Organization forms made of combinations of different coordination mechanisms is actually what we would expect in the presence of conflicting coordination requirements such as those posed by large size coupled with complex activities.

Pay-off size

Beyond the size of the system and the complexity of the information to be processed, the importance of activities has an impact as to which alternative means of coordination is more cost-effective. Decisions that have important consequences may justify the costs of more wide-sweeping decision processes and the investment in information-processing capacity. For even where, in principle, all members of a group have the right to be decision-makers (such as shareholders, or members of associations, unions, and cooperatives), only important decisions are actually discussed and evaluated by everybody. On the other hand, even where activities are coordinated primarily through the use of authority, such as in classical authority-based firms, complex and important decisions are taken jointly and directly by those actors holding the relevant knowledge and interests (for example, shareholder assemblies on capital variation issues, committees of divisional directors on strategic diversification problems, project groups for developing new products).

Conflicts between interests

Group coordination is prone to failures due to the differentiation and contrast between members' interests – which frequently goes hand in hand with growth in size and the differentiation of specialized activities. The experience described in Box 5.4 gives an opportunity to appreciate the reasons and

Box 5.4
Group failures: the Rainbow
case

Those nights spent in the hospital in his town had left Luke with bittersweet memories. During the silent nights he realized how much could be done to mitigate the suffering of the elderly. That's how, a few days after the death of his grandfather, Luke came to the decision to return to the hospital and work as a volunteer aiding old people during the night. In the first two months Luke was there, he was joined by eight other people: four youths and four adults, all of whom happened to come to the hospital because of a sick relative.

In 1995 the Rainbow association was established to bring non-medical assistence to elderly people.

Once a month the group of volunteers met to make operating-type decisions. A system of rotation was set up so that at least one person covered each night. It was fairly simple to divide up the work. There were relatively few skills required, and this, among other things made it easy to substitute people. The volunteers helped the old people to eat and to get around and generally worked to mitigate their suffering. The monthly meetings were very important and almost entirely dedicated to exchanging impressions and experiences. The group seemed to have no need for rules or procedures to work. They all shared the same objective and this made the relationships among the members easy. Those monthly meetings allowed the members to share small innovations in the art of helping others, an art at once difficult and easy.

As the months passed, Rainbow began to assume an increasingly important role in the hospital: both the medical and paramedical personnel considered them a valid and reliable help; the relatives confided in them in order to know the course of the illness or to be comforted; the old people undoubtedly benefited greatly from the service. Rainbow began to become known throughout the city. People talked about the association and soon many residents in the town, especially young university students, asked to join that small group; at the end of 1995 the association could count on more than 50 volunteers.

During the course of 1996 a few changes began to occur. Dividing the workload and coordinating the members required more attention, so much so that one of the "founders" took over the responsibility systematically. The monthly meetings were always well attended and became bimonthly, but it became apparent that their real purpose was being eroded: for some, they had become the occasion for socializing for the sake of socializing; for others, being present was important in order to say that one belonged to Rainbow (more than for assisting the old), also because this experience had become familiar to the local labor market. The veterans tried to continue governing the association democratically, but it was increasingly difficult. Beyond appearances there was no longer a common ideal: Rainbow had become a disorganized group that the founders could no longer manage by example and professional competence. With some frequency, shifts began to be left uncovered and complaints from medical and nursing staff began to be heard with regard to the lack of reliability of some of the members. At the end of the year a meeting of four of the founders was held, together with some doctors and the department head. Despite the affection and gratitude felt for Rainbow, the founders were presented with an alternative: either re-establish order and control over the volunteers or cease cooperating with the hospital.

A few days later, the original nine members held a very long meeting. Luke was convinced that, in order to work with the number of current members, the association needed some form of organization, some common rules and perhaps even a more finely tuned division of roles and the introduction of some supervising figures. However, he knew that an association like Rainbow also needed to be permeated with individual initiative and had to be based on shared objectives that might be destroyed by excessive supervision and division of labor. He also was evaluating the introduction of training courses for new volunteers to unite and make the group's initiatives more homogeneous at the expense of curtailing innovation. Another alternative was to dissolve the association and start again with a smaller group. This would mean sacrificing the heritage represented by the name of the association, which alone was able to attract and keep new volunteers. By the end of the meeting some important decisions for the future of Rainbow had to be made.

A brief training course for new volunteers was instituted. Members were divided into small subgroups, and in each of these one of the more experienced volunteers was assigned the role of group tutor, supervisor for the night shifts, and stimulus for the behavior so appreciated by the hospital and the patients. They tried to replicate the original organization in small groups, attempting to recapture the spontaneously desired behavior. However, the illusion that everybody could have the same calling had vanished. An administrative meeting of the nine founders, where all operative decisions were made, was added to the general monthly meeting. In this way, a type of hierarchy was added to the small groups structure.

Source: By Silvia Bagdadli.

processes of the likely hybridization of group coordination with coordination by hierarchy, rules, and negotiation as activities expand. It also introduces the control dimension of group coordination, treated in the next section.

GROUP CONTROL

As with other modes of coordination, using groups to make decisions can be distinguished from using them to control activities. A decision can be made by a group, and guaranteeing its execution can be entrusted to an authority or accomplished through the use of incentives. For example, a group can decide what characteristics a new product

must have, but the production of the new item can be carried out by an operating structure based on authority, rules, and planning. Moreover, a group can be called upon to control the execution of activities that the group itself did not decide. For example, a group assembling office machines may follow pre-defined activities; yet, given proper incentives to deliver a collective output, group members can reciprocally control each others' working behavior.

In general, if group members' activities could be separated and each action could be unambiguously connected to specific outcomes, no control activity would be necessary, because people could be motivated to contribute through results-based rewards. This would be more of an incentive than a control mechanism, and it would establish a price-like coordination in which each actor is guided to choose appropriate actions by considering their pay-offs. Potential candidate activities for group control are those where individual contributions are not discernible in the collective output (*"team production"*).

However, not all team production situations are manageable by team control. Let us specify the conditions under which a team can effectively control its members, and through what mechanisms, by examining the three basic operations of a control process: gathering information on performance, evaluating that information with respect to desired performances, and correcting actions through feedback.

Gathering performance data

Reciprocal observability

Group control requires that group members be able to observe each other. All members must have access to performance information, must be able to ascertain which contribution each member makes.

This requirement makes it feasible only under certain circumstances: members should have the competence and the technical opportunity to observe performance indicators. *Group size, work autonomy, the specialization and the complexity of activities are all obstacles to effective and efficient group control.* The larger the group, the more difficult and costly direct observation among group members becomes. The activities of a newspaper editorial staff numbering fewer than a dozen people who do a little bit of everything, could be observed and comprehended effectively, but not those of a large editorial staff with several dozen people working on different

activities. Therefore, in addition to the number of people, the degree of the division of labor and the diversity of group members' specializations also obstruct control by the group.

The complexity of activities poses a problem too. Consider, for example, research activities. If they are conducted in a laboratory, with physically visible experiments, and with the directly observable results of these experiments, then group control will be effective. If, by contrast, research is conducted in the field, or is in a conceptual phase so that it goes on in the mind, behaviors, and often results, are difficult to ascertain. So, if activities are complex in the sense that there are few standards of correct behavior or there are few indicators that these standards have been followed, the control capacity of groups is rather limited.

Evaluation

Competence

Group members must be able to evaluate the quality of the contributions made. For example, in the case of problem-solving groups, members are usually able to judge the quality of contributions in terms of dedication, preparation, seriousness, respect of discussion rules, absence of shirking. They will not always be able to evaluate the technical quality of the analyses and the information supplied, especially if the differentiation of specialist knowledge within the group is high. An important condition for the effectiveness of the group as a control mechanism is the relative *diffusion and homogeneity of the relevant competences* for the group's activities.

Roles

Shared expectations regarding the respective and specific models of behavior to be assumed by each member (*roles*) are common features of groups (Katz and Kahn 1966). A function of roles is to enable group members to make homogeneous judgments about the appropriateness of the contributions of each individual member. For, if there were many divergent opinions on the behavior that each member should assume, the group would not be able to apply sanctions in a consistent way in order to correct behavior.

On the other hand, this process in never perfect. An important part of social psychology literature on groups has focused on the origin of various types of imperfections in forming those reciprocal expectations of behavior that are the basis of social control processes. This theme is normally identified as a problem of "*role stress*" (Katz and Kahn 1966). The studies on role tension have been useful in identifying a series of sources of distortions in the processes of assuming certain models of behavior in response to group expectations.

An initial type of problem may emerge in the process of communicating expectations. Communicating role expectations involves transmission of poorly codified information: the message may lack clarity or the receiver's perception or interpretation may not conform to that of the sender (*role distortion*). For example, the role of a door-to-door cosmetics salesperson could be unclear because the salespeople have not had the time or the opportunity to form reciprocal expectations, because no time has been devoted to communicating, interacting, training, socializing, and exchanging experiences regarding customer behavior and usable techniques. The behavior of the salespeople will turn out to be largely unpredictable and uncontrolled simply because they *don't know how to behave.*

If people do not have the technical and professional resources to satisfy expectations,

the problem of scarcity of information and knowledge about expected behavior may assume a more serious, structural dimension. A frequently observed organizational dysfunction is expecting people to perform certain activities without giving these people the means to assume that role (competences, incentives, jurisdiction, status, time, or appropriate opportunities) (*role incongruence*). For example, a marketing group may expect a product manager to coordinate their requirements with those of production, but the person may be too young or know too little about production to satisfy the group expectations.

Lastly, *role conflicts* may emerge. People normally belong to several different groups, even as regards their work-related activities alone. One result of this is that the control mechanisms of any single group intersect with those of other groups. Moreover, if the various groups to which the actors belong have different expectations for the same activities, that role will be conflictual and ambiguous. This is characteristic of many "boundary-spanning roles" (Aldrich 1979). For example: the intermediate boss's role is likely to be stressed by the conflicting expectations of subordinates and upper management; salespeople of complex goods/services who have significant client contact are likely to feel the conflict between client expectations and those of the employing firm; interfunctional integrating roles, such as a product-manager or process-responsible role, typically receive different demands from the different functional units they are called to coordinate.

Deviance and conformism

On the other hand, role theory has neglected some important positive elements in role stress and the loss of control in groups. For groups cannot be equated with living organisms where the organism's organs and parts perform functions which are perfectly aligned with one another. Group members could deliberately refuse to conform to expectations, they could deviate from the expected roles – as occurs in control processes governed by authority as well. Groups usually tolerate a certain degree of deviance, not only because a perfect control process is impossible, but also because it is counterproductive. Behavior stretching and action slippage with respect to normal expectations, by chance or purpose, can lead to learning new behavior (Aldrich 1979; Weick 1979a); or they can allow adjustment to unforeseen changes in the activities. Perfect conformism, therefore, is rarely an advantage, although it would be the sign of perfect group control.

Stability

However, group control will be more effective the more the role system is clear and shared. If this is true, then *stability* is among the conditions necessary for a group to exert social control over its members: stability in the composition of the group, and stability in the activities of the group. In other words, team members should have the time to get to know each other, to form mutual expectations, to define models of acceptable behavior that are not already obsolete before they are put into use.

Dynamic and innovative activities are, instead, bad candidates for group control. Consider the case of a group which represents an engineering firm and must negotiate a project for building a nuclear plant in a third world country where that firm has had no previous work experience. Further, assume that the firm does not know of any similar experience by other firms that could serve as successful models for negotiation. The group has very little information available on possible effective behavior models it could use to evaluate the contributions of the participants. It is a fairly unique event, unrepeatable, and there would be no way of learning them in time. In contrast, in more traditional and familiar situations, the delegation would have had its coordinated strategy for negotiating, and its habitual roles and fair-play norms against which to evaluate behaviors.

Rewards and sanctions

What tools can groups use to exert influence? Why should the members of a group bother to take the time or make the effort to check up on each other, especially when it can be very expensive, materially and psychologically? Given a common interest in group performance, the group can allocate the rights to participate in the created benefits in various ways, illustrated in the next paragraph. In addition to the allocation of various categories of property rights over activities to group members, group control is distinctively sustained by the possibility of using social rewards.

Social rewards and sanctions

In fact, the group is inevitably a place for social interchange. Even when it is created to run economic activities, the interactions between members of the group imply social transactions. Hence, groups create social benefits and costs that can be granted or withdrawn for governing task-oriented behaviors. The following are examples:

- *Status:* commitment, cognitive capacities, ability to mediate and resolve problems, level of experience in group activities, are all recognized by group members; this recognition confers status within the group and gratifies individual members.

- *Power:* competences, control over information and critical resources, ability to discuss and manage relationships are bases for exerting influence on other group members; this possibility represents a benefit for many people.
- *Esteem:* an important part of the utility that many people draw from work comes from being valued by others; groups award or take back esteem as a function of the quality of individual contributions.
- *Belonging:* isolation, exclusion, being marginalized, or ridiculed are social sanctions that people generally have a negative perception of: the more a single work group is important in the life of a person, the less diversified her commitment is, and the fewer possibilities she has to be rewarded by participating in other groups.

TYPES OF GROUP-LIKE COORDINATION AND THE "GROUP PARADOX"

The group paradox

The different properties of the group as a decision mechanism as compared to the group as a control mechanism, can lead to an important conflict over how groups should be used as a mode of coordinating. Effective decision processes require variety and mobility in membership, diversity in knowledge, and difference of opinion. On the contrary, effective control processes require stability and affinity among group members, and conformity in judgments on and expectations of group actions and members' behaviors.

In principle, it is not impossible to think of groups as capable of wearing two hats, depending on which of the two functions,

control or decision, is being performed. Yet in practice it is not easy to develop such sophisticated contingent behavior. Moreover, the structural characteristics of members – orientation, personality, diversity in information and knowledge, variety of cognitive styles – that sustain effective processes are different in the "creative" group as compared to the "normative" group.

As a result, in coordinating by group there is a fundamental *trade-off between investing in decision-making capacity and investing in control capacity.* This trade-off is relevant for identifying different types of group coordination and to understand when to employ them. In fact, in the reality of organizational life, many groups clearly favor one or other dimension.

The "primitive group"

There are in fact teams in which neither decision nor control is problematic. The team members have sufficient competence to decide actions, can observe the behavior of each member perfectly and instantaneously, the common output is clear, and the purpose shared. Then, expected deviations are small and largely due to chance and error rather than to free-riding; and social and/or economic sanctions can be easily invoked anyway in response to behavior that deviates from what is expected. This situation has been identified since the very first studies on the nature of cooperation: "the mass problem" – how a group of people coordinate themselves to move a mass which no one could carry individually – (Barnard 1938) being its prototype. It was later referred to as a "*primitive group*" (Williamson 1981a). As the size of this type of group grows, this is the typical situation in which it may be efficient to centralize control and residual reward rights as the members of the group can no longer observe each other well but a central agent might. (Alchian and Demsetz 1972; Chapter 4).

In situations where the are complexities – in knowing and assessing one or more aspects of contributions, or even in devising which actions are superior – other forms of team coordination are effective.

Clans and relational teams

For example, the much celebrated "clan-like" groups in Japanese business organization are primarily oriented to control behavior, having been described as a blend of group control and cultural control mechanisms (Ouchi 1980; Ouchi and Wilkins 1985; Chapter 7). These scholars have considered situations in which it is difficult to assess the value of each particular actor's contribution every time it takes place. For example, in the construction processes of cars – or of other technology intensive, standardized consumption products in which Japanese industry excels – what is the value of each act of care and intelligence leading to correct a production defect? How can these contributions be sustained? A possible solution is to stretch out over time performance evaluation: the "longevity" of the relationship, evaluating performances and distributing compensation on the basis of a long series of episodes, enables contributions to be balanced and equity to be restored among members in a "serial" way, even if each single contribution is not precisely measured and not instantly rewarded. The theorists of "clan" have themselves admitted, however, that based as it is on stability, longevity, repeated action and observable contributions, clan control may entail costs in terms of change and innovation capabilities.

Communities

There may be situations in which contributions cannot be observed or evaluated even in the long term, because they are based on too complex, too specialized, too actor-specific, too distant knowledge. Consider an inter-functional project team in charge of designing a technical plant in such a way as to solve some particular production problems for a client. Group coordination is still highly effective on the knowledge sharing and problem-solving side. But group members can observe each other's relevant behavior only indirectly, let alone evaluate it. How intensively did the engineer work in devising possible alternative technical solutions? How well informed are they of similar, applicable experience, generally known or described in technical literature? How deeply did the raw material buyers look for the materials that could have solved the problem? How much does finding the solution depend on the effort of the group members and how much on external factors? The quality and quantity of the contributions can only be evaluated rather imprecisely.

This situation was encountered earlier when examining the limitations of agency relationships. Cooperation and exchange under *these conditions cannot be managed by control processes – either by a central agent or by a group – but must be regulated by the use of incentive systems or self-control mechanisms. It is a matter of realigning objectives rather than behavior.* This can happen in at least two, not mutually exclusive, ways, *both diverging from group control.*

• Team members can become the controllers of themselves through incentive mechanisms, such as profit sharing and gain sharing (Avadikian *et al.* 1993; Chapter 9). This is, in fact, what largely happens in professional and knowledge intensive work.

- Team members can become controllers of themselves thanks to cultural mechanisms, to sharing the same basic values and cognitive frames, to identification with common purposes (and eventually with the group), to reciprocal expectations of adhering to group norms that are the same for all members (Ouchi and Wilkins 1985; Chapter 8). Professional groups (whether professional associations, certified professions, professional firms, or groups within them) are once more a case in point: codes of conduct and a reputation for adhering to them, severe selection, and intense socialization and training are fundamental means used by these groups for controlling members.

In spite of these mechanisms, the more a peer group is oriented to problem-solving, creativity, innovation, and members' autonomy the less it is likely to solve control problems completely. For example, groups in professional partnerships (from project groups, to professional forums, to partners' committees) are often closer to the model of a problem-solving team than to a shirking reducing and behavior aligning clan. But these firms – from management consulting to software houses – have few defenses against the loss of members, and of the relations with clients that those members have cultivated; or against the private appropriation of information or other resources by the individual participants.

SUMMARY

This chapter analyzed teams as a distinct mode of coordination. To this end, the group was *not* considered as a generic small community where collective action can be coordinated in many ways – for example, by authority and leadership, culture and institutionalization of common norms, and negotiation. Instead, we tried to identify the distinctive mechanisms of "group decision-making" and "group control": knowledge sharing, confrontation, and mutual persuasion, the possibility of exerting influence based on balanced and diffused competences, control based on reciprocal observation and evaluation. The limits of the effective and efficient application of these mechanisms have been discussed, as contingent upon the *complexity of activities, the structure of interests, the importance of decisions, and the number of actors to be coordinated*. It has been shown that it is necessary to distinguish between the use of groups for decision-making purposes and for control purposes. In fact, there is a trade-off between the need for internal differentiation and slack resources in order to achieve innovative and high quality decisions, and the need for cohesion and pressure on results in order to align behaviors and control them effectively (*the group paradox*).

Three different types of groups were defined in light of the different possible control and incentive mechanisms: the "*primitive group*," the "*relational team*" and the "*community of peers*." Other conditions being equal, the effective use of these three forms of team coordination is related to increasing levels of information complexity.

Regarding both group decision and group control, the configurations of the social and *interpersonal processes* that can favor or inhibit group effectiveness were examined. Key elements to be addressed in this perspective are: governing group composition, supporting participation and the generation of variety, governing the process and relational dynamics and not only the problem-solving dynamics, managing role conflicts.

Exercise: PlastiSav

Before

PlastiSav is a European chemical firm, specializing in the production of special plastics for food use. The firm's leading product has by now entered a stage of maturity. Market competition has been growing over the last few years owing to the entry of certain East European countries which, exploiting factories built in the 1960s, run very aggressive price policies in a market where the basic product is substantially the same. Currently, the firm faces the problem of diversifying its production by developing new products capable of making best use of the technical and managerial abilities that PlastiSav has built up over the years. The new general manager has come from a large firm in the sector and is aware of the fact that, in view of the nature of PlastiSav's products and production processes, the project for developing a new product must be entrusted to the firm's in-house resources, relying on outside consultancy only for very particular aspects. He also thinks that the project should not be the exclusive responsibility of the research and development department, because in the past many innovations that were introduced, while interesting from a technical point of view, found no response in the market – this, *inter alia*, because their implications for production were not sufficiently taken into consideration. Before a product in the special plastics sector can be launched on the market, it must have been carefully studied and developed in all its aspects. In particular:

- detailed study must have been made of the chemical process leading to production of the material, in order to understand all its anomalies, quantity of waste, consumption, and return;
- all the problems involved in safety and control of discharge into the atmosphere must have been studied, in order to avoid severe penalties;
- testing and certification must have been performed of the material produced and the modalities of use (also because PlastiSav's special plastics are intended for food use;
- it is necessary to understand the market potential, the possible clients and the uses of the material, the competitors, other materials that may substitute for the one in question, and all the aspects of marketing the product;
- it is necessary to define the economic aspects of the project, the investment required, volumes, margins, and all the financial aspects;
- the organization problems must be understood, with regard to the repercussions on the organization of factory and office work, clarifying the responsibilities and the resources available.

   The general manager is thinking of entrusting the perfecting of the product to the main figures responsible in the firm, namely:

- production and safety manager
- factory management
- research and development manager
- laboratory and quality control manager
- sales manager
- marketing manager
- administration, finance, and control manager
- organization and personnel manager
- purchasing
- logistics

While preparing for the first meeting, the GM jotted down on a sheet of paper some fixed points of the project he wanted to set forth:

Original paper used by the GM (General Manager) to note the points to be set forth at the meeting

1   We must hurry up, we can't go on like this, the project must be in place in as short a time as possible, the market doesn't leave us much room, whoever performs this task will be responsible for the future of the firm;
2   The people I need don't have to like each other, I need well-prepared people, specialists. Rather than a department head who knows little, I should prefer a technician who can show he knows a lot. The concept is specialization. I don't want "general" experts, each specialist must bring his own knowledge to the project.
3   I am well aware that you may have very different ideas and objectives as regards which path to take, but I'm not concerned with that. All I want is for each of you to bring his own stock of knowledge to the project.

After

A working group was set up, which included all ten of the main responsible figures in PlastiSav. The first meetings immediately brought out some basic problems. The group worked with great difficulty; the initial meetings, held on Saturdays, lasted right through the day, and one was left with the feeling of merely wasting time. The various interventions brought out the conflicts between people and their functions, and frequently the meeting lapsed into discussions on topics that had little to do with the project. Some people appeared to view the project as a means of undoing the existing power balances, and many hoped "to get rid once and for all of that lump of a Production Manager or R & D Manager," while others glimpsed threats and hazards in the project.

No coordination roles, beyond that of a simple secretary, were set up to facilitate the working of the group. The agenda for each meeting was drawn up by the secretary, the youngest element, who confined himself to collecting proposals from the members with most influence and putting them in order. The result was chaotic and repetitive. After the initial meetings, the GM decided to take no further part, not wanting to seem to boss the group. But he began to get informal and cross-wise feedback; some people used the meetings to pass judgments on their colleagues to the GM. Some thought the project was purely a "wheeze" on his part to "flush out" his opponents and keep tabs on them. These rumors, many of them unchecked, increased the group's difficulties. At a later stage, many people opted out of the discussion, preferring just to listen, with the cynical comment: *"it will all blow over and things will return to being as they were before".*

By Giuseppe Soda

Questions

- How can you account for the failure of the group solution?
- What different options in the composition of the group, definition of the objectives, and government of the process might have led to a better result?

Appendix 5.1

Solution to the jeweler problem

Income	*Payments*
	39
100	100
	22
———	———
100	161
———	———

Loss = $61

Chapter 6

Negotiation

· ·

Implicitly inviting a comparative perspective, Raiffa (1982) observed: "There are many ways for settling disputes: traditions, rules, courts, markets and negotiations." What is the distinctive domain of the application of negotiation? It would seem that almost everything is or can be negotiated. The exchange of many goods and services is negotiated. Work contracts and the organization of work are negotiated. Interfirm and interunit relationships are negotiated . . . The relationships between professor and student, husband and wife, parent and child . . . are negotiated . . .

Even etymologically, the term negotiation has a very broad meaning: *Nec otium* in Latin identified economic activity itself, "the negation of idleness," dedicating oneself to business. The technical significance given to the term today is, however, much more specific. The necessary and sufficient conditions to define a process of coordination as a negotiation can be stated as follows:

- the process implies communication among identified parties having different interests and preferences;
- the process implies an exchange of material or immaterial resources among parties (money, information, rights, behavioral commitments);

- the process implies searching for ways of exchanging resources that will match the interests of the parties involved as much as possible;
- the process is concluded, if it is, by a joint decision or agreement among the parties.

Experts have defined it as "a process of interaction in which two or more parties try to reach an agreement about a mutually acceptable outcome" in a situation where there are conflicting interests (Druckman 1977); a form of decision in which two or more parties talk to each other in an attempt to settle opposing interests (Pruitt 1981); a joint decision between two or more parties who do not have the same interests (Bazerman and Lewicki 1983).

These definitions highlight the characteristics which distinguish negotiation from other methods of coordination, and help to characterize the domain to which it can be successfully applied: it is not based on unilateral decisions but *entails communication* – in contrast to pricing and voting; the right to decide what actions will be undertaken is shared by the parties rather than transferred – in contrast with authority and agency; actors are "parties," i.e. they have, and are aware of having, conflicting interests, in contrast with team coordination.

Two characteristics of negotiation make it similar to authority and group decision, but differentiate it from forms of unilateral decisions: not only is negotiation based on voice, it is a communication process that takes place between specific actors; it is also a search process, an attempt to find solutions, a process in which alternative courses of action are generated throughout. Negotiation is therefore capable of managing unstructured problems, where action alternatives are not pre-defined – although it is applicable also to structured problems.

Negotiation is not, however, an effective and efficient process for managing any type whatsoever of exchange or cooperation problem. It is an extremely costly process, as far as it requires direct discussion among the parties with different concerns. Consequently, compared to other kinds of coordination, it can be highly inefficient in some situations. In addition, depending on the configurations of interests, negotiation may be impossible, ineffective, or useless. The first section addresses the question of when to negotiate, being more precise about these cases. Subsequent sections treat some of the principal issues of how to negotiate: which offer/counteroffer strategies are and should be used in different circumstances? how and when should information be exchanged? how should social dynamics be managed so that negotiations do not degenerate into interpersonal conflicts?

The general structure of the argument, specifying the profile of the negotiation mechanism, the type of relations that can be effectively governed by it, and some salient sub-types of negotiation processes are summarized in Figure 6.1.

TO NEGOTIATE OR NOT TO NEGOTIATE?

Variable sum games

The first key question concerns the structure of the game. As was seen in the Introduction to Part II, there is no room for negotiation if two or more parties have interests that are diametrically opposed, i.e. if the game is a zero sum game.

For example, if two candidates are interested in the same position as director, and there is nothing else that can be used as compensation, they have nothing to negotiate. One will win and the other will lose, as a function of their unilateral moves. But zero sum

NEGOTIATION	
CONDITIONS	• Distributed knowledge • Unhomogeneous preferences • Unequal resources • Small number of actors
MECHANISM PROFILE:	• All to all communication • Resource exchange • Joint decision making • Hostage-based control
TYPES:	• Distributive/integrative/generative • Two party/multiple parties

Figure 6.1 The negotiation mechanism

games don't occur very often in economic activity. This is true even in particularly competitive relationships. For example, in buyer–seller relations, the discussion is focused on a rate of exchange or price that one side wants to reduce and the other to raise. Even in this case, there is room for negotiation, and the game is not zero sum, if the parties prefer some agreement to no agreement at all, compromise to exit. In this way, a door for negotiating has been opened.

Imperfect markets

The example of negotiated buyer–seller relationships shows other important aspects of situations where negotiation is useful. To say that two parties negotiate a price implies a situation in which price is not determined externally by the law of supply and demand, in which actors can assess which particular value an item has for them, in which prices do not supply all the information relevant for an efficient allocation of resources.

To say, moreover, that two or more parties to a certain extent prefer any agreement to none implies that there are some elements of monopoly, that there is no perfect substitution between parties. This may happen because one or more actors control scarce and valuable resources not available elsewhere. These elements of bilateral monopoly may be due to natural causes, market size, or public intervention; or to the fact that the resources exchanged are specific to the parties – i.e. they have a lower value when exchanged with alternative partners. Consequently, the purchases of new cars, detergent, or lots of bolts are not negotiated to a significant extent; but those of vintage cars, industrial plants, or lots of special composite materials are.

From this point of view, negotiation is an effective mechanism for regulating certain types of relationships for which price-based competition fails. Other situations where negotiation can be used effectively coincide with those where other coordination mechanisms – authority, group, and rules – fail.

Negotiation, authority, and imposition

For example, the governance of work relationships in the large firms of the western world have evolved from an authority-centered system to a negotiation-guided relationship. Two general reasons for this apparently long-wave retirement of authority to the advantage of negotiation may be the fact that wider sets of economic actors have matured and expanded their capacity to define personal interests and preferences as far as the use of work (a shrinking of their "indifference zone"); and the increased information complexity and uncertainty of many activities that undermine the effectiveness and efficiency of centralized decisions.

However, one could observe that eroding the base which legitimizes authority could also lead to "imposing" preferred actions by one side over another, whenever the elements of a monopoly (which are always present in negotiations) lead to situations of unilateral control of relevant resources and capacity for compensation, threat, and punishment. In effect, this observation helps to clarify that negotiation is a process based on promises or threats to give or do something in exchange for something else, which could be more or less symmetrical. If one of the parties finds it difficult to leave the relationship, has few or unattractive alternatives, and is unilaterally dependent on the resources supplied by the other party, then imposition is likely. This process, however, appears as an extreme form of negotiation: as found, for example, in the case of monopolistic firms imposing trading conditions on their suppliers or clients. These conditions have in fact been considered as calling for additional or alternative co-ordination mechanisms – such as third party arbitration and regulation, pledges and guarantees, or even some form of economic integration among trading partners if feasible. Though probable under conditions of unilateral monopoly, imposition and extremely asymmetrical allocation of resources do not always occur, even if they are possible. It has been empirically shown that reasonably fair allocations often occur, even then, for a variety of reasons (Kahneman *et al.* 1986a, 1986b), including the possible losses of reputation, the suspension of calculative rationality for following rules of fairness (Brusco 1999), and the possibility that the extra profits gained by one side in the phase of contract definition are taken back by the other side by adjusting actions in the ongoing process of implementation of agreements (Friedberg and Neuville 1999). On the other hand, whenever actors can choose whether or not to enter a negotiation, they should not be particularly attracted by highly asymmetrical relationships, especially when these asymmetries are information asymmetries rather than other kinds of resource asymmetries. This should seem obvious but is not, as the experiment described in Box 6.1 shows.

Information asymmetries

In Box 6.1 problem, the vast majority of decision-makers concentrate their answers on values between 55 and 75 per share; the reasoning being that: given that all the values between 0 and 100 are equally probable for the buyer, the expected value is 50. However, the value for the buyer of the firm, once acquired, increases by 50 percent – which leads to a maximum offer from the more generous students of 75. But this reasoning takes no account of the problem of assymetry of information.

In effect, any positive offer X the buyer makes, will be accepted only if the value of the study, known only to the seller, is less than or equal to X. Therefore, the expected value of the deal for the buyer is $\frac{x}{2}$ and not $\frac{100}{2}$. Even taking synergy into account and increasing this value by 50 percent, once acquired, the

---

Box 6.1
An acquisition problem

Consider the hypothesis that a leading firm in a given industry sector wants to buy a study on the labor market in that sector, conducted by a little known, specialized firm. Suppose that the study, for the market leader, is worth 50 percent more than it is worth to any other firm in that industry, thanks to the higher capacity to act on the results (let us also suppose that should others also buy the report, it would have no impact in terms of cost for the market leader). However, the real value of the information contained in the study is known only to the firm selling the report, and the company buying the report can only know the results after having bought it. Let us suppose that this report could have a value varying between 0 and 100. What price between these two extremes should the seller set?

Source: Adapted from Bazerman (1986).

expected benefit is ¾ X with an expenditure of X – in other words, a loss.

The standard recommendation is, therefore, not to enter into negotiations that are heavily and unfavorably marked by information asymmetry. It can be seen, however, that a wise negotiator could find a way out of the dilemma between experiencing a loss or losing a potentially interesting deal. For example, he could propose a contingent claim contract in which the payment made would correspond to a base payment for the resource as evaluated at the time of the transaction, and a second payment of an amount to be established at the outcome of the uncertain projects once it had been observed (Williamson 1979; Raiffa 1982).

More generally, for any negotiation to begin and end positively, the envisaged exchange or cooperation must have some kind of advantage for the parties: in other words, a "zone of agreement" should exist. For example, if in a buyer–seller relationship the highest price that the potential buyer of a good was willing to pay, perhaps due to budget constraints, was, say, 30 million, and the seller's minimum price was 50 million, because s/he had had other offers around that level, negotiation could not solve the problem. That exchange is not advantageous for those parties, there is no agreement zone, and probably no trade would take place (nor would it be efficient if it did).

Number of parties and opportunism potential

Another classic comparison helping in deciding whether or not to negotiate is that between rules and negotiation as alternative means of coordination.

Why do automobile drivers not negotiate who should pass through an intersection first? Or why do citizens not negotiate how much to pay in taxes? Or why does not each professor negotiate his lecture calendar with everyone else? These coordination problems will be discussed in greater detail in Chapter 8 on rules and conventions. For, in such situations, using rules is much more effective and efficient.

One of the motives is the number of interdependent relationships to be coordinated. Two, three, maybe ten parties can negotiate, but it would be difficult with 100.

Another reason, not unrelated to the number of interdependent actors, is the potential for opportunism with respect to whatever agreement can be reached. For example, if an agreement is not implemented at the same time as it is signed – as frequently happens – there may be incentives to betray the promises made when the agreement is realized. The greater the advantages in not cooperating, and the less the behavior of the parties can be observed and controlled during the realization phase, the less efficient negotiation, or negotiation alone, will be.

For example even when the residents of a community can negotiate directly the taxes they are to pay, the absence of inspecting authorities and sanctions makes it improbable that the resulting contributions will be sufficient to cover the need established (this coordination problem has the structure of a multi-person Prisoner's Dilemma) (Schelling 1960).

The number of partners is also connected with the process costs of negotiation. The value of the exchanged resources should also be considered in assessing the attractiveness of negotiation with respect to other modes of conflict resolution. It would not be worthwhile to employ resources in the process of joint decision-making which have a greater value than those which are being negotiated. Rules and arbitrating authorities may respond less precisely than negotiation does to all the various, particular configurations of the interests of the parties involved, but these costs of imprecise representation of actors' interests may be offset by the lower process costs.

BASIC NEGOTIATION STRUCTURES

Negotiation was said above to be a useful process for resolving conflict between diverse interests . . . but how diverse? Different types of conflicts can be solved effectively and fairly by different types of strategies. But how can the structure of interests in an uncertain situation be identified? By definition, in a situation that could be resolved through negotiation, parties do not know with certainty the constraints, alternatives, and preferences of the other side (if they know their own).

For this reason, the first steps in an effective negotiating process are always exploratory and tentative. There is no bargaining as yet; ideas and information about the basic goals and purposes motivating negotiation are exchanged. Why are we here? Why do we need what we are here to negotiate for? From what contexts do these needs emerge?

These simple, fundamental questions on the origins and sense of negotiation may be extremely valuable and helpful. Indeed, one of the best-known pathologies of negotiation is the overestimation of conflict. Since negotiation contains some highly visible elements of conflict (the parties are vying for or dividing resources), then it is assumed that the parties have completely opposite interests – that is, it is assumed that for one party to obtain a larger share of the pie, the other must obtain a smaller one. But this is a very particular type of conflict, and it is important to explore and recognize ways to "enlarge the pie" before cutting it up.

Interests and positions

An often quoted example of how negotiations may seem to be highly conflictual, when actually they are not, is the famous Camp David negotiation between Egypt and Israel over the strip of territory that the two countries contended in the 1970s (Raiffa 1982). What game can appear more conflictual than this one? The pie seemed to be of an unmodifiable size, a given territory; and it appeared to be merely a matter of dividing it up, each side hoping to get the larger share (really the entire territory). Questioning the underlying interests behind these positions (Fisher and Ury 1981), these claims over territory clarified that the really attractive resource was not the territory itself, but secure frontiers for the Israelis and the principle of sovreignty on the Egyptians' part. The solution of a demilitarized zone under the Egyptian flag satisfied both sides.

This lesson can be very instructive with regard to the governing of many situations of economic conflict. For example, two people may wish to be appointed director, but for different reasons. They may be interested in doing different activities and gaining access to different rewards among those offered by the position. In this way the resource, the "director's position," could be disaggregated in different, desirable resources (activities, rewards) and each claimant be eventually assigned the items more valuable to him/her. Or, two firms having similar products can compete to steal market share from each other; until they eventually discover that their competences are complementary – for example, making them strong in related but different product lines and sales channels. In this way, they can find convenient ways to cooperate, e.g. through commercial agreements (such as an agreement between a bank and an insurance company on distributing long-term financial products). And so forth.

The negotiator's dilemma

One might wonder whether disclosing information and communication is not excessively risky, given the presence of a potential, serious conflict among interests and the possibility that the information be used hostilely in negotiation. Or that once one has disclosed one's own information, the other side will not do the same. The dilemma over whether "to communicate or not to communicate" where the game structure is unknown and the counterpart's willingness to communicate is unknown, has the structure of a prisoner's dilemma (Lax and Sebenius 1986). For both parties, the outcome would be better if they both communicated; but for each, not knowing what the other will do, it is better to conceal as much as possible about their own interests. This could explain why many negotiations never get off the ground or are played in highly adversarial ways even when it would be better for everybody if they were not. Among the possible ways out of this situation, as in every prisoner's dilemma, is to transform a one-shot game into a repeated game: a series of small steps, of small openings in this case, that may be confirmed and followed by other openings only if the counterpart reciprocates (Axelrod 1984). Another possibility is to have access to partner-specific knowledge, to be able to assess his/her specific propensity to cooperation, thanks to long-standing relations and past experience.

'Batna'

Searching for and analyzing the *alternatives* each party might have to concluding an agreement with a specific counterpart, is a second, fundamental strategy for understanding the nature of a negotiation. This step is so important and so frequently taken into consideration when analyzing negotiations, that it is identified by negotiation experts with the acronym, "*batna*" or "best alternative to a negotiated agreement."

For example, it would be useful for two divisions negotiating transfer prices to ask themselves what the consequences would be if no agreement were reached, what the pay-offs of the alternatives to the agreement would be. One option could be to deal with external firms; another to have the price set by a higher hierarchical authority; yet other may be represented by postponing the transaction, or giving it up all together. Looking for or imagining some of the principal alternatives and evaluating their consequences and their overall utility enables one to understand whether different hypothetical agreements are acceptable or not. When the costs and benefits of a negotiated agreement can be evaluated in monetary terms, this level is called the "reservation price" (or "walk away price"). However, even when it is not easy to appreciate a monetary value and there are no "prices" in the strict sense, it is often possible at least to arrange the various alternatives according to preference. If negotiation is to be used for coordinating economic exchanges meaningfully, the relative attractiveness of different possible contracts or agreement should be visible and recognized, with the value of the most attractive alternative agreement as a minimum acceptability level and reference point.

Returning to the example of two divisions, the purchasing division could believe the alternatives to be: a hierarchically imposed transfer price with an expected value of, say, $1 apiece; using the least expensive external supplier (say $1.5); postponement, judged to be extremely costly. The best alternative to a negotiated agreement or reservation price is therefore $1. Let us now suppose that the supplier division expects that a price set by authority will be $1.3 apiece, and estimates that its output could be sold at $0.9 on the open market. The structure of this negotiation is shown in Figure 6.2.

This type of analysis allows two essential elements to be diagnosed or estimated: the agreement zone within which the contract negotiated with the counterpart is acceptable and the type and degree of conflict of interests.

As far as the agreement zone is concerned, if the two divisions do not correct their estimates of the imposed price (both cannot be right and probably both have a view biased toward their own advantage) there is no zone of agreement with respect to the best alternatives for each party. In this case they will have to consult an arbiter. Let us suppose, however, that headquarters, knowing that the divisions have a wide margin for negotiating with respect to market prices, does not accept fixing the price centrally. This hypothesis is

not unrealistic: it is well known that the more exchanges between divisions involve specific, complex resources, which have a lower price or a price that is difficult to estimate outside of that relationship, the more effective it is for transfer prices to be negotiated rather than set hierarchically or anchored to market levels (Spicer 1988). If market prices are used as reservation prices, there is an ample zone of agreement: both parties prefer an agreement, of whatever kind, between $0.9 and $1.5, to no agreement at all.

Distributive and integrative negotiation structures

As to the structure of negotiation, if price is the only consideration, if other compensative material is not wanted or cannot be found, then a negotiated exchange is, indeed, characterized by diametrically opposed interests with regard to *the point* of agreement (although interests may converge with regard to the convenience of reaching an agreement rather than going for alternative partners or remaining with no agreement).

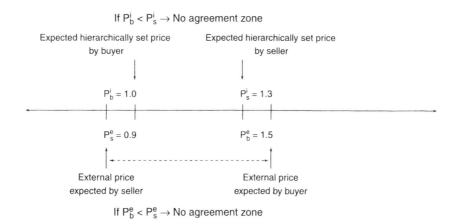

Figure 6.2 Negotiating a transfer price

This negotiation structure is called a "distributive structure" (Raiffa 1982; Walton and McKersie 1965; Pruitt 1983). The other principal possible negotiation structure is an integrative structure. In these situations, it is possible to find "integrative agreements," i.e. combinations of exchanges in which both gain with respect to other combinations. The example previously cited of Egypt and Israel provides a clear, comprehensible explanation as to how this can come about. Actually, it represents an extreme case in which the parties contend for 100 percent of a resource and both are able to obtain it (all of the territory to Egypt as far as sovereignty is concerned, and all of the territory to Israel as far as demilitarization is concerned). A similar point of agreement would be represented by point M in Figure 6.3: it leads to both parties appropriating a value that corresponds to winning the entire pie. The choice of such a contract, if it can exist and once it has been glimpsed, is actually conflict free. The same thing would happen if the point S (see Figure 6.3) were discovered: the two parties, by cooperating, can obtain larger pay-offs than either one could by appropriating the entire pie. That means that their agreement creates new value or "synergies," as in the

case of many collaborative agreements between firms with complementary competences. Therefore, these types of negotiations and agreements could be called "*generative.*"

In most situations, however, it will not be possible to find points of agreement that entail only net advantages and no sacrifices. Conceding "sovereignty" on political negotiations (or property, decision, and action rights in economic negotiations) may not be at "zero cost," but it may cost less than other concessions. For example, suppose that in labor negotiations, management is more interested in retaining the right to decide on personnel mobility and in the continuity of service, while the workers are more interested in pay and employment security. Contracts that allow flexible work organization, good pay levels, and long-term employment may be better for both (Pareto-superior) compared to contracts providing for low pay, rigid job descriptions, scant internal mobility, and short-term employment.

Graphically, one can see that among integrative agreements such as A, B, C, and D, points like B and C are created by small concessions from actors 1 and 2, respectively, that allow their counterpart to realize substantial gains. As a result, they are typically generated by giving up resources that have little value for those who relinquish them and high value for those who receive them.

Approaches to the construction of agreements

Hence, negotiated agreements and contracts are not independent from the processes that lead to them. A useful distinction for understanding those effects is that based on the degree of separation versus integration between the items to be negotiated. Three salient configurations or approaches are

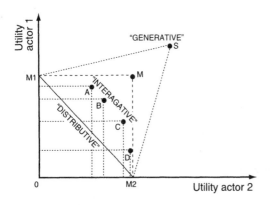

Figure 6.3 Alternative negotiation structures

usually distinguished on this "continuum," each with distinct advantages and disadvantages.

- *The item-by-item approach.* Negotiating the individual matters sequentially has the big, often decisive disadvantage of limiting the possibilities of seeing their complementarities in the actors' preferences and the possible trade-offs between them. The approach is more suitable for distributive negotiations where there are few possibilities for exchanging items between the sides. An item-by-item approach can be tempered by sequential reciprocal concessions: A having conceded on item X, already negotiated, will want a concession from B on item Y, which has yet to be negotiated. However, the item-by-item approach is sometimes the lesser evil in negotiations where there are many sophisticated and highly diverse technical issues to deal with. Even at the cost of neglecting the interdependences among issues, the item-by-item approach allows specialized competences to be applied and reduces the time and costs of the process.
- *The single text approach.* According to this approach, the negotiators do not proceed from opposite platforms but work from the very beginning on a single document which covers all issues on the table, modifying and developing it until a mutually satisfactory document is reached. It is an ambitious method because, since the text of departure is likely to influence the final agreement, it must meet high standards of rationality and fairness from the outset; rarely can it be developed without an unquestionably competent and balanced third party intervening; it always requires the investment of significant resources in analysis and

preliminary studies; it entails a high degree of formalization and institutionalization of the negotiation. This approach is therefore most attractive in innovative and complex negotiations, such as far-reaching collective industrial relations negotiations aiming to devise new orders on important matters.
- *The "packaging" approach.* This approach has the widest range of possible applications. In fact, in all negotiations of average complexity, where there is no need to proceed item by item, or there are not the conditions or the resources to proceed with a single text approach, the issues to be debated could be grouped so as to negotiate them together. It is useful to underline that there are at least two criteria, often in conflict with each other, according to which "intelligent" packages can be created. The first is to group *interdependent issues*, i.e. those issues that are expected to be weighted in complementary ways by the parties, so as to be able to find efficient exchanges of resources within each package. A second criterion is the need for *specialization*. Since it is not economical to maintain a delegation complete with financial analysts, production specialists, market experts, contracters, lawyers and all the other specializations that could serve in complex negotiations throughout the process, it may be necessary to group issues according to the technical specialization required.

Efficient agreements and fair agreements

The term efficient agreements indicates that they achieve Pareto-efficient or Pareto-optimal allocations of resources: these solutions are said to be "not dominated" by others, because improvements for all sides are not possible with respect to them. The weaker term "Pareto-superior" agreements is meaningful also in relatively unstructured negotiation problems: it indicates solutions that entail improvements in utility for one or more parties, without losses for others, with respect to other known or generated alternatives (which cannot be said to cover "all the possible alternatives").

The process of search for efficient agreements will usually lead to identifying more than one (for example, agreements A, B, C, and D in Figure 6.3, if the alternatives M and S were not available, would all be Pareto-efficient). Negotiation experts speak of Pareto-efficient "frontiers" to indicate those sets of undominated solutions, if they can be thought of as a continuum.

The negotiation, therefore, cannot be limited to a search for Pareto-superior solutions; it typically requires search and judgment processes that enable one of these to be selected. The processes and the procedures followed help and at the same time constrain that choice. For example, a "single text" procedure will tend to explore only balanced, central zones of a Pareto frontier and will tend to neglect allocations that are very advantageous for one side and very disadvantageous for the other. Figure 6.4 shows two possible paths of agreement development that lead to two different but equally efficient and procedurally fair agreements, named "single text 1" and "single text 2."

In addition to these fair processes and procedures that may lead directly to fair and efficient agreements, there are more analytical and "substantive" approaches that compare the various possible solutions in terms of "distributive" or "substantive" justice (Greenberg 1987; Chapter 2).

Figure 6.4 shows how contracts selected through different substantive and procedural

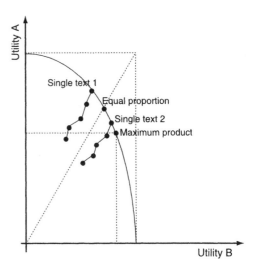

Figure 6.4 Effects of different procedural and substantive approaches to fairness on negotiation outcomes

fairness criteria may end up on different points of a Pareto frontier. For example, given the particular shape of the curve of efficient contracts in the figure, the maximum product of utilities is relatively more favorable to player B. Another fairness criterion, frequently used in theory and approximated in practice, "the equal proportions rule" (each side gets the same percentage of the maximum to which it could aspire) would be more favorable to player A. Given this variety of solutions, actors have room for choice and for strategic behavior, even when supposing they accept fairness criteria in addition to those of efficiency. To a large degree, therefore, the opportunity for the actors to influence the final agreement is tied to their cognitive abilities to propose solutions that are elegant, advantageous for both sides, efficient and fair, especially if the negotiation is conducted with sophisticated and prepared counterparts.

NEGOTIATION STRATEGIES

Strategies for distributive negotiation

Imagine being a collector of a particular artist's paintings and finding one of his latest paintings in an art gallery. You contact the gallery director to whom the artist has delegated the sales of the paintings. What would the most effective strategies for conducting this negotiation be, for both buyer and seller?

In reply to this question many people say that the first thing they would do would be to ask the gallery director what the value of the painting is. However, on second thoughts, they realize that this strategy is reasonable only if the price is not really negotiable – for example, because the pictures were evaluated by expert authorities, or because they belong to a class of art works that has standard evaluations. Let us suppose that neither is the case, and the price is negotiable.

Given that the good exchanged is not modifiable and that interests are opposed on price, the negotiation structure is distributive. Empirical research conducted on negotiating behaviors and their consequences has shown that the most effective negotiation strategies in distributive negotiation structures are proactive and assertive, as described below.

Background information

Information is an important base of negotiating power (Bazerman 1986; Fisher 1982). The more parties know about the context, market, sector, operating conditions, and alternatives, the better they will be able to estimate the minimum and maximum values that could be obtained from the other side. Naturally, these external limits to negotiable values may be more or less stringent. For example, the value of a painting by a living artist could be uncertain, but, given the technical nature, the subject, the size of the picture, the market could indicate reasonable upper and lower limits. Or, it would not be sensible to present oneself at a work-related negotiation without having an idea of what the upper limit to the exchange value of the competences that are being offered is, and making requests that are completely "out of the ballpark." On other matters, problems are less structured, items may not be traded on markets and may have very subjective and partner-specific values. For example, the barter of research-related new information between two firms or people working in the same technical area is likely to be implicitly or explicitly negotiated, but the rates of exchange will be highly specific to the relationship and will not be clearly bounded by external information or alternatives.

Looking for alternative partners before entering a negotiated exchange is, however, always important, even if only to discover that there are none. In many economic negotiations it is the essential move in order not to remain "trapped" in a negotiation process with a less attractive partner than others; in other words, in order not to risk one's specific investments and not to let a bilateral monopoly be formed in the "wrong transaction." For example, interfirm negotiated alliances (such as joint ventures) have been shown to be unstable and to have relatively high failure rates – and the above may be one of the reasons. In fact, sparing the search for alternatives causes two related types of inefficiencies. First, there are opportunity costs due to undertaking an economic relationship which generates less value compared to others. Second, not exploring other alternatives and what they can offer, weakens the capacity to propose solutions and formulate correct estimates about "batnas" and the values of one's contribution.

First movers' advantages

The most likely point of agreement – in a symmetrical distributive negotiation – is the average between the *first two offers declared* (Raiffa 1982). This is not the average between the true reservation prices, but between the offers out in the open. For example, if the gallery director initially speaks of a value around 2.5 million lire and the buyer declares that he intends to spend 1.5 million at the most, it is probable that the negotiators will settle at 2 million. This fact has important practical consequences, such as that, in distributive negotiations, the pay-off for each side is positively correlated with the ambitiousness of the first move (at least within reasonable limits set by context information); and that there are advantages in "moving first" (Hamner and Yukl 1977), since first moves "anchor" the range of negotiable values (Bazerman and Carroll 1987).

Concessions

The "ballet" of concessions is an incremental game of reciprocity (Raiffa 1982; Axelrod 1984). Through a series of steps, one can adjust expectations about future concessions based on observation of the magnitude and rate of variation of obtained ones. Stiffening and reducing the generosity of concessions can be used both in response to a stiffening of the counterpart and as a "signal" that the negotiators' pay-offs are approaching their reservation prices.

Arbitrating third parties

In distributive negotiations third parties may have a mainly arbitrating function (Sheppard 1984). In other words, arbitration-based authority can be employed to solve the pos-

sible impasses of resource division problems. In conditions where there is no clear technically superior solution, however, conflict resolution by authority can be felt as arbitrary and tends to create a sense of dissatisfaction in both parties, after the fact. This and other negative aspects of pure arbitration have led to identifying more refined techniques of arbitration which keep the players' commitment and participation in the negotiation alive. For example, "final offer arbitration" – having the arbitrator choose one of the two final offers each party formulates (Notz *et al.* 1983). Other ways in which third parties can maintain effective and fair distributive negotiations are brokering among the parties, moderating extreme positions, facilitating non-aggressive interpersonal relations, helping to construct reservation prices in a competent and responsible way (Bazerman and Lewicki 1983).

Integrative negotiation strategies

Consider the negotiation described in Box 6. 2. There are many opportunities for reaching integrative agreements in this negotiation. In fact, both sides have highly complementary resources: the ability to supply information of national interest on the one hand, and a local distribution network, on the other. The alternatives to a negotiated agreement are not represented by alternative partners, because the *Quotidiano* is the region's only significant local newspaper, while the national newspaper has the rather peculiar characteristic of not being present in the north-east market. As a result, the alternatives to a negotiated agreement are mainly unilateral actions (expanding direct distribution for the national paper and developing one's own capacity to cover national news for the local paper) or continuing the status quo.

Box 6.2
The local daily

A local daily, *Quotidiano*, was created out of a commercial agreement between a group of entrepreneurs operating in north-eastern regions of Italy and an important national newspaper.

Producing and selling a newspaper is no simple matter, even when you can count on a potential readership of cities with almost 200,000 residents plus the surrounding province. Either it must be able to supply the reader with national news, political and economic information – and this means setting up a specialized and costly editorial staff – or you must target that market which is willing to buy two papers a day, or is willing to give up national news. In any case, even with minimal structural costs it is difficult to reach the break-even point. Considering that in the Triveneto region, on average, one newspaper per every 11 residents is purchased, for a new editorial initiative to succeed it meant reaching a 25 percent market share in a brief period of time.

For this reason it was thought that the only solution could be to offer two papers for the price of one, selling the local daily together with a national newspaper.

Analyzing the industry sector, the *Gazzetta d'Italia* was identified as a possible partner. This newspaper had a significant share of the market (84 percent) in central regions, but – despite name, ambitions, and structure – sold only a couple of thousand copies in the rest of northern Italy, including the Triveneto region. As a result, national advertising had to be offered at regional rates, because the advertisers were not willing to pay full price for so few contacts in some of the principal economic areas of the country.

Cooperation was of interest to both parties. The *Gazzetta d'Italia* could increase its penetration in an area where it had little presence and experiment with a new marketing formula; if it succeeded, repeating the same idea in other areas would be sufficient to resolve the prickly question of advertising rates without having to invest in local pages and peripheral infrastructures! The local *Quotidiano* could become part of a complete product, while the authoritative support of an important national newspaper, for its part, would succeed in maintaining initial investment low and in concentrating its energy on the editorial work, targeting the problems of the local territory.

The two newspapers would be distributed together, in a single, transparent package, with both names visible. The price was increased over the regulated price of Italian daily newspapers at the time (1,500 lire instead of 1,300); in this way, the *Gazzetta d'Italia* was able to recuperate its own variable production and distribution costs, while the *Quotidiano* was able to earn a price close to the full one. To judge from the success of the initiative, it would seem that the readers were willing to pay a modestly higher price to have the two papers.

During the negotiations, besides dividing the profits of sales, it was necessary to place limits on the advertising collected. Both newpapers were, in fact, interested in advertising and resolving this problem appears to be more difficult. Nonetheless, the managers of the two newspapers were aware that the type of advertising is different for the two papers and decide that the *Gazzetta d'Italia* would have the exclusive agency for advertising by the large firms in the region, while the *Quotidiano* could act more freely with respect to the small and medium-sized firms and lesser advertising.

The potential of the integration was taken advantage of in the best way thanks to the long-standing relationship between the director of the *Quotidiano* and the marketing manager of the *Gazzetta d'Italia*, who had been former colleagues at an important press agency. The market analysis and launch plan for the new project were developed also with the collaboration of the marketing staff of the *Gazzetta d'Italia* who also contacted some of their suppliers to get better prices for the equipment, machines, and printers required to produce the new newspaper. The agreement had a three-year contract and contained options for the *Gazzetta d'Italia* to become a shareholder in the *Quotidiano*.

Source: By Francesco Paoletti.

Complementary preferences

A large integration potential in the above situation arises from the fact that the intensity of the preferences that the sides attribute to various resources is different and complementary. This is a fundamental characteristic of integrative negotiations. The basic question that actors may ask themselves is: how useful for oneself and for the counterpart is each resource or issue (Pruitt 1983)? For example, the share each of the two papers earn from sales on each issue could appear to be a distributive item. However, for the national newspaper those earnings are small, and the sole need is to cover costs; while for the *Quotidiano*, those earnings are significant, representing almost its entire income. It is therefore efficient for the *Quotidiano* to retain its earnings and for the *Gazzetta d'Italia* to take only what is necessary to cover its costs (efficient for the two sides as well as for consumers). The issue of advertising and advertising income is of extreme interest for both sides. The case shows how they were able to transform a distributive negotiation aimed at dividing that resource into an integrative negotiation by identifying two sub-resources. The *Gazzetta* is in fact primarily interested in large company advertising, whereas only small and medium-sized advertisers will, realistically speaking, seek out the *Quotidiano*.

Generating alternatives

As illustrated by the experience of the two newspapers, generating creative hypotheses for agreement is a particularly important negotiating strategy in an integrative negotiation. This approach to negotiation is essential both within the relationship – to take advantage of the possibilities for creating value for all sides as much as possible – and outside the relationship – to discover, analyze, construct, and even to invent alternatives of creative action. For, while distributive negotiations typically concern few and measurable items (such as prices and quantities of exchanged goods) the parties' best alternatives to a negotiated agreement being typically represented by alternative counterparts, in integrative negotiations precisely those resource complementarities that create synergies and a surplus, simultaneously make it difficult to find attractive alternative partners. Often the best alternatives are other courses of action and types of agreement – to be developed creatively – rather than different parties.

All techniques for supporting creativity in problem-solving (Chapters 2 and 5) are applicable to sustain creativity in negotiation. However, with particular reference to negotiation, some guidelines for formulating contract hypotheses with a higher probability of being accepted have been identified.

- *Contingent contracts.* In the negotiation of a contract, say, for professional services (for example, a consultancy or advertising services) the parties may find it difficult to agree on a lump sum compensation fee. Suppose that the service provider perceives a high chance of success and therefore expects the value of his/her services also to be high, while the buyer makes more prudent estimates. Contingent contracts resolve the differences in parties' divergent estimates of the value of the transaction and of the probability of uncertain events that could affect it, by distinguishing different possible levels of outcome and compensating each according to which one will be observed. This type of solution belongs indeed to the repertory of contracts for regulating transactions subject to uncertain external contingencies (as in the case of commercial services).
- *"Bridging."* Bridging between the interests of parties is useful when the characteristics of an object or of a joint action can be defined in the process of negotiation, and consists in constructing them in such a way as simultaneously to satisfy the most important preferences of both sides. Consider the case of two firms in the same industry sector that are negotiating a merger and have somewhat overlapping product lines, with each company striving to maintain its own products in production and eliminate those of the other in the new joint company. A bridging solution would gradually redesign the products that the two firms have in common, incorporating the strong features of each in a common new product line.
- *Introduction of new matters.* The more issues are included in a negotiation, the more varied the combinations for exchange are, and the greater the possibilities of inte-

gration become. The variety of matters can be increased by introducing new ones – that is, by enlarging the negotiation to encompass aspects that previously were excluded from the negotiations – or by disaggregating the matters under discussion into sub-issues. Time and money are two topics that deserve special mention. Compared to almost all other resources, they have a general value in exchanges and therefore can be easily introduced into any negotiation.

Time is an important variable because it is improbable that the sides will have exactly the same deadlines and needs as far as the use of time is concerned. Therefore, it often happens that a concession is impossible if negotiated all at once – for example an increase or reduction in staff – but it becomes acceptable if rationed opportunely through time.

Money, besides being one of the matters directly negotiated, can also be used as a collateral *or side compensation* matter. Even if integrative and bridging solutions be found, they may entail residual imbalances in the allocation of resources that call for compensation. For example, renegotiating the design of a product will involve to taking into account production costs simultaneously with the need for modularity/adaptability toward the client. A design that responds to all these demands may not always be technically or economically feasible. In these cases indemnities could be used – that is, side monetary payments made to the disadvantaged party. A typical example of this technique, and indeed of its limits, is giving dangerous work monetary indemnity, where no technical improvements in work conditions can be devised. Resorting to side payments implies a refusal to improve the quality of solutions to substantive matters, and therefore should be used cautiously.

Integrative third parties

Third parties in integrative negotiations should not involve the use of authority, because there is a need to find creative solution on the basis of complex and distributed knowledge; and because interests are not opposed. The role of third parties can range from fact-finding and the construction of a basis of shared judgments; to intermediating communication especially in cases in which there are language or cultural differences, as in international and interfunctional negotiations; to mediating between diverse interests by receiving confidential information from each side and drawing agreement proposals to resubmit to them.

The variety of "integration roles" that help to coordinate both inter-unit and interfirm relations can be better understood by using these insights on how to integrate knowledge and interests coming from negotiation theory (Part III).

MULTI-ACTOR NEGOTIATIONS

This paragraph is intended to supply some basic ideas for interpreting multi-sided negotiation situations. The increase in the number of interdependent actors that are coordinated through negotiations does indeed imply substantial complications and qualitatively different dynamics as compared to two-party negotiations. The principal source of these complications and differences is the possibility of forming coalitions (Raiffa 1982).

Coalition formation

Where coalitions are prohibited, multi-sided negotiations are more complicated than bilateral negotiations, but qualitatively similar to them. For example, a negotiation between an environmental association, a firm, and a workers' union on a pollution problem in a specific geographical region, may not be fundamentally different from the negotiations on multiple issues described in the preceding paragraph. There are common interests, such as the well-being of residents in the area. It is a matter of finding technical configurations and cost allocations that satisfy the minimum acceptability levels of all sides and reflect the intensity of each actor's preferences on each issue or aspect under discussion, as much as possible.

Where coalitions can be created there is, in addition, the possibility of agreeing with one of the actors and not with the others, depending on the relative advantages different coalitions have. These situations are frequent in economic relations: for example, firms located in the same geographical area, depending on the same clients and infrastructures, can compete or coalesce; economies of scale can be realized by setting up common marketing structures for similar products both within and between firms; different workers by uniting their efforts and competences can achieve results that would otherwise be unattainable. There are common interests, a surplus created by cooperation or exchange with similar or complementary actors, but there is a fair division and cost allocation problem as well. Hence there is a negotiation problem.

Some of the essential characteristics of multi-party negotiation clearly emerge in the following stylized coalition-formation problem (Box 6.3), which is in fact frequently proposed as a basic exercise in negotiation behavior (Hall *et al.* 1982; Raiffa 1982). Players make reciprocal offers. But what offers are

Box 6.3
Exercise of coalition formation

The participants are divided in threes, in which each assumes the role of a player, A, B, or C (the role is randomly assigned by the coodinator).

The objective of each player is to associate himself with a coalition that can guarantee a positive result and negotiate his own share of the resources that the coalition can win.

The system is such that the three sides playing can gain a share of the total resource available according to the following scheme:

A, B, and C alone get	0 points
Coalition AB gets	118 points
Coalition BC gets	84 points
Coalition ABC gets	121 points

Each coalition must decide how to divide its share among the partners. Naturally, the value of the shares also depends on how much each party can obtain by aligning himself with the third player instead of with the one with whom he is negotiating.

The objective of each side is to maximize his own share, which will be compared to that obtained by the other players playing the same role (A, B, or C) in the other threesome.

The sides can communicate, given a reciprocal invitation, two by two, or all three together. The game begins with the three people in each threesome in a symmetrical position. Each one sends the other a written message on a folded sheet with the message he deems appropriate (proposal, request for a meeting, etc.). If, as a result of this exchange, the two sides want to discuss "face to face" privately they can do it when they want, for a period of three minutes maximum. In this case, it could happen that:

- the third player is also invited to participate
- he can have a private discussion with only one of the other players
- all three players can break off oral discussions and recommence written ones.

In summary, the discussions can be conducted in written or oral form, either privately (between two) or openly among the three players, private oral discussions cannot be interrupted by the third party for at least three minutes.

The maximum time allowed for the negotiation is 30 minutes, but an agreement can be reached before hand. Prior to beginning the negotiations, the negotiators have about 20–30 minutes to prepare a strategy.

An agreement is considered to be concluded when the contracting sides pass a written and signed declaration to the game coordinator, describing the identity of the parties and the total amount of the resources each realizes.

Source: Constructed on the basis of an experiment described in Raiffa (1982).

reasonable? Which are excessive? Which run the risk of being rejected? Which put the collective resources to their best use? What is a fair division of the pie?

In the process of offer and counter-offer among different dyads or triads the basic different ways of answering these questions are usually discovered by trial and error. They reflect different efficiency and fairness criteria, such as apportioning the shares of resources according to the differences in the contribution and/or in the substitutability of each actor in the various coalitions. The experiment shows that not only different fairness criteria can be applied, but also different efficiency criteria. In fact, it is possible that each actor will strictly maximize the size of its own share, which, if sub-coalitions pay well enough with respect to all-ways alliances, may result in leaving some resources unutilized and some players excluded. In terms of the efficiency of the whole system, no resource should be "left on the table," hence, all value creating partners should associate and find a fair rule for eventually dividing the "sacrifice" with respect to their sub-coalition shares. The results obtained by role-playing the experiment can be compared with the analytic solutions reported in Appendix 6.1.

COGNITIVE AND SOCIAL DYNAMICS AND BIASES

Negotiation is primarily a heuristic decision process. However, the degree of structuration in negotiable problems can vary a lot. Pertinent information may be more or less ambiguous and quantifiable, alternatives more or less easy to find, objectives and interests more or less clear. These varying states of information lead to adopting more or less ambitious decision strategies and to relying more or less on ex ante analysis or on learning during the

process (Chapter 2). In addition, applied to the interactive joint decision setting of negotiation, some of the basic heuristics and biases of judgment under uncertainty (Chapter 1) generate peculiar consequences in negotiations with significant effects on the types of contracts and organizational solutions devised.

Cognition and negotiation

- *Distributive frames* tend to be over-applied, as schemes for interpreting what a negotiation is (Bazerman and Neale 1983). The diffusion of such frames generates inefficiencies because resources are underutilized, and value that could be created is lost owing to unjustified ruptures and to agreements that are inferior to those obtainable. Another widespread, often damaging interpretative scheme in negotiation is a *negative frame* – that is, a way of looking at the consequences of negotiations as "losses" and "concessions" relative to the maximum obtainable and desired, rather than as gains with respect to the alternative of not reaching an agreement or of having to resort to an agreement with a less attractive partner.

  The diversity of frames, understood as diversity between partners' cultures, visions of the world, meanings and values that can be attributed to events and actions, can also complicate negotiations, making it more difficult to communicate, and may add other sources of conflict to the conflicts of interests: misunderstandings, difficulty of interpreting signals, involuntary offence, and ideological conflict (Gulliver 1979). To reduce and manage the distortions of "competitive perception," experts in negotiation advise tactics for breaking out of the competitive spiral such as: knowing the counterpart's culture; putting one-self in the other's shoes; behaving in a way that does not conform to the stereotype that others may have of us; discussing reciprocal impressions and interpretations; looking for and utilizing "objective" (or neutral, supplied by third parties) information as much as possible rather than following one's own subjective intuitions (Fisher and Ury 1981).

- The obligations and actions already taken, and the resources already invested in a negotiating process may create *commitment traps* and have *conflict escalation* effects on the prosecution of the process. In the negotiating process, decision-makers tend to commit the sunk costs decision error with particular frequency and intensity: "I have invested too much to give up now," "Since we've already reached this point, let's go on."

- A negotiator's *possible alternative partners can be particularly inaccessible alternatives.* This is so because in order to know if a firm or person is an interesting partner, in many cases, it is necessary to begin a relationship, and test the alternative, at least in part. But to begin many negotiating relationships on the same object ("keeping one's finger in many pies") is extremely expensive, if not simply an incorrect, unfair process of interaction for many economic relationships (and the reason could be precisely the loss of relational investments and the sunk costs that this procedure would entail for many sides). Therefore, while evaluating one's "batna" in relatively simple, structured negotiations – where one offer is enough to understand the alternatives available – may be fairly easy, in complex negotiations, the effects of the availability, chance, and occasions are enormous. Potential partners to be taken into consideration are often

sought among the contacts one already has, among actors directly known, among those that one has had the opportunity of meeting (Granovetter 1985). Negotiated relationships are begun on the basis of limited knowledge, and deliberate effort should be dedicated to reducing opportunity costs, even though it may entail higher negotiation process costs (Ring 1999).

Motives and negotiation

Other studies have tried to model the effect of the *contents of motives* on negotiation behavior (Walton and McKersey 1965; Fisher and Ury 1981). Some prescriptions that have been developed are rather general, such as seeking to save the fundamental needs or primary interests of people, whatever the specific issue of the negotiation. Such needs include parties' security, identity, and esteem within one's own group. Highly conflictual negotiation can give rise to objectives and needs to assert oneself, to win, and to dominate the others as motives – which are usually detrimental to economic efficiency and equity of agreements.

The extent to which an actor's motives and objectives are stated in clear, explicit, quantified terms is also an important variable, with twofold effects. On the one hand, the *clarity and precision of objectives* tend to make conflict between interests stronger, agreement more difficult to find. On the other hand, actors are forced to search harder for better solutions.

Conflict about problems and between people

The conflict between interests can transform itself, all too frequently, into a conflict between people. This is the most widespread and obvious pathology into which a negotiating process can fall. Fisher and Ury (1981) have formulated this prescription by suggesting adopting, as a professional negotiating behavior, an attitude "soft toward people" and "hard on problems"; and they have outlined a variety of stratagems for sustaining this attitude: allowing others to let off steam without reacting; making symbolic gestures (such as offering excuses or symbolic goods); treating the positions expressed with force by the counterpart as hypotheses to which there are a number of alternatives; asking questions and asking the counterparts to justify their affirmations rather than reacting with counter-assertions; using pauses and delays; opening negotiative sub-processes on the rules of the game, the communication procedures and the acceptable interaction processes – on the fairness of procedures rather than on the fairness of substantive agreements (Chapter 2) .

Long-lasting relationships

The longevity of relationships, the expectation of repeated encounters or of a relationship that continues in time, is a facilitator of integrative negotiating relationships (Axelrod 1984; Barney and Ouchi 1984). For, whenever the actors keep track of a series of interactions, they will be interested not only in the short-term result, but also in not putting future results at risk. Therefore, the longevity of a relationship results in a positive value assigned to maintaining a good relationship. Moreover, it increases the interchange of information, the possibility of verifying another's affirmations, the creation of common languages, thereby discouraging opportunism and limiting the possibilities of using information strategically ("bluff").

NEGOTIATION CONTROL

In concluding this examination of the characteristics of negotiation as a coordination mechanism, we must ask what properties of control it may possess. Is there a "control through negotiation" as there can be control by a central agent, by a group, and by exit ? What are its mechanisms?

Negotiated action certainly needs controls: agreement on the actions to be undertaken does not imply a homogenization of preferences. Only in very particular situations will actors modify their own objectives and how they perceive their own interests to the point of defining common preferences, as the result of the learning processes during the negotiation. *For the most part, interests remain in conflict and this may create a potential for opportunism in the contract application phase.*

Some types of agreements can be controlled by *reciprocal observation and surveillance*. Each side has an incentive to ensure that the counterpart's performance conforms to its interests as stipulated in the agreement. In a long-lasting relationship, each side has, moreover, the capacity directly to sanction eventual inadequacies, by conditioning its own performance to correct behavior on the other side. In other words, in the process of putting a negotiated contract into effect, the sides hold each other hostage (Williamson 1983).

Hostages, guarantees, and pledges

The use of hostages, guarantees, and pledges is a fundamental mechanism in control by negotiation. It can also go beyond a game of reciprocity in contributions and consist in purposefully making allocations and reserves of resources that represent a potential indemnity for the sides that might be offended or damaged by others' failures. Examples are fund deposits guaranteeing some commercial transactions; or the systems of penalties established for specified cases of non-compliance.

Hostages, pledges, and guarantees may also be symbolic and immaterial. For example, public declarations and publicly made commitments (through mass media or on public occasions by representatives) "tie one's hands," by putting at stake the reputation and the image of the actor.

Reciprocal checking is, however, only effective under the condition that the actions and contributions of the partners can be reciprocally observed and evaluated by the actors, even if at the cost of specific investments in control structures (for example, inspectors). Reciprocal observability can, however, be jeopardized both by the high number of parties involved and by the information complexity of activities. For example, if two financial services firms commit themselves, in their relationships with clients, to commercialize an array of services including some but not all of the services of each, it would be rather difficult to check whether or not sales agents are pushing the various services as agreed. Or, it could be that the process of transformation to be realized following the negotiated agreement consists of too many elements and requires very specific and complex competences, making it rather difficult to check up on the counterpart and ensure it is upholding the spirit of the agreement (that s/he has used all and only those types of materials agreed upon, that s/he has fully followed a certain transformation formula and not another, that s/he has fulfilled the due commitment and diligence in brain-intensive activities, etc.). *In these complex situations the negotiation may resolve the decision problem (which actions to undertake) but not the problem of controlling actions.*

Third party authority

To that end, other mechanisms would be more effective and efficient – mechanisms that quite frequently help the negotiating mechanism during the realization phase. In the first place, a third party authority, who can perform control activities more efficiently on many actors or act as a competent "guarantor" in those cases where the sides cannot have direct access to the information and relevant competences in order to judge the performance of the others, for technical reasons and privacy and confidentiality problems.

Property rights

Alternatively, or in addition to the investment in bilateral control or in third party control, it is possible to invest in incentive systems. For example, in very complex activities, neutral authority does not have better access to the information relevant for checking that the parties themselves have. In these cases, implementation can be protected and guaranteed by having the parties become partners in the implementation activities. For example, the formation of joint ventures between firms to realize complex activities – such as research and development, or production based on sophisticated complementary activities – with pre-established rights on residual rewards, performs a hostage function and discourages opportunism, realigning the objectives of the sides in the implementation of the coordinated action (Hennart 1988; De Laat 1999).

SUMMARY

This chapter considered three basic questions regarding negotiations: when to negotiate, how to negotiate, and what to negotiate.

In answering the first question, the distinctive conditions under which this kind of coordination mechanism is applied have been identified. Among them, a "mixed-motive" game structure, with *elements of competition as well as of cooperation*, and the presence of elements of bilateral or multilateral monopoly creating *rents or surpluses to be divided* were highlighted.

The second and third paragraphs tackled the question of how to negotiate, distinguishing two primary types of negotiation structure and of effective strategies contingent on them: *distributive negotiations* (in which the surplus to be divided is fixed); and *integrative (and generative) negotiations* (in which the "pie" can be enlarged). More competitive strategies – information closure, ambitious initial proposals, first mover advantages, third parties' arbitration – are generally more effective in the first contingency. More cooperative strategies – open information sharing, single text negotiation, use of integrators rather than arbitrators – are more effective in the second instance. A further paragraph was devoted to expand the analysis to multi-actor negotiations, tied to the possibility of forming coalitions.

A paragraph on negotiation strategies answered the question on how to negotiate from the point of view of governing and improving the cognitive, motivational, and relational processes typical of negotiating. These processes can have a paramount effect on the economic efficiency of the reached agreement, for example: local search and commitment traps can reduce information costs but can generate very high opportunity costs; negative frames and interpersonal conflict can prevent advantageous contracts being concluded; dominance motives can substitute value-increasing motives; the lack of goal explicitation and operationalization can reduce negotiation costs but lead to accepting inferior solutions.

Hostages, pledges, and guarantees have been highlighted as negotiation-based control mechanisms, widely used for controlling performance for instance in complex commercial contracts or supply relations. Their effectivess is bound to reciprocal, albeit indirect, performance observability. Other mechanisms which can support the implementation of negotiated agreements are guarantors (rather that just guarantees) or property right sharing over the realization of agreements (as in interfirm joint ventures).

Exercise: Canavelas

The formation of consortia for developing large hydroelectric works occurs fairly often among the firms in the sector.
   In the case in point, there are three firms called respectively:

- Firm A: general contractor in the electromechanical sector;
- Firm B: civil engineering constructor;
- Firm C: general contractor, but tending to be a "business developer" rather than an industrial firm.

As is the usual practice in the sector, the process leading up to the consortium agreement starts with circulation of information and hearsay regarding an imminent competition for tender. This involves the construction of a medium-sized power station (costing about $400 million) in the United States.

Indeed, although firm A is active in 150 countries, it has never worked in the American market.

By the time firm A learns of the commission the deadline is very close and the initiative looks very dodgy.

For the commissioner is a regional authority concerned with drinking water, and its requests for tender involve some oddities. First, although this firm figures as a public company in the USA, it is actually constituted, legally speaking, as a private firm and can therefore fail.

In addition, the contract lays down very extensive conditions of responsibility, including indemnity for "indirect damages" or loss of other activities on the part of the commissioner that may result from any future faulty working of the plant.

The search for a partner

The competences demanded and the degree of risk connected with the performance of the commission in question left no doubts as to the need to take part in the competition jointly with other firms. In particular, since firm A has electromechanical competences, it was necessary to make an alliance at least with a local firm experienced in civil engineering and installation. Moreover, since firm A has no operating bases in the US and no easy way of entering the market – since it has never worked in the US – a second criterion adopted in the search for a partner was that the latter should be present, directly or indirectly, in the US.

Concerning the nationality of the partner, or partners, the orientation was toward European firms. For the Americans were already in the running with their consortia, and it was known that a couple of Japanese firms had already come in with them.

In view of all this, the not very extensive range of European firms in the sector was studied, firms that already had links with firm A and personal contacts at a high level.

The choice fell on a German civil construction enterprise (which had a majority shareholding in a US construction/installation firm); by now, it was realized, there were really no alternatives, for the large European firms of the sector were, just then, already either themselves engaged in the competition or had decided not to take part owing to the aforementioned risks.

The partner is a coalition

The contact with the German firm (hereafter called firm B) was actually a matter of meeting half way, since the latter was itself already starting to look for a partner with electromechanical competences. Firm B had, indeed, already stipulated an exclusive agreement with another German enterprise (firm C): this was an engineering company with plenty of experience in trading and a commercial orientation, a good international reputation, and varied experience as general contractor.

For firm A, as it prepared to become the third member of the coalition, this state of affairs clearly involved serious problems in how to proceed, which can be summarized as follows:

- a conflict of interest between A and C, firms with competences that largely overlap: a certain number of plant sub-systems could actually have been designed and supplied by one or the other firm; in addition, firm A, too, had experience as a main contractor;
- a conflict between two sometimes "mistrusting" cultures, Italian and German (A being Italian, B and C both being German);

- a sharing of the contracted risks that would be somehow limited and would anyway turn out to be in proportion to the amount eventually supplied.

Consortium or subcontracting?

When contacts have been started for reaching an agreement for the joint acquisition of the order, the problem arises as to what specific form the agreement should take. For the activity in question the formation of a joint venture is not usually contemplated, but there is a real debate on whether to opt for a consortium or subcontracting. The construction firm is all for assuming the role of main contractor, and often tries to achieve this, especially because the value of civil works is often very high and because it tends to view the contributions of the other firms as merely tiny pieces in a mountain of concrete. The same was true for firm B, too.

On the contrary, a firm taking part in an agreement with a weaker position in terms of volume of resources controlled – in this case, firm A – is concerned with reaching the most equal possible agreement. In the end, it was agreed to set up a consortium.

Internal negotiation

The formation of a consortium of this kind for participating in a competition for tender is generally regulated by a dual agreement: an external agreement known to the commissioner and an internal agreement among the partners. Focus thereafter is on the second type of agreement and on the internal negotiation between the firms potentially involved.

1   Leadership naturally represents a point of primary importance in an alliance in which the commissioner needs a single interlocutor. Which of the firms of the coalition will be the leader? Commercial leadership, however, is not the sole type of coordinating function required; for, since the cooperation among the firms involved is of a largely technical nature, it will be necessary also to define a technical leadership. In our case, the solution was to ascribe responsibility for commercial coordination to firm C and technical responsibility to firm B. The reasons were mainly that, in the first case, C was known to the commissioner and in the USA, and in the second case, the fact that the commission largely entails works of civil type.

2   Firm A agreed to be responsible for coordinating the other two partners. However, it insisted that its contribution be acknowledged to be indispensable at the level of decision-making rules, demanding that all the consortium's decisions be taken unanimously. A very long discussion ensued and the principle was felt to be very hard to follow. In the end, it was decided to establish the unanimity rule, but with the addition of a somewhat unusual and original clause in order to resolve possible deadlocks before having recourse to lengthy, expensive arbitration procedures. In case of failure to agree, the clause involved submitting the decision to a committee extended to include the presidents and managing directors of the firms in the consortium, but with the committee still subject to the unanimity rule in decision-making.

3   A central aspect in defining a consortium is the allocation of the tasks to the individual firms, i.e. determining what share of the total business to assign to each partner. In our case, the main problem was between A and C who, by direct production or subcontracting, could be responsible for supplying products/systems of similar nature. Firm A laid down as an essential condition that it be entrusted with all the supplies that its factories were able to produce. In other words, C would not be able to subcontract to outside firms any items that could be produced by A. This condition of being responsible for the largest share of production in its own factories was posed in the context of A's having anyway only a minority share in the consortium in question. Determining along general lines which task to allot to which firm also depends on other criteria, mostly of a technical nature:

- First, the tasks are assigned to the various partners according to the specific skills involved.
- Second, the share of specific tasks, plus the eventual share of tasks in which the partners can substitute each other, must reach a minimum level such as to justify the cost of participation in establishing and maintaining the consortium structure.
- Third, owing to the "separate" nature of the task responsibilities, as envisaged in the consortium agreements, it is important to allot work areas that are clearly demarcated and defined, above all in terms that enable the identification of errors and the resulting responsibilities for delays or failure to comply with technical guarantees and standards. In addition, wherever possible, the tasks should be split up "horizontally" rather than "vertically," in such a way that economies of scale can be exploited by all: the production of a number of similar machines will be divided among the partners by types of components or machine parts, rather than each firm producing a certain number of whole machines.

In consideration of all the above-mentioned criteria, the volume of business was shared between A, B, and C as follows: A 25 percent; B 60 percent; C 15 percent.

4   The *penalties* are a well-known sword of Damocles in the performance of large-scale industrial commissions. It is easy to delay and the client is not interested in arguments as to "whose fault it is." Within the consortium, there are two schemes by which potential conflicts as to who shall pay the penalty are regulated. Let us suppose that the maximum penalty for delays is 10 percent of the value of the plant.

Scheme A

The firm causing the delay pays the entire penalty.

Scheme B

The firm responsible pays the penalty applied on the amount of its supplies (10 percent of its share) and the remainder is covered by all the partners (including the firm responsible for the delay) in proportion to their share in the consortium. This second scheme, or principle of "mutual aid," was adopted in our case.

5   Regarding *compensation* for damage among the partners, it was decided that only direct, documented costs should be compensated, according to the principle of not additionally burdening the partners with the indirect costs and lost profits deriving from eventual delays or problems inherent in the commission.

6   If the head office of the consortium is, in practice, the headquarters of its formal leader, the place of arbitration and the law applicable are a matter for discussion (each firm would prefer its own place of operation). In the end, Switzerland was chosen as a "neutral place."

7   Last but not least, it is necessary to negotiate the *selling price* of the plant and the concessions that, in negotiation with the client, one is willing to grant. The problems arise mainly at two levels. First, a target price is established on the basis of a series of market considerations such as: the information on the budget available to the client, the minimum and maximum market value, the precedents, etc. As against that, by summing the market prices of the individual firms for their own products, a total selling price is reached that is almost always, not to say always, higher than the target price. How much, when, and by whom, must the prices of one's own components be reduced in order to reapproach the target price? In effect, a firm belonging to a consortium of this kind may refuse to bow to the other partners regarding its prices and walk out.

The consortium decided as follows: a price of $440 million was settled, which practically coincides with the sum of the prices of the member firms; decision on the amount of the necessary overall discount was adjourned till the stage of negotiation with the client, and it was agreed that the partners would all reduce their prices by the same amount.

To complete the picture, it is useful to add that three consortia took part in the competition: ours, a consortium made up of an American and a Japanese firm (for the civil engineering works) and a consortium involving an American and a European firm (supplying the machines).

By R. Bertolini and A. Grandori

Questions

- On the basis of what element can a preliminary decision be taken to participate in the competition or not?
- Which strategies of coalition were possible for A, supposing that the agreement between B and C was not binding?
- Which aspects of the negotiation are of distributive type and which of integrative type?
- Which negotiating tactics and behaviors enabled a "minority" partner to obtain a form of agreement that was largely equal in the organizational rights and, partly, in the volume of business?
- How was it possible to deal with the negotiation on the selling price otherwise than by "summing" the prices set by the parties?

Appendix 6.1

Analytic solutions to the coalition formation game

In analytical terms, the values of the shares that satisfy simultaneously the conditions: $X_a + X_b = 118$; $X_b + X_c = 50$ and $X_a + X_c = 84$ are $X_a = 76$; $X_b = 42$ and $X_c = 8$ (Raiffa 1982). These shares are empirically approximated by the players by trial and error, if they form two-way coalitions. In fact, these shares can be appropriated only by dividing the two-way pies; for the association of three actors can only realize 121 (and not 126). If the three-way coalition were to command a pay-off equal or greater than the sum of the maximum shares obtainable in the sub-coalitions, there would be no incentive to form them. A fair solution that is also efficient for the system could be that of proportionally reducing earnings so that each actor maintains the same proportion in the 121 pie as those they could gain in the two-way coalitions. Another possibility would be to divide the losses in equal parts ($-\frac{5}{3}$ points each).

Other more egalitarian rules, rather than being proportional to contributions, can reflect more the criticality of all partners for not leaving resources on the table and are often used in practice. For example, in the exercise, part of the agreements reached in the class-room end up close to a value of 20 rather than 8 for the "weakest" C player. Analytically, that value would result from a fairness rule such as: each actor receives the average value of the marginal contributions it brings to all possible all-way coalitions formed by each player joining in as first, second, third, (or nth) member, giving a value of 23.33 for the C player in the case (Raiffa 1982).

Chapter 7

Norms and Rules

A system of collective action which necessitated making decisions on each action, every time it was undertaken, would be a near-paralyzed system. Here we consider those coordination mechanisms which substitute for ad hoc decision-making, foresight and calculation: norms and rules guiding behaviors through a logic of appropriateness (Chapter 2).

- "Equal pay for equal jobs." "It's not right to go over your boss's head." These behaviors are prescribed or prohibited by norms: socially accepted behavior models, valid for all members of a system (and in some cases *formalized in laws and rules*).
- "In March the budget cycle begins." "In our industry, we add a 10 percent mark-up." "When the price of A's shares rises, that's the time to buy B's shares." "Before assigning a contract, at least three suppliers' offers must be taken into consideration." Also these types of rules and norms allow case-by-case decision-making to be avoided, even though they are, by nature, less general and more operative than the previous ones. They are action programs which explicitly prescribe which action is to be undertaken in a given decision area and under what conditions.

Therefore, there are differences between types of rules, among which the *degree of formalization* and the *degree of generality* (versus action specificity) make important organizational differences. However, rules and norms share the even more important common feature and distinctive property of guiding behavior in a non-calculative fashion. This chapter considers first the advantages of this general property of rules; then, treats separately the particular features of coordinating by social norms and cultures, and by formal rules and procedures.

The basic argument of the chapter, specifying the common and different attributes in the profile of those mechanisms, the type of relations that can be effectively governed by them, and some salient sub-types of norms and rules systems is summarized in Figure 7.1.

THE ADVANTAGES OF NORMS AND RULES

The rules of the road, the rules of politics, corporate plans, reward systems, even common language, all are systems of rules that can be justified as "convenient" for all participants in a system of collective action. Various advantages of rules and norms have been examined, will be briefly summarized below and used afterward in the chapter to assess various types of regulatory systems. Some of

	NORMS	RULES
CONDITIONS	• Common knowledge • Repeated action • Epistemic complexity • Confidentiality	• Computational complexity • Transparency and defensibility
MECHANISM PROFILE:	• Identity judgments • Situation recognition • Rules of appropriate action • Autonomous non-calculative decision	
TYPES:	*Internal/External* • Principles • Codes of conduct • Routines	• Constitutions • Procedures • Programs

Figure 7.1 Norms and rules

these advantages can be expressed (and used) as reasons for (calculatingly) adopting a rule; some as deriving from heuristic learning; and some as properties selected by the positive functions that rules perform. All these processes of rule formation are compatible with the assertion that to "adopt a rule" means to suspend calculative judgment on a case-by-case basis.

• Joint decision-making may be extremely costly. One of the more frequently cited examples to illustrate why some decisions should not be taken case by case is traffic. Regulating it by any form of concerted decision-making, coordinating traffic flows by mutual adjustment among all concerned, deciding who has right of way at an intersection, who has the right to pass first, who must stay to the right or the left, would be extremely inefficient. Nor would unilateral decision-making be an efficient or effective way for ensuring traffic coordination – for example, being the first to enter an intersection or binding oneself to a lane and thereby forcing others to deviate (Schelling 1960). Adopting a rule is clearly a superior mode of coordination for economic action problems similar to

the traffic problem (Brennan and Buchanan 1985).

• All participants may be better off if a rule is adopted: any rule, rather than no rule at all. For example, adopting a particular language or communication standard – natural or artificial – is a matter of "*convention.*" In the case of conventions, economists would say that there are many possible equilibria, and that the establishment of any particular solution may be a matter of path-dependency and first mover advantages (the more actors adopt a standard, the more it becomes convenient for others to adopt the same standard among the many possible ones); symmetry and cognitive availability (as in the case of equal division conventions); or unambiguity and clarity of interpretation (Sugden 1985). Consistently, although in a different language, analyzing conventions at the macro-level of the prevailing institutions of societies – as laws, monetary, and other exchange conventions and languages – sociological research has increasingly shown the variety of possibly "functionally equivalent" sets of norms that can regulate effectively similar activities (Whitley 1992; Delmestri 1998).

- The choice of rules is usually a less conflictual game than the choice of actions within defined rules, because each actor does not know what his/her position will be as a result of the application of the rule. For example, will s/he be coming from the right or the left? Will s/he be part of the majority or the minority? Will s/he be a high or low performer? Traffic rules, voting rules, or resource allocation rules, can be more easily accepted to the extent that they are accepted behind a "*veil of ignorance*" (Rawls 1971), in a state of uncertainty (Brennan and Buchanan 1985), concerning one's own position in the system. In addition, they can be more easily accepted because, by definition, a rule applies to many moves or interactions, and it can be accepted as "*serially fair*" over time (Barney and Ouchi 1984): that is, capable of distributing costs and benefits equitably among several actors, if not in each single interaction, on average over a long series of interactions.

- A large part of the norms that regulate behavior are not the result of calculated acceptance, because this type of foresight and judgment would be too demanding (Chapter 2). They are not blind though. Rather, they are the result of a learning process, a process of trial and error that leads to defining rules, and rule content, in certain areas of behavior. Many *routines, habits, and programs are the sedimented result of a series of past decisions and past experimentation* (March 1978; Nelson and Winter 1982; Schein 1985). Experiential learning is the source of their wisdom. For example, in an activity such as hiring personnel, history shows there has been a transition from subjective evaluations that

differ from case to case to systematic evaluation and selection practices that have been learned to be superior and that codify methods of search for candidates, interviewing and structured evaluations of candidate profiles. These routines do not represent optimal solutions; but they are not arbitrary solutions or "conventions" as well. They are good solutions among possible ones, and their configuration depends on the particular path followed in the learning process, on the particular history of errors committed and solutions found.

Hence, rules, and especially learned rules, *save enormous amounts of cognitive effort, both in terms of search and calculation costs and in terms of negotiation and conflict resolution costs*. (March and Simon 1958; Nelson and Winter 1982; Simon 1990). Actors capitalize on decisions made in the past, building a base of learned, programed actions, behavior that is conducted in a relatively automatic way, freeing attention and cognitive resources for new areas of action. These learned actions, programs, and norms can be reviewed periodically, at intervals, when there are signs that they are obsolete, that they no longer work well, when they no longer meet the expectations of the parties involved.

- If actors were free to consider any type of action or technically feasible behavior in a given situation, the problem of coordination would be much more difficult to resolve than it actually is. For the alternative behaviors actually taken into consideration in a given situation are much less varied than they might be on principle. This happens because actors "inherit" a repertory of action and behavior models, a stock of knowledge, that they have neither the tools nor the convenience to put in question (Chapter 2). As has been emphasized by the study of organizational cultures, actors may be largely unaware of how they acquired these models of behavior. Even in this case, rules and conventions do have the *property* of decreasing the likelihood to incur the paradoxes of choice due to a "free-actor," "free-preference" situation (Miller 1992).

• Compared to other coordination systems, rules and norms are often considered to be a higher order or embedding mechanisms or institutions – for example, national laws regulating corporate action, or the rules of a multinational concerning the behavior of subsidiaries. As rules of the game and paradigms of what could be considered good or bad behavior, they act as dispensers of legitimacy and agents which select ways of organizing, enabling only systems that are "isomorphic" to them to survive (Powell and DiMaggio 1991). For example, the affirmation and acceptance of laws and conventions concerning accountability and quality certification act as selection factors which favor those firms incorporating those principles (Hannan and Freeman 1989). However, there can be competition between different types of rules. In this case, rules themselves may be subject to a process of natural selection, of "regulatory competition" (Bratton *et al.* 1996). For example, firms force regulatory systems to compete with one another and influence their relative strength and survival by choosing where (e.g. in what country) to make their investments, or by choosing which commercial law regime they want to be regulated by, among those in use in various countries. In the same way, companies can choose to place their units in local environments where the prevailing set

of norms and cultural conventions is supportive and well suited to the way the company characteristically acts and organizes. For example, Hewlett Packard has sited a production unit in the region surrounding Bergamo, justifying their decision in terms of fitness between local culture and the cognitive and interaction patterns required in the activity; or Tetra Pack moved many research and development activities for the whole group close to Modena, where a "packaging" valley rich with relevant competences and norms sustaining outsourcing relations has been flourishing. Also for this reason, systems of norms and rules are not treated here as a "given context, " but as a mode of coordination which can be co-designed with other mechanisms.

NORMS AND CULTURES

Norms are prescribed models of behavior, valid for all actors within a system of action, accepted as legitimate by the participants, and relevant for the purposes of social and economic action. Norms have been considered as the key constitutive elements of "organizational cultures." In fact, the distinctive feature of cultural coordination and control can be traced in its peculiar cognitive nature: it plays the role of a "programming the mind, " of a software of the human brain (Hofstede 1980, 1993).

Considering norms relevant for economic behavior, an organization culture can be characterized by responding, for example, to questions such as: How do actors define their identity? To what extent is it considered legitimate to pursue one's own economic interest if this is detrimental to others? Is it considered neglible if a deadline is postponed and when? Is it considered legitmate that a man leave work to assist his ailing son, or attend a religious function? Is it considered legitimate that the ratio of the minimum to the maximum salary derived from work be, say, 1 to 100?

Other authors have distinguished the different components within this general culture construct (Trice and Beyer 1984). These components are usually grouped into different levels, according to the different cognitive elements and functions that they incorporate: from basic, founding principles and values to more superficial, operative, and applied norms (Duncan and Weiss 1978; Schein 1985). Therefore, the analysis of the structure of organization culture has led it to be considered as a form of collective knowledge, hierarchically organized like any knowledge (Chapter 2), and has focused on its peculiar traits as a social and collective mechanism for generating aligned action and controlling behaviors.

The stratified structure of cultures

Values

Any norm incorporates, or descends from, some framing value. Even in the dry example of traffic conventions, saying that it is convenient for everyone to adopt them, implies a judgment of the desirability to reduce time and errors. In the obvious rules of day-to-day behavior, such as "when it is cloudy, take an umbrella with you, " it is implied that getting wet has been given a negative connotation (not in all cultures would this norm be deemed as sensible). Organizational norms such as "don"t go over your boss's head" or "always consult with your peers" include values, or desirability judgments, as well as precepts for particular behaviors that realize said values.

The set of distinctive shared assumptions, cognitive frames, basic principles, and core values of a community is then identified as a first founding stratum of cultures. The type of knowledge that is incorporated in these norms may be shared by entire societies, or by lower-level systems like industries, regions, or firms: for example, a company's "mission" (Westley and Mintzberg 1989), or the "unwritten constitution" of an industrial district (Sabel 1993), or the basic values of a functional group (Ouchi 1980).

Given their generality, values leave actors with high degrees of freedom and discretion on how to realize them. Hence, being able to *control highly complex and variable activities is one of the distinctive properties of this level of cultural coordination.* For example, in complex service activities, such as consulting, a common culture in terms of common values and shared general purposes is often called for. In fact, in those activities, it is neither possible nor effective to ensure predictability of behaviors through predefined models, either formal or informal. The actors involved should be able to solve problems using their discretion case by case, client by client, order by order. At the same time, they should be motivated to select behaviors that are correlated to system efficiency and effectiveness. If neither behaviors nor their results are observable and measurable, mechanisms oriented to aligning preferences rather than to controlling behavior and results are particularly valuable. Organization culture is one of these mechanisms, if it is conceived as a set of values and mental schemes and not as a set of operational behavioral precepts and recipes. Box 7. 1 describes a situation of this kind.

Routines

At the other end of the spectrum of norm

Box 7.1
A visionary culture

The Los Angeles Organizing Committee of the Olympic Games was a somewhat original organization with a peculiar task. Its goal was to set up and manage the 23rd Olympic Games from July 28 to August 12, 1984. Shortly after that date, the body ceased to exist.

Their efforts commenced on March 26, 1979, 1,051 days before the opening of the games. Starting at the time with a handful of workers, the organization later grew enormously and rapidly from 200 employees to 2,500 at the beginning of 1984. At the time of the games, the Los Angeles Organizing Committee could count on 20,000 employees and 50,000 volunteers.

One of the biggest challenges was to hire and train this enormous workforce in a very short time. Interest and prestige in working for such a high visibility event played a positive role in the effort and made the task easier. In a situation where time was a factor, the staff learned from informal experiences coming especially from the stories and behavior of other colleagues. Shared myths and rituals emerged fast for an organization that was so young, even though it was operating on a long tradition of modern and ancient Olympic Games.

All in all, the staff of the Organizing Committee was extremely young and brilliant. The 42-year-old manager could have been a senior. Though the staff were all so young and this was probably due to the willingness and the flexibility of younger personnel, the organization took on an unusual characteristic. There was a lot of social activity among the staff and personal relationships were often the topic of discussion. In addition to that, an interest in sports shown by the majority of the staff was also quite noticeable.

Integration and collaboration among the large number of departments and groups within the organization were encouraged and made possible by the importance of the event and the strong feeling of belonging of the staff.

Source: Adapted from McDonald (1991) by Luca Solari.

---

generality, we can locate programs, procedures, routines, habits, and business recipes. They have been widely described empirically and thoroughly analyzed in their heuristic cognitive nature. "Routines" – regardless of whether or not they have been formalized – are operational norms prescribing what action to take in a specific area in response to what stimulus (Cohen *et al.* 1996). The sequence of actions a clerk automatically undertakes in processing a cheque in compliance with his bank's practices, or the oper-

ations an artisan performs in producing a handmade product following regional traditions, are examples.

Routines and programs align behaviors rather than underlying interests and values. Consequently, their effectiveness as a coordination mechanism is conditioned to stable activities, though not necessarily to particularly simple activities. For example, Mintzberg (1979) has highlighted that the routinization of know-how is a diffused mode of coordination in activities and relationships that are relatively ambiguous, not easily guided by calculations, not readily controlled by authority, markets or other means, such as teaching and health care (see Box 7.2).

Various components of cultures are geared to homogenizing, diffusing, and preserving behavior models, for example: languages, rituals, myths, and ceremonies (Meyer and Rowan 1977; Trice and Beyer 1984). They are the appearance, the form, the externalization, and communication of the routines accepted by a system to both an internal and external public. Examples are the ritual of electing the President, the ritual of hiring staff, promotion and reward ceremonies, the specfic language used in communications not only in different countries but in different industry sectors, in different firms, even in different functions and groups within the same firm.

The more this layer of operational precepts on how-to-behave is developed in a normative system, the less discretion is left to actors and the more rigid the type of coordination achieved. This effect is independent from the degree of formalization of social norms into formal rules.[1]

Codes of conduct

An intermediate level of rules is represented by empirical laws and rules of thumb that are believed to generate correct actions in specific fields. In other words, there are *"heuristic norms"* incorporating *procedural rather than substantive knowledge* (Simon 1976) and leaving more to the discretion of actors than routines (Winter 1993). Examples may be the unwritten, procedural laws on how to divide staff among university departments; the procedural rules on how to do good experimental research in a firm's laboratory; the codes of professional conduct that hopefully constrain the behavior of lawyers or physicians, while at the same time allowing them the necessary discretion. Perhaps the term *codes of conduct*,[2] is the most appropriate for identifying this type of procedural norm with respect to the other levels. The three layers of organizational culture are represented in Figure 7.2

In order to appreciate how these notions and distinctions can be used in organization analysis and the prediction of economic behavior, consider the example of a procedural norm identified as one of the core rules, informal but precise, sustaining cultural coordination in the now famous case of Emilia-Romagna's industrial districts (Box 7.3).

The analysis of organization culture as a hierarchy of norms enables one to go beyond simple-minded ad hoc explanations of these successful stories as consequences of a particular cooperativeness or other unique content of the local culture; and to enhance the capacity of norm engineering. The efficiency and effectiveness of the system of cultural coordination described rely, at least in part, on an appropriate deployment of rules of a different order of generality; on the richness of an intermediate layer of procedural rules that produces a high degree of predictability of behavior without constraining them too much; and on the lack of contradiction between the content of norms at different

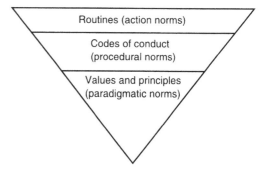

Figure 7.2 Layers of organization culture

Box 7.2
Know-how routinization
in hospitals

Most of the necessary coordination between the operating professionals is then handled by the standardization of skills and knowledge, in effect, by what they have learned to expect from their colleagues. "the system works because everyone knows everyone else and knows roughly what is going on." During an operation as long and as complex as open-heart surgery, "very little needs to be said (between the anesthesiologist and the surgeon) preceding chest opening and during the procedure on the heart itself: lines, beats and lights on equipment are indicative of what everyone is expected to do and does – operations are performed in absolute silence, particularly following the chest-opening phase." The point is perhaps best made in reverse, by the cartoon that shows six surgeons standing around a patient on the operating table with one saying, "Who opens?" Similarly, the policy and marketing courses of the management school may be integrated without the two professors involved ever having even met. As long as the courses are standard, each knows more or less what the other teaches.

Just how standardized complex professional work can be was illustrated in a paper read before a meeting of the International Cardiovascular Society. The author noted that "Becoming a skillful clinical surgeon requires a long period of training, probably five or more year." An important feature of that training is "repetitive practice" to evoke "an automatic reflex." So automatic, in fact, that Spencer keeps a series of surgical "cookbooks" in which he lists, even for "complex" operations, the essential steps as chains of thirty to forty symbols on a single sheet, to "be reviewed mentally in sixty to 120 seconds at some time during the day preceding the operation."

But no matter how standardized the knowledge and skills, their complexity ensures that considerable discretion remains in their application. No two professionals – no two surgeons, or teachers, or social workers – ever apply them in exactly the same way. Many judgments are required, as Perrow notes of police officers and others:

> There exist numerous plans: when to suspend assistance, when to remove a gun from its holster, when to block off an area, when to call the FBI, and when to remove a child from the home. The existence of such plans does not provide a criterion for choosing the most effective plan ... Instead of computation the decision depends upon human judgment. The police patrolman must decide whether to try to disperse the street corner gang or call for reinforcements. The welfare worker must likewise decide if new furniture is an allowable expense, and the high school counselor must decide whether to recommend a college preparatory or vocational program. Categories channel and shape these human judgments but they do not replace them.

Source: Mintzberg (1979).

Box 7.3
"Norms of caution" in
industrial district coordination

"As already pointed out by Lorenz in the case of the Lyon steel workers, the practice of apportioning contracts among various suppliers and soliciting orders from various clients is also widespread within Italian districts. This is done in order to prevent damage to the firm's viability in the event of a betrayal or a defection, thus leaving the contractor without his habitual tried and tested subcontractors who could be quickly assigned the work that was previously assigned to the offending party, or alternatively leaving a subcontractor without a reliable client. "Never put all your eggs in one basket" is the oft-quoted saying. It must be noted that this turns out to be an expensive rule to observe. In fact, building trust among various suppliers and contractors requires more time and effort than dealing with only one or two opposite parties. The additional costs inevitably involved with this method represent a kind of insurance against possible defections or betrayals. . . . It is a good thing to trust those who deserve it, even though prudent attitudes are legitimate and allowed. These attitudes are not necessarily evidence of a lack of trust in and esteem for the opposite party; rather, they merely represent precautions, typical of any careful entrepreneur. The true significance of the rule can be appreciated only by contrast, i.e. by reflecting on how often this norm is not applied and when prudent behavior is not deemed desirable and legitimate. For example, this procedure is felt to be normal and fair in Emilia-Romagna and Tuscany, but is interpreted as a sign of blinkeredness in the Veneto, where it is normal for an entrepreneur to ask his subcontractor to work exclusively with him/her. At the same time, in southern Italy only those who trust others unconditionally, through total commitment, have the right to ask for special treatment and support in case of need. These two different behaviors, unusual as they may seem, are actually quite similar. Indeed, in both cases the relationship is based on very strong dichotomies: either we are friends or we are enemies. If we are friends, we are expected to give and get back; any refusal will be interpreted as a betrayal typical of Aeschylus. If we are enemies, any unfair behavior is possible and all interactions will be characterized by fear and suspicion of cheating."

Source: Brusco (1999).

levels of regulation: in the case described, the firm level, the district level, and the regional level. This leads us to consider the role of the *content* of norms.

The content of norms

Many organizational studies have contributed to creating typologies of cognitive and emotional orientations of people and connecting them to their effectiveness in performing various kinds of tasks. Some of these studies have referred to firm cultures, others have studied the various subcultures that can exist within firms and be effective in diverse subsystems (for example, typically, the various technical functions).[3] The main value of these studies is not however to classify in general norm content – which would be an endless game (Chapters 1 and 2). These "models" become instructive as they enable us to *assess the degree of "fit" between a set of norms and a set of tasks*, and to measure the *cognitive differentiation or distance among normative systems*. In fact, differentiation in the "programmed" part of collective minds can become a barrier to knowledge flows and transfer among systems, requiring specific integrative mechanisms to be overcome (Grant 1996).

For example, it has been shown that the cognitive profiles in the research and development functions within the most effective and efficient firms in dynamic industries (such as plastics and composite materials) are significantly different from those found in other functions, in terms of the amount of attention allocated to innovation, longer time horizons, and the adoption of behavioral norms that include a propensity toward innovation and a positive outlook on change (Lawrence and Lorsch 1967; Galbraith 1982). Considering entire firms, it has been found that externally oriented (rather than inside looking) and "proactive" (rather than reactive) firms or units obtain superior results in dynamic and turbulent industries (Burns and Stalker 1961; Miles and Snow 1978; Lawrence and Dyer 1983) and in boundary-spanning activities involving interactions with other firms, other units, and consumers (Thompson 1967).

Among other things, these results show that *interfirm and inter-unit cultural differentiation is effective and efficient, to the extent that tasks' complexity and specialization between action systems differ*.[4]

The importance of a differentiated corporate culture has emerged even more forcefully in the management of multi-national companies. In these companies the cultural diversity of subsystems is not only derived from different professional and technical cultures,

but also from the diversity in the deeper layers of culture deriving from the diversity of national cultures encompassed by the firm.

For example, a famous study on the problems encountered by the prototypical large American multinational, IBM, in coordinating on a worldwide scale (Hofstede 1980) found that employees in different national subsidieries held quite different work-related values, along dimensions as: (1) the degree of *individualism* or collectivism (people are only concerned with their own interests or people identify with larger groups); (2) the extent to which *power distance* is accepted as a legitimate; (3) the *tolerance for uncertainty* (people can live in undefined situations or need order); (4) the assumption, by both men and women, of *"masculine" values* (money, strength, assertiveness, growth) as against "feminine" ones (cooperation, relationships, balance, sympathy for the small dimension). Again, these findings lead us to wonder whether large firms face a problem of untransferability of knowledge and organizational know-how matured in different cultural backgrounds, a problem of lack of communication between different paradigms (Hofstede 1980); or a problem of finding suitable integrating mechanisms among different cultures, leveraging on their differences (Avadikian *et al.* 1989; Bartlett and Ghoshal 1990; Chapter 11).[5] The next section on the evaluation of cultural conditions should help in answering the question.

THE COMPARATIVE EFFECTIVENESS OF CULTURAL COORDINATION

Given the above, a scheme for evaluating the effectiveness and efficiency of normative coordination can be proposed. The courageous notion of an efficient culture was put forth in studies on organizational culture in an economic perspective (Ouchi and Wilkins

1985; Casson 1991). It is called courageous because evaluating a culture in terms of economic efficiency may sound difficult and overly simplistic.

However, the task is not impossible and the results are useful, provided that the appropriate aspects of a culture are considered and that the evaluation does not consider culture in a lump (as, after all, it has been necessary to do for other mechanisms, as in the case of different types of authority or market) but is applied to different types of cultural coordination. In particular, as emerges from our treatment so far, systems of norms at different levels of generality versus action-specificity have quite different coordination properties.

Coordination efficiency

Cultural coordination is efficient to the extent it is capable of orienting actions toward desired results – i.e. of realizing Pareto-improvements (Casson 1991) – where alternative coordination mechanisms cannot or would do so at a higher cost.

Ouchi and Wilkins (1985) hypothesized that cultural coordination outcompetes the alternative coordination modes of price-based exchange and authority when information complexity involves difficulties in observing performances, in terms of both behaviors and results. It could be added that in those conditions it may also be superior to group control – which requires that peers be able to observe behaviors; and that using agency contracts to align objectives still requires that outputs be measurable, even if not perfectly attributable to single actors.

Epistemic complexity

Cultural coordination and control, then, is an alternative method for aligning values and

preferences that is particularly interesting, or even indispensable, if cooperation and exchange is to take place in highly complex activities, where the evaluation of inputs and outputs is difficult and causal relations between actions and consequences are unclear. "Ambiguity," "vagueness," or "epistemic uncertainty" are definitions that have been employed to characterize this state of uncertainty (Cohen *et al.* 1976; Barney and Ouchi 1984; Orlean 1989): the parameters used to define an activity as good or bad are not clear (for example, the quality of theater, peace proposals, or of research projects); nor are the causal relationshipsis between inputs and outputs clear (as for example, in management and professional activities that require complex problem-solving).

The creation of a common culture has been emphasized, for example, as a means of sustaining successful interfirm cooperation in research and innovation (Ouchi and Bolton 1988) and the regulation of the exchange of services that are hard for the buyer to evaluate (such as medical or legal services) (Arrow 1963; Karpik 1989). These examples illustrate how shared norms can effectively coordinate interdependences created by exchange, cooperation, or even competition among firms or actors that offer the same type of service or product.

The paradox of change

The thesis that culture is an efficient and effective coordination mechanism if complex knowledge and ambiguous preferences are involved runs, however, up against a paradox. Where can change come from, in those systems of activity that are coordinated thanks to the internalization of common values and norms, through intense reciprocal socialization processes among members or even through the hereditary transmission of a region- or industry-specific culture? And is not change obstructed exactly in those complex activities where it is often highly desirable (Ouchi and Wilkins 1985)?

Flexible and rigid cultures

The resolution of this paradox seems to reside partly in the particular *content* of norms, and partly in their *degree of generality.*

As said, some cultural conventions include fruitful pro-change biases: norms of "creativity," long time horizons, high tolerance of uncertainty, low acceptance of power distance, proactiveness.

In addition, by containing norms at the constitutional or paradigmatic level, a maximum degree of flexibility can be achieved. *These norms will mainly perform a function of uncertainty reduction (by framing decisions), rather than of information cost reduction (by substituting for case-by-case decision-making).* The arbitrary and conventional element of the contents of norms at this level of base knowledge is partly justified by the fact that they can be configured in many different ways, all equally effective (such as languages).

Functional equivalence

At this level of cultural regulation, then, we should also expect a significant degree of *"functional equivalence" among the content of adopted norms*: i.e. different norms perform the same coordination function and can be combined with organizational solutions that are similar in other respects. Box 7.4 synthesizes research showing how the different institutions and conventions, leading to the differentiation of some organization traits in the machine-tool industry in Germany and Italy, are combined with otherwise similar

economic behaviors and organization structures.

More applied, detailed, and action-specific norms layers, have a different domain of efficiency. The more intense the use of lower level norms – especially action programs and routines – the more economic action will be preceptively and rigidly restrained. *These types of rules reduce information costs and computational complexity* (March and Simon 1958) *rather than cognitive or epistemic uncertainty*, and their effective application will be contingent on the possibility of *stabilizing and repeating actions and interactions in the same conditions* (Galbraith 1974). It is not difficult, and is actually almost commonplace, to find situations in which the over-production of routines, customary behaviors, and habitual pratices make economic action too inertial, too rigid, too change-averse, and permanently obsolete with respect to a world which changes inexorably more rapidly.

LEGAL-FORMAL SYSTEMS

Stable systems of action, explicitly described in documents, private or protected by law, characterized by a specific model of division of work and coordination, have been defined as formal organizations (Blau and Scott 1962). It has been maintained that the attribute of formalization enables one to distinguish, in a useful and significant way, for example, a trade union from a social movement, a partnership from an informal group of peers, a set of production units coordinated within a firm from an industrial district. On the basis of the analysis of social and cultural norms conducted in the first part of this chapter, it can be noted that the difference between these systems does not reside in the fact that informally coordinated action is necessarily rule-poor. The difference lies in

Box 7.4
Functionally equivalent
institutions in the European
machine-tool industry

In the 1970s and 1980s the proponents of the institutionalist Societal Effect Approach (for a summary, see: Sorge 1991) discovered in studies comparing German, British, and French firms that: (1) the overall pattern of the organizational configurations showed German companies as less laterally and hierarchically differentiated; (2) in Germany higher professional continuity existed across layers, together with a lower split between technical and managerial competence, and with practical knowledge and theoretical knowledge being conceived as strictly intertwined; (3) the lines of differentiation (works-staff, production-maintenance, technical-managerial and line-expert) were less pronounced in Germany than in the other countries. The explanation for the German results was found in the roles of: (1) the education system which emphasised the collection of practical knowledge right at the beginning of a career, and strongly supported its merging with theoretical knowledge; and (2) the trade unions which pushed for the preservation of integrative organization structures. The prevalence of a purely theoretically oriented educational system in France had the opposite effect on careers, so that different hierarchical levels were reached more according to educational qualifications. This result was confirmed in another study, where Sorge and Maurice (1993) compared the French and German machine-tool industries.

In the 1990s a replication study, comparing nine pairs of firms, was conducted in the machine-tool industry between Italy and Germany (see Delmestri 1997). Emphasis was laid on a wider consideration and control of strategic contingencies, in order to test the prevalence of an institutional or contingent influence on organization structures. A significant societal effect was not evident at first sight. A convergence of the Italian and the German organizational arrangements toward a similar or functionally equivalent form was apparent. A strategy of leadership or followership was the variable that best explained both the internal configuration and the level of outsourcing. Asset specificity and task uncertainty affected internal process features, the intensity of interfirm coordination mechanisms, and the type of interfirm coordination modes. On checking for contingencies, differences in organization structure in the two countries appeared marginal and mainly functionally equivalent. In both countries, entrepreneurs and managers had to invest in: (1) the multiskilling of the workforce in order to reduce job and functional specialization; (2) the decentralized and integrative introduction and use of MRP systems; (3) the definition of organizational configurations and outsourcing levels consistent with the strategy of technological leadership or followership; (4) the coordination of internal and external processes according to the technological complexity, the exceptionality and variability of clients' requests, and specificity of assets.

Germany and Italy indeed present similar institutional and economic features (late political unification from a situation of regional fragmentation; late industrialization, both regionally and dimensionally dualized economies; similar political histories) and differ as regards the education system, which in Italy is more similar to the French one. This paves the way for the following questions: (1) How have the Italian firms studied succeeded in reaching the same organizational profile in the absence of the institutional provisions identified as necessary for successfully competing in the machine-tool industry? (2) How can the Italian industry, which relies on an exclusively theoretical French-type educational system, be successful in the same market niches as the German one?

The following explanations emerged. At a general level, the Italian machine-building industry has been internationally successful because, despite the lack of formalized institutional provisions, firms have been able to rely on traditional attitudes toward skill formation and the operation of organization structures, which have had a supportive effect on their competitiveness. The way qualifications were shaped in the two countries was similar to the extent that practical experience was at the basis of individual careers. In Germany, the cooperation between regional and national states as well as between trade unions and employer associations, did find unity within the institutionalization of the dual education system. In Italy, where such a formal path had not been instituted, single individuals were expected to gather the relevant qualifications and assume an entrepreneurial attitude toward their own education. Moreover, in Italy, in the absence of a formalized system, a higher respect for age favored the transmission of knowledge from one generation to the other.

Thanks to the Italian traditional attitude of combining firm-specific tacit knowledge with theoretical knowledge acquired from the educational system, a system functionally equivalent to the German dual one has come into being. This means that Italian companies have based their success on integrative organization structures, as in Germany, but according to an institutionally specific logic.

Source: By Giuseppe Delmestri.

---

the fact that *formal rules explicitate and codify knowledge about how economic actions should be performed and state it in documents that are accessible, controllable, and defendable*. This operation means not only accepting and stabilizing, but also transforming into laws – guaranteed by some type of legal system – some traits of the models of action and interaction. Actors can make decisions case by case, at their own discretion, only in the space that has not been predefined by accepted rules and conventions as stipulated in regulatory documents. An analysis of the coordination properties of formal regulation can be usefully organized by taking various types of documents into consideration.

Documents

An important conceptual distinction has been drawn between *"externally" enforceable documents* that stipulate reciprocal obligations by two or more actors to behave according to rules that are a subspecies of externally enforceable laws (*contracts*), and *"internally" enforceable documents* that reflect internal agreements made within the system of actors and are legitimized and enforceable within that system only (for example, *job descriptions, organization charts and procedures*) (Stinchcombe 1985; Williamson 1993a,b). The principal types of "external documents" and "internal documents" and their coordination properties will be illustrated below.

"External" and "internal" documents

Contracts

A contract, in law and in the economic theory of contracts, is an agreement with patrimonial consequences for the parties which institutes or modifies a relationship of reciprocal obligation. Strictly speaking, agreements that result in juridically relevant obligations do not necessarily imply formalization, i.e. do not imply that the contract is formalized in a document. For example, contracts derived from the exchange of goods and services in which the passage of ownership is readily identified, frequently are not formalized: for example, the "buy" declarations on the stock exchange, an order in a restaurant, self-service in a supermarket – all of these create the obligation for payment and are under the legal jurisdiction of an external legal system, but they are not formalized. Nonetheless, it is useful to recall that the law, if called upon, in the absence of explicit contracts, has recourse to that which norm, habit, and conventions state could be expected as "normal" behavior in a given action context. A contract therefore, in contrast to a simple exchange, always refers to a system of rules, formal or, if necessary, informal.

Here we shall deal with *formal contracts*, that establish and incorporate exchange and cooperation rules and explicit conventions for relationships. The typology of contracts that Williamson outlined (1975, 1979), integrating economic and legal notions, is a good point of departure for understanding the reasons for contracts and the varying content of rules and conventions in a contract.

An *instantaneous contract* defines the allocation of resources in "*substantive*" terms: what and how many resources are transferred among subjects – e.g. how many tons of copper for how much money. No process aspect would be included, hence the procedural intensity of this type of contract is very low.

A *contingent contract* is a more complex contract that recognizes that the relationship is not instantaneous, but takes place over a time during which conditions may change; and that the value of the exchanged or shared resources is not known in advance, but will be known only at a later point in time. For example, the price paid for copper, if delivery takes time and involves risks of price variations or material being damaged, could be transformed into a *contingent rule* according to which different prices will be paid depending on which "states of the world" will obtain among the possible ones.

However complex they may be, contingent claim contracts, in their common definition, concern allocations of resources (a *substantive* issue) and not obligations of behaviors to be respected (a *procedural* issue). A contract's content of rules changes substantially if contracts are not limited to setting the substantive content of an agreement, but establishes procedural obligations for behavior. These contracts have been called *obligational contracts* (Williamson 1979). A simple example of a contract that almost exclusively establishes behavioral obligations – albeit with potential patrimonial consequences – could be that of two firms that underwrite a document in which they commit themselves to exchanging all information acquired, or to coordinating strategic planning, on a certain product/market combination. Much more complicated contracts, may have tens or even hundreds of clauses to regulate more complex exchanges – as in the example of the obligational contract regulating the contracting out of maintenance activities by an elevator constructor to maintenance technicians, reported in Box 7.5.

The wider the matter regulated in the contract and the greater the variety of items of which it is composed, the more numerous the possible uncertain contingencies are, and the more a complete contract should be expanded in a series of clauses, conditions, job descriptions, conflict resolution procedures, and right assignments. Therefore, *information complexity*, understood as variability and unpredictability of circumstances and as number of elements to be regulated, *puts obligational "external" contracts under strain as a coordination device* (as was the case at Kauffmann) (Williamson 1975).

A possible response is to complement and integrate the formal regulation of relationship by extracontractual means; in particular, by norms and conventions that can be accepted as a frame of reference in the matter on hand, or also by a negotiated order agreed upon by specific parties but not formalized into and defensible by a contract. This possibility of combination of formal rules incorporated into contracts with informal norms and informal negotiated agreements has been referred to as *"relational contracting"* (McNeil 1978; Williamson 1979; Ring and Van de Ven 1992) and has been much studied as one of the most fruitful approaches to the regulation of long-term recurrent economic relations involving complex goods or services (Chapters 9 and 12).

Another possible response to the incompleteness of external documents, is to stipulate "internal contracts" which complement and integrate the regulatory function performed by external contracts where they do not suffice (Williamson 1993a). In this perspective, *formal regulation internal to a particular system* (an association, a consortium, a firm) *is seen as a "continuation" of the external regulation system under the shadow of a different "court":* an internal arbitration hierarchy, performing a function analogous to courts in the external legal system (Williamson 1993b).

Internal documents are, in fact, very rich in job descriptions, procedures, programs, and rules, that regulate a wider area of behaviors than do "external" contracts. But, it may be wondered, why the difficulty in predicting uncertain circumstances should be less severe in internal contract writing than in external ones (as is usually asserted in the analyses mentioned)? In fact, it is not. The use of rules and formalization, even if internal to a specific system, even in a firm, is effective and efficient only to the extent that the activities are relatively stable, predictable, and not very complex (Burns and Stalker 1961; Lawrence and Lorsch 1967; Pugh et *al.* 1969b) and *internal contracts soon become as incomplete as external ones, as the complexity and variability of the regulated matters increase.* The employment contract is the clearest example (Chapter 10). It follows that the regulation by contracts and formal pacts fails where uncertain and complex activities are concerned, whether in the case of internal or external regulation. Uncertainty is an important factor for resorting to ad hoc decisions (by authority, group, or negotiation) rather than to rules, not for choosing between internal and external rules – as it is not relevant for discriminating between formal and informal rules. The need for rules that are internal to a particular system of action, in addition to external contracts, can be better explained in terms of *the degree of specificity* of the regulated matters to particular actions or actors. The matters and models

Box 7.5
Kauffman's obligational
maintenance contract

Re: Mandate for the right to represent the firm in the performance of maintenance or installation activities in the —— territory.

General Conditions

Art. 1 Defining the Boundaries of the Territory

The territory is bounded by the geographic references indicated in the current mandate. Places located between two adjacent territories will be assigned to the territory with the nearest provincial capital (in kilometers), except when logistical reasons impose a different decision.

Art. 2 Exclusivity

Both the installation concession and the mandate to sign maintenance/repairs contracts are conferred and accepted by the parties in reciprocal exclusivity, except as allowed for in the last part of Article 6, the last part of Article 8, or Article 23 . . .

Art. 3 General Norms

The Agent must be a member of the Chamber of Commerce in the provincial capital of the territory. The Agent must comply with all the employment and tax laws. Serious noncompliance that causes material or reputational damage to the Company will be considered reasonable and sufficient cause for the dissolution of this contract.

The Agent further agrees to remain open for business in the territory of the concession, and to maintain an organization that is adequate to perform the average work required there. An adequate organization must include transportation, telephone services, tools, and an administrative service for billing, correspondence, etc.

For all reports concerning the present contract (installation, maintenance, repairs, etc.), the Agent agrees to use letterhead, rubber stamps, or similar means of identification immediately under the official name of the firm, in the following form: *Concession for installation*, or else *Mandate for maintenance and repairs* of the ——.

Art. 4 Duration

The present contract has an indefinite duration . . .

Art. 8 Withdrawal by the Agent

Upon six months advance notice sent in the form of a registered letter, the Agent can withdraw from this contract at any time.

In case of withdrawal, the Agency is expected to indicate to the Company names of persons or firms that could take its place in the agreement.

If the Company judges that the subject indicated has the necessary moral, technical, and administrative characteristics, it may confer the concession on an trial basis for a year, based on the rules in Article 6.

Art. 9 Withdrawal by the Company

a. The Company can withdraw for just cause without any requirement for advance notice. In addition to the hypotheses not specifically specified in advance, the following definitely qualify as just causes for the withdrawal by the Company:

i. The failure on the part of the Agent to precisely follow even one clause of the present contract.
ii. Bankruptcy, or economic or financial difficulties suffered by the Agent that are serious enough to compromise the efficiency of the service and the reputation of the Company.

b. Upon six months advance notice, the Company can withdraw in the following cases (*in the complete contract, six contingencies listed are listed here, n.t.*) . . .

Art. 11 Post-agreement Ban on Competition

In case of dissolution of this contract, the Agent agrees to refrain from direct or indirect (under a different name or using mediators) competition with the Company for three years from the date of dissolution. This ban applies to all the activities and territories specified in this contract.

In exchange, the Company agrees to avoid any direct or indirect action intended to take away the maintenance equipment remaining under the responsibility of the Agent . . .

Specific Conditions for Installation

Art. 13

When installing the equipment, the Agent agrees to comply with the technical and administrative instructions of the Company.

Art. 14

At the conclusion of the sales negotiations, the Company agrees to grant to the Agent a series of single orders for installation contracts in the assigned territory.

Art. 15

The installation activities will be compensated according to the installation price list, which is to be considered an integral part of the present contract, and can change in the following circumstances:

a. In the case that installation time decreases as a result of improvements introduced by the Company in the construction of its own equipment and in its installation technique.

b. In case of variation in the amounts specified in the supply contracts, according to the application of the clause referring to price variability.

Specific Maintenance Conditions

Art. 16

The Company will inform its clients that the Agent has been given a mandate for the territory, although it makes no promises that all clients who have purchased its equipment will entrust the maintenance of that equipment to the Agent.

Art. 17

The Agent agrees to offer its clients the maintenance services at the prices indicated in the Company's price list, except when authorized by the Company to modify those prices for competitive reasons. These prices are susceptible to continuous change at the discretion of the Company, as foreseen in the section above. The Company will include the prices for parts in the maintenance price list furnished to the Agent.

Art. 18

The relationships with clients for maintenance services will be taken care of directly by the Agent, which has the following obligations:

- Stipulate the relative contracts.
- Insure the equipment for liability toward third parties with the Company's reliable insurance company for a sum that is not inferior to that communicated and purchased by the Company.
- Take care of billing and charges as well as bill collection from the receivers of services.
- Communicate eventual accidents to the insurance company and the firm within 24 hours of their confirmation.
- Send its personnel for technical, administrative, and organizational training about the service by the Company.

Art. 19

The Agency agrees to respect the restriction of exclusivity, to maintain trade secrets, to observe the legal norms and rules, and to grant certificates of competence and training to the employees entrusted to perform services. Further, the Agency agrees to use the maximum diligence and care to the end of earning and maintaining a trusting relationship with the clients.

Art. 20

In maintenance and repairs of equipment, the Agent agrees to exclusively use the following construction materials (——)
   The Agent is prohibited from selling parts directly to third parties.
   The company agrees to supply parts only for the duration of the contract. Supplies of parts will therefore end at the expiration of the contract.

Art. 21

It is agreed that the Agent will pay the company an annual fixed sum to be cashed on the 31st of December of each year, as compensation for trademark and other general services provided to the Agent by the Company.

Art. 22

In case of dissolution of the contract, the Agent is committed to return to the company, at no extra cost, the following percentages for equipment being maintained: (*ten contingent payment clauses are listed below*)

Source: A. Colombo, Caso Elevatori Kauffmann; SDA Bocconi 1985.

---

of conduct considered by the law of a larger system – for example, national or international law – must be recurrent across application contexts. The arbiters of these norms, judicial courts, will not hear cases relative to infringements of rules that are not pertinent to their level of jurisdiction. A rule belonging to a more specific and particular level (for example, a firm) can detail the parties' commitments and reciprocal obligations to a greater extent. This interpretation of internal rules as more action-specific and actor-specific than external rules helps to explain why they are in fact more detailed, less general, and more operative than external rules – why, therefore, they do have a function of completing external uncomplete contracts when their application requires time and involves behavioral obligations, and why, at the same time, they get into trouble when uncertainty increases. Thus this perspective also helps in understanding and designing a proper "degree of formalization" of – either internal or external – organization as a function of the state of uncertainty.

Levels of formalization

The more activities of an economic system are explicitly described and prescribed ex ante

in organization charts, job descriptions, procedures, and programs, the more formalized that system is (Pugh *et al.* 1969). The fact that the system's rules are formalized does not make them privy to the logical order already analyzed regarding social norms and cultural conventions. A constitutional framing level of ruling, a set of procedures on how to apply those principles and how to reach desirable actions, and a body of programs of actions directly prescribing what to do in given circumstances can in fact be usefully distinguished also in internal formal systems of rules.

Constitutions

North (1990) observed that the distinction between constitutional law, statute law, and common law may be useful for understanding the stratified nature of institutions in general, and the different rate of change at the three levels. Consistent with their nature of paradigmatic knowledge and embedding frame, constitutional rules are (and should be, in this perspective) difficult to change. In the "internal legal systems" of firms and other collective economic actors the constitutional level of ruling is represented by founding acts and statements, and by the allocation of property, decision, and control rights constitutive of the basic internal organs, represented in organization charts and internal constitutional charts.

Systems of action founded on contracts of association, rather than exchange, and non-profit organizations are led to define themselves more explicitly in terms of aims, goals, and constitutive organs by means of statutes and constitutions. In classic firms less consideration has been traditionally given to this "constitutional" level of regulation. However, recently, the growing needs for what may be called "flexible formalization" in dynamic industries and "advanced tertiary" sectors have stimulated more interest in governing by *"charts of rights"* and *"mission statements."* Organization charts and constitutive acts specify only the fundamental rules of correspondence between actors and rights; they are not very informative about the "real functioning" of the action system – something that has sometimes been lamented as a sort of drawback, but that appears to be totally healthy if the different cognitive functions of rule levels are considered.

Job descriptions, programs, and procedures

Organization charts and statutes are usually accompanied by job descriptions – that is, the description of the activities assigned to each individual job position. With respect to the general indications supplied by the organizational chart, job descriptions are, therefore, a more detailed and constraining coordination instrument. Box 7.6 presents the job description of a publishing company's estimating office as an illustration.

Typically, job descriptions include: the placement of the position in the vertical division of work (in the case, a hierarchical dependence on the technical sales manager);

the content of action rights and obligations (writing up job plans); the objectives and the responsibilities according to which activities are evaluated (techno-economic feasibility, correspondence to price policies, entry completeness); the methods of work and the procedures that regulate the activities (in the case, the job planning process begins with a request for an estimate by the sales department; it should be based on a techno-economic handbook and is supported/recorded in client folders; estimated data must then be checked with other units in a series of pre-defined circumstances).

The example illustrates a particularly detailed job description, and shows a fairly high level of formalization, especially due to the variety of procedures and action programs that are specified. Is that degree of detail effective and efficient? What would it be necessary to know for responding to the question?

As in the case of cultural coordination, there is no universal response to the question of whether the above degree of specificity of rules is correct. In this case, the estimates office of firm A ran into problems – resulting in high error rates. A plausible explanation is exactly that activities were too extensively and precisely prescribed in advance, trying to predict all possible circumstances, in a situation that in fact would have required ad hoc and timely adaptation to very frequent clients' variation requests. In fact, the organization of work was later modified so as to form small teams responsible to follow entire editorial projects, rather than different phases of the estimate process, and to adjust estimates as variations arised. Under these circumstances job descriptions are inflated by clauses and contingent provisions without being able to keep track of variations.

In sum, formal-legal systems, as much as cultural systems, can be usefully conceived

Box 7.6
Job description of an
estimates office in a graphics
firm

Reporting

Staff of the estimates office report to the director of services

Description

The main role of the estimates office is to support the sales activity by providing, in a timely fashion, the compilation of estimates and ensuring that they:

- meet prices on the price lists
- are based on the most convenient option for the firm, both technically and financially
- include technical and timely conditions that can be easily met in case of acceptance of the order.

In order to fulfil their role efficiently, the estimates office staff are supported by:

- detailed estimates requests issued by the commercial division indicating, in complex situations, the basic categories of the estimate
- the professional support of the director of services
- the technical support of other staff or units (foreman, planning office, purchase division, paper division, etc.) that will be responsible for verifying their section of the estimate.

Internal environment conditions that would ensure maximum efficiency are:

- a suitable technical-professional background
- availability of detailed and current price lists
- availability of specific technical-economics manuals in order to best evaluate all alternatives.

There are two additional roles of the estimates office that complement the primary one:

- reports compiled in the estimates office constitute files. It is requested that specific methods be used to compile those reports in order easily to convert report data into estimates
- the estimates represent the basic elements on which to issue invoices later. Therefore, the estimates office will receive any modifications or communication relative to the issued estimate before the invoice is drawn up.

Responsibilities

The staff at the estimates office are primarily responsible for:

- compiling fast estimates
- monitoring and interpreting the price list correctly

- making the best use of the technical data on the estimate based on available resources
- ensuring that any changes to the estimate prior to the issuing of the invoice have been recorded
- maintaining a professional attitude and confidentiality both toward the public and the rest of the staff.

Tasks

The issuing of an estimate is required for all jobs. This is true even when complete information or details are missing. In that case, a "temporary" estimate will be compiled based on "average" or "routine" hypotheses; later the estimate will be updated.

The issuing of an estimate is also required, even if in simple form, for "partial" jobs; to this end the estimates office is responsible for looking for the "balance" orders usually addressed to the foremen.

In the case of estimates issued by other departments (commercial division, sales people) the staff at the estimates office must verify that they conform to the firm's rules and regulations.

Information on the estimate is verified in advance in all cases when the job for which the estimate is being drawn up:

- has a high chance of becoming an order and/or
- is particularly complex from a technical standpoint and/or
- is particularly urgent and/or
- is particularly relevant in terms of internal work load and/or
- is particularly relevant in terms of work load to be contracted out.

The advance verification is requested by the staff at the estimates office from the foremen and/or the planning office and/or external relation office and/or purchase office based on the critical, most important steps of the job. In the case of a technical check the two production phases taken into particular consideration are the preparation line and the finishing line. A positive acknowledgment implies a commitment from the production division and the purchase office . . .

As regards updating the estimates/files/invoices, the estimates office follows the enclosed procedures; based on them, the person responsible for the estimates office must fill out the "invoice change" form. This form is the "draft invoice" that, originating from the estimates, is constantly updated on the basis of the relevant contract variations, financially speaking.

Source: Constructed on material provided by G. Airoldi.

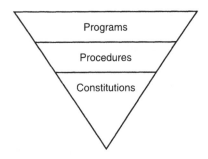

Figure 7.3 Levels of formal regulation

and engineered as stratified systems, as visualized in Figure 7.3. The three logically distinct levels of regulation, found in analyzing norms, can also be found by considering the different regulatory properties of formal rules. This is not by chance, of course, because we ordered the components of these systems according to the type of knowledge they embody: core, procedural, and declarative knowledge about action respectively, in order to be able not only to describe cultural and formal systems but also to evaluate their respective coordination properties.

The basic rules of the game and the attribution of objectives and responsibilities are less rigid and deterministic than rules that extend pervasively down to the level of procedures and the programs. Hence, the more the regulated activities can be predicted (are relatively stable, or governed by known variance models) the more detailed and action specific a rule system can be; a proposititition that has been widely confirmed empirically, as applied to firms' internal formal systems of rules (Burns and Stalker 1961; Blau and Schoenherr 1971; Galbraith 1974).

THE COMPARATIVE EFFECTIVENESS OF FORMALIZATION

The law just mentioned has been however argued to be valid for both for formal and informal rule systems. Why then are some rules formalized and some are not? How can we design this feature of a regulatory system, whenever possible?

Formalization does remain a relevant issue, for many reasons. The damages generated by excessive rule production, and especially by excessive proliferation of low level rules, has led many to throw out the baby with the bath water – the advantages of formalization with the defects of bureaucratization.

At least four major factors justify formalization.

Justice

A first reason for formalizing is the need to equitably handle multiple contracts of the same kind. For example, a hospital that does not have explicit rules for accepting patients, or a university that does not have formal and transparent admission systems, would be suspected of opportunism. Similarly, work contracts for regular employees solicit judgments of "perceived equity" by those who sign them and therefore should be highly transparent (Chapter 9). Or again, a franchising contract which binds only two parties, the franchisor and the franchisee, could be largely implicit; by contrast, if there are many franchisees, the contract should be standardized and equal for all. More generally, the widely documented fact that actors assign positive valence to procedural justice (Bazerman and Lewicki 1983) militates for the transparency and formalization of rules.

Justifiability and accountability

Formalization makes action systems easier to read, more transparent, more accountable (Hannan and Freeman 1989), more capable of reconstructing their own actions and justifying them in the face of third parties. As a result, for example, firms are obliged to produce a series of formal documents according to transparent procedures (such as balance sheets). Some kinds of companies must be more formal than others: for example, the fact that the organization of banks and insurance companies, or of hospitals, is highly formalized is at least partly attributable to the particularly strict requirements of control and record actions and transactions regarding their clients' patrimony or health.

Defensibility and interest conflicts

Both in the face of internal authority and of the authority of courts, explicit and formalized commitments and agreements make evaluating the degree to which they have been respected easier. There will always be a problem of vulnerability due to the problem of discovering what parties' actual behaviors have been, but expected behaviors at least will be clear. In the case of informal agreements and commitments, the "spirit of the contract" must, if necessary, be examined and reconstructed if there is a conflict. Hence the greater the conflict potential, and the larger the size of possible consequences, the more advantageous it will be to formalize them.

Computational complexity

An important advantage of formalization is the capacity to extend memory through the use of documents and other formal supports (such as information technology supports). Where a state of "uncertainty" in the actor is principally due to the quantity of information to be processed (rather than to the difficulty in interpretation), codifying information

allows memory capacity and information processing speed that would be otherwise unrealizable (Galbraith 1974; Simon 1977; Helylighen 1992). The advantages of formalization in managing computational complexity, i.e. a high number of elements, can explain why, other conditions being equal, the degree of formalization of activities is positively related to the number of actors and materials to be coordinated – that is to say, to an *action system size* (Pugh *et al.* 1969b): large groups get formalized into organizational units, large firms are more formalized than small ones (Chapter 11), large networks formalize into associations (Chapter 12). The case described in Box 7.7 allows these variables to be applied dynamically to interpret the processes of formalization and deformalization over time and on different areas of activities in a firm.

SUMMARY

The chapter showed first the common properties and advantages of rule-based coordination. The basic distinctive feature of this type of mechanism is to substitute case-by-case calculative decision-making for automatic compliance. This mechanism has advantages in *reducing conflicts*, in *reducing information costs*, as well as in *reducing the epistemic uncertainty* which would otherwise surround any action (and complex action in particular).

Both social norms and formal rules were analyzed as stratified structures of prescriptions of a varying degree of generality, embodying more or less operationalized knowledge. Different layers of cultural components are in fact frequently identified in cultural studies – here distinguished in basic "values," procedural "codes of conduct," and substantive routines. In formal rule

Box 7.7
Formalization and
de-formalization at
Drehmaschinen AG

Drehmaschinen AG is a German firm producing computerized numerical control (CNC) lathes. In the 1980s, the firm grew rapidly owing to the combination of a very rich market – demanding technical and design developments – and a weak Deutschmark that made it easy to export. Among German firms in the sector, this climate increased the power of those technical functions with workers who possessed a strong engineering background and training. Because the traditional German vocational education system emphasizes the training of highly qualified workers within firms, the technical orientation of positions within Drehmaschinen AG generated a spotty distribution, with areas of heavy formalization mixed with areas lacking any formalization.

This situation is clearly explained by the comments of the production director of an Italian lathe-producing company who had the opportunity to visit Drehmaschinen during those years:

"At my company the technology office A sends incomplete designs to the prep-worker (the worker who sets the machine up for the customer) because they know that the worker is very competent and is able to modify possible errors by himself. This also occurs because if the designer realizes that the worker changes what he has taken a long time to prepare, he becomes demotivated and sends the worker more incomplete designs, in a sort of vicious circle. The head of technical office B, on the other hand, does not create such a situation with his workers because he has great experience in mounting and is thus able to communicate better with his prep-workers. At Drehmaschinen however, the prep-worker receives a written note listing all necessary tools and all the elements of the finished design; if the design has some problems, the prep-worker sends it back with a note indicating where the problem is, and the communication continues interactively until the problem is solved. In the meantime, though, the machine sits idle. All this seems absurd, but perhaps it encourages the technology office to learn from its mistakes."

This hypothesis turned out to be wrong. The management of the formal system of coordination between production and technical offices increased the number of personnel in the latter, but this increased number could no longer be sustained during the sectoral crisis in 1993. The CEO explained the situation as follows:

"We had created a division in charge of the mechanical processes with a very large time and methods office which, in truth, was useless. The growth of that office was supported by tradition – it reflected the Taylorist approach. It derived from the view of the engineers who had become used to a certain type of organization and had the opportunity during the 1980s to implement a certain set-up. I already knew at the time that it would not work, but we needed the recession in order to make the necessary changes. At that point we totally externalized the mechanical processes in order to eliminate the reason for their existence."

This reorientation of the configuration of internal power within the firm cannot be understood separately from the strategic reorientation that happened simultaneously.

According to the CEO, "In the past, we had been proud to be able to accomplish everything all at once and then start over again." Parallel to the reduction of formalization, there was an increase in the standardization of the offer. However, this was not easy: "Our employees," said the manager for the ISO 9000 project for quality certification, "think that they are still manufacturing special equipment. For each new order there are meetings with several participants which turn out to be a waste of time when the product to be produced is actually a standard one."

The solution was therefore to reduce the formalization in the relationship between production and technical offices and increase it for the function of interfunctional coordination. However, the balance between formalization and mutual adjustment needed to be reset also in other areas:

"We combined the purchasing office with the planning office, both in terms of the organization and the space," said the purchasing manager. "In the past, tons of written notes would be exchanged between offices; now it is much more efficient if those offices actually talk to each other."

"At times we exchange the designers within the research and development area with those of the design of special tools for customers area so that the former can understand the issues that people below them face," explained the director of the planning office. "Similarly, when we run into unsatisfied customers, we send the designer on a visit to the customer together with the sales representative."

The externalization of the mechanical procedures ended by being problematic, both because it was impossible to ensure an acceptable level of quality by external suppliers, and because of problems related to insufficient formalization. When the mechanical procedures occurred within the company, changes to the designs would not be recorded but the production workers would know from experience what the designers meant with the sketch of a piece because they were familiar with its use and would understand the requested details. Now this know-how needed to be formalized if the company wanted various suppliers to make offers.

Concluding the interview the following statement was made by the CEO:

"About a year and a half ago we were certified ISO 9000. This happened before the big crisis which almost led us to bankruptcy. Now we have been certified again. By whom? By the same institute. Certification is just a formality, it is no indicator of economic efficiency."

Source: By Giuseppe Delmestri.

systems the coordination properties of "constitutions" (such as statutes and charts of rights), can be distinguished from those of "procedures" and those of "programs."

In general, effective and efficient coordination by rules requires conditions of *stability and replicability* of those elements of action crystallized in the rule. Therefore, *the paradoxes and difficulties of coordinating innova-tive and dynamic activities by norms and rules* have been examined. It has been argued that *"flexible cultures"* are focused on values and principles rather than on routines. Similarly, *"flexible formalization"* can be achieved by rules centered on "consitutional" objectives and responsibility and on the basic "rules of the game" rather than on detailed plans, programs and procedures.

The *content of rules and norms* also influences their coordination properties. For example, rules can incorporate pro-innovation statements, cooperative postures, and long term commitments which make them more adequate than others to survive in dynamic situations. The differentiation among systems of actors characterized by rules and norms of different content is also relevant: as is the case in the differentiation of collective (and memorized) knowledge and preferences, it poses requirements for the type of coordination systems that can be employed between those collective actors (that will be examined in Part III).

The analysis and design of an effective, efficient and fair *degree of formalization* has been finally addressed. The importance of the four following variables was underlined: *justice* and the transparency of organizational processes; *justifiability and "accountability"* of actions in the face of third parties; the degree of confict among interests and the *defensibility* of actors' interest before either internal or external third parties and authorities; *computational complexity* and the number of interdependent activities and actors to be coordinated.

Exercise: Industry Self-regulation in the Italian Construction Industry

The construction industry in Italy provides an interesting example with which to study the interrelationships between formal and informal regulation: the former refers to the legislation governing the certification of the competence of the companies to undertake particular types of building activity and the regulation of competition; the latter to the industry self-regulation (ISR) that can be substantially related to the informal norms governing the behavior of competition and cooperation.

A historical reconstruction of the legislative interventions aimed at regulating the industry (Soda and Usai 1999) has highlighted the production of formal regulations on the part of the state. The construction industry in Italy still seems to be characterized by the fact that it has the largest number of legal provisions governing the way in which it works. It is an industry that enjoyed almost forty years of continuous growth in Italy until it was struck by a profound crisis in the 1990s. Before this crisis, the large Italian construction enterprises had developed a system of cooperative relationships aimed at building large public works. The legislation favored the formation of coalitions and the companies gradually constructed a system for self-regulating competition that was based on rules that were unwritten because they frequently involved illicit behaviors. Industry self-regulation was complementary to rather than substitutive of state regulations. It was a kind of peaceful (even collusive) coexistence of formal public and informal regulation. In practice, the state had created conditions in which industry self-regulation was particularly profitable for the companies (for example, by creating a mechanism that allowed groups of companies to qualify for particular contracts by summing the individual certifications of the different partners).

No bankruptcies occurred for many years because the enterprises colluded with each other simply to divide the resources made available by the state by means of its financing of public works. But this distributive logic was not the only option for growth generated by ISR. Over the long term, fed by industrial growth, ISR led to the institution of a mechanism that actually modified state regulations. There is a lot of evidence to suggest that the construction companies exerted pressure on the legislative power in order to formalize the tacit norms already existing as industry rules or to create new norms that would be useful for strengthening ISR.

Actually, in principle, single firms could have participated in bidding processes alone and in competition with others. But this option was not even taken in consideration. The first question to be answered was: "With whom are we going to set up a consortium?," rather then "Should we ally or go alone?."

Now the situation has radically changed due to an institutional crisis, largely linked to the many and substantial illicit relationships between the public administration and the large construction companies. The social norms that governed the industry have been upset, the clash among institutional powers has led to the lapse of the rules and praxes that had governed the industry for over thirty years. The institutional crisis has, in fact, caused the crisis of a whole economic system based on formal and informal rules and practices which used to keep the industry functioning. The institutional earthquake was accompanied by a strong retrenchment of the resources given by the system (both economic and "legitimation" resources). The consequence was the paralysis of economic activity, causing serious financial problems to the firms. The network of cooperation that had long governed the industry dissolved over a period of a few years, many companies have gone bankrupt, and many others are currently finding themselves in considerable difficulty. A wave of mergers and acquisitions is transforming the industry. All are now looking for a new season of rules.

By Giuseppe Soda, adapted from Grandori et al. (1999)

Questions

- What were the characteristics of the described system of rules and norms?
- What were the assets and liabilities of the system?
- Discuss what traits of the industry self-regulation system could make it more effective, efficient, and fair, using the dimensions of formalization, of the extension of intra-industry and firm-specific norms, and of the level (generality) of rules.

Conclusion to Part II

Comparing and Combining Coordination Mechanisms

•••

Considering Part II as a whole, the meta-decision problem of how to choose among, or apply in combination, coordination mechanisms can be addressed. Each chapter has specified the conditions under which each mechanism can be effective, efficient and fair. In concrete problems, these conditions often occur in an intermingled fahion, so that, normally, combinations of mechanisms are superior to one-sided solutions. Consider, for example the situation described in Box II.5.

The effectiveness of the full range of cordination mechanisms can be assessed in the

---

Box II.5
The Credit Sud case

You are the president of a small but growing bank located in a southern region of your country. The headquarters of the bank is located in the capital of that region, but there are several other branches in several other southern cities. The location and the kinds of services that the bank offers reflect a traditional style of banking that is not very innovative at any level. When you became president five years ago, the bank was not in good financial health. Under your leadership, however, things have improved a lot. This progress is the result of a policy of selecting and promoting managers who are well known and respected in their local communities, as well as a series of prompt decisions on your part that have enabled the bank to grow during a time when the economy was going through a slight recession. Because of this, the managers highly respect you.

You have recently been granted the necessary loans and authorizations to open a new branch office. Your problem is to decide on the proper location. You are convinced that there is no magic formula that would allow you to choose the perfect site. The choice is based on "common sense," and intuition about what feels right. You have asked your managers to keep their eyes open for any commercial building that could fit your purpose. Their knowledge of the local situation, and their close relationships with leaders in their local communities may be particularly useful in helping you to make a wise choice; on the other hand, however, these factors may also distort the choice based on the managers' local interests.

Getting support from your managers is very important, as the success of the new branch office will in large part depend on their willingness to provide staff resources and assistance during the initial period of activity. In addition, your bank is small and you believe that input from all your managers is critical for the prosperity of the bank.

The success of the project will benefit everyone. In a direct way, everyone will benefit from an increased number of transactions, while in an indirect way, everyone will have personal and economic advantages in taking part in a successful business.

Source: Constructed on the basis of Lau (1975), Vroom and Yetton (1973), and Hall *et al.* (1982).

Table II.1 A coordination failures' framework

Mechanisms Failure condition	Pricing	Voting	Agency	Authority	Negotiations	Teams	Norms	Rules
Computational complexity:								
• Variability						X	X	
• N. elements and actors				X	X	X		
Epistemic complexity:								
• Unclear outputs	X	X	X					
• Distributed knowledge				X				
• Unclear inputs				X	X	X		
Conflicting preferences:								
• No collective preference order		X				X		
• No substantive zone of agreement	X	X	X	X	X	X		
• No procedural zone of agreement	X	X	X	X	X	X	X	X

described problem. Would an internal bid for different projects in competition be viable? Would a central decision be effective and acceptable? To what extent members can and should contribute with their opinions and analyses? Is the issue negotiable? Can all the above decision processes and costs be avoided by following an established routine or procedure? A core component of managerial and leadership competence is the capacity to respond to these questions and design the appropriate governance structure within which decisions will be made and actions undertaken. In Part III, on organization forms governing economic actions and interactions, it will appear that many organization design problems and models involve the structuring of effective mixes of the coordination mechanisms examined so far, in order to connect properly individual and collective economic actors holding different knowledge and preferences.

In order to summarize the analysis conducted in Part II, albeit neglecting a variety of contingencies and distinctions treated in each chapter, Table II.1 offers an overall synthesis of the main conditions of coordination mechanisms effectiveness. As it appears from the table, there is no one-to-one simple correspondence between knowledge and interests configurations and coordination mechanisms. The implications of Part II for the design of coordination structures is that certain states of knowledge and structures of interests "eliminate" certain coordination mechanisms from the feasible set. Therefore the link can be expressed as a set of "*coordination failures*" conditions.[1] Some combinations of these conditions are easier to handle – that is they are compatible with a wider set of mechanisms – eventually all. For example: almost any mechanism can coordinate a small numbers of actors, holding simple codifiable knowledge and homogeneous preferences. It is just a matter of avoiding redundant communication costs, if

---

Box II.6
A garbage can problem

Mr Frank Belts, Administrator of the Giuseppe Verdi Residence on 37th Street, was facing a serious problem: the new rules set by City Hall on recycling imposed a strict discipline and a tight control on all the families and residencies in town.

Each residence was expected to put out garbage after previously sorting it into five different categories: black bags for wet compost, grey bags for glass, white bags for paper, reds bag for plastic, and green bags for all other garbage. Residences that put out paper, for example, mixed in with the compost garbage would receive a $300 fine for each bag if caught.

Mr Belts had therefore intelligently set up an area within the court where the sorting could take place and where families could find different containers for each type of garbage. Unfortunately though, families did not sort the garbage correctly: one free rider had in fact not done his or her job. The result was a hunt for the lazy one, which led to the concierge threatening to quit: "I am not a detective!" he complained.

Giuseppe Verdi was a nice building complex set in a very green area; it consisted of six buildings of five stories each and four apartments per floor. There was a central receiving area where the concierge worked sorting mail and attending to the daily responsibilities of managing an apartment complex. The recycling policy was perceived in very different ways by the families. There were, for example, large families who employed maids, so the sorting not only took some time but was also assigned to people whom the families would have to check. There were also single people living in the residence: in their case the sorting would not take too much time, except that they were often away from home. Basically, except for a few tidy senior citizens, the majority of families could have been perfect "suspects."

Mr Belts wondered if the guilty parties could be caught red-handed, or if there was another solution, or perhaps the town had imposed a rule that could never be applied.

Source: By Ferdinando Pennarola.

they are relevant. Other combinations are very difficult to govern, the set of feasible mechanisms shrinks – eventually to a void set. The coordination puzzle decribed in Box II.6 is a basis for discussing what these condi- tions are and how to get out of them (Blend mechanisms? Tolerate control losses? Modify some parameters – cost/benefit perceptions, information available to the different actors?).

Part III

Forms of Organization

....

Introduction to Part III

A Definition of Organization Form

· ·

The last part of this volume is concerned with the analysis, explanation, and design of organizational forms. The problem is addressed on the basis of an integration of the main models of organization analysis and design in a unitary and more general framework. This overall approach is presented in Chapter 8, which is dedicated to the definition and explanation of the key variables that will be used in all the following chapters. The next chapters confront design and assessment issues at three different levels: Chapters 9 and 10 examine the organization of human resources and work relations. Chapter 9 focuses on the systems of performance evaluation, reward, and governance of mobility that combine work services with those provided by other resources (technical and financial). Chapter 10 deals with the forms of organization of work, focusing on the models of division of labor and on the coordination mechanisms among jobs held by individuals or groups. Chapter 11 deals with organization forms at the firm level, addressing the design of boundaries and coordination mechanisms among the firm's organizational sub-units. Chapter 12 considers the assessment of organization forms at an even more macro level, that of the boundaries and coordination mechanisms among firms.

Despite the peculiarity and the specific nature of the tools that each of these levels of analysis requires, the scheme of analysis shown in Chapter 8 is applicable at all of the various levels. Each chapter in Part III will provide two essential elements, although not always explained in the same order: a *procedure* for *finding* (devising, constructing, engineering) solutions that are *effective, efficient, and fair*; and a *substantive assessment* of which forms are superior in what circumstances within a given portfolio of known organization solutions. *All "organization forms" are described as configurations of rights and obligations – rights and obligations of action, decision, control, and ownership – and of coordination mechanisms among actors holding different rights.*

Both the definition of an organization form as a configuration of rights and coordination mechanisms, and the distinction between design as a search for forms and design as the evaluation of forms, are crucial for realizing the type of integration between different perspectives sought in this book. In fact, a difference between the organization design approaches prevailing in organizational and economic models respectively is *the focus on the heuristic search for superior solutions in the organization theory and strategy tradition, and on optimizing the comparative evaluation of given structural alternatives in the organizational economics tradition.*[1]

Chapter 8

The Configuration of Organization: A Generalized Model

In this chapter we develop an approach to the analysis and the evaluation of organization forms that is sufficiently general to encompass the main propositions from the main corroborated theories in the field. To do this, we present and discuss the main variables which have been found to systematically affect economic performance through the organizational forms adopted. This approach will allow us to see how many of the more widely known and taught propositions in the field of organizational design can be understood as particular cases valid under particular circumstances.

This approach to organizational analysis can be defined *enlarged* or *generalized* primarily because of the effort to integrate various existing analysis and assessment models The list of design variables used in this chapter includes factors highlighted by different models, eliminating overlaps and showing the effects of interaction between variables where they are relevant.

It is enlarged, moreover, because it takes seriously the fact that the design of organization is often (1) an unstructured problem, and (2) a problem characterized by significant conflicts among the interests of different actors.

The first condition implies that the process of deciding among organization forms consists of more than a calculation of costs and benefits of known organizational forms; a prior step normally consists in heuristic processes of search for combinations of resources, activities, and structural alternatives which might prove to be convenient. In most existing approaches, organization design is considered as the choice among *given types of structures* for governing a given type of activity and relation. However, this approach to the analysis of organizational forms ignores the opportunity to evaluate the extent to which the set of current activities may be inefficient with respect to the resources from which they are derived and to the relations of interdependence that link these resources. This type of inefficiency would generate high organizational costs whatever coordination mechanisms were chosen to manage the relationships between the activities.[1] In addition, the *construction of structural alternatives that are specifically tailored for governing the particular combinations of resources and activities may be more important than the comparative assessment of which "standard" organizational "form" is superior in the circumstances.*

The second condition implies processes of negotiations between actors with different interests about which, among the identified alternatives, would be relatively superior. In this way, the approach presented here aims at overcoming two opposing limitations of the existing models of organizational analysis.

For, on the one hand, there are models that maintain the capacity to prescribe one or more efficient or effective solutions but at the price of concealing the indeterminacy of the problem and the conflicts about the solutions to adopt;[2] and on the other hand there are models that highlight both problems but eschew prescribing one or more organizational solutions that are effective, efficient, and fair.[3]

Another sense in which the model proposed in this chapter is generalized is that the procedures and propositions of analysis and design are abstract enough to be *independent of the particular level of analysis chosen (micro, meso, or macro)*. In other words, it will be shown how most of the variables and procedures of analysis are applicable at the level of job design and the microstructure, at the level of the internal macrostructure of a firm, and at the level of the design of efficient boundaries and integration mechanisms among firms.

This chapter will thus require the effort by the reader to think at various levels of analysis: in concrete terms this could require a focus on the most elementary micro-activities (such as attaching one prefabricated piece to a passing automobile frame on an assembly line), or a focus on more aggregated macro-activities (for example, under what conditions is it efficient for two firms to merge or to remain divided, and what coordination mechanisms should they use?).

The benefits of this effort at abstraction can be seen in terms of saving cognitive time at interpreting different phenomena: we hope that the model offers a clear understanding of a few essential interpretative keys that open many doors. The organizational literature offers a great variety of concepts and similar variables, in part overlapping and as a whole certainly redundant, to respond to the same

basic problems – how do we assign a collection of rights of action, decision, control, and ownership on activities and resources to actors (or why they are effectively assigned in certain ways), and how do we manage the relationships of interdependence so as to obtain a coordinated result (or why they are effectively coordinated in certain ways)? In this chapter these variables are reduced to a manageable set of actors *that, taken together, are necessary and sufficient to explain and predict the main observed organization forms as well as to design new and original ones.* It should be stressed that no single variable can be properly used for actually designing anything; this can only be done by sets of variables – as shown in subsequent substantive chapters. Therefore the logic of this chapter is that of a "partial analysis" of the direction in which each variable affects organizational solutions, holding every other variable constant.[4] The key variables and the general logic of the chapter are outlined in Figure 8.1.

ACTORS, RESOURCES, AND ACTIVITIES

Resources and activities

Resources are the potential for action that can generate different streams of services (Penrose 1959). Resources are normally structured as discrete entities, or as bundles of possible services, that are much broader than the particular use that might have originated the development of the specific resource. There are many ways to use a particular machine or instrument, especially very flexible tools such as a hammer, just as there are many ways to use the competence and energies of a person.[5]

This factor helps us distinguish between resources that are more specialized and therefore capable of furnishing a more restricted set of activities, and resources that are more

Key variables

- Economies of specialization, of scale and scope, of complementarity
- Uncertainty and interdependence
- Unsubstitutability and value of resources
- Structure of interests

Organizational configurations

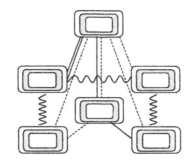

- Nexus of unit boundaries
- Nexus of coordination mechanisms

Evaluation parameters

- Effectiveness
- Efficiency
- Equity

Figure 8.1 Configurating organization: a general framework

flexible and polyvalent. Different potentials and paths of evolution and the growth of firm activities can be derived from the choice of reducing cost and creating value based on the specialization of resources on single activities (*economies of specialization* and *scale*), or based on the full utilization of the array of capacities of the firm's resources on many activities (*economies of scope*), or based on the joint application of complementary resources to a single activity (*complementarity advantages*). These dimensions or variables will be defined and illustrated below, focusing on their (partial) effect on the efficiency and effectiveness of various organizational solutions.

Resources and actors

Further, the notion of the firm as a collection of resources highlights another important distinction – between *resources* and *actors*. A single physical or legal person or an organizational unit can "possess" many types of resources. In addition, the nature and the intensity of that possession of or control over resources can and must be clarified in terms of the bundle of rights to which an actor has title. *The design of organizational units can therefore be seen as the allocation of these rights, including the right to use resources, the right to make decisions, the right to monitor activities, the right to appropriate the residual economic results derived from their economic use, and the right to transfer the above rights to other actors.*[6] Figure 8.2 visualizes the basic distinction and relationship between the notions of actor, resource, and activity.

Human, technical, and financial resources

The centrality of the concept of resources makes it necessary to distinguish between different types of resources with different organizational implications. A theoretically relevant distinction between resources is based on the different type of relationship that a resource can have with actors and activities respectively. The frequent distinction between human and social resources, technological resources, and financial resources can be justified on this ground, because these classes of resources are linked to actors on the one hand and to activities on the other in different ways, thereby entailing different implications for organization design.

*Human resource*s are primarily constituted

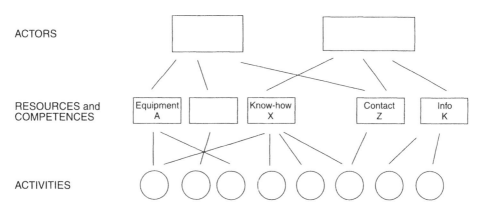

Figure 8.2 Actors, resources, and activities

by collections of *competences* (Chapter 2). *Human resources should not be identified with people – who are actors possessing those resources and allocating them according to preference.* The extent to which human resources can be separated from the actors that possess them by right or by fact, and the extent to which it is possible to completely define property rights over this type of resource (Barzel 1989) are very important design variables in the organization of work (Chapters 9 and 10). Therefore, the analysis and the design of work relationships must rely on some peculiar hypotheses with respect to those applicable to other types of resources.

Technical resources are machine embodied energy and knowledge. Many early studies on technology and its relationship with work and organization have stressed the function of substitution for, and amplification of, human energy and activity (Bright 1958). Current conceptions have stressed the growing import-ance of knowledge as a source of perform-ance, and of technology as reified knowledge (Dosi *et al.* 1990; Cantwell 1998a, b).

If technologies are conceived as forms of knowledge and competence, the analytical dimensions relative to knowledge should be applicable to both human resources and technical resources. We can speak of human or technical assets that are more or less spe-cific to a use or user, more or less specialized, more or less complex. Adopted technologies will influence the degree of specificity, special-ization, and complexity of the comple-mentary human intervention (Bright 1958). On the other hand – if technology does con-strain the feasible organizational solutions – one cannot predict efficient and effective organizational solutions exclusively on the basis of adopted technology (Trist *et al.* 1963; Williamson 1980). For, as the distinction between resources and activities should clar-ify, *technical resources are compatible with various configurations of activity, and in turn each configuration of activities is usually com-patible with more than one effective organiza-tion structure.*

Financial resources are those most independent of specific uses and specific act-ors. To that extent, they are the type of resources that are most easily transferable. However, the allocation of financial resources to the highest and best uses requires informa-tion that might not be easily available, and in this case it contributes in creating needs for complex coordination and decision mechan-isms (Chapters 11 and 12). For this reason,

223

the relationship between financial resources and their possible uses can contribute to explaining organizational configurations, and, in particular, the diversification and growth of the firm.

Inter-actor relations

The variables hitherto introduced have to do with the relations between resources, activities, and actors. Further organization design problems regard the coordination between different actors, endowed with given resources and performing given activities. As known from Part II the coordination of these relationships can be achieved through different means, involving different types of *exchange and sharing of information, decision and property rights.* In designing these coordination mechanisms, *the variables* of *information complexity* and *conflict of interests* have a role that is as important as that of economies of scale, specialization, and scope (Thompson 1967; Williamson 1980; Conclusion Part II).

Let us turn to define all these key variables.

ORGANIZATIONAL ANALYSIS AND DESIGN VARIABLES

Economies of specialization

Adam Smith long ago and vividly described the advantages of the division of labor among different actors, or their *specialization,* as reported in Box 8.1. The phenomenon documented by Smith is that of the spectacular increase in productivity that one can obtain through the specialization of workers in more and more focused activities to the point where they are no longer technically divisible. Below we discuss the sources of that increase in productivity.

In-depth learning

The great motor of economies of specialization is *learning by deepening* competence. The focus on an activity based on a single technique and its repetition trains the worker to perform that technique better. One discovers all the "tricks of the trade" building a repertoire of effective and efficient work procedures that permit one to solve production problems in order to obtain the best results in the shortest time without spending further time on analysis and decision-making. But there is more. The processes of discovery and growth of knowledge are never limited. To that extent, learning may sustain technical improvement and *economies of experience* over time indefinitely. The complexity of the competences required in the activities reinforce this effect. The more difficult activities are, the longer the learning cycle required to master them, the greater the importance of specialization and experience. Where activities are very difficult, it is unlikely that a single person, a group of people, or even a firm, who succeed in mastering that set will be capable of performing equally well in another set of activities. A high division of labor and specialization, therefore, does not necessarily imply the "deskilling" and job-impoverishment with which it has been associated in the so-called "Fordist" or "Taylorist" applications of specialization in mass production industries. Highly specialized *and* professionalized forms of organization of work are common in modern economies (Chapter 10).

The economies generated by the division of labor do not derive exclusively from the process of learning relevant techniques, but also from the learning and the development of cultural traits, cognitive, and emotional orientations that sustain performance in that activity (Lawrence and Lorsch 1967; Chapters 2

Box 8.1
Smith on specialization

To take an example, therefore, from a very trifling manufacture, but one in which the division of labor has been very often taken notice of, the trade of the pin-maker, a workman not educated to this business (which the division of labor has rendered a distinct trade), nor acquainted with the use of the machinery employed in it (to the invention of which the same division of labor has probably given occasion), could scarce, perhaps, with his utmost industry, make one pin a day, and certainly could not make twenty. But in the way in which this business is now carried on, not only the whole work is a peculiar trade, but it is divided into a number of branches, of which the greater part are likewise peculiar trades. One man draws out the wire, another straightens it, a third cuts it, a fourth points it, a fifth grinds it at the top for receiving the head; to make the head requires two or three distinct operations; to put it on, is a peculiar business, to whiten the pins is another; it is even a trade by itself to put them into the paper; and the important business of making a pin is, in this manner, divided into about eighteen distinct operations, which, in some manufactories, are all performed by distinct hands, though in others the same man will sometimes perform two or three of them. I have seen a small manufactory of this kind where ten men only were employed, and where some of them consequently performed two or three distinct operations. But though they were very poor, and therefore but indifferently accommodated with the necessary machinery, they could, when they exerted themselves, make among them about twelve pounds of pins in a day. There are in a pound upwards of four thousand pins of a middling size. Those ten persons, therefore, could make among them upwards of forty-eight thousand pins in a day. Each person, therefore, making a tenth part of forty-eight thousand pins, might be considered as making four thousand eight hundred pins in a day. But if they had all wrought separately and independently, and without any of them having been educated to this particular business, they certainly could not each of them have made twenty, perhaps not one pin in a day; that is, certainly, not the two hundred and fortieth, perhaps not the four thousand eight hundredth part of what they are at present capable of performing, in consequence of a proper division and combination of their different operations.

Source: Smith (1776).

and 7). For example, in a firm, the division of labor between those who produce and those who sell is not only a function of the technical differences that characterize the two types of activity. The production activities usually require and generate an allocation of attention, interest, and even a passion for the details, for the data, for ingenious and optimal solutions. Production activities also require and generate an orientation to short-term results and an adverse attitude toward risk. In contrast, sales activities usually require and generate strong orientation toward people and relationships, tolerance and acceptance of different mentalities and a plurality of solutions, an orientation toward medium-term results, less risk-averse attitudes and the capacity to confront and manage uncertainty. These specialized orientations are efficient in the performance of different work activities, and once formed in a particular person, they can produce *diseconomies of variety*. Although a variety of different *techniques* can be learned by one individual, it is increasingly difficult for one individual to acquire more than one *mentality*.

Specialized equipment

Economies of specialization are not generated exclusively from the division of labor and the focus on a technique by human resources, but also thanks to the specialization of technological resources. Machines, as well as humans, can be specialized. We need only think of the productivity gains caused by the change from universal tools (such as the hammer) to machines dedicated to a particular class of operations (such as the lathe), and then to machines specialized for only one type of transformation process and one output (such as an automatic assembly line).

Stability

For both human and technical resources, the great limit to specialization is the lack of *flexibility*, i.e. the inability to adapt to changing needs and demand. Flexibility implies, in fact, the opposite of specialization: generalism, the redundancy of competence with respect to the activity currently being performed, and the polyvalence of resources. A specialized economic actor is an actor exposed to risk; he "bets" on an activity and invest in resources that limit his capacity to become reconverted. He or she will win the bet only if the state of the future world remains favorable to the activities that can be performed with those resources – that is, if other actors demand those activities (Hannan

and Freeman 1977). As a consequence, even if there are economies of specialization in an activity, the opportunity to realize them and the incentives for actors to specialize in them depend also on other factors, such as the uncertainty of the demand for that type of activity. The advantages of specialization will be actually captured only if we can see a stable demand for that type of activity, or at least a demand that is cyclically and frequently favorable (Hannan and Freeman 1977).

Finally, the mere presence of economies of specialization should not automatically lead one to adopt an organization form based on a massive division of labor, for another reason too – the effect of other key variables on the degree of and type of division of labor that is effective and efficient, among which are the *interdependences* among activities (which is often the most important rival variable). The more activities are specialized and the more they are interdependent, the more they need to be coordinated.

Economies of scale

One of the factors traditionally considered most important for the explanation of the growth of the main unit of economic action (the firm) is the presence of economies of scale. Economies of scale are defined as the reduction of unitary costs of production of goods or services as the scale at which production factors are employed increases. The presence of economies of scale is therefore considered a factor in the expansion of the boundaries of productive units. In Box 8.2 Chandler describes the role of economies of scale in the concentration of the petroleum industry.

It makes sense to speak of economies of scale with reference not only to processes of physical or material production, but also to processes of transformation of symbols and

Box 8.2
Chandler on scale

In 1882 the Standard Oil alliance formed the Standard Oil Trust. (Its successor, Exxon, is still the world's largest oil company.) The purpose was not to obtain control over the industry's output: the alliance, a loose federation of forty companies, each with its own legal and administrative identity but tied to John D. Rockefeller's Standard Oil Company through interchange of stock and other financial devices, already had a monopoly. At the time, in fact, the members of the alliance produced 90 percent of America's output of kerosene. Instead, the Standard Oil Trust was formed to provide a legal instrument to rationalize the industry and exploit economies of scale more fully. The trust provided the essential legal means to create a central or corporate office that could do two things. First, it could reorganize the processes of production by shutting down some refineries, reshaping others, and building new ones. Second, it could coordinate the flow of materials, not only through the several refineries, but from the oil fields to the refineries and from the refineries to the consumers.

The resulting rationalization made it possible to concentrate close to a quarter of the world's production of kerosene in three refineries, each with an average daily charging capacity of 6,500 barrels, with two-thirds of their product going to overseas markets. (At this time, refined petroleum products were by far the nation's largest non-agricultural export.) Imagine the *diseconomies* of scale (the increase in unit costs) that would result from placing close to one-fourth of the world's production of shoes, textiles, or lumber into three factories or mills! In those instances the administrative coordination of the operation of miles and miles of machines and the huge concentration of labor needed to operate those machines would make neither economic nor social sense.

The reorganization of the trust's refining facilities brought a sharp reduction in the average cost of producing a gallon of kerosene. In 1880 the average cost at plants with a daily capacity of 1,500 to 2,000 barrels was approximately 2.5¢ per gallon. By 1885, according to the industry's most authoritative history, the average cost for plants of that size had been reduced to 1.5¢. Data compiled for the trust's manufacturing committee showed that the average cost of processing a gallon of crude for all its works had dropped from 0.534¢ in 1884 to 0.452¢ in 1885 with a resulting increase in profit margin from 0.530¢ in 1884 to 1.003¢ in 1885. (That profit margin was the core of four of the world's largest industrial fortunes, those of the Rockefellers, Harknesses, Paynes, and Flaglers.) As these averages indicate, the unit costs of the giant refineries were far below those of any competitor. To maintain this cost advantage, however, these large refineries had to have a continuing daily throughput of 5,000 to 6,500 barrels, or a threefold to fourfold increase over the earlier daily flow of 1,500 to 2,000 barrels, with resulting increases in transactions handled and in the complexity of coordinating the flow of materials through the processes of production and distribution.

Source: Chandler (1990).

the production of "immaterial" outputs. For example, if the cost of supplying an insurance service decreases as the company combines the risks of many insured parties, one can say that there are economies of scale. Alternatively, if the activity of administration in small firms does not saturate the capacity of the administrative structure that is necessary to perform them, more small firms can entrust their administration to a firm specialized in it or to an industry association that performs that activity for all. In this case, too, one can say that there are advantages in terms of economies of scale.

Alternatively, one can speak of economies of scale at a more micro level, with reference to human resources, and not only technical ones. This is the case when there are lower costs obtained by saturating the capacity of a person with specialized capacity in a given activity (e.g. a worker specialized on a particular type of lathe), instead of leaving that resource partially unused because the volume of activity is not sufficient to keep that person busy full time.

Although it is possible to speak of economies of scale in administration, or in the supply of services or in the use of know-how, usually economies of scale are more evident in capital-intensive rather than in labor-intensive transformation processes. For example, economies of scale are more intense in manufacturing and extractive industries rather than in service industries; within services, they are more manifest in sales, distribution, and transport, but less so in personal services; in the production of standardized goods and services (such as household appliances and bank accounts) and less so with non-standardizable goods and services (such as jewelry or management consulting). To find out why this is so, we next discuss the sources of economies of scale.

Discontinuities and inseparabilities

Resources often come in discrete entities. This implies that they cannot be varied in continuous ways, that there may be "discontinuities" in technical as well as human resources (Marschack 1965). For example, steel lamination equipment has a certain minimum efficient size and requires a certain amount of production in order to be fully utilized. Furthermore, if we consider the link between the melting and lamination phases in steel-working, we note that these are technically inseparable because it is not known how to transport melted steel. In this case, inseparabilities are truly "technical" because they derive from a lack of knowledge about how to conduct separate processes. In other cases, the separation might be technically possible, but would raise the costs of production to extremely high levels. As argued by Penrose and shown by Chandler with reference to the petroleum sector, the full utilization of technically connected resources, with different minimum efficient size, makes it convenient to dimension production according to the scale required by the most discontinuous technologies. In that way, economies of scale are realized at the level of the entire production cycle. Hence, the higher the costs of dividing activities and creating stocks are, the more there are incentives to integrate activities.

This observation allows us to specify that economies of scale can occur at different levels: in particular, they can be specific to a production phase or manifested over a series of phases. This distinction is important for the organization of the firm. In fact, the existence of economies of scale over several phases generates incentives to the integration of several phases in one organizational unit, or at least the strong coordination of the activities of different units through planning mechanisms, as in the petroleum chain case.

On the other hand, the existence of economies of scale internal to one phase or activity generates incentives to the expansion of that activity as a specialized activity, that can reach high volumes thanks to the fact of being able to serve many other organizational units. To that extent, economies of scale specific to a single activity or phase favor the division of labor among organizational units rather than their integration. For example, in contrast to the petroleum industry, in the textile industry there is a high vertical disintegration among firms. Spinning and carding, sewing and distribution, are activities that are not only technically separable but characterized by internal economies of scale. The output of each phase is stockable. Each activity tends to be performed not only by different specialized workers but often even by different firms that buy and sell to various other firms upstream and downstream in the value chain (Mariotti and Cainarca 1986).

Market size

The presence and configuration of economies of scale contribute in explaining – but it is neither necessary nor sufficient to predict – the type and degree of division of labor among actors, and firms in particular. For example, to say that the activities in the textile cycle can be efficiently allocated to different actors who realize economies of scale, implies that such actors can also efficiently transfer their respective inputs and outputs across their boundaries. The variables influencing transferability do not coincide with those influencing economies of scale, however, and the level of transferability depends on the type of coordination mechanism used for the transfer, as illustrated below.

Furthermore, like each type of economy generated by technology and each value generated by competence, economies of scale can be realized only if the economic conditions permit it. In the case of economies of scale, it is necessary that market size be sufficient to absorb the output of production on a vast scale. As economic history shows, the economies of scale realizable in sectors such as automobiles, household appliances, oil refining and large-scale distribution were only realized in steps with the rising level of wealth and the growth in consumption capacity.

Economies of scope

It could happen that the unitary cost of production diminishes, the more types of goods and services are produced jointly, utilizing the same resources (equipment, know-how, human resources with certain competences). Economies of this type are defined as economies of *scope*. If there are economies of scope, the sum of unitary costs of production of a good P1 (if this is the only output of the resources employed) plus those of production of a good P2 (also produced separately) is greater than the sum of the costs of the production of P1 and P2 produced together using the same resources. The presence of economies of scope is therefore considered one of the factors able to explain the *diversification* of a production unit. As occurs for specialization and scale economies, not all types of activity present economies of scope. What are the sources of these productive synergies? When do they occur?

"In-breadth" learning

As for specialization, learning is fundamental in the generation of economies of scope. However, in the first case, it is a learning of means and methods that are better in one type of activity (we have said that economies of specialization imply "in-depth learning" and may result in process innovations). Instead, in the case of economies of scope, learning is oriented toward discovering which other activities could be undertaken synergistically with those already being performed, often toward inventing new activities that allow a better utilization of resources (we can therefore say that economies of scope involve *"in-breadth" learning* and typically result in product innovations).

Excess (slack) resources

The opportunity to use certain resources in the production of more than one good or service springs from the fact that the technical and human resources that are applied to an activity, or that have been accumulated in time for that activity, are or become redundant with respect to that particular use (Penrose 1959). Teece (1981) describes, for example, how the technologies and the know-how developed in the activity of oil discovery grew beyond the specific needs of their original field of application, became precious and common factors of production for a vast array of activities in the field of energy research (see Box 8.3).

Another common example of how economies of scope can lead to diversification is that of activities undertaken as auxiliary, or in service to the main business activity, in which the competences and resources accumulated prove to be sufficient to develop that area into an autonomous business one. For example, IBM, as a sideline to its main activities of computer manufacturer, took advantage of its competence in electronics to develop a telecommunications network that connects practically every country in the world. Although this was done originally in order to manage their own affiliates better, it turned out to be a new and very profitable line of business – renting this channel of communication to other firms.

Core resources and competences

These reflections lead us to identify a second characteristic of technical and human resources that can provide opportunities for economies of scope. Economies of scope do not exclude the presence of economies of specialization in a single activity. Rather, normally it is exactly the learning in one activity that permits the accumulation of resources and competences that are applicable in other activities. However, it is important that the technology, the know-how, the competence have some components that are relatively universal, flexible, basic, and potentially common to many activities. For example, Rosenberg (1976) describes some typical development trajectories of firms that were technologically advanced in the nineteenth century, who passed from the production of firearms, to sewing machines, to bicycles, and then automobiles. What advantages, opportunities, and logic can explain such an evolutionary path? As Rosenberg highlights, there was a know-how, then highly innovative, that was accumulated by those firms and that could be applied in all those sectors involving components such as the techniques of reduction of friction (for example, ball bearings) and the techniques of metalworking.

This type of competence with multiple potential areas of application, is usually defined as *"core"* in the resource based theory of the firm (after the fortunate contribution by Prahalad and Hamler 1990).

Box 8.3
Economies of scope in
energy research

The task to be confronted now is the analysis of the extent to which petroleum industry technology is relevant to the production of alternate fuels. In locating alternate fuel sources such as coal, oil, shale, and uranium, exploration techniques developed by the petroleum industry are often useful. Mineral deposits are found in sedimentary formations similar to oil- and gas-bearing formations, so that geological and geophysical expertise is valuable. For example, geophysical techniques developed for oil and gas exploration (such as wire-line and well logging) have been directly applied to the location and definition of deposits of lignite coal. Similarly, uranium deposits can be identified by classical techniques used in oil exploration. In exploring for geothermal energy, sources can be located and identified using geophysical techniques such as electromagnetic, seismic, and gravity methods. Computer-assisted evaluation of geophysical data, pioneered by the oil industry, can facilitate the interpretation of geopressure levels and other data. Tying the results of mineral exploration together is a comprehensive data bank accumulated by oil companies from their exploration activities, including data highly valuable to the search for alternate fuels.

In the field of resource extraction the same techniques are also used in the recovery of a number of different fuels. For instance, technology developed in the petroleum industry can be used directly or with modification in geothermal energy recovery and for *in situ* production of shale oil and coal fluids. Dry rock geothermal energy recovery, now being investigated as a potential production technology, will require extensive utilization of petroleum technology, including hydraulic fracturing and sophisticated directional drilling. *In situ* coal or oil shale production, requiring a large number of closely spaced wells, draws largely on well drilling experience derived from petroleum exploration and development. In addition, the operation of an *in situ* process requires detailed knowledge of fluid and heat flow that is common to the extensive reservoir engineering knowledge developed in connection with oil production.

Similar examples abound in the area of resource processing. Coal conservation and shale oil recovery can involve extensive application of conventional refining technology and extensions of existing processes, so much so that in many respects a coal or shale oil conversion plant may have a number of features in common with an oil refinery.

High temperature and pressure treatment of hydrocarbon fluids, catalytic processing of hydrocarbons, fluidized bed design and hydrogenation processes, as well as conventional separation processes have applications common to oil processing in coal conversion and shale oil recovery. Indeed, many scientists believe that developments in the science of catalysis – a science crucial to petroleum refining – will be the key to whether gasoline can be made economically from coal. Also worthy of special mention is the considerable technology developed for treating and handling liquid waste streams. Especially important is the removal of sulphur, a problem in the forefront of many current developments in petroleum technology. The significance of these generic similarities becomes even more apparent when attention is focused on the specific fuels identified below.

In the later stages of the nuclear fuel cycle, technological complementarities with the petroleum industry are apparent. Conversion of ore to uranium oxide, uranium hexafluoride, or uranium metal, and the processing of spent fuel utilizes processing techniques such as solvent extraction, distillation, and physical separation similar to those encountered in petroleum processing.

Source: Teece (1980a).

Appropriability

Finally, also for economies of scope, just as for economies of specialization and scale, it is not sufficient that technical conditions produce a reduction in costs; these savings must be transformed into economies that produce income for the firms involved. One specific limit to economies of scope due to innovation is constituted by the difficult appropriability of common or basic resources. For example, the possession of know-how related to the reduction of friction in wheeled mechanisms might have been a proprietary or exclusive know-how in the nineteenth century, but it would not be so today, because such know-how has become widely diffused, eventually it has become a public good. In effect, the more difficult it is to define or defend property rights over techniques developed in one activity, the less the developer is able to sustain a competitive advantage over imitators in the development of new applications. The history of management is full of tragic legends of firms that developed very useful and versatile techniques that were easily imitated (e.g. photocopying by 3M that was overtaken by better development and distribution carried out by Xerox).

But even appropriability is not a sufficient condition for integration. The resources must not be easily transferable across the boundaries of organizational units (Teece 1980a). For example, in the case of a firm owning resources such as land, an informational network, patentable knowledge, the partial use of

unutilized capacity of the resource can be sold. Only if the resources are hard to transfer to other actors can economies of scope actually lead to organizational consequences that often are attributed to them – that is, the growth by diversification of the economics actor. This leads us to examine other key variables that have a fundamental impact on the transferability of resources employed in economic activities: the specificity of resources (and more generally their unsubstitutability) and the information complexity of the activity. Before addressing them, let us deal with another feature of resources that sustains the creation of value through new activities rather than just the reduction of costs in existing activities – the complementarity of resources

Complementarity

Most often, resources can generate flows of valuable activities in combination with other resources, rather than in a stand-alone fashion. If this is the case, these resources can be called complementary.

The importance of this variable has recently rediscovered to explain the great expansion of alliances between firms with different competences – alliances oriented to research, development, and production of new products based on complementary resources (Richardson 1972; Alter and Hage 1993). Complementarity between competences is equally important and analogous in its effects within firms. For example, it has been long known that product innovation can and must be sustained by a complementary application of the competences from different functional departments within the firm – research and development, production, sales and marketing, realized in inter-departmental work groups (Lawrence and Lorsch 1967).

Whatever the level of analysis – between or within firms – the search for complementarities among resources can be made systematic with the help of analytic supports forcing and sustaining an evaluation of the relationships between each resource and any other, and between resources and activities. One possibility for conducting this type of analysis is to apply some methods of relational analysis such as constructing matrixes of relationships between resources. A resource-resource matrix in which the cells are filled out by the activities that can be conducted by using those resources is represented in Figure 8.3.

This type of relational analyzes may help in translating into an empirical and design-oriented language some of the research questions that may be drawn from a resource based view of firms and other economic perspectives: Which are the principal resources and competences present in an action system? Which are the activities that currently require each type of resource? What

combinations and complementarities among resources are currently exploited? What new activities could more completely exploit the existing resources, either singly or in various combinations? Which new resources, if developed or purchased and applied in combination with the existing resources, could generate outputs of greater value than those already produced, or could produce existing output at lower cost? The matrix offers a framework within which to apply most of the variables illustrated above in responding to the above questions. Economies of specialization, scale, and scope, are readable in the cells along the diagonal, indicating which and how many activities can be performed using one given resource; or, if activities are attributed a value, the value of the activity obtainable by the aggregation of resources of the same type. Outside of the diagonal one can find which and how many activities can be performed by combining different resources. In Box 8.4, it is shown how a resource matrix can be constructed and how it can help in the generation and organizational partitioning of activities.

Unsubstitutability of resources

Organizational economists have stressed the impact of assets specificity and unsubstitutability on efficient organizational solutions.

Among the "defendable" sources of unsubstitutability (or monopoly) there are the *natural possession of rare and valuable resources* (such as sports talent); the relationship between *market size and the minimal efficient size of firms* in that market; *the innovation and differentiation of outputs*; and the *specificity of resources invested in a relation*.

All these forms of resource unsubstitutability create *rents* – economic return exceeding those realizable in alternative uses – (Barney 1991); in addition there are their

	R_1	R_2	$\cdots$	R_k	$\rightarrow$ R_n
R_1	A_1 A_5 A_7	?	$\cdots$	A_{31} A_4	
R_2		A_2	$\cdots$	A_2, A_5 A_8	A_8
			$\cdots$	$\cdots$	
R_K				?	
$\downarrow$ R_n		A_n			

Figure 8.3 Resource–resource matrix

Box 8.4
Resources and activities at
Mobil Green

Mobil Green produces and markets particle board, a type of intermediate good that is widely used in the furniture and building industries. The boards are produced with very complex and expensive equipment operating in continuous cycles. Production is done in various phases. The raw material, wood, comes from cutting (in limited amounts) and recycling actual timber. The wood purchased by Mobil Green is stocked in large open-air areas waiting to be shredded (i.e. reduced to chips of no more than 3–4 millimetres) and cleaned of residues (metal, paints, etc.). The shredding and cleaning processes are carried out using an electromechanical machine designed by Mobil Green and symbolically called "Dracula." After being cleaned, the wood must be dried to reduce its level of humidity within precise limits; this is done in a large drying machine. The shredded and dried wood is mixed with a special kind of glue so that it can be placed in the molding machines and later pressed at high temperature. During the formation of the layers, the thickness and size of the board are defined (there are various thicknesses and 10 different types of products if we consider length and width). The pressing occurs at a very high temperature, takes only a few minutes, and produces a cauterized surface layer about 5 millimeters thick that is eliminated through a polishing process.

The unfinished board is then either sold as it is or alternatively is subjected to another process called "nobilitation" (finishing). This process involves gluing a special kind of treated paper onto the board; the paper gives it the chosen color or the desired aesthetic effect (there are about one thousand different kinds of paper). The choice of paper is usually made according to fashion trends and obviously follows the specific request of the customer (i.e. the furniture makers). The vast majority of the product sold is finished – only 15 percent of gross sales are accounted for by the sale of unfinished boards.

At Mobil Green the whole process consists of very specific phases as defined in the list below (although not necessarily in the order listed):

A1 Purchase of the raw material (wood)
A2 Purchase of the glue
A15 Purchase of the paper
A3 Shredding of the wood and elimination of residues (metals, paints, etc.)
A4 Drying
A5 Mixing and molding
A6 Pressing
A7 Polishing
A8 Quality control
A9 "Nobilitation" (finishing)
A12 Purchase of supplies for the equipment
A11 Management of sub-contracted work on the equipment
A13 Production planning
A16 Marketing planning
A10 Maintenance
A14 Order receiving and customer service

There are also resources used in the carrying out of the firm's activities. At Mobil Green the following types of resources have been identified.

1   Wood
2   Glue
3   Energy
4   Technological platforms
5   Operational know-how (starting procedure, use and maintenance of the equipment)
6   Knowledge of the finished product
7   Knowledge of the supplier markets
8   Papers
9   Negotiation skills
10 Technological skills
11 Unfinished board
12 "Nobilitated" (finished) board

From the resource/activities matrix it is possible to construct a resource/resource matrix by assuming the resources with shared activities to be related and an activity/activity matrix by defining the activities using the same resources to be related.

Graph representation of the resource matrix (1 = existing relation)

	A1	A2	A3	A4	A5	A6	A7	A8	A9	A10	S11	A12	A13	A14	A15	A16
1			1	1	1	1										
2						1										
3			1	1	1	1	1		1							
4			1	1	1	1	1	1	1	1	1					
5			1	1	1	1	1		1	1	1					
6													1	1	1	1
7								1					1	1		1
8	1	1										1		1		
9									1					1		1
10	1	1										1		1	1	
11										1	1					
12									1				1	1		
13	1	1											1	1		

The resource/resource matrix can be employed in a "generative" way, to discover what new activities can flow out of them. For example, considering that the paper resource is already conveniently available to Mobil Green in large batches, one could think that it could be used for supporting other paper transformation processes, provided that complementary resources are accessible. A case in point would be the impregnation of paper, which could reduce the production and transportation costs of inputs for the finishing phase of board nobilitation conducted by Mobil Green. In addition, it could be eventually possible to sell competitively impregnated paper to producers of other finished goods. A complementary resource would be an impregnation machine. Mobil Green has captured this opportunity through an agreement with a multinational firm specialized in paper impregnation. Mobil Green has made an investment in a machine which can perform the specific activities in which MG is interested. The machine is, however, located under the roof of the multinational, who possess and contribute the relevant specialized technical and commercial know-how and can produce and sell a range of impregnated paper products more economically. The price paid by MG for the impregnation service is conventional and largely inferior to the market price.

Source: By Giuseppe Soda.

generating *transaction costs* (Williamson 1981a) – the costs of searching for partners, costs of negotiation of exchange or co-operation conditions, costs of control that contracts and agreements are respected. Therefore unsubstitutability almost by definition calls for coordination mechanisms other than price- and exit-based exchange. Such other mechanisms, however, depend on other variables (like uncertainty), as well as on the type of rent created.

Is an economic surplus earned a rent due to plain scarcity or is it a rent due to the generation of new value through innovation or combination among specific resources? For example, in the case of market size problems, *external regulation* is generally called for to contain the transaction costs of monopolistic pricing and quality decay for the customers. In the case of innovation and specific investments – leading to output differentiation – rents are a reward without which the necessary investments would not have been made, and reflect a value for customers and external users that should be compared with the eventual costs (Williamson 1987; Chapter 12). Rents deriving from specific investments are particularly diffused and organizationally relevant (Milgrom and Roberts 1992).

Specificity

A resource is said to be specific to a relation – with an activity or other resources – if it generates a higher value in that relationship than in alternative relationships. For example, if a salesman develops a particular relational competence in dealing with a group of clients of the firm in which he is employed, based on personal knowledge and experience, it can be said that his sales competence is "firm specific." If a textile entrepreneur develops a particular know-how that is applicable only for carding activities, it can be said that his competence is "phase-specific" in the production process. If two firms, understood as single actors, develop technical knowledge and relationship capabilities that may be of particular value only within their own reciprocal relationship, it can be said that they have developed partner-specific competences.

The specificity of competences is related but not identical to their specialization. Specialization expresses the degree of the division of labor. A secretary's competence can be fairly unspecialized, to the extent that s/he is able to perform many different office tasks. However, such competence can be very specific to an office, or to an assisted person, if it is not merely the generic competence of a

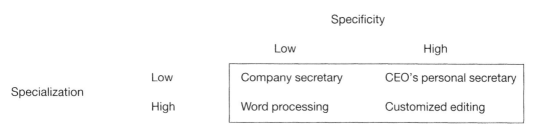

Figure 8.4 Specialized and specific competences

secretary, but also includes knowledge of the particular characteristics of the practices of that office, or the behavioral habits of the people with whom s/he interacts, and the ability to undertake adequate actions in that environment. Since the distinction between specialization and specificity can be confusing, try to generate examples of competences that can be placed in the four squares of a matrix defined by the intersection between high and low specificity and high or low specialization, in addition to the examples that appear in Figure 8.4.

Quasi-rents

Where value is generated by the specific investments of parties in a relation, the appropriable value is lesser or equal to the full rent (Milgrom and Roberts 1992). Therefore, it is called "*quasi-rent*": *the difference between the value created by a resource in a particular relation with respect to the value created in its best alternative relation or use (rent), minus the cost of search for and transfer to these alternative relations.*

Quasi-rents are particularly important in organized action because they are likely to be generated by stable or repeated cooperation itself. Once a relation of cooperation and exchange is started and maintained over time, the relation is likely to become specific (Williamson 1993a). One can imagine this with regard to the supplier of components to a car

manufacturer. Before and in addition to the eventual peculiar traits of competences or components that are valuable in those relations and less so in others, the reciprocal knowledge that is developed by actors – the jargon shared, or else the knowledge of the other party's reliability, administrative procedures, and action or reaction times – makes their resources specific to their relation.

The fair division of rents

To the extent that rents are created by more than one actor in conjunction, there is the problem of how to divide them between the parties that jointly contributed to them.

In general, this is a problem that can be solved and *is* solved through *negotiation* (Chapter 6). The value for each party of the next best uses of its resources – minus the costs of searching for these alternatives and mobilizing the resources for the transfer – provides "reservation prices" that delimit the "zone of agreement" or quasi-rent to be divided. Within it, parties can negotiate on price and other conditions of exchange, so as to expand as far as possible the total value created, and to divide it according to some fairness criterion (e.g. apportioning rents according to parties' relative contributions, if measurable, or to other criteria) (Chapters 2 and 6).

Organizational economists have noted that if an actor were to invest *unilaterally* in assets that are specific to the relationship with one other particular actor, he/she becomes exposed to a risk of having the other expropriate almost all the quasi-rent created by the exchange or common action (Klein *et al.* 1978). For example, a franchisee who unilaterally makes a specific investment to join a distribution chain has a disincentive to leave that chain unless the franchisor reduces the franchisee's income below the level of the potential alternative use of those specific resources (Rubin 1978). The franchisor, knowing this, can reduce the payments to the franchisee to that level, thus expropriating most or all of the surplus from the specificity of the resources used jointly. Box 8.5 reports the famous illustration of the problem by Klein, Crawford, and Alchian.

A possible solution to the problem is that a resource specific to other resources or activities is owned by the same actor owning those other resources, or performing those activities (see the Mobil Green case for an illustration). However, in many cases this "integrated" solution is not adopted, or not adopted in defense toward the opportunistic expropriation of rents. The actual possibilities and convenience of expropriation are in fact often limited by various factors. First, there is often uncertainty about the "reservation price" of a counterpart: the value of the resources of a counterpart in possible alternative agreements with alternative partners is never so easy to judge and even harder to quantify. Second, the size of joint gains: the greater the pie, the less competitive the game. Third,

---

Box 8.5
The printer problem

Imagine a printing press owned and operated by party A. Publisher B buys printing services from party A by leasing his press at a contract rate of $5,500 per day. The amortized fixed cost of the printing press is $4,000 per day and it has a current salvageable value if moved elsewhere of $1,000 (daily rental equivalent). Operating costs are $1,500 and are paid by the printing-press owner, who prints final printed pages for the publisher. Assume also that a second publisher C is willing to offer at most $3,500 for a daily service. The current quasi-rent on the installed machine is $3,000 (= $5,500 − $1,500 − $1,000), the revenue minus operating costs minus salvageable value. However, the daily quasi-rent from publisher B relative to use of the machine for publisher C is only $2,000 (= $5,500 − $3,500). At $5,500 revenue daily from publisher B the press owner would break even on his investment. If the publisher were then able to cut his offer for the press from $5,500 down to almost $3,500, he would still have the press service available to him. He would be appropriating $2,000 of the quasi-rent from the press owner. The $2,000 difference between his prior agreed-to daily rental of $5,500 and the next best revenue available to the press once the machine is purchased and installed is less than the quasi-rent and therefore is potentially appropriable. If no second party were available at the present site, the entire quasi-rent would be subject to threat of appropriation by an unscrupulous or opportunistic publisher.

Source: Klein *et al.* (1978).

the capacity to attract new partners and reputation losses. Therefore, it is not very likely that the user of a specific resource will offer to his/her partner only one dollar more than his/her reservation price (Chapters 2 and 6).

In conclusion, *the presence of specificity and quasi-rents is important, and it is a sufficient cause for the relations to be regulated extensively by negotiation.* Admittedly, this is a movement away from a pure market regime, and may lead to some form of inter-firm alliance (Chapter 12). Instead, it does not seem that the presence of specificity and quasi-rents is in itself sufficient to justify the recourse to the integration of the parties through unified ownership or arrangements close to it.[7] Figure 8.5 summarizes the principal sources of unsubstitutability as relevant to organizational analysis.

Uncertainty

The concept of uncertainty used in organization theory is distinctly broader than that used in classical decision theory, from which it originated and subsequently distanced itself (March and Simon 1958). The distinction in classical decision theory is between situations of *certainty, risk,* and *uncertainty.* In all cases the decision-maker is supposed to be able to list the possible actions and the various scenarios or exogenous conditions. Under certainty, the results of all combinations are known for sure; under risk the value and probability of occurrence of these results can be assessed; and a state of

uncertainty is defined as one in which the actor is not able to estimate probabilities.

The construct of uncertainty that is used in organization studies includes that used in classical decision theory, but it has become broader and broader. Uncertainty is a state of incomplete knowledge, which can regard all the different components of a decision process. Its *sources* can be traced into different types of *information complexity.* It is useful to distinguish among these sources and components because each has distinctive implications for some traits of effective organizational solutions.

Knowledge of the various scenarios

Uncertainty does not regard only the possibility of assigning a probability to a series of events, but also regards the difficulty of identifying a complete list of possible events or scenarios, due to the influence exerted by other contextual factors. For example, when considering the possible situations that might result from an action by the marketing department, one would have to consider also the recent moves of the competition, the contingent needs of the clients, the price of raw materials, the level of quality achieved in production, etc. The list may seldom be exhaustive.

Variability

Variability in these factors, even if identified as such, can also contribute to the level of uncertainty (Williamson 1975). Variability can stem from the more or less stable nature

Figure 8.5 Sources of unsubstitutability with different organizational implications

of the objects or raw materials subject to transformation during the activity, or the more or less stable nature of the transformation processes (Perrow 1967) or by the rate of change and the volatility of the needs of consumers (Hannan and Freeman 1977). For example, registering accounting data is a stable activity, while marketing a new product is a variable activity. Or, the transformation of the competences of human beings is a more uncertain activity than the transformation of wood. Or again, the activities of production and sales in a sector characterized by rapidly changing consumer tastes and competences (such as personal computers) are more variable and uncertain than production and sales activities in a more stable sector such as shelving for offices (at least until "griffed" shelving becomes a status symbol) and so forth.

Knowledge of cause–effect relations

Another component of uncertainty is constituted by the extent to which knowledge about cause–effect relations (action–result relations) is available or should be generated in the process of search. The nature of materials or transformation processes can require problem-solving processes, the production of new knowledge, and the search for more or less innovative solutions. For example, the activities involved in defining and completing an aerospace project are much more uncertain, in this respect, than the activities involved in defining and completing a hydro-electric project. Analogously, the activity of psychiatric care involves a more intense research process than teaching a foreign language to adults (Perrow 1967).

Clarity of preferences

The lack of complete *a priori* knowledge and

the necessity to produce knowledge during decision and action processes can also affect the ends of the actors (Lindblom 1959; Thompson and Tuden 1959; Cohen *et al.* 1976). There can be new fields of activity (or new for the actors) where objectives are set in an experimental or incremental mode; and there are fields in which they never become clear or explicit (Chapter 2).

Observability

A further source of uncertainty derives from the difficulty of observing and evaluating economic actions and consequences even ex post. In other words, with reference to the basic elements in decision processes, uncertainty can appear not only at the levels of information gathering, alternatives, and objectives, but also at the level of the evaluation of actions after they have been taken. It may be difficult to observe resources, actions, results or all these elements. What has been done in a research laboratory yesterday? Could it have been done better? Who has contributed more or less? These might be untestable observational propositions in complex activities.

The extent to which actions, results, or the resources themselves can be known and attributed to identified actors is of great importance for the organization of work and for the nature of contractual relations (Chapters 9 and 10).

Number of elements

A last component of uncertainty derives from "computational complexity" (Simon 1962; Galbraith 1974; Chapter 1). The higher the number of elements and combinations in an activity (number of actors, possible moves, relevant data), the more computationally complex it is. For example, an activity involving sales of an industrial good (e.g. a turbine) is usually more complex than sales of a consumption good (e.g. a cabinet). For, even if both are supposed to be "standard" products, the sale of a turbine involves many more exchange issues and items than simply the discount and the delivery time.

The presence of uncertainty on all these levels has important consequences for the efficient boundaries of economic units and on coordination mechanisms among them.

The possibility of dividing work horizontally and vertically between units (between firms themselves or between internal units) is linked to the clarity of objectives or output sought, and of the means for reaching them. Lack of knowledge on these elements makes the definition of separate property rights problematic.

As to coordination mechanisms (Part II), neither pricing nor voting would be able to deal with most of the sources of uncertainty described in this section. Authority, as well as group and control mechanisms, fails when actions are not observable; agency, when results are poorly observable or it is not known how much action affects them. Norms and rules are effective in conditions of scarce variability.

Figure 8.6 summarizes the principal sources of uncertainty and the basic direction of their effects on effective organization.

Information asymmetry

Further, when we refer to relationships of cooperation or exchange, uncertainty (like unsubstitutability) can generate asymmetric situations, with their own specific organizational implications. For example, it has been seen (Chapter 7) that when one party in an exchange has much more information than other parties on the good or service being exchanged, then not only does market coordination not work well, but also negotiation is not a very attractive alternative (Akerlof 1970; Bazerman 1986). If a party in a prospective exchange is uncertain about the value of the good or service to be exchanged, but the other is not, the informed party may accept the deal only if the "true" value is lower than the settled price (*adverse selection*). After an exchange has taken place, if one party is uncertain about the actions taken by another (unobservability), but the latter knows what the relevant and more convenient actions are for her, then the latter has incentives to take those actions even if otherwise

Computational complexity		Organizational implications
Unknown probabilities	→	Failure of complete plans and complete contracts
Variability		Increasing costs of centralization
Number of elements		Increasing need for formal and technological information supports

Epistemic complexity		Organizational implications
Unknown cause–effect relations	→	Failure of clear division of labor
Unknown possible states of the world		Generalist, high discretion units
Unobservability and unmeasurability of events		Property right sharing
Unclear preferences		

Figure 8.6 Basic effects of the sources of uncertainty on effective organization

agreed (*moral hazard*) (Milgrom and Roberts 1992). Information asymmetries would prevent fruitful exchanges and cooperation events from taking place unless unilateral or even joint decision-making were integrated by other mechanisms, especially norms, rules and conventions, and third party guarantee (Arrow 1963; Karpik 1989).

In conclusion, it should be noted that, as also holds for unsubstitutability, the "conditions of uncertainty" are not inescapable or "given" but are created by actors themselves, in particular through the choice of activities (Tosi *et al.* 1970; Child 1982). For example, the strategic choice between competing on cost or competing on product innovation and differentiation has a great impact on the level of uncertainty that will be faced. Despite the relatively simple technology involved and the mature nature of the markets, the degree of uncertainty faced by a firm producing cookies can be high for firms that strive to innovate their product or distributive channels. The same can be said for the recent revolution in the textile and clothing sector by the fashion houses, that have transformed stable and cyclical activities with few variations into activities with very high uncertainty and volatility.

Forms of interdependence

Interdependence is a very much used variable in economic and organizational models of design. In effect, the need to coordinate economic activities stems from the fact that many of these are "interdependent": the diffused local possession of information and resources and the division of work create opportunities for exchange and cooperation among different activities and actors. Though it is a particularly concise and close predictor of organizational solutions, interdependence is a composite and intermediate variable that

depends in turn on the variables already examined. Four basic types of interdependence, very useful in organization design, can be distinguished as shown in Figure 8.7.[8]

Sequential and reciprocal interdependence

A first fundamental distinction between types of interdependencies comes from the type of link between activities that the resources can imply. Resources can be *exchanged* (implying the physical transfer of resources) or *shared* (implying common or shared use of the same resources (Pfeffer and Salancik 1978). We can call the first type *transactional interdependence*, referring to the "transfer of goods or services through a technically separable interface" (Williamson 1981a). In other words, the activity A generates an output that is transferred as an input to activity B. A good is produced, then transferred to a warehouse, then distributed; or a division or a firm produces components that are transferred to another division or firm for the assembly in a final product (such as a car or a computer component). This is a relatively simple type of interdependence, characterized by a unidirectional flow from A to B, that has also been defined as *sequential* (Thompson 1967). Thompson hypothesized that sequential interdependence could be efficiently regulated through programming mechanisms, implicitly assuming that transfers are subject to time constraints and problems of balancing resource flows and resource utilization in the different stages of activities. Without these implicit additional assumptions, we can observe that sequential interdependence can also be regulated by transfer prices and inventories (Lorsch and Allen 1973; Galbraith 1977).

According to Thompson's initial analysis, transactional interdependence can also be symmetrical: that is, the input of A is the

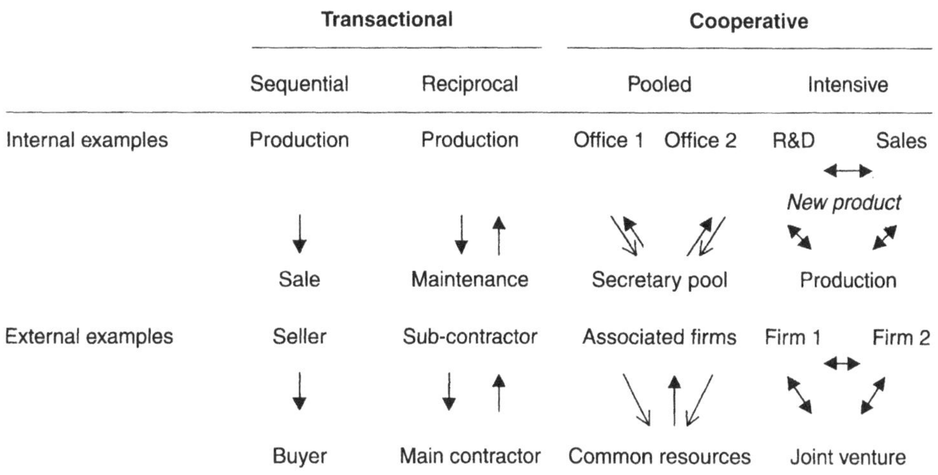

Figure 8.7 Types of interdependence

output of B, and the output of B is the input for A. His example of this is the relationship between maintenance and production. However, one can ask why bidirectional transfers of goods or services create problems of coordination that are qualitatively different from uni-directional transfers? Why cannot the former be regulated through more sophisticated planning or pricing mechanisms? In effect this is what happens in the regulation of many maintenance activities. Whenever these can be anticipated, as in preventive maintenance based on statistical failure rates of components, a mix of activity programs, cost attribution procedures, and spare parts inventory management is usually effectively applied (either in the case of internal maintenance offices or of external maintenance firms). What complicates and makes the effective coordination mechanisms qualitatively different is not the bidirectionality of the relationship per se, but the non-predictability of the relationship and the need to resolve new problems – that is, the *information complexity* of the relationship (Perrow 1967). For example, one needs communication between the production and maintenance divisions to resolve unexpected breakdowns from causes that are difficult to diagnose. Therefore effective coordination mechanisms should permit such interaction, such as *lateral relationships, boundary-spanning roles, or even groups* (Thompson 1967; Galbraith 1977). The conditions under which such mechanisms are effective are usually defined as *reciprocal interdependence*: the meaning of this term is that of *transactional interdependence complicated by information complexity and specificity* (and not simply the bidirectionality of the transfer). This includes many important examples of reciprocal interdependence, such as all those where one output is produced by A "ad hoc" according to the specifications given by B: A furnishes adequate output for B only if B furnishes the specifications which serve as an input for A. This type of relationship involves some information complexity – such as the variability of requests and low predictability of production processes – that may become quite high for complex industrial goods or services. It also involves some resource specificities in that the outputs of each unit are configured according to the needs of particular other units – otherwise the above information exchanges would not be relevant and uniform outputs could be sent to any other unit requiring them.

Pooled and intensive interdependence

There are forms of interdependence that do not involve transfers of goods or services between actors or activities, but that involve unified efforts, aligned behaviors, or common action. These could be generally defined as *cooperative interdependence* (from the etymology of the word: "cooperate" or "to operate together").[9] Thompson (1967) gave us the first description of one possible type of cooperative interdependence, which he called *pooled interdependence*. This occurs when several actors constitute and use common resources, such as the same offices, equipment, secretaries, marketing services, brands, know-how, thereby generating interdependence in the use of common resources. The internal units of a single firm are usually linked by this type of interdependences, while associations of firms (often in the same sector) occasionally decide to pool financial resources to generate common services. The analysis of these situations of "aggregation" or "pooling" can be enriched by considering not only the *aggregation of resources* but also *the aggregation of activities*. For example, some activities can only be performed in teams (some work on power lines requires one person on the ground and one in the air, for example), which are a form of pooled interdependence (Barnard 1938). Once again, however, the coordination of these inter-

dependencies that are rooted in economies of scale and specialization might not be problematic in the absence of information complexity. Mechanisms that are similar to pricing – such as "*fees*" and "*queues*" – can govern the access and allocation of the services of the common resources. These coordination mechanisms based on unilateral decisions are, however, no longer sufficient, instead, if information complexity increases in its various components. For example, when the contributors and actions are not observable, and, when the size of the team creates incentives for the improper use of common resources or "free riding" on the part of team members, the use of *authority or agency* relationships has been suggested, and if there are timing constraints and priorities among activities some *programming* is in order.

Situations of cooperative interdependence complicated by even higher information complexity can occur if the parties must define their individual actions by mutual adjustments based on the information that emerges from the performance of every other action in real time. Using another term from Thompson (1967), this type of relationship can be defined as *intensive interdependence*. Thompson used the example of the team of medical specialists performing a surgical operation. In the business world, we can think of the interdependence between production, marketing, and research in the activity of defining a new product, or the interdependence between mother firms in the creation and management of a joint venture. The organizational implications of this type of interdependence are the aggregation of the resources and activities in *common units* (albeit not necessarily stable or exclusive units) within which one can perform the required reciprocal adjustments, and the design of *incentive schemes that are capable of aligning actors' objectives.* Figure 8.8 locates the candidate coordination mechanisms in the four classes of interdependence.

Although it is an intermediate and composite variable, even interdependence by itself is not sufficient to explain, except partially, the observed effective forms of division of labor and coordination. For one thing, the implications of interdependence for coordination mechanisms hold for both internal and external organization: in other words, interdependence per se does not discriminate between an intra- or interfirm use of the predicted mechanisms. Further variables should be considered in conjunction for defining or evaluating this particularly complex aspect of organization:[10] in particular the structure of interests, as illustrated in the next paragraph.

Conflict among interests and opportunism potential

Conflict versus complementarity of interests

The degree of conflict among the interests of actors who possess different resources and perform different activities (or its opposite, the degree of complementarity or identity of interests) is a very important and surprisingly neglected organization design variable (Marshack 1955; Hill 1990; Grandori 1991).[11]

In organizational economics it has been claimed that, more than conflict among the interests per se, it is the *opportunism potential* that may stem from it that influences the efficiency of various organizational forms (Williamson 1975; Olson 1965). Opportunism is defined as "self-interest-seeking with guile"; a disposition to take advantage of any circumstance, even at the expense of others and against the spirit of agreements made. It is supposed that when parties are poorly substitutable and uncertain about how external conditions may change during their relation of exhange or cooperation, they should protect themself either through complete obligational contracts through credible commitments (as hostages) or by grouping under the roof of one single proprietary hierarchy.

In some approaches[12] "opportunism" is seen as a universal characteristic of economic behavior and a "behavioral assumption." More precisely, it is "assumed" that the best strategy to deal with the possible presence of opportunistic actors is to assume that all are so, because it is difficult to discern which actually are (Williamson 1975). However, this contention is in contrast with the implications of other economic approaches, such as game theory, as well as with behavioral research. In fact, there are situations in which it would be more advisable to "assume" that no one will

Pooled
Communication and decision procedures
Mutual monitoring or supervisory hierarchy
Fees and queues

Sequential
Prices and stocks
Programming
Hierarchical decision-making for inter-unit adjustment

Intensive
Group decision-making
Mutual monitoring or property-right sharing

Reciprocal
Integration and liaison roles
Authority by exception and residual arbitration

Figure 8.8 Types of interdependence and effective coordination mechanisms

behave opportunistically, because little or no occasion is built into the situation or is likely to be perceived; and there are situations in which the knowledge of a specific partner enables him to make individualized predictions on his reliability – as briefly illustrated below. Hence, there are situations with an either high or low potential for opportunism. The potential of opportunism should be treated as a variable, not as an "assumption" (Introduction II). Let us illustrate the possibility of situations of either high or low opportunism potential both in case of transactional interdependence and of collective action interdependence, and examine some possible remedies.

Collective action with high and low potential for opportunism

For example, the cooperation among oligopolistic firms that produce the same type of product (e.g. oil) on the definition of prices is a relationship with a high potential for opportunism. There is a common interest in aligning action (without which there would be no cooperation at all). However, there is also a significant incentive for the parties to unilaterally disregard the agreement and "free ride", which gives the game a Prisoner's Dilemma structure. Firms have a common interest in maintaining a high general price, but each single firm has an interest in lowering its own price just below that of the others, to gain market share. In this situation the coordination of "conspiring oligopolists" is difficult to sustain without particular guarantees and reciprocal monitoring against free riding (Williamson 1975). On the contrary, it is much easier to sustain cooperation among firms that operate in complementary activities (for example, products with demand that is positively correlated instead of negatively correl-

ated); in such situations, even prices can be coordinated tacitly (Pfeffer and Salancik 1978).

Consider cooperative relationships in the field of research and development. The nature of collaborative agreements varies widely, from highly formalized associational contracts, characterized by recourse to authority relationships for conflict resolution (such as joint ventures) to informal cooperation agreements (Ouchi and Bolton 1988; Schrader 1991). The degree of conflict among interests and the potential for opportunism built into the structure of the game can contribute in explaining these differences. For example, there are some types of know-how and competences that grow in value for both parties if exchanged or put in common, rather than involving a concession to be compensated. This may be the case of pre-competitive and basic research. On the other hand, it is not always easy to protect knowledge, and this may be hazardous, especially if such knowledge is critical for competitive advantage or survival. We can think of two firms that see an opportunity to put together their contacts and client relationships in a given country and their technical know-how about particular processes of chemical transformation. Once conferred or communicated, these resources can be reciprocally expropriated and the cooperative relationship can become transformed into an extreme competition for survival. Therefore, the governance of such cooperative relationships, *ceteris paribus*, involves the creation of structures allowing heavy monitoring and the exchange of guarantees, pledges, and "hostages."

Transactions with high and low potential for opportunism

One can make an analogous distinction for transactional interdependencies. Consider the relationship between the production and sale of equipment on contract. Suppose that production is oriented toward cost reduction and thus to the standardization of processes and outputs, and suppose that selling is oriented to customizing the equipment to meet the client's needs. The two activities have conflicting goals, and if the sales phase must pay for the activities of the productive phase by monetary transfers, they also have conflicting interests over the transfer price. If the game is really so distributive in nature, then this can generate a high potential for opportunism, if the parties cannot write complete contracts or control each other completely, and if the circumstances in which the exchange occurs can change during the execution phase (Williamson 1975).

However, even this is not completely true; it depends on the type of variations that may occur. Suppose that the uncertain or unforeseeable variations in the transfer agreement are favorable to both. For example, the client requests a delay in the delivery date because the building to house the equipment is not yet complete. This variation generates greater resources, more comfort, and as such is not subject to being used opportunistically. If variability is expected to make the context more generous and the game less conflictual, it is likely to lower opportunism potential rather than the reverse (Cyert and March 1963; Williamson 1970).

Effects of longevity and unsubstitutability

Furthermore, the actual risk of opportunism in a relationship depends also on the extent to which actors can be expected to adopt a calculating mode of decision, on the longevity and frequency that the parties expect regarding their relationship and on the possibility of assessing/signaling one's reliability (Axelrod

1984; Barney and Ouchi 1984; Lindenberg 1990, 2000). Repeated and long-lasting relationships that involve frequent interactions, discourage opportunism because parties take into account future interactions, and because learned behaviors (efficiently) displace calculative behaviors in many aspects of the relation, thereby reducing the potential for opportunism (*Revue Economique* 1989; Sabel 1993; Chapter 7).

Finally, the possibility of taking effective opportunistic action and exploiting one's contractual partner depends also on the degree of substitutability of both parties – that is, on the level of credibility of the threat of exit from the relationship (Williamson 1975).

In sum, the potential for opportunism can thus become high *if it is difficult to write complete contracts owing to various sources of information complexity, if the interests are conflicting instead of convergent, and if actors cannot be easily substituted*. Neither unsubstitutability per se nor uncertainty per se nor conflicting interests per se will create a high potential for opportunism, but their combination will. In addition this combination of factors is *not a necessary cause* for the growth of integrated proprietary units (which can occur also in response to other combinations of the explanatory variables considered in this chapter). It can be considered *a sufficient cause for transaction cost-driven integration* (Chapter 12). As such, the relationship between conflict of interests and potential for opportunism as mediated by other variables is shown in Figure 8.9.

Incompatibility

The relevance of conflicts among interests as a variable for organization design does not stop here. The differentiation between interests and the objectives prevailing in different

Rules and routines
Guarantees and guarantors
(Authorities, hostages, and pledges)
Interest realignment
(Property rights sharing)

Figure 8.9 Opportunism potential: antecedents and organizational consequences

activities is not only ubiquitous but usually functional (Chapters 1 and 11). It can be managed and even protected by the separation of those activities. In this case "conflict of interest" means *incompatibility*, and even though its importance for organization design is usually acknowledged where "public interest" in the wide sense is at stake, it is important and should be taken into account in organization design in general. For example, there are incompatibilities between the controllers (e.g. quality inspectors) and the controlled (the production manager responsible for quality), between activities undertaken for social purposes versus profit (out of which the "non-profit" category has emerged), between activities of asset management on behalf of depositors and asset management in the interests of financial intermediaries (from which came the separation between savings banks and investment banks).

Conflict over organizational solutions

Finally, different persons, organizational units, or firms might have different prefer-

ence orders about organizational solutions themselves. This means that there could be conflicts about the organization form to adopt and that the method of resolving that conflict could influence the form eventually chosen. Normally, this problem can be represented as a negotiation problem (Grandori 1991). If a "solution" or organizational form is a particular allocation of rights and obligations over resources and activities, and a particular configuration of coordination mechanisms, it is reasonable to expect that, among the various feasible and Pareto-optimal solutions that can be found, the various actors will prefer those solutions that guarantee them greater rights and resources. These actors must therefore come to some agreement about a "fair" solution to the problem of organizational form. The hypothesis that the actors have an interest in obtaining more resources and rights often means something more, and often something different, than a mere accumulation of resources and rights; the hypothesis proves more robust if it is taken more broadly as meaning that actors are interested in being free to choose which and how many resources to acquire and which and how many activities to perform (Sen 1992). Put differently, actors are usually interested in increasing their own degrees of freedom (Crozier and Friedberg 1977). With this qualification, it is possible to represent a generic structure of the negotiation over organization forms, as shown in Figure 8.10 for the case of two actors.

Examples of the content and process of negotiations about organization form at various levels (e.g. firm macro-structure, inter-firm relations, or job design) will be further developed in later chapters. To begin to illustrate the significance of the model and the relevance of the problem, it is useful to think about how difficult and contentious it is

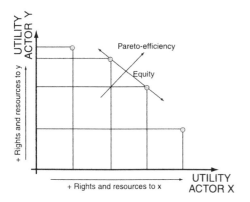

Figure 8.10 Generic structure of a two-party negotiation about organization forms

for a firm to make the transition from a functional or unitary form to a divisional form, owing to the fact that this implies a substantial transfer of rights of decision and control from the general managers or even from owners to the directors and managers in the various divisions. Typically in that type of transition (as in the development of small firms directly managed by the entrepreneur to a "managerial" firm) the need for informational efficiency has tended to coincide with the managerial interests in greater decentralization, and has often prevailed.

The organization of work is almost always a controversial issue and for this reason it is often explicitly regulated by negotiation. Workers are rarely "quasi-indifferent" about the use of their labor. In addition they tend to prefer solutions or agreements that add greater compensation, greater freedom in the workplace, and greater opportunity for development than not. More generally, workers often prioritize these objectives differently from the way employers do (Chapters 9 and 10).

Finally, at the inter-firm organization level, the conflicts of interests about organizational forms are even fiercer, given that the negotiation does not occur in a single firm, which is often a system that is characterized by more

homogeneous objectives, information, and language. The selection of an organization form usually includes the choice of a legally defined type of contract plus the definition of a series of formal and/or informal agreements designed to regulate the relationship. For example, a set of firms can come to an agreement on an opportunity to form an association to complete a complex project such as a new subway line, taking advantage of economies of scale and complementarity of competences. However, it often happens that one or more firms, usually those that get the largest part of the contract (in construction, for example), prefer to take overall responsibility as general contractors, subcontracting parts of the work out to the smaller or more specialized firms. These subcontracting arrangements would usually allocate to the general contractors a larger share of profit and risk, with respect to more parity-based possible alternative agreements, such as consortia or joint ventures. On the other hand, the specialized and/or smaller firms may resolve the trade-off between more risk and more profit by preferring to become partners in these parity based agreements rather than being put in the position of subcontractors (Grandori and Neri 1999). There is no single efficient solution. There are some superior alternatives among which a choice should be made with the help of fairness criteria.

SUMMARY

This chapter outlines the basic variables that can be used for analyzing, designing, and assessing organization forms. These basic variables are: *economies of scale, of specialization, of scope, and of complementarity, with the main effect on production costs; and information complexity, unsubstitutability, and conflict of interests, with the main effect on information and transaction costs.* We have also shown how some of these variables can be combined to construct some basic types of interdependence considered in the literature as particularly close predictors of effective and efficient coordination mechanisms. Further, we have shown that it is necessary to consider and resolve the conflicts of interests of various actors about the actions to be taken and about the ways of organizing them. The main effects on the efficient organization of each variable, other conditions being equal, have been outlined already in the chapter (Figures 8.2 to 8.9). Such relationships will be more completely and precisely developed in later chapters, in which the variables will be used together to resolve specific organizational problems. Here we can close by repeating that *none of the variables examined has, by itself, the capacity to explain and predict effective and efficient coordination mechanisms, let alone organization forms.* Each variable has only a partial correlation with some trait of organization forms, that have been highlighted at the end of the various sections in this chapter.

Exercise: CartoMed

CartoMed is a firm specializing in the production of machines for making and printing paper serviettes and labels for commercial use (on paper and plastic film). The firm was set up twenty years ago by Jene Akoret who, after working for ten years as technician in another firm, decided the time had come not only to return to his home town but also to venture into entrepreneurship. Many years have passed now since the first machine, manufactured with great financial and logistic difficulties, in an economic and social texture very different from the one in which Amoretti had developed his technical skills.

CartoMed is today a solid firm, able to compete, thanks to a flexible model of organization, with the leaders in the sector (German, Japanese, and American before all). The firm's size continues to be medium (60 billion lire turnover) but the quality of its products and its technological leadership site it in the forefront. At a certain point – owing to a series of coincidences and a period of prolonged crisis in the machine sector – CartoMed began producing ball bearings for industrial use. The ball bearing business did not develop as it should, but the ten billion lire the firm earns from this kind of production are an extra guarantee, despite the reduced margins. In time, the production of machines for serviettes was accompanied by production of machines for printing labels. The reason for this diversification is well explained by the entrepreneur himself:

We went into labels, which for us are a very different market from serviettes, for a reason regarding technology and basic know-how. Our machines work thanks to two technological platforms that represent, respectively, the heart and the brain of our products: the mechanical platform and the electronic platform. In developing these technologies for our serviette machines, we realized that we could apply them successfully and without excessive adaptation to the production of label machines. Practically speaking, it was a means to quicker amortization, and with greater margins, of the research and development costs we had borne for the serviettes.

Today, the firm must tackle problems of reorganization. It actually operates over three distinct areas of business, two of which have important technological links but with important differences in marketing and after-sales service. The third area is marginal as compared to the other two, the clients are different, even though a part of the ball bearing production is employed in making the machines for serviettes and labels. Hitherto, the firm has operated with a functional organization with some adjustments:

1   By distinguishing two departments (or mini-factories, as they are called at CartoMed) in the production area, "machines" and "bearings". This division stems from the absence of technological similarity between the two production processes. In addition, the tasks performed by the workers in the two production areas are specific, and therefore there can be no rotations or substitutions between one department and the other, except after suitable programs of training and education. In the "machines" department, the activities in the workshop and in assembling the different types of machines demand a high degree of coordination. Many technical workers are ordinary, only 15 percent of the workers and 10 percent of the production technicians can be called specialized by typology of machine (serviettes or labels). Production teams are usually made up according to the individual commission (called commission group) which comprises workers and technicians who happen to be "free" at that moment. This determines a model of organization that is very flexible and able to respond quickly to market requirements.

2   The work of the design office is divided into two distinct units under the supervision of the person responsible for "research and design." These two units are "machine design" and "bearings design." Between the machines for producing serviettes and those for producing labels there exist many homologous design activities. The software used for technical designs is the same, as are the simulation program and the test room. These programs demand continual innovation and adaptation to the specific requirements of the client firm. In the area of the machines, professionals are now available in the firm who are able to ensure a constant orientation toward innovation and personalization of the products. These are technologists whose technical specialization regards, rather than the type of product (serviettes or labels), the design and simulation softwares they have in common. These professionals are very important for the firm since they enable high levels to be reached in the personalization of the finished products. Personalization may be CartoMed's main strategic weapon. In the case of the ball bearings, the design work is simpler and requires less specialized technicians and standardized backup technologies (hardware and software), in line with the products.

3   The marketing activities are articulated, instead, by geographical area and, inside the area, the sellers specialize according to type of product sold. Selling a machine is not easy, and the marketing staff need to have thorough technical knowledge and to develop relations of trust with their clients. The latter, generally speaking, differ according to the three lines of product, but there is some overlapping between machines and bearings. Currently there are six geographic areas within which a high number of sellers operate, specializing in the three product lines.

4   The work of purchasing and performing production stages, which is subcontracted, shows much overlapping between the three areas. Nowadays, purchases are distinguished by the types of product to which they refer, so the Buying Office is organized as though it were divisionalized into three distinct units. In actual fact, on examining the product categories, one notes that there is a lot of overlapping between serviettes, labels, and ball bearings. In practice, the three areas of the firm's business have 80 percent of suppliers in common, only 20 percent being specialized suppliers.

5   One element to note is that within the firm fierce conflicts are developing between the bearings area and the machines area, and also within the latter. The head of ball bearing production recently threatened to resign. He is convinced that the firm could achieve much

better results, if only it wanted to. His main criticism is of the marketing manager, who is accused of favoring the machines at the expense of the bearings. It is no accident, says the head of the bearings, that in proportion to the turnover achieved the firm spends far more on training and incentivating the marketing staff of machines than it does on bearings. For that matter, a conflict is fomenting in the machine department that looks much more alarming. The sector of the future, according to many, will be labels, not serviettes, where there may no longer be much scope left for radical innovation. The serviette machines are entering a phase in which, according to several of CartoMed's managers, the advantages will be with the large firms that can manufacture more standardized products. In order to withstand the competition, CartoMed would be compelled to make a great reduction in its rate of innovation in favor of standardization. In view of the technological and organizational interchanges between the two areas of business, all this would end by creating problems for labels – which are, however, currently in a stage of great expansion (also technological). If this were indeed the case, the logical solution would be to sever the connection between serviettes and labels, in order to give the latter more autonomy in design and production.

By Giuseppe Soda

Questions

- Identify which of the key variables for analysis and organizational design are important in the situation described.
- What are the implications for a reconfiguration of the organization?

Note: In order to protect privacy, the names have been invented.

Chapter 9

The Organization of Work and Human Resources: Systems and Contracts

Actors, both individuals and groups, are considered here as possessors of "bundles" of human resources (competences); and as holders of preferences, and of rights and obligations deriving from the more or less complex contracts that regulate their work relations.

- A secretary is hired by a firm for an indefinite period of time.
- A migrant farm worker sells his labor for a season.
- A professional sells consulting services.
- A lawyer specializing in employment law is hired by a firm's legal office.
- A ceramics craftsperson works for several firms in an industrial district.
- A jazz guitarist plays in a series of nightclubs and restaurants on an evening contract basis.
- An independent weaver works exclusively on materials and designs furnished by a single fashion house.
- A firm rents contingent work for discharging activities from a work agency.
- A group of masons form a work cooperative.
- A group of professionals form a partnership.

The contracts that regulate these work relations are very diverse. Each of these different contracts can be effective, efficient, and fair in specific circumstances. This chapter aims to explore these various circumstances and the contracts appropriate for them. It explores the different mechanisms governing work contributions, grouped into three main classes: *evaluation, reward, and mobility/ development*. The fourth and concluding section examines and evaluates the combinations or configurations of these mechanisms that are embodied in some salient forms of *work contract,* and explores the conditions under which these can be considered effective, efficient, and fair. Enlarging the usual focus of human resource management, and integrating organizational economics contributions, the treatment encompasses both the "internal" and "external" organization of human resources and labor services with respect to the firm. The general scheme of the chapter, applying the general framework outlined in Chapter 8 to the problem at hand, is summarized in Figure 9.1.

To introduce the theme, consider the exercise in Box 9.1. What criteria can be used in deciding on the wage increases for the employees in the exercise in Box 9.1? There are many answers that are legitimate, in principle. Here are some typical criteria that can be identified and used in resolving the exercise.

- A performance evaluation, by superiors or peers, based on results or behaviors.

KEY VARIABLES USED	CONFIGURATION OF HRM SYSTEMS		TYPES OF WORK CONTRACTS

HUMAN RESOURCE
• Specificity
• Specialization
• Saturation/
  generative potential
  (scale and scope
  economies)
• Criticality
 	
COMPLEXITY OF
ACTIVITIES
• Observability of
  behaviors/results
• Knowledge of
  cause–effect
  relations
• Variability
	EVALUATION
	
	REWARD
	
	MOBILITY and
	DEVELOPMENT
		• Performance
		• Job
		• Competence
		• Potential
		
		• Job related
		• Contingent to
		  performance
		• Competence-based
		
		• Perfomance-based
		• Seniority-based
		• Competence-based
		• Potential-based
		
		• Internal/externals
		• Labor markets
		• Learning through
		  teaching/doing/
		  networking
		• Seniority/performance
		  based; single multiple
		  track planned/
		  competitive careers
			• Long-term/
			  short-term
			• Obligational/
			  relational/
			  associational
			• Internal/
			  external

Figure 9.1 Configurating human resources organization

- A competence-based evaluation of the level and substitutability of employee's skills and professionalism.
- A job evaluation, in terms of the cost and value for the person performing it, and for the system of action in which it is embedded (How difficult is the work? Is it dangerous? Does it involve responsibility and discretion?).
- An evaluation of the employees' preferences and needs relative to the amount and form of compensation (in this case monetary).

Even the simple information given in the exercise opens a fairly wide range of possible evaluation methods. The above questions also show the possibility of conflict between different criteria (e.g. results, behavior, type of work performed, personal situation, starting pay). The relative weight of each criterion can of course vary in different compensation systems. We start with the analysis of the evaluation system because an evaluation of the contribution of the human resources constitutes an anchor and an input for effective and fair compensation and career and development systems. Furthermore, the responses to the question of "what" and "how" to evaluate – performance or results,

Box 9.1
Motivation through
compensation

You have to make salary increase recommendations for eight managers that you supervise. They have just completed their first year with the company and are now to be considered for their first annual raise. Keep in mind that you may be setting precedents and that you need to keep salary costs down. However, there are no formal company restrictions on the kind of raises you can give. Indicate the size of the raise that you would like to give each manager by writing a dollar amount next to their names. You have a total of $17,000 available in your salary budget to use for pay raises. Current net salaries are indicated next to each profile.

$——*A.J. Adams.* Adams is not, as far as you can tell, a good performer. You have checked your view with others, and they do not feel that Adams is effective either. However, you happen to know Adams has one of the toughest work groups to manage. Adams's subordinates have low skill levels, and the work is dirty and hard. If you lose Adams, you are not sure whom you could find as a replacement. Salary: $20,000.

$——*B.K. Berger.* Berger is single and seems to live the life of a carefree swinger. In general, you feel that Berger's job performance is not up to par, and some of Berger's "goofs" are well known to the other employees. Salary: $22,500.

$——*C.C. Carter.* You consider Carter to be one of your best subordinates. However, it is quite apparent that other people don't agree. Carter has married into wealth, and, as far as you know, doesn't need additional money. Salary: $24,600.

$——*D. Davis.* You happen to know from your personal relationship that Davis badly needs more money because of certain personal problems. As far as you are concerned, Davis also happens to be one of the best of your subordinates. For some reason, your enthusiasm is not shared by your other subordinates, and you have heard them make joking remarks about Davis's performance. Salary: $22,700.

$——*E.J. Ellis.* Ellis has been very successful so far. You are particularly impressed by this, since it is a hard job. Ellis needs money more than many of the other people and is respected for good performance. Salary: $23,500.

$——*F.M. Foster.* Foster has turned out to be a very pleasant surprise to you, has done an excellent job, and is seen by peers as one of the best people in your group. This surprises you because Foster is generally frivolous and doesn't seem to care very much about money and promotion. Salary: $21,800.

$——*G.K. Gomez.* Your opinion is that Gomez just isn't cutting the mustard. Surprisingly enough, however, when you check with others to see how they feel about Gomez, you discover that Gomez is very highly regarded. You also know that Gomez badly needs a raise. Gomez was just recently divorced and is finding it extremely difficult to support a house and a young family of four as a single parent. Salary: $20,500.

$——*H.A. Hunt.* You know Hunt personally. This employee seems to squander money continually. Hunt has a fairly easy job assignment, and your own view is that

Hunt doesn't do it particularly well. You are, therefore, quite surprised to find that several of the other new managers think that Hunt is the best of the new group. Salary: $21,000.

Source: Lawler (1975).

what one does or what one knows, past performance or expectations about the future – allow one to answer questions about how to compensate whatever has been evaluated – what mix of monetary and non-monetary benefits are to be provided? should benefits be related to jobs or performance? should they be provided immediately or deferred? should they be provided according to the absolute contribution of the individual or to his or her contribution relative to others? These questions are formulated in a prescriptive way (i.e. how human resource systems should be configured) but they could equally be formulated in a descriptive way by asking why certain solutions are adopted and are effective in certain circumstances.

EVALUATION

Types of evaluation

What forms of evaluation are theoretically possible and applied in practice? Figure 9.2

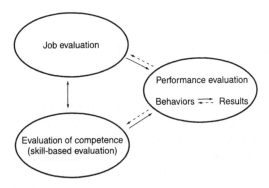

Figure 9.2 The causal attribution chain in evaluation systems

illustrates the difference between evaluation systems, based on the distinction between human resources, actual activities performed, and the expected activities relative to a work position or job. The main forms of evaluation considered in the Human Resource Management (hereafter abbreviated to HRM) literature are evaluations based on *positions*, *skills* (or *competences*), *performance*, *and potential* (Costa 1997). These elements can be ordered in a causal attribution chain that runs from resources and competences through behavior to present and future results.

The evaluation of results and behaviors is defined globally as *performance evaluation*. One of the core problems in designing a mechanism of performance evaluation is the choice between the evaluation of behaviors, that constitute the input in productive processes, and the evaluation of results, that constitute the output. The scheme proposed here highlights *the knowledge problem and the causal attribution judgments underlying the choice between evaluating results or behaviors, or competences and professional qualifications.* The problem consists in the fact that the further one moves away from the characteristics and attributes of actors toward results, the less the performance is clearly attributable to the actor being evaluated. This is especially true in activities subject to high levels of uncertainty. This recurrent problem explains many of the actual choices made in the design of effective evaluation systems.

The basic function of performance evaluation is that of revealing and measuring the value of the contribution of identified actors (single or groups) to the system of action. This data base is then, if necessary, used to make decisions about reward and mobility based on the contribution of each specified actor. Implying a problem of empirical measurement of a complex concept ("performance"), for which valid and reliable indicators are not always easily available, performance evaluation can be very difficult and often biased, as will be illustrated.

An alternative type of evaluation, that can complement or substitute for performance evaluation is the *evaluation of work positions or job evaluation.* For, even from a historic point of view, job evaluation has become diffused, often with the involvement of trade unions, as a mechanism to make the evaluation system less arbitrary and more transparent, through a standardization of the judgments and rules linking work and reward. More specifically, the contribution that is made by a position, without regard to the specific person who occupies it, has been considered a fair and efficient basis to design the structure of wages across jobs in an employment system. A possible justification for this belief is that the evaluation of a job, in terms of the competences and responsibilities it implies, can be seen as a measure of the average contribution expected from a given collection of activities (i.e. "the job") to a system. Thus, this can be seen as a substitute (or proxy) variable for a more specific and precise but more difficult and unreliable evaluation of the actual performances of each single actor.

Another important function of job evaluation is its capacity to consider important aspects of work that do not depend on the worker's actions, but on the context or the nature of the job. If evaluation were not done (also) on the basis of jobs, these contextual

factors would not receive sufficient attention and care, and the lack of specific incentives and compensation for certain types of work would make the work unattractive for job-seekers. In fact, the responsibilities and risk that some activities can require of a person to the advantage of the system are job attributes rather than performance or people attributes. For example, the driver of a school bus may be perceived as being in a position of high social responsibility, involving substantial risk, even though it involves competences that are commonplace. If school bus drivers were paid only for their driving skill or performance, this would be neither fair nor efficient for the system (in the long run, it would be hard to find and motivate good school bus drivers willing to assume the necessary responsibility and take the necessary care) (Lazear 1995).

On the other hand, the competences and the responsibilities of an actor cannot be adequately evaluated only from his position. Even in role systems that are highly prescriptive and formalized, competences may be underutilized or hidden. The more jobs involve discretion about how to interpret one's own work, the more difficult an appraisal of the value of a work role independently of how it is played becomes. A response to these difficulties can be provided by *competence-based evaluation*, to the extent that it is intended as an appraisal of *actor-specific competences* and not of the standard competences required by a job description.

Finally, if evaluation processes were oriented only to existing positions, existing resources, and observed performances, they would shape a very static and past-oriented action system. Such a system would not generate very relevant information for the governance of mobility even in static structures (hiring and promotion decisions), much less for the development of new competences or new activities. In response to this problem, a series of instruments has been developed for the analysis and appraisal of human resources' *potential*. This is a future-oriented evaluation, involving conjectures and expectations about the possible performances of a person in new roles, rather than something observable such as performance or competence. Measuring a person's potential involves estimating the possible variations and future development of this actor's competences and performance in different tasks and positions, even if these positions cannot be (or have not yet been) completely defined. Therefore the evaluation of potential is generally more subjective and less reliable, based on hypotheses and judgments under strong uncertainty about possible future combinations of resources and activities. Because of this, when evaluating potential, it is particularly important to rely on validated techniques and methods to minimize the likely errors. Upon this premise on the nature of evaluation and appraisal processes, we can enter into the merits of each system.

Performance appraisal

Some form of performance appraisal is implied in all types of work relations. Evaluating past and expected performance is necessary for a variety of reasons: to establish the price for a given package of work services so that those services can be purchased on a labor market; to allocate rewards across employees inside a firm, to hire personnel, or to staff a work group.

Observability

To the extent that evaluation is primarily a process of acquiring knowledge and informa-

tion, the efficient and effective use of the evaluation of behaviors or of results is conditional to the *observability and measurability of the inputs and/or the outputs* (Ouchi 1979). As widely pointed out in Part II, many economic behaviors are not directly observable and measurable either for logistical reasons or owing to asymmetry of information and competence (e.g. the behavior of a salesperson or a highly specialized lawyer). Many types of results may also be difficult to judge or evaluate, because they can only be seen over a long period, or because they are multidimensional or because the information is very difficult to obtain (e.g. the results of a trainer of executives).

The mere observability of behavior or results, however, should not lead the design of evaluation systems. For results may be observable but not causally attributable to certain actions, while actions may be observable but the causal relation with results may not be well known. In general, the advantage of using behaviors as performance indicators is their greater correlation with the resources that generate them; while the advantage of evaluating by results is their greater correlation with the final objectives of the action system.

Knowledge of input–output relations

If behaviors are observable and the link between actions and results is known, then performance can be evaluated on behaviors. Evaluations can be based on the deviations from standards and expectations, because it is known what the best model of action is. For example, one can evaluate how "good" the activities involved in producing beer cans are, because it is known what operations will produce good results.

Imputability of results

On the other hand, even if results are observable and measurable, a further problem is represented by the extent to which they can be *causally attributed* or "imputed" to the evaluated actors. For example, in sales, the results are, typically, easily observable and measurable via the generated income, market shares, client portfolios etc., while the behaviors are hard to observe and often not well understood and not standardizable. This contingency should not lead to exclusive evaluation on results, unless the *level of external uncertainty*, and of *dependence on other actors' behaviors* allow these results to be attributed to the salesmen's actions and efforts. The effects of these variables are explored below.

If difficulties in causal attribution originate from the fact that there is significant variance in measured results, potentially due to exogenous factors, or from the fact that results are observable only after considerable time, the appraisal of result performance can be operated over an extended time series of observations – averaging out random variations (Campbell 1969; Milgrom and Roberts 1992) – or over extended time periods (Lawrence and Lorsch 1967).

If difficulties in assessing performances stem from dependence on other actors and actions, they can be responded to in yet other ways.

Suppose that actors can behave independently, but that their results are influenced by what other actors have done. An example is the sale of new and used cars described in Box 9.2. This condition makes an evaluation of the results of each actor difficult. The problem can be responded to in various ways:

- by integrating the evaluation of results with an *evaluation of input behaviors*, if they are observable (for example, in sales activities, the respect of territorial zones, the use of specific sale techniques, the delivery of specified post-sale assistance services).
- by *widening the considered result parameters* so as to make the composite result indicator more clearly attributable and more specific to each actor considered (for example, by considering qualitative parameters as served client satisfaction).
- by *evaluating the collective results* of the interdependent actors (through indicators at the group or even the firm level).

Interdependence among inputs creates further problems. Suppose that activities are linked in a series with others upstream and downstream (e.g. different operations involved in a continuous-process technology such as rolling steel) or are linked in parallel with other activities performed on the same object being transformed (e.g. operations performed by different maintenance specialists on a large production machine). In these linked activities, the main objective is often not to maximize productive results, but instead to optimize a composite process, which will involve quantitative, qualitative, and time elements. In these cases, evaluation of behaviors is also called for.

In general, therefore, effective evaluation systems will often be mixed and composite in situations of interdependence rather than one-sidedly based either on inputs or on outputs.

There are also activities that involve very high information complexity in which neither inputs nor outputs are observable and causally attributable at reasonable cost. In these circumstances a resource-based evaluation (see below) can substitute for a performance-based evaluation.

The combined application of the above design criteria can be experimented upon by discussing the case illustrated in Box 9.2, describing an automobile dealership. The example also enables one to see how developing evaluation parameters is an exercise in the "operationalization" of the concepts of "results" and relevant "behavior" into observable indicators.

Evaluation processes

A good architecture of an evaluation system according to the above criteria does not guarantee that the system functions well. The process and technical instruments are also important. Especially in cases where the evaluation parameters are not "objective" (i.e. they are completely dependent on the estimates and judgments of an evaluator), the process may be subject to strong biases. In the most frequent cases, the evaluation is done through questionnaires directed to an evaluator containing items about the performance of the employee being evaluated. The evaluator is usually the employee's superior, but could be, and increasingly is, a user of the employee's services, or a colleague who has worked with the employee on a project or activity.

As in all research based on questionnaires, evaluators should be concerned with the *validity* of the performance measures (do they actually measure what they are intended to measure?) as well as with the *reliability* of the scales (do they yield stable results over repeated administrations in the same context?).

In addition, it should be remembered that the responses to the evaluation questions may be subject to specific distortions due to underlying conflicts of interests, which are particularly strong if appraisal is linked to reward. In the specialized research on evaluation processes, the inventory of biases includes:

"*representativeness biases*" (allowing stereotypes and prejudices to influence the evaluations of the employee's performance in a role or position); "*availability biases*" (giving greater weight to emotionally charged events and interpersonal familiarity); *anchoring errors* (evaluating based on small changes to previous evaluations, or giving similar judgments on all the evaluation parameters); and *moral hazard errors* (deliberately distorting judgments either to damage or to avoid damaging the employee being evaluated).[1]

With reference to the management of the intrinsic conflicts of interest underlying the evaluation process, procedural justice has naturally been stressed, given that an evaluation system is, in an aspect, a judicial system. The essential characteristics of a procedurally just evaluation system have been specified as shown in Table 9.1.

Job evaluation

Jobs are partitions of activities of a larger system that can be "held" by people or groups as collections of rights and obligations to perform certain actions. Job evaluation is a comparative judgment of the relative contribution of these collections of activities, independent of the performance of the specific job incumbents.

The first problem to resolve in a job evaluation is to obtain accurate and comparable job descriptions of all the jobs in a given system. This might seem simple, but the activity of obtaining job descriptions may require extended and systematic organizational research, based on a specialized repertoire of investigative techniques such as interviews, questionnaires, and field observation. These job descriptions generate a certain level of formalization and are considered particularly important in large systems (or in interfirm

Box 9.2
The Matt dealership

Matt has been for twenty-five years the dealership of Beta – one of the largest automobile manufacturers in Europe.

Mattioli is a typical auto dealership operating on four "lines": the "new" line, the "used" line (used vehicles purchased or traded in for new ones), the "parts" line (parts, accessories, and oils used by the internal repair shop or sold to clients), and the "repair shop" line made up of two sections: the "mechanical" one and the "body shop" one (prepares new vehicles for sales, performs repairs on clients' cars – both under guarantee and not – and reconditions used cars before selling them).

Because of the numerous conflicts among the company's employees, the top priority seems to concern clarification of responsibilities and thus the criteria for performance evaluations of the various divisions. Examples of conflicts among employees include: the used car salesmen, who often sell at a loss, claim that the repair shop raises the price of the car too high by performing too many reconditioning touch-ups, while at the same time the repair shop manager blames the parts division for the high prices it imposes. Below are the characteristics of the divisions of Matt.

The "New" Line

The strategy of this line is relatively rigid given that products, markets, and prices are set by Beta. On new vehicles there is a fixed gross margin of 14 percent so the division's profitability needs to be evaluated mostly in terms of efficiency. In order to stay competitive it is very important that the dealership maintains a good image, based on continuous and intense work by the salespeople, who must grant small discounts and above-market prices on vehicles traded in (which makes it harder for the "used" line to make a profit), as well as additional services such as financing options and free maintenance (which jeopardize the repair shop's profitability). The management of these tools is assigned to the salespeople; it is therefore necessary to set specific rules and check that they are implemented properly.

The "Used" Line

The management of the "used" line allows for more reasonable actions: purchase and sales prices are not set by Beta, and product quality depends on the reconditioning and guarantee policy followed. Because there is not the minimum demand "guaranteed" by the trade mark on new vehicles, the marketing strategies are of crucial importance. However, a large percentage of purchases of used vehicles comes from "trade-ins" for new vehicles; this means that the estimated value of the used vehicle made in such instances influences the profitability of the line very heavily. Another important cost element – which determines the quality of service – is the reconditioning phase (besides the possible guarantee). The cost of repairs determines the financial result of both the "used" line and the repair shop (which fixes the amount). Finally, in order to better understand this activity, it would be correct also to consider the cost/opportunity ratio of the inventory of cars from the date of their purchase to the date of their sale.

The Repair Shop

In the Matt dealership, the repair shop works on new cars (preparing them for delivery, inspections, and guarantees), on old cars (reconditioning and guarantees), and on vehicles not necessarily bought there (repairs on external customers' cars). The management of the repair shop directly influences the profitability of the other lines, and is influenced by them, so there are strong interdependences across lines. Income earned by working on new cars should therefore represent a revenue for the repair shop, and a cost for the new line. The same is true for reconditioning work: in these cases, though, the determining factor is the transfer price that the supply room applies to parts. While internal transactions represent a "captive market," the repair shop can be more reasonable with external customers and the profitability of this division depends on the marketing strategies that are adopted.

The Parts Department

The management of the parts department may be quite different depending on whether its main objective is providing service to the internal repair shop or to the "external" market made up of auto parts dealers and mechanics. When dealing with the outside market, the parts department can operate as a "separate enterprise" (in this case the key to success consists in always stocking a very large selection of parts), while when dealing with the internal repair shop the goal is always to stock the most frequently used parts (ordering stock from the distributor based on single orders). As far as the relationship between the supply room and the repair shop is concerned, it is important to keep in mind that profits generated for the parts department are costs for the repair shop. In addition, in evaluating the results of the auto parts division, one must keep in mind the cost/opportunity connected to the rate of turnover on parts, which is currently too high compared to the average of the Beta dealerships. One must also keep in mind the quality of the service provided, which does not always correspond to the expectations of the internal and external customers.

Given the interdependences among the four lines (summarized in the Figure below) and the different parameters of reference of the activities, putting some order into the management of the dealership appears to be no easy task. The existing relationships among the lines of the Mattioli dealership are as follows:

Note: Arrows indicate transfers of goods, services, or information.

Source: Adapted by Massimo Neri from Airoldi (1979).

Table 9.1 Due process and its relationship to the practice of performance appraisal

Element of due process	Descriptions relevant to performance appraisal
Adequate notice	Objectives and standards are established in advance, published, widely distributed, and explained.
	Employees have input into formulation of objectives and standards, or at least opportunities to question the content of the standards and objectives, the process whereby they were established, and the manner in which they will be implemented. Feedback is given on a regularly recurring and timely basis.
Fair hearing	Standards for the admissibility of PA "evidence" include the appraiser's familiarity with the appraiser's performance based on sufficiently frequent observation of behavior or work products.
	Employees have means to indicate their own viewpoint concerning their performance.
	Employees have opportunities to explain their own interpretation of PA "evidence" and present arguments supporting that interpretation.
Judgment based on evidence	Steps are taken to have the appraiser apply standards consistently, without external pressure, corruption, or personal prejudice.
	Evaluations show efforts to use principles of honesty and fairness (employees have opportunities to question evaluations, and the explanations provided reflect such principles).
	Evaluations withstand scrutiny, including that which might be engendered by an appeal or other type of opportunity for recourse provided to employees.

Source: Folger et al. (1992).

systems, such as a franchising structure)., both for reasons of transparency and fairness and for reasons of informational efficiency in making comparisons among several jobs.

The second problem to solve is the identification of the evaluation parameters. The relevant question should be: what aspects of the job are more correlated to the creation of value by that activity, independently of the particular job incumbent? As already observed, there are at least two components to be distinguished in this respect: *knowledge* *and competences* on the one hand, and *responsibilities and risks* on the other.

The most common method of identifying relevant parameters and for attributing them a weight or value is based on empirical correlations among the presence of certain dimensions or factors and the level of compensation generally observed. On this basis the evaluator can construct a scale on which a position scores more points (and is thus eligible for higher compensation) to the extent that the particular dimension or factor is present. The most widespread and applied method has been developed by the consulting company Hay: it has identified in the *competences required to cover a job*, understood as knowledge to be mastered, *the intensity of problem-solving capabilities required to perform the job, and the level of responsibilities* – the three main parameters on which to assess the value of a position. These are in turn operationalized in very detailed measurement scales that are supposed to be sensitive to variations over hundreds of points.

After a period of notable diffusion, this type of approach came in for criticism. Beyond the criticisms addressed to the content of parameters – which can be remedied through the addition of other dimensions – there are more methodological caveats. One criticism is that the use of points to express standard values to assign to the contents of a job type, conceals the differences in value that similar or identical activities may have in different systems – that is, standard scales tend to confound job specificities. A second criticism is that whenever the construction of the points in the job evaluation scale is based on statistical correlation analysis among various types of positions and the average compensation observed for those positions, a circularity problem arises if job evaluations are used to determine pay levels. One way around this second criticism is to use the average market compensation for the job to establish a *lower bound* on the fixed compensation for a generically defined job, since it is a good indicator of what a job incumbent could get in a similar alternative job, without consideration of any possible quasi-rents or specific value of that job in the focal system. In practice, in fact, wages are partly determined on the basis of job evaluations and the average salaries for similar jobs, and partly negotiated based on the particular surplus created by the particular contribution of jobs and people in the specific context.

Competence-based evaluation

The *evaluation of human resources as collections of competences* can constitute an alternative to job evaluation, especially in dynamic or complex activity systems in which the contents of jobs depend largely on actors' competences rather than vice-versa. Techniques of skill-based evaluation are in fact being more and more widely used. An important distinction in these techniques is the extent to which they are geared to capture the advantages of the specificity and specialization of competences in given tasks; or the potential of competences in the generation and definition of tasks (Chapters 1 and 8).

"Task-driven" approaches

One approach – developed in the field of human resource management (Spencer and Spencer 1993) – has aimed at discovering which mix of competences can be linked to superior performance in a *given* activity. The method of competence analysis generally involves the use of observations and structured interviews[2] that reveal which knowledge, behaviors, and action procedures the employee has used to get the best results. These elements are then used to construct a *model of competence* that can be copied and diffused, and with respect to which the level of competence of job incumbents can be measured. It is supposed that these evaluations can be used for staffing, hiring, and promotion decisions, as well to match reward with competence levels. The effectiveness of this procedure, however, involves certain conditions. It implies an imitative learning process, that is appropriate for fairly large systems of stable and similar activities.[3] It is *"task-driven"* – that is, it requires that tasks are given in order to define relevant competences. It offers a "standardized" approach to the problem, that may be successfully applied if competences are codifiable and it is known that they are common to many jobs.

"Resource-driven" approaches

Knowing that imitation and diffusion is not the only model of learning possible (Chapters 2 and 3), one can envisage modes of learning of superior practices that are better suited to complex and differentiated activities. Instead of simply "cloning" models of competence, one can construct causal models of the results obtained, specifying the conditions under which certain competences and actions produce certain effects, and taking into account the effect of exogenous and specific factors. In this way, these models may help to generate new profiles of competence instead of transferring models that are already observed. Hence they may be defined *"generative"* and *"resource-driven."* For example, if a consultancy firm has to organize a project group for a specific client/issue, the process, explicitly or implicitly, involves these evaluations:

- assessments of who possess relevant competences.
- estimates of which of these competences can develop more effectively and efficiently in providing relevant services (generative potential).
- judgments on which combinations of competences can manage the problem (combinative capability).
- calls for participation to relevant competence owners, who may evaluate the interest of the project (or participate according to previously set agreements and plans).

The case of competence-based evaluation described in Box 9.3 gives some material for identifying elements of both approaches, and for discussing some of the prospects and problems of approaching and using competence assessments in a non-standardized and generative way. In particular, it shows that – if evaluations are used for compensation purposes and not only for resource development – this may require a move toward a non-standardized, negotiated, and ad hoc approach in reward systems too.

Assessment of resource potential

The *evaluation of human resources potential* is aimed at estimating the capacity of the development and future performance of people in activities that they have not previously performed. It is an exercise in estimating the generative potential of resources (Chapters 1 and 8). As applied to human resources, this constitutes an important input for the design of mobility and development systems.

The difficulty of precisely and reliably evaluating potentials increases with the complexity and uniqueness of the past and future activities. In fact, when the contents and the characteristics of the job tasks are known in advance, so that the causal relationship between competences and results is clear, then it is possible to predict future performance with valid and reliable indicators. For instance, university admission tests can be based on correlations between the presence of certain capabilities and obtained grades, for very large numbers of subjects. Large hiring processes in banks and insurance companies or promotion plans within the same functional area are also examples. Objective indicators such as the possession of titles or degrees or professional qualifications can be combined with measures of past

Box 9.3
Competence-based evaluation
at Andersen Consulting

Human resource management at Andersen Consulting is characterized by the company's focus on the concept of competence, which is defined by the firm as *the collection of know-how and skills necessary to successfully carry out activities related to business objectives*. Each individual's personal growth is focused on the acquisition of competences that are in line with Andersen Consulting's marketing strategy, and is personalized in a way that takes into account various interests, orientations, and individual needs.

Once the five core competences had been defined (Architecting Business Processes, Architecting Technology, Setting Business Direction, Changing People and Organizations, and Managing Complexity) the first step was to evaluate the portfolio of competences existing at the time.

In the Andersen case, unlike the classic method by Hay-McBer of analyzing the "best performer" in order to identify winning competences for the organization, the competences that were taken into consideration were "drawn-up" by the partners. The reason for choosing a "deductive" method is explained by the need to change the direction that the company was going to take; the best performers of yesterday would not necessarily be the best performers of tomorrow.

Once the collection of best competences had been defined by the Competency Head, the next step was to survey the existing portfolio of competences. The method used starts with each professional filling out a self-assessment questionnaire about his or her competences. These data are then double checked and standardized by the Competency Head, who aggregated and tabulated them.

The analysis of the gap between the actual competences currently possessed by the organization and the future needs (then defined as strengths and weaknesses) has made it possible to develop personalized training programs and competence schedules.

At the individual level, there is a "performance appraisal." At the beginning of each project, roles and objectives are defined, and every four months there is an evaluation of the skill domains that have been developed on the job. This performance appraisal thus leads to the determination of the proficiency level reached, along with additional comments in case the evaluation differs from the standard level of proficiency expected (i.e. what the company expects a person "to know and to be able to perform" in order to qualify for a specific position).

The method of using an evaluation scale consisting of seven levels (where $0 =$ no competence and $6 =$ acknowledged leader in the area in question, even considering experts outside the company) seems to be an attempt to introduce a quantitative element in a company where everything is based on qualitative evaluations by one's boss – evaluations that are influenced by his/her expectations.

In addition, one could wonder what actually counts more in an evaluation – having accomplished a task or having demonstrated specific competences?

As to compensation implications, at Andersen Consulting the "pay for competence" concept is not strictly applied even if the actual competences are used when

deciding on bonuses. The fixed component of pay is strongly anchored to one's hierarchical position, while the variable component depends on the level of proficiency
that the individual has demonstrated in the projects in which he or she has taken part.
They refer to *proficiency* rather than results because the profile of the person changes
in line with his/her *competence* (both content skill domain and professional qualities)
independently of the results of the project.

Just before promotion times (September and March), area manager meetings are
called and the final personnel evaluations take place. Based on such evaluations,
people are categorized into four bands (top performer, full performer, performer, and
major problem) to which correspond specific compensations and career plans.

Careers are closely dependent on the performance bands; if someone is a junior top
performer it will take him/her two years to become senior, while if he/she is in a lower
band it may take him/her longer. Although compensation is also influenced by the
bands, the linkage is not deterministic; not necessarily do all top performers receive
the highest compensation. In this case, in fact, variables such as age, seniority, and the
importance of the work performed play an important role in distinguishing one
person from another within the same performance band.

In summary, at Andersen Consulting performance evaluation is done by the line
managers, and the salary raises by the practice managers even though they need to be
approved by the partners. However, the partners decide the compensation for each
position while the positioning of the single individual within a band is some kind of a
negotiation between partner and human resource manager.

As to the compensation, given that the "market" does not pay for competences,
Andersen Consulting relies on benchmarking, looking at a set pool of companies (not
necessarily all consulting companies) and within them at specifics such as the earnings
of a college graduate of the same age in a certain position. From data revealed in a
small survey, it does not look as if the staff are unhappy about their compensation.

However, once it is recognized that additional competences need to be rewarded
financially, the problem remains to decide whether to pay for the competences actually
used in job performance (as happens in, Deloitte & Touche, for example) or to pay for
the additional competences developed, even if not used on the job (as for Andersen
Consulting USA for very specific and specialized professional figures). The choice of
Andersen Consulting Italy seems to lie in between the two positions.

Source: By Christian Montermini.

performance, and tests designed to measure
one's expected performance in a job or a pro-
gression of jobs.

However, things are not so straightforward
when the job is difficult, the competences are
complex, and the activities are very different
from anything performed by a particular subject in the past. If the evaluation of potential
regards newly created jobs or involves a different context such as a new firm, a new work
group, or new markets, difficulties proliferate.
In these cases the evaluation of resources'
potential becomes more subjective and is
based on complex certifications and professional judgments. Informed judgments about
the competences and the general characteristics of the subject will carry more weight
in the evaluation process. Such informed

judgments will often be based on direct observation and field experiments, or on in-depth interviews, assisted by "clinical" and "expert" judgment as well as by referees and presentations (as in fact is the custom in admission to post-graduate studies) and on the self-assessment of the persons themselves.

REWARD

The *evaluation* of competence and performance is an input that – combined with an appraisal of *preferences* – enables us to define rewards. Keeping their competences and performances constant, different actors may attribute different values to different reward packages. In particular, people can attribute a value to both monetary rewards (or rewards that are easily convertible to money) and non-monetary rewards such as the possibility of professional and career development or the intrinsic content of the work (Herzberg 1953; Chapter 2). The rewards derived from career and development will be treated in the next section, while those deriving from the contents of jobs will have to wait until the next chapter. Here we concentrate on the monetary or quasi-monetary elements of the reward system.

Job-related compensation

Consistently with the major distinctions among types of evaluation systems, monetary compensation can be linked to jobs and time (also called "fixed" pay) and/or contingent to performance (also often called "variable pay" or "incentives").

The efficiency and the effectiveness of a pay scheme linked to a job (rather than contingent on performance) rest on several assumptions. The most important of these are (Chapter 4): that the actors contributing work are risk averse; that they sell to other actors (work employer) their work services and some rights to decide on their use over time; that the employers can either observe the workers' behavior or confidently infer it from the results. In other words, *job-related salaries* can be justified as *part of an exchange-based authority relation or "dependent employment relation."*

The problem of designing or explaining the appropriate *levels* of these kinds of wage can be solved in steps, considering the different *variables that may affect pay levels* and the *different decision processes* (Chapter 2) that may lead to their determination.

Optimal fixed pay levels

A minimal requirement that an efficient wage level should satisfy is that it be sufficient to motivate a worker to *enter the transaction* and to *produce at the desired level*.

This problem can be solved as an optimization problem if certain information requirements are satisfied. If the worker assigns a positive utility to monetary compensation and some negative (and/or positive) utility to the effort expended, and he can compare them; and if the employer can foresee the expected utility that can be derived from different actions and levels of efforts of the employee, then an efficient level of pay should satisfy the following conditions.

- The net utility for the worker – the positive utility of the salary minus work-related costs (opportunity costs, effort, transportation, material consumed) – must be a positive value.
- The worker's net utility should be greater than or equal to the net utility offered by alternative jobs available to him or her.
- For the employer, the optimal set of actions

to demand from the worker, is that for which the difference between expected earnings for the firm and the cost of labor required to obtain it is maximized (Levinthal 1988; Douma and Schreuder 1992).

Uncertainty, quasi-rents, and negotiated salaries

The above conditions are far from providing a complete framework for predicting or calculating wage levels.

In the first place, it is probable that in most situations this type of calculation will be done more heuristically, owing to the difficulties involved with the required evaluations and predictions. For example, it is not likely that the worker will know how to explicitly compare the costs of production of work services with the utility of rewards. In general, it is difficult to compare work contributions and rewards, because while benefits come partly in money, it is hard to think of effort in monetary terms. Empirical research has shown that workers evaluate the acceptability of their compensation more on the basis of comparisons with the compensation received by similar workers in similar jobs (Lawler 1971, 1973) than of comparisons with their own costs – that is, based on equity judgments more than on efficiency judgments.

In addition, the above criteria would set pay close to the best alternative salary that a worker can get, or at least do not provide guidelines on how much higher a fixed pay can be over that minimum level. To that extent, they neglect the likely presence of firm-specificities and quasi-rents in the long-lasting work relations in which fixed pay is typically efficient (Marshall 1890; Aoki 1984). In Marshall's words,

the point of view of the employer however does not include the whole gains of the business: for there is another part which attaches to his employees. Indeed, in some cases and for some purposes, nearly the whole income of a business may be regarded as a quasi-rent, that is an income determined for the time by the state of the market for its wares, with but little reference to the cost of preparing for their work the various things and persons engaged in it. In other words it is a *composite quasi-rent* divisible among the different persons in the business by bargaining, supplemented by custom and by notions of fairness.

In the labor relation context, a *rent* is *the proportion of compensation that a worker receives in excess of the minimum necessary to be induced to accept a particular job*. Quasi-rent is defined, instead, as *the portion of compensation that the worker receives in excess of the minimum necessary not to leave a particular job* (Milgrom and Roberts 1992).

Rents and quasi-rents derive from the presence of some monopolistic elements (Chapter 8), which, in the case of work, can be the possession of very scarce and valuable competences and talents, or to competences that have a very high value in a particular relation (specificity). For example, the compensation of opera singers involves rents derived from the possession of scarce and useful resources (i.e. talents that can create value in the marketplace). A different source of surplus compensation is specificity. A carpenter with firm-specific competences can enjoy a quasi-rent that includes the greater value he generates in that firm with respect to alternative candidates, minus the costs of search for and transfer to a new job.

Wages should include and often do include part of the quasi-rents that work contributes to creating (Masini 1978; Aoki 1984). It would not only be unfair, but is unlikely in practice, that these quasi-rents will be appropriated entirely by employers. The more uncertain reservation prices are, the less controllable is workers' behavior; and the more long-lasting the relation is, the less likely it is. If the parties lack clear information on counterparts' reservation prices, they are unlikely to get very close to them (Chapters 6 and 8). In addition, workers can win back what they lost in accepting a deemed unfair contract, by raising the level of free-riding and non-compliance at work. Therefore *a fair division of work-related rents has self-enforcing properties that other allocations would not have.*

Transactional advantages of unions

These conditions seem to apply particularly well to firm-specific human resources, that in fact usually enjoy highly protected and negotiated work conditions. One can ask, then, why wage negotiation, assisted by unions, within long-term employment contracts, is such a widespread system of industrial relations governance and is not confined to firm-specific and poorly monitorable work.

Among the reasons are the following.

- If there are significant information asymmetries (e.g. the value of alternative jobs for the worker is known to the employer but the value of alternative workers to the employer is not clear to the worker), or resource asymmetries (e.g. the relative amount and specificity of resources invested in the relationship are much lower for the employer than for the worker) then there is a substantial risk of unilateral appropriation of value by the employer. Hence, the formation of a *"countervailing power"* coalition on the side with less bargaining power is rational (Galbraith 1952; Goldberg 1980).
- The negotiation of labor contracts has high transaction costs; therefore the unification of job requests and the interaction with

one unionized counterpart rather than with many individuals, *especially if jobs are similar and standardized*, makes the process much more efficient (Freeman and Meadow 1984; Costa, 1990).

- In negotiations likely to involve a lot of conflict such as those between workers and employers, the *longevity of the relationship* with the same counterpart facilitates an agreement (Chapter 6). So even if many individual workers do not have a long history with the firm, the union can represent a stable negotiating partner for the firm.
- The value assigned to a contract, especially in the case of labor contracts, and its acceptance, depend not only on the amount of rewards obtained, but also on the *justice of the procedure* through which the agreement is reached. Trade-union bargaining over pay can be justified as a fair voice-giving procedure on the matter.

Reward contingent on performance

"Incentives" and "variable pay" elements refer to those components of compensation that are contingently determined by rules of correspondence between pay and performance. Its distinctive contribution to the regulation of work transactions is that through adequate incentives it enables motivation of work activities that (1) cannot be, at least in part, governed under an authority and job-related wage regime; and (2) cannot be totally regulated by instantaneous exchange contracts. Typically, therefore, variable or contingent pay is useful in compensating work services *that are to be delivered over time, in which workers have discretion about what action to take, when these actions cannot easily be observed and evaluated, provided that performance can be reliably measured and can be confidently attributed to the worker's behavior.*

In fact, pay based on results is especially relevant in compensating those work services that are provided under an agency relationship both within and across firm boundaries; and the determination of the level of incentives has been one of the areas of application of agency theory. From this perspective, the problem is solved with a value maximizing strategy.

Optimal incentives

The core problem is that compensation contingent on results *transfers risk* from a less risk-averse actor (the employer) to a more risk-averse actor (the worker). The employer can generally be supposed to be better able to bear the risk owing to more diversified investments and the lower impact of any single action and contract on total wealth; while the agent, for the opposite reasons, is supposed to be typically risk-averse. There is thus a *trade-off* between greater incentives to produce, generated by the risk transfer, and greater labor costs, due to the greater sums required to compensate for risk acceptance. The basic formulation of the problem supposes, in addition, that the agent evaluates possible actions according to the costs and benefits they yield, where costs are operationalized as "efforts" and benefits as compensation. The optimal intensity of performance-related pay will then be a function of the following variables (Milgrom and Roberts 1992):

- the value created by the extra effort;
- the incidence of exogenous variables (not under the control of the agent) on results;
- the degree of risk-aversion of the agent;
- the rate at which the marginal cost of effort increases for the agent.

The basic structure of the argument can be summarized in the trade-off between the two functions shown in Figure 9.3. The marginal benefits from the greater effort, net of the costs of these efforts, is a function that decreases as the incentives increase (because the marginal costs of the intensity of work increase while the marginal effects on the results decrease). The marginal cost of the incentive is instead a function that rises with greater risk transfer to the agent, and rises more steeply the more the worker is risk-averse and the greater the variance of results due to exogenous factors.

This formulation and solution to the problem can be extended and qualified in various ways. In the first place, the assumption of a strictly quantitative and continuous shape and content of utility functions can be modified. Agents, and managers, in particular, are likely to order business actions according to utility scales that are different from those of their principals, for example shareholders (Marris 1964, 1997). However, managerial preferences are usually linked not so much to the level of effort required, as to qualitatively different views of business policy or to social and power returns rather than monetary ones.

In addition, the feasible decision process may be less close to an optimizing strategy

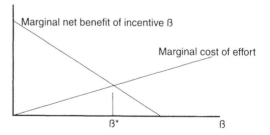

Figure 9.3 Optimal intensity of result-based incentives

Source: Adapted from Milgrom and Roberts (1992).

than the agency model expects and prescribes. Firms and managers do take into account the types of variables highlighted by agency theory, but they do so in a more heuristic way, based on levels of aspiration and performance targets to be reached, especially for complex and poorly structured activities involving a high level of discretion. A brief illustration of some of the most widespread practices and forms of result-based compensation, and of the conditions under which they have been found to be effective, supports this argument.

Management by objectives

One of the most common systems applied at the managerial work level is *management by objectives (MBO)*. In MBO specific levels of outputs to be reached are forecast and then used as criteria to evaluate the levels of performance reached by the responsible actors. MBO is based on a tight linkage between three subsystems: the planning and control system (that formalizes the quantitative economic objectives to be reached); the performance evaluation system (based on a comparison between planned and achieved results); and the compensation system (a contingent incentive scheme). From a cognitive point of view, MBO can be seen as a systematic and formalized version of *goal-setting* (Locke 1996; Chapter 2), that is particularly suited to activities with a lot of discretion about the type of objectives to reach and the best ways to reach them.

An important feature in MBO is the requirement that the process through which objectives are set be participative. A specific and economic justification for this requirement, if activities are uncertain, is that participation can help in overcoming the information asymmetries and the opportun-ism potential that are typically present in MBO. For, if both the amount of variable incentives and the formula to calculate them are established in a participative way, the incentives to set easily reachable targets, on the part of managers who enjoy exclusive information about the difficulty of reaching various possible objectives, could be diminished. The process of joint definition of objectives and of the rules for contingent pay can indeed be seen as the result of a proposal made by the employer of *a "menu of contracts"* and of the choice from that menu by the manager of the contract that s/he expects will lead to the best result (Milgrom and Roberts 1992). If the manager is confident of reaching a difficult objective, then s/he will choose a risky contract (i.e. with a higher variable compensation component); otherwise, s/he will choose a more conservative scheme (i.e. with less incidence of incentives).

Although compensation on results is particularly important for employees in positions with wide responsibilities and decisional autonomy, various forms of incentive can also be used effectively for operative positions, especially those involving discretion about work sequences and procedures and the use of time.

Piece-rate pay systems

One form of contingent pay traditionally used for blue-collar workers is the piece-rate system. Piece-rate systems aim to create an incentive for individual workers to an efficient use of time and resources so as to maximize the number of units produced and compensated for. The rise of this form of incentive has been connected with the diffusion of Taylorism, as a complement to jobs that were parceled out and studied to find the most efficient method of obtaining the greatest productivity in the shortest time. Its decline can be attributed partly to the diffusion of automation in industrial transformation processes, partly to the vicious circles inherent in the system, and partly to the shrinking of the set of industrial activities that can be "Taylorized." For while, on the one hand, automation has often reduced the control on work paces and systems on the part of workers, on the other hand, vicious circles have stemmed from the incentive for employers to raise normal production standards in response to increases in productivity, thus leading to an escalation of the efforts required to obtain premiums contingent on the high productivity generated. Finally, less specialized and individual models of labor organization, such as job enrichment and teamwork, have come into more widespread use. With less work being divided among individuals and more work done by teams, the efficient worker must not only be efficient in the use of time, but must also learn to manage relations with co-workers, solve problems, and work effectively in a team.

Gainsharing

A form of contingent reward that is more appropriate to work taking place in teams and requiring problem solving is *gainsharing*, which involves paying members of a group a share of the productivity gains earned from the increased performance of that group. Gainsharing can be claimed to have positive effects if group members have concrete chances to influence results through the exchange of relevant information and participation in decision-making – for example, through "quality circles" and other applications of group problem solving to production quality improvements (Mitchell *et al.* 1990).

Profit sharing

The two forms of incentive just analyzed (piece rates and gainsharing) are based respectively on individual and group results. It is also possible (and becoming more common) to offer compensation contingent on the residual economic results realized after sale by an economic unit. Mostly known as *profit sharing*, this compensation method is often applied at the level of entire firms or of sub-units for which profits are measurable (e.g. divisions or profit centers). Many of the debated conditions for an effective application of profit sharing have to do with the cost of transferring risk to employees. Also on the basis of the previous discussion of this issue, it can be hypothesized that profit sharing is efficient (beyond a symbolic function) when:

• the group is not too large, in order to reduce free-riding problems and to distribute notable benefits;
• workers have enough responsibilities and ways to affect the firm or unit results;
• profit sharing does not also involve loss-sharing, so that the problems of inefficient allocation of risk may be attenuated;
• it is possible to agree on fair and transparent procedures on what profit indicators to use and how to measure them.

Reward policies

The combination of job-related and performance-based pay elements as distributed across work positions can be represented synthetically as a function of the type shown in Figure 9.4. The curves plot the distribution of compensation levels as a function of the evaluation of the positions held.

The different shapes that these compensation curves can assume, as well as their comparisons across units or firms, or with

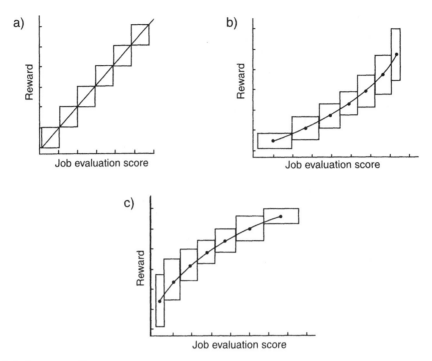

a)

b)

c)

Figure 9.4 Compensation curves

learning and productivity curves, yield useful information about what compensation policy is followed and indications on what should be followed. For example, a slowly rising curve describes a policy of pay increases that responds slowly to increases in the competence and responsibility represented by the job evaluation ratings on the x axis. This type of policy creates a "hostage effect" because employees must make investments in their competences and produce value today in order to be compensated in the future (Itoh 1994). This system is therefore sustainable if the firm is prepared to invest in the formation of those competences and if both parties are adequately protected from sudden termination of the work contract. By contrast, compensation curves that respond more elastically to the growth of experience and responsibility are compatible with systems involving greater job mobility.

Lastly, the compensation curves of single firms or units can be usefully compared with the average curves for their sector, or with comparable firms and units, especially in order to diagnose whether their compensation schedules over jobs are sufficient to hold and attract the desired types of human resources.

Procedural justice of reward systems

The use of explicit compensation criteria that are transparently connected to jobs, competences, and/or performances should increase both the procedural and the substantive fairness of a compensation system (Folger and Greenberg 1985). Procedural justice research (Greenberg 1987; Folger and Konovsky 1989) found that providing opportunity for employee participation in pay determination can be expected to lead to a perception of fairness and satisfaction with the pay system. Miceli and Lane (1991) applied the general procedural justice framework to the reward system such as:

- performance appraisals used to determine merit pay should be uncontaminated by unfair discrimination or personal bias
- when pay surveys are used to set rates, data should be complete, representative, and up to date in relecting other organizations' pay rates
- employees should have the opportunity to provide information that is used by the supervisor to adjust pay rates
- members of the compensation committee should be selected from a variety of locations, units, and stakeholders.

The case described in Box 9.4 enables one to apply the conceptual tools on evaluation systems and reward systems discussed so far, to assess the shortcomings of the proposed scheme of performance appraisal and contingent pay as applied uniformly to all the employees of a bank, and to devise a differentiated system that takes into account the different values of the relevant variable for reward system design in the various units.

MOBILITY AND DEVELOPMENT

Processes of mobility and development can be usefully viewed as those of match and co-evolution among individual actors, the resources they command, and the activities they generate. The effective, efficient, and fair configurations of these matching processes and the systems that govern them, depend heavily on the characteristics of the human resources and of their possible employments

---

Box 9.4
The CRC incentive system

The CRC is a bank which is being forced to drag itself out of a difficult situation brought about by a policy which has placed little emphasis on competitiveness and proved short-sighted with regard to internal organization. The management's strategy for recovery therefore involves a large commitment to customer relations (contacts, visits, and advertising initiatives to back up the relaunch of the bank's image) and with staff (efforts to improve competences and increase involvement in the bank's new approach). As part of this strategy, the bank has created a system of incentives with varying remuneration levels, in line with the strategy of customer-orientation, to be applied to the whole of the bank's staff of just under one thousand, who are subdivided between central functions and branches in a proportion of 30 to 70.

The objective of the system of annual incentives proposed, in the words of the General Director, is "*to create a strong team spirit amongst staff and to provide executives with a means of direct dialogue with their subordinates, without creating orders of merit since each branch only has to measure its results against its own previous performance; it must reward those who deserve it, those who have attained special heights during the year, stimulating dedication without guaranteeing anything else; it must allow clear communication of the bank's annual targets, facilitating their achievement.*"

The incentive applies to each organizational unit (branches and central departments) individually and is awarded (in differing measures, see Table 2) to the executives and clerks working there; however, clerks are not awarded the bonus unless their individual performance (evaluated annually by their respective managers) is rated at least as *good.*

For the branches, the incentive system is based on the comparison between budget targets and results with regard to the following parameters

- direct collection of funds (current accounts)
- indirect collection (securities and investment funds)
- lending
- overall profit margin, including a share of overheads.

The system is therefore closely linked to the planning and control system. The levels of the target parameters, ambitious but realistic, must be set so that the incentives system is self-financing and a proportion of profit is redistributed to employees. On average, the bonus envisaged is between 10 percent and 40 percent of gross salary.

The variations over each target parameter are translated into scores (see Table 1).

Table 1 Ratio between parameters and scores

Target parameters	0/+4%	+5–15%	+16–25%	>+26%
Direct collection	5	10	15	20
Indirect collection	3	6	9	18
Lending	2	4	6	8
Branch margin	2	4	6	8
Total score	12	24	36	54

As can be seen, in order to receive the bonus, the branch must have achieved a score of over 12. The score is then converted into the bonus sum on the basis of the following table.

Table 2 Calculation and distribution of the incentive

Ranks \ Scores	12/23	24–36	36/50	50/54
Branch manager	×	2 ×	3 ×	4 ×
Deputy manager	×	2 ×	3 ×	4 ×
Clerk with evaluation *"good"*	1/6 ×	2 1/6 ×	3 1/6 ×	4 1/6 ×
Clerk with evaluation *"very good"*	1/3 ×	2 1/3 ×	3 1/3 ×	4 1/3 ×

Note: Where x is the basic level of the incentive bonus.

So for clerks, a positive evaluation by their superior is the essential precondition for "getting a piece of the action," the size of which is established in close connection with the planning and control system.

For Central Department staff, participation in distribution of the bonus depends on the results achieved by the branches. So, for example, if not all the branches have achieved their minimum increases, this affects the internal departments in terms of a smaller bonus. On the other hand, if the results are positive, the distribution of the bonus to the internal departments reflects the split in staff numbers between the center (30 percent) and the branches (70 percent), while the allocation in relation to rank follows the procedures already described above. This solution means it is possible that not all staff with the same evaluation (better than "good") will receive the bonus, and so the HR management will have to make a choice on the basis of the comments on the evaluation forms.

In conclusion, although it has been introduced with a fair level of success the incentives system leaves two important questions open. The first concerns the attitude of the trades union; opposed to the differences which the system institutionalizes, the union suggests that it should be modified through the creation of a productivity bonus identical for all, to be calculated on the basis of a single performance parameter.

The second relates to the feeling of frustration expressed by some central department clerks, whose statements can be taken as representative:

"In the same city, some of our branches may tend to compete with each other."
"In the internal departments there is more uncertainty about the bonus; for example, here in the HR department we may do a good job, but if the branches don't sell successfully we don't get a penny, is that fair?"
"And what about the managers' final word over who receives the bonus in the internal departments?"

Source: By Luigi Golzio, adapted by Massimo Neri.

(as well as on people preferences). Two characteristics are particularly important: *the specificity of resources to uses and users, and the complexity of activities*. All systems that are relevant to mobility and development (*search, selection, training, career, exit*) are considered here together, in their interrelationships and in their aspects internal and external to firms.

Systems of search and selection govern the access of resources to jobs. The problem is often rather unstructured, involving questions as: How can relevant alternative candidates be defined? Where and how to look for them? Should the allocation and use of resources be thought of as a single job that currently exists, or a series of jobs (defined or to be defined), or a set of connected jobs such as a firm in its entirety?

Search, selection, and labor markets

Personnel searches involve, in principle, a huge number of alternatives. To make it even more difficult, the desired results and the criteria by which the alternatives should be evaluated regard future performances in as yet inexperienced combinations of people and activities. To that extent, it is reasonable to expect that personnel search and selection are heuristic processes, where learning by trial and error is not pathological but rather a way to discover effective combinations. On the other hand, exactly because of their heuristic character, research and selection processes can be highly improved by debiasing techniques and decision support systems. In addition, an appraisal of the different types of difficulties and uncertainties faced in searches for different types of resources helps in accounting for the differences between the systems that govern search and selection processes.

Internal labor markets

A basic distinction among systems of search, selection, and allocation of human resources runs between "internal labor markets" and "external labor markets" (Doeringer and Piore 1971). An internal labor market is constituted by a finite and definite system of jobs the application for which is reserved to people that belong to the system.[4]

The use of the term *internal labor market*, intentionally or not, effectively conveys the idea that the processes of reallocation of resources that occur internally to a firm or other contractually closed system, can still use "market-like" mechanisms: an internal labor market is a system of competition between internal candidates for possible jobs, regulated by a system of negotiated prices that are only weakly connected to the external system. Among the reasons why these protected labor markets arise, it is supposed that internal candidates are more likely to possess or be able to develop competences that are *specific* to the job system considered. Internal candidates also have the advantage of being easier to evaluate, because of the availability of direct information about past performance, especially if it is not easily quantifiable and if it can be observed only over the long term.

Therefore, the *complexity of work*, especially in terms of low measurability of performance, is also expected to favor the formation of internal labor markets; and even the formation of several internal labor markets, with limited mobility between one and another, in the same system, to which only groups of candidates with comparable competences have access (Milgrom and Roberts 1992).

Information costs

Even if they are generally costlier than the external market in the case of specific and complex labor transactions, internal labor markets are also not without costs, which in some circumstances can surpass those of external markets. The usually underlined costs of internal search and selection include the possible loss of control and loss of access to performance information as the number of system members increases, the cost of internal personnel management services, the costs of renegotiation of contracts especially if they are "typical" employment contracts incorporating extensive formalization of procedures and job descriptions; the escalation of pay and staff size.

Learning costs

A probably more important but less considered cost of internal labor markets, however, derives from the likely reduction in the sources of innovation, the higher organizational inertia, and the risks of obsolescence of the system's competences, no matter how much linked by specificities, due to the long-term stability of people, the homogenization and routinization of organizational culture and know-how, and the lack of input variety.

As a result of all the costs of internal labor markets, it happens that one turns to the external labor markets not only to acquire simple or standard resources, but also for complex and/or co-specialized resources. For example, innovative firms, or firms under pressure for change, extensively use the external labor market for executive and professional positions.

The tools and actors of effective and efficient search and selection processes, even if external, will however be different from those of an external market of standard and simple labor. The configuration of the system in the latter case is nearer that of a classic market: the generation and comparison among alternatives is feasible owing to the availability of good objective indicators of the competences required (e.g. a diploma or professional training) or by reliable tests; the encounter between demand and supply is facilitated by intermediary institutions that operate on large numbers of candidates; and finally the expected consequences of performance differences are often relatively low in standard and simple jobs, thereby providing an economic criterion for limiting the investment in the search and evaluation of candidates.

In the case of reliance on external markets for complex or specific jobs, instead, the effective instruments usually constitute a hybrid between an external and internal market, as can be expected given that the process should exploit some advantages of external acquisition of resources while respecting the internal need to evaluate candidates on the complex competences and their capability of performing synergistically within the context of the existing system.

Selection

While search represents a phase of variety generation, *selection* is a process that reduces variety by the elimination of candidates until an acceptable set is chosen. This process of evaluation is characterized by substantial uncertainty on both sides. In most cases the employer, at the moment of selection, lacks certain information about the productive and professional capacity of the candidate (Spence 1973), even if that employer is using the internal labor market. On the other hand, the candidate does not possess all the useful information about the real nature of the job. Both face the risk of adverse selection biases. Both are faced with the trade-off between investing ex ante in analysis or relying on ex post learning that experience will provide.

The structured instruments to evaluate human resource potential and competences partially reduce the uncertainty owing to the lack of *ex ante* information. As already observed by examining evaluation systems, these instruments will be more effective to the extent that the job descriptions are clear and specialized and to the extent that the evaluation concerns a specific job rather than a career or development path. For specific and complex jobs, owing to the lack of reliable predictors about the job performance in single activities, it will be more effective and efficient to focus the ex ante evaluation on competences and professional capabilities and to emphasize an ex post evaluation in the internal labor market, about performances and the degree of fit between specific people and specific jobs and activities.

Independently of the nature of the job, there are various reasons why efficient and fair search and selection systems should be quite structured and formalized.

- Selection interviews conducted in an intuitive and narrative mode are likely to be subject to strong and systematic cognitive biases. To that extent, the depersonalization and codification of the process should improve the quality of decisions.

- The application of transparent criteria to the evaluation and selection processes is a principle of procedural fairness that is highly appreciated by the candidates, and is in some aspects required by laws designed to ensure equal opportunities (Singer 1993).
- A decision process based on valid and reliable research and data gathering methods (such as questionnaires and simulations) yields better and more comparable knowledge, and permits economies of scale if selection activities occur on a regular basis.

Furthermore, a clear and precise declaration of the rules and administrative procedures that regulate an internal labor market (including the systems of evaluation, compensation, careers, training, etc.) activates mechanisms of *self-selection* that help in finding good job–people matches (Salop and Salop 1976; Milgrom and Roberts 1992). For example, if it is made clear that the spirit of a labor contract with a firm includes willingness to change the place of residence, to accept some compensation contingent on performance, to study to acquire new competences, this "offer" is more likely to be accepted by people whose resources and preferences are consistent rather than diverging. This mechanism permits the system to economize on the cost of search and to better use the information that both parties possess.

Nevertheless, this effect is by no means automatic. Its functioning depends especially upon demand/offer ratios. Box 9.5 illustrates the failure of self-selection mechanisms in both the opposite conditions of almost full employment and high unemployment.

Training

Training has an important role in the generation, development, and maintenance of individual and collective competences. For the firm, or other system of action, it is a possible source of distinctive competences and competitive advantage (Itami 1987), and for the people it is a form of reward, a capital increase that will remain forever in their possession (Pfeffer 1994).

The nature of the training system is tightly linked to the specificity and complexity of the competences that it is intended to develop. One of the reasons why competences are specific to a use or user is because they are formed through direct experience or learning by doing that can only be accumulated in specific contexts (Doeringer and Piore 1971). As to complex competences, they are by definition characterized by long learning cycles and multi-dimensional development paths (e.g. multi-functional, multi-firm, multi-sectoral, and international).

These propositions can be used as guidelines for assessing or designing an effective and efficient training system, in terms of the allocation of training costs, the effectiveness of in-house training versus external training, and about the level of training (e.g. individual or group, intra-firm or interfirm).

Locus of training

Using the distinction between specificity with respect to the uses (activities) or with respect to the user (e.g. a particular firm), one can predict that firms have an interest in investing in training that is to some extent specific to the user firm, and not in undifferentiated abilities that can benefit all firms (or all firms in their sector) and can be furnished by external training institutes. However, firms are often

Box 9.5
Selection systems and levels
of employment

The Agensud case. A group of teachers at a successful management school in northern Italy is engaged in founding and launching a management training institute that can be developed and will in time operate independently in the south of the country. Among the various activities, the most critical is the constitution of a group of local teachers. The first problem is the selection of people of sufficient potential who will then be trained and assisted in the first years of activity. The qualifications required, the type of motivations and abilities felt to be suitable to the kind of activity, the characteristics of the work, and the prospects offered for professional advancement – all these are carefully predefined. Considerations of transparency and fairness require a public competition for access to the admission concours. Despite the purposely restricted criteria used in defining the figures sought, the result is disconcerting: 2,000 applications for 5 places.

The Agensoft case. Specialized engineers, with some years' experience and qualification, are rarely encountered "at large." They are very hard to find and very easy to lose. They possess high, very specialized skills, which can be applied in several contexts and several firms. How to attract them? Various consulting firms have begun to offer support in "candidates' marketing," where the personnel is treated as a consumer to be attracted in highly competitive conditions. Market studies and analyses of the motivational profiles of engineering graduates are performed, they are segmented by branch of specialization and nationality, "employment packages" are offered, designed ad hoc on the basis of expectations as well as employment prospects. For example, the French firm Altex has perfected a solution that offers the engineers a permanent contract, high investment in training and development and variegated international experience through detached work on projects with firms requiring the specialized services of the engineers. The search for candidates is done through channels differentiated by country and by field of specialization, so as to maximize the probability that the message will reach its audience (for example, the periodicals most read). But even in this way – as Altex's research and selection staff emphasize – in this "hunting" the "quarry" will scarcely select itself; and one can never really be certain of having "caught" it.

Thanks to University of Modena trainee Federico Mazzoli for information on the Altex experience; and to Massimo Pilati, Bocconi University, for information on the Agensud experience. The names of both companies have been changed.

(and increasingly so) interested in investing in the formation of flexible knowledge that is not very specific with respect to particular uses within them, but in core competences that can generate economies of scope and can support learning and diversification processes.

Further, analyzing the level of the action system to which competences are specific one can assess what is the best level at which training can occur. For example, if certain competences and professional skills are specific to clusters of firms, rather than single firms, for example regional clusters of firms specialized in particular transformation processes, they can be acquired efficiently through processes of knowledge sharing and exchange at the interfirm level, for example through associational structures (Provan and Heimer 1999).

Training, learning by doing, and learning by networking

The complexity and innovativeness of the know-how to be transfered or generated in the training process, is the single most important variable for designing an architecture of knowledge transfers. Traditional school-like training is a mechanism of one-way knowledge transfer by means of communication. As such, its effectiveness is bound to codify well established knowledge. The more the relevant expertise is tacit, the more effective transfers call for *learning by doing*, or by observing other people doing. The more the relevant knowledge is innovative and should be generated within the formation context itself, the more a critical and selective sharing of experiences and knowledge becomes a superior mode of learning. For example, the recent diffusion of *learning by networking* in multinationals or professional firms – realized by connecting people with differentiated experiences – can be explained by a need not only for vicarious learning and imitation processes, not only for the transfer of sophisticated techniques, but also by processes of confrontation and exchange of knowledge, problem-solving, and reciprocal learning. Box 9.6 describes only some of the varied mechanisms for knowledge sharing and knowledge generation

that are present in one of the most notoriously innovation-oriented companies in the world. As can be seen, "training" systems in the traditional sense become a part of a wider set of "knowledge management" mechanisms for transferring and developing knowledge and competences.

A useful way to discuss the case is to locate the *different mechanisms governing knowledge transfer and sharing as a function of the characteristics of actors' knowledge* (as noted, sophistication and computational complexity, tacitness and discovery intensity – Chapter 1) *as well as of the configuration of interests*. In fact, barriers to knowledge exchange and sharing do not come only from knowledge complexity and lack of proper channels, but also from the risks of expropriation and competitive use and lack of proper incentives. Electronic networks are set up but sometimes poorly nurtured. Inter-divisional groups or supplier–customer mixed groups are constituted, but members retain jealously their most relevant information. The higher the conflict potential and the risk of hostile expropriation, the more explicit incentives to exchange and protect property rights on information and knowledge are required (see, in the case, the internal patenting system, the knowledge sharing awards, the "pathfinder program").

As to the *processes* of design of training and learning systems, some form of "*training needs*" analysis entered early in the repertoire of techniques is widely used in this area of management. On one hand, training and development needs analysis can be anchored on the expected and desired evolution of activities and competences. For this (just as for the selection process), it is important to identify the method of action that the system is aimed at sustaining (e.g. a specific job, a career, a firm, or a profession). On the other

Box 9.6
Knowledge management
systems at 3M

3M has over 80,000 employees, including almost 9,000 researchers in more than 60 countries. How do they keep such a machine together? How do they transfer innovation, ideas, technologies and competences? How can distant and often anonymous contacts among experts (with problems, unrealized opportunities, and solutions). become transformed into close relationships? There is the need for pollinators – small bee "integrators" able to distribute pollen.

Space

All the functions within the New Life Sciences (mainly health products). have been gathered under one single roof for the first time. More generally, in the Austin, Texas, facility, all the units of a single business are located on the same floor. 3M considers space very important; and provides plenty of well-equipped meeting places in order to encourage people to take breaks from their routine for conversation.

Mobility

The most important way that knowledge is spread is definitely through the mobility of human resources. In R&D, mobility is considered a company tradition, with exchange programs on various levels. Some job assignments involve formal education or training but others are aimed at establishing comparisons and collaboration among diverse research units. These assignments can vary from a quick visit to a two-year commitment; but it is the people who assess the quality of the relationship and value of prolonging it.

However, 3M has recently taken a relatively unusual step further, by giving new meaning to the word "self-development" as a process to be valued and sought within every individual. There is a program called EJIS that displays on every European employee's computer the current vacancies in continental Europe. This program exists in the US as well and forces each boss who needs to fill a vacancy to advertise the position through EJIS. The announcement contains a description of the position, the job responsibilities, goals, and objectives, position site, etc., and remains on the system for 15 days. Any person interested in applying for a position can simply press a key on the keyboard, without having to inform his/her boss, and is then automatically included in the selection process. The ultimate goal of EJIS is to fully exploit a system that is marked by broad-ranging and trans-national competences.

Forums

Space and mobility are not enough. For this reason, 3M is set up as a spider web of functional forums, including some Technical Forums (TF) and Lab Forums (LF). The Technical Forums include the entire technical "macro-family" – researchers, product developers, and technicians. The purpose of the Technical Forums is to provide informal and formal communication tools to encourage the cross-fertilization of ideas. Activities developed by the Technical Forums are all carried out on a voluntary basis and include (for example) organizing specialist seminars with Nobel Prize Winners to bring all technicians up-to-date with the latest scientific knowledge.

Technical Coordination

Corporate-level technical coordinators exist to support the sectors and divisions, but remain under the direction of the senior vice president for R&D. Technical coordinators provide internal consulting. They manage a huge database, providing all 3M employees with access to the various experts in the scientific disciplines and functional fields. The database is fed by all the work carried out by 3M researchers around the world (e.g. Internal Technical Reports). The feedback time of the Technical Coordinators is estimated to be an average of two working days.

The Pathfinders

Within 3M there is a program called Pathfinder whose goal is to encourage the development of ideas into industrial and commercial products.

- The original Pathfinder is aimed at all business units that develop new activities based on the creation of new market opportunities based on innovations. To be considered for the prize, products must generate profitable gross sales of over $400,000 or 25 percent of the total local annual gross sales. In 1995 there were 654 nominees for the Pathfinder program, 82 of which won a prize.
- The Pathfinder Merchant is reserved for companies that have successfully adopted Pathfinder programs that were originally developed in other countries. Although not explicitly stated, the objective of this program is to improve "listening skills" and thereby improve the potential to assimilate existing ideas and avoid the *not invented here* syndrome. The goal is to improve the capacity to combine markets and products in new ways by stimulating the diffusion of winning solutions.

Source: C. Turati, *Minnesota Mining & Manufacturing*. Case study SDA Bocconi 1997.

hand, a survey of preferences and expectations of potential participants has been revealed as crucial. Successful training requires a receptivity to communication and a willingness to change the structure of one's knowledge, skills, or even values and motivation. Hence, expecially in adult training, people should perceive that it is in their interest to accept training or to invest in learning or to exchange knowledge.

Analyze, for example, the intersection between the competence needs of the firm and people needs in the "guest courtesy program" at Walt Disney, described in Box 9.7.

What incentive structure is at work? What motivational structure can be hypothesized? What difficulties could be anticipated if the same program were offered, say, to aged life-long employed traveling personnel in a state-owned railway or post office?

Careers

Career systems regulate horizontal and vertical development of the people/jobs matches toward superior responsibilities and competence, and usually also toward superior rewards.

Box 9.7
How to make dreams come
true

Walt Disney said that it takes people to make a dream come true – dreamers as well as doers – and he founded Disney University as a place for developing Disney people. When Disneyland was launched in 1955, its creator wanted customers to feel like invited guests. Disney believed in training staff people to have good guest relations practices – and Disney pioneered a highly successful concept.

Today, guest relations programs in service companies are common –and Disney is working to build on its experience to maintain its service edge. Disney University continues to play a key role in this process, with its focus on "cast members," Disney's term for employees who are expected to play their part, and play it well.

"Disney University serves multiple functions," Bill Ross, manager, Disney University, said. "HR planning and development, cast communications (internal publications, formal communication programs), cast activities (social, recreational, and interpersonal communication programs), and audio visual programs are all handled out of the University.

"Each Disneyland unit has a dotted line relationship to Disney U, so that we can provide centralized HR services, yet have a strong link to individual entities. At Disneyland, we have about 6,000 employees."

International Focus

"Putting together our PHRM planning group is one of our newest HR efforts. Within the last two years, we've computerized information on our salaried employee population so that we can submit the criteria for a particular position, and generate the names of candidates through the computer. This system has also allowed us to pinpoint some of our development needs.

"We've found this capability particularly helpful since we've launched Tokyo Disneyland and our Euro-Disney project.

"We relocated about 200 executives to Japan – some for short stays, some for long. Given the expanded scope of our operations, we need to know all we can about the talent we have to draw on.

"We've been focusing on our need to become more internationalized. We are undertaking extensive training of Japanese managers, and our managers in the US, so that we can better understand cultural issues. We know that we can cross cultural lines – but we want to understand the issues to enhance our chances for success. We have established an International Fellowship with that goal in mind.

"We've also worked on providing a support system for those who return to the US after a tour abroad. We recognize them for their efforts, we listen to their descriptions of their experiences, and we review what took place here while they were gone. After all, they are not returning to the same organization that they left – things change. And the manager who has served abroad has changed, too.

Guest Courtesy – inside Disney

"We believe that, for our cast members to treat our guests in a friendly and helpful way, they themselves must be treated that way. We look at guest courtesy as something that must extend to those within the organization, too.

"When cast members join Disneyland, they are treated as VIPs – they are personally greeted, and everyone is on a first-name basis. We reinforce good guest relations through our orientation process, training, performance appraisal system, and we circulate guest compliments and complaints. Our biggest challenge is to stay in touch with the changing values of both our guest and our cast members.

"We look at how our guests define service – both first-time visitors and repeat visitors. We look at the environment itself, since elements such as temperature have a definite effect on people's perceptions of their experience. We encourage those behind the scenes to be conscious of courtesy, too – for example, we have a campaign called 'Put a Smile in your Voice' that emphasizes telephone courtesy. And for our Christmas party, cast members and their families come to the park – and management mans the park for that day. Cast members experience the park as a guest – and management experiences the cast members' jobs. There is a management program that focuses on guest courtesy, as well.

"We have a two-person team whose sole job is to evaluate the level of courtesy that exists in the organization. We poll guests daily, and circulate results.

"We show examples of good and bad guest relations in our training program, based on the information we gather. We teach cast members to understand outcomes – their goal is to focus on what they want the guests to experience. There are many ways to get to that goal – but the end result is what counts.

"Our training teaches them to enhance skills to initiate a relationship, to take the first step in approaching guests who might look puzzled or in need of help. In the service business, we are fortunate to get a second chance when something goes wrong: a guest may have an unfortunate experience in the ticketline, but a helpful interchange in a restaurant that helps compensate. We want to avoid the first mistake – but make sure we take advantage of all opportunities for a second chance."

Source: "Making dreams come true," *HR Reporter* (Jan. 1987).

Internal careers

If a career system is governed as an internal labor market, it contributes to increasing the longevity of the work relationship, through requests for contributions that will be rewarded – in terms of position and/or connected superior compensation – at a later time. The prospect of a career thereby allows contributions and incentives to be balanced over the long term instead of in every single transaction.

However, considered as an internal labor market, careers are only partially isolated from external competition for jobs. As Milgrom and Roberts (1992) have noted, workers that perform extremely well in one activity can make themselves visible and attractive for alternative employers, who might offer salary increases in order to convince them to change jobs. External offers therefore create incentives for the current employer either to use variable pay as a reward for high performance, or else to promote the worker. Promotion is often an attractive alternative compared to increases in incentives, for several reasons. First, as discussed above, there are limits to the efficient use of incentives (e.g. the difficulty of accurately measuring performance, variable risk aversion, etc.). Second, particularly high performance constitutes a signal that the competences and capacities of the person might be greater than those required by the current role, and therefore the full use of human resources would require activities of greater complexity and responsibility. To that extent, using promotions as a form of reward contains an element of organizational learning that monetary compensation does not include. Further, it is likely that employees with high goals and good results might assign a higher value to the intrinsic rewards represented by the increased opportunities to assume responsibility and apply competence that a promotion offers, than to pay increases.

External careers

The external labor market may however be better able to reallocate human resources to their best uses, especially in the case of jobs involving general rather than specific skills, or competences that can no longer be combined with other skills to create value in a specific system. For example, if a firm concludes that this is the situation for a given employee, it would be in that firm's interest to invest some resources to help that employee to look for better suited alternative jobs in other firms. To give this support may be convenient for several reasons: first, it may cost less than side compensating exits in other ways (for

example, with lump sum money); second, it can make the firm more attractive to people who are either employed elsewhere or looking for work, and to those who remain within the firm (Ulrich and Lake 1991; Pfeffer 1994). The recent diffusion of individual and collective *outplacement* processes can be explained by these advantages. Outplacement normally involves the firm in providing consulting services, logistical support, and useful contacts to its employees so that the latter can more accurately evaluate their own competences and expectations, and more easily find a job that is congruent with these.

Performance is not the only criterion on which mobility is based. The practice of adding other criteria, most commonly job tenure and the evaluation of potential, can be explained on the basis of the complementary properties of efficiency and fairness that such other criteria possess.

The seniority system

Internal promotions can be based on criteria of seniority. These tend to be related to other variables such as experience and competence, although not necessarily in a deterministic way. As a form of deferred time-based compensation, the seniority system has the property of creating disincentives for turnover by rewarding those employees who stay longer. In addition, the criteria underlying a seniority system are objective and non-discretionary, which makes such a system both efficient and fair. Because it is applied more or less automatically, the so-called "*influence costs*" are reduced. In fact, influence costs are incurred when people have the incentive to dedicate time and effort in presenting and misrepresenting information and in negotiating so as to influence the decisions of the evaluators; this is likely to occur when the promotion system is subjective and not transparent (Milgrom 1988). In contrast, a seniority system implies a standard rule for promotion that lowers the managerial discretion in career choices, thus reducing the efforts directed to influencing promotion decisions.

Performance-based promotions, following repeated positive performance evaluations, can generate also other types of distortions, that can be reduced with the use of other mechanisms.

The Peter principle

It can happen that the person with the best performance at his or her current level might not be the best candidate for the position at a higher level. In other words, it is not always the best blue-collar worker who could be the best production manager, and the best product manager is not always the best marketing director. Promotion on the basis of performance in the preceding role can lead to the so-called "Peter principle" where everyone is promoted to their level of incompetence, and for which many firms under- or mis-utilize talents and competences.

The evaluation of potential and the design of multiple career paths can contribute to the correction of these biases. In the first place, merit-based careers can and should be fed by the evaluation of resource *potential*, where people are promoted not only according to the level of performance at their current level, but based on their possessing the best potential for achieving at the next level.

Multiple careers

In the second place, it is possible to create more than one career path, even within one firm or unit. For example, in a practice originating in service firms, it is possible to follow a *professional* career path (e.g. researchers, teachers, doctors) or a *managerial* or *administrative* career path (e.g. project manager, sales manager, controller). Among the advantages of these *dual ladder careers* (Heskett 1986), are the capacity to facilitate synergies among employees and tasks. For example, dual career paths allow people with strong technical and professional competences such as researchers and scientists to continue to develop these competences, instead of reaching a "plateau" and being required to learn management competences in order to win further promotions. Dual career paths also can reduce the level of competition in promotion games multiplying and differentiating responsibility positions, at the same time making good career opportunities compatible with less hierarchical and vertical organizational structures.

Random careers

Furthermore, when the performance information that would be relevant for promotion is multidimensional and estimates are uncertain, complex performance and resource potential appraisal may give only an illusion of control. The evaluation data may turn out to be weakly correlated with actual performances and competences, making performance-based promotions subject to a significant random factor (March and March 1977).

Tournaments

A partial remedy to this problem may be to institute "tournaments" among people under reasonably controlled conditions, so that it is not necessary to measure absolute performance, but only the relative performance of the candidates (Milgrom and Roberts 1992). These races have disadvantages, however, such as prospecting zero-sum games that may damage the organizational climate and demotivate the losers, who may have had good performances anyway, and end up being underutilized.

Career and risk

Seeing a career as the assumption of a series of positions with greater responsibility and requiring more competences implies not only higher compensation due to the increased contribution, but also a change in the form of compensation. In fact, an increase in responsibility implies more decision rights and obligations, greater discretion, and greater consequences of choices. Therefore, career development may imply, beyond certain levels, an increasing *assumption of risks*, a change from the status of employee under authority relations to a status of an agent, or to a status of a partner or of an internal (or independent) entrepreneur (Pilati 1995). It is also likely to imply a change in the form of compensation, toward a greater incidence of rewards that are contingent on results, due to higher discretion. However, it is likely that positions of greater responsibility will also involve greater uncertainty about results and greater dependence of results on exogenous factors. Furthermore, the results are likely to become more complex and multidimensional and observable only over long time periods. Therefore, the relation between the level of a position and the form of reward that can effectively be attached to it is not likely to be linear and straightforward. A heavy reliance on variable compensation can either paralyze managers with excessive risk transfers, or at least distort managerial actions and investments in favor of short term and conservative policies; or, alternatively, cause executive pay to skyrocket.

Among the possible remedies to this problem are the following. First, it is possible to propose variable compensation that is only contingent on particularly positive results and not also on negative results. As Milgrom and Roberts (1992) have observed in their analysis of managerial compensation, stock options offered to managers can be interpreted as such – i.e. as opportunities to participate only in increases of the value of the firm.[5] If managers are given an option to buy their firm shares at a pre-defined price, they are encouraged to work in ways that can increase the shares' value, and buy them when this is conveniently better than the old fixed price they have to pay. If such a win-win system were thought to be too indulgent, it should be considered that there are other systems beyond compensation that can discourage errors and incorrect investments in high-level positions. One of the most important resources that is usually at stake for a manager is, for example, his or her *human and relational capital*, that can exhibit very sensitive variations as a function of observed performance. Prestige is very sensitive to failure, and it can seldom be salvaged by parachutes based on subtle caveats about where the "real" causes of success or failure were lying. Box 9.8 shows the notable and tangible importance of this factor, in a case in which a manager explicitly put his own human capital at stake, offering in advance to conduct action in a very public way and to accept the losses of prestige and reputation (and even of position) in case of failure of an important industrial restructuring project, as a pledge and guarantee offered to the shareholders that the investment that he was proposing was in effect a good one.

A more radical solution, used in cases where it is particularly hard to measure performance, is that of reducing the distinction

The interview in this case focuses on the restructuring of the Fabbrica Pisana, an Italian firm owned by a French MNC. Mr Scaroni was CEO and General Manager of the company at the time.

Q: What was the company's economic situation when the restructuring took place?

A: Fabbrica Pisana produces flat glass for uses in floats, cars, and the construction industry. It is fully owned by the St Gobain Group, which has been operating in Italy since 1881. Fabbrica Pisana faced the 1980s after living through a decade of labor union battles (all lost) that, in addition to forcing them to go on a hiring spree, had created delays and obstacles in launching the process of restructuring the firm.

To make things worse, foreign investors, still feeling insecure and uncertain after the unusual economic climate of the 1970s, did not feel comfortable about making further investments. As of 1981, the productive assets of the firm had been seriously compromised.

The French shareholders were seriously considering the possibility of leaving Italy and selling the company to the state (at the time this kind of transaction was still possible). Over the summer I prepared a restructuring plan that was then presented to the shareholders in September.

Q: How were the relationships with shareholders and headquarters handled?

A: Both shareholders and headquarters are located far away in Paris and did not have specific details on the situation. As far as they were concerned, the investment in Italy represented only one alternative among many different kinds of investments in different countries.

Q: In practical terms, how was the situation handled with headquarters?

A: First of all, by carefully working out all the technical details of the restructuring plan, and by explaining all possible investments alternatives, and the reasons why some were eliminated. Second, by carefully analyzing the evaluation criteria of headquarters and demonstrating that the proposed project met those criteria. In addition, we involved all offices (sectoral divisions, finance departments, and human relations) and we committed ourselves to "maintaining" the agreement by fostering continuous relationships, involving all parties in further developments of the plan, etc.

Q: Were there different positions with regard to the necessary investments to be made?

A: Conflicting interests existed on at least two dimensions:

- Headquarters was interested in choosing the investment that was the most profitable while to the Italian CEO the critical issue was that his project be accepted at any rate;
- Once the investment was approved, the Italian managers' main goal was to expand the plant and make use of the unexploited resources, while headquarters' aim was to reduce the gap between resources and results.

Q: How did you persuade headquarters that your project was the best, or at least better than the others?

A: Headquarters in Paris was initially particularly sceptical due to the labor union climate in Italy. My first task was to explain that Italy was changing fast especially as far as unions were concerned and because of my Italian background I could understand those changes better than they did. How did I persuade them that I was right? Well, I was betting on the project more than I was asking them to do; my name and my head were at stake with it.

At the end of the restructuring process, which lasted four years and called for over 150 billion lire worth of investments, the cost of labor to the company – which in 1985 had gross sales for about 220 billion lire – had decreased to about 65 billion. Such reduction contributed to shift the negative margin of 25 billion per year in 1981 to a positive margin of 15 billion per year in 1985, even after taking into account the high financial burden of paying for the new investments. The gross margin of the company went from −8 percent in 1981 to +22 percent in 1985 thanks also to a substantial reduction in transportation costs.

Source: Scaroni and Grandori (1989).

and the possible diversity of interests between principal and agent actors through a more intense sharing of property rights. Particularly common in professional firms, such as consulting companies, advertising agencies, and accounting firms, and generally typical of activities conducted through long term projects, this solution often implies that to make a career means to become a partner in the firm.

Procedural fairness in career systems

In practice, the career system is one of the organizational processes that is most influenced by unwritten norms and habits, and by implicit contracts (Pfeffer and Salancik 1978). Moreover, it has been shown that these are greatly influenced by the capacity of managers to strategically construct and manage their own "social capital" of relationships and contacts (Burt 1990). One could ask the extent to which these characteristics of career systems are justifiable.

From an efficiency standpoint, a promotion process based on criteria that are not very clear and explicit is extremely costly in terms of influence and negotiation costs. The quality of promotion decisions made without structured supports is surely threatened by strong availability, representativeness, and anchoring biases, even if these are only involuntary. The occurrence of stereotypes and discriminations (whether based on race, gender, or other prejudices) threatens not only the fairness of the process, but also an efficient and full use of human resources. All these considerations support the position taken by scholars of organizational justice, who have argued the superiority of personnel systems that are as explicit and transparent as possible.

On the other hand, it is fair to note that, both in promotion and compensation decisions, games are often very competitive, both because they involve dividing scarce resources and because people have a tendency to over-estimate their own contributions with respect to others and to believe that they receive an unfair share of those resources even if the system is well designed (Lawler 1966). To that extent, it is likely that rules and procedures alone, even if clear and fair, are not sufficient to govern these processes, and that it is inevitable that there be a component of discretional judgment, especially on the part of arbitration authorities. Another possibility, more applicable in compensation than promotion decisions, is to communicate the procedures clearly, but to maintain a certain confidentiality on single decisions (for example, the job responsibilities and compensation of single employees).

Manpower planning

If this is the nature of the main processes whereby job mobility and career development are managed, it follows that even in cases in which these are regulated inside the firm, they can be regulated by "planning" only to a very limited extent. *Even if internal, labor markets behave to a considerable extent like markets* – i.e. a system of decentralized, interactive, and multilateral decisions. The mechanism of negotiation, whether it is collective or individual, institutionalized or not, is required to define both the procedures and the individual decisions involved. This assessment of the effective mechanisms that can coordinate human resource mobility and development would suggest de-emphasizing the importance and applicability of "personnel planning" techniques, which received considerable attention in the 1970s. Managerial recipes during that period were in fact celebrating integrated, systemic, and strategic approaches to management in all areas. In personnel management, these approaches sought to foresee the evolution of the overall human resources of firms, through accurate estimates

of turnover (both departing and entering personnel) among various positions and professional families, across organizational units and the boundaries of the firm. However, the idea of being able to plan the evolution of the firm – from strategy to personnel management to information and control system – over long time periods has been revealed as being at best only possible in particular situations where development is linear or predictable, typically in large firms with protected markets, and where the firm is governed primarily by programs and plans and by hierarchy. This vision has not stood up particularly well, even in large firms, to the challenges posed by competition through innovation and through people and competence.

However, it is possible to identify some types of useful planning instruments, limited in scope, valid for the short term, and applied to systems of moderate dimensions and complexity, for which it is possible to estimate reliably the information inputs required. Those inputs are fairly numerous and include:

- a selection of activities to be performed and of positions entitled to conduct them;
- the type of competences required for sustaining those activities;
- estimates of the average man-time required for perfoming the various activities;
- the modes of acquisition of the human resources (internal or external labor market; times and costs; channels);
- the training interventions required;
- the normal exit rates from positions (turnover);
- a planned promotion or tranfer rates across positions;
- the availability of candidates.

On these bases it is possible to calculate or simulate, eventually for various possible business scenarios, the evolution of the population in the relevant organizational layers or families of positions and to assess the needs for hiring or staff reductions. Box 9.9 provides an example.

FORMS OF EMPLOYMENT CONTRACTS

The systems governing work relations shown above can be combined in various modes, thereby configuring different types or forms of work contracts. Some characteristics of human resources, and work activities and relations have been shown to be particularly useful to explain and predict which configurations of human resources organization are effective, efficient, and fair: the *specificity of human resources* with respect to other technical and human resources with which they are combined in transformation processes; and the *information complexity* of the activities and relationships, in particular the *observability of performance* and the *knowledge of its causes and consequences*. In addition, the variables more directly affecting the structural costs of organizing labor internally or externally (the economies of scale in the utilization of resources, the economies of specialization that can be achieved by the focal firm or other firms, the frequency of transactions) should be taken into account. Therefore, it can be expected that different effective forms of work contracts are correlated with those dimensions. Figure 9.5, illustrated below, proposes a typology of contracts based on these dimensions.

Contracts can be *complete or incomplete*, primarily because of the variable amount of *uncertainty* (unforeseeable circumstances) that they are designed to regulate (Chapter 7). These can incorporate complex clauses, procedures, rules, and systems to manage inter-

dependence and resolve conflicts, including authority (*obligational contracts*) without necessarily taking the form of a permanent internal dependent employment contract. In the presence of uncertainty about changing circumstances and of difficulties in the evaluation of performances, contracts can become very incomplete in their written and formalized part, and are integrated with agreements and expectations of "good faith" and "good conduct" according to the norms that are prevalent among those who practice certain activities. This informal regulation of behavior is also assured by mechanisms such as reputation, social control, and mutual adjustment (*relational contracts*). In situations of maximum complexity of activities, characterized by difficulties in evaluating both input and output performances as well as the value of positions, contracts arranged around a logic of exchange – based on the measurement of some of those values – cannot be effective. In these cases, contracts implying the association of resources (*associational contracts*) can be effective because they create direct incentives for the actors to behave effectively in their own interest, such as partnership and gain sharing contracts. Objective alignment and intrinsic motivation can be sustained by the sharing of property rights in their various forms (the rights to decision, control, and residual compensation), and by a strengthening of the coordination mechanisms that rely on shared values and fundamental objectives. These conditions tend to occur frequently in brain-intensive and personality-intensive systems.

In a second dimension, contracts can be ordered according to their *time frame* and to their *degree of "internality"* or "*externality*" (Chapter 7). These features of contracts are particularly related to the comparative *administrative and productive economies of*

Box 9.9
Why does everybody run away from InfinityNet?

Mr Morrison, Sales Director of InfinityNet, the third leading cellular phone operator in the country, could not understand the reasons for the increasing turnover in the call center, which was worrying him. The call center was the main organizational operating unit within the company.

Once signed-up, the customer was managed through a call center, a complex center for receiving customer toll-free calls that is equipped with the latest technology and is open 24 hours per day all year round. It should be able to solve all customers' problems, and at InfinityNet employees were proud to have created procedures that would guarantee the so-called "one call solution," where the customer's problem was solved in the first phone call.

The call center was also at the heart of the marketing and sales strategies of InfinityNet: with a toll-free call, anyone could receive a complete and polite answer about any of the now 20 charge plans or the 50 additional services (some included and others not) in the contract. The call centre was therefore overwhelmed by customers' or potential customers' calls any time the company launched a new promotional campaign or a new calling plan. This strategic choice was what differentiated InfinityNet from the other two cellular phone network providers.

The third task performed by the call center staff was one of support to the sales activities. Specifically, this involved telemarketing (for promotional activities toward customers or potential customers), sales management (recording of new contracts and set-up of new phone lines), payment solicitations, and the management of notices.

The call center employed 1,200 people who were organized on various shifts that would guarantee staff coverage 24 hours per day, 365 days per year. The typical staff person was a young college graduate or a college student in his or her last years of study. The motivation for hiring staff with these profiles was that the company wanted to convey a sense of safety and competence, as well as an image of dynamism and freshness. Because of the complexity of the procedures, training costs for new staff were on the increase: the minimum length of training was now 6 weeks. Shifts were scheduled with a maximum of 7.5 daily working hours 4 of which (all continuous) were spent providing phone assistance. Task rotation was ensured by the fact that, when traffic permitted, operators could be re-directed by their supervisors to different kinds of tasks: the recording of contracts, telemarketing, payment solicitation, assistance to business customers, sorting of recorded calls.

It is because of this variety of tasks that Mr Morrison could not understand why the annual turnover had gone from an acceptable 35 percent to a worrisome 70 percent. This meant that, lately, staff at the InfinityNet call centre had actually worked there for barely over a year. Even though a percentage of the turnover was explained by the fact that many students would finish their degrees and then find less stressful and better paid jobs in other companies, Mr Morrison thought that the rate of turnover was still high. In order to study the problem, he created a task force.

The task force concluded that it was necessary to improve the selection process and the overall management of the call center staff which accounted for half of the total number of company employees. The task force made the following suggestions:

- after a two year period at the call center (or earlier for those students who finished their degree) all staff would receive a performance evaluation. If the evaluation was positive, there would be an offer to work in a different division within the company. The human resources manager had stressed that the professional profiles of the call center staff were the same as the people sought by the other divisions of the company (network engineers, business managers, corporate lawyers, etc). Being able to count on the call center as the human resources candidate pool for the whole company would certainly reduce overall recruitment and selection costs.
- all call center staff would receive more in-depth training on all other company divisions with the goal of creating more competent and prepared staff when dealing with customers. The additional training would be of an informational nature in order to encourage the staff to consider other jobs in other divisions of the company in the future.

Mr Morrison accepted these recommendations, but stated that they would complicate the management of the call center because the scheduling of shifts (modified now to allow for attendance at training courses) had become extremely complicated. At the same time, Danny Scott, VP for Finance, was worried about the increasing personnel costs and in particular those of the call center, as it employed a large number of company staff. On the other hand, decisions about call center staff directly impacted those about customer service strategy: fewer staff means longer waiting time for the customers in receiving services. Hence, it was absolutely essential to find a tool that would allow for an annual human resource planning among the numerous tasks in order to be able to forecast the human resource budget. This is the reason why a human resources planning model was created (and nobody would have accepted it at the beginning) that, based on certain technical parameters necessary to provide the service required, would allow them to determine the staff needed, excluding those staff who were attending training sessions. Examples of parameters include: a standard number of minutes spent speaking with a client on the phone, the time necessary to activate a new contract, and average number of incoming monthly calls.

Source: By Ferdinando Pennarola.

---

scale and specialization that can be realized through a continuity of association, and to human resources' *specificity* to the system.

Even considering, simplifying, only some combinations of the two dimensions (and of their sub-dimensions) one can explain some relevant forms of efficient contract, such as those indicated in Figure 9.5.

If *competences are not specific or co-* *specialized, or the scale at which activities are conducted do not saturate the resources generating them,* then contracts are likely to be *short-term*:

- almost *complete* and *obligational*, if information complexity is also low, and activities can be clearly defined (as in the case of "temporary work");

LABOR CRITICALITY AND COMPLEXITY	ECONOMIES OF SPECIALIZATION SCALE AND SCOPE IN HR CONTINUOUS ASSOCIATION AND HR SPECIFICITY		
	LOW	HIGH	
SIMPLE COMPETENCES • Observable outputs • Observable inputs	• External contingent contracts (seasonal work) • Internal short-term contracts (temporary workers)	• External long-term (insurance or car agents) • Internal long-term (clerical work)	OBLIGATIONAL
COMPLEX COMPETENCES • Observable outputs • Observable inputs	• External short-term (purchase of advertising services) • Internal short-term (project-based engineering work)	• External long-term (insurance co-makership outsourcing of components) • Internal long-term (complex production work, managerial work)	RELATIONAL
HUMAN RESOURCES CRITICAL • Unobservable inputs and outputs • Human capital principal asset at risk	• External associational contracts (profit sharing association of work-service providers, e.g. "contract managers")	• Internal associational contracts (property sharing association of work providers, e.g. professional partnership)	ASSOCIATIONAL
			↑
	SHORT-TERM OR EXTERNAL	LONG-TERM OR INTERNAL	← TYPES OF CONTRACT

Figure 9.5 A typology of employment contracts

• *incomplete and relational*, but *external* or *short-term* if competences are complex but standardizable, and can be more efficiently employed in many firms rather than one (as in the case of a contract for advertising services or in the temporary employment of engineers in complex projects);

• *associational, but external or short-term*, if the work services are highly discretional and poorly observable (as in "contracted out" managerial work).

If *human resources are firm-specific or co-specialized, or there are economies of scale and scope in employing them in multiple activities, efficient employment contracts tend to be long-term:*

- if *uncertainty is low* (work conditions are foreseeable), then contracts can be *obligational*; internal and linked to behavior and time if those are observable (as for "typical" "dependent" blue- and white-collar work relations) or external and linked to results if those can be evaluated (as in the case of the outsourcing of material handling services, or of agency contracts in insurance or car sale);
- if *uncertainty is high*, contracts will be *relational* rather than obligational; internal if processes and inputs are observable and critical for obtaining good results (as in research, complex production, staff activities), external if good results are clear and could be achieved without tight process integration (as in the outsourcing of industrial good maintenance or sale activities);
- if *information complexity is high in all its components*, *associational contracts* entailing property rights sharing would be appropriate (as in professional partnerships).

Notwithstanding the variety of employment contracts considered here, these do not exhaust the variety of possible effective modes of regulation of work relationships. Other combinations are also possible. For example, can temporary work be combined with property right sharing? This is what happened to govern highly professional but highly standardized work in the case described in Box 9.10.

SUMMARY

This chapter focused on the "nexuses of contracts" linking actors contributing their work to the economic action systems in which they participate.

The final section of the chapter explored the variety of contractual structures that can provide the link. The typology of work contracts proposed there highlights the peculiar features of work contracts, and their varying degree of "completeness" in formal terms, as well as the different configurations of the basic human resources management systems that they incorporate – evaluation, reward, and development systems. The proposed framework enables one to assess the conditions under which different types of contract can be expected to be effective (in particular, the conditions of information complexity, and the conditions of specificity, specialization and scale economies).

The first sections of the chapter were devoted to analyzing the various systems governing human resource contributions. In addition to exposing some core and corroborated tenets from human resource management research, the conceptual framework for describing and designing these systems has been developed also with the help of other perspectives and contributions. In particular, it has been shown how evaluation systems provide the cognitive foundation for human resource organization, through the observation and appraisal of resources, performances, and activities (jobs). The relative effective use of the different methods of evaluation has been shown to be dependent on the clarity of available information and possible causal attributions relative to resources, behaviors, or results. Compensation methods and forms related to jobs, to performance, or to attributes of human resources themselves (competences) have been linked to evaluation methods and assessed as a function of the levels of uncertainty and competence complexity, of discretionality, of added value and

Box 9.10
Microsoft, freelances, and
stock options

In one of Microsoft's latest appearances in a court of law the debate centered on *freelances*, who work in the computer sector as independent entrepreneurs. The reason for the law suit was stock options, which play an important part in the remuneration for employees in both hardware and software sectors. If a product is especially successful, the value of the shares will rise, as, at the same rate will the remuneration of the engineers and programmers, who have elected to be paid partly in shares. Some of them have even become millionaires overnight.

Microsoft USA introduced its program in 1986. Every six months, all the employees can exercise the option to be paid partly in shares at 85 percent of their current value. This program led eight foreign collaborators, who had been "hired" as freelances between 1987 and 1988, to file a suit. At the time, they had been told that owing to the limited duration of their residence permit they had no right to this option. The court ruled in their favor, to the effect that freelances with a fixed term residence permit must also be considered as full employees. Microsoft and the entrepreneurs' association tried to take a tough line, but in vain.

In actual fact, anyone in the sector requiring specialized workers tends to find them through firms specializing in information technology and electronics. These firms offer very flexible contracts, by which the programmers can be "rented like cars: they don't need to be filled up with petrol on return" (says the advertisement of a firm in Seattle). It may be understandable that Microsoft didn't care to use these firms, but the court did not forgive it for obtaining the same result by creating two sets of rights, for first-class and second-class employees.

Thanks to the development of the Internet, these problems will probably sort themselves out. For some time now, many software houses have been letting programs be written in other countries. In numerical control programming, the offshore programming share may have already reached 85 percent. But the use of such tele-collaborators is not without its disadvantages: they are not available for the marathons that go on for several days and in which a team of programmers creates software under terrible time pressure in order to deliver to the client on the stipulated date. Projects of this kind require group work and the carrot-cum-stick of shares.

Source: By Giuseppe Delmestri, adapted from Detlef Borchers, *Die Zeit: Bulkware*, February 1998.

of the costs of efforts. Development and mobility systems have been examined in their dimensions of internal and external labor markets; of learning by formal training, by doing and by networking; of performance-based, potential-based and seniority-based promotion; linked to knowledge complexity and innovativeness, human resources specificity,

and specialization, scale and scope advantages.

For each system, we have examined *both effectiveness and justice issues*, and applied them both to the system *architecture* (for example, the optimal incidence of contingent reward) as well as to the *process* through which evaluation judgments and compensation and mobility decisions are made.

Exercise: The Chimney Sweeps of Finance

Pursuit Credit Sp.A., based in Rome is a debt recovery agency. Through the Istituto della Cessione del Credito it purchases high insolvency loans from the banks and starts the procedures allowed by law for at least partial recovery of the sums owed.

The managing director is worried about the activities of the section responsible for preparing the client's file for debt recovery, a crucial function. This activity precedes the judicial one (that is, the representation in court by lawyers or prosecutors) and consists in preparing the briefs (analysis of the debtor's situation, evaluation of the mortgaged property, verification of conditions required for legal action) and in contacting the debtors (verification of debtor's willingness to repay part of the debt). Profiting from the firm's growth over the last few years, the idea had been to upgrade the professionalism of this activity by hiring young graduates in jurisprudence, on training contracts. But the atmosphere in the briefing department seemed very fraught.

What follows is the text of some interviews performed with operators in the aforesaid unit:

"Well, I studied hard for four years. There's a crisis in the market, so I took the first thing I was offered. Of course, I didn't want to be a clerk. Now that thirst for cash I felt immediately after university has faded. I've saved up a bit of money, and I'm going to wait for better times and then leave. Soon, I hope. But I certainly shall leave." "Work is a problem, and this job isn't at all interesting. Of course, I never expected to become a manager on taking my degree. You can accept an apprenticeship, as you can make do with 1,570,000 lire a month – if you have prospects, a future, the chance to grow. But that's the salary, and the prospects of getting anywhere are non-existent. Will anyone tell me why I should come happily to work, and sometimes stay on till eight in the evening, with no overtime pay?"

"But there's no career here. In order to become a prosecutor you must first pass the exam, and to have access to the exam you need two years' practice in an office and presence at a certain number (prescribed by law) of court cases. Here, none of us has ever set eyes on a court, a judge, a conciliator. Letters, yes, we write tons of letters."

"It's plain," says one of the firm's lawyers, "that if we had more motivated staff, not only would we be able to recover more debts, but we could also reduce our costs. Very often I find myself before the conciliating judge who wonders why there is all this bother with legal recovery when heavier pressure on the debtors would have done the trick. Moreover, the briefs that are sent to me by the unit are often inaccurate or quite wrong, and I sometimes have the feeling that they conceal something like a taste for making life difficult."

By Giuseppe Soda

Questions

* What is the present configuration of the systems of selection, training, career, assessment, and remuneration in the situation described?
* Under the assumption of maintaining and enriching the work content in the department, and to continue staffing with recent graduates, what would be a better configuration of the system?

Chapter 10

The Organization of Work: Structures

The problem examined in this chapter is the "division of labor" and the coordination between divided activities, which a person or group can be responsible for ("*job*"), on the basis of a set of rights and obligations. This level of analysis is often defined as the *microstructure*, as opposed to the *macrostructure* – the higher order aggregation of jobs in organizational units. The microstructural problem has sometimes been defined as the problem of the *organization of work*: forms of organization analyzed at the level of what people do and have the right to do (Friedmann 1963; Butera 1979; de Terssac 1992; Williamson 1980). *A form of organization of work will be defined here as a particular configuration or distribution of rights over the domains of action, control, decision, and ownership.* In this way, the discussion can integrate the classic contributions from the sociology of work and the socio-technical systems approach – focused mainly on the allocation of tasks and the rights of decision and control – and the tenets of organizational economics – looking principally at the allocation of property rights and the incentive mechanisms associated with a given distribution of tasks.

There are three parts to the chapter. In the first section, the principal problems that have drawn attention to the theme are recalled in a historical perspective. The second section offers a procedure for designing job boundaries and work coordination mechanisms, based on all the key variables that have been suggested by relevant research, as indicated in Figure 10.1. As also evidenced in the figure, in the third section, an overview of some particularly important alternative forms of organization of work, and a framework for their comparative assessment are given.

A LONG HISTORY OF ACTION RESEARCH PROJECTS

Job design is probably the oldest theme in organization studies. Perhaps also because of this, history is particularly important in this field. Early studies in the organization of work emerged from the problems posed by the diffusion of "Taylorism." Notwithstanding the productivity gains permitted by the specialization of jobs and in many industrial sectors during the first half of the twentieth century, many exceptions to the rule, important unintended consequences, and some changes in conditions, have stimulated work redesign studies and interventions. Among the problems dealt with in early studies there were: the loss of attention and productivity linked to fatigue and boredom; the disaffection and alienation toward work linked to

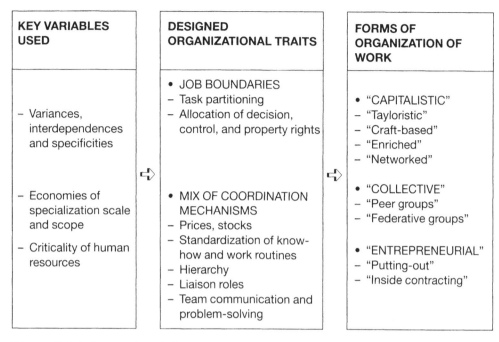

KEY VARIABLES USED	DESIGNED ORGANIZATIONAL TRAITS	FORMS OF ORGANIZATION OF WORK
– Variances, interdependences and specificities	• JOB BOUNDARIES – Task partitioning – Allocation of decision, control, and property rights	• "CAPITALISTIC" – "Tayloristic" – "Craft-based" – "Enriched" – "Networked"
– Economies of specialization scale and scope – Criticality of human resources	• MIX OF COORDINATION MECHANISMS – Prices, stocks – Standardization of know-how and work routines – Hierarchy – Liaison roles – Team communication and problem-solving	• "COLLECTIVE" – "Peer groups" – "Federative groups" • "ENTREPRENEURIAL" – "Putting-out" – "Inside contracting"

Figure 10.1 Job analysis and design

the lack of a sense of contribution; the low "quality of working life"; and the union opposition that Taylorism sparked from the very beginning.

Despite these numerous problems, the first wave of studies attempting to redesign the organization of work was characterized by many difficulties and failures (Trist 1981). It may be that these early studies, in the 1950s and early 1960s, were characterized by an approach that some later claimed was too "universalistic," attempting to diffuse new "philosophies of management" valid for all seasons and giving scant consideration to the different productive needs of various sectors. In addition, the economic conditions may not yet have been mature, while, later, the conditions that had favored the success of the Tayloristic model changed in many if not all sectors. Furthermore, research and intervention were initially focused precisely on those mass industrial production sectors where

tasks could be divided and programmed profitably.

Later, some instructive studies started focusing on technologies and sectors that were either impermeable or unsuitable for the implementation of the principles of Taylorism, with its massive division of labor (both vertically and horizontally), and extreme formalization and programming. Examples include steel transformation, the chemical industry, and continuous processing technologies (Miller and Rice 1967; Murray 1960; Trist and Bamforth 1951).

Furthermore, even in sectors with divisible technology and standardizable processes, the 1960s saw the emergence of conditions of uncertainty caused by changes in the characteristics of demand, competition, and competitive strategies. This cluster of factors led to conditions – to use the label of the time – of *environmental turbulence* (Emery and Trist 1963). In sectors such as automobiles and household appliances, the increase in the number of competitors, the increasing buying power and needs of consumers and the acceleration of the innovation of processes and products all implied productive systems very different from Taylorism, with its standardization and specialization of technical and human resources.

In addition, some of these studies and others highlighted how the development of automation enlarged the spaces of discretionality and *"organizational choice"* on how to organize work even under the same technological and market conditions, hence the likely *"equifinality"* of different models of work organization (Touraine 1955; Rice 1958; Trist *et al.* 1963).

Finally, in practice and history, the second postwar period was marked by a generalized development and legitimization of unionization, or otherwise in the weight of workers' interests in firm decisions in work-related matters, and the extension of the labor relation issues regulated by negotiation with respect to those submitted to a regime of authority. In organization theory and method this led to the recognition that *organizational arrangements at the microstructural level have a particularly strong and systematic impact on primary individual interests,* and to the inclusion of explicit surveys of the preferences of job incumbents in job analysis and design models (Hackman *et al.* 1975). More recent models have also typically included an analysis of the impact of the organization of work on the *quality of working life* (Davis and Cherns 1975), as inclusive of the broader consequences on health and family life.

Together, these studies have generated a fairly coherent body of knowledge and methodologies for work analysis and design. These will be discussed in the next sections, together with other more economic design models of work arrangements.

KEY VARIABLES AND ANALYTICAL STEPS IN JOB DESIGN

"Primary work system" and "unit operations"

A basic error that one could make in a job analysis would be to start from job descriptions as they are currently constituted, and/or to consider each of them as isolated from neighboring ones (both vertically and horizontally). For example, if we are interested in understanding how the job of a secretary could be efficiently and effectively designed, we should go beyond the activities that are currently assigned to the position, identifying which other activities these are interdependent with (even if they are currently assigned to colleagues or superiors), and understanding what criteria for aggregating these activities are currently applied and what alternative criteria could be used. To that extent, the two initial levels of analysis are the super-ordinate level of the *"primary work system"* that comprises the job being redesigned, and the subordinate level of the *elementary unit operations* that can be comprised in the job.

Primary work systems

A *primary work system* is a collection of interdependent activities that leads to an identifiable result – typically a unit of product or a service provided (Susman 1976). The reason for using this unit of analysis derives from the following hypothesis: if a system of activities is potentially able to regulate itself, an effective and efficient organization of this system should use this self-regulatory capacity. By doing so, the costs of coordination and control can be reduced and at the same time the level of satisfaction of the workers' identity need can be increased. A system that is capable of self-regulation should "contain" within its boundaries the main sources of interdependence and uncertainty that can significantly influence its output. Therefore, a primary work system would typically have to include at least the following two types of related activities:

- The interdependent transformation activities that are involved in the realization of an identifiable and valuable output (for example, all the assembly activities that lead from the components to a finished automobile; or all the administrative activities that are needed to process a request for a bank service on the part of a client).
- The activities of support, maintenance, control, and regulation of the transformation process (for example, maintenance activities if we are analyzing a production process; human control by exception of numerical control machines in an auto-

mated process; decision and planning activities regarding the type and sequence of operative activities).

Unitary operations

If the primary work system bounds job design externally, *unit operations* set a lower bound beyond which tasks are no longer technically separable. The question is to what extent and according to what criteria these elementary operations should be aggregated; i.e. what the *"efficient boundaries" of jobs* are. Figure 10.2 shows a simplified matrix of the unit operations in a work system, identified by researchers in one of the most well-known large-scale socio-technical job design projects, the Shell project (Hill 1971; Trist 1981).

Once a work system and its unit operations have been identified, some key attributes of activities and of their relations can be analyzed. Among the variables that generally

Variances		1	2	3	4	5	6	7	8	9	10	Unitary operations
Temperature	1	K										Bitumen storing
Gradation	2											
Level	3	*		K								Mold filling
Mold position	4				K							
Speed of flow	5	*										
Extraction of separators	6	*		*		*	K					Extraction of separators
State of separators	7					*	*					
State of blocks	8			*			*					
State of molds	9						*			K		Cleaning
Action of cleaning agent	10	*					*		*	*		

K = key variance;
* = interdependence

Figure 10.2 Example of variance matrix

303

influence effective economic unit boundaries and inter-unit coordination mechanisms, the following have shown themselves particularly relevant at the micro-structural level.

Variances, interdependences, and specificities

Variances

In job analyses, the exceptions, the unforeseen events, and the uncertainties that can affect a transformation process are usually called "*variances.*" Enriching the statistical meaning of the term, in job analyses "*a variance" is defined as a deviation with respect to a "normal" transformation process, that has a non-negligible effect on the output, and that creates a need for human intervention in the form of corrective action.*

For example, in the Shell case, for each elementary operation, some characteristics of the material or the processes can involve unforeseen variations in the conduct of the activity, affecting outputs and through them, eventually, other activities. The temperature and the other characteristics of bitumen such as the level of fill in the molds and the positions of separator grids could become abnormal and turn out to be key variances in the process. In fact, if that happens and someone does not intervene, the effect of the variance is felt on output through a waste of materials and wrongly shaped blocks.

Interdependences

The unit operations in the example of the formation of bitumen block molding may seem at first sight linked by simple sequential interdependence. However, the presence of a high level of variance in the process complicates and intensifies interdependences with successive operations, conditioning aspects such as the speed of flow, the withdrawal of separators, and the action of cleaning chemical agents at the end of the process. The analysis of downstream transmission of variances highlights how the operators upstream need a considerable amount of information about downstream activities in order better to regulate variances. The type of interdependence between activities can therefore be defined as reciprocal rather than sequential. In turn, this implies that effective coordination mechanisms should be based more on mutual adjustment between parties, than just on programming.

In general, *holding other conditions constant, the greater the variance and the more intense the interdependence between unit operations, the less efficient and effective it is to divide work into specialized jobs assigned to different workers.*

Initially, in the Shell molding unit, the work was divided in various different jobs, assigned to different people with different training and professional qualifications, including: a "filler" position (specialized in the mold filling operation), a chargehand role (responsible for storage tanks), an electro-magnets operator (removing the separator grids), and cleaning personnel. There were no mechanisms built into the process for the upstream workers to regulate the sources of variance ex ante; instead, the downstream workers would try to fix the problems how and when they could ex post, and many of the problems that they could not fix were transformed into defects in the final output.

Specificities

An additional factor that raises the level of interdependence and therefore the need for integration between technically separable activities is the reciprocal specificity of the resources generating those activities. *In general, holding other conditions constant, the more activities are linked by specific transactions, the less efficient it is to divide these activities into different jobs.* For example, if the activities needed to operate a particular set of machines, to maintain and repair them, and to decide how to allocate them to different productions all require reciprocally specific competences, then the activities of production, maintenance, and production planning can be effectively and efficiently conducted by the same worker or by the same group of workers. In certain studies some evidence can be found to support the hypothesis that where there are job-specific competences, jobs tend to be richer and wider than otherwise (e.g. O'Reilly 1993).

Variance, specificity, and interdependence therefore favor relatively more "integrated" jobs.

Specialization, scale, and scope

Horizontal specialization

If interdependences between elementary activities typically work in favor of the aggregation of tasks in wide jobs, then often economies of specialization, and sometime also economies of scale, work in the opposite direction. Herbst (1976), in particular, has specified this important step in job analyses.

He proposed analyzing various matrices of people and tasks such as those illustrated in Figure 10.3 (they could be also constructed as competences/activities matrixes) (Chapter 8).

The situation defined as "maximum specialization" indicates that significant economies of learning and specialization in single tasks are present and that the "bundle of resources" of a single individual can be fully used in a single task. For example, in a surgical operation, it is efficient and effective that the tasks of cutting, sewing, and anaesthetizing be done by different people with specialized jobs, both because they require very different knowledge and learning paths and because the operations must be done in parallel.

A situation of maximum polyvalence can be derived either from the facility and from low "entry barriers" to different tasks, or from the presence of economies of scope among different activities. For example, one who has acquired competence in a task (for example, writing a computer program to automate a procedure) may be the best candidate to use this acquired know-how in other work (e.g., programming other procedures).

Vertical specialization

The same type of analysis is also relevant for the vertical dimension of the micro-structure – that is, for the choices of vertical aggregation

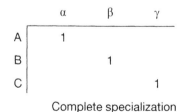

	α	β	γ			α	β	γ
A	1				A	1	1	1
B		1			B	1	1	1
C			1		C	1	1	1

Complete specialization   Complete polyvalence

Figure 10.3 Specialization matrices

Source: Adapted from Herbst (1976).

between operative activities and related activities of decision, control, and regulation. For example, the operative activity of traditional manual work at the lathe did not create barriers to the aggregation of decisional activities concerning the sequence of work and the re-equipment and maintenance of the machine. Rather, the knowledge and skills regarding the state of use and the performance characteristics of the machine and the materials generated many of the competences relevant to the programming of production and the regulation of variances. This is different for numerically controlled machines (for example, the automatic lathe), and even more for complex automated equipment, where the activities of surveillance and feeding of the process require low level and fairly generic competences, while the activities of planning and regulation of the variances (possible problems and production anomalies) require high-level and very specialized (electronic and electro-technical) competences. These competence and specialization problems can explain some of the observed consequences of automation in terms of "polarization" of occupational and job structures between a band of execution and machine surveillance jobs and a band of planning and designing jobs (Pollock 1956; de Terssac 1992).

For other types of activity, we find, on the contrary, that it would be absolutely ineffective and inefficient to separate the operative activities from those of decision and control: because operation and control activities are based on the same competences; because operative activities involve very high variance and cannot be planned; or because activities are hard to inspect and guide without actually doing the work (Alchian and Demsetz 1972; Susman 1976; Butera, 1979).

Observability and criticality of work inputs

It may be noted that the vertical aggregation of action, decision, and control rights could create problems of conflict of interest that might make it inadvisable even where it responds to the need to control uncertainty and the existence of common competences. Leaving the agent to decide what actions to undertake can lead to his or her reducing effort and following particularistic objectives, whereas allowing the agent to control his or her own actions could lead to self-serving biases and moral hazard problems (Milgrom and Roberts 1992). As distinct from the horizontal aggregation of tasks with different specialization, therefore, the vertical aggregation of the activities has implications for the allocation of property rights.

Agency theory studies (Levinthal 1988) have been paying particular attention to jobs in which significant decision and regulation rights are associated with the right and obligation to take action. In fact, by definition, an agent is not only entitled to act but also to decide which action to take.

In the case of observable activities, a possible solution is a division of rights: an allocation to the agent of the rights of action and decisions over activities, but an allocation to the principal of the rights of control (for example, the activities of a skilled worker with high qualifications and discretionality, such as a chief laminator in a non-automated process, or the activities of a nurse in a hospital). If activities are not observable, then incentive- rather than control-based solutions to the problem are in order (as it is often the case in sale activities). This result can be obtained through a reunification of the rights of action, decision, and control with a more or less ample quota of residual reward rights and other property rights (Chapters 4 and 9).

A corollary of the previous proposition on the diversity of efficient and effective systems of work organization with activities with high or low observability is that *activities with different levels of observability should not be united in the same job* (Milgrom and Roberts 1992). The integration of tasks differentiated in that respect is likely to bias behavior toward those aspects of performance that are measured and rewarded at the expense of other tasks. Corrective measures should be taken if the aggregation is advisable for other reasons.

With regard to the conditions of efficient allocation of property rights to the workers, other studies in organizational economics have underlined the importance of other variables, beyond the degree of observability of work. Further elements are:

• the degree of substitutability of human resources
• the value added by work contributions with respect to other inputs
• the risk to which human capital is put with respect to other resources
• the extent to which the knowledge and competences on which activities are based have been accumulated by the workers and are tacit and poorly transferable.

If this set of variables is synthesized in an indicator of *human resources criticality*, keeping other conditions constant, it holds that if human resources are critical, a fair and efficient form of work organization should involve the allocation of property rights to the actors contributing those resources. In fact, arrangements under which "*work hires capital*," or associational contracts among the providers of different types of human, technical, and financial capital (Williamson 1980;

Grossman and Hart 1986; Hart and Moore 1990; Milgrom and Roberts 1992) are often observed in human-capital-intensive firms (law, consultancy, education, health care, etc.).

Analysis of preferences

A complete procedure for job analysis and design should either make assumptions on worker preferences or empirically survey them. Organizational economists usually opt for the first methodology – making assumptions. For example, some important economic treatments of job design and the organization of work assume that workers' preferences are distributed randomly and therefore do not affect efficient arrangements in a systematic way (Williamson 1980). Others, like agency theorists, assume that workers preference orders over actions and work arrangements conform to a principle of maximum economic benefit with minimum effort.

However, this approach has important methodological drawbacks: first, it binds solutions to a particular configuration of preferences, and second, it does not provide evidence that interested people would actually "vote" as assumed if requested to express preferences about work organization arrangements.

In this respect, the socio-technical tradition, in tackling the practical problems of implementing redesigned jobs, ended by developing an empirical approach to the analysis of preferences that can be claimed to be more rigorous not only in the terms of scientific research standards (it is more falsifiable) but also in terms of its accuracy in the representation of interests (a utility theory criterion).

Socio-technical research has shown, first, that the preferences that workers define regarding their own work activity *consider not only the actions to undertake, but also the modality by which such activities are organized*, and second, that *these preferences are not distributed randomly* but that their configurations are to a great extent predictable. Below, the main job attributes that are systematically used by job-holders to evaluate their jobs are reviewed, together with some substantive results on how they might be rated under what circumstances.

Variety

Individuals usually have definite preferences about the variety of activities that their jobs allow. That does not imply that in all cases more variety is preferred to less variety. For example, it has been found that in cases of uninteresting work with little autonomy, the horizontal aggregation of more tasks to augment the variety and reduce the monotony may not be appreciated by the workers. In fact, the increased variety in these situations augments the levels of attention required and fatigue for work that remains, which is in any case, uninteresting, and reduces the possibility of dedicating one's mind to other activities while one works in an automatic mode (for example, social relations, planning one's family life). On the other hand, more variety is often appreciated in the activities that have a high discretional content – for example, by line managers (Mintzberg 1973).

However, the horizontal aggregation of different activities assigned to the same person can be judged positively, even in situations of low discretion, where monotony reaches health-damaging levels. Conversely, variety can be judged negatively in high discretion and rich activities where high concentration and specialization are needed for problem-solving (such as for planners or researchers instead of line managers).

Autonomy

The degree of autonomy characterizes the vertical dimension of a job. Autonomy is the extent to which decision, planning, and control activities are attributed to the job. The degree of autonomy therefore expresses the element of discretion, self-control, self-determination, and the degree of freedom possessed by an actor in a job. For example, the job of a salesperson is usually characterized by a greater level of autonomy as against that of a production worker.

It has already been emphasized that the degree of information complexity and of variance in activities is positively related to the effective amount of autonomy in the job. Workers' preferences can be expected to act in the direction of extending the level of job autonomy required by task characteristics, because people fairly systematically prefer more autonomy to less autonomy, especially if they are currently in positions that are highly constrained and formalized (Crozier 1964; Crozier and Friedberg 1977; Salvemini 1977).

A dynamic factor and the starting level of autonomy explain the exceptions to this rule. If a very large increase of responsibility and autonomy is planned with respect to a preceding situation, and if the initial job is already challenging, then workers may perceive excessive risk and stress – especially if self-confidence and self-efficacy in the task are not yet high. For example, a young person in a staff position in a personnel department might not appreciate the premature assumption of personnel management responsibility. Or again, there may be a perception of too much autonomy and over-stress in very flexible organizational systems, where jobs are not well defined (Lawrence and Dyer 1983).

Identity and identification

The need for identity, for a positive image of oneself and the meaningfulness of one's contribution, is considered one of the basic needs of human beings. In work contexts its realization is influenced by the possibility of identification: with the output of work or with reference groups. Research shows that the lack of significance perceived in what a person does negatively affects job satisfaction (Hackman and Lawler 1971; Grunenberg 1976) and that a perception of significance is sustained by the clarity of connection between workers' contributions and identifiable and valuable outputs. For example, a job that is limited to monitoring an electric circuit in an assembly line for an office machine would be classified as a low meaningfulness job; while a polyvalent job inside an assembly group that has an identifiable output, such as a typewriter, would give the worker a greater sense of contributing something meaningful.

Studies on the meaningfulness of contributions have highlighted how this can be enhanced by either increasing the interest, image, and identifiability of the output (Bergami 1996) or by increasing the clarity of the relationship between the worker's individual and partial input and the final result (Salvemini 1977).

In a wider perspective, identification is however possible even where outputs are ill-defined. Identification with a social group – a craft, a firm, a profession – can perform this function (Gouldner 1957/8; March and Simon 1958). A work position belonging to a system with high identification potential (high social status, strong cultural identity, "a name") may be preferred to positions similar in tasks and better rewarded in low identification systems (Albert and Whetten 1989).

Social interactions

The possibility of engaging in social relationships and satisfying needs for closeness, sociability, power, and emotional or affective exchange at work is not uniformly appreciated by people. Factors that can influence the preferences of a worker for relationships with colleagues are diverse, and include age, cognitive style, how interesting and technically difficult the job is, and the interpersonal "chemistry" – how well people get along who are not free to select each other merely on the basis of personality fit (Tosi 1992).

However, even the early studies on job satisfaction revealed that extreme conditions such as isolation (the technical impossibility of speaking and interacting with others) can be systematic causes of dissatisfaction and stress (Walker and Guest 1952).

Development

A job attribute that is often under-defined is that of the dynamic prospects for professional development, which prepare the job-holder to assume other more qualified or attractive jobs in the future. Most workers assign a positive preference to good prospects for career development (meant in the sense of progressive development of the individual either within or outside the current firm), but the type of development sought is not uniform. For example a classic empirical distinction between employees with regard to the preferences for different career development paths is that between "locals" and "professionals": the former are people identified with a particular organizational system and oriented to the career within that system, while the latter are people identified with a profession, in search of career development within that profession – such people tend to have a much stronger propensity to geographic and organizational mobility (Gouldner 1957/8).

In addition "development" may refer to the content of jobs or also to the type of contract and the type of rights attached to it. For example, in traditional or handicraft industries in areas with strong local identity (e.g. in some industrial districts), people attribute a positive value to tradition, and to the continuation of social relationships and of craftsmanship. To this extent, the evolution in the content of work is not of primary interest. Instead, people often look for development from the point of view of the rights of control and ownership over their activity, with the objective of doing the same activity "on one's own behalf" instead of "working for others' (Inzerilli 1991).

Self-actualization

Both theory and empirical research have demonstrated that work can be a source of intrinsic reward for those who do it, rather than merely a means, and an expenditure, for receiving extrinsic rewards. Such intrinsic rewards, and the sense of self-fulfillment that these lead to, often consist of the psychological benefits from doing one's job, which can be manifested as interest, amusement, a sense of competency, or merely using all of one's capacities for a useful purpose. The primary characteristic of the job that can feed these intrinsic rewards from work is the correspondence of the job's activity with one's individual competences, capacities, tastes, and values.

It should be noted that, among all job characteristics, this one is the most volatile and subjective. Even if full recognition is given to the subjectivity of actors' preferences, one must note that it is very difficult for individuals to evaluate in advance how interesting an activity is likely to turn out. To that

extent, for this characteristic of the job even more than for the others, not only should preferences be empirically elicited, but actors must have the time to acquire and learn about them in the course of action. It is not by chance that many projects of job analysis and design have taken an "action-research" approach, based on long processes of collective field learning about cause–effect relationships and the objectives and preferences of actors (Elden and Chisholm 1993).

Health, safety, and quality of work life

This collection of factors is more relevant to the external conditions and the context of the job than to job content. Emphasis has recently been placed on the opportunity for designing not only jobs, but more ample change packages oriented to a more comprehensive improvement of the quality of work life (Hackman 1977).

This need derives primarily from the impact that job design has on safety, health, and the work environment. For example, jobs that are extremely fragmented with little variation can have negative effects on one's psychological health; and jobs that are not sufficiently rich and coordinated can increase the risk of errors and accidents (Golzio 1985). In addition, the organization of work obviously affects private and family life, through the availability of free time and energy, the richness of stimuli, the influence on social identity and prestige, and on psychological equilibrium. The characteristics of jobs also have important consequences on the possibilities for two-career families and on equal opportunities for men and women. In the *Quality of Working Life (QWL)* programs (Davis and Cherns 1975), the "comprehensive well-being" of the person is treated as relevant.

Another enlargment of perspective

proposed in QWL studies is to ask explicitly not only workers but also employers about their preferences for different job design solutions (Tosi *et al.* 1986). In traditional socio-technical studies, in fact, the "preferences" of the entrepreneur or manager were assumed to coincide with the technical needs based on the analysis of elementary operations and their interdependence – which is not necessarily the case. Lastly, technology and technical needs themselves are seen as an element that can be re-designed and co-designed together with jobs, rather than as a given and unmodifiable independent variable (Davis and Taylor 1973; Edberg and Mumford 1978).

Approaches to "joint-optimization"

Designing or assessing a micro-structural arrangement is, as is evident from the above discussion, typically a multiple-actors multiple-objectives problem. In the socio-technical tradition, this was early acknowledged and some rules for a "joint optimization" of the frequently contrasting "technical and social requirements" were devised to solve job design problems.

Operatively, it was proposed to assign utility points to each alternative organizational solution identified, both in terms of "satisfaction" and in terms of "efficiency." Each utility evaluation should be the sum of grades obtained by a job design on each relevant job dimension, such as variety, autonomy, the meaningfulness of the contribution, etc. Then the solution with the highest score could be chosen (Lupton 1975). For example, suppose that a particular arrangement, say an autonomous working group solution, receives the following "votes" on a 5 point scale from workers and management respectively: 2 and 3 on variety, 2 and 4 on autonomy, 4 and 4 on meaningfulness, 2 and 5 on development and

career implications. The work group solution would be evaluated with 26 total points $((5 \times 1) + (4 \times 3) + (3 \times 1) + (2 \times 3))$.

As an applied example, we can consider the implications that this would have in the Shell case, introduced earlier in this chapter. The analysis of variances and interdependences highlights how a recomposition of activities in larger and richer jobs would have many advantages: fewer errors, better final output quality, and a better utilization of personnel. On the issue of specialization, the filling phase and the electro-magnetic removing of grids required different training and timing, so that they could not be easily aggregated. To that extent, a technically efficient solution might have been to enlarge job boundaries to coincide with the two technically different phases of the process, to be assigned to two different small groups. Coordination tasks could be assigned to the most competent figure (the filler), whose status in the group was at stake.

The approach described employs a fairness criterion based on the sum of utilities. As such it could be criticized for implying inter-personal comparisons of utility – as well as for being an "armchair" integration of interests.

Indeed, both in theory and in practice these issues are conducive to solution by negotiation (or voting). If organizational solutions are negotiated, we could expect the parties to "weigh" their own utility for different jobs' attributes and find efficient exchanges between them (e.g. a greater flexibility in the allocation of people to tasks could be exchanged with greater task autonomy and meaningfulness); and that they would appraise their reciprocal "weight" or bargaining power through the negotiation process. A stylized reconstruction of a process of negotiated design of the organization of work in a harbor is presented in Box 10.1.

Box 10.1
Negotiated organization of
work in a harbor

In 1987 a long series of strikes led to the closure of Genoa harbor. This action was taken by the Autonomous Group of Harbor Workers – a quite unusual organization which is a combination of a trade union and a cooperative which "sells" its work force time to the harbor authorities – a consortium of enterprises. The group of harbor workers was created from the older corporations typical of commercial harbors and with time it acquired a series of privileges, the most important of which was an exclusive right to perform work related to harbor activity. The group is organized as an association, its members share the profits and have a kind of job security in the form of a fund to ensure everyone a minimum salary. Among members there are clan-like relationships with strong norms of mutual social assistance, which turn out to be useful in the coordination of various stowage jobs that are sometimes considered dangerous.

The Genoa harbor authority had been recently restructured, changing from a single functional hierarchy to a consortium of autonomous enterprises, with the goal of increasing awareness of local demands to utilize specific competences and reduce structural costs. The organizational change included the transformation of the role service system from an "on call" structure to one based on shifts. In the "on call" structure (which had been established when harbor traffic was much less intensive), workers were on duty and were called when a ship came in, based on the estimate of the number of people and skills needed to load or unload the cargo in question. Thus the group would work by the hour until the job was completed. The central figure of the group was the "caporal" who, usually, was the natural foreman; then there were the members of the group, who usually had worked together for some time. The foreman would assign jobs, supervise safety procedures and deal with the clients in order to ensure that a priority system was respected for loading and transportation. Both the "on call" structure and the role of the foreman were subjects of dispute by the recently organized harbor authorities. Management claimed full right to exercise control as far as relationships with clients were concerned, as well as the right to choose the foreman. In addition, management wanted to introduce a shift-based structure that would ensure the availability of resources present at the harbor, 24 hours a day.

Negotiations were difficult for both parties. The four different projects originally presented were nothing but the four combinations of "on call" and shift structures, and internal or external foreman (see line A–D in the figure). The negotiations finally failed and the harbor suffered a dramatic loss of traffic which was picked up by other ports.

It might have been possible to explore some Pareto-superior solutions (some of them were actually recently studied) to try to separate the issues in order to find efficient trade-offs, thus modifying negotiations from distributive to integrative ones. For instance, by separating the role of the foreman into its various components, it would have been possible to realize that the workers are actually interested mainly in an internal allotment of jobs and in the pursuit of safe working conditions; on the other hand, harbor management gets the most benefits from controlling the external components of that role. A specific redesign of the role of the foreman, properly negotiated among the parties, could have led to splitting the role into two parts; the first part would be assigned to a foreman chosen by the workers' association, thus responsible for the internal organization of the group; the second part would be assigned to a shift representative appointed by the port authorities, who would be responsible for job planning and customer relations. This project could be associated with a shift-based structure in which the group members are reliable and selected in order to preserve an efficient social coherence. However, this organizational structure implies gains by both parties and is thus Pareto-superior compared to the majority of other solutions that are based on negotiating the distribution of a fixed sum. In addition, it involves minimal losses in terms of cost efficiency, given that 24-hour service, together with management control and the planning of the stowers' jobs based on direct contacts with clients (the lack of which in the past increased costs and caused an arbitrary and uneven service) were guaranteed.

As the figure shows, this is only one part of the story. If we do not take for granted that a quasi-internal system, currently protected by the law, lasts forever, there are conflicts of interest that are much more fundamental as well as cost efficiency problems. As a matter of fact, management could consider the idea of paying the price of a unilateral action aimed at repealing the statute that protects the exclusive right of the group of workers to the harbor work so as to reinstate a free work market. However, the market mode of management of the transactions would not represent a point of agreement given that the game would be a zero-sum one. If the choice were between a free market and any form of internal regulation of work relations, both parties could only act unilaterally to try to win.

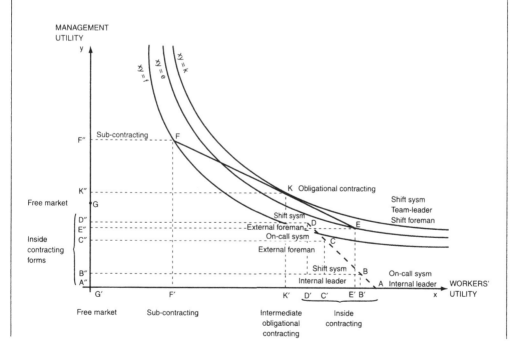

Another solution is, however, applicable. The harbor workers group would have to assume that it is improbable that the workers could maintain such a highly protected organizational structure in an environment where there is strong competition among European ports. On the one hand, it is true that it could be difficult for the harbor workers to sell their labor to organizations other than the port authorities. On the other hand, owing to the high costs of replacing them, the former would have the right to fight for a highly integrated solution. The port authority (1) prefers a free market because the harbor workers' skills are not sufficiently complex or specific to distort or block competition in dealing with loading and unloading procedures; (2) can count on a stronger negotiation position, being less replaceable and being supported by the increasing pressure of competition. If the harbor workers considered the risk of the port's declining, they might decide an acceptable sub-contracting formula. In the case of such a solution there would not be any additional statutory rights of monopoly: rather, we would notice privileged long-term contracts and an enduring relationship as long as the needs of both parties were totally satisfied. The port authority, however, could prefer this alternative to that of the free market, given that it would have to take into consideration the long experience at the port and the social cohesion of the various groups of workers..

All this said, the structure of negotiations on organizational forms can be described as shown in the figure. Among Pareto-efficient forms, two are particularly interesting; solution E (the mixed form of internal contracts) and F, the subcontracting solution. According to the equity criterion (the product of utilities) they both rank high, as is shown by the position of the hyperbola touching those points ($xy = e$ and $xy = f$). The truth is that the inside contracting E form is "more equitable" (given that $e > f$) and reflects more closely a principle of balance among the parties; whereas the sub-contracting form is more cost-efficient and reflects more closely the relative structural power of the parties. Also, if we assume that there is evidence of a continuum of possible contacts, between E and F, each of them representing various degrees of intensity of commitment of the parties (based on merely informal agreements) we can interpret line $E - F$ as a continuum of contract forms that are binding to various extents. Assuming hyperbole $xy = k$ tangent to this line, we can thus determine the degree to which the contract is binding as well as the specific internal organization form which tends to maximize the product of utilities (point K in the figure).

Source: Grandori (1991).

A critique that economists and games theoreticians would make about both the sociotechnical approach and the negotiation approach to job joint optimization, is that many of the conflicts between preferences about the configuration of the jobs could be simply resolved through side payments and monetary indemnities paid to workers in exchange for their acceptance of non-preferred jobs and tasks. In effect, this happens in part. Monetary aspects are in fact usually negotiated and defined in close connection with job characteristics. It happens that jobs that are unpleasant, or dangerous, are compensated for with extra bonuses. However, the effective use of payments for this function has limits for at least three important reasons. First, the monetization of the imbalance in the distribution of other desired resources would reduce the incentive to seek solutions that would be qualitatively superior. Second, not all the characteristics of the organization of work can be monetized without creating ethical problems and affecting the human rights of a worker (such as health). Third, compensation is typically a tool that is already overloaded with functions. Hence, compensation structure may send too many conflicting signals: payment should be correlated to the level of discretion and decisional responsibility; it should also (on the contrary) be an indemnity for jobs that are poor or hazardous; it should also guarantee a decent quality of life for everyone; it should also be correlated to results. The result of all this could be that of weakening the readability, the perceived fairness, and the transparency of any compensation system.

ALTERNATIVE FORMS OF WORK ORGANIZATION

In this section some salient discrete configurations of work organization, that have been shown to be effective under specified conditions, are reviewed. Such solutions involve different combinations and allocative configurations of the rights and obligations defining a job: the rights to action, decision, control, reward, and ownership; as well as different combinations of coordination mechanisms. *These are only a few combinations among the many that are theoretically possible.*

Williamson (1980) has proposed a distinction among forms of organization of work based on the allocation of property rights that can provide a useful starting point. The classification identifies a few broad types of proprietary structures: capitalistic, entrepreneurial, and collective. Within these general classes, various subtypes can be distinguished characterized by different allocations of other rights and obligations,[1] with the support of empirical organizational research.

Capitalistic forms

In the forms of work organization traditionally defined as "capitalistic," ownership over all of the technical resources – raw materials, intermediate products, finished goods, facilities, equipment, and know-how – is allocated to a single party. This actor or group of actors own the capital and "hire" the labor of others using various types of contracts. Primarily, then, within capitalistic forms, jobs are characterized by work assignments carried out wholly or in part "for" (in the interest of), and "according to the instructions of," actors who are not the agents themselves. In general, the effectiveness of this broad class of forms is linked to contingencies such as: the greater criticality of technical and financial capital with respect to human capital; large teams; and the measurability of agents' performances (Alchian and Demsetz 1972; Hart and Moore 1990; Chapters 4, 8, and 9).

However, many variants can be identified inside this general class, characterized by different degrees of division of labor, different allocations of decision and control rights, and different coordination mechanisms.

The "Taylorist/mechanistic" model

This model of organization of work is characterized by a maximum division of labor between different workers and by an allocation of the tasks of decision, coordination, and control to a super-ordinate authority. Conceptually linked to the thought of Taylor and Weber, it has been and still is widely diffused in manufacturing sectors with stable technologies and competition based on costs, such as traditional metalworking or food processing.

It is often said, especially in organization and sociological studies, that the "Taylorist" model is out of date, and that by now we are living in a "post-Fordist" epoch. This is probably true as regards many cultural and ideological traits of Taylorism and Fordism. However, if we consider the more technically organizational attributes of a configuration "with maximum specialization and programming," we may doubt whether it has disappeared or whether it may not be efficient in some circumstances. Thus, just as "Taylorism did not stop at Prato" (and in many other technological "places") – i.e. it did not spread everywhere – so in others it has been preserved or has been rediscovered. Specialization may also be associated with the deepening and excellence of knowledge and skills in sophisticated activities (Chapter 9). The case in Box 10.2 illustrates the possibility of a professionalized, post-industrial Taylorism.

"Craftsmenship" models

Historically antecedent to Tayloristic models, "craftsmenship" forms still provide an interesting, more decentralized, alternative. Consider the type of organization described in Box 10.3. Specialization and qualification are both high. The material and know-how are not standardizable, knowledge is to a large extent tacit and embodied in specific people, and workers' discretion has a paramount impact on product quality. Knowledge is diffused and technical resources are not clearly owned by any "one side." Actually it would be rather irrelevant whether the craftsmen are "hired" by the entrepreneur

who accumulated the commercial know-how or they were collaborating with him on the basis of long term contracts. In every case, property rights configuration would not change much and the key coordination mechanisms would remain the same: the standardization of know-how, work routines, communities of practice, norms, and codes of conduct.

Examples of this "craftsmenship" arrangement can be found wherever high-quality products must be made from non-standard raw materials, such as in the leather or woodworking industries and are particularly diffused and performing effectively in Italy and other European countries.

"Enriched" models

Many organizational change projects at the microstructural level have been aimed at modifying Tayloristic systems of work so as to make them more flexible and more motivating (Butera 1984). Three types of interventions about job descriptions have become widely diffused: *job rotation*, *job enlargement*, and *job enrichment*. Job rotation is aimed at increasing the knowledge of the worker about the entire cycle of work, increasing the worker's sense of offering a meaningful contribution, and the equivalence of resources through the periodic assumption of different jobs on the part of the same worker. Job enlargement is aimed at increasing variety through the aggregation of different tasks at the same decision level. Job enrichment is aimed at "vertically loading the job" with activities of decision, control, and planning, so as to guarantee a better regulation of variances, an improved capacity for local adaptation, and a better satisfaction of the workers' needs for autonomy and self-actualization.

Box 10.2
Professionalized Taylorism
in eyeglasses

Optissimo is a young commercial distribution firm (not more than six years of age) selling eyeglasses (sight and sun, with more than three thousand frames per sales point) and contact lenses of the best makes, through a network of its own shops located throughout the country.

The Offer

The offer combines customization with rapid service. Optissimo holds rapidity to be an important competitive factor because it enables the customer to exploit the time of the visit to the shopping mall (average 2.5 to 3 hours) to best advantage, avoiding further visits that may be needed. The formula of Optissimo's offer is proposed to the market through the opening of the first four sales points in a like number of malls.

Subsequently, Optissimo proposes the same offer to the customer going into the town center, in the opinion that the value of time is a crucial element also for this second segment of its clientele.

The Shop: the Contact Area

At the Optissimo sales point, frames are displayed in transparent cabinets, with interposed mirrors, for ease of access and choice by the client. The cabinets are lit so as to enhance the frames and decorate the shop walls.

The customer is welcomed at a reception point at the shop entrance (provided with cash register, telephone, and counter sales items). In the center are little tables (the counters), each furnished with chairs and personal computer, where the client is assisted by the *sales optician*. This person (holding an optician's diploma and suitably trained by Optissimo in-house) has the job of choosing and advising suitable lenses and counselling/confirming the best frames, from the technical point of view (correction of visual defect). In choosing the frames, the client does not consider (not being competent to do so) the aesthetic and functional effects of the lens needed (more or less thick) on the spectacles when it is mounted.

If the client arrives without a prescription, the *optometrist* (holding a diploma) proceeds to test the client's sight in the refraction room, a specialized part of the shop.

Staff (men and women) performing the two above roles wear a dark-colored uniform and a tag showing their first name.

The Shop: the Back Rooms

Behind the counters are the laboratory for lens construction and fitting, and the refraction rooms and rooms for application of contact lenses. The laboratory uses advanced electronic equipment enabling many operations to be effected automatically and in quick time. The laboratory is *open to view*, so that the customer can personally follow all the stages of construction and fitting of lenses as they are performed by the *laboratory technicians* wearing white coats. In the shopping malls, the Optissimo sales point is located in such a way that passers-by can see inside the laboratory.

The Process of Purchasing and Production of Service

While conversing with the customer, the sales optician uses the computer to input the customer's data in the data bank of the sales point; to look for the correct lenses and items regarding the frames. The duration of the conversation depends on the customer's needs, perceived or implicit. The sales optician's skills in listening and asking the right questions are aimed at understanding the use value of the spectacles for the client and thus advising on the most suitable kind of lens; for example, a bifocal lens instead of two distinct lenses. The sales optician has to manage both the client at the counter and those waiting (through visual contact and welcoming or orienting speech), especially at peak moments.

If eye testing is needed, the sales optician accompanies the client to the optometrist, who does the test in the refraction room. Testing is done with a state-of-the-art machine (the electronic Phoropter), equipped with measuring lenses. The machine changes the lenses rapidly in front of the customer's eyes and guarantees very precise measurement. As against the manual equipment traditionally used in family-run opticians' shops, the electronic test halves the time needed (15–20 minutes compared with the usual 40 minutes), and has much greater precision. The results of the test are entered by the optometrist in the "technical" prescription that contains indications about the value and type of lens and is passed to the sales optician.

The latter adds to the prescription the type of frame and places the document (together with the frame selected by the customer) in a numbered box which is then handed to the lab technician for construction and fitting of the lenses in the frame to complete the spectacles. Standard working occurs in mounting the "finished" lenses, already having the correct power (for visual correction) in the "closed" frame (that entirely surrounds the lens). The lab technician is responsible for the following operations:

- Extracting the finished lens from the relevant drawer and finding the focal point of the lens manually instead of electronically – because the operation is then more precise. Time for both lenses: two minutes.
- Inserting the frame in the "electronic scanfor," which reads (by means of the palpator) electronically the shape of the frame and transfers it to a display. The technician introduces in the display the data needed to obtain correct centering and then superimposes the centered lens so that the points coincide. The technician then inserts the lens in the grinder. This shapes the lens and marks the border, making it round so that it can be fitted in the frame. Time: for each lens two minutes, for both lenses four minutes.
- Manual fitting of lenses in frames. Time for both lenses: two minutes.
- Final check of the spectacles, consisting in verifying the centering, and checking the setting (the earpieces must have correct inclination with respect to the front piece, must sit neatly against the temples, and the lenses must be flush with each other). This synthesizes all the work performed for the client's satisfaction. Time: four minutes.

Work on the closed spectacles therefore takes 12–15 minutes. Variations are due to some not strictly technical operations (e.g. fetching lenses from the stockroom, or calls from the counter).

Special working consists in constructing special lenses (diopter power, type of lens, bifocal, gradual, or type of material) in the laboratory at the sales point. Particularly as regards special working, Optissimo undertakes to deliver the spectacles within one hour after the frames have been chosen (and, if necessary, performance of a test). The special working represents the distinctive element in Optissimo's offer as compared with competitors. In constructing the lenses, the lab technician performs the following operations:

- Choice of the ideal *blank* (the unground lens) and defining the work plan. The technician inputs the technical prescription data into the computer, which performs the necessary calculation to define the curve of the lens and gives the work plan (border and center of lens), tools (grinders), and setting for the work. The data are transmitted automatically to the machine that carries out the work. Traditionally the work plan is made by the optician who does all the calculations manually. Use of the computer, however, requires that the plan be verified by the lab technician, who, on the basis of experience, may make necessary modifications to it. Time: two minutes.
- Working the *blank*. This involves operating only on the back of the blank, in order to obtain the necessary rear curvature. The working consists of the stages of finding the inner curve that will give the diopter power), lapping (eliminating the furrows left by smoothing the surface) and polishing the lens. Time: smoothing for both lenses, 15 minutes, lapping and polishing both lenses, 11 minutes.

The subsequent operations depend on the choice of frames and are those of standard working.

Source: By Luigi Golzio.

This model is widely and effectively used in sectors and activities with high variance and high uncertainty, high interdependence among elementary operations, and relatively low requirements for specialization in single activities. A combination of these conditions has also occurred in some sectors that have been traditionally organized according to the Tayloristic model, such as the automobile or office equipment sectors. Richer or enriched jobs are more widely diffused in sectors of activity strongly exposed to variable market demands and competition based on differentiation and innovation of products; in activities involving white-collar workers, in many service activities, in activities in which the work is qualified and firm-specific.

"Networked" models

A more radical solution aimed at a more "flexible" organization of labor is to allocate a job to a group rather than to an individual (Salvemini 1977). These solutions are effective in the simultaneous presence of specialization economies in single activities and high variance and interdependence. Positive preferences for social interaction and group work, and low individualism concur. The success of Japanese group-based organization of work in sectors such as electronic equipment can be taken as an emblematic example.

Various configurations may be conceived and are diffused in practice. Herbst (1976) for example, early identified some "alternatives

Box 10.3
Castello pipes

Pipa Castello was founded in 1932 by Carlo Scotti in Cantu' for the production of a top quality smoking pipe that could compete with the best producer of the time, the English *Dunhill*.

Over more than sixty years, *Pipa Castello* has become known for being the only producer that directly performs all the phases in the construction of the pipe, including the research, the work on the briar wood, and the construction of the mouthpiece. Every pipe is carefully hand-made from one single piece, owing to the characteristics of the raw material (the briar wood).

Vertical integration distinguishes the Castello Pipe from its competitors, who assemble and sell pipes worked by small artisanal subcontractors.

Among smokers, the Castello Pipe is a true cult object which is often purchased for the simple pleasure of owning one, or for a collection. The firm is managed by Mr Scotti's son-in-law, who also owns it.

The Product: the Smoking Pipe

At the beginning of the century, the pipe was used by lower income people to smoke tobacco. Apart from those made with briar wood, pipes were therefore manufactured with poor raw materials, e.g. cherry wood, terracotta, and meerschaum. Cigarettes, on the other hand, were in limited production and were reserved for a wealthy elite of smokers.

Italy soon became the largest producer of pipes in the world, with 35–40 factories located mainly in Lombardy, many of which worked as subcontractors for distributors, often British, who then would put their trade mark (the "punzone") on the finished product.

The importance that Italy gained in the pipe making industry is explained, among other things, by the fact that the raw material, briar wood (a form of tumor of the roots of heather) is a Mediterranean plant typical of the Italian and French coastal areas.

The Woodworking Process

A good quality pipe is obtained by processing the briar wood (the "stick") which ages in the stockroom for nine years from the date when it is picked. Briarwood is the most appropriate material because it conducts heat very well. The wood of the internal walls burns, while the external walls stay fresh. Briar wood is also a very variable material: only at the end of its processing can one tell whether the finished product is worthy or not, as the owner of Castello Pipe comments: "When I start producing fifty pieces, I know how much manual labor is necessary; however, I do not know what I will get out of it, whether they will be first or second quality pipes."

The pipe's mouthpiece is made of plexiglass, which is a material that is exclusively guaranteed and is a result of a secret formula created by an established supplier.

The pipe production process consists of several phases: sketching and shaping of the bowl, hollowing and creation of the smoke channel, working the mouthpiece, polishing it, etc.). These steps are easily definable and can be carried out by individual workers (each worker may build a whole pipe or all the workers may specialize in one step) or by teams (all workers jointly build the pipe and are accountable for the production of the pipe).

The Organization of Labor

In the owner's opinion: "Each artisan feels a little bit like an artist and wants to work on his own. It is very important to respect this individuality, hence each worker is responsible for one detail, not the entire piece, because the Castello pipe is purposely the result of team work. The seven artisans who work for me need to be able to carry out each step of the process: they are perfectly interchangeable and I rotate them often. This allows them to check on each other's work. The team ensures the best quality: fourteen eyes see better than two. If each worker works on one detail, the pipe belongs to Castello and not to Joe or Tom; this way no jealousies are created. When I sell an exceptional piece, I show it to all the workers for the last time. They all know which pieces are the best, so they remember those and keep them in their minds as examples, and so they work well together.

In truth, it is the group that controls the entire production process of the pipe. Each morning the group decides who is doing what. In addition, it is always the group who regulates the behavior of its members. In the mornings, there are workers who come in at 8.00 and others who come in at 8.15. At noon some go home for lunch and others stay in the factory. During the day, if someone is bored with his job, another agrees to do it. As the owner states: "Everybody knows each other for a lifetime (the youngest artisan has fifteen years seniority) and one look in the morning is enough to figure out who is in good shape and who is not. They all are asked to give their best every day and I think this is the best system to meet my needs." The group even decides on new employees to hire. The owner proposes the potential new members and the group, after an apprenticeship period, chooses and decides the new hires. Lastly, it is the group that controls the quantity and the quality of its own work, as the owner confirms. "I cannot interfere and control the work of my artisans. I can only check the final results, which is very subjective. The pipe must be weighed in the hand, touched, felt in the mouth, to see what emotion it sparks in you."

About five thousand pipes are produced annually, of which there are not more than thirty of the highest quality. The production of a single pipe is difficult to plan because it depends on the condition of the raw material – the stick.

The wage for each artisan is personal, and is paid in cash every fifteen days. The wage level is much higher (almost double) the average of the artisans in the area. The cost of labor counts for 85 percent of the sales price. There is no formal checking on the work hours; individual statements are enough, and those who want, work also on Saturday. The artisans are not unionized. As the owner summarises: "We are a family. The pay, which I decide, is varied, because there are real differences among my artisans and they know it. They are masters over whom one cannot lord it, but only reason. I have to know how to stimulate them, to work on their own love for their craft, because from them I expect new shapes and lines for the pipe."

> The customer of Castello pipes, after the first purchase, becomes a pipe collector and is then certain to buy more pipes throughout his life.
>
> *Source*: By Luigi Golzio.

to hierarchy" in the organization of work, including *"autonomous work groups"* and *"matrix groups"*. An autonomous work group should be capable of regulating all relevant variances and interdependences internally. Therefore, it is effective if the external interdependences with other groups are not too high. Classical examples of this are "islands" of production or assembly (see Box 10.4a). The group is typically autonomous also in the flexible assignment of tasks to its members; ideally also in the selection of members. A more stable and specialized division of labor among the group members, by technical qualification and by type of output they contribute to, would configure a matrix structure at a micro-level, as is often used in the internal organization of the R&D function.

Finally, a fully networked form of organization of work can be even less pre-defined and more ad hoc. Work groups can be responsible both for assigning tasks internally *and* also endowed with the right to regulate external interdependences with ad hoc decisions (such as some experiences inspired by the *just-in-time* approach, as described in Box 10.4b).

Collective forms

The team-based forms of work organization considered hitherto are only so in a partial way. A more radical alternative is a group of associated workers entitled not only to rights of action and decision but also to rights of ownership of complementary resources. In collective forms of work organization, the workers share property rights over resources, including technical, commercial, and financial resources. Legal forms under which *peer groups* are actually constituted and play an important role in market economies include *cooperatives* and *partnerships*. They are diffused in sectors ranging from semi-artisan to professional work; and even in large and globalized firms – like professional partnerships with thousands of associates all over the world (Greenwood *et al.* 1990; Pfeffer 1994).

As with any other group of forms, a certain configuration of ownership rights is compatible with very diverse configurations of division of work and coordination. The case that follows can be used to reconstruct a discrete range of these, and also to introduce the discussion of certain *raisons d'être* of collective forms (see Box 10.5).

If the case of the institution and design of the cooperative structure is conducted like role-playing, various groups reach solutions that in different ways combine modalities of division of work, allocation of decision and control rights, and forms of reward. At least two salient alternative configurations can be compared.

Peer groups

In the extreme case, the peer group members are equally entitled to all the decision, control, and property rights and obligations associated with a certain action (Marglin 1974; Williamson 1980). Internal democracy can be representative rather than direct, in large size groups. Administrative responsibilities are

Box 10.4a
Semi-autonomous working groups: the Nobo Fabrikker AS case

In the 1960s and early 1970s, a team of researchers led by Prof. Einar Thorsrud of the Industrial Sociology Institute of Trondheim, Norway, completed a research project on "new organizational labor" experiments that many local enterprises were carrying out.

The goal of the research was to:

- get a picture of the top (in terms of the hierarchy) level workers and the various labor organizations they belonged to;
- carry out research on the possibility of the evolution of workers' participation in the job.

Among the various cases studied, some more successful than others, the best organization innovation experiment was that of Nobo Fabrikker AS. The main objective of this experiment was to increase opportunity for participation in the job among the workers and at the same time to empower those unutilized resources within the existing organizational structure. In doing this, there was an attempt to create a gradual transition from an organization based on principles of fragmentation of work to one based on autonomous groups.

The experiment took place in 1965 in the electric heater division of the headquarters of Nobo Fabrikker AS, located near Trondheim. Before the experiment, each worker was assigned a specific set of tasks with a high degree of redundancy.

In order to complete the experiment the workers involved had to be trained to be able to carry out at least three other tasks in addition to their own. All production was structured in five groups, each developing a significant portion of the task. Thanks to the close collaboration among groups (transfers of workers among groups was quite frequent and occurred based on the respective work loads), the workers managed to learn about the entire production chain.

Within the groups, each member was not assigned a fixed task, rather, all of them helped with the common task based on criteria of need and their own personal preferences for certain assignments. As a result, after about three years, half of the workers were able to carry out all tasks related to a certain division. Each year, each group elected the person who would coordinate relationships with the other groups and with the local management. The five contact people, who worked full-time just like the other workers, represented, together with local management, a committee in charge of overseeing a number of issues: production plans, budget, organizational and technical development, suggestions, etc. The main responsibility of the top management was to oversee boundaries between each group – that is, maintaining relationships with the top management itself as well as the other staff, and supplying materials as well as technical equipment and information.

The workers agreed that the new organizational model and the new technical and social working conditions were a definite improvement over the previous ones; they displayed a high degree of involvement in their job, as was shown also by the increased number of suggestions that were made by the groups.

The electric heater division had a minimum turnover thanks to the excellent relationships established between the workers and the local management. In terms of industrial democracy, the most interesting aspect of the experiment was that the workers were very eager to carry out the project.

The experiment has shown a dramatic change from individualistic behavior to a group oriented attitude; this change can be explained by the improved knowledge of the work and the working structure. In addition, while earlier workers were involved in the planning of labor from day to day, now they actually participated in a three-month planning horizon.

Thanks to all this the workers reached a level of competence that allowed them to be totally confident of handling any problem internal to their unit. On its side, the management stopped checking up on the individual workers and its relationships with the work groups started to be regulated by the payment system, by sales schedules, and by production techniques. Even quality control became a responsibility of the workers, that led to a reduction in customer complaints.

Source: Martino (1982).

Box 10.4b
Networked jobs: the Toyota kanban case

The kanban system represents an example of production organization in which the central office coordinating the transfers of materials among divisions is lacking; such an office is however a typical structure in western countries.

Kanban, which in Japanese means "wooden sign" (those typically put outside a store), identifies a form. At the end of the daily production, the divisions in the final assembly phase communicate their production orders – or kanban – for each kind of component or semi-finished product they need (engines, transmissions, headlights, etc.) to an office located within the warehouse. The kanbans report the kind and quantity of the goods picked up, as well as the schedule for future re-supply. The divisions that supply these components pick up the kanbans based on regular schedules at the warehouse office – a few times per day. Therefore, the kanbans work as order forms and are returned to the warehouse together with the actual delivery of the products ordered. In short, kanbans have two functions: order forms and delivery slips. The division that receives the kanban during the final phase of assembly communicates its orders – or kanbans – to the divisions directly above it; thanks to such circulation of kanbans, the relationship of orders to deliveries among divisions working closely in the production process is extended to external suppliers who have long-term contracts with the firm.

Such a system assumes that the divisions at the beginning of the cycle match their production based on the demand coming from the divisions below them which are written up in the kanbans. In such a circumstance, the single divisions do not have to strictly follow the orders given by the central offices which can easily be overridden owing to issues arising between the planning and the revision process; rather, they can make necessary adjustments in a timely and coordinated fashion thanks to the use of kanbans.

A second and important prerequisite for meeting high levels of productivity (possibly linked to the use of the kanbans) is the development of flexible and multi-functional workers' skills; in fact, workers are assigned to various phases of the process based on work loads. The result is the reduction to a minimum of dead time for each worker.

A third important aspect is quality control: this occurs along the whole cycle and is not limited to the end of it. The divisions at the end of the cycle have the choice of refusing the semi-products that are produced by the divisions above them.

Finally, the direct link with the order issuing phase enables the company to substantially reduce investments in stock, justifying a "zero-stock" system. Such a structure resolves the hierarchical problem as well, given that production levels and product mix adjustments occur without any interference by the central offices within the factory.

In addition, thanks to team work, the interdependence of the phases and the typically Japanese culture, the kanban system enables potential opportunistic behavior typical of any non-hierarchical structure to be reduced.

Source: Aoki (1988).

---

allocated by election (and occasionally by rotation).

Specifying the conditions for the effectiveness and efficiency of these forms is not simple, to the extent that the debate on these has been strongly polarized by positions with an ideological or universalistic character in favor or against (especially between radical and neo-institutionalist economists). On the basis of the available empirical and theoretical research, it is, however, possible to outline the following variants of collective forms and the following evaluative considerations.

Employee-owned firms persist and are efficient in both productive and motivational respects in activities where human and social capital is the critical input, from the cooperatives of masons and construction workers to those of professionals and consultants (Zan 1992). In the case where the work is specific and not easily monitorable, there are even stronger reasons to align the interests of participants through the diffusion of

property rights (Fama and Jensen 1983a, b; Chapter 9).

Federative groups

A milder version of collective organization is that of a group of co-workers who collectively possess some or all of the main means of production, but who hold separately the right to the rewards deriving from their own work (Demsetz 1967). This can be defined as a *federative group* to evoke the community of resources or property but the retention of the rights to residual rewards and self-regulation. In this case the activities must be separable, even if there is participation in the use of common resources (e.g. the commercial contacts, the plant, a brand name).

For instance, a training firm whose partners own the brand name and the offices, but where each selects his/her own collaborators, uses a partly personal network of contacts, draws on partly self-owned, not communal

Antefact

Twenty women living in a small community in southern Italy have decided to put an end to their permanently unemployed status and start a business. The motivations leading these women to take this initiative are as heterogeneous as their personal characteristics, educational backgrounds, and political ideologies. To some of them, work is a livelihood, due to the unemployed status of their husbands or fathers; to others work means dignity and autonomy as opposed to a situation of dependency on other relatives; to still others work enables them to build on their own emancipation in a social and economic context that is still very backward; for all of them, work is a dream come true. The business idea involves offering (at a very low price) to perform all the finishing work on knitwear produced by large firms in northern Italy.

Doing finishing work on knitwear is a very expensive process because it is considered high intensity work and a high quality clothing item is made of good quality collars, cuffs, etc. (the so called finishings). The worker-entrepreneurs know that the lower prices which northern Italian firms demand in order to offset the transportation costs will limit their personal earnings (to the point of being lower than the salary of a hired textile worker). However, as they like to say "it is better than nothing." There are two problems facing these women today: first, it is necessary to find the best arrangement for the management of the new company; second, it is necessary to define an organizational model and a compensation system. There are several questions that need answering. How do we allocate property rights? How do we distribute decisional rights? Who will decide whether or not to accept a contract? On what basis will employees be compensated?

The cost of the equipment, and the start-up costs of the firm have been divided equally among the twenty women, and there is an agreement that property rights should also be distributed equally. The new company is thus set up as a cooperative in which each "partner-worker" has the right to vote on company decisions. The first conflict among the twenty partner-workers arose when it was time to discuss for which decisions it would be necessary to opt for a democratic vote. Some partners proposed the creation of a few new positions (a director, a production manager and a customer service manager) who would be responsible for operative decisions and who would oversee contracts that required a working commitment of over 10 days. Others maintained that given the small size of the company, decisions needed to be made within some kind of a permanent "Agora." The second issue that led to a conflict is more serious and deals with the compensation policy. Again, there are two "groups" having conflicting opinions.

The first group proposes a form of compensation for individual labor based on the average number of knitwear items produced in a month. This hypothesis also implies that each worker would have to perform all necessary production steps in order to complete one clothing item. Unanimously, at the beginning of each week, the workers would decide how to "rotate" themselves within the various tasks in order to ensure fairness. The second group instead believes that it would be better to specialize work among groups with homogeneous tasks, thus creating a sort of assembly line. The partners-workers would therefore be compensated on the basis of the work performed individually (here again by counting the items produced).

Epilogue

The St Francis Cooperative – the name was chosen for the "women's firm" to remember St Francis who would protect them along the road – became a shining example for many other initiatives in the area. In 10 years, twenty cooperatives have been created, supporting unemployed women. The St Francis Co-op decided to adopt a collective method for decision-making: all decisions took place through a voting process and were made based on a majority vote. No Director was nominated. The organizational model chosen was the assembly line one, characterized by high workers' specialization within the various tasks. In order to ensure continuous work, the co-op invested in keeping stock available at all times. However, this created some problems when the co-op accepted small contracts or when the customer requested a quick turnaround. Compensation was calculated based on the hours worked and not the number of items produced. Quality control was a group assignment given the close working relationships that the women had with each other. A sum of money necessary to pay ongoing expenses was deducted from each pay check.

This solution worked very well for the first few years. Quality control, the hourly based compensation, and the choice of accepting even barely profitable contracts permitted the co-op to work full-time for a few years. However, once the initial motivation died, conflicts arose concerning the company strategies. Some partners wanted to expand the range of activities which would, in addition to doing finishing work, also include higher value activities that would increase profitability. Another group wanted an increase in the hours of work. The system of compensation based on hours worked led to the co-op splitting into two factions: those who wanted and could afford to work long hours and those who by choice or need could not be away from home for more than 6–8 hours per day. This, together with the initial and irreversible choice of opting for specialization, led to conflicts among the partners-workers and to delays in the delivery of contracts.

The cooperative attitude that had made this dream come true disappeared. Besides more conflicts, there were boycotts, sabotage, and factions were created with little "bosses." The St Francis Co-op ceased to exist on December 31, 1997 without being able to celebrate its tenth birthday. The equipment, bought by an entrepreneur from the Marche region, is today being used in a small firm in Albania.

None of the partners became rich but all of them are convinced that it was worth the experience.

Source: By Giuseppe Soda.

knowledge, and has the right to the economic results of the projects performed, after allotting a percentage to the common structure, would be an example of federative group.

In the real case of the St Francis Cooperative, a solution was adopted having some features of the peer group, others of the federative group, and yet others of a classic Taylorist-bureaucratic model. The outcome of this was not positive. The solution of work organization adopted, beyond distribution of ownership rights, envisaged an impracticable combination of highly divided labor and the absence of coordination mechanisms, burdened by incentives to maximize the number of hours worked rather than the quantity and quality of the outputs.

Entrepreneurial forms

A possible alternative for organizing the work of finishing garments could be an entrepreneurial form instead of a collective one. For example, the firm producing the garments could hand over the finishing stages to independent outside workers. If there exists a

sector where these forms have always been widespread, it is indeed the textile-clothing sector.

Entrepreneurial forms can be conceived as mixed arrangements, where actors owing and contributing technical and financial capital also contribute work, and actors who contribute work are also owners and contributors of human and technical capital (competence and task-specific equipments).

Among entrepreneurial arrangements, one more "external" and one more "internal" form can be identified as particularly relevant.

Putting out

This has been analyzed as an archaic and outdated form of organisation by some scholars (Williamson 1980). In their view, the advantages of flexibility are overridden by the costs of free-riding, negligence, waste, and delay. Ironically, the retention and revitalization of putting out in the textile sector has been a factor in the success story of Italian fashion worldwide (Box 10.6). The advan-

> **Box 10.6**
> Putting out in the fashion industry: the Benetton mills
>
> The 80,000 clothing items that Benetton sells can be categorized in three groups: wool, cotton, and outfits and Capi Spalla. Their production occurs partially in Benetton's own factories, partially at subcontracting factories, but also at a number of independent factories: the mills. Over the years, the number of mills has increased based on the growth of Benetton itself. Today, the mills number about 500, if we exclude those directly managed by firms owned by Benetton. Their dimensions range from very small to medium, based on the production phases that they specialize in, and the technology they employ. Generally, each mill carries out only one phase of the production process, realizing economies of scale in that single phase. Within the entire transformation process (which for wool starts with the production of the fiber itself) the mills fit at the beginning, in the phase that starts from the thread or the material, transforming it into the final product. The mills concentrate their activity in tasks that demand high intensity labor such as cutting, outfit-making, ironing, and embroidery.

From a juridical-formal point of view, each mill is autonomous and independent. Today, as in the past, there are no written contracts between the mother factory and the mills. Relationships are managed through some tacit and informal rules that are the result of selection, inclusion, and dismissal procedures that the parties have developed over the years and that allow the mother factory to directly monitor the single mills without any binding contracts.   The rules pertaining to the management of the relationships are very simple. Benetton acts as central agent and controls the entire production chain; it sets quality standards, the ratio between prices/costs, and the quantity to be produced. The mills are not asked for any planning commitment; the issue concerning production comes down to respect for the standards and the delivery schedules. Since production is fragmented among so many factories, it is critical that the mother factory be in charge of quality control, keeping statistics for each of the middle products; to this end, each lot is brought to Benetton before then being sent on to the mill that will perform the next working phase. Mills work exclusively for Benetton (except those specialized in embroidery and printing) who usually keeps them fully operational all year round. Together the mills can be considered as a relatively stable group of factories even though there is some rotation among them, which is encouraged by Benetton itself. Each mill is free to end the relationship at any time. The same can be said about the mother factory even though the stability of the system gives advantages to both of them..

The mother factory does not guarantee the mills a constant level of work; however the now commonly used practice of accepting more contracts then one can complete, has allowed the development of confidence about the reliability of the relation. In fact, what characterizes this group of factories is the strong and tight collaboration among them, around which also rotates the flexibility that the fashion industry demands nowadays. Collaboration however also brings competition among the mills to be "the best" – think for example at the "Benettoniadi" – true battles between different mill teams. The overall positive feeling that the success of each mill is based on the overall system facilitates collaboration and a sense of belonging, thus creating improvements to efficiency.

Source: S. Bagdadli, F. Buttignon, and D. Montemerlo, "The Benetton Case," in Airoldi and Ruffini (1993).

tages of specialization and flexibility in productive combinations as a function of demand, as against integrated capitalistic forms (Sabel and Piore 1984) have been concretized thanks mainly to coordination through very clear sectoral/local rules and routines, though not very formal ones (Brusco 1999) – which were probably absent from the putting-out systems of the nineteenth century (Kieser 1993).

Inside contracting

Instead of a commissioning firm entrusting production of proprietary materials (and, if necessary, with proprietary equipment) to outside entrepreneurs, one can envisage a situation where a firm lacking the technical equipment and knowledge specific for a given activity may make use of "inside entrepreneurs" able to perform the production –

by supplying complementary resources such as finance capital, buildings, or structures and competences for marketing and distribution. Thus, not only decision and control rights but also ownership is diffused and mixed, rather than entirely held by any single party. One party, the employer, owns some tools and resources such as the buildings, central facilities, sales outlets, and commercial brands. Despite this, the transformation and the generation of products or services are carried out by actors who own complementary assets, such as competence, technical instruments, software, and relational capital. In addition, they may hire and manage their own co-workers and are compensated on results according to an agreement negotiated in advance. Even though this system has been diffused in agriculture in an economically distant past – for example, in the farms of the beginning of the century, the milling of grain or milking of cows were entrusted to specialist entrepreneurs who went from one farm to another – it is not difficult to find modern and highly efficient examples, when economies of specialization and the differentiation of knowledge for conducting the different activities are coupled with site specificities and other sources of interdependence.

Box 10.7 describes the case of a professional service firm, but inside contracting has been resurrected also in industrial production, for regulating the outsourcing of material handling, maintenance, and other activities that are carried out "under the roof" of the externalizing production firm by independent entrepreneurs.

SUMMARY

The theme of the organization of work was introduced by recalling some elements of the history of the interventions and projects in this "contested terrain."

A basic model of analysis and design was displayed in the second section, including and combining both socio-technical and economic model variables. In particular, economic models have been useful for reintroducing concerns and concepts relevant for appraising the importance of *production costs and learning economies*, and of the *specificity and criticality of human resources*, among the antecedents of work organization forms – in addition to the much debated impact of *variance and interdependence* – and of *property rights* among their dimensions – in addition to *action, decision, and control rights*.

In the last section, a range of discrete forms of work organization – characterized by different ownership structures, different decision and control structures, and different mixes of coordination mechanisms – have been described and assessed. The relative superiority of "capitalist," "collective," and "entrepreneurial" proprietary structures is connected mainly to the relative criticality of technical and financial resources, or instead of human resources. Among capitalistic forms, the specialized and programed "Taylorist-like" organization – especially effective in divisible and sophisticated tasks – has been joined by "enriched" models (with more "generalist" and discretionary jobs, better suited to adapt to varying demands and to solve new problems), network models (providing flexible combinations of specialized competences and activities as conditions change). When human capital is critical (add more value, is more exposed to risk, is poorly transferable) "group-like" arrangements are effective, in the federative group form – if contributions are discernible – or in the full peer group form – in "team production" and

The Taj Business School was founded in the early 1980s by Peng Lee, a leading man in the electronics industry who believed that a top training school was vital for the economy of any country. The school owned a beautiful post-modern building facing a small artificial lake with ducks and lotus flowers and was equipped with the latest technology. Facilities included two auditoriums and 50 classrooms, each equipped with multiple sliding blackboards, video-beam, video camera, and personal computer, an excellent snack bar-restaurant and a gym with a heated swimming pool. All this infrastructure represented the "hardware" of the school. What the school lacked was faculty members and researchers. They were the actual "software" of the school, the people who held the scientific and technical knowledge to produce and deliver the service in question: training.

The division of labor reflected (or at least should have reflected) the specialized competences of individual faculty members. Each course was planned and coordinated by an internal faculty member (usually an expert on the course topic) who would choose to staff the course with assistants who were the most knowledgeable on the course material and were therefore a good match; for example, an executive training course required more experienced faculty whereas a basic course could be taught by junior members of the staff. When a faculty member was thought to be an expert on a topic, there was a true competition for his/her expertise, with the consequence that some faculty members were overloaded and others much less so. The products that Taj offered on the market were courses, research studies, and other projects that were planned with large (though not total) autonomy by the various faculty members who would "hire" the best resources for the job.

Shared norms and mechanisms facilitated the coordination of courses and faculty as well as standardization of the product. Faculty members were compensated based on specific categories. Teaching had a different rate of pay than other activities such as the preparation of course material. A fixed portion of the course was the responsibility of the coordinator, who was thus paid based on his/her planning and management activity. Compensation based on the success of a certain product could also be awarded. The remaining part of the profit was awarded to the "department" or "client group" of which the coordinator or the course were part. The school faculty was in fact grouped on the basis of professional families or sometimes client groups at whom the courses were aimed. Each similarly defined "area" consisted of a series of common structures that everybody had access to and its objective was to standardize knowledge though the development of material and specific know-how later made available to other faculty. The margins (profit) obtained from the different courses were used to pay for general and shared costs (advertisement of courses, research, faculty training) and anything left over was added to the central budget. In fact, in order to standardize ways of delivering services, as well as to safeguard the "Taj, training for the future" trademark, some central services in charge of marketing and communication were created. With the same objective, logistics, copying, and scientific research offices were established. These structures would guarantee, more or less in general terms, equity among the clients, economy of scale within the services for the delivery of activities, and integration with the market.

The image of matrioska fits Taj well, even though the external shell started to be a little heavy and, with the increase of training, the client integration was not always total.

Source: By Silvia Bagdadli.

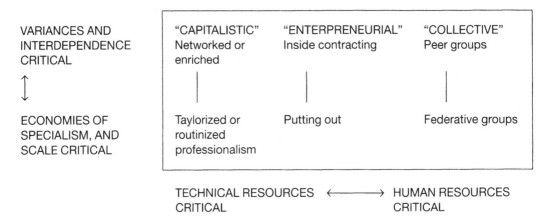

VARIANCES AND INTERDEPENDENCE CRITICAL	"CAPITALISTIC" Networked or enriched	"ENTERPRENEURIAL" Inside contracting	"COLLECTIVE" Peer groups
↕			
ECONOMIES OF SPECIALISM, AND SCALE CRITICAL	Taylorized or routinized professionalism	Putting out	Federative groups

TECHNICAL RESOURCES ⟷ HUMAN RESOURCES
CRITICAL   CRITICAL

Figure 10.4 Comparative evaluation of work organization forms

"intensive interdependence" situations. In entrepreneurial arrangements, the same actor is the assets owner and provides critical work services. In the putting-out system, external entrepreneurs process materials which are owned and delivered ("put out") by another firm, thereby realizing phase-specific economies of specialization and scale. In the inside contracting system, entrepreneurs are "internal," in the sense they use common resources and structures owned by a firm, but they produce effective specialized services too thanks to their proprietary assets (knowledge, electronic equipment and programs, tools and instruments).

In very synthetic terms, some of the main variations between the considered forms can therefore be captured by a two-dimensional space of human resource criticality and task interdependence, as indicated in Figure 10.4.

Exercise: Westa I

The story

The Westa publishing company was set up in 1989 in St Petersburg. It consisted of three people: the director and two young women, Natasha and Marina. The only equipment was a computer and a laser printer. Westa's activity involved typing new books on file and printing one copy.

The division of labor was very simple. The director was responsible for seeking new clients; Marina typed the texts on computer and Natasha dealt with the editing and printing. They were paid for each printed page of the original copy. Payment was documented by part-time accountants.

As from 1980, the demand for this kind of service began to grow very quickly. Many daily newspapers and periodicals were springing up, and there was a large, constant request for thrillers, love stories, and Russian literature. New firms also wished to print advertising prospectuses and headed letter paper.

There were plenty of firms like Westa in St Petersburg, but there was work for all of them.

Early in 1990, it became plain that one computer and two operators were no longer sufficient. Marina hired three part-time typists; Natasha could no longer deal with all the work – editing the files, printing them, correcting the errors, and then printing them again; so she took on a part-time girl to correct the errors.

At the end of 1990, Westa rented three rooms, five computers and two laser printers. Marina headed the group of six typists; Natasha was responsible for editing and printing the copy; two girls worked with her; an accountant was hired. The director was responsible for the marketing and administration; and the group now included an engineer, who provided technical backup.

In 1993 there were two groups of operators headed by Marina and Natasha.

Marina's group dealt only with typing the texts on computer. There were three computers, with three girls working in the morning and three in the afternoon of each day. This group produced the files, indicating only the chapters, with no form of editing.

Natasha's group saw to editing the files, using appropriate software, printing them, correcting errors, printing them again and producing the text. They used a further three computers and two laser printers.

At a certain point, the group's productivity began to decline. Clients found many errors in the finished products and were dissatisfied. "We should like the files transcribed without errors, and we should like to have them by the deadlines fixed. If you cannot do a good job, we shall find another firm," said an angry client to the director on receiving his order two days over the deadline and with various errors on the first page.

The decision to reorganize the work

"What can we do? Who is responsible for all these errors? Why can't we ever deliver on time?" the director asked Marina and Natasha.

"The errors are typos, nothing to do with us," replied Natasha.

"Your job consists in finding and correcting them, and you're responsible for the time lost," retorted Marina.

"That will do, thanks. We used to be friends. Let's try and make some changes. We are losing customers and lots of money; if you don't want to return to poverty, put your heads together and think up something," said the director.

By Silvia Bagdadli

Question

* How would you reorganize the work in order to recover productivity and increase the workers' perceived benefits?

Chapter 11

The Organization of the Firm

Whether we should have first gained an understanding of what goes on within firms – the theme of this chapter – in order to understand interfirm boundaries and coordination – the theme of the next chapter – or, vice-versa, to understand first how it happens that firms are constituted and grow, is uncertain. In either case we would have needed to rely in part on the content of the other chapter. In fact, the models of analysis and design of firms' efficient boundaries are based on an array of properties ascribed to internal organization with respect to external organization. On the other hand, the solutions of division of labor between organizational units and of inter-unit coordination employed with a firm depend on which activities and relationships have been internalized within the firm's boundaries and why. Aware of this inter-action between the problems addressed in these last two chapters, let us start with internal organization, just to keep track of our itinerary from the more micro level of human resources and work organization; to the meso level of the pattern of division of labor and of coordination between the most important organizational units of the firm; to the more macro level of the boundaries and coordination mechanisms between firms.

The analysis of organizational units and coordination mechanisms inside firms is a field of study that is central to the discipline of organization and thus rich with models.

Studied together, the most well-known and tested of these models can help us to resolve the two fundamental organization design issues at the firm level:

- how to explain and design effective, efficient, and equitable boundaries between organizational units, both in terms of criteria by which to divide and allocate activities (for example, by product, by technical specialization, etc.) and in terms of the degree of specialization (which and how many activities to assign to which units);
- how to explain and design effective, efficient and equitable mechanisms of coordination and control between units.

These elements and the key variables used in this application of the general design framework (Chapter 8) at the firm level are highlighted in Figure 11.1.

In this chapter, it is assumed that firms – as collections of differentiated resources and activities and as nexuses of contracts allocating rights and obligations over them among relevant actors – exist. This very fact can be taken as problematic, but here this will be done fully only in the next chapter.

The structure of this chapter is analogous to those of the former chapters in Part III. In

KEY VARIABLE USED	DESIGNED ORGANIZATION TRAITS	INTERNAL ORGANIZATION FORMS
- Information complexity - Interdependence - Conflicts of interest and control losses - Economies of specialization, scale and scope	• UNIT BOUNDARIES: - Type of specialization - Decision and control rights - Ownership of assets • INTER-UNIT COORDINATION MECHANISMS: - Prices and incentives - Direct communication - Programs, routines, and procedures - Supervisory and decisional hierarchy - Liaison roles and integration units - Meetings, committees, and team work	• "UNITARY" - Mechanistic - Loosely coupled (e.g. professional bureaucracies) - Integrated - Networked • "DIVISIONAL" - Mechanistic - Integrated - Networked - Loosely coupled (e.g. H-forms and M-forms)

Figure 11.1 Organization analysis and design at the firm level

the first part, the above two issues will be dealt with by providing a general *procedure* or *method* of analysis and design. The underlying logic, then, is one of organization design as heuristic problem-solving, where the main task is the search for and the construction of ad hoc solutions, suitable to govern a firm's activities and resources. In the second part, a set of known organization forms diffused and successful in practice under certain circumstances will be assessed. They will be described as salient combinations between modes of partitioning of action and property rights and obligations and modes of coordination, and will be comparatively evaluated in terms of their superiority in governing certain economic activities and relations. The focus there is therefore not on the search and construction of organizational solutions, but on the choice of a superior form among given

structural alternatives (conceivable even as an optimal form within the set).

UNIT BOUNDARIES AND INTER-UNIT COORDINATION: A PROCEDURE FOR ANALYSIS AND DESIGN

One of the most obvious and central organizational problems for a firm is to determine whether its organization is "right" or "wrong." Consider for example the problem described in Box 11.1.

In solving this type of problem, one could easily make the error of seeking to deal with the symptoms and the obvious dysfunctions by investing in better mechanisms of coordination between organizational units. The costs of the resulting structure could be particularly high, in case of basic problems in the configuration of units and their

> **Box 11.1**
> The organizational problem
> at Silca
>
> A few years ago, the CEO of Silca, a medium-sized firm specializing in the production of machinery for paper mills, was struggling with a problem. The problem was the organization of the company. The firm had experienced organizational problems in the past, but these had become more serious when a sectoral crisis hit orders and gross sales to the point where a re-organization was needed. The costs of organizational changes at that time were judged to be lower than the negative consequences of keeping the current structure.
>
> The problems showed themselves through routine symptoms: information was being lost or distorted on its way from one department to another (sometimes causing machines to be built with different characteristics from the original project), there were staff conflicts at various levels, there were no-shows at meetings because people were too occupied with routine tasks, work schedules were being constantly moved back with the excuse that "more urgent orders" were coming in, and there were situations of over- and understaffing in various offices.
>
> The firm, with about one hundred employees and ten operational units – all reporting to the CEO – was perceived as being too "heavy."
>
> *Source*: A. Grandori and P. Susani, Caso Silca in Decastri (1986).

responsibilities. In effect, in this case one would incur the double cost of an inadequate division of work and of an excessive coordination effort, largely absorbed by the necessity to mediate the conflict and the dysfunctions generated by that partitioning of tasks. Therefore it makes sense to start from an analysis of the effectiveness and efficiency of the boundaries of organizational units, before examining the coordination mechanisms.[1]

To understand what the efficient boundaries of an organizational unit can be, it is necessary to start with a smaller and more elementary unit of analysis. As in the case of unit operations and jobs, when analyzing the boundaries of organizational units, we should consider more elementary activities that may or may not be aggregated in an organizational unit. However, to analyze the effectiveness and efficiency of a complete system of firm activities starting from technic-

ally inseparable activities is usually an extremely expensive process which tends to yield benefits that decrease sharply with increasing distance from the level of the unit being analyzed.

In the case of Silca, we ran a field experiment analyzing 45 elementary activities. Those 45 elementary activities were internally homogenous both from the point of view of the techniques employed, and from the point of view of the relevant market (export or domestic). Although they would have been further technically separable, it was judged not efficient to make the analysis more detailed. Some examples of the firm's definition of elementary activities include the following: "*domestic marketing; foreign marketing; promotion and publicity; domestic sales; export sales; coordination of domestic agents; coordination of export agents; technical project implementation; commercial project* implementation; drafting of domestic order contracts; drafting of export order contracts". To keep the task manageable here the exemplified analysis will be conducted on 11 activities, rather than 45.

Having identified the elementary activities, the following variables have been considered: *task complexity and environmental uncertainty, specialization, scale and scope, interdependences, control costs, and conflict of interest.* In fact, among the variables generally relevant for organization design (Chapter 8) these have been shown to have a particularly significant impact on effective internal firm structures (Chandler 1962, 1977; Thompson 1967; Lawrence and Lorsch 1967; Williamson 1970; Galbraith 1974, 1977; Teece 1980a; Child 1984; Becker and Murphy 1992). To the extent that many of these key variables are attributes of the relationships between activities – owing to the resources they use or to external factors – a good basis for analysis is a matrix that displays them both in rows and columns (Chapter 8; see Figure 11.2 for the Silca case).

Uncertainty analysis

Elementary activities can be characterized by a relatively greater or lesser degree of information complexity, including both task complexity and environmental uncertainty. Differences in the degree of information complexity of the activities is a barrier (which becomes a source of costs) to their combination. For, to the extent that accomplishing a particular task is certain or predictable – without important exceptions with respect to a regular process or normal pattern – that activity can be governed in the long term by using rules, programs, and standard operating procedures. On the other hand, to the extent that an activity involves exceptions and requires ad hoc research for new solutions, that activity requires local discretion and problem-solving. This difference in the organization of elementary activities with a low and a high degree of uncertainty makes the combination difficult for at least three types of reason.

First, programmed tasks tend to remove

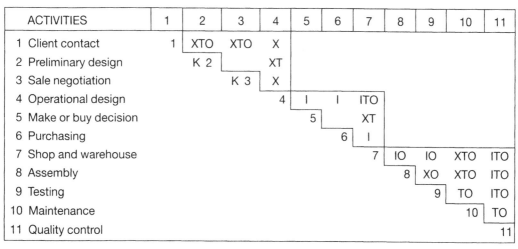

ACTIVITIES	1	2	3	4	5	6	7	8	9	10	11
1 Client contact	1	XTO	XTO	X							
2 Preliminary design		K 2		XT							
3 Sale negotiation			K 3	X							
4 Operational design				4	I	I	ITO				
5 Make or buy decision					5		XT				
6 Purchasing						6	I				
7 Shop and warehouse							7	IO	IO	XTO	ITO
8 Assembly								8	XO	XTO	ITO
9 Testing									9	TO	ITO
10 Maintenance										10	TO
11 Quality control											11

Legend: T = Technical similarities   O = Orientation similarities
         I = Sequential interdependences   X = Reciprocal interdependences
         K = Critical uncertainties

Figure 11.2 Activity matrix at Silca

unprogrammed activities from attention, if carried out by the same actor (Simon 1960). Second, tasks that are very risky and need a lot of research can be effectively accomplished only under a particularly "free atmosphere": low formalization, high integration, infrequent controls, emphasis on rewarding successful innovations rather than on punishing errors (Burns and Stalker 1961; Lawrence and Lorsch 1967; Galbraith 1982; Popper 1989; Milgrom and Roberts 1992). Lastly, task complexity influences many aspects of the professional and technical knowledge and the cognitive and emotional orientation that may lead to high performance. For all these reasons, the separation of activities generating different degrees of information complexity in different organizational units often creates *learning and specialization advantages*.

For designing unit boundaries properly, it is also important to evaluate the intensity of variances and the importance of their consequences on other tasks. Whenever the more or less successful problem-solving and uncertainty management in an activity has important consequences for the effective conduct of other activities, the activity is said to entail *"critical uncertainties"* (Lawrence and Lorsch 1967). The analysis of critical uncertainties is important for the *assignment of coordination tasks*: the fact that a transformation activity entails critical uncertainty implies that – other conditions being equal – it will be effective and efficient to assign coordination tasks to the unit performing it: this unit has the best knowledge of the problems to be solved and will be able to take responsibility for communicating the relevant information to other centers of activity with greater precision and at lower costs than any other unit.

In the Silca case, the main sources of uncertainty are situated on the client's side, more than on the technical-productive side or the purchasing side. In fact, the materials and the production techniques are traditional enough to make production an activity with low variance; the parts purchased on the market are standard components and do not involve particularly unusual or complex relationships with the suppliers. On the contrary, the clients are the source of continuous variations not only between off-the-shelf and custom system designs, but also in the course of delivering an order, with requests to change delivery times and specifications. Hence, in the matrix of Figure 11.2, critical uncertainty is attributed to the activities of bid preparation and client negotiation.

Specialization analysis

A first aspect of specialization is the knowledge and cognitive orientations that have to be mastered by the specialists performing each task; and an important implication for the relationships between activities is the degree of *diversity between these competences* (Chapter 1).

The profile of competences correlated to performance in each activity can be constructed by referring to the array of disciplines and professional specializations, as well as to the tacit components and routines, distinguished, if need be, by product, phase, or relevant market outlet. For example, considering a sales activity, one would have to distinguish in what measure performance in that activity depends on public relations techniques and/or interpersonal relations competence and/or specific negotiation techniques; or on a knowledge of specific products, a knowledge of the technology (e.g. engineering, chemistry) implied by the complexity of the product, a knowledge of the suppliers' markets, a knowledge of the economic context, etc.

The analysis of the softer components of effective cognitive profiles in the different activities can draw upon all the dimensions of organizational culture, and in particular the difference between rigid and flexible cultures (Chapter 7): an orientation to standardization or innovation, to tasks or people, to the short or long term.

In the Silca case, the activities of the shop floor can be conducted with exclusive attention to the technical aspects of each work cycle: the orientation is to be concentrated on reducing the cycle time, on the reproducibility of the cycle, and on its technical quality. On the other hand, customized equipment sale and design requires much broader competences and sensitivity: to costs, internal productive capacity, the make-or-buy decision, cashflow, the profitability of the contract, the firm's public image and relationship with clients, etc.

On that basis, the *relationships between activities* in terms of *affinity or diversity of competences* can be evaluated. For example, preliminary design and operational design activities, in the Silca case, involve the application of the same competences at different degrees of detail. The two activities therefore have technical affinity – that is, they require the same or similar modalities of calculation, the same basic knowledge of the productive process, a certain level of common knowledge of the techniques and of the productive processes of the client firms, although these competences are more important in the technical-commercial activities of preliminary design. However, in regard to people orientations, the preliminary design requires contact with the client and implies sensitivity to interpersonal relations, sensitivity to the economic aspects as well as the technical

ones, the capacity not to get lost in the details, and creativity. The development design, on the other hand, requires precision, attention to details, and concentration on technical aspects.

In Figure 11.2, the presence of technical or orientation affinities between competences is indicated by the presence of a T or an O in the corresponding box (if there is no affinity, the box is blank).

Interdependence analysis

Activities involving complex interdependences of the *intensive* or *reciprocal* type require coordination by mutual adjustment and therefore should be either aggregated in one organizational unit, or linked by fully connected communications networks, or at least connected through "linking-pin" or liason roles – other conditions being equal. Activities involving *sequential* interdependence can be effectively regulated by programming, pricing, and inventory mechanisms between different organizational units. *Pooled* interdependences arising from the use of common resources can in most cases be efficiently governed by regulating the access to common resources and by establishing communication procedures among users (Chapter 8).

In the Silca case, the most important interdependences that link the different activities are of the *transactional* or vertical type. Figure 11.2 indicates with an "I" the interdependences that are strictly *sequential* (also for the diminished possibility of using remaining stock in producing goods with highly variable components) and with an "X" the interdependences that are *reciprocal*. For example, the designs and documents produced by the planning department (activity number 4) constitute direct inputs for make-or-buy decisions (activity number 5), both for the issuing of purchase orders and for production according to the desired specifications.

The whole process of defining client needs, including the type of equipment that could satisfy them and the feasible modes by which these can be installed, links the first four activities of the matrix into a block of reciprocal interdependences. In contrast, between planning and the shop floor, there is only sequential interdependence in the specific case of equipment for the paper industry: once planned and defined in detail and passed on to the production department, the job does not show important variance because it involves traditional materials and a well-established body of knowledge (in this case, mechanics). Note that this could be different for contracts that involve more complex technologies, materials, and components than those used by Silca; in such cases, intensive interdependences are conceivable.

Limits to unit size

In the choice of efficient organizational boundaries, we need to compare not only the economies of scale and specialization and the costs of coordination, but also the *costs of controlling* the units proposed. The upper limit to unit size is significantly higher if the activities can be strongly programmed or regulated by formal mechanisms, if the style of supervision is not centralized, if the objectives of the actors are not in conflict with each other or with those of the firm, if communications are clear and quantitative rather than complex and qualitative (Woodward 1965; Williamson 1970).

There are also limits to unit size connected to the problem of resources saturation, given the scale in which each activity is concurrently performed. The key questions in this respect concern the capacity of each single activity to fully utilize human resources and equipment entirely dedicated to it. When the aggregation of more activities permits full utilization of human and technical resources that otherwise would remain under-utilized, then an expansion of the organizational unit is favored by the opportunity to realize *economies of scale and scope* (Penrose 1959). For example, in Silca small and highly variable batches of activity mean high costs due to the under-utilization of bidding and implementation resources if these are separated in two different offices. In fact, given the small dimensions of the firm, it is likely that the planning employees may not have enough work in periods when orders are declining; at the same time sales employees might be overloaded with work doing market research, contacting clients, and preparing bids.

Conflict of interest and incompatibility

Assigning two activities with different and conflicting objectives to the same people can interfere in the performance of both these activities. Separation among organizational units is advisable in the case of *incompatibility* between objectives and *conflicts of interest*.

An incompatibility problem often encountered in organization design is between controlled and controlling activities. For example, in Silca, there was the problem of whether to entrust quality control to the production department. Because in that case quality control implied exercising discretion and judgment and not a mere application of standard procedures, the unit responsible for control was separated from the production department and attached to general management.

In addition, the problem of the location of

the "make-or-buy" decision involved aspects of conflict of interest – the production department having its own interests in "making" rather than "buying." In spite of the technical affinities and interdependences with production, this consideration led to the allocation of the make-or-buy decision activity to the purchasing department, in coordination with the production unit.

Comparative analysis of unit boundaries

The variables analyzed in the preceding sections – uncertainty, interdependence, specialization, unit size limits, and interest conflicts – provide criteria and constraints to the feasible and effective aggregation of activities and resources into organizational units, that can be summarized as follows:

- Activities and resources should be aggregated so as to maximize the interdependence inside each organizational unit and minimize the interdependence between units. This criterion reflects a principle of reducing coordination costs.
- Activities and resources should be aggregated so as to minimize the differentiation inside each organizational unit and maximize the differentiation between units. This criterion reflects a principle of seeking to achieve economies of scale and specialization and to support the growth of knowledge that the constitution of groups of specialists can bring about.
- The dimensions of any organizational unit should not exceed the limit beyond which the increase in the internal costs of controlling and coordinating the unit exceeds the reduction in inter-unit coordination and production costs due to the first two criteria above.
- Activities with conflicting or incompatible

interests should not be put in the same organizational unit, in order to avoid biased behaviors with respect to some or all of the relevant interests and objectives.

Why exactly should the aggregation of activities and resources in a single unit realize these advantages? It depends on what precisely to "aggregate" means. A unit is a pool of shared or unified rights over the resources and activities, usually consituted by more than one person. In the context of this chapter it is assumed that ownership is unified or shared at the firm level. A unit then can unify to a greater or lesser extent the right to act, decide and control with respect to a defined class of resources and activities. The sharing of these rights may be realized by the *constitution of a team*, in which more frequent, free and dense interactions can take place and support knowledge sharing and growth. In addition, these rights can be unified through the insitution of a "principal" (the unit's head). Therefore a unit can bring about at least three interesting properties: it sustains continued association among members in a group-like fashion; it can be made accountable for the assigned resources and activities and therefore it is likely to direct them more consciously and responsibly; third, it has the chance to more consciously *self-design* its own organization, i.e. internal task partitioning and coordination, adapting them to changing circumstances.

It is clear however that only in particular cases will all the above criteria dictate the same solution for every pair of activities. In many cases, there are advantages and disadvantages for each boundary hypothesis. Hence, it will be wise to weigh the advantages and disadvantages achieved on the different dimensions under the various possible organizational designs. Figure 11.3 offers an

Hypotheses on organizational units	Economies	Diseconomies	Choices on organizational units
Technical sales: Client contact + Preliminary design Sales negotiations	• Economies of specialization (T, O) • Economies of coordination costs (X)	– –	Yes
Production and maintenance Shop and warehouses + Assembly + Quality control + Maintenance	• Economies of specialization (T, O) • Economies of coordination costs (X)	• For maintenance: ignores customer post-sales assistance interdependence with the sales department	Yes
With production / *Purchasing* \ Independent	• Coordination economies in make or buy decisions	• Differences of technical specialization (T) and of orientation (O) • Sequential interdependence only • Very high costs to control the organizational unit	No
		• Coordination costs with production department on make or buy decisions	Yes
With production / *Make or buy decisions* \ With purchasing	• Economies of coordination costs (X) and specialization (T)	• Interdependencies and similarities with purchasing are ignored • Diseconomies due to the interest of production in making rather than buying • Costs of controlling large and diverse production units (CO)	No
	• Economies of coordination costs (X) and specialization (T, O)	• Interdependencies and affinities with production are ignored	Yes
	• Economies of technical specialization (T) • Economies of coordination (X) • Economies of resource saturation (S)	• Orientation affinities with production are ignored	Yes

With technical sales / *Independent operational design* \ With production	• Economies of technical specialization (T) and orientation (O)	• Efficient minimum dimensions are not reached (under-utilized resources)	No
		• Interdependencies and affinities with sales are ignored • Costs of control of large organizational units (C)	No
Independent / *Quality control* \ With production	• Economies of specialization (T, O) and scale (S)	• Inferior economies of specialization (T, O) and resource saturation (S)	Yes
		• Conflicts of interest between monitor and monitored (CI)	No

Legend: T, O = Similarity in techniques and orientations; X = Reciprocal interdependences; S = Economies of scale; C, CI = Control and conflict resolution costs; CO = Control costs

Figure 11.3 A comparative evaluation of hypothetical alternative ways to aggregate activities

illustration of this exercise, associated with some hypothetical redesigns of the Silca structure. The evaluations here are expressed on simple ordinal scales (more or less), thereby demonstrating how ordinal judgments about relative costs and benefits can be used in organizational design. A quantitative evaluation is, however, in some cases possible.

Some groups of activities are clearly candidates for aggregation in a new organizational unit, given that practically all the variables run in the same direction. This is the case for three commercial activities (client contacts, sales negotiation, and preparation of bids) that share affinities both in technical knowledge and in cultural orientations. In addition, these activities are highly interdependent in the process of defining the technical and economic characteristics of the equipment to be provided. The same is true for the activities in the technical field (shop floor and warehouse, installation, testing, and main-

tenance) that share the same orientation and a common core of technical knowledge. The only problem is post-sales maintenance and technical assistance: because of the need for contact with the client and feedback, they have some affinities and interdependence with the commercial activities. In fact, in other types of firms, post-sales assistance is often allocated to the commercial unit. However, in this case the activity is mostly composed of technical maintenance and assistance, while the contact with the client for broader purposes is already covered in the commercial area under the activity of "customer relations."

The solutions emerging from Figure 11.3 for the remaining activities are less clear. Regarding purchasing, there are two alternatives: one independent unit, or its combination with the technical-productive unit. The first alternative is judged superior to the second in terms of overall costs, because the only significant cost associated with a separate unit is the cost of coordinating the make-or-buy decision (e.g. meetings, contacts, and decision procedures).

The most complex trade-off between different categories of costs and benefits is the allocation of the activities of operational design. In practice, observed solutions are quite varied in equipment-producing firms owing to the different characteristics of contracts and demand. For example, the lower the percentage of bids that turn into orders, the less convenient it is to draw up a detailed design of the project during the bid preparation phase, and therefore the greater the differentiation required between activities of bid preparation and operational design. Furthermore, the technical detail required during the bidding is also a function of the complexity and technical sophistication of the contract and the materials and processes required to execute it. On the one hand, such complexity creates interdependence between commercial, planning, and production activities, while on the other hand the technical sophistication creates the need for specialization and division of labor. For this reason, the most common solutions adopted in large industrial equipment firms involve very differentiated organizational units (e.g. the operational design plus production in one unit and the bid preparation and the commercial division in another unit, or where dimensions permit, the separation into three distinct units – commercial, engineering, and production). Such firms also adopt powerful coordination mechanisms (e.g. project managers).

In Silca, the low technical complexity of the contract, the small size of the activities and the high percentage of bids turned into sales all favor a solution of direct integration

of operational design inside the technical-commercial unit.

The resulting design of units' efficient boundaries in the Silca case (actually adopted) is portrayed in Figure 11.4.

Types of specialization of organizational units

In the preceding sections, the analysis of units' efficient boundaries was applied to the case of a single product firm, where the basic activities differ primarily according to the techniques used in the different phases of contract preparation and execution. In this section, we generalize the analysis to the case where specialization has different possible dimensions. Traditionally only two basic types of specialization were contemplated, namely by technical function or by product/market combination. In principle, however, these are by no means the only possible and interesting alternatives, and in practice applied specialization criteria have multiplied. Acknowledging therefore that there is no

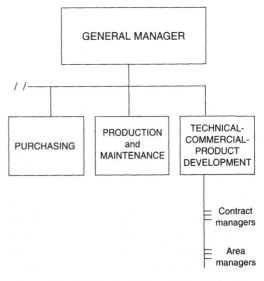

Figure 11.4 Efficient unit boundaries in the Silca case

reason for considering the list exhaustive, currently important specialization criteria include the following.

- Specialization by *function* is the most commonly used criterion, implying a specialization by type of *input*. The definition is usually applied either to clusters of similar competences or clusters of similar activities. It implies a division of the transformation processes in groups of activities that are homogenous in terms of the techniques used. At the firm structure level, it typically leads to the constitution of departments of production, marketing, research, organization, control, finance, etc.
- Specialization by *product* – that is, by *output* – has long been considered the most important alternative to a functional criterion, and implies grouping different activities and transformation phases (e.g. production and sales) when they are related to the same product or product line (e.g. detergents versus perfumes), or when they are related to the same contract or development project with a recognizable output (e.g. a hydroelectric dam).
- Organizing by "*processes*" is the now very popular option of creating organizational units that include or coordinate the *processes linking inputs to outputs*. This involves identifying the chains of activities leading to valuable outputs, even though they may not be "products" in the traditional sense but are internal outputs to be delivered to "internal clients." In that sense, it is an opposite and rival criterion with respect to dividing transformation processes by phases or sub-processes, in that it prescribes governing together sequentially linked phases in order to reduce stock and time buffers and the slack between them.

- Specialization by "*market*" has become more common as firms have grown more "market- and client-oriented," and reflects a focus of firm structure on the very final link of the value chain: not even output, but *output recipients*, customers. These of course may be segmented in various ways: different markets can be separated by *geographical areas* with different customer preferences and institutional rules; by *market segments* in a strict sense (groups of consumers with different profiles and buying behaviors); or by *distribution channels* that work in different ways (Gerloff 1985).
- Specialization by *relationship* or *partner*. Firms maintain a growing number of external relationships that are not "market relations." They often do not relate directly to the final customer or do not experience the customers as a mass or average, but as specified partners. These relationships include managed and negotiated relationships with other private and public institutions, sometimes in the context of broader networks of actors (Chapter 12). Where the governance of external relations with other organizations is crucial to a firm's success, it could be advantageous to specialize at least some units by type of partner or type of relationship. For example, in the case of a computer or car manfacturer, it could be effective to entrust the management of all relationships of a certain type (e.g. the governance of the supply chain, of the subcontracting network, of the franchised outlets or the licensees) to a stable group of people, with competences specific to that relationship, and/or specialized in the type of contract and governance mechanisms typical of that relationship.

Considering that a large firm, beyond using a variety of techniques (e.g. production, sales, administration, and personnel management), usually produces a variety of products and offers them in different markets, the analysis of the relationships between activities should in principle be conducted on activities that are elementary and disaggregated enough to distinguish whether different competences and specialization advantages are present in any of the above dimensions. Such an analysis should reveal whether the strongest interdependences and affinities are between technically different activities in the same product or market; or are between different products or markets with technically similar activities; or are between different phases in a process, etc.; thereby guiding the choice between different specialization criteria (or the blend of them). Rather than choosing among different criteria, in fact, combining them is most often a superior strategy, capable of capturing different types of economies simultaneously. The types of unit that can be found in the "new economy" forms are telling examples.

Designing inter-unit integration mechanisms

Even though many problems of diversity and interdependences between activities can be governed by group and authority mechanisms within self-contained organizational units, many *residual interdependences* will usually remain between units, even if units have been designed to minimize them (Thompson 1967). The inevitable presence of such interdependences creates further needs for coordination through mechanisms of integration across different organizational units. *The need for (and costs of) inter-unit coordination will be positively related to the degree of interdependence between units' activities* (Van de Ven *et al.* 1976) *and to the degree of unit specialization and differentiation in terms of orientations and culture, knowledge and competences, objectives and interests* (Lawrence and Lorsch 1967; Becker and Murphy 1992).

The main mechanisms of coordination and control that are typically and specifically applied at the firm macro-structural level were summarized in Figure 11.1.

If inter-unit interdependence is "simple" – involves only the sharing or transfer of resources – then a set of mechanisms capable of regulating it at low cost on the basis of structured information includes programs and procedures, prices, inventories and hierarchical interventions based on information transmission and decisional efficiency.

If inter-unit interdependence is "complex" – complicated by exchanges of complex information and knowledge sharing – then differentiated units should know more about each other's activities. Knowledge exchange and reciprocal adjustment call for mechanisms such as liaison roles, integration units, or problem-solving and negotiating groups (meetings, committees, task forces, focus groups, etc.). Residual hierarchical interventions based on arbitration and monitoring can usefully complement the mix. The sharing of at least some categories of property rights, especially access to residual rewards generated by a unit's actions should be also be included for poorly controllable activities.

Note that this "ordered listing" of coordination mechanisms – from the less tight and integrating, to the more intense – should not be read as a set of one-to-one correspondences, such that for every situation of interdependence one type of effective and efficient mechanism exists. *The more tightly connecting mechanisms do not necessarily substitute for, but are most often found in addition to simpler ones* in effective and efficient organizational configurations. They are overlaid to govern, and with mutual adjustment where needed, over a stratum of programmed or unilateral actions and decisions. Therefore, we should expect that *the more complex interunit relations are, the wider is the efficient set of coordination mechanisms.* Consider for example the case shown in Box 11.2. Which coordination mechanisms are used between organizational units? What other mechanisms would it be useful to introduce?

In the case described, the mechanism supporting almost all the weight of coordination activity is the full hierarchical power of the facility director. Even in the first phase of the life of the firm, characterized by high stability and low uncertainty, a more intense use of programming could have improved the ratio of results to resources spent for coordination.

At a later stage, characterized by uncertainty, more innovative technologies, expansion of activities, and reciprocal interdependence between the functions of production, sales, and development, it is important to add mechanisms for mutual adjustment. In particular, one could use a significant decentralization of decisional power to the directors of the functional units, the opening of lateral (horizontal) channels of communication such as meetings and work groups, the institution of integration units, such as the "contract managers" that were in fact introduced at Card. These managers were responsible for the planning and monitoring of the entire process of contract realization and were engineeers from the R&D function, consistently with the criticality and particular uncertainty associated with that function.

Negotiating over internal structural alternatives

In this section, as in all others in Part III, we offer an extension of the procedure of analysis and design that includes instruments for dealing with differences and *conflicts between the preferences of the organizational actors that regard not only what actions to undertake but also the form of organization with which to regulate their action.*

If the costs and benefits that different internal actors can derive from various organizational solutions are quite distinct, the cost and benefit analysis conducted earlier becomes more difficult and should be done in a discrete fashion. One possible procedure could be to construct a collective utility function as a weighted sum of parties' utilities (if the different costs and benefits are thought to be "objectively" and clearly measurable and comparable, or if voting among structural alternatives is applicable). A less bold, usually more appropriate and empirically more common procedure is a negotiation approach.

Consider a situation in which the negotiation over internal structure is particularly clear and admitted as a post-merger restructuring. In fact, the unification of ownership of technical resources is relatively simple to accomplish compared to the unification of organizational structures. Often, after a merger, the firm finds itself with a juxtaposition of the two pre-merger structures, with all the duplication and incongruence that this implies. To ask which is the "best" structure in a situation of this type also begs the question "best for whom?," given that the interests of the actors typically diverge. The case in Box 11.3 narrates the story of the negotiated formation of the structure analyzed and redesigned in the first section of this chapter.

By applying the negotiation analysis concepts developed in Chapter 6, the reader can interpret and assess to what extent the

Box 11.2
The Card case

During the 1950s and 1960s Card was leader in Italy in the supply of combinations of addresses and biographical information to public administration offices: 3,500 municipalities in Italy used these combinations (and some of them still use them today). Punch card machines would emboss data on the citizens on special zinc plaques; printing presses would then transfer the information from the plaque to forms or documents.

A great opportunity for growth came round when, in the 1970s, especially in the US there was a boom in credit cards and badges.

The punching technology on zinc plaques was almost totally transferable to these new needs and Card took advantage of this opportunity thanks to its founder and president who realized the implications of such a business.

Today (1984) Card employs 380 people, 200 of whom are employed in the design and the construction of two lines of office equipment which represent direct descendants of the two lines of punching and printing machines.

The factory. This operational unit was always very autonomous from the other areas within the firm. Since 1980 it has expanded to the commercial, export, administrative, financial, and technical divisions (the last one with customer assistance responsibility in the technical-commercial areas).

The independence of the factory, up to the 1970s, had been possible, according to current director, Mr Attilio Sala, thanks to the long-standing personal and professional relationship between the founder/president and the person who for decades had headed the factory.

"The figure of the former director, who left the firm in 1980, right after the passing of the principal," says Mr Sala, "was, and in a way still is, very difficult to substitute. He was very charismatic, both in the way he cared for the firm and for his skills in always thinking of ways to build innovative machinery (. . .). The "technology boom" of the 1970s played a key part in the changes in responsibilities and organizational structure within the firm. In 1975 the firm started to develop an electronic design area: various designers were hired, I myself came from that area. A new function was therefore created and, like the others, it reported directly to the factory director".

The strong technical profile of the product makes some of the design and production phases very critical such as, for example, the step between the creation of the prototype and the subsequent mass production. This step is nothing but an engineering phase in which several operational functions overlap and at times are in conflict with each other. Specifically these functions would include design, production and sales. This is particularly true for the mechanical parts that have significant production and purchase problems; for electronic parts the relationship between design and production is not as complex in that, after the design phase, the production does not present many technical difficulties.

Despite the rapid development of the firm – or perhaps because of it – there are still problems, old and new, that remain to be solved.

For example: "Often we don't know in which direction we are going. We say 'the competition has built this new machine, let us build one too.'" "At times, we don't even know what we are doing – we cannot quantify results because there is no management control system in place. The result of this situation is that people often find themselves solving difficult, unpredictable problems in somewhat of a personal way."

"We are too open to our customers; sales people tend to accept any kind of order to the point that sometimes they bring the customer to the factory to discuss the order directly with the designer."

"The 'factory' and 'customer assistance' are managed as 'independent units.' Requests from customer assistance were always interpreted as 'demands' for offering suggestions to people who are instead quite competent in their work. On the other hand, in the past there was a real 'direct line' between the former factory director and the president of the firm. This personal relationship has always either substituted or overridden any form of coordination between the factory and the administrative, technical, and commercial departments."

Source: E. Arduino and A. Grandori, *Case of Card*, Bocconi University, Milan, 1986.

agreement reached was efficient and fair, with respect to the parties involved as well as with respect to the economic sustainability of the agreement. The core problem of that negotiation was that the two interest groups tended to enlarge the pie by maintaining the bundle of resources they formerly had, and to split rights either in equal shares or in proportion to contributions where measurable. That this negotiation procedure might have been too indulgent became clear a few years later, when the same actors undertook the more resource-saving design process described in the first paragraph of this chapter, in order to respond to a sectoral crisis that reduced the sustainable level of slack resources.

ALTERNATIVE INTERNAL ORGANIZATIONAL CONFIGURATIONS

The possible variety of internal organization forms is at least as wide as the possible combinations of coordination mechanisms and the possible partitions of action and property rights among the main sub-units of a firm.

Despite the peculiarities of the solutions adopted by different firms, some models and forms have been identified as particularly important, notable, used, or effective at internal organization. Here we present the main structural alternatives that research on business organization has proven to be diffused as effective configurations.

The comparative analysis of internal structures is usually conducted over pairs of alternative schemes. A very basic distinction is between "*unitary*" structures and "*divisional*" structures. This partition is based on the traits of the governance system connecting units – especially on the degree of division of responsibilities and the mechanisms of control (Williamson 1975). Within each of these broad structural families, various sub-types can be distinguished, even remaining oriented toward identifying discrete structural alternatives. In particular, the type of specialization of units – by function or by product/market – generates salient variations.[2] All these structural alternatives will be described according to the common

Box 11.3
The Silca case II: history
of a merger

The supply structure in the paper machinery industry is characterized by the presence of a small number of firms that compete in the Italian market. At the moment, three major firms share about the 90 percent of the market; the rest is covered by very small-sized firms that mainly operate in local markets.

This asset is typical of the situation of lesser concentration which characterized the previous sector in 1979–80; those were the years when two of the four major firms merged with the result that the market rate of the smaller competitors dropped dramatically.

The following are some of the characteristics of the major firms: they are fairly young companies, usually small to medium sized, that sell, design, and in part produce machinery for the paper industry. All activities are based on contracts drawn based on specific conditions set by the clients.

A proportion of the production of machinery parts is done in house, either because they are are hard to find on the market – based on a specific design requested by the client – or they are difficult to produce without violating quality standards; finally, there may be confidentiality issues related to the pieces necessary to produce them. Thus there is always a constant need for communication between production, design, and sales.

In turn, the general design and sales activities need to be carried out together during negotiations for the acquisition of orders.

Silca, a firm founded in 1989 from the merger of firms A and B, manages all these activities through a very well specified organizational structure, described below.

The process leading to the merger was led by Varetti, general manager of firm A. Varetti knew that firm B was quite small in size and somewhat "out of the turmoil" (not involved in the commercial wars at the time) and should be dealt with as such. Due to his personal involvement, he is also aware that this firm has a problem with the lack of executive and organizational resources and that it runs the risk of "structural extinction" if this need is not filled. He also knows that the firm is trying to resolve this problem by hiring a general manager, because this position was offered to him by the owner and the president some time ago. What better opportunity, thinks Varetti, to take that offer and become the general manager of both firms?

Besides his personal goals, Varetti realizes that firm B (managed by Moretti) has some strengths and weaknesses that are complementary to those of his own firm. Firm B is very strong as regards commercial visibility and client base. Firm B stands, in fact, in the medium-high range of the market in which firm A is relatively weak. On the other hand, firm B lacks a production division to the point that it subcontracts out; firm A, instead, has a production division and enjoys greater opportunity for product innovation. Mr Varetti then calls Mr Moretti to propose the deal. Both of them are convinced that there are four critical points to the deal: the internal organization of the new firm, problems with the labor unions, the overlapping of products, and the definition of the value of the two firms.

The initial perception on the first point is that the division of positions based on a new organizational chart might not be easy. As far as the product overlapping problem is concerned, the basis for negotiations seems to be that there are neither technical criteria to verify the superiority of either firm's products nor many analogies among them. The issue of the value of the two firms is obviously separable into two parts: a "material" one, based on the size of the gross sales, the inventory, and the profits (in which firm A is stronger) and a "non-material" one, based on the image, the patent quality, the product range, and the value of the patents (in which firm B is stronger). Both firms are perfectly aware of this situation. Lastly, the problem with the labor unions is perceived as potentially critical given that the two firms are located on two different sites, about 40 kilometers apart. Staff would therefore have to travel back and forth. However, the executives of firm A feel that the problem can be dealt with through a legal agreement between the executives of firm B and their employees. The merger agreement reached in 1980 between firm A and firm B created the following structure:

- *Organizational structure:* The organizational chart of Silca S.p.A. resulting from the merger of firm A and B, retained almost all the management positions which existed previously. Varetti is the general manager, Moretti the president, Vanni, former president of firm A, resigned, declining any formal position in the new company, but remaining relative majority shareholder. Bosi (ex-GM of B) became director of administration. The two former commercial directors became co-directors of the commercial department of the new firm.
- *Ownership structure:* Owners of the former firm A control 65 percent of the new company, while Moretti and his two former partners in firm B control 35 percent.
- *Product range:* The new company considers some new products with additional characteristics compared to single products produced earlier by either firm A or B. For all overlapping components for which this is possible and profitable, an agreement has been reached for a gradual replacement of products A and B based on the willingness of the clients to accept them.
- *Site:* All offices have been moved to the headquarters near Milan, where firm A used to be: firm A has therefore been expanded. All employees of firm B living far from Milan were granted the following benefits: financial support for commuting purposes, a private shuttle service, and cafeteria service on site.

Source: A. Grandori and P. Susani, *The Silca Case II: History of a Merger*, Bocconi University, Milan, 1986.

language developed in the first part of the chapter, so that their full range – rather than just two extremes – can be appraised. Four variants of unitary structure and four variants of divisional structure will be described and evaluated here.

Unitary forms

Not all firms grow, but if the economic and organizational bases for efficient expansion of the firm's unit boundaries are present, then a first class of growth strategies involve integrating within one firm the main processes and functions related to a certain type of product. This kind of firm would be specialized in a single product or product line but would be a generalist in terms of the different functions performed about that product: that is, each firm would be capable of carrying out many or all of the main different functional processes related to a certain product – research and development, production, sales, purchasing, as well as the auxiliary "staff" functions such as finance, data analysis, accounting, organization, and human resource management. These technically homogeneous areas of activity are clustered into the main first level units of the organizational structure as functional departments and directions. The size and articulation of the system (that usually involve hundreds of employees, dozens of sub-units, and various hierarchical levels) imply a relatively high degree of formalization and stability in departmental units. This path of development has been diffused in industrial enterprises, but it is by no means unique. Figure 11.5 contains an example of an organizational structure in a service firm.

The displayed organization chart (Figure 11.5) illustrates how, even in unitary forms, a functional criterion of specialization is often mixed with a product criterion, where the "product" offered tends to coincide with the "process" of transformation applied. Service activities typically show this overlap or coincidence (Norman 1984; Chase 1978). Therefore, the distinction between catering and accommodation in hotels, or between damage payments and patrimony management in insurance companies can be seen both as different functions or processes and as different lines of services. However, these structures are *unitary, because the rights and*

obligations of the main units are specified in terms of rights of action, decision, and control, and do not involve residual reward rights or property of assets.

From the point of view of the ownership structure, the growth of the firm is often connected to the differentiation among the actors holding different types of property rights in it (Jensen and Meckling 1976; Chandler 1977; Marris 1997). This can be explained by considering that the need for financial resources and for decentralization of decision-making in relatively large systems of economic action makes it efficient to differentiate between internal and external financing, and between decision and control and to use incentives.

In terms of type of differentiation between functions and the mix of coordination mechanisms used, different configurations are possible. Here we present four functional forms that are particularly important in theory and in the real world: two relatively rigid forms – "mechanistic" and "professional" – and two flexible forms – "high differentiation and high integration" and "network."

Mechanistic forms

A first type of functional organization has merited the title of "machine bureaucracy" (Mintzberg 1979). It is defined by the specialization by competence of the main units, the depersonalization of roles and organizational responsibilities, the formalization of tasks, a pronounced division of labor not only horizontally between functions but also vertically between strategic, directional, and operative units. To these characteristics one must add a set of inter-unit coordination mechanisms represented by the combination of formal communication procedures, standardized and programed transformation and transaction processes, hierarchical supervision and

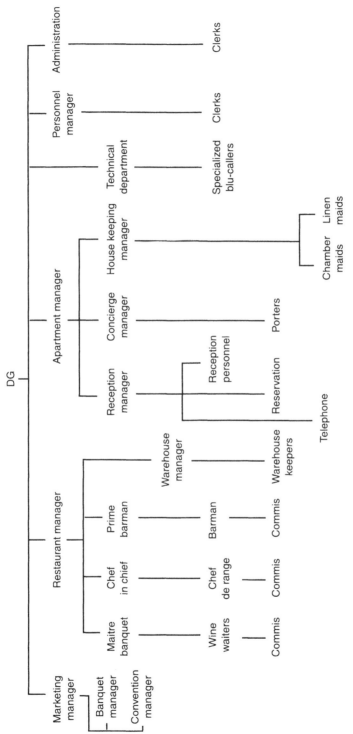

Figure 11.5 Example of a hotel organization chart

decision-making interventions (Lawrence and Lorsch 1967).

Such a predefined and specialized organizational machine can be effective and efficient (compared to more flexible forms) when activities – the goods and services to produce, the clients to serve, the competitors' behaviors to be responded to, the suppliers' conditions, the technologies and transformation processes – are all essentially *stable* and *known* (Lawrence and Lorsch 1967; Galbraith 1973). These conditions can occur, for example, wherever firms compete in large markets with clients that can be satisfied with products with long life-cycles and standard qualities, if the firm actually chooses to compete on costs and standardized goods quality. These conditions were much more common in the past: after World War II firms were able to respond to the development of mass consumption in the Western industrialized world. However, similar conditions can still be found today, although often with more emphasis on quality and the substitution of machines for human labor, as linked to the "globalization" of demand for certain classes of products – pocket electronic products, automobiles – and services – banking and insurance services.

This solution, also defined as a "mechanistic organizational system" (Burns and Stalker 1961), is usually replicated inside each functional unit without important differences, both in its structural aspects (high division of labor and formalization) and in its process aspects (types of decision-making processes and coordination mechanisms). For example, within all functions, leadership style will tend to be rather centralized, controls to be frequent, and result targets to be precise and short term (Lawrence and Lorsch 1967).

Loosely coupled forms

A second type of unitary form is differentiated but loosely coupled. Each department is largely autonomous. The basis for this autonomy is usually a high level of specialization and differentiation between sophisticated competences. If interdependence among units and specializations is sufficiently low, as in the case of pooled interdependence, coordination mechanisms can be reduced to common rules, procedures, and routines and to ad hoc negotiations for specific problems on which joint decision is required.

A configuration of that sort has been found in some large firms in the professional service sectors. Due to this contingency, this configuration has been defined as a "professional bureaucracy" (Mintzberg 1979). They are distinguished from machine bureaucracies by the lighter and different mix of coordination mechanisms, centered on the standardization of knowledge and competences, and on negotiation between units rather than on hierarchical and programmed integration. Thanks to these mechanisms the large systems of complex but relatively stable services (such as schools and hospitals) can deal with extremely variable raw material to transform (health or competences) on a very vast scale, without addressing the very difficult enterprise of entering into each other's knowledge domain.

This organizational form would seem particularly linked to service rather than to industrial activities, and more precisely with professional services. At the same time, in more than a few types of industrial activity the service component is becoming essential, and it is possible to hypothesize the presence of a tendency for the diffusion of this form also in some industrial sectors. For example, some recent organizational restructuring in large firms in the electronics and telecommunication sectors (such as AT&T and IBM) has been based on ideas like reducing the number of hierarchic levels and lightening the use of supervision as a coordination mechanism, and on the distinction between managerial roles (supervising people, programming, deciding) and professional roles (developing and applying specialized knowledge, solving technical problems) because of the actual and prospective growth in the number and importance of professionals. Therefore, it is possible that these industrial firms will assume some of the organizational characteristics of professional, loosely coupled bureaucracies, such as a dual ladder structure and career system (administrative and professional), the decentralization of decisions based on the application of professional know-how, and certified competence-based selection and training criteria.

Differentiated and integrated forms

Do unitary forms governing distributed and differentiated specialties through knowledge sharing and joint decision-making exist? There was an intense search, in both theory and practice, for the organizational answer to the problem of making the unitary structures more flexible, in the 1960s and 1970s. The organization literature of those decades (as is still substantially true today) is full of examples of lack of communication and difficulty of understanding among firm functions that became "watertight compartments," chronic conflicts between sub-objectives that had become too divergent, sub-optimizations of partial aspects at the expense of the final quality of the products, and so on.

The main structural "reforms" that have been identified as a response to these problems refer to fundamental aspects of structure, processes, and organizational mechanisms. In particular, it has been shown that organizational efficiency is correlated to changes in the internal organizational profile of functions that have to govern the subsystems of activity that are most influenced by information complexity, and in the mix of mechanisms used to coordinate and control the functional units.

Competence differentiation and organizational differentiation

Specialized organization units do not only differ in terms of knowledge and objectives. They differ also in terms of task complexity, hence in effective internal organizational structuring. According to Thompson (1967), the subsystems that are most affected by exogenous variables and the requirements of adaptability and flexibility are often constituted by boundaries spanning roles in contact with the organization's environment (clients, suppliers, competitors, and public actors) rather than by inward-looking roles (e.g. administration). Alternatively, they are subsystems where activity is intrinsically complex and rapidly evolving (such as research and development or, recently, finance and high tech production. These researches have empirically shown that high-performing firms have adopted "flexible" organizational structures at least within those units that are most critical for business success: low formalization, heuristic decision processes, decentralized leadership styles, long-term oriented controls.

Integration

In conditions of high differentiation and high interdependence between units, and high complexity of at least some unit tasks, effective and efficient firms are expected to use fewer predefined and centralized mechanisms such as procedures, planning, standardization, and hierarchy, and to use more flexible, ad hoc, and participative means such as direct lateral relations, shared interfunctional decision-making, task forces, or roles and units dedicated to interunit coordination activity (Lawrence and Lorsch 1967; Galbraith 1973; Van de Ven *et al.* 1976; Chapter 8).

Integrating organizational units as instruments of coordination is worth deeper analysis. For, not only do they represent an important subject in organizational design literature, but they are important and widely utilized instruments in practice. They are used to create product-, project-, or process-oriented organization, that cuts horizontally across functional units and has been the subject of much talk in the business and consulting worlds. With specific reference to *functional structures*, it is possible to distinguish between different classes of integrating units, that have been historically used in response to *critical uncertainty* emerging in different functional areas.

A collection of interfunctional integration units was originally developed to resolve problems generated by the evolution of demand and competition in the marketing function, which were becoming critical factors for effectiveness, efficiency, and the long-term survival of the firm. The most well-known organizational unit is the *product manager*, aimed at integrating the main line functions, development, production, and sales, with the aim of optimizing the marketing mix of products. Product managers are usually used in firms that offer a wide array of products in the same sector: for example,

food, cleaning, drugs, and other consumer products.

Other important integration units with similar characteristics to product managers are *brand managers* and *account managers*. In these cases, the critical needs around which to integrate the functions are not products but brands or clients (or client accounts). For example, firms that produce and sell standard types of industrial goods that are sold with many variations under different brands (for different market segments or geographic zones) can effectively use brand managers in the sales organization (as in companies with many brands of household appliances). Account managers are, instead, roles devised to coordinate line functions so as to orient them to the relations with other firms, suppliers, or distributors, in negotiated environments when relatively few partners have high negotiating power (such as in the sales organization of firms distributing through supermarkets).

The integration units with a commercial orientation are often assigned to be supervised by the top management of sales and marketing. In situations of particular complexity and interdependence, they might take a more generalist orientation and report directly to the divisional or corporate headquarters management. These integration units take advantage of the support and status conferred on them by their nearness to top management, but do not have authority as a tool to coordinate across the functions. Their role is typically as mediators in the process of interfunctional negotiation.

Project managers are responsible for a team-based unit created to resolve complex problems between different functional specializations. The *project* might be developing one product, bringing home and/or realizing an industrial contract, or developing and implementing an automation program.

The project group employs people either full- or part-time hired from the functional units (and today often complemented with people from specialized staff agencies, or even from other firms) for the duration of the project. These are under the hierarchical authority of the project manager (a very residual authority, given that the leadership style of a project manager should be participative).

Other types of integrative unit are responsible for process optimization and control. Figures of "*process owners*" are widely used in large functionally organized firms so as not to lose control of the efficiency of passages of inputs through the various stages of internal value chains till a deliverable output is generated (for example the processing of a bank operation). *Contract managers* are used even in medium-sized or small firms that work on many contracts, with critical problems of interdependence between sales, purchasing, and production planning. The contract manager is responsible for planning, cost control, scheduling, and for managing processes of interfunctional and inter-contract negotiation. The contract manager can perform activities of supervision and control over the work of members of functional units according to rules and programs, but usually does not have discretionary authority over them.

Organization structures that on the one hand preserve specialization by input competences and differentiate organization units accordingly, while on the other hand use a complex mix of integration mechanisms and units, of the type described above, have been called *high differentiation and high integration*

forms (Lawrence and Dyer 1983). The firms that have adopted this organizational solution with the best success are those that have developed generalist strategies of adaptation to demand and revitalization of their markets by product differentiation and innovation, in dynamic or potentially dynamic sectors. Some examples of industrial and commercial firms where this is most common and important are the producers of computers, radios, and telecommunication equipment, composite plastics, and market-oriented firms in non-industrial goods sectors (food, household appliances, drugs).

Unitary network forms

Matrixes

The "new form" of organization of a system of economic activity that attracted the most interest in the 1970s is the *matrix form* (Galbraith, 1971, 1974; Davis and Lawrence 1977). The matrix structure was the natural development and institutionalization of a "dual" organizational logic, founded both on functional specialization and integration between the functions oriented to and specialized by product. A matrix structure by function and product makes permanent the dual membership of all participants in the system, both in an area of technical specialization and one or more sub-systems of activity producing one specific product or service. This scheme can be and has been generalized to types of unit specialization. For example, within a research and development unit, the two dimensions of a matrix can be different scientific/technological specialties and different product development projects.

Matrixes are effectively applied in many firms in the advanced third sector, such as consulting companies or management training institutes. In fact, the technical sophistication and the length of the learning cycle for the functional activity (for example, the disciplinary areas involved in economics and management) make it effective to maintain groups of specialists and experts in single functional areas. On the other hand, the delivery of effective service to the client (courses or high-level consulting) generates significant interdependence between the specializations that can be resolved only with direct collaboration among specialists, aimed at solving problems in the specific product or service. In the industrial sector, the matrix form is widespread in the regulation of activities that are technically highly sophisticated and innovative, such as aerospace firms or engineering and machine tool firms.

Matrix structures have been described as uncertain and ambiguous worlds, in which it is difficult to orient oneself. In fact, the "double-sidedness" of that form affects – and should affect – not only task partitioning but also coordination mechanisms and human resource management: hierarchy, that becomes two-sided (product and functional); functional planning that intersects and conflicts with products/services/project planning; rewards contingent to products and results overlaid on job and competence evaluation and reward systems; shared decision processes that often require negotiations between several conflicting parties .

Although it has been said that matrix structures extend the capacity to handle information (Galbraith 1974), this is true only with respect to the information processing capacity of a hierarchical structure, and only to a limited extent. A matrix structure seeks to predict and govern a dense network of relations, assigning responsibilities, formalizing, prescribing which contacts of what type it is necessary to have on which problems. As such, it is likely to go under strain, as the computational and epistemic complexity of the web becomes high (number of possible connections, uncodifiability of knowledge, complex qualitative messages, unmeasurability of performances).

Internal networks

A structural alternative with even higher information processing capacity enables but does not predefine the relations between multiple units with different specializations. In the 1980s, the "new forms" of organization that polarized many debates and caused concrete efforts at reorganization were defined as *internal network forms*. The basic idea that distinguishes these forms from matrices is traceable to older contributions about the organization of highly innovative and professionalized work under the label of the *organic* and *adhocratic* organization forms (Burns and Stalker 1961; Mintzberg 1979). This basic idea consists of de-emphasizing and weakening the structure as a stable system of assigned activities – either single or double – and replacing it with a system of nodes competence that can be flexibly aggregated as necessary.

An organizational form of this type is necessarily very *flat*; at the extreme, it is a network of units that are all on the same plane. The predominant integration mechanisms are direct communication, shared decision-making, and negotiation among peers, an incentive-based rather than control-based coordination (Pettigrew *et al.* 1995; Jones *et al.* 1997; Volberda 1998).

Examples of economic activities that are regulated in this mode are those oriented to research, innovation, and knowledge creation (Nonaka and Takeuchi 1995). Often these are divisions or sub-systems of large firms in very innovative high-technology sectors, such as information technology, research institutes and laboratories, or small firms in research-intensive sectors (such as biotechnology) (see Box 11.4).

Problems and costs associated with unitary forms

The main advantage of unitary structures is efficiency gains from economies of scale and specialization that are possible owing to the aggregation of technically similar activities. This should bring absence of duplication, better utilization of resources, and growth of technical proficiency. The main problem associated with unitary structures is that they tend to generate behaviors oriented to sub-unit objectives, and they make it hard to distinguish responsibilities and performances in the final firm's "team production." These problems and costs pose limits to the size and complexity of the activities that can be governed by a unitary form.

Sub-goal pursuit

Unitary governance implies assigning partial objectives to the different parts of the whole. For example, the systems of evaluation and compensation of a unitary functional structure encourage the pursuit of partial and different objectives, such as reducing production costs, increasing sales, sustaining product quality, and innovating. In order to pursue those objectives effectively, the different functions develop different jargons, cognitive schemes, objectives, information, and even values. Therefore "departmentalization" based on particular objectives and delegation of responsibility to bureaucrats and managers is likely to create local and managerial

interests that are particularly strong and potentially conflicting with the effectiveness and the efficiency of the general system (Selznick 1957; Williamson 1964). For example, the production department usually develops an interest in expanding internal production capacity, the information systems department in increasing the sophistication of the information technology applied, the sales and marketing department in increasing the sales force, and so on.

Measurability of outputs

Another source of crisis of unitary structures is the difficulty of measuring performances according to outputs, as the number of outputs grow. Business history documents (Chandler 1962) the rising difficulty of firms organized according to a unitary functional scheme to control the performance of different products, as the degree of diversification increased.

Both these types of difficulties contribute to generating diseconomies of growth in unitary systems. The more the number of functional, product, and service units increases, the more inter-unit conflict tends to grow out of control; general management units become absorbed by activities of control, coordination, and conflict resolution within the system, and do not dedicate the necessary attention to strategic decisions and the external world (Chandler 1962).

Divisional forms

A large and much respected tradition of research in business history and organization studies has shown how the divisional form has spread, although with different times and rhythms, in all industrialized countries (Chandler 1962; Scott 1971; Teece 1980a;

Box 11.4
Oticon: an internal network structure

Oticon, one of the leading manufacturers of hearing aids, has tied its recent competitive success to a radical redesign of structures and systems that has led to faster decision-making, increased support to individual initiative and creativity, and better integration between the different departments in the organization. The changes have affected 150 people in the headquarters, engaged in administration, research and development, and marketing activities. The old functional structure has been replaced by what the newly appointed CEO Lars Kolind has called a "knowledge-based organization": a structure designed to leave ample freedom to the development, the application, the combination and the recombination of individual knowledge and skills.

One of the core principles around which the new organization has been designed is the elimination of any relationship between positions and tasks. In the new organization, the concept of position itself has gradually lost meaning. Traditional jobs have been replaced by a multi-job system: everyone is responsible for the development of a portfolio of jobs – corresponding to the activities performed in the different projects in which he or she takes part – according to his or her own attitudes, skills, and personal aspirations. In the beginning, employees were not only encouraged, but even required to include in their portfolio of activities something outside their specific competence or professional area, so now most employees perform several different activities, some of which lying outside their formal competence or education.

Such a "job destructuration" reflects a related revolution in the organizational structure. The formal structures regulating the task system, in fact, have been completely dismantled. Representing the organization once and for all, though, it is not possible, as projects are initiated and terminated, responsibilities shift, roles modify and no formal structure, no precise division of labor or authority provide a stable point of reference over time. Dismantling functional barriers has brought great benefits to the product development process. The abolition of functional membership and the establishment of project teams spanning the former functional boundaries has substantially improved communication between functional areas, and research and development activities have regained touch with the market.

Most of the previous department heads have become "professional managers" – specialists whose task is to coordinate the diverse professional skills involved in product development and other activities. Most professional areas do not correspond to the old departments: Marketing and Audiology, Quality Assurance and several technological development groups, called "competence centers" (Integrated Circuit, Mechanical Engineering, etc.), have replaced the old functions. Professional managers are responsible for securing physical, technological, and human resources for the projects. They are responsible for selecting, hiring, and training people and coordinating the development of internal skills in order to maintain sources of competences for the different projects. Professional managers have a coordinating role, but no functional authority over a specified group of people. They do not manage anybody, in a traditional sense. Hierarchical structures have lost meaning: titles have disappeared and now there are only two levels: the top management team (five people with responsibility for strategic direction and general coordination) and all the rest. Relationships do not run vertically along the traditional chain, but in a circular/horizontal way, within project groups. "The new organization is not based on a hierarchy," says Lars Kolind, "but on a network of experts with informal relations between them; a team of people guided by common strategies, values and objectives; free to take initiatives and to make things happen."

The functioning of the structure is based on individual responsibility. The basic idea is that everyone is responsible for filling his or her own days with useful projects. "If people don't have anything to do," Kolind says, "they need to find something – or we do not need them." People are free to decide about their working hours, vacation days, and time allocation between the different projects they take part in. There is no explicit supervision: it is left to group control and self-regulation.

Such a radical change should have been accompanied by an equally radical change in people's values and attitudes. The new corporate culture should stimulate communication, participation, and cooperation. Important, in this respect, have been the changes in the physical lay-out. "Traditional offices," says Kolind "create emotional barriers and prevent free movement and spontaneous interaction." In the new headquarters, then, offices and corridors have been replaced by open spaces filled with uniform workstations, consisting of a drawer-less desk equipped with computer, telephone, fax, etc. Everyone, including the CEO, has been assigned a "trolley," a personal file cabinet on wheels, and encouraged to freely move to and from common workstations, changing location according to his or her project work. Using the CEO's words: "The office layout allows product groups and task forces to be formed, to act, to work and to become dissolved quickly and flexibly." As people work in close contact with one another, then, occasions of casual encounters and transfer of information and ideas are increased.

Internal communication, finally, has been greatly improved by a "paperless company" campaign aimed at reducing the use of paper by 90 percent. Paper communication of any sort (memos, reports, forms, etc.) was discouraged. Informal dialogue was to replace memos as the accepted mode of communication. The anti-paper campaign was based on the idea that the more paper employees accumulate, the harder it is for them to leave their office and move around. Furthermore, information kept in physical files in a closed office is accessible only in theory, not in practice. A new information system helped to liberate information and people. All organizational and individual information is now stored in an advanced electronic archive. All incoming mail is scanned into the system and hardcopies are shredded for recycling. Filed documents are either scanned in or directly typed in. Everyone has free access to the central archive holding all the information available to the company, the only restriction being on salaries and confidential records from board meetings. People, then, have real-time access to all the existing information regarding people, products, strategies, markets and technologies in the company. Information flow is not restricted and delayed by physical or organizational infrastructure: information is available when needed and where needed.

"The immediate effect of the restructuring has been chaos," says Kolind, "then again it takes time to change working attitudes 87 years old and a whole corporate culture." Soon though, the dialogue between the functions and a strong stimulus to creativity led to the development and marketing of two highly innovative product lines, based on a new philosophy that privileged attention to people and quality of life rather than the purely technical aspect. In the following years, the company has almost doubled its sales, maintaining a high profitability. Sales growth was based fundamentally on new products, whose contribution to the overall turnover passed from 20 percent in 1991 to 50 percent in 1997. A further proof of the improved innovative ability are a halved time to market and the doubled rate of new product introduction.

Source: By Davide Ravasi.

Whittington and Meyer 1997). At its origins in the first large firms that adopted this form in the United States (such as General Motors, Dupont, Sears, and Standard Oil), divisionalization was discovered as an organizational response to the problems caused by a growth in the number, diversity, and complexity of products and markets managed by single large diversified firms. If this was the historical path through which it was discovered, the divisional form is now a well known and codified solution that does not necessarily follow from a "functional stage." For example, there are groups of financially connected entrepreneurial firms that are governed by some variant of a divisional structure, and there are also cases of "return" from divisional to unitary forms for purposes of structural cost reduction (or even waves of functional rationalization after periods of diversification in certain moments, places and sectors – for example in the Italian insurance industry in the 1980s). Nor is a divisional form of governance incompatible with a specialization of units according to a "functional" criterion, as illustrated in Box 11.5.

With respect to unitary forms, divisional forms are based on a radically different organizing principle: whereas the former is an attempt to unify and integrate as many different but strongly interconnected areas in the firm as possible, the divisional form is an attempt to divide the firm into combinations of resources and activities that are as independent as possible, so as to enable each division to operate with the transparency of results, innovative capability, and autonomy of a (quasi-) independent firm. We can therefore think of the divisional form as a collection of units that are specialized by a marketable output – a product, service, commercial and distribution activity in a geographical area – each of which aggregates the principal resources and competences pertaining to that output. Divisions can be made responsible for and rewarded according to the residual economic results relative to that output, and are comparable in terms of profit and income indicators as if they were independent firms.

In terms of *ownership structure*, the divisional form is characterized by an allocation of some property rights to the divisional units. This has led to the hypothesis that managerial objectives and behaviors are more oriented toward the overall performance of the firm in divisional rather than in unitary structures (Williamson 1970). A division should also be endowed by the discretionary power for taking profit-maximizing actions according to circumstances, thereby implying an agency rather than an authority relation with the firm's principals. This separation and diffusion of different types of property rights – decision rights, control rights, residual

Box 11.5
Lambda: divisional
governance of "functional"
units

Lambda is a multinational operating in the maintenance service sector for data systems. The firm has grown in an exponential way following the crisis of so-called closed systems.

Two of the firm's managers are commenting on the new hierarchy, and an argument has arisen over the type of structure. One of the two is convinced that this is a functional structure, the other a divisional structure.

At central level there is a holding articulated in two large units: commercial directorate; production and research directorate. The commercial directorate is articulated by geographical area through nation units or clusters of homogeneous countries. Within the country or the clusters, the structure is further split up geographically by regions and regional branches. For instance, a salesman in Italy operating in a branch is hierarchically dependent on the head of the branch and answers to the head for the region, who, in turn, answers to the head for the country or the cluster. The commercial head for the country or cluster answers to the commercial manager of the holding. The production and research area is articulated in the same sort of way, though with higher levels of centralization. This would in effect appear to be a functional structure (the first-level units are specialized in the "techniques"), were it not for one of its special characteristics, described by the manager arguing for the divisional structure as follows: "All right, let's suppose that this is a functional structure. In that case, I wonder how the prices of transfer between production and commercial come into it." For the customer is contacted by commercial which works out a project and requests the resources necessary for the local "production and research" unit. Commercial is responsible for the profit generated by the project. Production is also a center of profit, whose returns are made up of the internal transfer prices paid by commercial for the resources made available. A simple system exists for attributing prices to the production unit. On the basis of the project, production works out an estimate (expressed in man-days and day-prices) that is discussed with commercial. After an initial period in which the agreement between the parties was the only solution possible, a radical solution has now been reached. If the estimate performed by production should turn out to be excessively expensive for commercial, the latter can apply to alternative suppliers. In the same way, production can offer the market its own competences and, at a pinch, work with a competitor. The manager who argues in favor of divisional structure remarks: "If it were a functional structure, I should expect commercial to be accountable on the earnings and production for the costs. But here everyone is accountable on profit, as if there were two divisions."

Source: By Giuseppe Soda.

reward rights and alienation rights (right of sale) – and the agency costs associated with that, contribute in explaining why the efficient ownership and financing structure of divisional firms is diffused and largely external (Jensen and Meckling 1976; Chapter 4).[3] In addition, in large multidivisionals the needs for investment and divestment in different branches of activity with relatively low reorganization costs and the diversity in the legislative and institutional frameworks in different countries in which the firm is present, make it efficient to keep divisions in the form of "subsidiaries" with the legal status of separate firms.

Different types of divisional forms can be connected to different reasons for the diversification of activities and to different types of interdependences. There may be economies of scale and specificity that link activities in different sectors positioned along the value chain, such as the production of raw materials, manufacturing, and distribution (Chandler 1990). There may be economies of scope that make it economic to produce several types of outputs simultaneously (Teece 1980a). There can be activities that can be known sufficiently well to undertake risky investments only if they are conducted directly by the firm (Williamson 1970, 1981b). All these reasons for a diversified growth of the firm will be examined in the next chapter. Here, we present different types of divisional forms, connecting them with the different configurations of diversification and interdependence between activities that are generated by different factors and paths of emergence of multi-activity firms. Four main alternative types of divisional forms can be identified: *mechanistic, integrated, networked, and loosely coupled (M-forms)*, which, under a different incentive and control system, in other respects

parallel the four described types of unitary organization.

Mechanistic divisional forms

Different divisional forms can be defined based on the types of relationships between the divisions and the resulting mix of effective coordination mechanisms. One configuration can be defined as a *mechanistic divisional form*, because, in spite of the differences in the allocation of action and property rights that distinguishes it from mechanistic unitary forms, the type of interunit interdependence and coordination mechanisms are similar.

Suppose that the reason why a firm operates in different sectors of activity is that it was efficient to integrate inside the same firm activities linked by transactional interdependence upstream and downstream in the value chain; for example, through acquisitions of suppliers or by directly entering into the business of distributing its products (Porter 1985; Chandler 1990). The internal organization thus finds itself with the need to regulate a series of *sequential interdependences* (Thompson 1967) connected along the value chain.

Given the specialization by product or output, and the different types of knowledge employed in the different stages of transformation, if it is possible to assign exchange values to the transferred goods and services, *transfer prices* are effective and efficient mechanisms for regulating the exchanges between divisions. These are supported by other mechanisms of vital importance for this type of divisions: *strategic plans* for division development and for regulating the utilization of resources in the different stages of the value chain; *central staff* of functional specialists who coordinate the divisions by furnishing specialized knowledge and defining common policies in the various functional areas – technology management, strategic marketing, human resource management, financial management, information systems, and accounting (Lorsch and Allen 1973).

Typical examples of large firms governed by this type of divisional structure are oil companies that are vertically integrated to include the extraction of oil, the refining of oil-based products, and their distribution. Another type of diversification that has been governed by bureaucratic divisional structures is the internationalization based on advantages of economies of scale in the globalized markets for standard goods. In this type of internationalization, in fact, the *pooled interdependence* that links the affiliates in different countries is generated by the massive use of common resources and by the exportation and replication of the know-how accumulated by the mother firm to the subsidiaries (Bartlett and Ghoshal 1989). Examples of this configuration typically include American consumer products firms pioneering the internationalization process and many internationalized Japanese firms.

Integrated divisionals

The basic explanation of the diversification in different but *related industrial sectors* has been identified in the efficient governance of complex transfers involving the re-learning and ad hoc application of accumulated know-how in new activities; and more generally, in the common use in various activities of *complex firm-specific* resources (Teece 1980a).

A divisional structure that is capable of effectively governing the *reciprocal or even intensive interdependences* generated by this type of complex transaction and joint action is not the classic and completely divided divisional structure that is generally identified as

the "M" form (discussed below). Nor would a bureaucratic mechanistic model of interdivisional coordination through planning, central staff policies, and transfer prices be adequate. The regulation of this type of interdependence between divisions requires coordination mechanisms through which knowledge can be transferred or shared. People from the new divisions should be able to learn from those who have already learned from experience and to receive technical assistance from other divisions.

The following examples of *integrated divisional structure* illustrate and support this theoretically derived proposition. Figure 11.6 illustrates different configurations of interdivisional integrators with technical, financial, or market orientations according to the nature of the critical resources that are shared across divisions.

For example, at Saint Gobain the diversification in various industrial activities based on a few core technologies and competences in glass transformation, especially developed in some firms of the group, was managed by assigning coordination tasks to these firms (*pilot firms*) as far as technological development and research were concerned; and to "*branches*" in order to govern sectoral commercial and product development specificities; while geographical coordination was overseen by *country managers* (who have recently lost importance, as in many multinational corporations).

A second example is a divisional structure integrated by *critical functions*. This solution was identified by Channon (1978) in his vast research on the organization of service firms. In particular, for insurance companies that have diversified into various types of financial activities in different countries around the world, the *functional activity* of financial management cuts across the different services

"Core product"

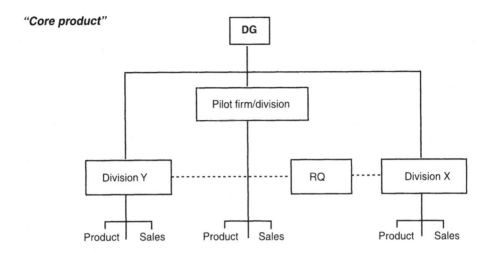

"Critical function"

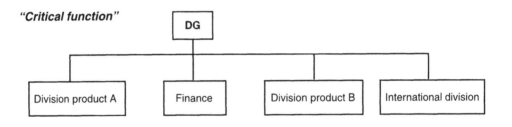

"Divisional matrix"

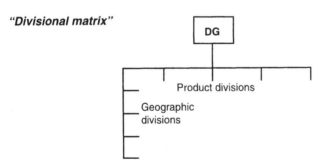

Figure 11.6 Variety of integrated divisional structures

and is crucial for the firm's success. Therefore, all financial management activities are centralized and the financial function has been granted the responsibility to coordinate between the geographic divisions.

A third configuration is that of product divisions integrated by area managers. In this case the efforts of the various product divisions in the same zone or country need be made compatible and adapted to the institutional and cultural specificities of the site.

Networked divisional forms

One of the most famous models of the evolution of multidivisional structures is shown in Figure 11.7 (Stopford and Wells 1972). Based on a large empirical study, this goes beyond showing two different possible trajectories of internationalization – reaching high product diversity and high internalization of sales developing first the one or the other dimension. It asserts that "dual" processes of diversification (e.g., by market or country and at the same time by product or service) can be governed by *matrix divisional structures.*

Divisional matrix

As in the case of the unitary matrix, these structures have a very high information processing capacity and can deal with complex problems, but are very costly in terms of decisionmaking and negotiation processes. In addition, in divisional matrix structures, managers of both geographic and product divisions are responsible for the profit results of their activities. Given the great inter-

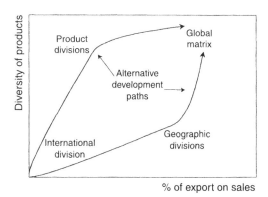

Figure 11.7 Paths of divisional development
Source: Stopford and Wells (1972).

dependence between directions specialized in different ways and the uncertainty of international competition, however, the results and the rewards of divisions tend to depend on factors well beyond their control: the influence of other divisional managers and exogenous factors is significant. In these circumstances, the efficiency of result-based incentives is limited and the level of structural conflict among divisions tends to rise, even though it can be partly restrained by some form of participation in the overall profit of the firm. Box 11.6 illustrates some of these problems and contributes to understanding the type of remedy provided by network divisional structures.

Divisional networks

A response to the "failures" of the divisional matrix solution has been a less predefined and rigidly specified – both in terms of the specialization of divisions and of the patterns of interdivisional interaction – network divisional form (Bartlett and Ghoshal 1990). Some large firms, often multinationals, present in both manufacturing and commercial sectors (e.g. Philips and Unilever) that in the past have experimented with more orthodox divisional matrix models, have been faced with the problem of coordinating activities on a world scale, while preserving the competences, identities, and local embeddedness of subsidiaries. In such a situation, these firms look for organization solutions that do not destroy the distinctive combinations of competences and resources characterizing each firm and its competitive advantage bases, even though these combinations do not fit into a clear-cut specialization by product or market in the overall picture of the diversified company.

Referring to the case of internationally

Box 11.6
Multidimensional organizing
in Bull

During 1992, Bull (the French information systems multinational) decided to adopt a matrix structure in each of the commercial divisions in France and abroad. Several reasons underlaid this decision, all linked to the previous organizational structure.

At the subsidiary level, the company had been structured functionally: on one side the commercial division and on the other a customer service one. The commercial division had been in turn divided between sales staff (in charge of all aspects of client relationships and transactions), and technical support staff (in charge of the installation of the equipment at the client's site as well as more technical issues). However, such a structure had two main problems: first, too much ambiguity in determining the contribution of the technical support staff compared to the sales staff (this ambiguity encouraged opportunism, conflicts, and negotiations); second, a significant investment in human resources, given that in this structure the number of technical-commercial teams increased proportionally to the number of clients to service. This dynamic had led to a even more dangerous resistance to the very strong pressure to reduce costs that the company was feeling due to the crisis that the information systems sector was going through at the time.

It was precisely to resolve these problems that Bull decided to adopt the matrix structure. In fact, this new structure was an attempt to resolve Bull's increasing inability to face more and more complex demands by clients with fewer resources. In order to achieve economies of scale in the use of technical support resources and, at the same time, increase the technological specialization and the flexibility of the system, it was decided to group the support engineers in separate functional areas from the commercial ones. This separation created two branches of the matrix: on one side the "business units" and on the other the "lines of business."

Business units (BU) represent a step up from the former sales divisions. They are divided according to the type of clients that they service: for example, wholesale, banks, public administration, etc. They therefore have a portfolio of clients. Their competences lie in the "proximity to the client," i.e. their ability to understand and meet clients' needs.

The lines of business (LOB) are, instead, a step up from the technical support structures (the "engineers") and the customer service. They have a portfolio of products (Networks, PCs, UNIX, software) or services (system integration, customer services, client training).

Both BUs and LOBs are profit centers, i.e. they are evaluated based on the margin resulting from the difference between revenues from their area of activity (billed to a client or related to a product/service) and the costs incurred to in their organizational unit. The objective is to promote a culture that is results-oriented and market-driven.

Another advantage of this structure lies in the possibility of using fewer resources for a larger number of clients: resources are used based exclusively on existing opportunities and based also on their appeal. Thus this system ensures (at least in theory) the best allocation of resources since, thanks to this internal market mechanism, the best and the most competences will be concentrated on the most profitable business opportunities. Finally, this structure, if well managed, should guarantee maximum flexibility since, through the creation of ad hoc multidisciplinary teams, it continuously changes and adapts itself according to the clients' needs.

This is the testimony of a manager: "An organization such as this one, that strives so hard to meet profit-margin goals for basically every employee, cannot help but reduce the degree of previous collaboration between the sales staff and the engineers in that it creates separate entities having distinctive objectives. In order to achieve the advantages linked to the matrix structure, the price to be paid is communication problems, conflicts, and different cultures. Once again, I think that all this is inevitable".

The truth about the relationship between BUs and LOBs is key because both areas' competences are complementary: this problem creates the need for *teamwork* which within a short time became the fundamental process on which the entire sales cycle focused. In fact, all clients, especially the big ones, need to be managed by an interdisciplinary team in order to ensure that they get access to the best combination of competences and their needs are totally satisfied. Thus, each team responsible for a client is made up by members of the BUs and the LOBs; if necessary, other staff from the marketing and finance divisions may work with them through decision-making processes.

For example, a team to whom an important bank is assigned requires the presence of a group composed of:

- an accounts manager from the BU division (branch Banks and Insurance companies)
- an expert system integration engineer member of the LOB division
- a Zenith personal computer specialist, member of the Zenith LOB
- a marketing specialist asked to improve the presentation of the project to the client's top management
- a finance specialist who will verify that the project has been an economic success
- an engineer from the customer service division in charge of the maintenance of the system
- other consultants or specialists.

Managing a team like this is certainly not an easy task. Rather, it is quite safe to say that the fundamental process on which teamwork is based is internal negotiation. In some subsidiaries the terms of negotiations are fixed by transfer prices: the account manager, evaluated on the margin, must pay the costs of the professionals called in to the LOBs; in fact, they sell their services as internal consultants. In other subsidiaries, instead, such a rigid system does not exist; in these cases, the entire process is based on negotiations among the different parties, that is, conflict resolution processes in which higher hierarchical-level staff are involved.

In practice, the final result of such an organization is ambiguous: although it has put all areas of the company "under pressure" because they are more exposed than before to the market and its economic ties, it certainly generates a large number of conflicts, to the point that one would wonder if it does not channel too many energies toward internal dynamics rather than the client.

Source: By Roberto Ravagnani.

diversified firms, in which these circumstances have typically occurred, such a model has been empirically identified. Bartlett and Ghoshal (1989) have called it a "*transnational*" model – or a *network* model (Bartlett and Ghoshal 1990) – and contrasted it with "*global*" and "*international*" models (which roughly correspond to the bureaucratic and integrated divisional form described above) and with a "*multinational*" model (which roughly corresponds to the classic decentralized multidivisional form that will be described in the next section). This research highlights how both technical and social capital is controlled in a diffuse mode in this structure, and the opportunities to combine such resources in different but advantageous modes vary and cannot and should not be planned and prescribed much in advance. Together, these circumstances make the decentralized formation and negotiation of flexible ad hoc coalitions and collaboration networks between affiliated firms more effective than sophisticated but predefined integration mechanisms. These organizational forms have therefore also been labeled "*heterarchies*" (Hedlund 1986) to underscore how, despite the centralization of property rights, in a vast group of firms it is very difficult to use hierarchy as a means of decision-making and control.

Multidivisional structures (M-forms) and holding structures (H-forms)

The more radical version of a divided enterprise is characterized by the allocation of almost all decision and residual reward rights to divisions and a maximum separation of decision-making among them, as well as by an extended application of market-like coordination and control mechanisms to guide division behavior. The divisions are largely autonomous in their choices and coordination is ensured primarily by rules and economic incentives: internal prices are negotiated and sensitive to external price levels for similar goods or services (rather than imposed); investments and financing toward divisions are based on returns on investment; few technical or functional issues are dealt with at headquarters, and control is based on economic and financial parameters. This logic of functioning of the multidivisional form has been defined as an "*internal capital market*" (Williamson 1970, 1975; Chandler 1977). The model can be taken to extreme points in *holding structures* (or *H-forms*) in which the divisions are juridically separate firms, controlled mainly in financial terms by a central firm.

The implicit hypothesis underlying the efficiency of the M-form, so defined, is that there are relatively simple interdependences between the different sectors of activities, so that they can be coordinated in a "market-like" fashion. This condition may be met in the *conglomerate firm,* which engages in a wide variety of uncorrelated activities (Scott 1971).

It may be worth noting that, this type of firm may be justified if and when the internally available knowledge about firm activities in different fields allows a better allocation of resources than the external market would, and allows financing of risky firm-specific investments that external financers would not endorse (Williamson 1981b; Chapter 12). If this is the case, then even in M-forms and conglomerates sufficiently rich information channels should be established, at least as star-like connections between headquarters and subsidiaries. If divided firms simulate markets too closely – taking the idea of avoiding non-financial communication too seriously – they would only entail higher

coordination costs without distinctive benefits with respect to independent firms.

Problems and costs of divisional structures

Hollow corporations

The just mentioned possible loss of knowledge and information advantages of large
groups of firms over independent firms are a
first core problem of diversified and divisionalized firms. The pathology of excess
diversification and firm over-expansion has
been empirically confirmed (Porter 1987).
The use of excess financial resources to
acquire other firms – even profitable firms – is
not justifiable at either the firm or the macro-
economic level, unless the acquirer has specific competences and/or information that are
transferable to the acquired firm (or vice
versa) so as to make investment decisions better than they otherwise would be. Of course,
investments may be undertaken for "diversifying risks" but ordinary equity investments can
satisfy this need, not involving the knowledge
and management of activities of other firms.

A second reason for which the central
structure of a divisionalized firm can become
a dead weight is simply the size of the system
to be coordinated. Any system of economic
activity with elements of central coordination
will sooner or later reach its dimensional
limits. Divisional forms make a limited use of
hierarchical and planning mechanisms and a
greater use of market mechanisms with
respect to other internal forms, so a divisionalized firm will find its size limit later (at
a larger size) (Williamson 1970).

Distributive conflicts

In unitary structures there is much interdependence and frequent occasions for con-

flict, but these conflicts often have the characteristics of integrative negotiations (i.e. there
is the possibility for both sides to win by finding a synergistic outcome). For example, in
interfunctional negotiations focused on the
configuration of a new product, there are
usually many ways of designing products so
as to satisfy, say, consumer needs and production feasibility and costs. In addition, functional specialization creates many differences
of opinion and judgment, that can be
resolved through confrontation rather than
through negotiation (Lawrence and Lorsch
1967).

In divisional structures there are fewer
occasions for conflict because the interdependence between units is much reduced,
but when it emerges, these conflicts often have
a more marked distributive component.
Examples of distributive conflicts include
disputes regarding transfer prices, or competition for the allocation of resources (Eccles
1985).

Agency costs

It has been observed that the level of pursuit
of local or private interests of managers in
divisional forms must be less than in unitary
forms, because these are evaluated on profit
results and not on partial objectives (Williamson 1970). On the other hand, this may
be offset by the fact that in unitary structures
the control over input behavior is less difficult
and costly than in divisional forms. Divisional structures are decentralized hierarchies, with high discretionary power assigned to
the divisions and little possibility to observe
or control the actions actually undertaken. In
this context, there will be much more investment in incentive mechanisms rather than in
control mechanisms, which will entail
significant transfers of the firm's risk to the

divisional managers, who will in turn demand a risk premium (Chapter 9). Hence, one could expect divisional arrangements to push chief executives' compensation to very high levels (a fact that used to be a very hot issue in large US enterprises, in fact). It is difficult to solve the trade-off between the cost of monitoring and the cost of incentives and all "solutions" in decentralized decision-making systems are likely to be quite imperfect and incomplete (Miller 1992; Radnor 1997). Divisional forms may entail fewer control costs but are likely to rank high on agency and incentive costs.

SUMMARY

In Chapter 11, we proposed a general method of analysis, design, and assessment of the internal organization of the firm. The configurations of units and of interunit coordination have been connected to the key variables of economies of specialization, scale and scope; uncertainty and interdependence; the possible confict of interest and incompatibilities; and the costs of controls and incentives.

The second section presented a repertory of particularly important organization forms, that are described as combining in distinctive modes the partition of rights that defines unit boundaries, and the mix of coordination mechanisms that govern their relations. Four configurations which present themselves under both a unitary and a divisional mode of definition of unit rights and boundaries were identified: mechanistic, loosely coupled, differentiated and integrated, and networked. The principal conditions of the superiority of each form (expressed as particular values of the key variables) have been discussed as theoretically expected and empirically observed, and are summarized in Figure 11.8.

Roughly speaking, the superiority of a divisional over a unitary form is affected by the relative similarities and interdependence linking the resources and capabilities generating the firm outputs. Different types of residual interunit interdependence allow us to explain the mix of coordination mechanisms employed among units. Hence, mechanistic forms – either unitary or divided – are expected when interunit interdependence is pooled or sequential, uncertainty and innovation rates are low, firm size is not very large. Integrated forms – either unitary or divided – have been shown to connect with dynamic and innovative sectors, interunit reciprocal or intensive interdependences, but bound to a known model of interaction. Networked forms, being informed by a principle of reconfigurability and self-design according to arising contingencies, have been found to be especially effective solutions in "hyper-competitive" situations, in which no long-lasting fitness – let alone competitive advantage – can be expected out of any particular combination of resources and competences. Knowledge and competences should be recombined continuously; the organizational capacity for doing so (or doing so more quickly) through a network arrangement may confer some advantage. Loosely coupled forms can govern high differentiation between unit resources and knowledge, and low interdependence (whereby no intense information and knowledge exchange among units is a necessary condition for an effective output). "Market-like" internal arrangements, such as M-forms and H-forms, in particular, are efficient solutions for coordinating clusters of very numerous, dissimilar, and uncorrelated activities. Still, the firm should possess a better knowledge or competence about the coordinated activities with respect to the market itself, for its presence to be justified (Chapter 12). Among unitary forms,

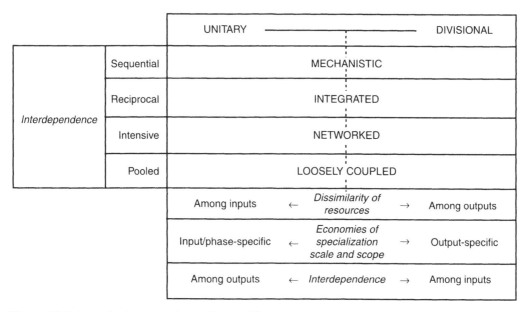

Figure 11.8 A synthetic comparison of internal forms

"professional bureaucracies" are loosely coupled systems coordinating very autonomous units, using completely different knowledge to provide their services, through the standardization of know-how and negotiation.

Exercise: Ediblu Publishers

Ediblu publishing company specializes in books concerning the sea: sailing and power boats, larger craft, competition fishing. Following its strong growth over the last few years, the firm has set up a working organization chart. The main activities are the following:

- selection of subjects and contacts with authors;
- editing – writing, graphics, proof reading, etc.;
- layout and printing, in the single production plant;
- marketing.

The firm's new general manager has proposed a plan of development based on the increase in production of books and the publication of some magazines. The first project, a bi-monthly review on period ships and the restoration of boats, has met with a very encouraging response in the market. In the organization of the firm, however, some problems have arisen:

- as compared to books, the production of magazines demands much shorter deadlines and a high capacity for work adaptation, that seems to be lacking in the firm at present;
- a worrying series of clashes has emerged between those responsible for the commercial sector and those in production, the latter being sometimes compelled to alter the set-up

373

of the plant several times in the same day. On the other hand, the commercial side is urging that delivery times be respected and production be more flexible (adding an article or simply a few photographs in a magazine means changing the whole layout);

- the quality of the magazine, in terms of misprints and layout, is very poor; sales have been initially stimulated by the novelty, but their volume must be kept up. The editorial staff complain that their work is very dispersive; despite hiring of more staff, the whole editorial personnel has to deal with both books and magazines.

The plan of development for Ediblu entails starting three new editorial projects in the following months: a series of books about fishing, and two new monthly magazines.

By Giuseppe Soda

Questions

- What further information would you look for in order to redesign the organizational structure? Formulate some hypotheses on the configuration of these variables.
- Propose a new design of organization for Ediblu.

Chapter 12

Firm Boundaries and Interfirm Organization

In this chapter, the problem of the efficient boundaries of organizational units and of an adequate mix of coordination mechanisms among them is dealt with at the level of the major and most important units in which economic activity is organized – the firm. As is increasingly recognized, however, it is by no means simple to define what a firm is. Some passages from one of the leading figures in the "theory of the firm" are instructively problematic in this respect, and are reported in Box 12.1.

FIRMS AND MARKETS

Demsetz's observations harmonize with the idea toward which we are led by considering the vast array of coordination mechanisms actually employed in firms, analyzed in large part especially and by non-economists, encompassing all those examined in the second part of this book. Firms are constituted by a nexus of rights and obligations, defined in external and internal complex contracts and treaties, incorporating systems of internal and external laws and norms, employing a vast and varying range of coordination mechanisms. The problem is to specify what cluster of contracts and coordination devices is classifiable as a firm. A minimal juridical definition for considering an institution to be a firm is that it "professionally conducts an organized economic activity" for the "production or exchange of goods or services" (specialization and continuity of association); and that in the case of "collective" rather than individual firms, is based on "conferments" of goods or services" and entails a common risk bearing and direction (Galgano 1974). Firms may or may not be characterized by profit-making purposes (only some types of incorporation contracts include this feature) but all are supposed to be "economic organizations" in the sense of being able to recover the costs of their own activity and create some value (Masini 1968). The "conscious" and "common" risk bearing and direction may or may not be ensured primarily by the mechanism of a hierarchy of authority relations (it is not so in cooperative firms, nor in large conglomerates) (Chapter 11).

If we were to summarize the common features of "firm-like" coordination of activities, independently of the particular organization structure adopted within the firm, it would be necessary at least to specify *a set of mechanisms, rather than just one*, and to define them in comparison with other nexuses of mechanisms that are not "firm-like." A classic comparison is with the nexuses of mechanisms that might characterize "markets," which in

We may recognize that we have no clear notion of firm-like contractual arrangements, especially since we now recognize the difficulty of distinguishing between coordination achieved "across markets" and coordination achieved "within firms." It might be useful to adopt legal notions of what a firm is and what it is not, for there do arise cases in which this determination has been called forth because of the important impact it has on which body of law determines the liabilities of the parties involved. I prefer instead to identify three aspects of the nexus of contracts that plausibly influence firm-like coordination. (At least two of them receive mention in case law.) These aspects of firm-like contractual arrangements brush aside the question of absolutes – "When is a nexus of contracts *a firm*?" – and substitute instead a question of relatives – "When is a nexus of contracts *more firm-like*?"

A common feature of corporate charters is a statement about the business of the firm. While this may change over time, one aspect that persists is that the firm produces goods that are to be sold. This implies an agreement to *specialize*, by which I mean to produce mainly for persons who are not members of the firm's team. The complement to this is self-sufficiency or production by and for the same persons, which, in the limit, is one person doing for himself without the cooperation of others. Specialization, which can differ in degree between firm-like institutions, is adopted as a characteristic of firm-like contracts in order to maintain compatibility with the theory of price. The firm in the theory of price does not consume what it produces, it sells to others.

The second aspect of the nexus of contracts is the *expected length of time of association* between the same input owners. Do the contractual agreements entered into contemplate mainly transitory, short-term association, which in the extreme would be characterized by spot market exchanges, or do these agreements contemplate a high probability of continuing association between the same parties? The firm viewed as team production exhibits significant reassociation of the same input owners.

The third facet is *the degree of conscious direction* that is used to guide the uses to which resources are to be put; this is minimal in spot market transactions, but more important in a context in which continuity of association is relied upon.[1] (. . .)

Our interest centers mainly on the cooperative efforts of more than one person, but the one-person firm is not ruled out by these characteristics. The financial advisor, working alone, offers specialized services. Continuity of association and directability of behavior would seem more difficult to imagine in the case of a one-person firm. Still, a person must deal with himself in a relationship that is continuous over a lifetime, and conflicts do arise between the capabilities and tastes of a person today, or in one set of circumstances, and the "same" person tomorrow, or in a different set of circumstances. Because of these conflicts, a person sometimes finds it desirable to restrict his activities by entering into binding precommitments that control his future behavior. Deadlines are often accepted as a self-enforcing device and costs are imposed on future errant (from today's perspective) behavior (as when Christmas savings clubs are joined). The agency problem resides within each of us as well as in interactions between us.

> *Specialization, continuity of association, and reliance on direction are characteristics of firm-like coordination.* They substitute for self-sufficiency and spot markets. These are frequently found characteristics of firm-like organization because they are productive in many circumstances. This productivity derives in part from transaction and monitoring cost considerations, but it also depends on other conditions. Particularly important are those that underlie the acquisition and use of knowledge.
>
> *Source*: Demsetz (1991).

FIRMS	MARKETS
• Unified property rights over assets (by shareholders, partners, or an entrepreneur)	• Separate property rights over assets
• Coordination and control mainly based on partner-specific communication	• Coordination and control mainly based on exit
• Information on different activities gathered directly and transferred ad hoc where useful	• Information encoded in price and profit signals
• Regulation of exchange and of cooperation through incomplete contracts, and system-specific rules for evaluation, compensation, and resource allocation	• Regulation of exchange and competition through complete contracts, in the frame of external regulation/legislation
• Residual resolution of conflicts mainly by resort to internal hierarchy	• Residual resolution of conflicts mainly by resort to external judiciary system

Figure 12.1 Firms and markets as nexuses of coordination mechanisms

turn are increasingly recognized as "highly organized events" (Buckley and Michie 1996). A possible description of the mix of mechanisms broadly characterizing the two institutions is given in Figure 12.1.

These profiles or configurations of coordination mechanisms, even though complex and comprehensive, are still rather extreme. They are by no means the only feasible or efficient combinations of mechanisms. In particular, it has been increasingly stressed that a combination between the feature of property rights held separately by different firms and the use of various subsets of coordination mechanisms – including those listed above on both sides – configures a variety of interfirm "networks" or "hybrid" organizations which can be superior to both "firm-like" and "market-like" arrangements (see later in this chapter). Before addressing the issue of how and when different salient

combinations of coordination mechanisms are relatively superior throughout the whole range of possible combinations, it is reasonable to present a basic model of comparative analysis applied to the alternatives of "internal" or "external" organization broadly conceived. One advantage of this type of comparison is that it is directly relevant for designing firm boundaries – that is, to respond to questions such as: Why and when to "outsource" an activity? Why and when to directly acquire the capability to make a new product (rather then, say, stipulating an alliance)? Why some firms grow gigantic while others seem to be efficient by remaining small?

The basic structure of the first section is outlined in Figure 12.2 at the end of the section; while the comparative analysis of interfirm coordiantion modes is outlined in Figure 12.3 at the beginning of the next section.

"Market failures" and "bureaucratic failures"

Why do firms exist? This embarrassingly fundamental question was not seriously posed in economics until Coase (1937) proposed a first answer. His perspective stimulated and informed much of the economic analysis of "market failures," to which the existence and expansion of the planned coordination enacted by firms (and by other central planners, such as the state) is supposed to be a response.[2]

Market failures

Information and resources should have fairly particular characteristics if a situation of economic interdependence is to be efficiently regulated by market mechanisms.

In the first place, as Coase stressed, markets are unable to effectively manage those exchanges which have an important impact, whether positive or negative, on third parties not involved in the exchange – that is, when there are "*externalities.*" For example, industrial pollution is a typical case of a negative externality. Even positive externalities can create problems: for example, suppose that a highly beneficial and effective product or process innovation could be easily imitated. The firm which sustained the costs of the innovation would reap few of the benefits, they would be enjoyed externally without any of them being tied to the initial investment. Therefore, it is possible that such innovations would not be undertaken in a market regime.

In the second place, economists analyzed a series of causes of market failures generated by the characteristics of the production process and by the ensuing configuration of *production costs*. The existence of *economies of scale and scope* has been considered a reason for markets to fail and an incentive to firm growth; as well as the *indivisibilities of resources*, combined with the variety in their possible uses and in the value-creating combinations of their services (Penrose 1959; Chapter 8). These factors have been seen as contributing to explaining the growth of integrated production units as a more efficient alternative with respect to many small units connected by market relations.

It has, however, been argued that these situations of technical indivisibility could, nonetheless, in principle be managed through ingenious systems of market contracting (for example, contracts for renting the technological infrastructure or licensing the use of know-how to third parties) (Teece 1980a). It has been underscored how a second category of "costs" – *transaction costs* – when combined with production costs, can give a more complete explanation of when market coordination will actually be substituted for other forms of coordination (Coase 1937; Williamson 1981a). Included in these costs are all the costs of transferring goods and services between economic actors and stages of activity: the costs of search for partners and information, the costs of acquiring the relevant knowledge for designing goods or services useful to the transferee or for utilizing the transferred items, the cost of quality and performance evaluations, the costs of negotiation of exchange terms and contractual provisions, the costs of control on the respect of established conditions. These costs are information costs, not production costs.

When will these costs be high under market coordination? Not when there are many possible partners, who offer comparable products or services of a standardized and observable quality, and when the knowledge for performing at one stage is not necessary for supplying inputs or using the outputs of that stage. These costs are potentially important, instead, where the partners become poorly substitutable because they offer differentiated, non-comparable products or services, when the value of a contribution is different in different relations, when the results of employing a resource in an activity are poorly observable, when for performing well in one activity one should know how other complementary operations are generated.

For example, think of selling or licensing complex expertise, such as the know-how of a business school. The costs of regulating this transfer through prices are very high. We are very far from the situation where they can convey all relevant information. Complex knowledge must be exchanged. Coordination mechanisms based on the direct communication between parties are required.

In order to make this analysis relevant for the design of firm boundaries, however, *it should be demonstrated that internal organization has distinctive advantages exactly in the coordination of these types of informationally complex and specific transactions, rather than being equally or even more troubled than market coordination by those contingencies.* It has been observed that organizational economics in all its branches, including transaction cost economics, has not offered an analysis of "bureaucratic failures" as rich and precise as that of "market failures."[3] Organization theory and research can offer the necessary complementary insights in this respect.

"Bureaucratic failures"

The relevant questions may be: does the internal organization of a firm enable better knowledge to be gained about the best use of specific resources in activities that are difficult to observe, action to be adjusted to unpredictable contingencies in a better way,

and the chances of opportunistic behaviors to be reduced?

The answers that can be drawn from organization theory (and from the examination of the internal organization of the firm conducted in the former chapter) are not straightforward: *they depend on which organization structure prevails in the firm.*

- An important advantage that is attributed to the firm is a more intense, pervasive and qualitatively rich circulation of information and knowledge with respect to feasible cross-boundary communication. This feature has been attributed to the continuity of association and the creation of a common language and culture, as well as to weaker threats that shared knowledge will be used competitively in harmful ways (Williamson 1975; Demset 1991; Grant 1996; Kreps 1996). However, information gathering and performance evaluations are far from perfect within firms, especially if they are large and divided. It could be hypothesized that *a firm will exhibit particularly high knowledge sharing capacity if its structure is of the integrated or network type*; while the more internal communication channels are segmented, specialized and formalized, the narrower will its advantages be over feasible external communication and exchange networks. In fact, horizontal all-to-all integration mechanisms are required if tasks are complex and different competences are to be actually combined in unitary firms (Lawrence and Lorsch 1967; Chapter 11); and network-like coordination is necessary if core competences are to be actually transferred and applied to new branches of activities in multidivisional firms (Bartlett and Ghoshal 1990; Chapter 11).
- *Environmental variability and unpredictable*

contingencies are a cause of bureaucratic failure as much as they are a cause of market failure. Just as economists have amply stressed that this type of uncertainty makes the writing of complete contracts difficult, organization scientists have amply stressed that it makes it difficult to write complete plans as well. In fact, the lack of predictability undermines the effectiveness of coordination by formalization and documents in general (Chapter 7), and not only of external documents or contracts. To that extent, in the presence of unforeseeable variability, only *"adhocratic" conscious direction* can be deemed superior. In addition, only if external relations are supposed to be adversarial and potentially opportunistic in the absence of complete contracts more than internal ones, could one conclude that variability favors internal organization. As noticed (Chapters 1 and 8) this cannot be a general assumption. In recent economic history, for example, the transaction costs of internal organization under uncertainty (especially due to internal staff rigidity in sticking to internal contracts) have been deemed sometimes to be more effective than those of governing relations with subcontractors, thereby favoring externalization processes.

- There is no question that internal organization is rich in diverging interests and opportunistic behaviors. This has been widely acknowledged by both organizational sociologists and organizational economists (Williamson 1964; Pfeffer 1981). Does internal organization enable the use of mechanisms for solving disputes and reducing opportunism which would not be employable between firms? The systematic use of arbitration and supervisory authority – the elimination of conflicts by the "fiat" of a central agent – has been

regarded as such a mechanism (Williamson 1975). Useful as it can be, arbitration authority is by no means a prerogative of firm organization. It can be employed and is increasingly employed among firms as well (Williamson 1979; Eccles 1981; Stinchcombe 1990). In addition, the effectiveness of arbitration authority is limited to situations of low information complexity (Chapter 4) and it tends to kill the search for more innovative solutions (Chapter 6).

In conclusion, three methodological suggestions may be drawn for conducting proper analyses of a firm's "efficient boundaries."

- *Firm boundaries should be co-designed with the forms of internal and external organization they aim to bound.* External competitive "markets" and internal "hierarchies," for example, (Williamson 1975) can compete for the organization of relatively simple activities and relations. If complex activities are considered, the relevant alternative will be between *internal and external network forms* rather than between *markets and hierarchies.*
- *Firm boundaries should be co-designed with the activities that they are thought to govern.* Effective firm boundaries depend on which activities can be effectively developed starting with available resources and competences, and not only on the comparative costs of ways of organizing *given* activities (Penrose 1959; Demsetz 1991; Dietrich 1993). Hence, a first step in analyzing the boundaries should consist of evaluating and, if need be, reconfiguring the activities and resources (Chapter 8).
- Firm boundaries are not precisely defined unless we admit that *there are various types of boundaries*: there are boundaries of property rights, boundaries of contracts,

and boundaries of resources and activities de facto possessed or directed by a firm, which are not coterminous.

In consequence, the treatment is here divided into a first point of dynamic analysis of the boundaries based on resources and knowledge; and a second point of comparative analysis based on the production and transaction costs of alternative set-ups. Figure 12.2 provides a synoptic picture of the relevant factors for designing and evaluating firm boundaries.

Growth based on the generative potential of resources and knowledge

The expansion of American Express activities (see Box 12.2) can be explained by economies of *scope* (Teece 1980a) along with effective learning curves starting from a given base of knowledge (Dosi 1984). The specific advantages of the internal governance of the newly devised activities lie, first, in the opportunity for generating appropriable value; and, sec-

ond, in being able to do so at low cost, through a better use of available resources, without bearing costs of definition or renegotiation of outside contracts, without having to define precisely the value and conditions of knowledge transfers. This explanation provides a conceptual foundation for the recommendation, often made in managerial literature, "not to externalize" activities and resources that stem from a firm's "core and distinctive competences." For the learning paths followed and the particular collection of resources built up through them are the source of those uniquenesses of configuration eventually generating sustainable and justifiable competitive advantages (Barney 1991).

From a more design-oriented point of view, one can think of ex ante analyses, and not only of ex post rationalizations,[4] of the possible development paths based on resources. These may consist of analyses of resources/resources/services matrices (Chapter 8) or resources/products matrices (Wernerfelt 1984) in order to identify combinations with maximum added value, or minimum learning

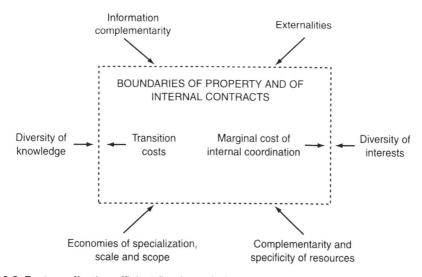

Figure 12.2 Factors affecting efficient firm boundaries

> **Box 12.2**
> From credit cards to
> travel-related services

The specialization and identity of American Express as a firm was founded on credit card business. This initial nucleus of activity led to the acquisition of financial resources and competences, information systems, knowledge of local conditions and contacts in various countries, and knowledge of money management problems connected with travel. This set of knowledge and resources was ripe for exploitation, and was indeed exploited in order to offer a vaster range of services, generated by the resources themselves; or by the same resources with marginal acquisition of new competences. Some of the possible development paths are shown in the figure. In time, the new activities directly performed by the firm have come to include accounting services and control of management of expenditure relating to travel for firms, travel agencies, and some information services.

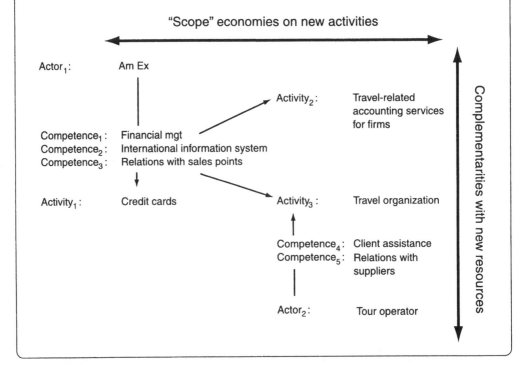

cost. These analyses favor growth of activities linked by common or connected underlying knowledge and resources, and discourage entry into activities where one has no advantages of information or competence. With that they supply an analytical justification for the idea that, normally, the profitability of products or activities (the value for the consumers) or the diversification of the risk are not sufficient reasons for embarking on different activities, and that a diversification on products linked by core competences is better founded (Williams *et al.* 1988; Prahalad and Hamler 1990).

Growth based on comparisons of production and transaction costs

Let us now suppose that there is a "given" set of "nodes" of resources and activities, not separable for "technical" reasons in the broad sense – there is no available knowledge on how to separate the activities or it is clear that they are unique and valuable combinations of resources. Suppose, too, that there is a "given" set of exchange and cooperation relations among them. For each relation, a comparative analysis question can be posed: is it better that the relation be governed inside a firm or through outside contacts?

A basic scheme

This "make-or-buy" problem has been well analyzed (Williamson 1981): (1) with reference to "transactional" or exchange interdependence; (2) with reference to hierarchical internal forms and external forms of "complete" contracting. The central proposition of the model is that *as the specificity, uncertainty, and frequency of the transactions grows, the internal organization becomes relatively more efficient than the external organization.*

It is argued that as the *specificity* of transactions increases, production and transaction costs under an external regime increase, while internal production and transaction costs decrease. For example, the unit costs of production of an industrial component in other firms rather than in the user firm are supposed to increase as the specificity and uniqueness of the component rise with respect to the needs of the user, because the supplier cannot realize economies of scale in producing for many users. In addition, to the extent that alternative partners cannot easily be found, an increase in the transaction costs of external organization is also expected, due

to the processes of communication of production instruction, of checking that standards are maintained, and of negotiating possible conflicts. Holding economies of scale constant, it is supposed that internal organization could maintain high levels of co-specialization between the production of components and other transformation phases at lower cost, and could better govern the opportunism potential among the different actors, thanks to the easier access to information, shared language and objectives, and the arbitration authority that internal hierarchy provides.

The effects of *uncertainty and frequency* of exchanges on production and transaction costs have been less deeply analyzed. These variables are speculated to be positively related to internal governance effectiveness for the following reasons: uncertainty creates difficulties in writing complete contracts; if contracts are incomplete, the conflicting objectives between transaction parties generate incentives for opportunistic behaviors (which may be actually adopted if substitutability is low, for the specificity of transactions); if transactions are frequent the costs of setting up an internal governance structure become sustainable. The response to these problems in governing transactions by external market relations is supposed to be their integration inside the same firm. The explanatory power of these basic propositions can be discussed by applying them to the case of Box 12.3.

Why did a crisis emerge over the internal governance of the transaction between the producers of components and the other actors downstream? Why did "outsourcing" seem a possible solution? The main reason for the problem in market procurement seems to be a crisis of demand that led to a reduction in the volume of activities and a consequent

> **Box 12.3**
> The Calor case

During the 1960s, the firm Calor, a producer of gas and oil heating furnaces, had developed a limited diversification strategy for its products and a clear vertical integration, thus producing all basic components of its products in its own factories. A leading firm in its sector in Italy, both in terms of productivity and commercialization, Calor had opted to produce its own optional pieces based on a number of considerations: it could always count on quality and quantity, something the market for components could not always guarantee; it could take first hand advantage of possible "opportunities" in the external demand for components; it created jobs, given the importance of the firm in its region; it could invest its cash from cash-flow liquidity.

For a while, thanks to market development and the consequent saturation of production, Calor reported very positive financial results. Facing a demand crisis, Calor's production structure, much less flexible than the competition's, was too rigid for any reconversion. A proposal was then put forward for a new strategy of internationalization in order to manage a now excessive production and avoid laying off workers.

One obstacle seemed particularly hard to overcome in this new foreign market strategy: production costs for components seemed way too high to the point that they had an effect on the competitiveness of the final products. This was mainly due to the fact that different countries had different specifications (based on various laws concerning safety and their different interpretations): Calor was not able to contain costs since its structure was best suited for standardized production; second, several other producers of components had settled in the area who, given their limited size and their specialization of brand and technology, had price/quality/reliability conditions that were better than Calor's production.

Faced with this obstacle, Calor first reacted with an ambitious "back to efficiency" program aimed at cost reduction; later, among other steps, the firm imposed more careful quality control, introduced bonuses based on performance, and opted for the limitation and reorientation of the duties of the project managers and the production technicians in favor of more concrete tasks aimed at strengthening the work flow. Even though these initiatives resulted in some benefits for the firm, workers and technicians reacted in different ways: the former were disoriented by quality control systems and the introduction of bonuses, neither of which had any precedent in the history of the firm; the latter were afraid of taking steps backward in their careers given the limitations in the creativity of their tasks. Despite these reactions and some noticeable positive results, the new strategy did not manage to reposition the firm.

At this point, the top management concluded that the only way Calor could finally achieve economic stability was to drastically reduce the workforce and begin purchasing components on the market; also suggested was a restructuring of the roles of the specialized technicians in various units, thus strengthening innovative skills in the "critical" technologies and better controlling the production contracted out.

Although conceptually clear and simple, this strategy met with very strong resistance both internally and externally, creating an obstacle to its implementation. A decision was then taken to apply this new strategy only to the new production lines, while the "old" or "traditional" structures and processes would be dealt with in the best possible way, keeping in mind the need to change whenever good opportunities arose. Obviously, the firm's profitability had been limited as compared with its potential: a suggestion was then made to improve it through a new diversification strategy.

Source: Rugiadini (1985).

reduction in economies of scale. In other words, the internal costs of production went up. In that situation, the external producers who can aggregate production over many clients have cost advantages over internal producers. At the same time, the components needed were not specific to the equipment produced by Calor. The situation was thus characterized by a combination of two circumstances – economies of scale for external producers and the absence of specificities – that could raise the costs of governing an external relation (such as unfilled or delayed orders, renegotiation of prices, etc.).

Up to this point the propositions of the basic model help. Some refinements can, however, expand the explanatory power of the comparative assessment framework and settle some anomalies and counterexamples. They are elaborated in the rest of the section.

Counter-effects

Uncertainty increases the expected costs of internal production

In the Calor case, as in many others, the increasing levels of uncertainty in the volumes and configuration of demand seem to have raised the expected costs of internal production. In effect, many examples of decentralized production similar to that described above are due to the need for flexibility: owing to the discontinuities and rigid-

ities of plants, and to the rigidity of long-term internal contracts with complementary human resources, demand uncertainty can be a source of high internal production costs (Mariotti and Cainarca 1986). Thus, the *uncertainty of transactions may have contrasting effects on firm boundaries: it raises internal production costs, while it may increase (under conflict of interest and low substitutability) the transaction costs of external governance.* A trade-off is required, and the solution depends on the shape of these costs functions. If we suppose that the difference between external and internal transaction costs increases with the uncertainty of transactions, but the difference between external and internal production costs decreases, then the sum cost function will have a minimum for an intermediate value of uncertainty – that is, *external organization would be favored by intermediate, not by minimal levels of uncertainty.*

Specificity creates surplus and reduces conflict among interests

The outsourcing and sub-contracting of components or transformation phases is quite diffuse even in the case of specific transactions, as in the textile-clothing sector, in printing and graphics, or in the transformation of plastic and composite materials. For example, many very successful Italian fashion houses externalize production activities that are very specific such as sewing "griffed" clothes (that often require specific techniques) or even waiving phases through techniques and on materials that enable identification of the stylist from the appearance of the fabric. The transactions in this case are specific and also uncertain; notwithstanding this, they are governed externally through very incomplete contracts and norm-rich market exchanges that are renegotiated only from time to time. This form is not only very diffused in the fashion sector, but has contributed to make it one of the most competitive Italian industries. These events can be explained by hypothesizing that the effects of uncertainty in increasing internal production costs are higher than the effects of both uncertainty and specificity in increasing external transaction costs, or even by questioning the hypothesis that transaction specificity favors internalization. The very fact that, say, a stylist and a textile producer are highly co-specialized, and that they have made specific reciprocal investments generates a surplus with respect to exchanges with alternative partners. Both parties have a strong interest in maintaining the relationship and if quasi-rents are high the fashion house can distribute part of them to its suppliers without high negotiation costs. Suppose further that all are interested in sustaining the image of the product, so that the best actions for the producer and for the stylist as to delivery time, quality, technical assistance, types of material to use, etc. are not very different. *The relationship will have a low potential for opportunism, despite – or rather, thanks to – its specificity and uncertainty.*

Therefore, the specificity of transactions (even if combined with uncertainty) does require communication-based coordination and concerted decision, but does not really justify internalization.

Transaction frequency diminishes opportunism potential

The frequency of transactions is also likely to have non-linear effects on make or buy decisions and the efficient boundaries of firms. It is supposed to favor internalization due to economies of scale and the reduction of contract negotiation costs. On the other hand, the frequency of interactions and the expectation of repeated exchanges create familiarity and common language among the partners, reputation effects, the possibility of serial equity among partners, and the creation of rules and routines that substitute for continuous contract negotiations. These effects are likely to reduce the expected costs of external organization (Brusco 1982, 1999). To that extent, *transaction frequency also has two counter-effects on production and transaction costs that should be evaluated: it tends to lower the costs of internal production because it permits productive and administrative economies of scale, but it tends to limit the costs of external transactions by containing the opportunism and error potential.*

Extensions

High information complexity and non-hierarchical firms

We have seen (Chapter 11) that complex and interdependent activites can be effectively organized within firms by integrated, networked, group-like – rather then hierarchical structures. Which forms of external organization could compete with these internal ones in the organization of activities and relations in innovative and complex fields? A type of organization that, in spite of being "external," or intercurrent between firms, is characterized by coordination mechanisms based on continuity of cooperation, direct communication, and joint decision-making. These forms (joint ventures, cooperation agreements, associations, certain forms of subcontracting) are analyzed in the second section of this chapter and belong in the vast spectrum of forms of interfirm organization. Here the following should be noted:

- High information complexity makes network forms (internal or external) superior to both authority and planning based firm-like arrangements and to unconnected market-like arrangements.
- Given that the internal and external organization forms effective in governing complex activities are quite similar in terms of coordination mechanisms used, the boundaries among them should not be very sensitive to relative coordination costs. Rather, they should be very sensitive to the economies in the acquisition of knowledge and the generation of new outputs; to the curves of experience on different but complementary activities; and to the cognitive feasibility of internal learning and investment. Moreover, it has been remarked that if a subject is not sufficiently knowledgeable in a field, it cannot learn very effectively and efficiently, it does not possess enough "absorptive capacities" (Cohen and Levinthal 1994). It follows that if firms do not invest, also directly, in the development of competences in a certain field, they are not likely to learn a lot from alliances in that field (Colombo 1999). Internal organization develops, on complex activities, not because external organization fails, but because external organization nurtures it – and vice versa.

Limits to firm size and the costs of change

Make or buy decisions need dynamic analysis.

Firms cannot grow indefinitely and remain efficient. In other words, it can be expected that *a limit to firm size exists beyond which it is no longer convenient to aggregate new activities inside a firm, independently of the characteristics of that activity and independently of the type of relationships with the activities already aggregated in the firm.* This limit has two properties: (1) it can be lower or higher depending on the organization form adopted by the firm (Williamson 1970; Chapter 11); (2) it always exists, by the fundamental principle according to which as a coordination system grows, all the coordination mechanisms based on communication lose effectiveness and efficiency: centralized authority or agency, joint decision-making, central planning and control, and reciprocal control (Arrow 1974; Part II).

Marginal coordination costs

In other words, this argument forces us to take into consideration not only the comparative internal and external production and coordination costs, but also the marginal costs connected with the aggregation of an additional activity. While consideration of the marginal costs of production has long been considered a criterion to evaluate the limits to the efficient expansion of internal production, consideration of the *marginal costs of coordination* has not been highlighted to the same extent.[5]

Transition costs

In addition, as is evident from more than one of the boxes in this chapter, the *history* of a firm, that has existed for a significant period of time, conditions the choice between internal and external organization in another way: the *process of transition* from internal to external organization or vice versa, is a process that is costly in itself (Nacamulli 1985; Rugiadini 1985). It is so for the transition toward externalization – or at least so it has been where and when actors have been strongly interested in job security and stability (such as in Europe and Japan). And it is true for the transition toward internalization, not only by the processes of search and negotiation that can lead to mergers and acquisitions but also by the long, delicate processes of negotiation and adjustment of internal structures after mergers and acquisitions.

It is therefore possible that the twin dynamic factors of the *diseconomies of size* and *transition costs* interact to block further evolution and adaptation of the boundaries of the firm and to render them, at least for certain periods, very stable. Undoubtedly they make efficient firm boundaries dependent on the past evolution of a firm.

Multiple objectives and fair boundaries

Production and transaction costs attached to a certain governance form may not be the same as seen by the different partners. The parties to an economic relation are not always equally substitutable. Critical resources are unequally distributed and specific investments may occur unilaterally. Third parties may bear unintended consequences. Various actors internal to the firm may rank alternative boundary designs differently. How to solve these problems? What "efficient" arrangements do we expect to observe – and what is an efficient arrangement – in such multiple-objectives situations?

External diverging objectives

Think of the case of an automobile firm that is one of the few present in a given country (due to economies of scale) that buys components from many suppliers. The suppliers can be substituted with only moderate costs in reconstructing the specific competences and capacities (i.e. specific ways of production that are adapted to the particular assembly processes of the constructor). For the constructor, the external relations thus present fairly low transaction costs, in addition to being convenient in terms of lower production costs. On the other hand, suppliers may experience high transaction costs owing to the greater negotiating power of their counterpart in prices, delivery times, quality standards, etc.

In these cases, the different parties in a transaction hold different cost functions; therefore, the problem of "designing efficient boundaries" will rarely be solvable by one cost-efficient solution for everybody, but would generally admit more than one Pareto-superior and fair solution (Grandori 1991).

A conceptually similar problem is the possibility that some costs, generated by the governance regime chosen, are born by third parties external to the transaction. Whatever the production and transaction cost savings for two or more parties involved in a merger, acquisition, or other form of internalization of exchanges, one needs to ask what *externalities* are generated outside of the relationship.

A concept of "fair boundaries" may help here – as it did in the design of job and unit boundaries – in addition to that of "efficient boundaries," for selecting from the possible better solutions. Box 12.4 illustrates.[6]

Internal diverging objectives

Frequently, make or buy decisions also have consequences for the interests of firm internal actors, that may require negotiation. For example, the Calor case shows what happens

---

Box 12.4
"Chinese walls" boundaries

Some years ago a discussion was started in Italy as well as elsewhere about whether or not to allow acquisitions of stock broker firms by banks. Obviously banks were favorable to this possibility because they could have extended their scope of activity and gathered from clients also the money currently intermediated by stock brokers. Clients might have reduced some costs too, by having only one counterpart offering a full range of alternative ways of investing their money. On the other side, banks have their own interest such as investing monery in stocks, which may very well differ from those of any particular client. So, if the agent who decides what bonds to buy knows this information internal to the bank which allows him to detect what purchase is in the best interest of the bank, he might find himself in the position of being an agent with two principals with different interests. Is there any organizational form which may solve the problem? Both the extreme forms of standard acquisition and complete separation between the two types of financial intermediaries seem to suboptimize. Then it can be hypothesized that an intermediate form could be (Pareto) optimal, tailored for satisfying the requirement of informational separateness between stock broker activities and other banking activities, plus the requirement of reducing the number of transactional partners for an investor, that of unified rights over the residual economic results of the two types of activities. That would be an H-form with restricted access to information between stock broker firms and other subsidiaries of the same financial group.

Looking for something of this sort "in nature," I discovered that this conjecture was proven to be right by the emergence of a form of quasi-integration between banks and stock broker firms operating at the London Stock Exchange called a "Chinese wall" solution, based on a reciprocal limitation of information rights.

Source: Grandori (1991).

– as more of a rule than an exception – when hitherto it is decided to externalize an activity.

In effect, an internal organizational structure, once constituted, creates interests directed toward its own maintenance (Selznick 1957). These interests may be due to simple inertia toward the maintenance of the *status quo* (Hannan and Freeman 1989). More frequently, and less conservatively, internal actors may be interested in the growth of the firm (Marris 1964, 1997). As many have observed, the growth of the firm beyond its cost-efficient boundaries in the strict sense can bring benefits of various types to the internal actors. First, it can permit the accumulation of *slack resources* with respect to those necessary for current activities. This element can diminish workload, improve consumption, and in general improve the quality of work life for the participants. In addition, it can create the conditions for innovation to take place (Cyert and March 1963). Further, the growth of the firm usually increases the prestige, the visibility, and the job security of those who work in it. In fact, it has been argued that the firms in which *managerial objectives*, or more generally the objectives of the employees, have an important weight will have *larger efficient boundaries* – efficient with respect to these broader utility functions – than firms where only shareholders' interests have weight (Baumol 1959; Marris 1964; Williamson 1970).

However, there is a problem of *sustainability*: all these possible effects of widening the efficient boundaries of firms due to objectives other than profitability require that the external conditions enable significant levels of organizational slack to be sustained (Williamson 1970). Innovation and unique, firm-specific combinations of resources certainly contribute to creating distributable surplus.

On the other side, those same internal interests can generate *restrictive effects* on the boundaries of the firm, instead of expansive ones. For example, if the expansion of firm boundaries is understood as rate of investment and capital accumulation, then a firm under managerial control can expand more slowly than one where investment decisions are taken with the sole criterion of return on invested capital (Jensen and Meckling 1976). Even if human capital investments are considered, internal actors may have an interest in restricting access of new entrants, who may be seen as competitors for revenues and positions (Mead 1972).

Collective action interdependence

Not all the important relationships between economic activities are of the "transactional" or "vertical" type (deployed along a chain of transfers from upstream to downstream). "Horizontal" and "diagonal" relationships are also important, between activities and actors that possess and use similar and/or complementary resources. From these are born relationships of interdependence that can be competitive or cooperative to a varying degree: such as relationships of "commensuality," "complementarity," "symbiosis," and aligned or joint action (Thompson 1967; Pfeffer and Salancik 1978; Hannan and Freeman 1989).

Much of the theory of the firm described in the previous sections was developed by reflecting on transactional interdependencies and the problem of vertical integration. However, many of the arguments and the variables can be extended to the analysis of horizontal and "cooperative" interdependencies, with some integration and specifications that can be adapted from other studies and relevant models.

Continuing for now to limit the discussion to the comparison between the two broad alternatives of markets and firms, a horizontal relationship coordinated through a market is a competitive one. Competitive relationships may become very costly and inefficient allocative mechanisms due to the same factors that make market exchanges costly. An example is the gradual substitution of cooperative relationships for previously competitive ones in the formation of a hotel chain, shown in Box 12.5.

This type of movement away from competitive relationships toward cooperation can be connected to uncertainty and economies of scale factors. For example, the independent offer of hotel services is affected by the problem of the utilization of invariable inputs and facilities under conditions of very uncertain and unpredictable demand. Furthermore, the hospitality business also presents problems of information asymmetry and difficulty in judging the quality ex ante on the part of clients (which hotel will offer the type of service desired in an unfamiliar location?). Under these conditions, the hotel owner or manager who looks at both the supply and the demand sides will realize that a strategy

---

Box 12.5
Emergence of cooperation
in the hotel industry

Best Western, one of the largest hotel chains in the world, was founded in California in the early 1940s as an informal network of hotel owners who would recommend customers to each other. Today this network has been formalized into an association of independent hotels whose staff offers a centralized and computerized reservation service that links some 3,500 hotels around the world.

The administrative savings achieved in the supply of routine services and the technical savings in the centralized use of the computer system have encouraged the widening of the activities of the association, especially as regards advertising the hotels under one brand name, compilation of statistics, and the regulation of new affiliates based on the vacancies of other Best Western hotels in a given location.

Best Western is an association, not a corporation or a franchising chain. This characteristic is attributable mainly to the kind of resources and activities undertaken by this coalition, as compared to other coalitions.

In fact, there are hotel chains managed by more integrated organizational forms such as, for example, many American hotel chains structured as franchises (Holiday Inn, Sheraton, Hilton). The most important Italian hotel chains are instead totally integrated and combined under one management and are usually organized as divisional structures (Ciga Hotels, Jolly Hotels).

The differences in organizational form can be explained in terms of different choices of services/markets and the different costs resulting from this. For example, the franchised hotel chains compete on the standardization and the quality of service that is guaranteed in a certain number of locations. This structure requires more pervasive information systems than those needed merely for reservations, given that it will work to support purchasing policies, staff policies, and accounting and planning policies.

The proprietary management of a hotel chain seems to be more efficient when the chain competes for excellent services, ones that are sophisticated and "unique" such as those offered by hotels located in historical buildings. In this case the number of affiliates to the chain cannot be high and information systems are (or should be) more oriented toward offering the hotel management better support in decision-making and flexible planning rather than to a standardization of the service (for example, decisions on the renovation of the site that would take into consideration architectural style and furnishings).

Source: By Anna Grandori.

---

of cooperation is preferable, in many cases, to one of competition: for example to standardize and guarantee the service offered and put in place common services of reservation and promotional programs can reduce the costs of search and potential opportunism for the clients, as well as reduce the expected production costs for the hotel through better use of the facilities and economies of scale in the common activities.

As in the case of transactional inter-dependence, and as the hotel chain case illustrates, the comparative assessments of internal versus external forms cannot be properly made without a specification of which these forms are. A range of possible combinations between coordination mechanisms and a set of "structural alternatives" for interfirm organization is examined in the next section (see also Box 12.6).

INTERFIRM ORGANIZATION

The service offered by an airport implies intense cooperative interdependences in terms of both *common resources* (building and infrastructure) and *activities* (the different activities contribute in the "transformation" of passengers and goods transported).

The intensity of these interdependences can be described through the key variables introduced in Chapter 8 and already used in the examination of the intensity of transactional interdependences. In the first place the common resources are in various aspects technically indivisible and come close to the characteristics of a "public good" for the actors that use them. There are economies of scale for many ground services such as materials handling, internal transport, supplies, etc. There are team production effects, to the extent that the marginal contribution of each single activity is not always visible in the quality of the total airport service. Many activities involve very frequent interactions. There is the potential for opportunistic behavior in the improper use of common goods and the supply of substandard services that exploit a captive market.

Notwithstanding all this complexity, it is not really sufficient to fully justify the constitution of a unique firm, for the following reasons: (1) the conditions of intensive and

complex interdependence are not generalized to all the airport services; (2) there are strong demands for local responsiveness of different services to diversified client needs; (3) the number of activities and services provided is very high; and (4) there are pronounced knowledge and technology differences between activities favoring specialization and division of labor among actors providing them.

All these factors act to discourage an aggregation of activities in a single firm, no matter whether that firm is coordinated via centralized planning, control, and compensation systems or coordinated by decentralized negotiation and joint decision-making.

These conflicting needs can explain the oscillation of the interested actors between a market solution and the constitution of a single firm. Which then is the best solution? The basic model hitherto considered pushes us toward weighing the relative costs and benefits of the two alternatives and choosing the solution that creates more value at a lower production and coordination cost. In so doing, however, one will probably choose a solution that is anyway costly and probably sub-optimal. An alternative strategy is to develop solutions that could be superior to both market-like coordination and an integrated firm. These interfirm "network-like" governance structures are in fact widely and increasingly diffused.

The coordination problem at the airport, like many other problems of cooperation and exchange, is characterized by simultaneous and conflicting needs for specificity and local specialization on one side and complex interdependence on the other side. One can ask whether or not organization forms can be devised that are capable of simultaneously satisfying these contradictory needs, instead of choosing the superior form between

Box 12.6
The Alpha Airport case

During the 1970s the Alpha Airport company was created to manage all activities related to the airport of the City of Alpha: expansion, modernization, maintenance of airport infrastructure, handling and catering, commercial ground activities (bars, restaurants, shopping centers).

The pre-existing situation was characterized by a different and partial organizational structure. The national airline, for which Alpha represented the hub, was managing its handling and catering directly ensuring good cost savings given the high volumes; other airlines managed their own handling, as well as the smaller ones, which, gathered in a consortium, managed to keep their costs relatively low. As far as catering, these airlines were supplied by a separate and independent company. The other commercial businesses were contracted out, without applying a standardized policy, to small and medium outside companies. The airport infrastructure, however, was under the responsibility of the public administration, based on criteria and rules that often did not meet high efficiency and service standards.

The new company Alpha Airport ended by substituting and combining this multitude of separate and independent activities, maintaining a priority in the improvement of the infrastructures.

As time went by, the objectives of expansion and reorganization were met; the centralization of the other activities did not allow for as significant an improvement in efficiency as had been hoped. Relationships with staff and other airlines turned out to be more difficult and costly.

Alpha Airport had in fact hired the staff previously employed in the other airlines and businesses. A difficult integration was soon noticed in the handling department, where staff and responsibilities did not fit well with one another. In the rest of the businesses, the change from small independent companies to a larger organization offering more job security and union support – and where it proved harder to check on the staff on a regular basis – allowed the employees to work more "loosely" with less commitment to the job. The consequence of all this was obviously lower efficiency and lower quality in customer service. Closed-shop unionization of some categories also meant higher personal costs: better salary conditions could not be ignored, and served as a basis for negotiations with other departments as well. In addition, the new centralized structure had created new organizational costs for Alpha Airport: training for professional staff, based on a company-wide program and the creation and launch of a new information system, totally automated, in order to provide support for a growing and more complex organization.

Serious problems started to arise with the other airlines as well. Their main complaint was that the larger integration was limiting their efforts to promote their own image. Some of them, for example, were demanding a better and more qualified runway service, together with the re-institution of the dedicated check-in service; meeting these particular requests would have meant reducing the efficient use of resources.

After about a decade of activity, Alpha Airport was still looking to answer some of these questions. A decision was made to contract out the majority of the commercial

> businesses. As regards the handling department, the decision turned out to be more difficult to reach: on the one hand, there was a need for global efficiency and, on the other, there was pressure from the other airlines; above all, the management of Alpha Airport was afraid that the company would lose its identity, given the reduced control on other activities, if indeed there were to be a lesser commitment on the infrastructure and the loosening of the centralized handling service department.
>
> *Source*: Rugiadini (1985).

market and firm coordination. Many effective and efficient organizational forms of this type have been discovered – some of them for a long time now, others more recently. All of them are based on two contradictory criteria that are applied simultaneously: the criterion of the division of labor and differentiation between firms according to specific local conditions and specialization advantages; and the criterion of integration through the more or less intensive use of coordination mechanisms that differ from pricing, exits and background regulation, applied in addition to them, or even in substitution for them.

In the case of the airport, for example, one solution could be the creation of a sort of "federation" of many independent firms, each specialized and motivated based on their individual contribution, but integrated by rules assigning them work, activity programs, quality controls, and penalties for failing to meet standards. Consortium structures, for example, are by now fairly common in the governance of differentiated systems of equally critical activities that are linked by intensive interdependencies. Such systems include ports and airports, the delivery of large industrial projects (hydroelectric dams, power stations, etc.) and joint research and development projects.

Consider the following other possible questions: What organization form could be effective and efficient in the regulation of a construction project? What organization forms are behind the term "chain" in sectors like retail supermarkets or shopping centers or hotels? What forms of cooperation usually link firms in the electronics and telecommunication sectors in order to develop new products and to bring them to market?

In the following paragraphs, the salient organizational attributes and variants of these forms will be illustrated. In general, all these network forms involve the alliance of two or more firms, in order to respond simultaneously to contrasting needs for differentiation and integration.

Interfirm coordination mechanisms and organization forms

Consider a set of firms linked by some form of transactional or collective action interdependence, and suppose that it would not be effective and efficient to fully integrate them in one firm. What are the possible coordination mechanisms between these different firms? The combination of proprietary separation and conscious coordination between firms has generally been identified as "hybrid" or "network" governance (Thompson *et al.* 1989; Powell 1990; Williamson 1991; Langlois and Roberts 1995). This classification is however very broad, catching in one category all types of relations among firms that are not market relations. In addition, it does not allow us to design or assess one form of network against another – a problem which is at least as frequent and relevant, and usually more difficult to solve, than the internal/external dilemma itself. In the following a typology of external organization forms is proposed (outlined in Figure 12.3), as a repertory of combinations among coordination mechanisms which can be employed among firms beyond prices, stocks and background regulation typical of market-like governance of competition and exchange.[7]

SOCIAL COORDINATION: small numbers and/or common interests

	POOLED	INTENSIVE
	Routines-based coordination	Team like communication
	(e.g. Marshallian districts)	(e.g. hightech districts)
INTERDEPENDENCE		
	SEQUENTIAL	RECIPROCAL
	Constellations	Informal mutual adjustment
	(e.g. textile filière)	(e.g. long-term industrial buyer–seller relations)

BUREAUCRATIC COORDINATION: large numbers, computational complexity and/or different interests

	POOLED	INTENSIVE
	Rule-based association	Team-like decision and control
	(e.g. associations, purchasing, or marketing consortia)	(e.g. industrial projects consortia, research consortia)
INTERDEPENDENCE		
	SEQUENTIAL	RECIPROCAL
	"Star-like" networks	Differentiated an integrated nw
	(e.g. licensing and concessions, one-way sub-contracting)	(e.g. co-makership sub-contracting, franchising)

PROPRIETARY COORDINATION: high information complexity, highly differentiated competencies and interests

	POOLED	INTENSIVE
	Team production	Team-like knowledge sharing
	(e.g. production JVF, JV contracts)	(e.g. R&D JV firms)
INTERDEPENDENCE		
	SEQUENTIAL	RECIPROCAL
	Hierarchical profit-sharing associations	Differentiated and integrated ventures
	(e.g. "Associazioni in partecipazione")	(e.g. capital ventures)

Figure 12.3 Comparing interfirm organization forms

Source: Grandori (1997b).

Social coordination

A natural mode for an actor to connect and coordinate with other actors is through direct communication, with the eventual end of making a common decision on the actions to undertake. This is true for individuals and also for collective actors such as firms (Evan 1966; Aldrich and Whetten 1979). Firms therefore create many informal, direct, and interpersonal links between their participants that have important coordination capacities (Granovetter 1983). Direct informal relations permit the acquisition of partner-specific knowledge in several dimensions: identity, behavioral habits, and degree of trustworthiness. This confidential information can constitute a base on which to identify opportunities to cooperate or to exchange with reliable partners (Granovetter 1985). These "weak ties" can then be strengthened and can evolve into stable relationships between firms with the purpose of regulating specific relationships of exchange and cooperation.

For example, some researchers who have studied relationships of exchange and cooperation in research and development have spoken of the resurrection of "barter" economy in activities of extreme information complexity for which exchange based on market values would be very difficult (Schrader 1991). Confidential information of potential economic relevance is exchanged directly through negotiated relationships without the help of a system of value measurement. Alternatively, a series of professional firms specialized in adjacent and complementary fields (such as management consultants or physicists in different sub-fields) can reduce the uncertainty and the costs of search for clients through cross-reference and recommendations.

These relationships between firms usually imply something more than simple lateral communication. They imply "strong ties" of social and normative control, keeping an eye on each other and if necessary referring to interested third parties inappropriate or opportunistic behaviors.

Overall, informal coordination between firms is feasible under some general conditions.

General antecedents

Two core barriers to information disclosure among firms are: (1) the risk of knowledge expropriation or of competitive use of information, due to *conflicting interests* (for example direct communication, if directly relevant for competitive advantage, is difficult among direct competitors); and (2) the *number of firms and matters* to be coordinated (the firm cluster size and the computational complexity of transactions or common actions) (Chapter 7). Conditions of perceived common goals, or at least low chances of defection from fair conduct, can however occur more frequently than one may expect among different firms, and even among competing firms on a variety of issues that have no direct competitive significance (such as the negotiation of sectoral work contracts, or lobbying for a sectoral law). The interested actors can clearly perceive common objectives as dominant, thanks to the perception of the surplus generated by the collaboration. Or they can at least conclude integrative agreements and stick to them because of reputation effects and the repeated and frequent nature of interactions. A moderate number of interdependent firms makes social control and informal governance of the relationships feasible. In addition, coordination may regard areas of action in which a non-calculative, rule following decision style is adopted, often thanks to common culture and proximity (as in local clusters of firms).

Forms

Partner-specific communication networks among firms can assume different configurations, according to the shape of the connections (all-to-all, star-like, chain-like) and to the extent they intermingle with other mechanisms (price, authority, rules and norms). In the following they are described and connected with different configurations of interdependence, according to the general scheme exposed in Chapter 8.

- A *routinized form* is the traditional variant of "industrial district" governance (the "Marshallian" industrial district) (Becattini 1979) and is commonly characterized by a reliance on shared routinized know-how, shared rules and norms, shared pro-collaboration values, and tacit coordination as prevailing and effective governance mechanisms of local systems of firms with similar or complementary specializations, especially in traditional sectors as leather or textile (Brusco 1982 and 1999). Intense direct communication is not necessarily a prominent feature of the functioning of this type of tradition-based clusters of firms.
- Instead, researches on "industrial districts" in technology intensive and dynamic rather than traditional industries document the existence and effectiveness in dealing with innovation and intensive interdependences of a *"team-like" model* of industrial clustering, based on competence differentiation and coordinated through much more intense processes of information exchange, confrontation and problem solving (Powell 1996; Lomi and Lipparini 1999).

- Transactional interdependence can also be managed successfully through informal task partitioning, and the simple set up of interfirm information and communication systems. The sequentiality of interdependence may however complicate the coordination activity, which may end up being taken on as a specialized task by one or more "central firms" (a form sometimes called *"constellation"*). For example, it happens that firms with commercial competences coordinate the level, timing, and type of output of clusters of producer firms so as to respond flexibly to demand – in sectors such as textiles or precision equipment (Lorenzoni and Ornati 1988; Lorenzoni and Baden-Fuller 1995).
- The sustainability of informal self-enforcing rules of cooperation in the regulation of transactional interdependence has also been demonstrated in a context where interests are aligned by belonging to sectoral and industrial communities that are not necessarily "local." Many long-term industrial goods buyer–seller relationships, even at an international level, are only weakly regulated by formal contracts and substantially regulated by joint decision making and shared sectoral norms (Johansson 1987). The considered transactions are repeated frequently so that reputation effects are important, and the goods exchanged are multifaceted and partner specific, where both elements contribute in generating integrative negotiation structures. Long-term industrial buyer–seller relations are thus examples of reciprocal interdependence, managed by a *differentiated and integrated arrangement* allowing mutual adjustment and monitoring.

Box 12.7 provides an illustration of the evolution of social network governance from a

---

Box 12.7
The evolution of Versace's
network in the 1980s

Question: How would you describe the relations with the producer firms working for you, now with respect to the beginning of the Italian fashion industry expansion and success?

Santo Versace, the managing hand of the family, remembers: "The take off, as for many other leading firms in the Italian fashion industry, was sustained by a constellation of small external producers. There has been a long period in which hand shaking was sufficient between us and our suppliers. My brother was the 'Designer,' for all of them. We selected the threads and tissues. We knew each other well for many years. It has never been a problem of trust. However a time has come in which these small suppliers were no longer sufficiently reliable. They were no longer able to learn quickly enough, to follow technological change, to be as precise as needed in realizing our models. It was for those reasons that we gradually chose to establish a much smaller number of connections with larger, more autonomous, more competent, more prestigious producers. Firms like Zegna, to make one name. Firms who did have an independent name."

Question: How did the coordination with these suppliers change?

"It became much more structured. Our group was split in three controlled firms: Versace S.r.l. – the fashion house; GV Moda S.p.A. – the unit coordinating distribution and marketing; and the brand 'Istante' – developing and commercializing all griffed non clothing products.

On the supply side, our fashion house dedicates a 'product manager' to follow the realization of the models entrusted to a particular producer. Our man worked most of his time at the producer's location, assisting their people and work processes."

Question: What changes accompanied this evolution on the commercial side?

"On the commercial side, we entered foreign markets, and we did so in differentiated ways. For example, in Japan, we made an agreement with a large distributing company. In the US, we started with multi-brand outlets trying to ensure that our griffe were dominating. In European countries, we privileged exclusive franchising contracts with shops, with a very close link with us: our professional training, identifying 'Versace' layout, visits and direct controls by our personnel, financial auditing."

Source: From "An interview with Santo Versace," Anna Grandori, Bocconi University, Milan, 1986.

---

tradition-based "constellation" to a more conscious differentiated and integrated arrangement, in which various obligational and proprietary mechanisms are also present, in one of the most successful Italian fashion houses.

The discrete salient forms of social networking illustrated above, are located in connection with the four general types of interdependence that they can effectively regulate in Figure 12.3.

Bureaucratic coordination

Interdependent firms can regulate their cooperation and exchange relationships through both obligational and relational contracts, that incorporate, in addition to patrimonial obligations, a series of behavioral obligations, reciprocal rights of information, decision, and control, including the division of tasks and responsibilities. These contracts are typically incomplete and the interested parties add to legally binding external clauses, interfirm agreements that specify procedures, activity programs, supervision systems, arbitration procedures and integrating structures. Such forms may be called "bureaucratic," if the word is meant to capture in one concept the ensemble of mechanisms sustaining conscious direction through rules and programs, hierarchy and joint decision-making, and planned task partitioning (Grandori and Soda 1995).

These mechanisms can govern interfirm relations in combination with price mechanisms or not. For example, suppose that two firms are neither competitors nor linked by the transfer of goods or services, but see some possibilities for future cooperation by joint exploitation or coordinated use of complementary resources. These firms might sign a contract in which they commit themselves to exchange certain information and to jointly decide some strategic moves. This would be a purely procedural contract not involving any "mixture" with price or market-like mechanisms.

General antecedents

As *the number of actors and activities to be coordinated increases computational complexity, and/or interests diverge calling for conflict resolution structures and procedures*, a shift is observed from informal and social coordination to contractual coordination in interfirm relations. The effect of network size on its degree of formalization is easily

observable and well documented. The needs for transparency, equity, and management of a large number of elements force groups of firms to become formal associations and to more formally define their exchange relationships. The possible incentives for free-riding, unobserved unfulfillment of commitments, substandard efforts, and the unilateral reduction of costs make it efficient to specify explicit guarantees in well-defined and legally enforceable contracts, and to appoint central agents with surveillance and arbitration functions.

Forms

Under the shadow of interfirm obligational and relational contracts, a variety of structural alternatives can be defined for the purpose of designing, or even only assessing, effective interfirm coordination modes.

- Trade *associations* are typically formed for regulating the *pooled interdependences* linking firms in the same industry, or for regulating the cooperation between firms who are technically similar or complementary on particular matters or projects, but who are and wish to remain autonomous or even competitors on most other matters. The regulation of these interdependencies is accomplished through rules of membership and member behavior, procedures of information and decision-making that specify the allocation of decision rights and the modes whereby they are exercised (voting rules, the power of the assembly of the associates, etc.), and a definition of common purposes. All these rules usually become formalized to a large extent in statutes. Central staffs are set up for the provision of common services – promoting sectoral interests with respect to the public authorities, generic promotion of the product, specialized training and information, and sectoral-level bargaining with unions – but are unlikely to go beyond this (Van Waarden 1992); in particular, control over members' behaviors is quite difficult in the framework of an association (Zan 1992).

More tightly coupled forms use a wider set of coordination mechanisms, capable of governing more complex exchanges or cooperations, under the legal umbrella of complex contracts such as consortia, franchising, and sub-contracting. At least two organizational forms – one more "mechanistic" and another more "team-like" and integrated – can be distinguished and evaluated for each type of contract.

- *Consortia* are based on associational contracts between firms regulating the joint realization of projects or transformation processes whereby sub-phases or sub-projects are carried out by different firms. Consortia are not dealt with in the same way by all legal systems (for example, Italian law is particularly favorable to this form of interfirm coordination).

The consortium usually maintains a separation of the profits, if any, that each firm independently earns on the activities assigned to it. On the other hand, the consortium can create a central organizational structure in the sense of assigning stable tasks, using programs of activity, time and quality evaluation systems, penalties in case of unfulfilled commitments, and internal authorities with the functions of inspection, supervision, and arbitration.

In horizontal relations, the consortium is a structural alternative to the association, allowing firms to *pool similar or complementary resources* instituting stricter quality *control over access* in the first place and over the maintenance of *quality and prod-* *uctivity standards* afterwards. Examples of this type of consortium are sale or purchasing consortium – for example a consortium for the commercialization of a regional wine.

A more tightly coupled, *differentiated and integrated type of consortium* is found in the governance of the realization of complex projects, e.g. the design and construction of industrial plants or complex civil constructions. In this case, firms realize the different "parts" to be assembled in a more complex service or product. The different production sub-processes are and should be technically separable in order to assign tasks and reward rights to the different firms. On the other side, firms are linked by various interdependences and the achievement of an integrated output of the desired quality in the desired time typically involves the coordination of programs and reciprocal adjustment. In fact, this type of consortium employs a wide mix of coordination mechanisms, including inter-firm planning, mutual control systems, incentive and penalty systems to deal with failures in respect of external commitments (see Canavelas Case, Chapter 6; Grandori and Neri 1999).

Other examples are problem-solving oriented groupings of firms (and eventually other institutions as universities and research laboratories) with highly differentiated competences applied to the exchange and development of research related information (Evan and Olk 1990). The computational complexity of activity and the possibility of signing commitments and being responsible toward third parties (e.g. public supporting agencies) seem to be the main factors accounting for the formalization of this type of cooperative relation into the consortium contract. The internal structure of these consortia is in fact described as rather undefined, peer group based and adhocratic, as we would expect on a research intensive task.

- *Franchising* is a form of complex obligational contracting regulating the relationship between one firm (the franchisor) that possesses know-how that is transferable to other firms through processes of technical assistance, training, supervision, and activity programs. These other firms (the franchisees) apply the know-how to the local business context, paying royalties to the franchisor. Franchising agreements normally include the right to use a trademark that is identified with that know-how. This organization form is widely used in the large-scale commercialization of a product or service with a strong identity, which is highly firm-specific, but standardizable. Examples include restaurants, the hospitality industry, retail distribution, clothing stores, and medical analyses laboratories.

The distinctive format of the franchising contractual relation contemplates that a central firm, the franchisor, is assigned both monitoring and decision-making rights over a large number of affiliate firms. Firm ownership remains independent and, even though there is no need to suppose that an agency contract *strictu sensu* is implied – e.g. that the franchisee is intended to act "in the interest" of the franchisor – the group or chain of cooperating firms is typically exposed to free-riding behaviors toward each other, that are thought to justify the creation of a central authority (Rubin 1978; Williamson 1985; Brickley and Dark 1987). A limiting condition is that the relevant managerial and technical competences are or can be effectively centralized in a single central firm, i.e.

that products or services are not so complex as to prevent information from being structured and processed by a single central actor. In spite of this centralization of common know-how, site, or market, specific critical information and competences are and should be diffused and controlled by the peripheral units, if the overall formula of franchising is to generate its advantages of specialization and local responsiveness on one side and of coordinated action and economies of scale on the other. Therefore franchising agreements can be classified as effective and efficient governance structures for reciprocal interdependences.

On the ideal continuum of obligational contracts that can regulate transactional interdependence, simpler structures, involving mainly one-way rather than two-way transfer of know-how, products, and services are *licencing and concession* relations, as found in the regulation of the relations between production and distribution of standardized products – such as cars or gasoline; or in the regulation of the transfer of patented and structured know-how – such as chemical and pharmaceutical formulas.

- *Sub-contracting* is, instead, an arrangement typically employed in the regulation of upstream rather than downstream activities, in parts or phases of the production cycle that can be efficiently entrusted to third parties by a central firm. Thus the subcontractors are not simple "suppliers": they work according to specific instructions from the user firm, at times using materials and equipment supplied by it, and normally under the supervision and the assistance of the central firm – as in the outsourcing of car components, the sub-contracting of sub-activities in construction projects, and the externalization of production phases in the textile industry. Typically, then, in a subcontracting system, the central firm manages a series of control, incentive, planning, and supervision mechanisms that have led the subcontracting firm to being defined as a "quasi-firm" (Eccles 1981) and the overall system as a "macro-firm" (Dioguardi 1987).

Also within sub-contracting arrangements, two distinct forms have been repeatedly observed, and recurrently present as two rings of relations around the same main contractor firms. An inner ring is constituted by "co-makership," "open-book contracting," "partnership-like" relations, and typically regulates the outsourcing of specific and complex components or phases of activities, involving reciprocal interdependence. An outer ring is composed of more competitive, one-way, hierarchical relations (Suarez-Villa and Rama 1996) and governs the procurement of more standardizable and codifiable items or activities, so that the resulting type of interdependence is predominantly sequential.

Proprietary coordination

The coupling of high information complexity and highly differentiated competences and interests can explain a good number of the reasons why even more tightly coupled interfirm governance structures emerge. In its strongest form – epistemic complexity – information complexity may be due to non-observability of performances and non-measurability of partners' contributions, unpredictability of the kind of results that can be achieved, high problem-solving intensity, even uncertain objectives and a level of differentiation and tacitness of the knowledge mobilized by parties that prevents full communicability. In these conditions, conflicts

may be very difficult and costly to solve on a case by case basis, authorities may not be competent, and rules too rigid. What alternatives are feasible and comparatively more effective and efficient?

There are many examples of activities and interdependences characterized by this level of information complexity: sharing complementary and poorly transferable for innovations purposes (such as new products); or pooling productive or commercial resources that can generate economies of scale or scope in production or distribution, accompanied by team production effects; or matching accumulated financial resources with accumulated know-how for sustaining highly innovative activities, too specific and risky to be financed by the conventional capital markets and financial intermediaries.

These situations do not permit a clear division of rights to actions and results on which to base obligational contracts between firms. The activities are difficult to observe and monitor, even among peers, and relational contracting would be difficult as well. As we know, in general these conditions suggest a shift from monitoring mechanisms to incentive mechanisms, and to property rights sharing, in particular.

Various forms of joint venture contracts allow a more or less complete sharing of property rights.

Corporate joint ventures

Two or more firms can contribute not only the financial capital but also the technical and human capital for the constitution of a new jointly owned and jointly managed firm – "*corporate joint ventures*" (CJV). These forms entail "full" sharing or property rights: residual decision and control, residual rewards and ownership transfer rights – albeit on portions of the mother firm's activities. Empirical studies show that CJVs are particularly diffused in dynamic high technology sectors (e.g. Mariotti and Migliarese 1984; Contractor and Lorange 1988), and that they are diffused in mature industrial sectors as well (Hagedoorn and Narula 1996). In both cases, the shared property rights resolve the difficulties in measuring the contribution of each party by assigning to each partner in advance residual reward rights according to the shares held in the new firm. Resource commitments create a hostage effect, incentivating the delivery of agreed upon contributions (Hennart 1988). However, our framework would predict that the internal organizational structures of CJVs and the relations with mother firms will be different in the two contingencies (Grandori 1997c): more hierarchical and rule-based (and with strong connection with mother firms) in production CJVs where there is team production but inputs remain rather separate; more team-like in innovation-oriented CJVs where the point is to share knowledge (whereby internal integration of the CJVs may be even stronger than communication with mother firms) (De Laat 1999).

Capital ventures

Venture capital relationships are usually considered as financial operations: a firm, usually a professional venture capitalist, furnishes risk capital to an existing but relatively new firm for innovative projects that are difficult to finance through the standard capital market. Just because this relationship is explainable as efficient for transactions involving high risk and risk sharing that may be difficult to regulate through normal capital markets, effective CV arrangements should set up organizational connections allowing thicker information exchange and should allow the investor to participate in the direction of the financed firm (Sapienza and Gupta 1994). Therefore, an effective venture capital relation involves a rather extensive property right sharing, not merely financial participation – the more intense, the more the financed firm's projects are risky and novel. More extensive knowledge transfers and joint direction are in fact often invoked in the specialized management literature for improving CV performance (Roberts 1991).

Limited property rights sharing

The full mingling of property rights is not the only mode of proprietary interfirm coordination. In principle, it might be possible to share only some property rights and not others – for example, share profits but not ownership. These forms exist, and are used, for example, for projects in which interdependence is limited in time or in the entity of resources absorbed, for which a common ownership structure is not justifiable. Here are several examples:

- "*Joint venture contracts*" are contemplated in international law, based on which firms participate in a share of the profits derived from a common action (for example, the common participation in an international bid for petroleum exploration) but do not consitute a new firm and do not involve common property of assets.
- "*Profit sharing associations*" (e.g. the "associazione in partecipazione" in Italian law), allow a firm which contributes technical instruments or other assets to an activity of another firm to participate in the profits generated by that activity (Galgano 1974).
- There are *federative groups of firms* based

on shared ownership but separate profits, used for example to regulate the use of common proprietary know-how in highly distinguishable settings and activities as a federation of professional service firms using a common blend (Daems 1983).

The case of the ATR Consortium, described in Box 12.8, illustrates several conclusive points.

First, it illustrates how interfirm networks effectively combine *social, bureaucratic, and proprietary mechanisms* to govern a variety of different interdependecies involved in their action, inside and across the broadly defined legal typologies of contracts.

Second, it allows discussion about whether a consortium structure was more or less effective than a joint venture structure for governing the type of complex collaboration involved.

Third it allows *a dynamic analysis*: through what sequence of arrangements – and through what changes in the state of uncertainty and of opportunism potential – interfirm coordination may evolve?

Fourth, it introduces a *combined analysis and choice of a governance structure* capable of properly coordinating a given type of activity and relations – a coordination cost issue – *with the choice of partners* themselves – an opportunity cost issue (Chapter 6; Ring 1999).

In the ATR case the trajectory was from a lack of experience and confidence and a partially integrated structure, to more profound knowledge of partners' assets and a proprietary agreement. This path would fit with a learning interpretation: firms may start with loosely coupled structures and "sample activities" for testing whether the partner itself was the right one. If the scale of activity is not easily divisible, and it is difficult to figure out incremental steps, firms might choose to bear higher coordination costs (adopting a loose, not highly protected agreement) instead of facing high opportunity costs (being tied to the wrong partner). This is not the only possible path however: firms may start with highly defensive, formal, if not proprietary contracts, for transforming their relation into an almost social one, upon successful experience (Ring and Van de Ven 1992).

Negotiating interfirm agreements

In the design of interfim organization, it is quite likely that the preferences of the potentially allied firms may diverge regarding the form of regulation of their relationship. For example, in the construction of complex high-technology projects (e.g. intelligent buildings, subways, dams, energy plants) that require both general construction and infra-structural competences, the construction firm often prefers to take the role of main contractor and manage the contributions of the other firms as subcontractors; however, the firms that have infra-structural competences would often prefer a more equal relationship such as a consortium. Similar problems of analysis and choices of organizational forms can be resolved by looking for organizational solutions that are Pareto-superior and fair, in a logic of multi-party negotiation (Jarillo 1988; Contractor 1985; Grandori 1991; Chapter 6).

Box 12.9 reports a semi-structured analysis of a process of negotiated design of the contract and the internal coordination mechanisms regulating the relation between an international delivery firm and its agent network.

Interfirm organization and firms' multiple boundaries

The analysis of interfirm coordination modes reinforces the idea that we can not talk

Box 12.8
The ATR Consortium

The ATR Consortium (*Avions de Transport Regionaux*) between the French Aerospatial and the Italian Alenia was created in 1981 through a GIE – Groupement d'interêt economique – and is today one of the largest manufacturers of aircraft for regional transportation. The agreement was the result of a project involving the equal collaboration of the French Aerospatial and the Italian Alenia (former Aeritalia), two companies that had never worked together before. Nevertheless, the production of the ATR vehicles was for both partners a great opportunity. For Alenia, it meant that the company would once again produce passenger aircraft, after being absent from that market for almost forty years. For the French, though, this was not the first project of this kind, as they had already taken part in numerous cooperative projects such as Concorde and Airbus.

The absence of previous relationships between the two companies, the complexity of the project, and its length combined to create problems in achieving a balance of cooperation and competition. The first model, the ATR 42, was tested in 1984 and deliveries of the first aircraft began the following year. In 1986 a larger version of that plane, the ATR 72, was launched and deliveries were scheduled to begin in 1989. The lack of previous collaboration between the two companies created uncertainty also about the potential behavior of both parties during the agreement. It seemed obvious that the first element to be taken into consideration was the partners' ability to exploit the complementary know-how developed by the two companies in the passenger/commercial and military fields. Both Alenia and Aerospatial had a common interest in exploiting their separate technical skills and experience. However, the same could not be said about tasks not requiring specific skills, which were therefore considered to be easily substitutable between the parties. Lastly, there was the issue of the definition of the areas of leadership of each partner, in terms of technical leadership (the role of the systems integrator), sales/marketing leadership (the relationships with the customers), and organizational leadership (i.e. internal coordination).

The cooperation agreement signed through the GIE called for the division, by "competences," of the industrial and the development activities of the two parties. The agreement was the result of a massive investment on the part of both parties. These investments in the relationship concerned industrial, personnel, and organizational aspects, through specific know-how. The agreement was designed to limit the risk of opportunistic behavior, in consideration of the complexity of the contract and the high specific investments. Among the numerous clauses of the agreement, one stated that both partners could invoice the consortium for all activities carried out, with specific price-setting mechanisms. The prices paid had a big impact on determining how income from the sales of aircraft was shared. This implied that a possible "opportunistic" increase in prices automatically would lead to an increase in profits, creating a disadvantage for the counterpart. On the other hand, unfair behavior by one of the two parties would lead to numerous benefits from it. The ATR Consortium therefore acted on two fronts: on the one hand, it tried to make all activities as transparent as possible through a sophisticated control and sanctions system while, on the other hand, it tried to establish a climate that would encourage both parties to expect the absence of opportunistic behavior. The agreement anticipated the total and full responsibility of the partners, the sharing of any damages and delays in the delivery process, and the impossibility of one party breaking the contract.

A common organization was defined and the two companies exchanged personnel. Social coordination and control mechanisms were easier to create because of the common features of the two companies, such as size, financial structure, and organizational culture. Even though they lacked an earlier relationship, both companies knew about each others' peculiarities from the start. One of the main sources of this knowledge was the indirect or cross-collaborative relationships. For example, long before the creation of the ATR plane, Alenia and Aerospatial worked independently with British Aerospace and with Dasa. This meant that the indirect networks of cooperation had contributed to the presence of strong and fast information flows, while at the same time serving as a channel for the communication of knowledge.

Further business development and the need to articulate an effective organizational control of the agreement laid the groundwork for increased intensity in the relationship between the two companies. At the same time, the number of social exchange opportunities also grew. With the increase in activity it became even more difficult to implement all contractual safeguards. The growth of targeted investments increased the risk of opportunism and "locked" the parties into the relationship. An efficient level of safeguards would have reached unsustainable levels of complexity and costs unless social mechanisms came into play.

Starting from January 1, 1996, the success of ATR planes and the entrance of a new partner (British Aerospace) led to a shift in the ATR Consortium to a proprietary agreement of a joint venture called Aero International Regional. With this new agreement the ATR experience became integrated with that of British Aerospace, thereby including new activities and new airplanes.

Source: By Giuseppe Soda.

meaningfully of "the boundary" of a firm, but we have to be precise in specifying what boundary we are talking about. Firms have multiple boundaries. Figure 12.4 visualizes firm boundaries as a set of demarcation lines, marked by property rights (the de facto possession of resources, especially knowledge, may draw another not coincident boundary); by internal contracts regulating the continued and co-specialized association with the owners of human resources; by external obligational and relational contracts, which also, to various extents, govern transaction and cooperation in a conscious way, in a regime of specialization and continued association.

SUMMARY

In this chapter a conceptual framework for the analysis, design, and assessment of firm boundaries and interfirm coordination has been presented, extending and integrating new institutional economics contributions with other strands of relevant organizational and sociological research.

The first part of the chapter centered on a comparison between the use of internal or external organization to regulate economic activities. This comparison was first made on the basis of explanatory variables proposed by transaction cost economics (*transaction specificity, uncertainty, and frequency*), though

Box 12.9
The International Delivery
case

ID is an international company providing door-to-door express delivery service in almost 200 countries. In order to serve its clientele by handling distribution of parcels and documents in almost every part of the world, the company created a network of locally owned branches, as well as of indirect unit agents. It should be pointed out that, as ID operates on an international level with a long-standing and consolidated image of reliability, it imposes quality standards that are well-nigh identical throughout the world. One example of this is overnight delivery guaranteed practically anywhere in the world. To achieve its declared objectives of quality, ID requires substantial organizational integration with its suppliers (agencies, indirect units, cooperatives), considered as partners – to all effects, members of the ID network. None of these partners, however, works exclusively for ID and therefore part of their turnover is independent of their relationship with ID.

The current solution is a *commercial agreement* between ID and partners. The commercial agreement is drawn up by headquarters but some margin of negotiability is left to the district managers. In fact, the standards of quality required are uniform throughout the ID network, but within each district there are different problems, particular operating conditions that necessitate negotiation: the relationship is constantly negotiated through a task force named "fair costs." The team's goal is the analysis of the ID–partner exchange in terms of *fairness*, determining, area by area, what is the actual contribution of the partners and of ID to the relationship and to the creation of the final value of the service, in terms of costs and investments, but also in terms of the quality of the service. As the output is measurable (delivery in the required time at the level of the service requested) and the ratio existing between inputs and outputs of the parties can be determined, it is possible to apply a criterion of rewards proportional to contributions.

As from 1994, ID compensates partners on the basis of the number of parcels handled by each employee (until then the co-ops were paid on the basis of the number of hours worked by each courier, regardless therefore of the number of parcels handled).

ID asks its partners to make specific investments (managerial investments and physical assets) and to respond to its needs, but at the same time it has made a number of concessions: on the one hand, these are standardized contributions for the use of cellular phones, uniforms, and logos on the vans (the advertising contract currently includes a fixed amount per day for each vehicle bearing the ID logo, for each courier who wears the uniform and is equipped with a cellular phone), on the other hand they are related to the particular necessities of the partners (special rates, material support, incentives). In addition, training (not only technical but also managerial) and management assistance are provided by ID.

In terms of procedural fairness, it should be noted that all the initiatives connected with the partnership are managed in collaboration with a considerable number of the partner companies, defined as "strategic," in respect therefore of the criteria of representativeness and voice. Until now there has been basically no turnover among the partner companies.

As to parties' utility, the ideal contract for ID is a contract in which there is a total variabilization of delivery costs. In this way, the fixed costs would be sustained completely by the partner. Related to this strategy is a tendency to become "brokers" of the transportation service rather than direct suppliers, and therefore to transfer the risks and costs of delivering to the partners. ID's best alternative to a negotiated agreement can be considered to be the internalization of distribution with an estimated increase in administrative and transaction costs.

As to partners' utility, the advantage that the partner companies derive from their relationship with ID is the possibility of synergizing their local distribution activity by means of their partnership with a major company known worldwide. However, the partners of ID aim to obtain a "platform" of fixed reward and contributions to specific investments, so as to reduce the risks borne and to appropriate a larger share of the surplus or rent created by the cooperation. The partners' best alternative can be considered as the possibility of entering into partnership with another delivery company.

If the existing type of contract were not taken for granted, it would be possible to explore *other feasible fair forms.* The creation of a network of *franchisees* has recently been taken into consideration. It would appear to be a superior solution in terms of substantial and procedural fairness. In substantial terms, it could allow ID to complete the process of organizational integration with its partners and decentralize part of the activities that are now managed by the central organization (for example, invoicing) without increasing structural costs. At the same time, the franchisees could reduce the risks currently born by participating in the performance of the whole chain to which they are contributing rather than being entirely linked to local fluctuations in demand. In procedural terms, equal and formalized treatment for all partners could be appreciated. On the other hand, it may be noted that a formal franchising contract may entail some loss of utility for the franchisees if the system – as is usually the case – included a clause of exclusivity. The "niche" activities currently performed by couriers locally would be lost without any benefit for the franchisor. Indeed, ID always has difficulties in accepting local deliveries with particular characteristics (weight, size, number, value) and therefore it might prefer to let its partner make this margin rather than working almost at a loss, or "making a present" of the client to the competition.

Therefore, a fair contract that seems to be Pareto-superior, in this case, would be, so to speak, a non-mechanistic "*tempered franchising,*" in which a greater organizational integration is associated with ad hoc contractual provisions tailored to the specific needs and preferences of local partners.

Source: Grandori and Neri (1999).

revising the hypotheses on the positive and linear effects of these variables on firm efficient boundaries in the light of relevant empirical research and conceptual criticism.

In the second part, comparative analysis was extended in regard both to the variables considered and to the forms considered. The variables added include: the *type of interdependence* (collective action as well as transaction interdependence); the *structure of*

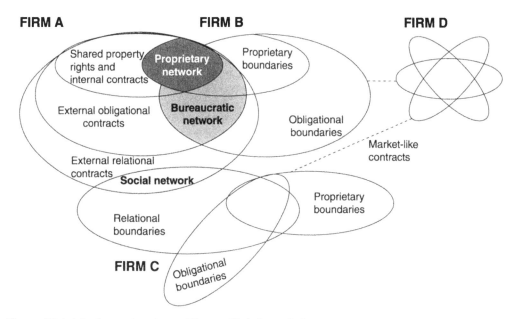

Figure 12.4 Interfirm networks and firm multiple boundaries

interests and the extent to which they can actually lead to significant opportunism potential; the presence of *different preferences over firm boundary designs* held by different internal and external actors; the *degree of differentiation and tacitness of the knowledge* on which activities are based; and dynamic factors, such as *transition costs* and the *marginal costs of internal coordination.*

Lastly, the analytical framework has been extended to analyze different forms of interfirm organization. Three broad families of coordination mechanisms were analyzed and assessed – *social, bureaucratic, and proprietary coordination* – effective under different combinations of information complexity and differentiation between interests and competences. Various contractual and organizational configurations have been distinguished within each of them so as to support interfirm organization design as a function of the type of interdependence (pooled, intensive, sequential, reciprocal): *procedural rule-based networks; team-like networks; star-like networks; and differentiated/integrated networks* (see Figure 12.3).

Exercise: Anchors and Airplanes

That day, in the hot summer of 1920, when Ariberto Sanpietro's grandfather stole a bamboo plant from Villa Hanbury, he could hardly have predicted that that act would change the life of his son and grandson.

At the end of World War II, Alfredo Sanpietro began making fishing rods for the fishermen on the western Ligurian coast, using the bamboo cane that had accidentally burgeoned behind his father's house. From being a secondary activity, the production of fishing rods gradually grew to be Sanpietro's main occupation. Ten years later, he opened the first factory of Imperia Pesca s.r.l., a firm specializing in equipment for competitive fishing: rods, reels, floats, etc.

In 1995, Sanpietro's son, Ariberto after his father, had inherited a firm with a noble name but in grave difficulties, for he had not been able to keep pace with the technological innovations that had involved the production of fishing equipment, above all in materials. Here he was at the crossroads: either innovate or resign himself to a slow but inexorable decline.

The opportunity for a fresh start came from the trials that were being successfully conducted by Imperia's renovated research and development laboratory: the production of a fishing rod that was super-lightweight but very long and strong, ideal for the surf-casting technique (performed from the beach with long casts out into the open sea). If this product could gain the approval of more and more demanding clients, Ariberto would launch a line of super-lightweights for all the other types of fishing. That would be the long-awaited turning point.

Sanpietro contacted a team of competitive fishermen from San Bartolomeo (Imperia) to carry out tests on the rods. After the tests, the most expert of them, Agostino Amoretti, Italian surf-casting champion, went to report the group's opinion to Sanpietro: "Well, Mr Sanpietro, the rod is extraordinarily flexible and sensitive, but there's one serious defect, the reels are too heavy for this kind of rod and, given its lightness, the weight is shifted too far backwards, and that impairs the length of the cast. Without long casts there's no fishing, and no fishing means no rods will be bought."

Sanpietro was well aware of this problem. The reels made by Imperia were too heavy owing to the materials used. For some time, Sanpietro had been toying with the idea of a reel using materials employed by the air industry (a special alloy), but he was alive to the fact that the firm would have to invest a lot of resources in order to produce a reel of this kind: they would have to purchase the plant, contact new suppliers, train or find an already trained workforce. Yet without a light reel the "super-lightweight" line would get the thumbs down from the market. Sanpietro decided to apply outside and found firms already in possession of the technology and knowledge required for the production of the reels. These were suppliers to the air sector. Sanpietro estimated that to launch the product in its first year he would need about 7,500 reels. Visiting the firms (three in Italy, two in Germany but with very high prices), he realized that in order to produce the 7,500 reels they would have to halt their production of components for about two months. But the factories were flexible and at 4,000 reels the minimum efficient scale could already be reached.

One of the owners of the components firms spoke very plainly to Sanpietro: "Look, if we produce 7,500 of your reels, you will pay for 7,500 and no mistake, so if the sales of your product go badly you'll pay up everything and immediately. Either we work for you at zero risk, or we don't work at all." Sanpietro was well aware that these entrepreneurs had the air industry literally breathing down their necks. So he didn't trust them, for he was convinced that the producer of components wouldn't wait a second to give up making the reels in order to meet an urgent order from a producer of airplanes. He trusted neither the production programs nor the prices fixed. Now, he had to have all the reels available in the first months of the year, before the summer, and this risk made him lose sleep. On the other hand, seeing that the product was unique in the market, he couldn't give a realistic estimate of its sales, since it would occupy a high price band. For some time there had been a lot of talk of a proposed law that would make it compulsory to have a license for sea fishing, which would drastically change the market for fishing gear; and he had no idea what his competitors (mainly American) would present the following summer. In this state of uncertainty, therefore, he could not offer the producers of air components anything more than his good intentions.

Yet he said to himself, while nervously fingering the report on the firm's indebtedness (which wasn't that much of a headache): "My workers would be perfectly able to make this reel, I'm sure of it." Meanwhile, one of the components manufacturers had made a proposal: the reels would be delivered in the month of April (apart from a small portion for the competition team and for the sector fair in March). Sanpietro had to take a decision.

It was November, and while Ariberto Sanpietro strolled along the deserted beach in the rain that heralded the arrival of winter, he thought he would get ready to launch the new line without having seen a single one of the reels except for the prototypes.

By Giuseppe Soda

Questions

- Would it be better to entrust the production of the reels to the Imperia workers or to outside producers?
- Which factors favor which solution?
- If opting for outside production, what mix of coordination mechanisms with the suppliers could effectively govern the relationship?

Economic Organization Beyond Divides: Polymorphism and Reconfigurability

This conclusion emphasizes certain innovative implications, in content and method, of what has been said on the forms of organization, and recall the link with the concepts developed in the first two parts (Conclusions Parts I and II).

An initial term that seems to capture the key message of the entire book is: multiplicity. Multiplicity of forms of rationality, multiplicity of coordination mechanisms, multiplicity of forms of organization, multiplicity of organization boundaries.

MULTIPLICITY AND POLYMORPHISM

Multiple rationalities

Part I started out from a reconstruction of the fundamental forms of rationality – optimizing, heuristic and automatic – as "decision strategies," renewing the traditional way of considering them, at least in the following respects (Conclusion Part I).

In the past, much has been said about alternative "models of man," about different "assumptions" or postulates regarding rationality. Various organization theories have been linked with one or other systems of assumptions and have, also or mainly for this reason, become non-communicating systems of thought. In addition, treating the forms of

rationality as "behavioral assumptions" hinders one from perceiving one of the most important properties of human and economic rationality – namely, its multiformity and its meta-rationality. People are able to activate different decision processes; more than that, they are able rationally to govern this meta-choice, as a function of the informational state in which they happen to be. This property is extremely important for understanding economic and organizational phenomena as the emergence of relations of trust between the parties in exchanges and cooperation; the differentiation of organization as a function of problems; the formation of rules; innovation in all its manifestations and, in particular, in forms of organization.

Three configurations of decision processes, that can be seen to recur, have been identified; but the multiplicity of possible configurations is much greater. The concept of multiplicity to which our anlyses have led is more radical than that of an observed variety of "types" consisting of different elements – as much for the "forms" of rationality as for the "forms" of organization. The "forms" are composite entities. The diversity among the forms is due to the diversity in the combinations among the elements themselves, rather than solely to the presence of different elements. Moreover, the fact that certain combinations are remarked upon does not imply that others could not be. Understanding the constitutive elements of "forms" and their possibilities of combination can enable us to perceive new ones. In the case of decision-making strategies, the effort to specify them precisely has led to their being reconstructed as salient configurations of rules of research, choice, and learning. They could be recombined differently, thus yielding mixed strategies, suited to different circumstances in different stages or subactivities of decision-making.

Multiple combinations of coordination mechanisms

In Part II a similar path was followed, in the attempt to identify the fundamental coordination mechanisms among several actors, considering those mechanisms in their distinctive, non-composite traits, in order to analyze their distinctive governance properties with sufficient precision. Attention was focused not on "markets" but on prices; not on "democracies" but, distinctly, on the mechanisms of voting and teaming; not on "hierarchies" but, distinctly, on the relationships of authority, agency, rules and plans; not on "cultures" but on norms, values, and routines. This approach has enabled clearer analysis of the conditions of *failure* and the possibilities of a combination of different mechanisms (Conclusion Part II).

The engineering of new organization forms

In Part III, reconstruction of the forms of organization starting out from combinations between mechanisms, and between mechanisms and decision processes, has supplied an extension of the *procedures* for describing, explaining, and designing organizational solutions; and an extension of the portfolio

of identified organizational solutions themselves. This perspective affords a possible answer to the widespread dissatisfaction felt by researchers and by many managers with concepts that are too aggregated, too macroanalytic, not very clear and not very (or no longer) useful in guiding action and organizational choice – as, for example, the firm as opposed to the market, functional as opposed to divisional structures, post-Fordism as against Fordism and Taylorism, capitalism as against collectivism, and so forth. The specification of forms of organization as combinations among various ways of allocating rights to action, decision, control, and ownership; the ways of exercising these rights according to different forms of rationality; and the nexuses of different coordination mechanisms – all this has opened out the range of different, potentially effective forms of organization to a far greater extent than those normally categorized in the theory, and in some cases even more than the possibilities exploited in actual practice. Hence, a further advantage of this mode of viewing organization is that it is better able to "predict new facts" (Lakatos 1976) – that is, new forms of organization – than is the case with perspectives that confine themselves to codifying ex post the association of organizational attributes and mechanisms as this has occurred in practice, and exhaust, in these classifications of empirical combinations, the repertoire of possible "forms of organization."[1] In this book, we take account of the utility of identifying "discrete" and "salient" configurations with the aim of comparative evaluation, but we also show the utility of a more creative, more generative approach, bent on seeking and finding ad hoc solutions to organizational problems, and on designing new architectures, working within a space of elements, rather than only observing, assessing and applying known archetypes. Among other things, to the extent that it is true that the relative uniqueness of the combinations of resources and activities is a source of competitive advantage, it is then precisely the particularities and differences in the form of organization adopted, rather than its typicalness, that can make a difference to a firm's performance. As a matter of fact, several of the forms of organization that have turned out to be interesting and effective, at least in the most recent conditions of competition, appear to be so precisely thanks to the employment of an especially ample, hybrid and "inconsistent" (rather than "coherent") mix of tasks and rights partitioning and of coordination mechanisms: unified property rights *and* price mechanisms, separate property rights *and* bureaucratic integration, hierarchy and plans incorporated in external contracts, common ownership of resources *and* separate rights to profits or vice versa; Taylorization of work *and* associative contracts of partnership among workers; team coordination *and* strict programming of work flows with "zero stock" and "zero defects."

Multiple boundaries

Among the manifestations of "organizational multiplicity," the analysis and design of "boundaries" of organization units ultimately led us to define "multiple boundaries." There are boundaries set by actual possession of knowledge and techniques, that could be termed "knowledge-based boundaries." The rights of ownership of resources define "proprietary boundaries." "Internal contractual boundaries" are defined by internal contracts, above all for acquisition of human resource services. A variety of external obligational and relational contracts marks an "area of influence" (to use another geographical-

military term like boundary) that is ampler ("external contractual boundaries").

It would appear, then, that one of the ultimate results of the work of "integration" among different perspectives performed in this book has been to "disintegrate" the broader concepts, the "ideal types" and "archetypes," which have too often been understood in a monolithic way and in contraposition – markets and firms, contracts and plans, internal and external, "informal" and "formal" regulation, "absolute" and "bounded" rationality – into more elementary components, alliance among which is possible and fruitful.

UNIVERSALITY, CONTINGENCY, AND POSSIBILITY

At a methodological level, the inventory of propositions of organization science reconstructed in the book includes three different types of statements, all with claims of legitimacy: "possibility theorems," "contingency propositions" and "universal laws."

Possibility – or, conversely impossibility – theorems specify the feasible or unfeasible combinations between conditions (the premises, the "ifs": for example, the state of knowledge and the configuration of interests) and organizational arrangements (the consequences, the "thens": for example, applicable decision strategies or coordination mechanisms). Statements of this type have been used to construct the "failures frameworks" of decision strategies and of coordination mechanisms (Conclusions Parts I and II).

"Contingency" statements specify a probabilistic rule of correspondence between a set of conditions (premises) and one or few relatively superior organization forms (the prediction is that this or these forms should be observed with greater *frequency* than other specified forms in conditions of effectiveness). The approach has also been used here in the parts concerning comparison between the given, recurring forms of organization in order to govern sets of given, comparable activities.

One might think that organizational solutions governed by means of "possibility" theorems are too undetermined; but the partial fungibility between elements of organization and the presence of degrees of freedom in using and combining them enables not only new and innovative organizational solutions to be designed, but also certain facts to be accounted for – facts which would indeed be "anomalous," if only a logic of organizational contingencies were contemplated. Some of these are represented by the differences of organization among and within the various sectors and countries. For example, the fact (Meyer and Whittington 1997) that in different countries one may adopt different conventions at the level of institutional arrangements, or that managers have different cultural backgrounds, and that these differences in norms and conventions can nevertheless combine with other similar organizational solutions for similar problems – like the adoption of multi-divisional structures in large diversified firms – all this is not an anomaly in the logic of organizational possibilities, whereas it would be so in a scheme of organizational contingency to national contexts. In like manner, a "possibility theory" of organization enables one to explain why, even in the same sector and same region, there exists a variety of organizational set-ups, based on the diversity among the combinations of resources and activities that characterize individual firms or clusters of firms, and why these set-ups are effective.

A third type of statement on organization is universal – that is, they are valid in all circumstances.

There are aspects of organization that are largely and increasingly "convergent," for which it is actually possible to express "universal laws." Indeed, these "universal" aspects of "good" organization seem to be more present now than formerly, owing to the closer interdependence of economic action and the diffusion of ethical principles and basic justice rules that find increasingly general acceptance (Pfeffer 1992). There appears to be a universal tendency of slavery to disappear as a form of work organization. It is universally asserted that forms of organization that discriminate by race, gender, religion, and other factors unconnected to the potential working contribution are always inefficient (wasting resources) as well as iniquitous. Universal, too, is the property of complex organization systems to break down into simpler ones. This type of statement has been found valid, for example, for devising procedurally fair traits of human resource management systems (e.g. transparency, possibility of appeal, anticipate definition of rules, etc.).

STRUCTURAL INSTABILITY AND RECONFIGURABILITY

The multiplicity in the forms of organization is also sustained by the multiplicity in the processes that govern their formation. Structural variations can be produced by conscious discovery of new solutions, but also by non-planned organization stretching by trial and error, or by serendipity (fortuitous discovery). On these processes the effects of "natural selection" of superior forms are overlapped. A combination of different processes of change enables a high rate of change in economic organization, which would otherwise be inexplicable and unsustainable; it also makes the instability of any form probable. For, however well any organizational arrangement may have been designed, it is hard for it be effective over a long period. Not only because the "external" or uncontrollable conditions change quickly – there are changes in available technologies, consumer preferences, and the responses of other actors to these changes. There are intrinsic reasons for instability in any form of organization, if it is to be effective, efficient, and fair for a given system, as argued below.

Organisational alternance

All forms of organization are imperfect and costly. Some are better suited to solving certain problems and generating certain results, but are weaker in other respects, for which different solutions work better. For instance, highly decentralized and multipolar network structures, either inside or outside the firm, appear to do better in generating product and process innovation, but in the commercial development of innovations they may yield ground to more centralized and planned structures (Nooteboom 1999). Thus, in time, *alternation between different forms* in one and the same system is probably healthy. Whatever the solution or form of organization chosen as superior at any given moment, subsequently it will probably be overtaken by another one, merely because it has been applied and has demonstrated its typical advantages and equally systematic shortcomings. Even in a distributive perspective, the imperfection of resolution of conflicts, the probable persistence of imbalances to the advantage of one or other group of actors, in any regime of organization, generates incen-

tives to change toward set-ups that, in time, will compensate the parties who were previously disadvantaged.

In time, moreover, learning and the growth of knowledge in the various areas of action of a system change the degree of complexity of the activities, the knowledge of the counterparts, the configuration of preferences and the potential for opportunism in the relations, the size of the system, i.e. of almost all the variables on which the effectiveness of organization forms depend. Hence, whichever arrangement may be efficient for a system at time t will probably no longer be so at time $t + 1$, which today is measured rather in months than in years.

Reconfigurability

This is one reason for maintaining that a desirable feature of an organization in conditions of change and rapid learning is *"lightness" and ease of reconfiguration* ("flexibility"). The modalities and procedures of organization design put forward in this book should help to outline a "light organization." Their prescriptions include not introducing explicit coordination mechanisms if tacit coordination is sufficient; not setting up figures of authority if this does not bring specific advantages in the costs of decision and control; not setting up groups if there is no demand for problem-solving based on diffused knowledge. On the part of managers and persons involved in the firm's life, who have commented on some of the design procedures described in the book, it has been remarked that they sound like a sort of organizational "Occam's razor":[2] tools for a "zero-based" analysis of organization, oriented to shave out structural redundancies. These procedures may nonetheless give a different response than the now popular ones to the problem of "heaviness" of the structures. For example, catchwords like "delayering," "downsizing," "slim," and "flat" organization, have been diffused as recipes and heuristics for lightening organization structures. However, these recipes have already shown the dangers of an approach fettered within a perspective of "cuts" and "reduction" (of times, persons, and levels and units of organization), rather than one that looks toward reconfiguration. To be sure, structures tend to grow heavier in time, but not merely, and not so much, because the number of persons or hierarchical levels increases, but rather because new activities are added to the pre-existing ones, new coordination mechanisms are added and overlaid on the old ones and the fundamental aggregations of resources and activities are seldom reviewed. If such "reviews" were performed in the spirit *of reconfiguration rather than reduction*, they would not only be less short-sighted but also less threatening and so more frequent.

Organisational discovery

Lastly, the structural instability of forms of economic organization stems from the possibilities of *organizational discovery*. Superior solutions are only so in a relative sense. There is no point in speaking of "optimal" solutions except within a set of alternative structures that have already been defined. Hence it is probable – and we may hope – that the best solutions and the best practices of today will be surpassed by those of tomorrow. The evolution of information and communication technologies contributes, for its part, to making feasible architectures of organization that were previously unthinkable. "Long-term equilibria" are irrelevant in organization – not so much because "in the long term we shall all be dead," but above all because, hopefully, new ideas and solutions will spring up, and some "old" and seemingly outdated ones will gain a new lease of life.

Glossary

....

Accountability   Explicit of responsibility criteria which enable an actor to justify its action in front of other interested parties.

Actor   Individual or collective subject endowed with homogeneous knowledge and preference with respect to a matter.

Adverse selection   Self-selection of exchange partners with worse rather than better attributes for the counterpart, due to the presence of advantages for the self-selecting parties and the lack of information for the other party. It is considered a form of pre-contractual opportunism.

Agency   Relation by which one or more actors ("principals") transfer to other actors rights to decide and act in their interest, within a defined "zone" of behaviors.

Agency costs   In an agency relation, all costs of information, of control, of diverging goals pursuit, and of compensation for risk transfer between principals and agents.

Agency theory   Set of models explaining and prescribing efficient types of contract and ownership structures for governing agency relations; on the basis of cost–benefit maximizing calculation and choice by both principals and agents.

Anchoring bias   Tendency to make estimates starting from a known value and adjusting (insufficiently) that value for a changed circumstance.

Asset   Potential for generating flows of revenues. See RESOURCE.

Authority   Relation by which one or more actors accept to follow the decisions of one or more other actors (thereby transferring decision rights to them) within a defined "zone" of behaviors.

Availability bias   Tendency to consider easily retrievable information.

Behavioral decision theory	Branch of cognitive psychology applied to decision-making, modeling empirically observable information processing behaviors and interpreting their differences with respect to the subjective expected utility model and to correct inference rules.
Bounded rationality	Property of human rationality, consisting of being limited in a computational capacity, fallible in constructing reliable and valid knowledge of the world, and imperfect in transferring (communicating) meanings interpersonally.
Bureaucratic failure	Inapplicability of hierarchical and planned governance, or relative inferiority of it with respect to other forms of governance. It is due especially to information complexity in all its components (variability, number of elements, observational and causal ambiguity).
Capital venture	Type of interfirm contract by which a firm, usually a professional venture capitalist, furnishes risk capital and specific management competence to other firms for innovative projects that are difficult to finance through the standard capital market. The degree of interfirm integration should be a function of the innovativeness and specificity of the undertaking.
Career	System regulating horizontal and vertical development of people/jobs matches toward superior responsibilities and competence, and usually also superior and eventually more variable (risk-loaded) rewards.
Centralization	The degree of centralization of an organizational arrangement is the extent to which property, decision, and/or control rights are allocated asymmetrically to a sub-set of the actors (at the extreme, one actor) comprised in the system.
Codes of conduct	Procedural norms of behavior.
Cognitive dissonance	There is cognitive dissonance when the human mind has to process inconsistent and incoherent information. It is supposed that there is a tendency to eliminate it, by discarding or even not seeing those elements which do not fit or have no significance according to one's own scheme of interpretation.
Compensation curves	The curves plot the distribution of compensation levels as a function of the evaluation of the positions held.
Competence	Ensemble of an actor's knowledge, skills, and energy. The concept can be applied to individual or collective actors.
Competence-based evaluation	Assessment of the value of the contribution of an actor on the basis of its competence (resource) rather than on the activities released or results reached.

Complementarity	Resources can be said to be complementary if they can be employed in combination for producing valuable outputs; or if an expansion of activities based on one resource raises the value of activities based on the other.
Computational complexity	Difficulty in information processing deriving from the number of relevant elements and connections.
Conglomerate	Firm with diversified uncorrelated activities; in particular activities not generated by employing the same technical and human competences.
Consortium	Associational contract between firms regulating the joint realization of projects or transformation processes whereby sub-phases or sub-projects are carried out by different firms, usually entitled to separate gain shares. Mechanistic and integrated organization forms of consortia are used for regulating sequential versus intensive types of interfirm interdependence.
Constellation	"Star-like" interfirm social network.
Contract	Agreement with patrimonial consequences for the parties, which institutes or modifies a relationship of reciprocal obligation. *Contingent* contract: in which different agreements are specified as a function of the possible situations that may arise. *Obligational* contract: incorporating behavioral obligations in addition to or instead of patrimonial ones. It can also include mechanisms for enforcing the agreement and coordinating behaviors. *Relational* contract: that is only partly formalized and complemented by informal agreements and norm acceptance. *Associational* contract: constituting and regulating a society rather than an exchange.
Control loss	Imperfection in the compliance of actors to expectations of other actors, due to various factors including language and communication ambiguity, adjustment to unexpected events, and diverging interests.
Convention	Norm or rule whose content is relatively arbitrary (e.g. a language).
Cooperation	Pooling of information, resources, or outputs, across technologically separable interfaces, to capture opportunities for collective action.
Coordination	The intended achievement of better configurations of activities and resources. These "Pareto-improvements" can be achieved through a variety of mechanisms, involving or not involving communication or joint decision-making.
Co-specialization	Specialization of resources in ways that make them complementary.

Critical uncertainty   Whenever the more or less successful problem-solving in an uncertain activity has important consequences for the effective conduct of other activities, the activity is said to entail *critical uncertainties*.

Cybernetic decision   Mechanistic decision strategy defined by the rule of applying appropriate actions drawn from a repertoire or tried at random, and by learning according to a PRINCIPLE OF REINFORCEMENT.

Decision strategy   Combination of search, choice, and learning rules.

Divisional form   Type of firm structure in which the main units in which structure is partitioned (divisions) are entitled to some firm property rights (rights to decide investments and divestments in technical assets, and residual reward rights) and are controlled on residual results parameters (profits, returns on investments).

Dual factor motivation   Differentiation of an actor's preference structure into a "motivational zone" (the set of factors perceived as surpluses – their presence generates positive utility but their absence is not perceived as a loss) and a "hygiene" zone (set of factors perceived as due – their presence is not perceived as a gain but their absence is perceived as a loss).

Ecological models   Models of behavior and organization studying the processes of change through substitution of misfit actors (*natural selection*) rather than through the learning of new actions.

Effectiveness   Property – of actions or action organization – of attaining desired consequences.

Efficiency   Property – of actions or of action organization – of generating benefits economizing on scarce resources. *Allocative efficiency*: Pareto-superior allocation of resources and rights among different actors.

Epistemic complexity   Difficulty in information processing deriving from the variety of possible interpretations of observations and cause relations.

Equity   Property of actions – or of action organization – consisting in a division of scarce resources that is acceptable by all actors, if they did not know in which position they participate to the division. It is used here as a synonym for justice and can be be operationalized in fairness judgments. Equity can be an attribute of a solution (in that case it is also called *"substantive justice"*); or an attribute of the process leading to select a solution (*"procedural justice"*).

Federative form   Organization form under which units (typically firms) own some assets in common but do not share gains or profits.

Federative group	Loosely coupled version of collective organization in which a group of co-workers collectively possess some or all of the main means of production, but hold separately the right to the rewards deriving from their own work.
Formalization	Codification of information into codified languages and documents.
Frame	Way of seeing facts and interpreting information. Framing a problem means defining what is inside and what is outside the focus of attention, what the relevant information is, and what it means.
Franchising	Form of complex obligational contracting regulating the relationship between one firm (the franchisor) that possesses know-how that is transferable to other firms through more or less intense and integrated processes of technical assistance, training, supervision, and activity programs.
Functional organization	Clustering of similar competences or of similar activities into specialized units.
Fundamental attribution error	Tendency to overweight actors and their conscious will as causes of social and economic events.
Gain sharing	Reward system by which the benefits (monetary or not) generated by a collective effort are distributed to the participants.
Goal setting	Model hypothesizing that actors can be motivated to select actions whose expected consequences for them are equal to or greater than a goal or target.
Governance	Used here and elsewhere in the broad meaning of the term, as a synonym for organization. The term originated in the study of corporate institutional and proprietary arrangements.
Group paradox	Contrast between the heterogeneity of inputs maximizing a group problem-solving capacity and the homogeneity maximizing its control capacity.
Groupthink	Pathology of group information processing consisting of the elimination of dissent and the homogenization of (expressed) judgments.
Heuristic decision	Decision strategy defined by the rule of choosing an alternative whose expected value is above an acceptability level (also called *aspiration level*), by the rule of searching until the hypothesis of finding an alternative with acceptable pay-off is verified, and by the rule of adjusting objectives (or other components of the decision process) according to what is found.

Heuristics	Rule on where and how to look for information, alternatives, or solutions relevant to a problem at hand.
H-forms (holdings)	Type of divisional structure in which divisions are financially controlled firms, fully endowed of property rights on their assets.
Hierarchy	Formalized chain of authority relations. As not applied to actors but to cognitions, the term is used in its more abstract meaning of a chain of logical command, in which there are superior entities governing inferior ones (for example a procedure for changing a program is hierarchically superior to the program).
Hollow corporation	Pathology by which large diversified companies may become devoided by differential and superior information or competence with respect to a cluster of independent firms with no central coordinating structure.
Incremental decision	Mechanistic decision strategy defined by a linear choice rule (in time t change action by a constant or a given proportion with respect of $t-1$ action), and learning by reinforcement.
Indifference "zone"	Set of an actor's behaviors over which he is indifferent. Basis for the suspension of judgment in authority relations and in the acceptance of conventions.
Industrial district	Cluster of firms taking advantage of "proximity" to one another in a defined territorial zone, sharing similar or technically inter-dependent competences (e.g. Silicon Valley, the Como silk district).
Information complexity	Ensemble of COMPUTATIONAL and EPISTEMIC COMPLEXITY.
Inside contracting	Entrepreneurial form of work organization in which an employer, owning some resources such as the buildings or sales outlets, contracts (in) transformation processes to internal worker-entrepreneurs owing complementary assets (e.g. expertise, technical resources).
Institutions	Sets of interrelated established (stable, accepted) rules and norms constraining and shaping choice-based actions and interactions.
Integrated forms	Forms of organization in which coordination is ensured primarily by direct interunit communication, teaming, and negotiation, and by dedicated intermediary and integrating roles.
Interdependence	Relation of transaction or cooperation between entities (activities, resources, or actors). *Pooled*: sharing of resources among activities or actors. *Sequential*: transactional link under time constraint. *Reciprocal*: transactional link involving the exchange of information on how to conduct action in the different stages. *Intensive*: cooperative link involving the sharing of information and knowledge on how to conduct parallel action.

Interest	Judgment on what courses of action, in a defined situation, brings positive consequences for an actor.
Job description	Description of the rights and obligations defining a job, formalized into a document.
Job enlargement	"Backward" or "forward" integration of activities into a job.
Job enrichment	"Loading" of a job with decision and control rights.
Job evaluation	Assessment of the value of a job independently from the attributes of the job incumbent. Usually operationalized as a function of required competences and assigned responsibilities.
Job	Partition of action, decision, and control rights and obligations which can be consciously assumed by a person or group with respect to others in a wider system of action.
Job rotation	Periodical reciprocal substitution among the people performing interdependent jobs.
Job sharing	Assumption of one job by more than one person, usually entitled to self-determine the particular time slots that they will cover.
Joint venture (corporate)	Jointly owned and jointly managed firm constituted by two or more "mother" (and owner) firms, contributing the financial, technical, and human capital. Under the shadow of that contract, a variety of organizational arrangements should be found, according to the patterns of resource and activity relations and their complexity.
Joint venture contract	Contract by which firms participate in a share of the profits derived from a common action.
Knowledge	Set of interrelated and interpreted information. *Paradigmatic*: out of discussion, accepted by convention or inheritage. *Tacit*: that cannot be expressed without loss of information
Knowledge-based view of the firm	Linked conceptually to the resource-based view, this perspective focuses on the effective governance of knowledge acquisition, sharing, and exchange and hypothesizes that firms have distinctive advantages in knowledge integration respects.
Loosely coupled forms	Forms in which the main units are connected by weak rather than strong ties, consisting in coordination mechanisms based on unilateral decision or on general negotiations and rules and norms.
Management by objectives (MBO)	In MBO specific levels of outputs to be reached are forecast – with more or less intense participation by the agents responsible to reach them – and then used as criteria to evaluate the levels of performance.

Market failure	Inapplicability of market-like governance, or relative inferiority of it with respect to other forms of governance, due to conditions of low substitutability of resources, externalities, technical indivisibilities, and information complexity in its various components.
Matrix	Variant of networked form of organization, in which there are units pooling similar resources (by technical specialization, by geographic area, etc.) that provide services into processes governed by other units responsible for the process output (product, project, service) or for the process itself.
Mechanistic forms	Forms of organization in which coordination is ensured primarily by rules, procedures, programs, and/or hierarchy. There are variants at the micro-structure level (e.g. Tayloristic forms); at the firm level (unitary and divisional mechanistic structures); and at the interfirm level (star-like bureaucratic networks).
M-forms (multidivisional)	Loosely coupled divisional structure coordinated by strategic planning, transfer prices, and incentives (profits, ROI, ROE, etc.).
Modeling (roles)	Learning approach geared to construct a causal model of success in a defined task. Provides a more creative alternative to best practice imitation.
Moral hazard	Risk that a contribution expected from a contractual partner is intentionally under-provided when the action or contribution is not easily observable by the other party. It is a form of post-contractual opportunism.
Need	Judgment of what categories of things and in what quantity are "necessary" for the equilibrated existence of an actor.
Negotiation	Mechanism of joint decision between two or more actors with differentiated information and interests, based on the exchange of resources. *Distributive*: the surplus generated by the actors' match is "fixed": a larger share allocated to one party implies a smaller share obtained by other parties. *Integrative*: the surplus generated by the actors' match depends on the type of exchanges of resources that are identified; some agreements generate larger surpluses than others.
Networked forms	Forms of organization in which the configuration of interdependence and coordination is not pre-defined, but selected ad hoc by the nodes of the network themselves according to changing circumstances. These extremely "flexible" forms have recently been applied not only at the interfirm level where firms form changing ad hoc alliances, but also at the micro level (e.g. in "just-in-time" production organization); and at the firm level (e.g. in "organic forms" and knowledge-based internal networks).
Norms	Models of behavior accepted by all actors in a system, which substitute for case-by-case decision-making on the behavior. In this

	book it is conventionally stipulated that norms are socially defined (norms are social norms), not formally expressed RULES.
Objective	Operational judgment on levels of results to be reached (also termed *goals*).
Opportunism	Self-interest seeking "with guile" Calculative behavior oriented to take advantage of any arising opportunities, without minding breaking the spirit of agreements made with specific partners or the commonly accepted rules and norms of fair conduct.
Optimizing	Decision strategy defined by the rule of choosing the alternative with maximum expected value in a defined set of alternatives, generated with a rule of search for information until the expected benefits offset the costs of search, and by rules of probability adjustment contingent to the availability of new information. These "rules" are all algorithms, computational rules for selecting the best solutions according to preference.
Organization	Mode of partitioning rights over action, decision, control, and ownership, and of coordinating those "parts."
Organizational differentiation	Difference or "distance" among the organizational profile of units (e.g. departments or divisions). The profile can be measured by various attributes; traditional measures consider the degree of centralization and formalization, the frequency of controls and the time horizon of decisions, and the dominant decision frames and decision strategies.
Overconfidence	Tendency to set too strict confidence intervals or to assign excessive probabilities of being right in making estimates under uncertainty.
Pareto-superiority	Property of an economic solution (allocation of resources and rights, contract, organization form), consisting in being "superior" or "un-dominated" by other solutions for a given set of actors: a Pareto-superior solution brings equal or greater benefits to all actors with respect to other solutions, and cannot be improved for at least some actors without losses for others. In structured problems the notion of Pareto-optimal or Pareto-efficient (in the sense of allocative efficiency) is employed. In unstructured problems a relative notion of Pareto-superiority can be employed.
Peer group	"Team-like" form of work organization in which member actors are fully and equally entitled to decision, control, and property rights and obligations.
Performance appraisal	Evaluation of behaviors or results of an actor according to qualitative or quantitative criteria.
Peter principle	Pathology of performance-based promotion consisting of people

being promoted out from positions in which they perform well, until they reach a position in which performance is low.

Piece-rate compensation

Reward system by which individual producers are paid an amount for each piece produced.

Potential appraisal

Forecast of the flow of services and relative results that might be generated by a resource in future types of employment. Typically used for assessing the expected performance of human resources in future jobs.

Preference

Evaluative judgment on the attractiveness of actual or potential consequences for self or others. It implies a more or less formal, more or less complete, more or less quantified assessment of the "*utility*" of these consequences.

Price

Codified exchange value of transferable goods or services. Can be expressed in money or other general comparative measure unit (e.g. time).

Primary work system

Collection of interdependent activities that lead to an identifiable result – typically a unit of product or a service provided.

Principle of reinforcement

Learning rule by which actors repeat actions (of self or comparable others) with a frequency proportional to that of the observed success of that action.

Prisoner's Dilemma

Game structure in which if all actors play their dominant strategy, they end up in a Pareto-dominated outcome.

Procedure

Rules prescribing what process to follow to select an action; for example: before granting a job to a supplier, examine a certain number of alternative offers, consult those responsible for purchases.

Product manager

Responsible for the performance of a product or service, and for integrating the objectives and competences of the specialized units intervening in its realization (typically different functions).

Profit sharing

Reward system consisting of a scheme of participation in the residual economic result of a profit generating unit (a firm, a division), reserved for categories (larger or smaller, internal or also external) of actors contributing work.

Program

Operational rule specifying what action or sequence of actions to take, eventually as a function of circumstances. For example: "first, grasp the piece and carry it to the machine," "second, place the piece on the chuck ...," "third, tighten the bit of the spindle," etc.

Project manager

Responsible for a group, endowed with human and technical resources conferred by differentiated specialized units, to which a design task (project) is assigned.

Prospect effect   Systematic difference in the perception of utility depending of whether it is defined over gain or losses. A loss of a certain amount is perceived to be greater than a gain of the same amount.

Putting out   Entrepreneurial form of work organization in which an owner of materials and other production inputs contracts them out for transformation to an external worker-entrepreneur.

Quality circles   Meeting of workers, in the original Japanese experience within regular working time, to improve production processes and outputs.

Quasi-rent   A rent diminished by costs of transfer of a resource from its current use to an alternative use.

Rent   Difference between the return on the use of a resource in an activity and in its best alternative use. This difference may derive from various sources of unsubstitutability, including innovation (Ricardian rent) and resource specificity (Paretian rents) having different organizational implications.

Representativeness bias   Tendency to underutilize base-rate information and privilege case-specific information for estimating the probability of events.

Residual control and decision rights   Right to a last word on the appropriateness of action taken or to be taken after and beyond delegated responsibilities.

Residual reward rights   Claims of compensation out of the returns from an economic activities after all input resources have been compensated for their services.

Resource   Potential for generating flows of services and activities. If a resource is more narrowly conceived as a potential for flows of revenues it is defined as an *asset*. For organization, competence-embodying resources are particularly relevant, i.e. technical and human resources and assets.

Resource-based view of the firm   Stream of resource dependence thinking, mainly in organizational economics and business strategy, explaining the mix and boundaries of firm activities (e.g. diversification) as convenient evolution trajectories starting from an initial resource collection.

Resource criticality   Composite characteristic of a resource used to express synthetically the ensemble of its degree of substitutability, the value added by its contributions with respect to other resources, and the risk to which it is exposed.

Risk aversion   Preference of a sure amount of resources over an uncertain one of equal expected value.

Role   Shared expectations regarding the respective and specific models of behavior to be assumed by each member of a group.

Routine	Operational and action-specific norm, prescribing what action to take in given circumstances; for example, if you need a computer, contact supplier X.
Rules	If–then propositions leading to select a behavior appropriate to an actor in a given circumstance, which substitute for case-by-case decision-making on the behavior. In this book it is conventionally stipulated that rules are formally expressed.
Satisficing	Variant of heuristic decision-making in which search is truncated as soon as one acceptable alternative is found.
Scale	Size at which resources are employed. If a larger size brings production costs and quality advantages (due to technological discontinuity or other factors) *economies of scale* are present.
Scope	Range of services and outputs generated by the same resources. If there are cost or quality advantages in employing the same set of resources (rather than separate sets) for producing differentiated outputs, *economies of scope* are realized.
Self-efficacy	Judgment on the probability of attaining a certain level of performance in a defined task.
Slack resources	Resources available to an actor exceeding in quantity and quality those applied in current activities. Albeit "costly" to maintain they constitute a potential for the development of new activities.
Social coordination	Coordination achieved by communication, teaming and negotiation, norms, and cultural elements, as distinct from that supported by formal/legal systems.
Specialization	Narrowing of tasks and of focus of attention. When it generates advantages in production costs and/or output quality (due to greater depth of knowledge or to greater dexterity), there are *economies of specialization*.
Specificity	A resource is specific to a relation with an activity, actor, or other resource, if it generates higher value when employed in those relations rather than in alternative ones.
Standardization	Crystallization of a behavior into a "normal" model, both in the statistical sense of the term and in the sense of transforming it into a norm or rule.
Stock options	Rights to buy shares at a pre-defined price when convenient.
Structural contingency theory	Set of models explaining and prescribing which structural arrangements to adopt within firms, on the basis of their theoretical capacity for information processing and of the observed correlations between organization form and firm performance in different settings.

Sub-contracting Class of arrangements employed for regulating the entrustment of parts or phases of the production cycle to third parties by a central firm. More hierarchical and mechanistic forms of sub-contracting can be usefully distinguished from more integrated and "team-like" forms, as a function of task complexity and interdependence.

Tayloristic The term is employed here to qualify a solution of work organization characterized by the maximization of specialization and by coordination through programs and hierarchy.

Team Collection of actors communicating all-to-all and deciding jointly through a mechanism of confrontation, characterized by homogeneous preferences and eventually differentiated knowledge. *Primitive*: action-oriented team, where actions are instantly observable and the relevant coordination problem is effective communication. *Relational*: control and relation-oriented team, where contributions can be evaluated on a serial, long-term basis, and the key coordination problem is effective reciprocal monitoring. *Communitarian*: decisions and task-oriented; where decisions are taken on a knowledge-sharing basis and the key coordination problem is to set up conditions and mechanisms for effective knowledge integration.

Team production Multi-actor production in which the contribution of each member is not discernible. It could also be said that the output of a team production is not separable into additive components and it is greater than the sum of them.

Transaction Transfer of information, resources, or outputs, across technologically separable interfaces, to capture opportunities of exchange.

Transaction costs All the costs of transferring goods and services: the costs of a search for partners and information, the costs of acquiring the relevant knowledge for designing goods or services useful to the transferee or for utilizing the transferred items, the costs of quality and performance evaluations, the costs of negotiation of exchange terms and contractual provisions, the costs of control on the respect of established conditions. These costs are information costs, not production costs.

Transaction cost economics Branch of economics explaining and prescribing efficient organizational forms as least cost devices (production plus transaction costs) for coordinating transactions.

Transfer price Term used to indicate internal prices employed to coordinate exchanges between administrative units.

Transition costs All costs of changing one organizational arrangement into another: costs of analyzing, generating alternatives, negotiating, designing.

Uncertainty Lack of relevant knowledge. It can regard some or all the judgments relevant for economic decision-making – on what relevant alternatives, outcome probabilities, observed events, and cause–effect relations are. A source of uncertainty is information complexity in both its computational dimension and its epistemic dimension.

Unitary forms
Type of firm structure in which residual rights of decision, control, and reward are "unified" in one central unit (rather than distributed to the main units in which structure is partitioned).

Unitary operations
Tasks that are not technically separable.

Valence/expectancy model
Model hypothesizing that actors are motivated to select the action with maximum expected valence for them.

Value
Basic judgment about what things are good and what bad, of what constitutes a benefit and what a loss; for example: is work effort a cost or a benefit?

Variance
In an analogy with the statistical parameter, the term is used in job design in the sense of a deviation with respect to a "normal" transformation process, having a non-negligible effect on the output, and requiring human corrective intervention.

Voting paradox
Impossibility of devising a voting scheme generating a collective preference ordering under some configurations of actors' preferences.

Wealth effects
Deviations from neutrality toward risk and from expected monetary value maximization due to the absolute level of wealth of an actor.

Zero sum game
Game structure in which the sum of the players' pay-offs is zero, because the gain for some parties are equal to the losses for other parties. An organizational property of zero sum games (and more generally of constant sum games) is that there is no incentive to communicate.

Further Reading

....

This selection signals works that are not too technical, recent (1990s), not already cited in the bibliography, and relevant to the strands of literature integrated in this book in an organization science perspective (organization theory, organizational and cognitive economics, cognitive organizational behavior, economic and "rational" sociology).

GENERAL

Sorge, A. and Warner, M. (eds) (1997) *International Encyclopedia of Business and Management. Handbook of Organizational Behavior.* London: Routledge.

MARKET AND/AS ORGANIZATION

Burt, R.S. (1993) "Market integration," in S. Lindbeberg and H. Schreuder (eds) *Interdiscplinary Perspectives on Organization Studies*, Oxford: Pergamon Press: 241–92.

Ménard, C. (1995) "Markets as institutions versus organizations as markets? Disentangling some fundamental concepts," *Journal of Economic Behavior and Organization*, 28(2): 161–82.

Swedberg, R. (1994) "Markets as social structures," in N.J. Smelser and R. Swedberg (eds) *The Handbook of Economic Sociology*, Princeton, NJ: Princeton University Press.

White, H.C. (1993) "Markets, networks and control," in S. Lindbeberg and H. Schreuder (eds) *Interdiscplinary Perspectives on Organization Studies*, Oxford: Pergamon Press: 223–39.

WORK ORGANIZATION

Greenberg, J. (1996) *The Quest for Justice on the Job: Essays and Experiments*, Thousand Oaks, CA: Sage.

Heller F., Pusic, E., Strauss G., and Wilpert, B. (1998) *Organizational Participation: Myth and Reality*, Oxford: Oxford University Press.

Knights, D. and Willmott, H. (eds) (1990) *Labor Process Theory*, London: Macmillan.

Stephen, F.H. (ed.) (1984) *Firms, Organization and Labor: Approaches to the Economics of Work Organization*, London: Macmillan.

Whitley, R. and Kristensens, P.H. (eds) (1997) *Governance at Work: The Social Regulation of Economic Relations*, Oxford: Oxford University Press.

FIRM STRUCTURES AND ORGANIZATION DESIGN

Butler, R.J. (1991) *Designing Organizations: A Decision Making Perspective*, London: Routledge.

Ciborra, C. (1996) "The platform organization: recombining strategies, structures and surprises, *Organizations Science*, 7(2): 103–18.

Huber, G. and Glick, W. (eds) (1993) *Organizational Change and Re-design*, New York: Oxford University Press.

Keidel, R.W. (1994) "Rethinking organizational design," *Academy of Management Executive*, 8(4): 12–30.

Wilson, D. (1992) *A Strategy of Change: Concepts and Controversies in the Management of Change*, London and New York: Routledge.

TECHNOLOGY AND/AS ORGANIZATION

Arora, A. and Gambardella, A. (1994) "The changing technology of technological change: general and abstract knowledge and the division of labor," *Research Policy*, 23: 523–32.

Davenport, T.H. (1993) *Process Innovation: Reengineering Work through Information Technology*, Boston: Harvard Business School Press.

Orlikowski, W.J. (1992), "The duality of technology: rethinking the concept of technology in organizations," *Organization Science*, 3(3): 398–427.

Rockart, J.F. and Short, J.E. (1989) "IT in the 1990s: managing organizational interdependence," *Sloan Management Review*, winter: 7–17.

Sproull, L.S. *et al.* (1990), *Technology and Organization*, San Francisco: Jossey-Bass.

COORDINATION

Camerer, C. and Knez, M. (1997) "Coordination in organizations: a game-theoretic perspective," in Z. Shapira (ed.) *Organizational Decision Making*, Cambridge: Cambridge University Press.

Radner, R. (1993) "The organization of decentralized information processing," *Econometrica*, 61: 1109–46.

Williamson, O.E. (1996) *The Mechanisms of Governance*, New York: Oxford University Press.

INTERFIRM COORDINATION

Alter, C. and Hage, J. (1993) *Organizations Working Together*, Newbury Park, CA: Sage.

Dyer, J.H. (1996) "Specialized supplier networks as a source of competitive advantage: evidence form the auto industry," *Strategic Management Journal*, 17: 271–91.

Dussauge, P. and Garrette, B. (1999) *Cooperative Strategy. Competing Successfully through Strategic Alliances*, Chichester: John Wiley.

Nohria, N. and Eccles, R.G. (eds) (1992) *Networks and Organizations*, Boston: Harvard Business School Press.

Oliver, C. (1990) "Determinants of interorganizational relationships: integration and future directions," *Academy of Management Review*, 15(2): 241–65.

CULTURE

Alvesson, M. and Berg, P.O. (1992) *Corporate Culture and Organizational Symbolism: An Overview*, Berlin and New York: De Gruyter.

Fiol, C.M. (1991) "Maintaining culture as a

competitive resource: an identity-based view of sustainable competitive advantage," *Journal of Management*, 17: 191–211.

Frost, P.J. (1991) *Reframing Organizational Culture*, Newbury Park, CA: Sage.

Frost, P.J., Moore, L.F., Louis, M.R., Lunbdberg, C., and Martin, J. (eds) (1985) *Organizational Culture*, Beverly Hills, CA: Sage.

Hofstede, G. (1991) *Cultures and Organizations: Software of the Mind*, London: McGraw-Hill.

Scheider, S.C. and Barsoux, J.L. (1997) *Managing Across Cultures*, London: Prentice-Hall.

Sorge, A. (1991), "Strategic fit and societal effect: interpreting cross-national comparison of technology, organization and human resources," *Organization Studies*, 12(2): 161–90.

KNOWLEDGE AND COMPETENCE

Argyris, C. and Schon, D.A. (1996) *Organizational Learning. II. Theory, Method and Practice*, Reading: Addison-Wesley.

Badaracco, J. (1991) *The Knowledge Link*, Boston: Harvard Business School Press.

Blackler, F. (1995) "Knowledge, knowledge work and organizations: and overview and interpretation, *Organizational Studies*, 16(6): 1021–46.

Boisot, M. (1998) *Knowledge Assets*, Oxford: Oxford University Press.

Brown, J.S. and Duguid, P. (1991) "Organizational learning and communities-of-practice," *Organization Science*, 2(1): 40–57.

Nonaka, I. (1994) "A dynamic theory of organizational knowledge creation," *Organization Science*, 5(1): 14–37.

Senge, P. (1990) *The Fifth Discipline*, New York: Doubleday.

Spender, J.C. (1994) "Organizational knowledge, collective practice and Penrose rents," *International Business Review*, 3(4).

Von Hippel, E. (1994) "Sticky information and problem-solving," in A.D. Chandler, P. Hangstrom, and O. Solvell (eds) *The Dynamic Firm*, Oxford: Oxford University Press.

Winter, S.G. (1987) "Knowledge and competence as strategic assets," in D. Teece (ed.) *The Competitive Challenge: Strategies for Industrial Innovation and Renewal*, Cambridge, MA: Ballinger: 159–84.

ACTORS' IDENTITY AND PREFERENCES

Acker, J.N. (1992) "Gendering organizational theory," in A.J. Mills and P. Tancred (eds) *Gendering Organizational Analysis*, London: Sage: 248–60.

Kay, J. (1997) "The stakeholder corporation," in G. Kelly, D. Kelly, and A. Gamble (eds) *Stakeholder Capitalism*, Sheffield: University of Sheffield in Association with Political and Economic Research Centre.

Kramer, R.M. (1993) "Cooperation and organizational identification," in K. Murnighan (ed.) *Social Psychology in Organizations: Advances in Theory and Research*, Englewood Cliffs, NJ: Prentice-Hall: 244–68.

Mintzberg, H. (1991) "Managerial work forty years later," in S. Carlson (ed.) *Executive Behavior: Reprinted with Contributions by Henry Mintzberg and Rosemary Stewart*, Uppsala: Acta Universitatis Upsaliensis.

Mitroff, I.I. (1983) *Stakeholders of the Organizational Minds*, San Francisco: Jossey-Bass.

Watson, T. (1994) *In Search of Management*, London: Routledge.

White, H. (1992) *Identity and Control: A Structural Theory of Social Action*, Princeton, NJ: Princeton University Press.

Whitley, R. (1996) "The social construction of economic actors," in R. Whitley and P.H. Kristensen (eds) *The Changing European Firm: Limits to Convergence*, London: Routledge.

GROUPS AND TEAMS

Advances in Group Processes, annual series, San Francisco: JAI Press.

Howard, J.R. (1995) "Peer control in the industrial workplace," *Sociological Focus*, 26: 241–56.

Johnson, D.W. and Johnson, F.P. (1991) *Joining Together: Group Theory and Group Skills*, Englewood Cliffs, NJ: Prentice-Hall.

Lindenberg, S.M. (1997) "Grounding groups in theory: functional structural and cognitive interdependencies," *Advances in Group Processes*, 14: 281–331.

Tyler, T.R. and Dawnes, R.M. (1993) "Fairness in groups: comparing in the self-interest and the social identity perspectives," in B.A. Mellen and J. Baron (eds) *Psychological Perspectives on Justice*, Cambridge: Cambridge University Press.

Weick, K.E. and Roberts, K.H. (1993) "Collective mind in organizations: heedful interrelating on flight decks," *Administrative Science Quarterly*, 38.

LEADERSHIP

Dansereau, F., Yammarino, F.J., and Markham, S.E. (1995) "Leadership: the multiple-level approaches," *Leadership Quarterly*, Special issue, 6(2): 97–109.

Popper, K.R. (1989) "The critical approach versus the mystique of leadership," *Human Systems Management*, 8: 259–65.

Simon, H.A. (1987) "Making management decisions: the role of intuitions and emotions," *Academy of Management Executive*," 1(1): 57–64.

Zand, D.E. (1997) *The Leadership Triad: Knowledge, Trust and Power*, New York: Oxford University Press.

RATIONALITY AND DECISION

Donaldson, G. and Lorsch, J.W. (1983) *Decision-making at the Top*, New York: Basic Books.

Egidi, M. (ed.) (1992) *Economics, Bounded Rationality and the Cognitive Revolution*, Aldershot: Edward Elgar.

Klein, G.A., Orasanu, R., Calderwood, R., and Zsambok, C.E. (eds) (1993) *Decision Making in Action: Models and Methods*, Norwood, NJ: Ablex.

Kleindorfer, P.E., Kunreuther, H.C., and Schoemaker, P.J.H. (1993) *Decision Sciences: An Integrative Perspective*, Cambridge: Cambridge University Press.

Shapira, Z. (ed.) (1997) *Organizational Decision Making*, Cambridge: Cambridge University Press.

Weick, K. (1994) *Sensemaking in organizations*, Thousand Oaks, CA: Sage.

Zey, M. (ed.) (1992) *Decision Making: Alternatives to Rational Choice Models*, London: Sage.

MOTIVATION

Dunnette, M.D. and Hough, L.M. (1991) *Handbook of Industrial and Organizational Psychology*, 2nd edn, Palo Alto, CA: Consulting Psychologists Press.

Kleinbeck, U., Quasst, H.H., Thierry, H., and Haecker, H. (1990) *Work Motivation*, Hillsdale, NJ: Erlbaum.

HUMAN RESOURCE MANAGEMENT

Abraham, K. and McKersie, R. (1990) *New Development in the Labor Market: Toward a New Institutional Paradigm*, Cambridge, MA: MIT Press.

Baron, J.N. and Kreps, D.M. (1999) *Strategic Resource Management: Frameworks for General Managers*, New York: Wiley.

Hendry, C. and Pettigrew, A. (1990) "Human resource management: an agenda of the 1990s," *International Journal of Human Resource Management*, 1(1): 17–44.

Itoh, H. (1994) "Japanese human resource management from the viewpoint of incentives theory," in M. Aoki and R. Dore (eds) *The Japanese Firm*, Oxford: Clarendon Press: 233–64.

Lazear, E.P. (1991) "Labor economics and the psychology of organizations," *Journal of Economic Perspectives*, 5(2): 89–110.

Nalbantian, H.R. (ed.) (1987) *Incentives, Cooperation and Risk Sharing: Economic Psychological Perspectives on Employment Contracts*, Totowa, NJ: Rowman & Littlefield.

Storey, J. (ed.) (1995) *Human Resource Management: A Critical Text*, London: Routledge.

Walton, R.E. and Lawrence, P.R. (eds) (1989) *Human Resource Management, Trends and Challenges*, Boston: Harvard Business School Press.

RULES AND INSTITUTIONS

Rogers Hollingsworth, J. and Boyer, R. (eds) (1998) *Contemporary Capitalism: The Embeddedness of Institutions*, Cambridge: Cambridge University Press.

Scott, R.W. (1994) "Conceptualizing organizational fields: linking organizations and societal systems," working paper, Stanford University.

AUTHORITY

Itoh, H. (1992) "Cooperation in hierarchical organizations: an incentives perspective," *Journal of Law, Economics, and Organization*, 8: 321–45.

Radner, R. (1992) "Hierarchy: the economics of managing," *Journal of Economic Literature*, 30: 1382–415.

Tyler, T.R. (1998) "The psychology of authority relations: a relational perspective on influence and power in groups," in R.M. Kramer and M.A. Nease (eds) *Power and Influence in Organizations*, Thousand Oaks, CA: Sage: 251–60.

NEGOTIATION

Lewicki, R., Bies, R., and Sheppard, B. (eds) *Research on Negotiation in Organization*, Annual Series, San Francisco: JAI Press.

Lewicki, R., Litlerer, J.A., Minton, J.W., and Saunders, D.M. (eds) (1994) *Negotiation*, 2nd edn, Burr Ridge, IL: Irwin.

EQUITY AND JUSTICE

Ottensmeyer, E.J. and McCarthy, G.D. (1996) *Ethics in the Workplace*, New York: McGraw-Hill.

Cropanzano, R. and Greenberg, H. (1996) "Progress in organizational justice: tunneling through the maze," in C.L. Cooper and I.T. Robertson (eds) *International Review of Industrial and Organizational Psychology*, New York: John Wiley: 317–72.

Notes

•••

**INTRODUCTION I ORGANIZATION: A
PROBLEM, A DISCIPLINE**

1 The following discussion path is by no means
the only possible one. Depending on the different initial ideas that people have in mind about
organization, there will be different ways to
reach an agreement on the basic defininition
proposed of economic organization.

2 On this issue, see Simon (1997), Sen (1992), and
Douma and Schreuder (1992).

3 Among the great economists interested in questions of methodology the first position was
argued by von Hayek.

1 KNOWLEDGE AND PREFERENCE

1 There has been an endless debate on whether
"organizations" can have goals and knowledge,
as individuals do. The debate has been marked
by rather naive, individualistic assumptions
about the nature of knowledge and self-
knowledge. If the question "Where do individual preference and knowledge come from?"
is asked, it appears that it is not more obvious
that individual preference and knowledge
"come before" collective ones. The notion of
identity, and its relation with the configuration
of knowledge and interests, has regained
importance in recent organization theory
(March 1994). In addition, the notion of
actor is usually too "substantive": a person, a
firm, or a group are decided to be classified
either as actors or not. Here the notion of
actor is "procedural": the same entity can be
conceived as an actor or as multiple actors

depending on how knowledge and preferences
are configured in a certain action field or
occasion.

2 The term "paradigm" was, notoriously, coined
by Kuhn (1962). Although it has been widely
and rightly criticized in the philosophy of science (about twenty-one definitions have been
found for it), here it is used in its meaning of
cognitive frame and temporarily unverified
assumptions, and it is not meant that all
knowledge is structured in paradigms.

3 This distinction has also been formulated by
contrasting "declarative" and "procedural"
knowledge. The term and the concept of
declarative knowledge, however, mix together a
dimension of substantiveness (knowing *what*
rather than knowing *how*) with a dimension of
explicitness (the possibility to declare). The two
dimensions have quite different organizational
implications: the former has to do with the
degree of discretion, the latter with the transferability of knowledge.

4 We leave aside "content" typologies of cognitive
frames (e.g. Myers and Briggs 1962), chiefly for
the general problems incurred by content typologies (see Introduction and section on
preferences).

5 As examples abound, no box is provided here.
To introduce the concept, one can use one of the
many situations described in the studies on
interfunctional differentiation.

2 DECISION AND MOTIVATION

1 The meta-model of decision processes presented
here is based on a comparative analysis of cogni-

tive processes originally presented in Grandori (1984).

2 Simon's model of "satisficing" decision-making, in the original version elaborated in contrast to the "optimizing" model that became widely known and used, is a particular case of heuristic decision-making as defined here (and eventually used in other and subsequent contributions by Simon on problem-solving as scientific discovery). "Satisficing" is a "conservative" version of heuristic decision-making, in which:

- only the levels of aspiration and the set of alternatives are allowed to change
- search is truncated by the finding of just one acceptable alternative.

3 There is a great variety of subtypes of rules that can be used to formulate these kinds of satisfaction or acceptability constraints. For example, there are "conjunctive" rules by which all of the constraints must be satisfied simultaneously. There are less ambitious, "disjunctive" rules in which an alternative must satisfy at least K constraints among N (for example, proposals for training programs which are financed on the basis of five desired effects but where the acceptability level is to guarantee results on at least three out of five aspects). Or, there are even simpler rules for eliminating the alternatives based on whether a particular attribute is present or not, without looking at the other characteristics (elimination by aspect) (for example, all candidates who do not have a university degree are eliminated, then all those who do not know a foreign language, then all those who are over 40, etc.) (Payne 1976; Tversky 1972).

4 As Locke (1996: 118) also notes, indeed, "the approach of goal setting theory is consistent with, although its beginnings somewhat antedated, the cognitive revolution."

5 On this issue, students or readers can be encouraged to find and report their own examples. Alternatively, examples about how exclusively quantitative and monetary targets – for example, profits, sales – can narrow the focus of attention away from anything else can easily be constructed or found.

6 The perspectives referred to here are principally: equity theory in social exchanges (Adams 1965; Walster and Walster 1975), the theories of just-

ice in economic exchanges (Rawls 1971; Raiffa 1982; Sen 1992), organizational justice research (Greenberg 1987), cognitive pyschology research on the role of fairness judgments in economic actions and relations (Kahneman *et al.* 1986a, b). The typology of fairness rules presented here is a revision and generalization of a classification originally set out in Grandori and Neri (1999).

PART II   COORDINATION MECHANISMS

1 Although not all zero sum games admit equilibrium solutions, communication among players about what action to take does not help anyway.

2 Game theory therefore contributes in explaining *when* opportunism is to be expected, and in linking market failures and the superiority of authority, hostages, and joint decision-making to the opportunism potential deriving from certain game structures. This is a different methodological option with respect to "assume" opportunism as a generalized behavioral trait, as done in transaction cost economics.

3 Among received theories, this classification draws and elaborates on various broad classifications of the fundamental mechanisms of coordination of economic and social action, namely Hirschman's (1970) distinction between exit, voice, and loyalty, Lindblom's (1977) distinction between market, authority, and preceptoral systems, Williamson's (1975) distinction between markets and hierarchies, and Etzioni's (1961) distinction between utilitalistic and normative control.

4   AUTHORITY AND AGENCY

1 The chapter draws on a contribution I have been asked to make for the *International Encyclopedia of Business and Management* to give a presentation of the subject integrating the sociological and organization theory of authority and the contributions of transaction costs economics and agency theory (Grandori 1997a).

2 The implications of agency theory for the design of incentives and of property rights are presented in Part IV on organization forms.

3 It is curious how social psychology has been traditionally concerned with the risks of leaders manipulating followers, while organizational economics has been seeing the opportunism of agents as the core problem.

4 On the other hand, this could be argued also for the other forms of coordination, to the extent they are really applied in a "pure" mode or in "high dosages."

5 TEAMS

1 See below for an illustration of the possible contrasting effects – accentuating biases – that may be produced by highly homogeneous and cohesive groups.

7 NORMS AND RULES

1 This is worth noticing considering the endless opposition between informal and formal organization and the properties of "flexibility" ascribed – wrongly – to informality as such. See also North (1990) and Friedberg (1993) for conceptualizations rejecting that unfirm opposition and hypothesis.

2 Recently used in the economics of conventions.

3 Even though they were, at least in part, studies on cultures, frequently these studies were not self-defining as such because the term "culture" was not yet of common use in the organization and management field.

4 That part of management literature, and even of the "theory of the firm," which has recently depicted the firm as the realm of shared and common culture and knowledge, has apparently forgotten or ignored these results, seeing only the reduced coordination and control costs that a strong and cohesive common culture can entail. Instead, organizational theory that has directly or indirectly studied cultures leads to questioning whether or not it is appropriate to sustain the costs of sophisticated integration mechanisms among differentiated cultures, rather than eliminate cultural diversity.

5 Hofstede's study and a number of related ones (Maurice and Sorge 1980; Hickson 1993a) led to a quarrel – especially in the 1970s and 1980s in European studies – on the so-called "culture-free" or "culture-bounded" views of organization. That debate has somehow obscured the fact that it is always possible to find "differences," but the interesting problem, at least for economic behavior, is whether or not they matter for performance, and to what extent they are functionally equivalent (Whittington and Meier 1993).

CONCLUSION TO PART II   COMPARING AND COMBINING COORDINATION MECHANISMS

1 An economic game-theoretic, comparative treatment of the failure of different mechanisms in the solution of conflicts can be found in Miller (1992).

PART III   FORMS OF ORGANIZATION

1 Actually there are models that are often classified as economic – as those in the resource-based view of the firm – that are oriented toward the heuristic search for innovative value-creating combination of resources, which will therefore be considered in the first part of the chapters of Part III; as well as there are models in the organizational tradition that are based on a cost minimization logic (e.g. Galbraith 1974) which will be considered in the sections devoted to the structured comparative assessment of given forms.

8   THE CONFIGURATION OF ORGANIZATION: A GENERALIZED MODEL

1 Some recent techniques are in fact characterized by the fact that they propose procedures for a "zero-based" review of all the activities that are "necessary" to produce value-adding outputs, through a critical re-examination of the various components of the transformation process that led to that output (*business process re-engineering* is one such technique). Without discussing the reductive aspects of these procedures, they are a sign of the need for rethinking the current activities.

2 This is the case for all the most important theories of organizational design, including structural contingency theories (in both the classical and "configurational" versions) and organizational

economics models (in both the transaction costs and agency theory versions).

3 This is the case of the more "critical" theories such as those of the self-designing organization, the political analyses of organization, or the "stakeholders's" views of the firm.

4 This chapter is largely definitional. For teaching purposes, suggestions for use are: not to "present" the chapter in a sequential way; propose a sufficiently rich case – such as that at the end of the chapter and reconstruct which variables are relevant for explaining/redesigning arrangements, defining them in the occasion; assign the chapter as an ex-post reading and a resource for consultation on the key variables.

5 Because they have a potential for action and the generation of value that are relatively independent of the specific use to which they are put, resources are often defined as "forms of capital" in the resource-based perspective (for a review, see Perrone 1996).

6 This view is consistent both with the modern theory of property rights and with the classic prescription of organization models of not assuming existing boundaries among actors and units when redesigning.

7 Klein *et al.* (1978) developed the thesis that specific and asymmetric investments and the possibility of expropriation of quasi-rents are remediable by vertical integration. This has been criticized and weakened by Monteverde and Teece (1980), who have argued that these situations can also be resolved by weaker forms of "quasi-integration," such as the ownership by the downstream firm of specialized tools and materials and the putting out of transformation processes. The argument developed here further weakens the impact of all specific investments – and asymmetric ones in particular – on effective and efficient organizational forms, by considering them *a sufficient cause only for the creation of a negotiated relationship*. The effective forms of governance of this negotiated relationship may vary widely depending on other factors, such as the level of information complexity and the distributive or integrative structure of negotiations.

8 The model in Figure 8.7 is an extension of that of Thompson (1967), integrated with organizational economics contributions as well as extended by analyzing not only vertical but also horizontal interdependences. Thompson (1967) proposed two typologies that, although overlapping, are not clearly and explicitly linked: a typology of "technical systems" (long-linked, intensive, and intermediary technologies) and a typology of situations of interdependence: pooled, sequential and reciprocal. In addition, Thompson's propositions on how to use interdependence configurations for design will be modified (in this chapter and in Chapter 11 on internal organization). For Thompson overstated the effect of interdependence on the boundaries of efficient organizational units, stating that, *ceteris paribus*, reciprocal interdependence should lead to integrating activities into one unit. This overstatement can be seen clearly if the models privileging different variables are connected, as we have done here. This overstatement is similar to that by organizational economists about the need for integrating into one firm, *ceteris paribus*, specific and uncertain transactions.

9 The choice of this word, as ever, has pros and cons. Among the pros, we may add that it can be contrasted with "competitive interdependence" to complete the description of possible horizontal or collective action relations, as contrasted with transactional or exchange relations. Among the disadvantages, there may be the different way in which the term is used in game theory, in which it is reduced to meaning a relationship in which there are incentives to communicate and communication is allowed. This meaning, although not unrelated to the one postulated here, mixes elements concerning the configuration of interests and resource flows with elements concerning how the relation is governed or coordinated, which is not good for purposes of organization design.

10 The choice between organizing within or across firm boundaries is complex because it involves the comparisons between institutions (such as firms and markets), each involving the use of many coordination mechanisms and each admitting quite different internal configurations or variants (see Chapter 13).

11 With the risk of simplifying, there is some truth in saying that organizational economics design model have tended to presume (or suspect) universal conflict among interests, while

organization science design models have tended to presume (or desire) universal convergence among interests.

12 In particular transaction cost economics (Williamson 1975).

9 THE ORGANIZATION OF WORK AND HUMAN RESOURCES: SYSTEMS AND CONTRACTS

1 Note that some procedures and corrective heuristics to these biases were discussed in Chapter 2 of this volume.

2 The main technique for revealing competences, developed initially by David McClelland, one of the best-known experts on motivation and spiritual father of the analysis of competences, is a technique of structured interviews through *critical incidents*. This also has a long and authoritative history in the analysis of the contents of motivation (see Herzberg 1966; Chapter 3). In the analysis of competences, the technique was named a "behavioral event interview" and consists of asking the interviewee to describe in detail, in the form of a narrative, what he/she has done in a few critical situations – some big successes and some big failures – in his/her activity.

3 In effect, it does show some resemblance to the procedure conceived by Taylor to diffuse the "best practices" of "first order workers" to the other workers in similar jobs.

4 The definition by Doeringer and Piore is not limited to that and states that the system is an "administrative unit" and that resource allocation is regulated by plan and command. Their definition is too strict, in that it does not allow one to apply their useful notion of internal labor markets to systems that are not firms (for example, there are labor markets that are internal to a franchise chain, or to an industrial district); nor to admit that the allocation of resources within firms can be regulated by competition and decentralized matching decisions, rather than by centralized plans, which is also possible.

5 In effect, this type of solution can be supported by cognitive and behavioral research that has shown how managers perceive and define risk as the possibility of high losses, and not as variance in consequences (either gains or losses), as risk is defined in finance and economics (March and Shapira 1987).

10 THE ORGANIZATION OF WORK: STRUCTURES

1 In the comparative evaluation of the forms of the organization of labor, we will use some particular elements of the evaluation framework developed by Williamson. However, we will not adopt the framework as a whole, because that assumes as constant some of the fundamental variables that influence the effectiveness of the forms of the organization of labor: namely, it assumes that activities are sequentially interdependent (semi-independent and semi-separable operations); that there are relevant economies of specialization in the elementary operations; and that individual worker preferences are randomly distributed and therefore do not systematically influence the superior form of work organization (Williamson 1980).

11 THE ORGANIZATION OF THE FIRM

1 The procedure presented in this section is a re-elaboration and extension of a framework originally developed in Grandori (1988).

2 In organization literature a main counterposition between "functional" and "divisional" structures frequently crops up. It derives mainly from the historical observation that the first appearance of divisional structures – that associated diversification by product with the division of structure in quasi-firms for each product – was an evolution of structures that associated a "unitary" governance with specialization by technique or function ("functional"). In principle, however, and nowadays also in practice, different criteria of specialization (by function, product, or other) may be combined with different systems of responsibilization and governance (responsibility for partial results and governance through strongly connected mechanisms, as in the unitary forms, or responsibility for final economic results and governance through weakly connected mechanisms, as in the divided forms). Hence we shall here use the distinction between unitary or divided forms, and the unitary functional

(or divided functional) configurations will be considered as subtypes.

3 The argument goes as follows. If differences are created between external investors (shareholders) as principals and managers-agents, then *agency costs* due to these different interests would arise (e.g. costs of control, free-riding, influence, and negotiation). The presence of agency costs will tend to limit the degree of efficient separation between ownership and control. Thus, in general, agency theory predicts that a *mixed ownership structure, with property rights allocated to a mix of internal agents and external shareholders* will usually be superior, as a result of the trade-off between the need for an efficient allocation of risk on the one hand and the need for incentives and objectives alignment on the other hand (Grandori 1997a).

12 FIRM BOUNDARIES AND INTERFIRM ORGANIZATION

1 Demsetz adds here the phrase "The direction of some by others catches the spirit of managed coordination." This extension of the concept of "conscious direction" to that of the direction of some by others is an undue restriction of the concept of a firm to a particular type of firm. Paraphrasing, "group-like" coordination can govern a firm as much as "authority-like" coordination. The passage is not coherent with the general spirit of the argument which is to give a definition of the firm as wide as possible, as illustrated also by the subsequent effort at not ruling out individual firms from the notion.

2 Coase noted that if economic actors could freely exchange resources and rights according to their expected utility, without "attrition," restrictions, "wealth effects," lack of information, and other possible limits to efficient exchanges to take place (Chapter 2), actors would arrive at a Pareto-optimal allocation of property rights regardless of the pattern of their initial distribution, there would be no externalities and no incentive to the growth of the firm, *beyond its technically efficient size*. This argument does not deny the relevance of production costs in determining what a firm does and what not; it mainly *adds* the category of transaction costs and

purports that firm boundaries may be enlarged (or cut down) with respect to technically efficient ones for transaction cost considerations.

3 An exception is Gary Miller's (1992) analysis of "hierarchical failures."

4 The interpretative utility (ex post) but the predictive weakness (ex ante) have been pointed to as a limit of the resource and competence based views of the firm based on resources (e.g. Foss 1996).

5 This criterion is present, although not emphasized, in Williamson (1975).

6 As mentioned also in the other chapters of Part II, a joint optimization exercise based on trade-offs and sums of utilities may be attempted, but it is not likely to be highly applicable nor very consistent with utility theory recommendations against interpersonal comparisons of utility. Williamson (1987) for example suggests approaching the problem as a trade-off: *the reduction of the production and transaction costs obtained by integrating formerly independent activities must be greater than the losses caused by negative externalities* (damage to consumers, suppliers, and all other actors caused by the reduction in the level of competition).

7 This section is based on specific essays (Grandori and Soda 1995; Grandori 1997b) in which we analyze the vast existing literature on interfirm networks with the objective of identifying some salient forms and some key explanatory variables of these organization forms, considering the configurations of property rights and of coordination mechanisms that they imply.

CONCLUSION TO PART III ECONOMIC ORGANIZATION BEYOND DIVIDES: POLYMORPHISM AND RECONFIGURABILITY

1 The perspective that emerges from this book may therefore be called "configurationist" and "relational." But it is so in a stronger sense than that understood by those who have already argued in support of the notion of "organisational configuration" (Mintzberg 1979; Miller and Friesen 1984; Meyer *et al.* 1993). They say: "Organizational structures, production systems, information-processing procedures, strategies and environments all tend to influence each

other. Our thesis is that they do so in a manner that gives rise to a small number of extremely common and sometimes discretely different configurations" (Miller and Friesen 1984). By contrast, our thesis is that the ability to find new and firm-specific combinations of organizational elements is one, if not the main, basis for better performance attributable to organizational arrangements.

2 The logical razor of the fourteenth-century philosopher prescribed to shave off all concepts and elements that were not strictly necessary, that were redundant or derivable from others ("entia non sunt moltiplicanda praeter necessitatem").

Bibliography

....

"Classics" or "core" contributions" in a disciplinary field or school of thought, "overviews" and "states of the art" of a field or perspective, "integrative" or "comparative" analyses across perspectives are classified or described in brackets:

Adams, J.S. (1965) "Inequity in social exchange," in L. Berkovitz (ed.) *Advances in Experimental Social Psychology*, New York: Academic Press: 267–299. (Classic on social psychology.)

Airoldi, G. (1979) "Caso Concessionaria Mattioli," in S. Salvemini (ed.) *Casi di organizzazione*, Milan: F. Angeli.

—— (1980) *I sistemi operativi*, Milan: Giuffrè.

Airoldi, G. and Ruffini, R. (eds) (1993) *Aspetti istituzioni e governo delle aziende e dei sistemi II: Casi*, Milan: Bocconi University.

Akerlof G.A. (1970) "The markets for 'lemons': qualitative uncertainty and the market mechanism," *Quarterly Journal of Economics*, 1984, August: 488–500 (Economic classic on information asymmetries.)

Albert, S. and Whetten, D.A. (1989) "Organizational identity," in L.L. Cummings and B.M. Staw (eds) *Research in Organizational Behavior*, 11, Greenwich, CT: JAI Press. (Organizational overview of the concept of identity.)

Albin, C. (1993) "The role of fairness in negotiation," *Negotiation Journal*, July: 223–44.

Alchian, A.A. (1970) "Information costs, pricing and resource unemployment," in A.A. Alchain, *Microeconomics Foundations of Employment and Inflation Theory*, New York: Norton.

Alchian, A.A. and Demsetz, H. (1972) "Production, information costs and economic organization," *American Economic Review*, 62, December: 777–95. (Classic in organizational economics and agency theory perspective, on the rationale for the "classic firm.")

Alderfer, C.P. (1972) *Existence, Relatedness and Growth*, New York: Free Press. (Development of Maslow needs hierarchy.)

Aldrich, H.E. (1979) *Organizations and Environments*, Englewood Cliffs, NJ: Prentice-Hall. (Organization theory classic, particularly interested in boundary-spanning roles and networks, and in an ecological/natural selection perspective.)

Aldrich, H.E. and Whetten, D.A. (1979) "Organization-set, action set, and networks: making the most of simplicity," in P. Nystrom and W. Starbuck (eds) *Handbook of Organizational Design*, Vol. 1, New York: Oxford University Press: 281–407.

Allison G.T. (1970) *Essence of Decision: Explaining the Cuban Missile Crisis*, Boston: Little Brown. (Political science classic on the plurality of rationalities.)

Alter, C. and Hage, J. (1993) *Organizations Working Together*, Newbury Park, CA: Sage.

Alvesson, M. and Lindkvist, L. (1993) "Transaction costs, clans and corporate culture," *Journal of Management Science*, 30(3): 427–52.

Anderson, J.R. (1983) *The Architecture of Cognition*, Cambridge, MA: Harvard University Press.

Aoki, M. (1984) *The Cooperative Game Theory of the Firm*, Oxford: Oxford University Press. (Organizational economics classic on the link between the configuration of interests and governance structures.)

—— (1988) *Information, Incentives and Bargaining in the Japanese Economy*, Cambridge and New York: Cambridge University Press.

Aoki M., Gustaffson, B., and Williamson, O.E. (eds) (1990) *The Firm as Nexus of Treaties*, London: Sage.

Argyris C. (1957) *Personality and Organization: The Conflict between the System and the Individual*, New York: HarperCollins.

—— (1964) *Integrating the Individual and the Organization*, New York: John Wiley. (Organizational behavior classic.)

Argyris, C. and Schön, D. (1978) *Organizational Learning: A Theory of Action Perspecitve*, Reading, MA.: Addison-Wesley. (One of the most influential and path-breaking contributions in the field of organizational learning.)

Armour, H.O. and Teece, D.J. (1978) "Organizational structure and economic performance: a test of the multidivisional hypothesis," *Bell Journal of Economics*, 9: 106–22.

Arrow, K.J. (1951) *Social Choice and Individual Values*, New York: Wiley. (Economic classic on collective choice.)

—— (1963) "Uncertainty and the welfare economics of medical care," *American Economic Review*, 53: 429–41.

—— (1971) *Essays in the Theory of Risk Bearing*, Chicago: Markham. (Economic classic on the theory of risk allocation.)

—— (1974) *The Limits of Organization*, New York and London: W.W. Norton and Company. (One of the earliest information economics treatments of organization.)

—— (1991) "Economic theory and the hypothesis of rationality," in J. Eatwell, M. Milgate, and P. Newman (eds) *The World of Economics: The New Palgrave*, London: Macmillan: 198–210.

Asch, S.E. (1955) "Studies of independence and conformity: a minority of one against a unanimous majority," *Psychological Monographs*, 70(9). (Organizational psychology classic on group pressure.)

Ashby, W.R. (1952) *Design for a Brain*, London: Chapman and Hall.

Astolfi, A. (1981) *Il contratto di joint-venture. La disciplina giuridica dei raggruppamenti temporanei di imprese*, Milan: Giuffrè.

Axelrod, R.M. (1984) *The Evolution of Cooperation*, New York: Basic Books. (Game theoretic contribution on the possible stabilization of cooperative strategies in Prisoner's Dilemma games.)

Bales, R.E. (1950) *Interaction Process Analysis*, Reading, MA: Addison-Wesley.

Bandura, A. (1986) *Social Foundations of Thought and Action*, Englewood Cliffs, NJ: Prentice-Hall. (Important research-based work on the cognitive foundations of social action.)

Barnard, C.I. (1938) *The Functions of the Executive*, Cambridge, MA: Harvard University Press. (Organization theory classic.)

Barney J. (1990) "The debate between traditional management theory and organizational economics: substantive differences or intergroup conflict?" *Academy of Management Review*, 15(3): 382–92.

—— (1991) "Firm resources and sustained competitive advantage," *Journal of Management*, 17: 99–120.

Barney, J.B. and Ouchi, W.G. (1984) "Information cost and organizational governance," in J. Barney and W. Ouchi (eds) *Organizational Economics*, San Francisco: Jossey-Bass.

—— (eds) (1986) *Organizational Economics*, San Francisco, Jossey-Bass. (Essays by leading figures in the various strands of organizational economic, including agency theory, transaction cost economics, and resource based perspectives.)

Bartlett, C. and Ghoshal, S. (1989) *Managing across Borders: The Transnational Solution*, Boston, MA: Harvard Business School Press.

—— (1990) "The multinational corporation as an interorganizational network," *Academy of Management Review*, 15: 603–25.

Barzel, Y. (1989) *Economic Analysis of Property Rights*, Cambridge: Cambridge University Press.

Bateson, G. (1972) *Steps to an Ecology of Mind*, Milan: Chandler. (Classic on cognitive theory.)

Baumol, W.J. (1959) *Business Behavior, Value and Growth*, New York: Macmillan. (Economic classic on firm expansion driven by sales rather than profit maximization.)

Baumol, W.J. and Quandt, R.E. (1964) "Rules of thumb and optimally imperfect decisions," *American Economic Review*, 54: 23–46.

Bavelas, A. (1951) "Communication patterns in task-oriented groups," in D. Lerner and H.K. Lasswell (eds) *The Policy Sciences*, Stanford, CA: Stanford University Press: 193–202. (Early classic experiments on group communication.)

Bazerman, M.H. (1986) *Judgment in Managerial Decision Making*, New York: John Wiley and Sons. (Overview of behavioral decision theory applications in management.)

Bazerman, M.H. and Carroll, J.S. (1987) "Negotiator cognition," in L.L. Cummings and B.M. Staw (eds) *Research in Organizational Behavior*, 9, Greenwich, CT: JAI Press.

Bazerman, M.H. and Lewicki, R.J. (eds) (1983) *Negotiating in Organizations*, Beverly Hills, CA: Sage. (Overview.)

Bazerman, M.H. and Neale, M.A. (1983) "Heuristics in negotiation: limitation to dispute resolution effectiveness," in M.H. Bazerman and R.J. Lewicki (eds) *Negotiating in Organizations*, Beverly Hills, CA: Sage.

Becattini, G. (1979) "Dal settore industriale al distretto industriale: alcune considerazioni sull'unità di indagine dell'economia industriale," *Economia e Politica Industriale*: 722.

Becker, G.S. (1964) *Human Capital: A Theoretical and Empirical Analysis, with Special Reference to Education*, New York: Columbia University Press. (Economic classic on human resources.)

Becker, G.S. and Murphy, K.M. "The division of labor, coordination costs, and knowledge". *Quarterly Journal of Economics*, 107(4): 1137–60.

Beer, S. (1972) *The Brain of the Firm*, London: Penguin.

Bell, D.E., Raiffa, H., and Tversky, A. (1988) *Decision making. Descriptive, Normative and Prescriptive Interactions*, Cambridge: Cambridge University Press.

Bergami, M. (1996) *L'identificazione con l'impresa*, Rome: NIS.

Bern, E. (1964) *Games People Play*, New York: Grove Press.

Blake, R. and Mouton, J.S. (1964) *The Managerial Grid*, Houston, TX: Gulf Publishing Co. (Organizational behavior classic.)

Blau, P.M. and Schoenherr, R.A. (1971) *The Structure of Organization*, New York: Basic Books. (Organizational theory classic.)

Blau, P.M. and Scott, B.R. (1962) *Formal Organizations: A Comparative Approach*, San Francisco: Chandler. (Organizational theory classic.)

Boisot, M.H. (1986) "Markets and hierarchies in a cultural perspective," *Organization Studies*, 7(2): 135–58.

Boisot, M.H. and Child, J. (1988) "The iron law of fies: bureaucratic failure and the problem of governance in the Chinese economic reforms," *Administrative Science Quarterly*, 33(4): 507–27.

Boudon R. (1977) *Effects pervers et ordre social*, Paris: PUF. (Influential sociological contribution in the "anti-bureaucratic" tradition.)

Bouwman, M.J. (1982) "The use of accounting information: expert versus novice behavior," in G.R. Ungson and D.N. Braunstein (eds) *Decision Making: An Interdisciplinary Inquiry*, Boston, MA: Kent Publishing Company.

Bower, J.R. (1970) *Managing the Resource Allocation Process*, Homewood, IL: Irwin.

Boyatzis, R.E. (1982) *The Competent Manager: A Model for Effective Performance*, New York: Wiley Interscience.

Bratton, W., McCarey, J., Picciotto, S., and Scott, C. (eds) (1996) *International Regulatory Competition*, Oxford: Clarendon Press.

Brennan, G.H. and Buchanan, J.M. (1985) *The reasons of rules*, Cambridge: Cambridge University Press. (Classic economic analysis of rules.)

Brickley, J.A. and Dark, F.H. (1987) "The choice of organizational form: the case of franchising," *Journal of Financial Economics* 18: 401–20.

Bright, J.R. (1958) *Automation of Management*, Cambridge, MA: Harvard University Press.

Brusco, S. (1982) "The Emilian model: productive decentralization and social integration," *Cambridge Journal of Economics*, 6: 167–84.

—— (1999) "Rules of the game in industrial districts," in A. Grandori (ed.) *Interfirm Networks: Organization and Industrial Competitiveness*, London: Routledge.

Buchanan, J.M. and Tullock, G. (1962) *The Calculus of Consent*, Ann Arbor, MI: University of Michigan Press. (Classic economic analysis of democracy.)

Buckley, P.J. and Michie, J. (eds) (1996) *Firms, Organizations and Contracts*, Oxford: Oxford University Press. (Overview of organizational economics contributions by reprints of classic papers in the field.)

Burns, T. and Stalker, G.M. (1961) *The Management of Innovations*, London: Tavistock Publications. (Organization theory classic.)

Burt, R.S. (1992) *Structural Holes*, Cambridge, MA: Harvard University Press. (Influential work in social network analysis. Applied to economic and organizational problems.)

—— (1997) "The contingent value of social capital," *Administrative Science Quarterly*, 42: 339–65.

Butera, F. (1972) *I frantumi ricomposti. Struttura e ideologia nel declino del Taylorismo in America*, Padua: Marsilio.

—— (1979) *Lavoro umano e prodotto tecnico*, Turin: Einaudi.

—— (1984) *L'orologio e l'organismo*, Milan: Angeli.

Buttrick, J. (1952) "The inside contracting system," *Journal of Economic History*, 12: 205–21.

Campbell, D.T. (1960) "Blind variation and selective retention in creative thought as in other knowledge processes," *Psychological Review*, 67: 380–400. (Methodological classic on the connections and differences between "selection models" in thought and nature.)

—— (1969) "Reforms as experiments," *American Psychologist*, 24: 409–29.

Campbell, J.P. and Pritchard, R.D. (1976) "Motivation theory in industrial and organizational psychology," in M. Dunnette (ed.) *Handbook of Industrial and Organizational Psychology*, Chicago: Rand-McNally.

Camuffo, A. (1996) "Competenze," *Economia e Management*, 2: 67–81.

Cantwell, J. (1988a) "Knowledge, capabilities, imagination and cooperation in business: introduction," *Journal of Economic Behavior & Organization*, 35, special issue.

—— (1998b) "Technology and the firm: introduction," *Research Policy*, 27, special issue.

Carroll, J.S. and Payne, J.W. (eds) (1976) *Cognition and Social Behavior*, Hillsdale, NJ: Lawrence Erlbaum Associates. (Applications and implications of cognitive psichology to interpersonal and social dynamics.)

Casson, M.C. (1991) *Economics of Business Culture: Game Theory, Transaction Costs and Economic Performance*, Oxford: Clarendon Press. (An economist's contribution linking economic perspectives with business administration problems.)

Chandler, A.D. (1962) *Strategy and Structure*, Boston: MIT Press.

—— (1977) *The Visible Hand*, Cambridge, MA: Harvard University Press.

—— (1990) *Scale and Scope: The Dynamics of Industrial Capitalism*, Cambridge, MA: Belknap Press. (All these three books by Chandler have become classics of business history and very influential in organization theory.)

Channon, D.F. (1978) *The Service Industries*, London: Macmillan.

Chase, R. (1978) "Where does customer fit in service organizations," *Harvard Business Review*, 56(6): 137–42.

Chen, H.T. and Rossi, P.H. (1981) "A multi-goal theory-driven approach to evaluation," *Evaluation Research*, 6: 38–54.

Child, J. (1982) "Organizational structure, environment and performance: the role of strategic choice," *Sociology*, 6: 1–22. (Classic on organization theory. Criticizing deterministic contingency models.)

—— (1984) *Organization: A Guide to Problems and Practices*, London: Harper & Row.

Cleland, D.I. (1990) *Project Management: Strategic Design and Implementation*, Blue Ridge Summit: Tab Books Inc.

Coase, R. (1937) "The nature of the firm," *Economica*, special issue 4: 386–405. (Founding essay of transaction cost economics.)

—— (1960) "The problem of social cost," *Journal of Law and Economics*, October: 1–44.

—— (1988) *The Firm, the Market, and the Law*, Chicago: University of Chicago Press.

Coda, V. (1988) *Orientamento Strategico dell'impresa*, Turin: Utet.

Cohen, R.L. (1991) "Justice and negotiation," in *Research on Negotiation in Organizations*, Vol. 3, Greenwich: JAI Press.

Cohen, M.D. (1996) "Routines and other recurring action patterns of organizations: contemporary research issues," *Industrial and Corporate Change*, 5(3): 653–98.

Cohen, M.D., March, J.J. and Olsen, J.P. (1972) "A garbage can model of organizational choice," *Administrative Science Quarterly*, 17: 1–25.

—— (1976) *Ambiguity and Choice in Organizations*, Bergen: Universitaetforlaget. (Selection of essays representative of the US–Swedish organizational perspective studying decision-making under radical uncertainty.)

Cohen, W.M. and Levinthal, D.A. (1994) "Absorbtive capacity: a new perspective on learning and innovation," *Administrative Science Quarterly*, 35: 128–152.

Cohendet, P., Avadikian, A., and Llerena, P. (1993) "Coherence, diversity of assets and networks," paper presented at the European Science Foundation EMOT Conference, Workshop on "Coping with complexity and diversity of assets, and learning and adapting to strategic change," Strasbourg, July 6.

Coleman, J.S. (1990) *Foundations of Social Theory*, Cambridge, MA: Harvard University Press. (Effort by a leading sociologist to give a clear cognitive foundation to social theory.)

—— (1993) "Properties of Rational Organization," in S. Lindenberg and H. Schreuder (eds) *Interdisciplinary Perspectives on Organization Studies*, Oxford: Pergamon Press.

Colombo, M. (ed.) (1999) *The Changing Boundaries of the Firm*, London: Routledge.

Contractor, S.J. (1985) "A generalized theorem for joint-venture negotiation," *Journal of International Business Studies*, 16.

Contractor, S.J. and Lorange, P. (1988) *Cooperative Strategies in International Business*, Lexington, MA: Lexington Books.

Costa G. (1990) *Economia e direzione delle risorse umane*, Turin: Utet.

Crozier M. (1964) *Le phénomène burocratique*, Paris: Editions du Seuil. (Sociological classic on strategic games played by organizational actors with knowledge and uncertainty. Translated into English.)

Crozier, M. and Friedberg, E. (1977) *L'acteur et le système*, Paris: Editions du Seuil. (Influential sociological contribution to the concept of organizational actor. Translated into English.)

Cyert, R.M. and March, J.J. (1963) *A Behavioral Theory of the Firm*, Milan: Prentice-Hall. (Classic of organization theory on firm behavior in a "bounded rationality" perspective.)

Cyert, R.M., DeGroot, M.H., and Holt, C.A. (1978) "Sequential investment decisions with Bayesian learning," *Management Science*, 24: 712–18.

Daems, H., (1983) "The determinant of hierarchical organization of industry," in A. Francis, J. Turk, and P. Willman (eds) *Power Efficiency and Institutions*, London: Heinemann.

Dahl, R. (1957) "The concept of power," *Behavioral Sicence*, 2: 201–15. (Sociological classic essay on power.)

Davenport, T.H. and Prusak, L. (1998) *Working Knowledge: How Organizations Manage What They Know*, Cambridge, MA: Harvard University Press.

Davis, L.E. and Cherns, A.B. (1975) *The Quality of Work Life*, Vols 1 and 2, New York: Free Press. (Handbook.)

Davis, L.E. and Taylor, J.C. (1973) "Technology, organization and job structure," in R. Dubin (ed.) *Handbook of Work, Organization and Society*, Chicago, IL: Rand-McNally.

Davis, O.A., Dempster, M.A.H., and Wildavsky, A. (1974) "Toward a predictive theory of government expenditures: US domestic appropriations," *British Journal of Economics*, 9: 587–608. (Point of reference on incremental decision-making.)

Davis, S. and Lawrence, P. (1977) *Matrix*, Reading, MA: Addison-Wesley.

Decastri, M. (ed.) (1983) *Organizzazione e cultura dell'innovazione in impresa: La funzione ricerca e sviluppo*, Milan: Giuffrè.

—— (1986) *Casi di organizzazione*. Milan: Franco Angeli.

De Laat, P. (1999) "Dangerous liasons: sharing knowledge in R&D alliances," in A. Grandori (ed.) *Interfirm Networks: Organization and Industrial Competitiveness*, London: Routledge.

Delmestri, G. (1997) "Convergent organizational responses to globalization in the Italian and German machine-building industries," *International Studies of Management and Organization*, 27(3): 86–108.

—— (1998) "Do all roads lead to Rome . . . or Berlin? The evolution of intra- and interorganizational routines in the machine building industry in Italy and Germany," *Organization Studies*, special issue, "The organizational texture of interfirm relations," August, 19(4): 639–66.

Demsetz, H. (1967) "Toward a theory of property rights," *American Economic Review*, 57(2): 547–59.

—— (1991) "The theory of the firm revisited," in O. Williamson and S. Winter (eds) *The Nature of the Firm: Origins, Evolution and Development*. Oxford: Oxford University Press. (A rethinking essay criticising and bridging cost-oriented organizational economics with an emerging knowledge-oriented organizational economics.)

de Terssac, G. (1992) *Autonomie dans le travail*, Paris: Presses Universitaires de France.

Dietrich, M. (1993) *Transaction Cost Economics and Beyond*, London: Routledge.

Dioguardi, G. (1987) *L'impresa nell'era del computer*, Milan: Ed. Sole 24 Ore.

d'Iribarne, P. (1989) *La logique de l'honneur: Gestion des enterprises et traditions nationales*, Paris: Editions du Seuil.

Doeringer, P.B. and Piore, M.J. (1971) *Internal Labor Markets and Manpower Analysis*, Lexington, MA: Heath. (Classic economic work on the segmentation of labor markets.)

Donaldson, L. (1990) "A rational basis for criticism of organizational economics: a reply to Barney," *Academy of Management Review*, 15(3): 394–401.

Dore, R.P. (1989) *Taking Japan Seriously: A Confucian Perspective of Leading Economic Issues*, London: Athlone Press.

Dosi, G. (1984) "Technological paradigms and technological trajectories," in C. Freeman (ed.) *Long Waves in the World Economy*, London: Pinter.

Dosi, G., Pavitt, K., and Soete, L. (1990) *The Economics of Technical Change and International Trade*, Hemel Hempstead: Harvester Wheatsheaf. (Overview.)

Douma, S. and Schreuder, H. (1992) *Economic Approaches to Organizations*, Engelwood Cliffs, NJ: Prentice-Hall. (Pioneering small textbook covering both organizational economics perspectives and some organization theory perspectives.)

Drucker, P.F. (1993) *Post Capitalist Society*, New York: Harper Business.

Druckman, D. (ed.) (1977) *Negotiations: Social-psychological Perspectives*, Beverly Hills, CA: Sage.

Duncan, R. and Weiss, A. (1978) "Organizational learning implications for organizational design," in B. Staw (ed.) *Research in Organizational Behavior*, Vol. 1, Greenwich, CT: JAI Press.

Dyer, J.H. (1996) "Specialized supplier networks as a source of competitive advantage: evidence from the auto industry," *Strategic Management Journal*, 17: 271–91.

Eccles, R.J. (1981) "The quasi firm in the construction industry," *Journal of Economic Behaviour and Organizations*, 2: 335–57.

—— (1985) *The Transfer Pricing Problem: A Theory of Practice*, Lexington, MA: Lexington Books.

Edberg, B.L.T. and Mumford, E. (1978) "La progettazione dei sistemi informativi atuomatizzati," in C. Ciborra, A. De Maio, A. Edström, and P. Maggiolini (eds) *Informatica e organizzazione*, Milan: Franco Angeli.

Einhorn, H.J. (1980) "Learning from experience and suboptimal rules in decision-making," in T.S. Wallsten (ed.) *Cognitive Processes in Choice and Decision Behavior*, Hillsdale, NJ: Erlbaum.

Einhorn, H.J. and Hogarth, R.M. (1978) "Confidence in judgment: on the illusion of validity," *Psychological Review*, 85: 395–416.

—— (1981) "Behavioral decision theory: processes of judgment and choice," *Annual Review of Psychology*, 32: 52–88. (Overview.)

Elden, M. and Chisholm, F. (1993) "Emerging varieties of action research: introduction to the special issue," *Human Relations*, special issue on Action Research, 46(2): 121–42.

Elster, J. (1983) *Explaining Technical Change*, Cambridge: Cambridge University Press.

—— (1985) *The Multiple Self*, Cambridge: Cambridge University Press.

Emerson, R.M. (1962) "Power-dependence relations," *American Sociological Review*, 27: 31–40. (Classic on a sociological resource-based perspective.)

Emery, F.E. and Trist, E.L. (1960) "Socio-technical systems," in C.W. Churchman and M. Verhulst (eds) *Management Sciences: Models and Techniques*, Oxford: Pergamon Press.

—— (1963) "The causal texture of organizational environments," paper presented to the

International Psychology Congress, Washington, DC, reprinted in *La Sociologie Du Travail*, 1964 and in *Human Relations*, 1965, 18: 21–32. (Organization theory classic on a "socio-technical" perspective.)

Engwall, L. and Morgan, G. (1999) *Regulation and Organization*. London: Routledge.

Erg, C. and Martin, J. (eds) (1985) *Organizational Culture*, Beverly Hills, CA: Sage.

Etzioni, A. (1961) *A Comparative Analysis of Complex Organizations*, Glencoe, IL: Free Press. (Organization theory classic on coordination and control modes.)

—— (1985) "Opening the preferences: a socio-economic research agenda," *Journal of Behavioral Economics*, 14: 183–205.

—— (1988) "Normative-affective factors: toward a new decision-making model," *Journal of Economic Psychology*, 9: 125–56.

Evan, W.M. (1966) "The organization set: toward a theory of interorganizational design," in J.D. Thompson (ed.) *Approaches to Organizational Design*, Pittsburgh: Pittsburgh University Press.

Evan, W.M. and Olk, P. (1990) "R&D consortia: a new US organizational form," *Sloan Management Review*, 31(3): 37–46.

Fama, E. and Jensen, M. (1983a) "Agency problems and residual claims," *Journal of Law and Economics*, 26, June: 327–49.

—— (1983b) "Separation of ownership and control," *Journal of Law and Economics*, 26, June: 301–25.

Feldman, J. and Kanter, H.E. (1965) "Organizational decision making," in G. March (ed.) *Handbook of Organization*, Chicago, IL: Rand-McNally.

Festinger, L. (1957) *A Theory of Cognitive Dissonance*, Stanford, CA: Stanford University Press. (Classic in cognitive psychology.)

Feyerabend, P. (1975) *Against Method*, London: New Left Books. (Classic on the philosophy of science and thought.)

Fiedler, F.E. (1966) *A Theory of Leadership Effectiveness*, New York: McGraw-Hill. (Classic on organizational behavior.)

Fisher, R. (1982) "Negotiating power," *American Behavioral Scientist*, 27.

Fisher, R. and Ury, W. (1981) *Getting to Yes*, Boston: Houghton Mifflin. (Point of reference on negotiation.)

Fishhoff, B. (1981) "Debiasing," in D. Kahnemen, P. Slovic, and A. Tversky (eds) *Judgment Under Uncertainty: Heuristics and Biases*, Cambridge: Cambridge University Press: 422–44.

Fishhoff, B., Lichtenstein, S., Slovic, P., Derby, S.L., and Keeney, R.L. (1981) *Acceptable Risk*, Cambridge: Cambridge University Press.

Folger, R. and Greenberg J. (1985) "Procedural justice: an interpretative analysis of personnel systems," in L.L. Cummings and B.M. Staw (eds) *Research in Organizational Behavior*, Vol. 7, Greenwich, CT: JAI Press.

Folger, R., Konovsky, M.A. and Cropanzano, R., (1992) "A due process metaphor for perfomance appraisal," in L.L. Cummings and B.M. Staw (eds) *Research in Organizational Behavior*, 14, Greenwich, CT: JAI Press.

Follett, M. Parker (1925) "The giving of orders," in H.C. Metcalf and L. Urwic (eds) (1941) *Dynamic Administration: The Collected Papers of Mary Parker Follet*, London: Pitman. (Pioneering contribution of a "mother" of organization theory.)

Foss, N.J. (1925) "Theories of the firm: contractual and competence perspectives," *Evolutionary Economics* 3(2): 127–44. (Statement of the main differences and "tensions" between the two main strands of thought in organizational economics.)

—— (ed.) (1996) *Resources, Firms and Strategies: A Reader in the Resource-based Perspective*, Oxford: Oxford University Press.

Francis, A. (1983) "Markets and hierarchies: efficiency or domination?" in A. Francis, J. Turk, and P. Willman (eds) *Power, Efficiency and Institutions*, London: Heinemann: 105–16.

Frank, R.H. (1992) "A theory of moral sentiments," in M. Zey (ed.) *Decision Making*, London: Sage.

Freeman, R.B. and Medoff, J.L. (1984) *What Do Unions Do*, New York: Basic Books.

Friedberg, E. (1993) *Le Pouvoir et la Règle. Dynamiques de l'action organisée*, Paris: Editions du Seuil.

Friedberg, E. and Neuville, J.P. (1999) "Inside partnership: trust, opportunism and cooperation in the European automobile industry," in A. Grandori (ed.) *Interfirm Networks: Organization and Industrial competitiveness*, London: Routledge.

Friedman, M. (1953) "The methodology of positive economics," in *Essays in Positive Economics*, Chicago: Chicago University Press. (Classic on the methodology of economic science.)

Friedmann, G. (1963) *Où va le travail humain?*, Paris: Gallimard (1st edn 1950). (Classic on the sociology of work.)

Friedmann, G. and Naville, P. (eds) (1961) *Traité de Sociologie du Travail*, Paris: Colin. (Classic on the sociology of work.)

Furubotn, E.G. and Richter, R. (eds) (1994) "The new institutional economics: bounded rationality and the analysis of state and society," *Journal of Institutional and Theoretical Economics*, special issue, 150(1): 11–17.

Gagliardi, P. (ed.) (1986) *Le imprese come culture. Nuove prospettive di analisi organizzativa*, Turin: Isedi. (Overview. Essays by leading experts on organization culture. Translated into English)

—— (1990) *Symbols and Artifacts: View of the Corporate Landscape*. Berlin: De Gruyter.

Galbraith, J.K. (1952) *American Capitalism: The Concept of Contervailing Power*, New York: Houghton, Mifflin. (Classic on the "old" institutional economics.)

Galbraith, J.R. (1971) "Matrix organization design," *Business Horizons*.

—— (1973) *Designing Complex Organizations*, Reading: Addison-Wesley.

—— (1974) "Organization design: an information processing view," *Interfaces*, 4: 28–36.

—— (1977) *Organizational Design*, Reading: Addison Wesley. (Classic on organization design.)

—— (1982) "Designing the innovating organization," *Organizational Dynamics*, winter.

Galbraith, J.R. and Cummings, L.L. (1967) "An empirical investigation of the motivational determinants of task performance: interactive effects between instrumentality-valence and motivation-ability," *Organizational Behavior and Human Performance*, 2: 237–57.

Galgano, I. (1974) *L'imprenditore. Il contratto di società. Società di persone. Società per azioni*, Bologna: Zanichelli.

General Accounting Office (1981) "Productivity sharing programs: can they contribute to productivity improvement?," *AMFD*, March.

Gerloff, E.A. (1985) *Organizational Theory and Design: A Strategic Approach for Management*, New York: McGraw-Hill.

Giddens, A. (1984) *The Constitution of Society: Outline of the Theory of Structuration*, Cambridge: Polity Press. (Founding contribution of the "structuration theory" in organizational sociology.)

Goffman, E. (1969) *Strategic Interaction*, Pittsburgh, PA: University of Pennsylvania Press.

Goldberg, V.P. (1980) "Bridges over contested terrain: exploring the radical account of the employment relationship," *Journal of Economic Behavior Organization*, 1: 249–74.

Golzio, L. (1985) *Economia ed organizzazione della sicurezza del lavoro in impresa*, Milan: Giuffrè.

Goodman, E. and Bamford, J. (eds) (1989) *Small Firms and Industrial District in Italy*, London: Routledge. (Research overview.)

Gouldner, A.W. (1954) *Patterns of Industrial Bureaucracy*, New York: Free Press. (Classic on organizational sociology.)

—— (1955) "Metaphysical pathos and the theory of bureaucracy," *American Political Science Review*, 49: 496–507.

—— (1957–58) "Cosmopolitans and locals: toward an analysis of latent social roles," *Administrative Science Quarterly*, 2: 281–306 and 444–80.

—— (1960) "The norm of reciprocity: a preliminary statement," *American Sociological Review*, April. (Sociological classic on norms.)

Grabher, G. (1993a) "The weakness of strong ties: the lock-in of regional development in the Ruhr area," in G. Grabher (ed.) *The Embedded Firm: The Socio-economics of Industrial Networks*, London: Routledge.

—— (1993b) (ed.) *The Embedded Firm: The Socio-economics of Industrial Networks*. London: Routledge. (Overview of "socially embedded" district firms.)

Graicunas, V.A. (1937) "Relationships in organization," in L. Gulik and L.F. Urwick (eds) *Papers on the Science of Administration*, New York: IPA. (Classic contribution on hierarchy and the span of control.)

Grandori, A. (1984a) "A prescriptive contingency view of organizational decision-making," *Administrative Science Quarterly*, 29: 192–208. (Overview of decision-making literature and prescriptive model of multiple rationalities.)

—— (1984b) *Teorie dell'organizzazione*, Milan: Giuffrè. (Overview. Translated into English in 1987.)

—— (1986) *Simulazioni di organizzazione*, Milan: Angeli.

—— (1988) "Analisi dei costi per la progettazione organizzativa," *Sviluppo & Organizzazione*, 195, January–February: 27–37.)

—— (1991) "Negotiating efficient organization forms," *Journal of Economic Behavior and Organization*, 16: 319–40.

—— (1993) "Notes on the use of power and efficiency constructs in the economics and sociology of organization," in S. Lindenberg and H. Schreuder (eds) *Interdisciplinary Perspectives on Organization Studies*, Oxford: Pergamon Press.

—— (1995) "Models of pluralistic organization: the contribution of European decision making research," in Sam Bacharach, Pasquale Gagliardi, and Bryan Mundell (eds) *Research in the Sociology of Organizations 13, "The European Tradition,"* San Francisco: JAI Press.

—— (1997a) "Agency, markets and hierarchies," in A. Sorge and M. Warner (eds) *International Encyclopedia of Business and Management: Handbook of Organizational Behavior*, London: Routledge: 64–78.

—— (1997b) "An organizational assessment of inter-firm coordination modes," *Organization Studies*, 18(6): 897–925.

—— (1997c) "Governance structures, coordination mechanisms and cognitive models," *Journal of Management and Governance*, 1(1): 29–47.

Grandori, A. and Neri, M. (1999) "The fairness properties of networks," in A. Grandori (ed.) *Interfirm Networks: Organization and Industrial Competitiveness*, London: Routledge.

Grandori, A. and Soda, G. (1995) "Interfirm networks: antecedents, mechanisms and forms," *Organization Studies*, 16(2): 183–214. (Overview.)

Grandori, A., Soda, G., and Usai, A. (1999) "Rules as a mode of economic governance," in L. Engwall and G. Morgan (eds) *Regulation and Organization,* London: Routledge.

Granovetter, M. (1983) "The strength of weak ties," *American Journal of Sociology*, 87(1): 1,360–80.

—— (1985) "Economic action and social structure: the problem of embeddedness," *American Journal of Sociology*, 89: 481–510. (Classic on the "social embeddednes" of economic action.)

Grant, R.M. (1996) "Toward a knowledge-based theory of the firm," *Strategic Management Journal*, 17, winter, special issue: 109–22.

Greenberg, J. (1987) "A taxonomy of organizational justice theories," *Academy of Management Review*, 12(1). (Overview.)

—— (1990) "Organizational justice: yesterday, today, and tomorrow," *Journal of Management*, 16(2). (Overview.)

Greenwood, R., Hinings, C.R., and Brown, J. (1990) "'P2-form' strategic management: corporate practices in professional partnerships," *Academy of Management Journal*, 33(4): 725–55.

Grossman, S. and Hart, O. (1986) "The costs and benefits of ownership: a theory of vertical and lateral integration," *Journal of Political Economy*: 691–719. (Economic classic on the allocation of property rights.)

Grunenberg, M.M. (ed.) (1976) *Job Satisfaction*, London: Macmillan.

Gulliver, P.H. (1979) *Disputes and Negotiations: A Cross-Cultural Perspective*, New York: Academic Press.

Hackman, J.R. (1977) "Work design," in J.R. Hackman and J.L. Suttle (eds) *Improving Life at Work: Behavioral Science Approaches to Organizational Change*, Santa Monica, CA: Goodyear Publishing: 96–162.

—— (1987) *Design of Work Teams*, New York: Prentice-Hall.

—— (1990) *Groups That Work and Those Who Don't: Creating Conditions for Effective Teamwork*, San Francisco: Jossey-Bass.

Hackman, J. and Lawler, E. (1971) "Employee reactions to job characteristics," *Journal of Applied Psychology*, monograph, 55: 259–86.

Hackman, J., Oldham, G.R., Jansen, R., and Purdy K. (1975) "A new strategy for job enrichment," *California Management Review*, summer. (Organization classic on a "socio-technical" perspective.)

Hagedoorn, J. and Narula, R. (1996) "Choosing modes of governance for strategic technology partnering: international and sectoral differences," *Journal of International Business Studies*, 27: 265–84.

Hall, D.T., Bowen, D.D., Lewicki R.J., and Hall, F.S. (eds) (1982) *Experiences in Management and Organizational Behavior*, 2nd edn, New York: John Wiley.

Hamner, W.C. and Yukl, G.A. (1977) "The effectiveness of different offer strategies in bargaining," in D. Druckman (ed.) *Negotiations. Social-Psychological Perspectives*. Beverly Hills, CA: Sage.

Hannan, M.H. and Freeman, J. (1977) "The population ecology of organizations," *American Journal of Sociology*, 82: 929–64. (Founding contribution to the organizational ecology perspective, by two leading sociologists.)

—— (1984) "Structural inertia and organizational change," *American Sociological Review*, 49: 149–64.

—— (1989) *Organizational Ecology*, Cambridge, MA: Harvard University Press. (Overview.)

Hanson, N.R. (1958) *Patterns of Discovery: An Enquiry into the Conceptual Foundation of Science*. Cambridge: Cambridge University Press. (Classic on the philosophy of science.)

Hardin, G., (1968) "The tragedy of the commons," *Science Magazine*, 13 December, 162: 1,243–48.

Hart, O. and Moore, J. (1990) "Property rights and the nature of the firm," *Journal of Political Economy*, 98, December: 1,119–58. (Economic classic on the allocation of property rights.)

Hedberg, B.L.T., Nystrom, P.C., and Starbuck, W.H. (1976) "Camping on seesaws: prescriptions for a self-designing organization," *Administrative Science Quarterly*, 21: 41–65.

Hedlund, G. (1986) "The hypermodern corporation: a heterarchy?," *Human Resource Management*, 25(1): 9–35.

—— (1993) "A model of knowledge management and the N-form corporation," *Strategic Management Journal*, 15: 73–90.

Hees, K. (1987) *Creating the High-performance Team*, New York: John Wiley.

Hennart, J.F. (1988) "A transaction costs theory of equity joint ventures," *Strategic Management Journal*, 5(9): 361–74.

Herbst, P.G. (1976) *Alternatives to Hierarchies*, Leiden: Martinus Nijhoff.

Herzberg, F. (1966) *Work and Nature of Man*, Cleveland: World Publ. Co. (Classic on the organization of work and motivation.)

Herzberg, F., Mausner, B., and Synderman, B. (1959) *The Motivation to Work*, New York: John Wiley.

Heskett, J.L. (1986) *Managing in the Service Economy*. Boston: Harvard Business School Press.

Helylighen, F. (1992) "Making thoughts explicit: advantages and drawbacks of formal expression," paper submitted to the *Journal of Applied Philosophy*.

Hickson, D.J. (ed.) (1993a) *Management in Western Europe. Society, Culture and Organizations in Twelve Nations*, Berlin: De Gruyter. (Research overview of culture-related differences in organization.)

—— (1993b) "Many more ways than one," in D.J. Hickson (ed.) *Management in Western Europe: Society, Culture and Organizations in Twelve Nations*, Berlin: De Gruyter.

Hickson, D., Butler, R.J., Mallory, G.R. and Wilson, D.C. (1986) *Top Decision*, Oxford: Blackwell.

Hickson, D., Hinings, C.R., Lee, C.A., Schnek, R.E., and Pennings, J.M. (1971) "A strategic contingencies theory of intraorganizational power," *Administrative Science Quarterly*, 16: 216–29. (Organization theory classic linking unit power to uncertainty and unsubstitutability.)

Hill, C.P. (1971) *Toward a New Philosophy of Management*, London: Gower Press.

Hill, C.W.L. (1990) "Cooperation opportunism and the invisible hand: implications for transaction cost theory," *Academy of Management Review*, 15(3): 500–13.

Hirschman, A.O. (1970) *Exit, Voice and Loyalty: Responses to Decline in Firms, Organizations and States*, Cambridge, MA: Harvard University Press. (Economic classic on alternative coordination modes.)

Hodgson, G.M. (1986) *Economics and Institutions*, Cambridge: Polity Press. (Conceptual discussion of the differences and complementarities between knowledge and cost oriented perspectives on economic organization.)

Hofstede, G., (1980) *Culture's Consequences: International Differences in Work-related Values*, London: Sage. (Vast empirical research which gave birth to a school on organizational cultures.)

—— (1993) "Intercultural conflict and synergy in Europe," in D.J. Hickson (ed.) *Management in*

Western Europe: Society, Culture and Organizations in Twelve Nations, Berlin: De Gruyter: 1–8.

Holmstrom, B. (1982) "Moral hazard in teams," *Bell Journal of Economics*, 13: 324–40.

Homans, G. (1950) *The Human Group*, New York: Harcourt, Brace and World. (Sociological classic.)

House, R.J. and Wohba, M. (1972) "Expectancy theory in mangerial motivation: an integrated model," in H.L.Tosi, R.J. House, and M.D. Dunnette (eds) *Managerial Motivation and Compensation*, East Lansing: Michigan State University, Division of Research, College of Business Administration.

Inzerilli, G. (ed.) (1991) "The Italian alternative: flexible organization and social management," *International Studies of Management and Organization*, 20(4), special issue, "The Italian alternative": 6–21.

Itami, M. (1987) *Mobilizing Invisible Assets*, Cambridge, MA: Harvard University Press.

Itoh, H. (1994) "Japanese human resource management from the viewpoint of incentives theory," in M. Aoki and R. Dore (eds) *The Japanese Firm*, Oxford: Clarendon Press: 233–64.

Janis, I.L. (1972) *Victims of Groupthink*, Boston: Houghton Mifflin.

Jarillo, J.C. (1988) "On strategic networks," *Strategic Management Journal*, 9: 31–41.

Jensen, M.C. and Meckling, W.H. (1976) "Theory of the firm: managerial behavior, agency costs and ownership structure," *Journal of Financial Economics*, 3: 305–60. (Founding essay on agency theory.)

Jaquemin, A. (1985) *Selection et pouvoir dans la nouvelle economie industrielle*, Paris: Economica.

Johanisson, B. (ed.) (1987) "Organizing: the network metaphor," *International Studies of Management and Organization*, 17(1), special issue. (Overview of the Swedish studies on interfirm networks.)

Jones, C., Hesterley, W.S., and Borgatti, S.P. (1997) "A general theory of network governance," *Academy of Management Review*, 22(4): 911–45.

Jorde, T.M. and Teece, D. (1989) "Competition and cooperation: striking the right balance," *California Management Review*, spring: 25–37.

Kahneman, D. and Tversky, A. (1979) "Prospect theory: an analysis of decision under risk," *Econometrica*, 47: 263–91. (Classic on behavioral decision theory by the two leading cognitive psychologists.)

Kahneman, D., Knetsch, J., and Tahler, R. (1986a) "Fairness and the assumptions of economics," *Journal of Business* 59(4): 284–300. (Article opening the applications of Behavioral Decision Theory to the analysis of fairness in economic behavior.)

—— (1986b) "Fairness as a constraint of profit seeking: entitlements of the market," *The American Economic Review*, 76(4): 728–41.

Kahneman, D., Slovic, P., and Tversky, A. (eds) (1982) *Judgment under Uncertainty: Heuristics and Biases*, Cambridge: Cambridge University Press. (Overview of behavioral decision theory.)

Karpik, L. (1989) "L'économie de la qualité," *Review Française de Sociologie*, 30(2): 187–210.

Katz, D. and Kahn, R.L. (1966) *The Social Psychology of Organization*, New York: John Wiley. (Classic)

Keeley, M. (1980) "Organizational analogy: a comparison of organismic and social contract models," *Adminstrative Science Quarterly*.

—— (1988) *A Social-contract Theory of Organizations*, Notre Dame, IN: University of Notre Dame Press.

Kelley, H. (1971) *Attribution in Social Interaction*, Morristown, NJ: General Learning Press.

Kerr, S. (1975) "On the folly of rewarding A, while hoping for B," *Academy of Management Journal*, 18: 769–82.

Kieser, A. (1993) "Why organization theory needs historical analysis," keynote speaker address, EGOS Colloquium, Paris.

Klein, B., Crawford, R., and Alchian, A. (1978) "Vertical integration, appropriable rents and the competitive contracting process," *Journal of Law and Economics*, 21: 297–326. (Economic classic on vertical integration and asset specificity.)

Klein, H.J. (1989) "An integrated control theory model of work motivation," *Academy of Management Review*, 14(2): 150–72.

Knight, K. (1976) "Matrix organization: a review," *Journal of Management Studies*, May: 111–30. (Overview.)

Komaki, J.L., Coombs, T., and Schepman, S. (1996) "Motivational implications of reinforcement theory," in R.M. Steers, L.W. Porter, and

G.A. Bigley (eds) *Motivation and Leadership at Work*, New York: McGraw-Hill

Kreiner, K. and Schultz, M. (1993) "Informal collaboration in R&D: the formation of network analysis," in R. Burt and M. Minor (eds) *Applied Network Analysis*, Beverly Hills, CA: Sage: 18–34.

Kreps, D.M. (1990) *Game Theory and Economic Modeling*, Oxford: Clarendon Press. (Classic.)

—— (1996) "Corporate culture and economic theory," in P.J. Buckley and J. Michie (eds) *Firms, Organizations and Contracts*, Oxford: Oxford University Press (1st edn 1986). (Bridging contribution between economic analysis and management issues.)

Kuhn, T.S., (1962) *The Structure of Scientific Revolutions*, Chicago, IL: University of Chicago. (Classic on the sociology of science.)

Lakatos, I. (1970a) "Falsification and the methodology of scientific research programs," in I. Lakatos and A. Musgrave (eds) *Criticism and the Growth of Knowledge*, Cambridge: Cambridge University Press. (Classic on the philosophy of science.)

—— (1976) *Proofs and Refutations: The Logic of Mathematical Discovery*, eds J. Worral and G. Currie, Cambridge: Cambridge University Press.

Lammers, C. (1993) "Interorganizational democracy," in S. Lindenberg and H. Schreuder (eds) *Interdisciplinary Perspectives on Organization Studies*, Oxford: Pergamon Press: 323–37.

Landy, F.J. and Becker, W.S. (1987) "Motivation theory reconsidered," in L.L. Cummings and B.M. Staw (eds) *Research in Organizational Behavior*, 9, Greenwich, CT: JAI Press.

Langer, E.L. (1975) "The illusion of control," in D. Kahneman, P. Slovic, and A. Tversky (eds) *Judgment under Uncertainty: Heuristics and Biases*, Cambridge: Cambridge University Press.

Langlois, R.N. and Robertson, P.L. (1995) *Firms, Markets and Economic Change*, London: Routledge.

Lanzara, F. (1992) *Capacità negativa*, Bologna: Il Mulino.

Latsis, S. (ed.) (1976) *Method and Appraisal in Economics*, Cambridge: Cambridge University Press. (Essays by leading experts.)

Lau, J.B. (1975) *Behavior in Organizations: An Experiential Approach*, Homewood, IL: R.D. Irwin Inc.

Lawler, E.E., III (1966) "The mythology of management compensation," *California Management Review*, IX(1): 11–22.

—— (1971) *Pay and Organizational Effectiveness*, New York: McGraw-Hill. (Classic on human resource management.)

—— (1973) *Motivation in Work Organizations*, Belmont, CA: Wadsworth.

Lawler, E.E. and Letford, G., Jr (1982) "Productivity and the quality of work life," *National Productivity Review*, winter: 23–36.

Lawler, E.E. and Suttle, J.L. (1972) "A causal correlation test of the need hierarchy concept," *Organizational Behavior and Human Performance*, 7.

Lawrence, P. and Dyer, D. (1983) *Renewing American Industry*, New York: Free Press.

Lawrence, P. and Lorsch, J. (1967) *Organization and Environment*, Cambridge, MA: Harvard Business School. (Classic on organization and structural contingency theory.)

Lax, D.A. and Sebenius, J.K. (1986) *The Manager as Negotiator*, New York: Free Press.

Lazear, E.P. (1995) *Personnel Economics*, Cambridge, MA: MIT Press. (Textbook.)

Leventhal, G.S. (1980) "What should be done with equity theory?," in K. Gergen, M. Greenberg, and R. Willis (eds) *Social Exchange Theory*, New York: Plenum.

Levinthal, D. (1988) "A survey of agency models of organization," *Journal of Economic Behavior and Organization*, 9: 153–85. (Overview by an organization and evolutionary economics expert.)

Lewicki, R.J. (1983) "Lying and deception: a behavioral model," in M.H. Bazerman and R.J. Lewicki (eds) *Negotiating in Organizations*, Beverly Hills, CA: Sage.

Lewin, K. (1948) *Resolving Social Conflicts*, New York: Harper and Row. (Classic on industrial psychology.)

Lichtenstein, S., Fishhoff, B., and Phillips, L.D. (1982) "Calibration of probabilities," in D. Kahneman, P. Slovic, and A. Tversky (eds) *Judgment under Uncertainty: Heuristics and Biases*, Cambridge: Cambridge University Press.

Likert, R. (1961) *The Human Organization: Its*

Management and Value, New York: McGraw-Hill. (Classic on organizational behavior.)

Lindblom, C.E. (1959) "The science of 'Muddling Through,'" *Public Administration Review*, 19: 78–88. (Leading contribution by a political scientist on incremental decision-making.)

—— (1977) *Politics and Markets*, New York: Basic Books.

Lindenberg, S. (1990) "Homo socio-economicus: the emergence of a general model of man in the social sciences," *J. Inst. & Theor. Econ.*, 146: 727–48.

—— (2000) "It takes both trust and lack of mistrust: cooperation and relational signaling in contractual relations," in A. Grandori (ed.) *Journal of Management and Governance*, special issue, "Rethinking the cognitive and relational foundations of governance," 4(1–2).

Loasby, B.J. (1976) *Choice, Complexity and Ignorance*, Cambridge: Cambridge University Press. (Classic on decision-making in a broad cognitive and economic perspective.)

Locke, E.A. (1968) "Toward a theory of task motivation and incentives," *Organizational Behaviour and Human Performances*, 3.

—— (1991) "The motivation sequence, the motivation hub, and the motivation core," *Organizational Behavior and Human Decision Processes*, 50: 288–99.

—— "Motivation through conscious goal setting," *Applied & Occupational Psychology*, 5: 117–24.

Locke, E.A. and Latham, G.P. (1990) *A Theory of Goal Setting and Task Performance*. Englewood Cliffs, NJ: Prentice-Hall. (Point of reference on goal setting.)

Lomi, A. (ed.) (1997) *L'analisi relazioale delle organizzazioni. Riflessioni tecniche ed esperienze empiriche*, Bologna: Il Mulino.

Lorenzoni, G. and Baden-Fuller, C. (1995) "Creating a strategic center to manage a web of partners," *California Management Review*, 37(3): 146–63.

Lorenzoni, G. and Ornati, O.A. (1988) "Constellations of firms and new ventures," *Journal of Business Venturing*, 3: 41–57.

Lorsch, J.W. and Allen, S.A. (1973) *Managing Diversity and Interdependence: An Organizational Study of Multidivisional Firms*, Division of Research, Graduate School of Business Administration, Harvard University.

Lorsch, J. and Morse, J. (1974) *Organizations and Their Members: A Contingency Approach*, New York: Harper and Row.

Luce, R.D. and Raiffa, H. (1958) *Games and Decisions*, New York: John Wiley. (Classic on decision-making in a game theoretic perspective.)

Lupton, T. (1975) "Efficiency and the quality of work life: the technology of reconciliation," *Organizational Dynamics*, autumn: 68–80.

Lysonski, S. (1985), "A boundary-theory investigation of product manager's role," *Journal of Marketing*, 49, winter: 26–40.

McClelland, D.C. (1961) *The Achieving Society*, Princeton, NJ: Van Nostrand.

—— (1965) "Toward a theory of motive acquisition," *American Psychologist*, 20: 321–33.

—— (1971) *Assessing Human Motivation*, New York: General Learning Press.

—— (1987) *Human Motivation*, New York: Cambridge University Press. (Reference points on motivation.)

McDonald, P. (1991) "The Los Angeles Olympic Organization Committee: developing organizational culture in the short run," in P.J. Frost, L.L. Moore, M.R. Lonis, C.C. Lundberg, and J. Martin (eds) *Reframing Organizational Culture*, London: Sage.

McGregor, D. (1960) *The Human Side of Enterprise*, New York: McGraw-Hill. (Classic in organizational behavior.)

Machlup, F. (1978a) "Theories of the firm: marginalist, behavioral, managerial," in F. Machlup, *Methodology of Economics and Other Social Sciences*, New York: Academic Press. (Classic methodological analysis by an economist and theorist of the firm.)

—— (1978b) "Ideal types, reality and construction," in F. Machlup, *Methodology of Economics and Other Social Sciences*, New York: Academic Press.

McNeil, I.R. (1978) "Contracts: adjustment of long-term economic relationship under classical, neoclassical and relational contract law," *Northwestern University Law Review*, 72: 854–906.

Maier, N.R.F. (1967) "Assets and liabilities in group problem solving," *Psychological Review*, 74: 239–49.

Malone, W.T., Yates, J.A., and Benjamin, R.I.

(1987) "Electronic markets and electronic hierarchies," *Communications of the ACM*, 30(6).

March, J.C. and March, J.G. (1977) "Almost rendom careers: the Wisconsin School superintendency, 1940–1972," *Administrative Science Quarterly*, September, 22: 377–408.

—— (1978) "Performance sampling in social matches," *Administrative Science Quarterly*, 23: 434–53.

March, J.G. (1976) "The technology of foolishness," in J.G. March and J.P. Olsen, *Ambiguity and Choice in Organizations*, Bergen: Bergen Universitetforlaget.

—— (1978) "Bounded rationality, ambiguity, and the engineering of choice," *Bell Journal of Economics*, 9: 587–608.

—— (1992) "Exploration and exploitation in organizational learning," *Organization Science*, 2: 71–87.

—— (1994) *A Primer on Decision Making*, New York: Free Press.

March, J.G. and Shapira, Z. (1982) "Behavioral decision theory and organizational theory," in G.R. Ungson and D.N. Braunstein (eds) *Decision Making*, Boston: Kent Publ. Co.: 92–115. (Overview linking decision-making research in cognive psychology and organization theory.)

—— (1987) "Managerial perspectives on risk and risk taking," *Management Science*, 33: 1,404–18.

—— (1992) "Variable risk preferences and the focus of attention," *Psychological Review*, 99: 172–83.

March, J.G. and Simon, H.A. (1958) *Organizations*, New York: Wiley. (Classic on organization theory.)

Marglin, S.A. (1974) "What do bosses do? The origins and functions of hierarchy in capitalist production," *Review of Radical Political Economics*, 6: 33–50. (Point of reference for radical economics.)

Mariotti, S. and Cainarca, G.C. (1986) "The evolution of transaction governance in the textile-clothing industry," *Journal of Economic Behavior and Organization*, 7: 351–74.

Mariotti, S. and Migliarese, P. (1984) "Organizzione industriale e rapporti tra imprese in un settore ad alto tasso innovato," *L'Industria*, 1: 71–110.

Marris, R. (1964) *The Economic Theory of Managerial Capitalism*, New York: Free Press. (Point of reference for managerial theories of the firm.)

—— (1997) "Managerial theories of the firm," in A. Sorge and M. Warner (eds) *International Encyclopedia of Business and Management. Handbook of Organizational Behaviour.* London: Routledge.

Marschak, J. (1954) "Toward an economic theory of organization and information," in R.M. Thrall, C.H. Coombs, and R.L. Davis (eds) *Decision Processes*, New York: Wiley.

—— (1955) "Elements for a theory of teams," *Management Science*, 1: 127–37.

Marschak, J. and Radner, R. (1972) *Economic Theory of Teams*, New Haven, CT: Yale University Press. (Classic economic analysis of teams.)

Marschak, T.A. (1965) "Economic theories of organization," in J.C. March (ed.) *Handbook of Organizations*, Chicago, IL: Rand-McNally: 423–50.

—— (1972) "Computation in organizations: comparison of price mechanism and other adjustment processes," in C.B. McGuire and R. Radner (eds) *Decisions and Organizations*, Amsterdam: North Holland: 237–82.

Marshall, A. (1890/1949) *Principles of Economics*, London: Macmillan. (Classic.)

Martino, F. (1982) ""Esperimenze di cambiamento organizzativo in Norvegia," *Sviluppo & Organizzazione*, 14: 11–14.

Marturana, H.L. and Varela, F.J. (1980) *Autopoiesis and Cognition: The Realization of the Living*, Boston: Reidel. (Classic linking cognitive and natural sciences with an interest in the concept of organization.)

Marwell, G. and Ames, R.E. (1981) "Economists free ride, does anyone else? Experiments on the provision of public goods," *Journal of Public Economics*, 15: 295–310.

Marx, K. (1867) *Das Kapital: Kritik der politischen Ekonomie*, Hamburg: Verlag von Otto Meissner. (Classic on the socialist economics and sociology of capitalism.)

Masden, S.E. (1996) "A legal basis for the firm," in P.J. Buckley and J. Michie (eds) *Firms, Organizations and Contracts*, Oxford: Oxford University Press.

Masini, C. (1978) *Lavoro e Risparmio*, 2nd edn,

Turin: UTET (1st edn, Turin: UTET, 1970). (Conceptual textbook integrating various fields of business administration.)

Maslow A. (1964) *Motivation and Personality*, New York: Harper and Row. (Classic on the psychology of work.)

Maurice, M., Sorge, A. and Warner, M. (1980) "Societal differences in organizing manufacturing units: a comparison of France, West Germany and Great Britain," *Organization Studies*, 1(1): 59–86.

Mayo, E. (1945) *The Human Problem of an Industrial Civilization*, and *The Social Problems of an Industrial Civilisation*, 2 vols. Cambridge, MA: Harvard University Press. (Classic clinical perspective on the psychology of organization.)

Mead, Y.E. (1972) "The theory of labor-managed firms and of profit sharing," *The Economic Journal*, March, special issue: 402–28.

Meindl, J.R., Ehrlich, S.B., and Dukerich, J.M. (1985) "The romance of leadership," *Administrative Science Quarterly*, 30: 78–102.

Merton, R.K., (1949) *Social Theory and Social Structure*, New York: Free Press. (Classic on structural functionalist sociology.)

—— (1965) "Structure bureaucratique et personalité," in A. Levy (ed.) *Psychologie sociale*, Paris: Dunod.

Meyer, J.W. and Rowan, B. (1977) "Institutionalized organizations: formal structure as myth and ceremony," *American Journal of Sociology*, 2: 340–63. (Path-breaking sociological contribution to the institutional analysis of organization).

Meyer, A.D., Tsui, A.S., and Hinings, C.R. (1993) "Configurational approaches to organizational analysis," *Academy of Management Journal* 36(6): 1,175–95. (Overview and classification of configurational approaches.)

Miceli, M. and Lane, M. (1991) "Antecedents of pay satisfaction," in G.R. Ferris and K.W. Rowland (eds) *Research in Personnel and Human Resources Management*, Vol. 9, San Francisco: JAI Press.

Miles, R. and Snow, C. (1978) *Organizational Strategies: Structures and Processes*, New York: McGraw Hill.

Milgrom, P. and Roberts, J. (1992) *Economics Organization and Management*, Englewood Cliffs, NJ: Prentice-Hall. (Systematic presentation of organizational economics contributions to business administration problems in textbook format.)

Miller, D. and Friesen, P.H. (1984) *Organization: A Quantum View*, Englewood Cliffs, NJ: Prentice-Hall.

Miller, E.J. and Rice, A.K. (1967) *Systems of Organization*, London: Tavistock.

Miller, G.J. (1992) *Managerial Dilemmas: The Political Economy of Hierarchy*. Cambridge: Cambridge University Press.

Mintzberg, H. (1973) *The Nature of Managerial Work*, New York: Harper & Row. (Organizational classic empirical study on management.)

—— (1979) *The Structuring of Organizations*, Englewood Cliffs, NJ: Prentice-Hall. (Classic on organization design.)

—— (1983) *Structure in Fives: Designing Effective Organizations*, Englewood Cliffs, NJ: Prentice-Hall.

Mitchell, D.J.B., Lewin, D., and Lawler, E.E. (1990) "Alternative pay systems, firm performance and productivity," in A. Blinder (ed.) *Paying for Productivity: A Look at the Evidence*. Washington, DC: The Brookings Institution.

Monteverde, K. and Teece, D. (1980) *Appropriable Rents and Quasi Integration*, working paper, Stanford, CA: Stanford University, Graduate School of Business Administration.

Morgan, G. (1986) *Images of Organization*, London: Sage. (Overview of organization theories.)

Murray, H. (1960) *Studies in Automated Technologies*, London: Tavistock.

Myers, I.B. and Briggs, K.C. (1962) *Myers–Briggs Type Indicators*, Princeton, NJ: Educational Testing Service.

Nacamulli, R.C.D. (1985) "L'efficienza fra economia e organizzazione," in R.C.D. Nacamulli and A. Rugiadini (eds) *Organizzazione & Mercato*, Bologna: Il Mulino.

Nash, J.F., Jr (1950) "The bargaining problem," *Econometrica*, 18: 155–62. (Classic exposition of the solution of bargaining problems with the criterion of the maximum product of utilities.)

Nelson, R.R. and Winter, S.G. (1982) *An Evolutionary Theory of Economic Change*, Cambridge, MA: Harvard University Press. (Classic on evolutionary economics, from a bounded rationality perspective.)

Neri, M. (1994) "L'equità nelle organizzazioni,"

Sviluppo & Organizzazione, 145, September–October: 33–44.

Newell, A. and Simon, H.A. (1976) *Human Problem-solving*, Englewood Cliffs, NJ: Prentice-Hall.

Nierenberg, G.I. (1968) *The Art of Negotiation.* New York: Simon & Schuster.

Nisbett, R. and Ross, L. (1980) *Human Inferences: Strategies and Shortcomings of Social Judgment*, Englewood Cliffs, NJ: Prentice-Hall.

Nonaka, I. and Takeuchi, H. (1995) *The Knowledge Creating Company*, Oxford: Oxford University Press.

Nooteboom, B. (1999) "Innovation, learning and industrial organization," *Cambridge Journal of Economics*, 23: 127–50.

Normann, R. (1984) *Service Management: Strategy and Leadership in Service Businesses*, New York: John Wiley.

North, D.C. (1981) *Structure and Change in Economic History*, New York: Norton.

—— (1986) "The new institutional economics," *Journal of Institutional and Theoretical Economics*, 142: 230–7.

—— (1990) *Institutions, Institutional Change, and Economic Performance*. Cambridge: Cambridge University Press.

—— (1993) "Institutions and credible commitment," *Journal of Institutional and Theoretical Economics*, 149 (1): 11–23. (North's works are classic and founding contributions in the new institutional economics.)

Notz, W.W., Starke, F.A., and Atwell, J. (1983) "The manager as arbitrator: conflicts over scarce resources," in M.H. Bazerman and R.J. Lewicki (eds) *Negotiating in Organizations*, Beverly Hills, CA: Sage.

Olson, M.O. (1965) *The Logic of Collective Action*, Cambridge, MA: Harvard University Press. (Economic classic on the problem of collective rationality.)

O'Reilly, J. (1993) "Neat prescriptions or untidy preactice? The use of functional flexibility in Britain and France," 11th EGOS Colloquium, Paris.

Orlean, A. (1989) "Pour une approche cognitive des conventions économiques," *Revue Economique*, 40(2): 241–72.

Osterman, P. (ed.) (1984) *International Labor Markets*, Cambridge, MA: MIT Press.

Ouchi, W.G. (1979) "A conceptual framework for design of organizational control mechanism," *Management Science*, 25: 833–48.

—— (1980) "Markets, bureaucracies and clans," *Administrative Science Quarterly*, 25: 129–1. (Point of reference on the concept of clan.)

Ouchi, W.G. and Bolton, M.K. (1988) "The logic of joint research and development," *California Management Review*, 30(3): 9–33.

Ouchi, W.G. and Wilkins, A.L. (1985) "Organizational Culture," *Annual Review of Sociology*, 11: 457–83. (Analysis of culture in a transaction cost perspective.)

Padgett, J.F. (1980) "Bounded rationality in budgetary research," *American Political Science Review*, 74: 354–72.

Paniccia, I. (1997) "One, a hundred, a thousand industrial districts: organizational variety of local networks of SMEs." *Organization Studies*, special issue, "The organizational texture of interfirm relations," 1964: 666–700.

Payne, J.W. (1976) "Task complexity and contingent processing in decision-making: an information search and protocol analysis," *Organizational Behavior and Human Performance*, 16: 366–87.

—— (1982) "Contingent decision behavior," *Psychological Bulletin*, 92: 382–402.

Penrose, E. (1959) *The Theory of the Growth of the Firm*, New York: John Wiley. (Classic and founding contribution on the resource-based view of the firm.)

Perrone, V. (1996) "Forms of capital," Academy of Management Meeting paper, Las Vegas.

Perrow, C. (1967) "A framework for the comparative analysis of organization," *American Sociological Review*, 32, April: 194–208. (Classic on organization theory.)

Pettigrew, A.M. (1973) *The Politics of Organization Decision Making*, London: Tavistock. (Point of reference on organizational decision-making.)

—— (1979) "On studying organizational cultures," *Administrative Science Quarterly*, 24: 570–81.

Pettigrew, A. and Whittington, C.R. (1995) *Organizational Strategy and Change*, San Fransico: Jossey-Bass.

Pfeffer, J. (1981) *Power in Organizations*, Marshfield, MA: Pitman. (Point of reference on organizational power.)

—— (1994) *Competitive Advantage through People*. Boston: Harvard Business School Press.

Pfeffer, J. and Salancik, G.R. (1974a) "Organizational decision making as a political process: the case of a university," *Administrative Science Quarterly*, 19: 135–51.

—— (1974b) "The bases and use of power in organizational decision-making: the case of a university," *Administrative Science Quarterly*, 19: 241–54.

—— (1978) *The External Control of Organizations: A Resource Dependence Perspective*, New York: Harper and Row. (Classic on resource-based organizational analysis.)

Pilati, M. (1995) "L'organizzazione delle reazione di lavoro," in A. Grandori (ed.) *L'organizzazione delle attività economiche*, Bologna: Il Mulino.

Polanyi, M. (1958) *Personal Knowledge*, London: Routledge.

—— (1967) *The Tacit Dimension*, London: Routledge. (Classics on the philosophy of knowledge.)

Pollock, F. (1956) *Automation-Materialen zur Beurteilung de ökonomischen und sozialen Folgen*, Frankfurt am Main: Europäische Verlagsanstalt.

Popper, K.R. (1935) *Der Logik der Forschung*, Vienna (tr. Eng. 1959, *The Logic of Scientific Discovery*, London: Hutchinson.) (Classic on the philosophy of science.)

—— (1989) "The critical approach versus the mystique of leadership," *Human Systems Management*, 8: 259–65

Porter, L.W. and Lawler, E.E. (1968) *Managerial Attitudes and Performance*, Homewood, IL: Dorsey.

Porter, M.W. (1980) *Competitive Strategy*, New York: Free Press. (Classic bringing industrial economic concept to bear on firm strategy.)

—— (1985) *Competitive Advantage*, New York: Free Press.

—— (1987) "From competitive advantage to corporate strategy," *Harvard Business Review*, 65(3): 43–59.

Powell, W.W. (1990) "Neither market or hierarchy: network forms of organization," in L.L. Cummings and B. Staw (eds) *Research in Organizational Behavior*, Vol. 12, San Francisco: JAI Press.

—— (1996) "Inter-organizational collaboration in the biotechnology industry," *Journal of Institutional and Theoretical Economics*, 152(1): 197–215.

Powell, W.W. and Di Maggio, P.J. (eds) (1991) *The New Institutionalism in Organizational Analysis*, Chicago: University of Chicago Press. (Overview of the new insitutionalist sociology approach through leading expert essays.)

Prahalad, C.K. and Hamler, G. (1990) "The core competence of the corporation," *Harvard Business Review*, 68(31): 79–91. (Point of reference on the notion of "core competences.")

Provan, K.G. and Heimer, S.E. (1999) "Organizational learning and the role of the network broker in small-firm manufacturing networks," in A. Grandori (ed.) *Interfirm Networks: Organization and Industrial Competitiveness*, London: Routledge.

Pruitt, D.G. (1972) "Methods for resolving differences of interest: a theoretical analysis," *Journal of Social Issues*, 28: 133–54.

—— (1981) *Negotiation Behavior*, New York: Academic Press. (Systematic treatment of the field.)

—— (1983) "Achieving integrative agreements," in M.H. Bazerman and R.J. Lewicki (eds) *Negotiating in Organizations*, Beverly Hills, CA: Sage.

Pugh, D.S. (1991) "The Aston program perspective. The Aston program of research: retrospect and prospect," in A.H. Van de Ven and W.F. Joyce (eds) *Perspectives on Organization Design and Behavior*, New York: John Wiley.

Pugh, D.S., Hickson, D.J., Hinigs, C.R., and Turner, C. (1969a) "The context of organizational structure," *Administrative Science Quarterly*, 14: 91–114.

—— (1969b) "An empirical taxonomy of structures of work organizations," *Administrative Science Quarterly*, 14: 115–26. (Classic piece of organization research.)

—— (1981) "The Aston research program," in A.M. Van de Ven and W.F. Joyce (eds) *Perspectives on Organization Design and Behavior*, New York: John Wiley.

Quinn, J.B. (1980) *Strategies for Change: Logical Incrementalism*, Homewood, IL: Dorsey.

—— (1988) *Beyond Rational Management*. New York: Jossey-Bass.

Radner, R. (1997), "Bounded rationality, indeterminacy, and the managerial theory of the firm," in Z. Shapira (ed.) *Organisational Decision making*, Cambridge: Cambridge University Press.

Radner, R. and Rothschild, M. (1975) "On the allocation of effort," *Journal of Economic Theory*, 10: 358–76.

Raiffa, H. (1968) *Decision Analysis*, Reading, MA: Addison-Wesley. (Classic teaching oriented contribution on decision theory.)

—— (1982) *The Art and Science of Negotiation*, Cambridge: Cambridge University Press. (Analysis of negotiation from a game theoretic perspective.)

Rawls, J. (1971) *A Theory of Justice*, Cambridge, MA: Harvard University Press. (Classic.)

Revue Economique (1989) "L'économie des conventions," special issue.

Rice, A.K. (1958) *Productivity and Social Organization: The Ahmedabad Experiment*, London: Tavistock.

Richardson, G.B. (1972) "The organization of industry," *Economic Journal*, September: 883–96. (Classic on the competence-based view of the firm and of interfirm organization.)

Ring, P.S. (1999) "The costs of networked organization," in A. Grandori (ed.) *Interfirm Networks: Organization and Industrial Competitiveness*, London: Routledge.

Ring, P.S. and Van de Ven, A.H. (1992) "Structuring cooperative relationships between organizations," *Strategic Management Journal*, 13: 483–98.

Roberts, E.B. (1991) "High stakes for high-tech entrepreneurs: understanding venture capital decision-making," *Sloan Management Review*, 1932: 9–21.

Rockart, J.F. and Short, J.E. (1989) "IT in the 1990s: managing organizational interdependence," *Sloan Management Review*, 1930: 7–17.

Roethlisberger, F.J. (1942) *Management and Morale*, Cambridge, MA: Harvard University Press. (Classic on organizational behavior.)

Rogers, E.M. (1962) *Diffusion of Innovations*, New York: Free Press. (Classic on industrial economics.)

Rosen, S. (1985) "Implicit contracts: a survey," *Journal of Economic Literature*, 23: 1,144–75. (Overview.)

Rosenberg, N. (1976) *Perspectives on Technology*, Cambridge: Cambridge University Press. (Classic encompassing business history, technological change, and organization.)

Rosengren, W.R. and Lefton, M. (1979) *Organizations and Clients*, Columbus, OH: C.E. Merrill Publ. Co.

Rosenkopf, L. and Tushman, M.L. (1994) "The coevolution of technology and organization," in J.A.C. Baum and J.V. Singh (eds) *Evolutionary Dynamics of Organizations*, Oxford: Oxford University Press: 403–24.

Rubin, J. and Brown, B.R. (1975) *The Social Psychology of Bargaining and Negotiation*, New York: Academic Press.

Rubin, P.H. (1978) "The theory of the firm and the structure of the franchise contract," *Journal of Law and Economics*, 21(1): 223–33.

Rugiadini, A. (1979) *Organizzazione d'impresa*, Milan: Giuffrè.

—— (1985) "L'efficienza delle scelte manageriali fra organizzazione e mercato," in R.C.D. Nacamulli and A. Rugiadini (eds) *Organizzazione & mercato*, Bologna: Il Mulino.

Russell, B. (1948) *Human Knowledge: Its Scope and Limits*, New York: Simon & Schuster. (Classic on the philosophy of knowledge.)

Russo, J.E. and Schoemaker, P.H. (1989) *Decision Traps*, New York: Simon & Schuster.

Sabel, C.F. (1993) "Constitutional ordering in historical context," in F.W. Scharpf (ed.) *Games in Hierarchies and Networks: Analytical and Empirical Approaches to the Study of Governance Institutions*, Frankfurt am Main: Campus Verlag.

Sabel, C.F. and Piore, M.J. (1984) *The Second Industrial Divide: Possibilities for Prosperity*, New York: Basic Books. (Point of reference on the concept of "flexible specialization.")

Salop, J. and Salop, S. (1976) "Self-selection and turnover in the labor market," *Quarterly Journal of Economics*, 90, November: 619–28.

Salvemini, S. (1977) *La progettazione delle mansioni*, Turin: ISEDI.

Sapienza, H.J. and Gupta, A.K. (1994) "Impact of agency risk and task uncertainty on venture capitalists/CEO interaction," *Academy of Management Journal*, 37(6): 1,618–32.

Scharpf, F.W. (ed.) (1993) *Games in Hierarchies and Networks*, Frankfurt am Main: Campus Verlag.

(Game theoretic perspectives applied to organizational problems.)

Schein, E.A. (1965) *Organizational Psychology*, Englewood Cliffs, NJ: Prentice-Hall. (Classic.)

Schein, E.H. (1985) *Organizational Culture and Leadership*, San Francisco: Jossey-Bass. (Point of reference on culture.)

Schelling, T.C. (1960) *Strategy of Conflict*, Cambridge, MA: Harvard University Press. (Classic on decision-making using game theoretic concepts.)

Schrader, S. (1991) "Informal technology transfer between firms: cooperation through information trading," *Research Policy*, 20(2): 153–70.

Schumpeter, J.A. (1912) *Theorie der Wirtschaftlichen Entwicklung*, Berlin: Duncker and Humblot.

—— (1942) *Capitalim, Socialism and Democracy*, New York: Harper & Brothers. (Economic classics.)

Scott, B.R. (1971) *Stages of Corporate Development*, Cambridge, MA: Case Clearing House, Harvard Business School. (Organization theory classic.)

Scott, W. R. (1995) *Institutions and Organizations*. London: Sage. (An original statement of the institutional approach to organizational analysis by a leading sociologist.)

Selznick, P. (1957) *Leadership in Administration*, New York: Harper & Row. (Classic on the sociology of organization, in the "anti-bureaucratic" tradition.)

Sen, A.K. (1992) *Inequality Reexamined*. Oxford: Oxford University Press.

Shapira, Z. (1993) "Ambiguity and risk taking in organizations," *Journal of Risk and Uncertainty*, 7: 89–94.

Sheppard, B.H. (1984) "Third party conflict intervention: a procedural framework," in L.L. Cummings and B.M. Staw (eds) *Research in Organizational Behavior*, 6, Greenwich, CT: JAI Press.

Simon, H.A. (1947) *Administrative Behavior*, New York: Free Press; 2nd edn, 1957/1961, New York: Macmillan. (Organization theory classic, outlining the theory of bounded rationality.)

—— (1951) "A formal theory of the employment relationship," *Econometrica*, 19: 293–305.

—— (1955a) "A behavioral model of rational choice," *Quarterly Journal of Economics*, 69: 99–118.

—— (1955b) *Models of Man: Social and Rational: Mathematical Essays on Human Behavior in a Social Setting*, New York: John Wiley.

—— (1960) *The New Science of Management Decision*, New York: Harper & Row (2nd edn, 1977).

—— (1962) "The architecture of complexity," *Proceedings of the American Philosophical Society*, 106: 467–82.

—— (1973) "The structure of ill-structured problems," *Artificial Intelligence*, 4: 181–201.

—— (1976) "From substantive to procedural rationality," in S.J. Latsis (ed.) *Method and Appraisal in Economics*, Cambridge: Cambridge University Press.

—— (1977) *Models of Discovery and Other Topics in the Method of Science*, Dordrecht: Reidel.

—— (1990) "A mechanism for social selection and successful altruism," *Science*, 250: 1,665–8.

—— (1997) *An Empirically Based Microeconomics*, Cambridge: Cambridge University Press.

Simon, H.A., Langley, P.W. and Bradshaw, G.L. (1981) "Scientific discovery as problem-solving," *Synthese*, 47: 1–27.

Sims, H.P. and Lorenzi, P. (1992) *The New Leadership Paradigm: Social Learning and Cognition in Organizations*, London: Sage. (Teaching oriented overview of social cognitive theory.)

Singer, M. (1992) *Fairness in Personnel Selection*, Newcastle: Avebury.

Sloan, A.P., Jr (1963) *My Years with General Motors*, Garden City, NY: Doubleday.

Smircich, L. (1983) "Concepts of culture and organizational anlaysis," *Administrative Science Quarterly*, 28(3): 339–58.

Smith, A. (1776) *An Inquiry into the Nature and Causes of the Wealth of Nations*. (Economics classic.)

Soda, G. and Usai, A. (1999) "The dark side of dense networks: from embeddedness to indebtedness," in A. Grandori (ed.) *Interfirm Networks Organization and Industrial Competitiveness*, London: Routledge: 276–302.

Sorge A. (1991) "Strategic fit and societal effect: interpreting cross-national comparison of technology, organization and human resources," *Organization Studies*, 12(2): 161–90.

—— (1993) "Management in France," in D.J. Hickson (ed.) *Management in Western Europe*.

Society, Culture and Organizations in Twelve Nations, Berlin: De Gruyter: 1–8.

Sorge, A. and Maurice, M. (1993) "The societal effect in the strategies of French and West German machine-tool manufactures," in B. Kogut (ed.) *Country Competitiveness: Technology and the Organizing of work*, Oxford and New York: Oxford University Press.

Spence, A.M. (1973) *Market Signalling: Information Transfer in Hiring and Related Processes*, Cambridge, MA: Harvard University Press.

Spencer, L.M., Jr and Spencer, J.M. (1993) *Competence at Work*. New York: John Wiley.

Spicer, B.H. (1988) "Toward an organizational theory of the transfer pricing process," *Accounting Organizations and Society*, 13.

Starbuck, W.H. (1976) "Organizations and their environments," in M.D. Dunnette (ed.) *Handbook of Industrial Organizational and Psychology*, Chicago: Rand MacNally: 1,069–123.

Staw, B.M. (1976a) *Instrinsic and Extrinsic Motivation*, Morristown, NJ: General Learning Press.

—— (1976b) "Knee-deep in the big muddy: a study of escalating commitment to a chosen course of action," *Organizational Behavior and Human Performance*, 16: 27–44.

—— (1980) "Rationality and justification in organizational life," in B.M. Staw and L.L. Cummings (eds) *Research in Organizational Behavior*, 2, Greenwich, CT: JAI Press. (Overview on retrospective rationality and its organizational implications.)

—— (1982) "Motivation in organization: Toward synthesis and redirection," in B.M. Staw and G.R. Salancik (eds) *New Directions in Organizational Behaviour*, Malabar, FLA: R. Krieger Publishing Company (2nd edn).

Steers, R.M., Porter, L.W., and Bigley, G.A. (eds) (1996) *Motivation and Leadership at Work*, New York: McGraw-Hill. (Teaching-oriented selection of essays on motivation theories.)

Steinbruner, J.D. (1974) *The Cybernetic Theory of Decision*, Princeton, NJ: Princeton University Press.

Stigler, G. (1951) "The division of labor is limited by the extent of the market," *Journal of Political Economy*, 59: 185–93.

Stinchcombe, A.L. (1985) "Organizing information outside the firm: contracts as hierarchical documents," in A. Stinchcombe, *Information*

and Organizations, Beverly Hills, CA: University of California Press.

Stopford, J.M. and Wells, L.T., Jr (1972) *Managing the Multinational Enterprise*, New York: Basic Books.

Streeck, W. (1992) *Social Institutions and Economic Performance*, London: Sage.

Suarez-Villa, L. and Rama, R. (1996) "Outsourcing R&D and the pattern of intra-metropolitan location: the electronics industries of Madrid," *Urban Studies* 33(7): 1,155–97.

Sugden, R. (1985) *The Economics of Rights, Cooperation and Welfare*, Oxford: Basil Blackwell.

Susman, G.I. (1976) *Autonomy at Work*, New York: Praeger. (Classic on socio-technical job design.)

Tannenbaum, R. and Schmidt, W. (1958) "How to choose a leadership pattern," *Harvard Business Review*, 36(2): 95–101.

Taylor, F. (1947) *Scientific Management*, London: Harper & Row. (Classic.)

Teece, D.J. (1980a) "Economies of scope and the scope of the enterprise," *Journal of Economic Behavior and Organization*, 1, September. (Point of reference on the concept of economies of scope and their organizational implications.)

—— (1980b) "The diffusion of administrative innovation," *Management Science*, 26: 464–70.

—— (1981) "The multinational enterprise: market failure and market power considerations," *Sloan Management Review*, 22: 3–17.

—— (1982) "Toward an economic theory of the multiproduct firm," *Journal of Economic Behavior and Organization*, 3: 39–63.

—— (1986) "Profiting from technological innovation: implications for integration, collaboration, licensing and public policy," *Research Policy*, 15(6): 286–305.

Thompson, G., Frances, J., and Mitchell, J. (1989) *Markets, Hierarchies and Networks: The Coordination of Social Life*, London: Sage. (Overview.)

Thompson, J.D. (1956) "On building an administrative science," *Administrative Science Quarterly* 1(1): 102–11.

—— (1967) *Organization in Action*, New York: McGraw-Hill. (Founding classic in organization theory.)

Thompson, J.D. and Tuden, A. (1959) "Strategies,

structures, and processes of organizational decision," in J.D. Thompson, P.B. Hammond, R.W. Hawkes, B.H. Junker, and A. Tuden (eds) *Comparative Studies in Administration*, Pittsburgh, PA: University of Pittsburgh Press: 195–216.

Tosi, H. (1992) *The Environment/Organization/Person Contingency Model: A Meso Approach to the Study of Organizations* Greenwich, CT: JAI Press.

Tosi, H., Aldag, R., and Storey, R. (1970) "On the measurement of the environment: an assessment of Lawrence and Lorsch environment uncertainty scale," *Administrative Science Quarterly*, 18: 27–36.

Tosi, H.L. and Gomex-Meija, L.R. (1989) "The decoupling of CEO pay and performance: an agency theory perspective," *Administrative Science Quarterly*, 34(2): 168–89.

Tosi, H.L., Rizzo, J.R., and Carrol, S.J. (1986) *Managing Organizational Behavior*, Boston: Pitman Publishing Inc. (Textbook.)

Touraine, A. (1955) *L'evolution du travail ouvrier aux usines Renault*, Paris: CNRS. (Classic on the sociology of work.)

Trice, H.M. and Beyer, J.M. (1984) "Studying organizational cultures through rites and ceremonials," *Academy of Management Review*, 9(4): 653–69.

Trist, E. (1981) "The socio-technical perspective," in A.H. Van de Ven and W.F. Joyce (eds) *Perspectives on Organization Design and Behavior*, New York: John Wiley. (Overview.)

Trist, E.L. and Bamforth, K.W. (1951) "Some social and psychological consequences of the Longwall method of coal getting," *Human Relations*, 4: 3–88.

Trist, E.L., Higgin, G.W., Murray, H., and Pollock, A.B. (1963) *Organizational Choice,* London: Tavistock. (Classic on the "socio-technical" organizational perspective.)

Tullock, G. (1967) "The general irrelevance of the general impossibility theorem," *Quarterly Journal of Economics*, May: 256–70.

Turk, J. (1983) "Power, efficiency and institutions: some implications of the debate for the scope of economics" in A. Francis, J. Turk, and P. Willman (eds) *Power, Efficiency and Institutions*, London: Heinemann: 189–204.

Tuschman, M.L. and Romanelli, E. (1985) "Organizational evolution: a metamorphosis model of convergence and reorientation," *Research in Organizational Behavior*, 7: 171–222.

Tversky, A. (1972) "Elimination by aspects: a theory of choice," *Psychological Review*, 79: 281–99.

Tversky, A. and Kahneman, D. (1974) "Judgment under uncertainty: heuristics and biases," *Science*, 185: 1,124–31

—— (1981) "The framing of decisions and the psychology of choice," *Science*, 211: 453–8.

Ulrich, D. and Lake, D. (1991) "Organizational capability: Creating competitive advantage," *Academy of Management Executive*, 5(1): 77: 77–92.

Van de Ven, A.H., Delbecq, A.L., and Koenig, R. (1976) "Determinants of coordination modes within organization," *American Sociology Review*, 41: 322–38. (Point of reference in the organizational analysis of interdependence and coordination.)

Van Waarden, F. (1992) "Emergence and development of business interest associations: an example from The Netherlands," *Organization Studies*, 13(4): 521–63.

Varian, H.R. (1990) "Monitoring agents with other agents," *Journal of Institutional and Theoretical Economics*, 146(1), special issue on *The New Institutional Economics*: 153–74.

Volberda, H.W. (1998) *Building the Flexible Firm: How to Remain Competitive*, New York: Oxford University Press.

Von Bertalanffy, L. (1950) "The theory of open systems in physic and biology," *Science*, January: 13.

Von Hayek, F. (1945) "The use of knowledge in society." *American Economic Review*, 35, September: 519–30. (Economic classic offering a knowledge-based interpretation of the the economic system and of prices.)

von Neumann, J. and Morgenstern, O. (1944) *Theory of Games and Economic Behavior*, New York: John Wiley. (Classic.)

Vroom, V.H. (1964) *Work and Motivation*, New York: John Wiley. (Core contribution on the valence/expectancy theory of motivation.)

Vroom, V.H. and Yetton P.W. (1973) *Leadership and Decision Making*, Pittsburgh, PA: University of Pittsburgh Press.

Walker, C.R. and Guest, R.H. (1952) *The Man on the Assembly Line*, Cambridge, MA: Harvard

University Press. (Classic on industrial psychology and the organization of work.)

Walras, L. (1874) *Elements d'economie politique pure*, Lausanne: L. Corbas & Co.

Walster, E. and Walster, G.W. (1975) "Equity and social justice," *Journal of Social Issues*, 31: 21–43. (Point of reference on equity theory of motivation.)

Walton, R.E. and Dutton, J.M. (1972) "The management of interdepartmental conflict: a model and review," in B.M. Bass and S.D. Deep (eds) *Studies in Organizational Psychology*, Boston: Allyn & Bacon.

Walton, R.E. and McKersey, R.B. (1965) *A Behavioral Theory of Labor Negotiations*, New York: McGraw-Hill. (Point of reference on labor negotiation as linked to negotiation theory and organizational decision-making)

Warglien, M. (1990) "Trasferimento di competenze e flessibilità dell'impresa," *Sviluppo & Organizzazione*, 121, September–October: 19–31.

Warner M. and A. Campbell (1993) "German management," in D.J. Hickson (ed.) *Management in Western Europe. Society, Culture and Organizations in Twelve Nations*, Berlin: De Gruyter.

Wason, P.C. (1960) "Reason about a rule," *Quarterly Journal of Experimental Psychology*, 20: 273–83.

Watson, W.E., Kumar, K., and Michaelsen, K.K. (1993) Cultural diversity's impact on interaction process and performance: comparing homogeneous and diverse tasks groups, *Academy of Management Journal*, 36: 590–602.

Watzlavick, P., Helmickbeavin, J., and Jackson, D.D. (1967) *Pragmatics of Human Communication*, New York: Norton.

Weber, M. (1922) *Wirtschaft und Gesellschaft*, Tubingen: Mohr. (Sociology classic.)

Weick, K.E. (1979a) *The Social Psychology of Organizing*, Reading, MA: Addison-Wesley. (Organization classic emphasising processes rather than structures and "variation/selection/retention processes" at different levels of analysis.)

—— (1979b) "Cognitive processes in organizations," in B. Shaw (ed.) *Research in Organizational Behavior*, Greenwich, CT: JAI Press.

Weiner, B. (ed.) (1974) *Achievement Motivation and Attribution Theory*, Morristown, NJ: General Learning Press.

Weiner B. *et al.* (1970) "Perceiving the causes of success and failure," in E. Jones *et al.* (eds), *Attribution: Perceiving the Causes of Behavior*, Morristown, NJ: General Learning Press.

Weiner, N. (1948) *Cybernetics*, Cambridge: MIT Press. (Classic.)

Wernerfelt, B. (1984) "A resource-based view of the firm," *Strategic Management Journal*, 5: 171–80. (Point of reference for the perspective.)

Westley, F. and Mintzberg, H. (1989) "Visionary leadership and strategic management," *Strategic Management Journal*, 10: 17–32.

White, H.C. (1981) "Where do markets come from?," *American Journal of Sociology*, 89, November: 517–47. (Seminal contribution in the structural sociological analysis of markets.)

—— (1988) "Varieties of markets," in B. Wellman and L. Berkowitz (eds) *Structural Sociology*, New York: Cambridge University Press.

Whitley, R.D. (1992) (ed.) *European Business Systems: Firms and Markets in their National Contexts*, London: Sage. (Point of reference for the economic sociology school on the cross-national comparison of business systems.)

Whittington, R. and Mayer, M. (1997) "Do institutions matter any more? Strategy and structure in France, Germany and the UK, 1950–1993," ESF–EMOT Final Conference, Stresa.

Wildavsky, A. (1964) *The Politics of the Budgetary Process*, Boston: Little, Brown.

William, J., Paez, B.L., and Sanders, L. (1988) "Conglomerates revisited," *Strategic Management Journal*, 9: 403–14.

Williamson, O.E. (1964) *The Economics of Discretionary Behavior: Managerial Objectives in a Theory of the Firm*, Englewood Cliffs, NJ: Prentice-Hall.

—— (1970) *Corporate Control and Business Behavior*, Englewood Cliffs, NJ: Prentice-Hall.

—— (1975) *Markets and Hierarchies: Analysis and Antitrust Implications*, New York: Free Press. (Classic and core contribution of transaction cost economics.)

—— (1979) "Transaction cost economics: the governance of contractual relations," *Journal of Law and Economics*, 22: 233–61.

—— (1980) "The organization of work. A

comparative institutional assessment," *Journal of Economics Behavior and Organization*, 1: 5–38.

—— (1981a) "The economics of organization: the transaction cost approach," *American Journal of Sociology*, 87: 548–77. (The most systematic exposition of the perspective.)

—— (1981b) "The modern corporation: origins, evolutions, attributes," *Journal of Economic Literature*, 19, December, 1: 537–68.

—— (1983) "Credible commitments: using hostages to support exchange," *American Economic Review*, 73: 519–40.

—— (1985) *The Economic Institutions of Capitalism*, New York: Free Press.

—— (1986) "Economics and sociology: promoting a dialog," 8th EGOS Colloquium, Antwerp.

—— (1987) *Antitrust Economics: Mergers, Contracting and Strategic Behavior*, Oxford: Basil Blackwell.

—— (1991) "Comparative economic organizations: the analysis of discrete structural alternatives"; *Administrative Science Quarterly*, 36: 269–96, and in S. Lindenberg and H. Schreuder (eds) (1993) *Interdisciplinary Perspectives on Organization Studies*, Oxford: Pergamon Press: 3–37.

—— (1993a) "The evolving science of organization," *Journal of Institutional and Theoretical Economics*, 149: 36–63.

—— (1993b) "Transaction cost economics and organization theory," *Industrial and Corporate Change*, 2(2): 107–56. (Bridging contribution by the leader of transaction cost economics toward organization theory.)

Williamson, O.E. and Ouchi, W.G. (1981) "The markets and hierarchies program of research: origins, implication, prospects," in A.H. Van de Ven and W.F. Joyce (eds) *Perspectives on Organization Design and Behavior*, New York: John Wiley: 347–70 (Overview.)

Winter, S.G. (1975) "Optimization and evolution in the theory of the firm," in R.H. Day and T. Groves (eds) *Adaptive Economic Models*, New York: Academic Press: 73–118. (Methodological discussion by a leading evolutionary economist on the difference between maximization logic and evolutionary logic.)

Witte, E. and Zimmermann, H.J. (1986) *Empirical Research on Organization Decision-making*, Amsterdam: North Holland.

Woodward, J. (1965) *Industrial Organization: Theory and Practice*, Oxford: Oxford University Press. (Organization theory classic.)

Wrong, D.H. (1961) "The oversocialized conception of man in modern sociology," *American Sociological Review*, 26: 182–93. (Classic critical essay by a sociologist on the assumptions about rationality in sociology.)

Zan, S. (1992) *Organizzazione e rappresentanza* Rome: NIS.

Zucker, L.G. (1987) "Institutional theories of organization," *Annual Review of Sociology*, 13: 443–64. (Overview.)

Index

Lightning Source UK Ltd.
Milton Keynes UK
UKOW06f2234130314

228022UK00001B/8/P